"ONE OPENS NOVICK'S BOOK WITH HIGH HOPES, AND AS CHAPTER FOLLOWS MASTERLY CHAPTER THE HOPES MATURE INTO ADMIRATION OF THE AUTHOR AND AWE OF THE SUBJECT." —*The New York Times Book Review*

"A TRIUMPH . . . NO BOOK COULD DO MORE TO BRING US INTO THE PRESENCE OF GENIUS."
—Mark Sagoff, Director, Institute for Philosophy and Public Policy, University of Maryland

HONORABLE JUSTICE

"ESPECIALLY ENLIGHTENING . . . Novick is an attorney, and not the least of his accomplishments is his clear explanation not only of individual cases, but of their political and social ramifications."
—*The Seattle Times*

"VERY READABLE . . . will appeal to the general reader as well as the scholar." —*Library Journal*

"THOUGH A WARTS-AND-ALL APPROACH, NOVICK'S WELL-DOCUMENTED BOOK nevertheless shows above all Holmes's singularity as a thinker and his influence on the direction of American jurisprudence." —*Booklist*

"RICHLY REWARDING . . . A DETAILED AND FASCINATING PORTRAIT OF HOLMES THE THINKER AND HOLMES THE MAN . . . [Novick] succeeds in presenting the man in his time, as he saw himself and was seen by his contemporaries."
—*Star-Tribune* (Minneapolis)

Also by Sheldon M. Novick

THE CARELESS ATOM

THE ELECTRIC WAR

HONORABLE JUSTICE

The Life of Oliver Wendell Holmes

by

SHELDON M. NOVICK

LAUREL

A LAUREL TRADE PAPERBACK

Published by
Dell Publishing
a division of
Bantam Doubleday Dell Publishing Group, Inc.
666 Fifth Avenue
New York, New York 10103

ISBN: 0-440-50325-6

Reprinted by arrangement with Little, Brown and Company

Printed in the United States of America
Published simultaneously in Canada

October 1990

10 9 8 7 6 5 4 3 2 1

RRH

For Carolyn

Style is thus a form of honor and courage, just as, Santayana tells us, is the pursuit of truth always. One cannot read these opinions without seeing honor and courage written down on every page.

— Justice Benjamin Cardozo,
"Mr. Justice Holmes"

CONTENTS

ILLUSTRATIONS

*(All pictures, unless otherwise noted,
are from the Harvard Law Art Collection.)*

PREFACE

This is the first full biography of Justice Oliver Wendell Holmes, one of the best-known and most honored Americans in this country's history.

A Lord Chief Justice of England called him the greatest judge in the English-speaking world; his successor on the Supreme Court, Benjamin Cardozo, thought him one of the greatest judges of any time. Justice Felix Frankfurter said of Holmes: "No judge of the Supreme Court has done more to establish it in the consciousness of the people. Mr. Justice Holmes is built into the structure of our national life and has written himself into the slender volume of the literature of all time."

John Dewey praised his philosophy, and Edmund Wilson placed him among the great literary figures of his age. His fame continued to grow after his death, and his name remains perhaps the best known of any figure in the history of American law. He was the "Magnificent Yankee," celebrated in a hit stage play that became a television film; he was the "Yankee from Olympus," in Catherine Drinker Bowen's 1944 best-selling, somewhat fictionalized, biography of Holmes's family.

Successive generations of law students have been raised on his stirring dissents, and his book *The Common Law*, still in print after a hundred years, has been called the greatest work of legal thought in American history.

Yet no biography of Justice Holmes has been completed since his death in 1935.

There has been no biography of Holmes, because the executors of his estate gave exclusive access to Holmes's unpublished work, for more than forty years, to a succession of authorized biographers, each of whom died or abandoned the task unfinished.

The first of the authorized biographers was Felix Frankfurter, a friend and admirer of Holmes. In order to protect the authorized biography, Holmes's executor, John G. Palfrey, gave Frankfurter exclusive access to Holmes's unpublished letters and diaries. Frankfurter was then a professor at Harvard Law School, but in 1939, he was appointed an associate justice of the Supreme Court, and it soon became plain he would not have time to write Holmes's biography. He selected a protégé, Mark DeWolfe Howe, who had been one of Holmes's legal secretaries, to succeed him as authorized biographer. Professor Howe died in 1967, with only a third of the biography completed. (See Appendix B, "A Note on Sources," below.)

Although he did not succeed in writing Holmes's biography, Howe did create an extraordinary scholarly resource. He retrieved many thousands of Holmes's letters, assembled the roughly 36,000 documents of the Oliver Wendell Holmes papers, interviewed many of those still living who remembered Holmes or his family, sent assistants into the records of courts and law firms, transcribed thousands of pages of Holmes's illegible manuscript, and published five volumes of meticulously edited and indexed letters. He provided valuable new editions of Holmes's *Common Law,* and of his collected speeches.

On Mark Howe's death, his widow and the Harvard Law School, which had succeeded to Holmes's literary estate, jointly chose Grant Gilmore, a distinguished professor then at the Yale School of Law, as Holmes's next authorized biographer. Professor Gilmore labored at this task, on and off, for the fifteen remaining years of his life.

There have since been other efforts to write a biography, some of which have been abandoned and two of which to my knowledge are still underway. Although they have granted me access to the Holmes Papers, the Harvard Law School and Mark Howe's widow, Mrs. Faneuil Adams, have not excluded other qualified scholars, nor is mine an authorized biography in any sense.

The eerie failures that dogged Holmes's biography have afflicted other works connected with his life. He left a large sum of money to the United States in his will, and there was a prolonged struggle among his political heirs for control of the bequest. A bill was eventually passed, providing for preparation of an edition of Holmes's collected papers (never published) and an authoritative history of the Supreme Court. Sadly, Alexander Bickel, who was to write the "Holmes Devise History" of the Court during most of the years in which Holmes was a member, died before writing more than a fraction of his assigned portion of the series; by the summer of 1988 the effort to write an authoritative history of the Court had apparently been abandoned, and a series of volumes, most of which would be much more modest, was planned. The volumes covering Holmes's tenure are scheduled for publication in two and three years.

One can only speculate why earlier efforts were not completed. Aside from bad luck, there was, of course, the sheer volume of materials. Holmes lived almost ninety-four years and wrote three books and more than two thousand opinions; he wrote more opinions for the United States Supreme Court than any other justice who has been on that bench. In an extraordinary variety of fields, from tort to copyright law, from contract to the Constitution, his opinions are leading cases. In his long lifetime, he was active professionally or socially at the highest levels of polite society and government in the United States and Great Britain. Palfrey, Frankfurter, Howe, and Gilmore all spent years assembling materials. (I had the immense good luck to begin when these materials had already been collected, and many of them had been transcribed and arranged in orderly fashion. I have also benefited greatly from Mark Howe's scholarly work.)

Still other difficulties faced the authorized biographers. Justice Holmes proved to be a shadowed figure, marked by the bigotry and sexism of his age, who in personal letters seemed to espouse a kind of fascist ideology. He was a violent, combative, womanizing aristocrat whose contribution to the development of law was surprisingly difficult to define. For Mark Howe and Grant Gilmore, laboring under the obligations of an authorized and authoritative biography, the task became difficult and even distasteful. I believe that both Howe and Gilmore came to regret having undertaken the biography of Justice Holmes.

I have come to this task, however, without obligations of any kind. I have tried to tell Holmes's story with sympathy, but without apology. I have tried to present Holmes in his own context and to avoid judgments drawn from a future he could not foresee. In a number of ways, I have been obliged to adopt the conventions of his time, which may now seem sexist or racist. I have called Holmes's wife "Fanny," for instance, while referring to him by his last name. "Mrs. Holmes" would have been hopelessly awkward, and not obviously an improvement; "Dixwell" would have been wrong.

The term *race* was used in Holmes's lifetime as we now might say "culture" or "nationality," and again there did not seem to be any way of avoiding the usage of his day in some cases, without awkwardness or constant explanations.

I have not tried to evaluate Holmes's contribution to present-day law in any systematic way, except as such assessments seemed necessary for the narrative of his life. As to Holmes's early work, I refer the reader to

Mark Howe's admirable writings, listed in the Bibliography below. As to Holmes's work as a judge and Supreme Court justice, the daunting task remains to be done. Holmes was remarkably prescient about the development of the law, and many of his opinions, even in dissent, marked the beginning of new lines of development. But, as Holmes said, each generation pretty well rewrites the law for its own time, and the importance of even those opinions is now principally historical.

If Holmes is of interest today to any but scholars, it is for his character, which shines through his writings even from the distance of a century or more. This book is the story of Holmes's life as a man, a life that he labored to make a work of art in itself. Perhaps the life, even beyond its intrinsic interest, will help others to understand better Holmes's elusive, tantalizing ideas.

South Strafford, Vermont
April 24, 1989

ACKNOWLEDGMENTS

Although I never met him, my debt to the late Mark DeWolfe Howe is considerable. Professor Howe did not live to complete his biography of Holmes, but his scholarship as much as Holmes's own work has given Holmes a place in history. Professor Howe's published and unpublished works were my starting point and the beacon to which I could always look back to keep my bearings.

My wife, Carolyn M. Clinton, through wisdom and patience, made this work possible, and her advice and suggestions have been valuable at every step. I am grateful, too, for my daughter, Melia Bensussen's, insight and suggestions, delivered with tactful skill. My son, Michael, age two, helped in his own way.

Jennifer Josephy's thoughtful criticism and meticulous editing are gratefully acknowledged. Elisabeth Gleason Humez rescued me from numberless errors. Thanks also are due to Peter Teachout, Jules B. Gerard, and Julian McCaull for their patient and careful reading of badly typed drafts and for their generous encouragement; to Claire Reinhardt, who did valuable and original work while bringing to life for me Holmes's Pittsfield and Boston, his circle of friends, and the revival of chivalry; to Mary Jane Warren, who among other valuable helps identified for me the labor leader with whom Holmes probably held private conversations in the 1890s; and to John Grzybeck, who generously helped me with the background to Holmes's Supreme Court years.

So many people in so many libraries have helped me that I cannot thank them all, but I must say a word of grateful thanks to Judith W. Mellins of the Harvard Law School Library Manuscripts Division, whose advice has been invaluable at every step and who for five years has patiently and graciously answered my requests; to Bernice Loss, curator of the Harvard Law Art Collection; and to Lisa Myer, of the Vermont Law School Library, whose intelligent researches greatly aided my work.

Early in this long project I was helped by advice from some of the old China hands of Holmes scholarship. Professor Saul Touster kindly shared with me his extensive knowledge of the Holmes literature and his then still unpublished work on Dr. Holmes. Erika S. Chadbourn, then curator of manuscripts at the Harvard Law School, was a helpful and skillful guide to the Holmes papers, who saved me many weeks of labor. Judge Harry Shriver (now unfortunately deceased) shared his bibliographical resources and his fund of anecdotes.

Morton J. Horwitz's words of encouragement at odd moments over the last ten years, probably now forgotten by him, meant a great deal to me. Fran Collin planted the idea of writing a biography; Cynthia Vartan gave early help and encouragement.

I am grateful to Mary M. Adams for permission to use the late Professor Mark Howe's unpublished Holmes materials, and to the Harvard Law School for access to the Oliver Wendell Holmes, Jr., Papers, as well as materials assembled for the never-completed biographies by Mark Howe and Grant Gilmore, and for permission to publish portions of the Holmes and Arthur E. Sutherland papers.

Among the materials assembled by Professor Howe were some contributed by Alexander Bickel, Eleanor Little, L. Kinvin Wroth, and Hiller Zobel (now Judge Zobel), all of which were helpful to me.

Dr. Franklin K. Paddock shared with me his knowledge of Pittsfield and his memorabilia of his great-aunt Carolyn Kellogg. The present owners of the Holmes house in Pittsfield, Mr. and Mrs. Arthur Stein, graciously opened their doors to my assistant, Claire Reinhardt. My thanks also to Dr. Howard Feinstein of Cornell University, who answered questions about the James family; and to Dr. Peter F. Stevens, curator of the Harvard Herbaria, who identified the century-old leaves pressed into Lady Castletown's letter.

Thanks are due as well to Professor Paul Freund and the Harvard Law School Library for giving me access to the Frankfurter and Brandeis collections there; to Jonathan Hand Churchill, Gerald Gunther, and the Harvard Law School Library for access to the Learned Hand Papers; and to the President and Fellows of Harvard College for permission to quote from Holmes's letters and speeches published by the Harvard University Press.

It is a pleasure finally to acknowledge my manifold debts to Dean Douglas M. Costle, the faculty, and the staff of the Vermont Law School, where I have been Scholar in Residence while completing this book.

PART I

A
NEW ENGLAND
BOYHOOD

1

FATHERS
AND SONS

T HE FIRST OLIVER WENDELL HOLMES WAS BORN ON AUGUST 29,
1809, in Cambridge, Massachusetts, a quiet country town near
Boston. There were a few grand houses in Cambridge, but the
Holmeses lived more modestly a quarter-mile to the east on the far side
of the Common, in a yellow clapboard house shaded by slender elms, on
an unpaved road. Beyond their house, open fields ran down to the distant Charles River. Young Wendell, as he was called, liked to wander
alone in the neighboring fields with a gun, shooting birds and rabbits.
The hills of Boston were visible in the distance.

He was a talkative, restless boy, the fourth of five children. At school
he was often punished for whispering in class. His father, Abiel Holmes,
minister of the First Congregational Church, reprimanded him constantly for playing his flute too loudly, for smoking cigars, for laughing
in church, and for every other infraction of the minister's numerous
rules.

The minister was a cool, distant, and implacably conventional man.
On the Sabbath, which in Puritan fashion began at Saturday nightfall,
even schoolwork was forbidden. Wendell hated the silence and inactivity.
When he was fifteen, his father sent him to Phillips Academy in Andover
for a year to improve his behavior, and like most of the other boys he

was whipped almost to maiming, whipped across his open palms on one occasion so that for a fortnight he could not close his hands without pain. But he returned to Cambridge still noisy and rebellious.

Until he was twenty-two years old he lived at home, attending Harvard College, which he could see from his kitchen garden, and for one unhappy year the Harvard Law School. Two older sisters — a third died young — married and moved away when he was still a child, but he and a younger brother, John, who was lame and cross-eyed, remained at home.

Their mother, Sarah Wendell Holmes, was a tiny, vivacious woman. Wendell, small and round-faced like his mother, had her striking blue-gray eyes. She was proud, and ambitious for her children. Despite the disapproval of the congregation, she bought a piano, saw that her daughters were taught to sing and that all her children were taught dancing and graceful manners. She spoke often to her children about her father's family, especially her grandfather Jacob Wendell — called "Colonel" by courtesy — who had owned six square miles in the Berkshires, most of what became Pittsfield Township, and a part of Boston. In the Great Boston Fire of 1760, "all the buildings on *Colonel Wendell's* wharf were burned." Sarah told her children that grandfather Jacob Wendell lost forty buildings in that fire,

> which always made [Wendell Holmes] feel pretty grand, as being the descendant of one that hath had losses. . . . Most people's grandfathers in Boston got their living working in their shirt-sleeves, but when a man's [great-grandfather] lost forty buildings, it [was] almost up to your sixteen quarterings.[1]

The yellow clapboard house had a big attic filled with old Wendell furniture, and a darkened bedroom where dim portraits of dead Olivers, Wendells, and Quincys were shrouded to keep off the light and where the long mirrors reflected shadows. At night, the house seemed inhabited by ghosts.

But in daylight it was cheerful enough. A visitor recalled:

> [The] house overflowed with books. Amid the lumber in the attic, one found Erasmus's *Colloquies* and queer old Latin works on alchemy. Sometimes, in the evening, Mr. and Mrs. Holmes and their sons and daughters gathered about the London-made piano, and one of the daughters, who was the family minstrel, sang the *Irish Melodies* of Thomas Moore.[2]

Oliver Wendell Holmes began writing light verse when he was a schoolboy. At college, he wrote comic songs for the Hasty Pudding Club, and when law school oppressed him, he found diversion and solace in writing occasional verse for the newspapers. He wrote skillful and, for the most part, unremarkable rhymes that were popular among his friends.

He turned more often to the distraction of poetry in his last year of college, when his father was caught in a violent upheaval of the church. The congregation had divided into two factions, one caught up by the revival of Calvinist orthodoxy, and the other by liberal, Unitarian reform. Abiel Holmes was of neither party, but, his son said bitterly, "The time having come when he stood in the way of the tacticians managing the church militant, he was sacrificed."[3] After two years of acrimonious maneuverings, Abiel Holmes was removed from his position. He retired to his study and his antiquarian works.

In the midst of his father's troubles, Wendell read a notice in the *Boston Daily Advertiser* that the Navy Department was planning to dismantle the famous Revolutionary frigate, the *Constitution*. He stood at an old-fashioned desk in a whitewashed room in his father's house and in a single burst of passion wrote "Old Ironsides," protesting the indignity that was to be done — to the old ship.

> *Ay, tear her tattered ensign down!*
> . . .
> *Oh better that her shattered hulk*
>   *Should sink beneath the wave;*
> *Her thunders shook the mighty deep,*
>   *And there should be her grave;*
> *Nail to the mast her holy flag,*
>   *Set every threadbare sail,*
> *And give her to the god of storms,*
>   *The lightning and the gale!*[4]

When the church struggles had at last ended with his father's dismissal, Wendell Holmes resigned from the law school, left Cambridge and home, and took a room in a boardinghouse at 2 Central Court in Boston. He began to study medicine.

> I have been quietly occupying a room in Boston attending medical lectures, going to the Massachusetts Hospital and slicing and slivering carcasses of better men and women than I ever was myself or am like to be. It is a sin for a puny fellow like me to mutilate one of your six foot men as if he was a sheep. . . .[5]

Poetry was forgotten for a time. Wendell Holmes attended the lectures of Dr. James Jackson of the Harvard Medical School and, at Jackson's suggestion, spent two years studying medicine in Paris. In 1835, he returned to Boston and hung out his shingle as a physician. He worked in the Boston Dispensary as well, where the sick needed food and warm clothes, not medicine. He found that a doctor could do little for his patients except to give them comfort and some relief from pain. But success in medical practice went to the humbugs who talked of cures. Within a few weeks after his return from Paris, Holmes was writing comic poetry again and composing songs that he would sing at dinners. Sometimes, because he was small, he would be lifted up on a table to perform.

He soon went onto the lecture circuit. Lyceum lectures were a popular new public amusement and paid well. Dr. Oliver Wendell Holmes gave lectures on France and on poetry, enlivening his talks with jokes and puns and snatches of his own verse.

When his father died in January, 1837, the youngest son, John, decided without apparent regret to remain at home to care for their mother. Wendell stayed on in Boston, and with three other young doctors started the Tremont Medical School in a room above an apothecary's shop at 35 Tremont Row. He lectured on pathology, introduced his students to the novelties of the microscope, and supervised their dissection of cadavers. He was happy in this work, but he refused a professorship that would have required him to practice surgery on living patients. He could not bear even to kill the rabbits that were needed for demonstrations; he begged an assistant not to let him hear the rabbits squeal.

Dr. Holmes's friendship with James Jackson steadily deepened through those years, and he came to think of Jackson as a second father. He visited often as well at the nearby house of James's brother, Charles, who would soon become his father-in-law.

Charles Jackson was a lawyer, a tall courtly man who dressed and spoke in the fashions of the eighteenth century, and was called "Judge" because he had served for a time as a justice of the Massachusetts Supreme Judicial Court.

Judge Jackson's law practice was devoted to obscure and technical property disputes, and he had written a scholarly and exhaustive treatise on the topic. The treatise was a work of self-effacing admiration for the English law of an older epoch. "I was well convinced," he said after the book appeared, "that the system of real [property] actions established by the common law [from the thirteenth to the sixteenth centuries] needed only to be known, to be universally approved." His book was flatteringly reviewed, and the great Chancellor James Kent of New York, whose *Commentaries* were called the American equal of Blackstone's, sent him a very gratifying letter about it.[6]

Judge Jackson and his wife, Frances — she was always known as "Fanny" — and their two children lived in Bedford Place,[7] in a large brick house with a walled garden behind. This garden, which held an old St. Michael's pear tree whose fruit was greatly prized, was the judge's special delight. His neighbors were all brothers, sisters, and cousins of various degrees. Dr. Jackson's house was a few paces away, and around them was a clan of Jacksons, Cabots, Higginsons, Lees, Morses, Gardners, and Lowells. The adjoining gardens seemed to make a little country village in the midst of Boston.

On June 15, 1840, Holmes married Judge Jackson's only daughter, Amelia, in King's Chapel. The judge gave his daughter a house, not far away at 8 Montgomery Place,[8] and the Holmeses were able to live comfortably there. Holmes's practice had grown, and with the fees from the Tremont Medical School and his Lyceum lectures, they were able with some difficulty to keep servants, a horse, and a carriage.

Amelia was inordinately fond of her husband. She had married late, and perhaps had married beneath her position in Boston society. Certainly Oliver Wendell Holmes was quite unlike the conventional youths she knew. Amelia was taller than he, not talkative, not intellectual, even a little dull; friends remarked that the doctor might improve her conversation.[9] But she was gentle and fond, doted upon her husband, and reveled in his brightness and energy. She said, "I think we are as happy a little household as you will meet with."[10]

On March 8, 1841, their first child was born, and Dr. Holmes wrote to his elder sister Ann:

Last evening between 8 and 9 there appeared at No. 8 Montgomery Place a little individual who may be hereafter addressed as
———— Holmes Esq.
or
The Hon. ———— Holmes M.C.
or
His Excellency ———— Holmes, President, etc.
etc.
but who at present is contented with scratching his face and sucking his right forefinger.

Amelia had a favorable time of it and is now remarkably comfortable.[11]

The little boy was named for his father and was called "Wendie." He grew quickly and it was soon apparent that except for his striking gray-blue Wendell eyes he would take after his mother's family, the tall and lantern-jawed Jacksons, rather than the little, round-faced Wendells and Holmeses.

Two more children followed at deliberate three-year intervals — a daughter, Amelia Jackson, and a son, Edward Jackson Holmes, soon known as Ned. The doctor struggled to support his growing family. With the assistance of Dr. Jackson he became professor of anatomy at the Harvard Medical School. No salary was attached to the position — Holmes received only the fees students paid to attend his lectures — but he was a skillful performer; his lectures were well attended and therefore lucrative. He kept up his medical practice, taught a summer term at the Tremont Medical School, and kept up his Lyceum lectures. But there was never enough money, and when in 1847 the post of dean of the Harvard Medical School came open — the duties were primarily clerical and administrative — Holmes took that on as well.

Even this did not exhaust his energy. The doctor continued to write poetry and to sing songs for every public occasion. He was an experimenter, a maker of improvements. He took up the new science of photography and took pictures of his family and friends. He tinkered with his microscope and designed a new and more convenient stand for it. He invented a hand-held stereoscope that soon was in wide use. He taught himself to play the violin, although he had no ear for music. And he turned his restless, combative, inexhaustible energy to the task of raising his eldest son.

2

IN THE DOCTOR'S
HOUSEHOLD

MONTGOMERY PLACE WAS A LITTLE PRIVATE WAY THAT OPENED on Tremont Street, opposite the Old Granary Burying Ground, ran for a single block, and ended with a flight of stone steps down to Providence Street. Those steps seemed to Wendie to be the very stones of antiquity, but the street was only a little older than he and was filled with young families and small children. Number 8 was second from the end and had a black iron trellis over its door.[1] There was a privy at the rear of the house, where squares of newspaper hung on nails, and a pump in the backyard for water.[2]

Beyond the mouth of Montgomery Place and to the right was King's Chapel, at the foot of Beacon Hill, and to the left was the Park Street Church. Beyond Park Street, an unbroken row of new brick houses on Tremont Street faced the Boston Common, and across the Common lay only marshes and the Back Bay, where Wendie fished with pin hooks. The air was fresh and smelled of the sea.

Indoors, in the winter evenings, there were candles, warm firelight, and whale oil lamps that were lighted by holding a glowing coal against the wick and blowing until one was dizzy. The furniture was stately, solid, and expensive. Carpets of English make covered the floors. Family portraits and European prints hung on the walls: colorless, dimly depicted scenes.

Dr. Holmes, although very liberal in his own views, kept the children to a strict orthodoxy in behavior, very much like the hated regime his own father had imposed. He chastised young Wendie as regularly as he himself had been corrected by Abiel Holmes.[3] Sundays in the doctor's house were as silent and constrained as they had been in Cambridge. On Sunday mornings, Wendie listened to the monotonous pealing of church bells and the sound of boots scuffing the uneven slate sidewalks. After services at King's Chapel, there was a ritual two o'clock dinner that always ended with tapioca pudding, which Wendie called "stick-jaw." Sunday dinner left the family stupefied, and afterward Wendie was not permitted to go outside or to play. "The Boston of my youth was the still half-Puritan Boston, with the 'unutterable ennui' of its Sundays . . . it was a Boston with no statues, few pictures, little music outside the churches, and no Christmas."[4]

He was thin, cheerful, gray-eyed. The dim quiet of Sunday was hard to bear, but in dark winter evenings his life expanded among books. The engravings enflamed his imagination. Ladies wore the court dress of another age, showing bare shoulders and round arms. There was Claude Duval, the highwayman, whose epitaph Wendie read with secret rapture:

> *Here lies Duval: Reader, if male thou art,*
> *Look to thy purse: if female to thy heart.*[5]

Another picture he recalled long afterward: "The cover of my copy of Jack and the Beanstalk — the beanstalk was cut off by the top of the cover and Jack was climbing — to one could not see what mysterious end."[6]

He read tales of chivalry: Sir Walter Scott's stories and tales of King Arthur, of Sir Lancelot with his secret sin; Sir Walter Raleigh — poet, soldier, gentleman — and Sir Philip Sidney, who died gloriously for the Virgin Queen. There was Captain Marryat's *Children of the New Forest*, filled with violent deaths and lingering romances and a noble son, hidden in a woodsman's hut, who was raised secretly to fight for the exiled king.

The Holmeses regularly drove in their carriage to Grandmother Holmes's yellow clapboard house in Cambridge. When the Fitchburg Railroad ran a line out to Harvard, they rode the exciting steam cars. Grandmother and Uncle John told Wendie their own romantic tales. Grandmother had stories of vanished wealth and of the Revolution. She remembered the British soldiers coming into Boston when she was a girl of six. Her family had fled to Newburyport — the Redcoats were coming, murdering as they went.[7] Great-grandfather David Holmes had fought in the French and Indian Wars, and again in the Revolution; there were his officer's sword and his powder horn.

Wendie did not attend the public Latin School, where the teachers beat the boys. At first he went to a dame school, and then, when he was seven, he began at Mr. Sullivan's little school on Beacon Hill. He was given a new composition book that year, its thin covers a shining bluish green, stamped with golden pagodas, bridges, phoenixes, and swans. Inside the front cover, Wendie wrote carefully, "O. W. Holmes. Oct. 18th 1848. 7½ years old."[8]

A week later, there was a celebration on the Common. Wendie wrote in his composition book:

> Introduction of pure water into the city.
> This work began two years and two months ago and the water was introduced into the city the twenty-fifth of October 1848. The procession was two hours passing one point there were 300,000 people assembled in the city.[9]

Wendie had watched the parade from Tremont Street.[10] At the head of the great procession rode veterans of the Revolution, old soldiers with their white hair, in uniform: "I was most impressed by a carload of veterans. I got the notion, which has persisted, that the glory of life was to be carried in a civic procession, in a barge, as a survivor."[11]

In the summer of 1849, Mrs. Holmes came into a legacy of two thousand dollars. She and the doctor decided to buy a beautiful piece of property just outside the village of Pittsfield, a 280-acre farm and woodlot, and to build a summer house there.[12] The land, farmed by a tenant, lay beside the former six-mile-square Wendell estate.

With a summer house, the Pittsfield farm became a country seat for the Holmes family, and the doctor became a country squire. He appeared with other distinguished local citizens at the annual Berkshire County fair, where he was chairman of the committee to judge the plowing contest, and wrote a poem, "The Ploughman," for it. He opened the fair with a little address full of self-deprecating humor. His clear tenor voice carried well; it was a good voice for singing and recitation.

The doctor and Mrs. Holmes built a spacious, generous house in Pittsfield. They called their property "Canoe Meadow," because a mark on the original deed seemed to show that Indians had used it as a resting place. Bay windows and dormers made cozy corners within the house. The floors were intricate parquetry, the walls paneled wood. Sunlight streamed generously through the windows.

The house sat on a knoll, and the veranda looked over a broad sweep of lawn to the Housatonic. Down the slope toward the river, the doctor built a reflecting pool and installed fountains with water jets. He built a grape arbor. Behind the house, he put a little clubhouse for billiards. He built a barn and kept a carriage and horses.

The expenses of maintaining this country establishment rose steadily, and the doctor expanded his lecture schedule accordingly. He could not bear to think of parting with the Pittsfield farm. He loved the big trees on the land, particularly an immense white pine that rose in front of his house. He went about the farm with a length of string in his pocket, to measure the thick boles of the biggest trees: "It amused me to see how meek one of the great swaggering elms would look when it saw the fatal measure begin to unreel itself. . . . I call all trees mine that I have put my wedding ring on, and I have as many tree-wives as Brigham Young has human ones."[13]

Wendie, too, loved Canoe Meadow. He remembered long afterward the granite rocks in the bright sun and the thorny dark-leaved barberry bushes. He fished in the river, among the tumbled rocks, and walked in the woods. The trees were chestnut, elm, birch, white pine, and hemlock. Their colors were luminous green, yellow, and brown. The sky was transparent blue.

> I am out of doors almost all the time, I row a good deal, and sometimes fish. Mr. Noble, the man who hires the farm, has some wheat, the seed of which came from Michigan. . . . We have a variety of birds out here, such as the red tail hawk, the hen hawk, wild ducks & pigeons, red headed wood peckers, Kingfishers, and smaller birds. Also of beasts such as Otters, Foxes, Woodchucks, Rabbits, Muskrats, Weasels.[14]

Wendie was learning to draw. He sat patiently in the doorway one afternoon, sketching a stone that pushed up out of the lawn, spotted with moss and shaped oddly like a lion's head; he tried to see and to capture its surprisingly profuse detail.[15]

> [Wendie] shoots, fishes, swims, draws. . . . Amelia, my next, is ten years old, is a nice little body, can swim across the Housatonic, and is a clever little scholar without being a wonder. Ned, aet. 7, is something of what we used to call a "buster" — great at practical jokes, red in the face, uproarious, aggressive, indomitable, loud in voice.[16]

On Sunday mornings, the Holmes family went into the village to attend church. On Sunday afternoons, the doctor walked back to the village with some lilies he had waded for on Saturday, and called on Mrs.

Kellogg.[17] The crushing burden of Sunday ennui was lifted; the children were allowed to play outdoors.

In the village, an old cart path divided around a great elm in Park Square. The tree, shattered by lightning and dying, still rose darkly in the center of the green. To the south, the delicate white steeple of the Congregational church, straight and logical and graceful, rose higher than the trees, and seemed to float in the white sunshine, a mysterious reflection of the shattered elm. The Herman Melvilles lived at Arrowhead Farm, three-quarters of a mile away; Wendie once came upon the gruff, taciturn Melville in the study at Canoe Meadow, consulting the doctor about his uncertain health.[18] The Nathaniel Hawthornes were nearby in Lenox.

For seven years, from 1849 until 1856, the Holmeses returned to Pittsfield every summer. They were never happier than at Pittsfield in those years. Life passed in a slow rhythm of alternation between country and city, bright summer and dark winter.

Boston meant a return to Sundays and to school. When he was twelve, Wendie left Mr. Sullivan's school, and went to Epes Sargent Dixwell's, across the Common. Mr. Dixwell, who was a Cambridge neighbor and friend of John Holmes's, made Wendie his favorite. But school did not count for much. Wendie's education was conversation and books; school was only a chance to be among other boys. Henry Adams, who was two years ahead of Wendie at Mr. Dixwell's school, said: "Most school experience was bad. . . . Boston at that time offered few healthy resources for boys or men. The bar-room and the billiard room were more familiar than parents knew."[19]

Wendie was thin and awkward, and shrank from new things. He did not learn to skate or to ride. He often waited for Mr. Dixwell after school and walked home across the Common with him, his hand in the older man's. His rebellious energy, like his father's, flowed into a stream of talk; Wendie's report card said, "Talks too much."[20]

The doctor was away a great deal in the winter evenings, giving lectures. These had become more profitable than his medical practice, and at last the doctor gave up the practice of medicine entirely — and with relief. Wendie remembered the day his "Governor" brought in the shingle that hung outside their house on Montgomery Place and sawed off the "Dr." so that it read only, "O. W. Holmes."[21]

When he was at home, the doctor presided over meals. The family were a nest of wrens; he and the children all talking at once. The doctor himself was a jolly, chirpy little man, whom friends often compared to a jackdaw, a hummingbird, a bumblebee.[22] The children, too, chattered on, each talking without listening to the others. The doctor enjoyed the talk and would give any of the children an extra helping of marmalade if he or she said anything clever.

'Melia and Ned talked loudly, but the doctor's attention was most often turned to his eldest son. Father and son had begun their rivalry, and, like Samuel Johnson, whom he admired, Dr. Holmes talked for victory. A visitor remembered:

> Holmes [talked] very nearly all the time. . . . There is a curious effect while he is conversing with you — arising from his continual *surprises* of thought and construction. He travels telegraph — . . . while you think him stagecoaching at your side — coming out upon you at every stopping-place.[23]

As Wendie grew older, he learned to hold his ground; but he was always under assault. A nephew remembered the two men years later: "I used to see both of them, sometimes together and sometimes separately, at least once a week, and heard the most brilliant conversation that I have ever heard or expect to hear, with absolutely fair give and take."[24]

But it was not always fair. The doctor teased Wendie about his appearance, especially his boyish, long thin neck. "The stately neck is manhood's manliest part: / It takes the lifeblood freshest from the heart," the doctor crowed. Great lawyers and orators, the doctor said, had thick necks: "You remember what they tell of William Pinckney, the great pleader: how in his eloquent paroxysms the veins of his neck would swell and his face flush and his eyes glitter, until he seemed on the verge of apoplexy."[25]

Wendell, with his thin neck, would never make an orator or a lawyer, his father said. Wendell became sensitive about his appearance, and the doctor could not resist teasing him about it.

> Was there ever a person in the room with you, marked by any special weakness or peculiarity, with whom you could be two hours and not touch the infirm spot? I confess the most frightful tendency to do just this thing. If a man has a brogue, I am sure to catch myself imitating it. If another is lame, I follow him, or worse than that, go before him, limping. . . .
>
> I have been worried to know whether this was owing to some innate depravity of disposition on my part, some malignant torturing instinct.[26]

Mrs. Holmes eased the tension. Wendie was her favorite, and he and she were set apart a little from the rest of the family. She and Wendie were tall, broad-shouldered, long-limbed. When the family stood together for a photograph she sat, or leaned and bent her knees under her full skirts, to conceal her height. Her face was full of life, but plain — eyes a little close together, long upper lip, square jaw, wide full mouth.

In the evenings, Mrs. Holmes would stare fondly at her son, admiring his handsome gray eyes, his thick shock of brown hair. When he was away from home, she sent little reports to him of their life.

> Mr. Emerson's lectures are just over & have been much liked — And now three times a week the ladies [go] to Prof. Blot to learn how to cook — & a great big French woman stands with her huge carving knife — her pots & pans — & carries out all his teachings — Then the ladies rush with their spoons to try his delicious compounds — come home — & try to be French cooks themselves. We may improve, but you will find us I think much as you left us.[27]

> Yesterday we had another pleasant word about you. . . . Perhaps you don't care for any pleasant words, you used to profess entire indifference to them — but your mother cares for them & is always made happy by them — ![28]

> There are 4 pictures of you on my writing table, and yet I cannot recall you — I mean the whole of you — just as you look when you dance into the breakfast room — & kiss me. . . .[29]

The moral upbringing of the children was left to Mrs. Holmes. She was no more orthodox than her husband, but she had strong views about duty. She taught her son to accomplish something each day. She was an Abolitionist, and refused to consider such questions complicated. Slavery was an evil, and must be eradicated. The preachers of Abolition — Charles Sumner, William Lloyd Garrison, Charles Francis Adams — were great figures in Wendie's life; cold, hard, solitary, determined men, he remembered them.[30] "The Abolitionists had a stock phrase that a man was either a knave or a fool who did not do exactly as they . . . *knew* to be right."[31] They preached defiance of the Fugitive Slave Law and even dissolution of the Union if necessary to free it of the slave-holding states.

The doctor was not an Abolitionist. The Constitution recognized slavery, and required that runaway slaves be returned. If slavery was an evil — and it was — the remedy was to be sought peacefully and lawfully. But Mrs. Holmes, when the time came, was prepared even for war.

> It is very hard to have our sons and brothers go off [to war], but we would not keep them at home if we could. I long ago learned that there is no happiness to be had in this world by avoiding duty. The sting of conscience never dies. I am now fearing that the manliness of the North is dying out, that there is nothing worth preserving among us. The rich are daily, hourly, almost, growing richer, and these big bags of gold fill their eyes and thoughts. . . . The antislavery feeling is not strong enough to conquer these fabulous fortunes that are rising up among us.[32]

A young black man, known as Shadrach, was arrested in Boston in 1850, charged with being an escaped slave, and taken before a federal magistrate.

> The doors [of the courtroom] which had been locked were suddenly burst open by a mob of negroes, the officers guarding them kicked, cuffed, and knocked about. . . .[33]

> . . . Down the steps came two huge negroes, bearing the prisoner between them, with his clothes half torn off, & so stupefied by the sudden rescue & violence of his dragging off that he almost sat down, & I thought had fainted, but the men seized him, & being powerful fellows, hurried him through the Square into Court St., where he found the use of his feet, & they went off toward Cambridge, like a black squall, the crowd driving along with them and cheering as they went. It was all done in an instant, & so successful was it that not only was no negro arrested, but no attempt was made at pursuit.[34]

The following April, another fugitive was captured and tried, and Chief Justice Lemuel Shaw chained the doorway of the courthouse. There were riots, but efforts to free the escaped slave failed, and he was returned to his owner. Again, in 1854, Abolitionists besieged the courthouse, and knocked down the door, but they were repulsed. Wendie, in his bedroom six blocks from the courthouse, may have heard the disturbances in the street; young Thomas Wentworth Higginson — "Bully Hig," who led in snowball fights on the Common — came to the doctor's door with his head bandaged.

But Wendie was still a schoolboy, and at home. He was drawing well and had begun to engrave in wood. He haunted the Old Corner Bookstore, and his principal companions were books and engravings.

At teatime, there was often company. Sometimes the literary men called. William Ticknor and James Fields, the publishers, and the historians William Prescott and John Lothrop Motley visited. The poets James Russell Lowell and Henry Wadsworth Longfellow came in from Cambridge. Ralph Waldo Emerson came often from Concord. To Wendie, he became "Uncle Waldo."

Emerson was tolerant of the Abolitionists. In his own youth his circle had been radicals, and Emerson was never troubled by contradictions. The world was a harmony of disparate ideas. At teatimes, at the Holmes household, when the children chattered and the doctor dominated the table, Emerson was composed and smiling and often silent. His silence and composure made a center, around which the room seemed to revolve. "O you jug without a handle!" someone cried out to him as he brimmed up with himself, self-determined.

No one affected Wendell so much or so strongly as this smiling visitor: "I saw him on the other side of the street and ran over and said to him: 'If I ever do anything, I shall owe a great deal of it to you,' which was true. He was one of those who set one on fire."[35]

3

EDUCATION

THE FIRST DEATH TO TOUCH WENDELL WAS HIS GRANDFATHER Charles Jackson's. The old scholar and judge died in 1855, when Wendell was fourteen.

In that same year, Dr. Holmes began to be famous. He had written a paper long before, in 1843, early in his medical practice, and published it in the short-lived little journal of the Boston Society for Medical Improvement. The subject of the paper was puerperal fever — childbed fever — which killed many women after childbirth. The disease would sweep through lying-in hospitals with devastating effect; mortality would sometimes rise to one hundred percent. A few doctors had begun to notice that the disease was carried from bed to bed on doctors' unwashed hands and bloody instruments. Young Dr. Holmes, fresh from his scientific training in Paris, carefully collected evidence that seemed to prove childbed fever was indeed a contagious disease, transmitted by doctors themselves.

In Europe, Ignaz Semmelweis published the same conclusion and was not content to let the matter rest, but traveled and spoke and fought for his discovery. His doctrine began to make headway against the angry denials of the older doctors, and by 1855 was widely accepted in Boston.

Dr. Holmes republished his own early paper, then, was bitterly attacked by the die-hards of the old order and praised by the more modern doctors. For the first time, his name became known outside Boston.

His new prominence as a medical scientist contrasted oddly with his popular lectures. He continued on the Lyceum circuit, sprinkling his talks with light verse and seemingly uncontrollable joking. In a lecture in New York City, he attacked Boston's temperance agitators and Abolitionists with acid humor that was gleefully exaggerated in the reports that eventually found their way home. Someone offered Harvard a substantial gift to endow the doctor's professorship — on condition that the occupant of the chair be prohibited from giving Lyceum lectures. The university declined the gift, but the doctor did give up most of his lectures.[1] The constant travel was affecting his health, in any case, and bringing on attacks of his chronic asthma. His income was much reduced, and with deep regret he sold Canoe Meadow:

> I couldn't bear to think of it or to speak of it for a long time. I loved the trees, and while our children were little it was a good place for them; but we had to sell it; and it was better in the long run, although I felt lost without it for a great while.[2]

The comfortable pattern of life in which his children had been raised began to shift and break up.

When a few Boston and Cambridge men met in 1857 to talk over the founding of a new literary magazine, the doctor was invited to join them. He suggested a name for the new magazine — *The Atlantic Monthly* — and became one of its first and most popular contributors. What he had expected to be only a modest new source of income to replace the Lyceum lectures became worldwide fame.

Until then, the doctor's literary efforts had been casual and sporadic. He had not even troubled to keep copies of his lectures or most of his verse. Now, however, at the age of forty-eight, he found his voice. As Emerson remarked: "Holmes came out late in life, with a strong, sustained growth for two or three years, like old pear trees which have done nothing for ten years, and at last begin to grow great."[3]

Essays seemed to pour from Holmes's pen. They appeared in *The Atlantic Monthly* each month, under the heading "The Autocrat of the Breakfast-Table." His own Boswell, the doctor recorded his breakfast and tea-table talk, interlarded with poetry, stories, jokes, and verse. He invented a boardinghouse breakfast table, and seated around it his neighbors and family. Among them was an earnest, slender, idealistic young man who strongly resembled the doctor's eldest son, to whom the Autocrat addressed a great deal of his conversation.

There is a divinity student lately come among us to whom I
commonly address remarks like the above, allowing him to take a
certain share in the conversation. . . .

The divinity-student looked as if he would like to question my
Latin. . . . He is a rather nice young man, and I think has an appreciation of the higher mental qualities remarkable for one of his
years and training. I try his head occasionally as housewives try
eggs, — give it an intellectual shake and hold it up to the light, so
to speak, to see if it has life in it, actual or potential, or only contains lifeless albumen.[4]

Wendell was sixteen years old, and ready for college, when his father
became the famous Autocrat of the Breakfast Table, displaying in each
month's *Atlantic* the doctor's wit and his son's frailty. The *Autocrat* series
ran for a year and was so successful — in Britain as well as America —
that the doctor went on with "The Professor at the Breakfast-Table." The
continuing series ran monthly through Wendell's first three years in college. The essays were collected into books, and became immense trans-
atlantic successes. The doctor was a celebrity, and Wendell found himself
the son of a famous man: a man as different from modest, retiring
Charles Jackson or silent, composed Emerson as a man could be.

A day before Wendell's sixteenth birthday, the Supreme Court of the
United States decided the Dred Scott case. The court found that Dred
Scott, who was then living in Illinois, was not a citizen of the United
States, entitled to the protection of the federal courts, but only the property of another man in Missouri, to whom he was returned. Federal laws
prohibiting slavery in the new territories were shown to have interfered
with the rights of property; the great compromise that had prevented
civil war over the territories was null.

New England's radical Abolitionists now prepared for war. The mill
owner Abbott Lawrence and other wealthy men organized the New England Emigrant Society to settle the contested Western territories with
antislavery whites. In Kansas, these emigrants founded little armed
towns and tried to make Kansas a free state without the aid of federal
law. Slave-owners tried to drive them off, and at least two hundred people were killed in raids and reprisals.

Thin, dark-haired Tom Higginson, now a Unitarian minister of
Worcester, was one of the stalwarts of the Anti-Slavery Vigilance Committee. A saber cut received in the futile effort, two years before, to rescue an escaped slave had left a scar on his chin. Now he went to Kansas
and smuggled guns to the settlers, carried supplies and propaganda. He
became an agent of the Kansas National Committee and wrote home
from Topeka, "Imagine me patrolling as one of the guard for an hour

every night, in high boots amid the dewy grass, rifle in hand and revolver in belt."[5] A few years later he helped John Brown plan his raid, and still later he led a regiment of black soldiers in the Civil War. He had graceful manners and wrote elegantly; he was one of the scholar-soldiers whom Wendell admired: a gentleman of the Elizabethan mold.

In the autumn of 1857, Wendell left home for the first time, to attend Harvard College. He did not go very far: the college was just across the Charles River from his parents' house. He went by horsecar — the old Fitchburg Railroad branch line had failed in 1855, and a new horsecar line now ran out to Cambridge. The cars were narrow, high-sided wooden affairs, with rounded roofs like scuttles, each drawn by a pair of horses. Straw was spread underfoot, in lieu of cleaning, and the cars were crowded, smelly, and cold on winter mornings.

The college was a few brick buildings around a muddy yard, overshadowed by dark elms. The students lived in three dormitories standing in the yard, plain red-brick Georgian buildings, in which the woodwork was painted white and there was no plumbing. Porters carried water to basins in the rooms, which were used to wash hands and faces; baths in winter were still rare. There was no heat in the dormitories, except an open fire in the common parlors: "In winter the place was ungainly and forlorn . . . the uneven undrained ground would be flooded with rains and half-melted dirty snow one day, and another day strewn with foul ashes over the icy pavements."[6]

The first-year students, however, who were fifteen or sixteen years old, were permitted to live in private rooming houses on the tree-shaded Cambridge streets, where there was a warmer family atmosphere. Wendell lived in a rooming house, with six other boys.[7]

There were fewer than one hundred students in Wendell's class, fewer than four hundred in the college. All wore the same clothes — black coats, white waistcoats, and gray trousers — the boys were disciplined if they wore any other costume. Freshmen could not wear hats or smoke pipes; none of the boys was permitted to smoke in public. In the evenings, they stood about the college yard, had snowball fights, broke windows. It was the duty of the president of the college to subdue the rowdiness. In Wendell's first year, the president was a mild Unitarian minister, James Walker. Dr. Walker taught ethics to the seniors, a course in which he warned them against the irreligious doctrines of Hobbes, Spinoza, Hume, Bentham, and Adam Smith. Deaf and arthritic, he reluctantly hobbled out into the yard when told there was noise. The students shouted, "Heads out!" when he came.[8]

Sophomores "hazed" the freshmen; throughout his first semester Wendell, like other new students, was threatened with humiliations, was insulted if he ate in a place from which freshmen were barred, wore a forbidden hat, or smoked a pipe. In his first and second years there were bloody football matches between the sophomores and freshmen, which became so violent that the faculty stopped them.

Each day of school began with chapel exercises at seven. At first, these were held in the college's little chapel in University Hall; then, in Wendell's second year, Appleton Chapel was completed and services were moved there. The minister was Frederic Huntington, who restored some of the old ritual, but he soon left the Unitarian church in Cambridge and became an Episcopalian in New York City. Services then reverted to sermons and Bible reading, unrelieved by any High Church embellishments.

Classes were held after morning chapel until nine in the evening: Latin, Greek, Greek history, mathematics, rhetoric, English literature. French and German were recent additions to the curriculum, offered without credit. Class hours were taken up with recitations; the boys stood one after another to answer questions on the day's work, just as they had in school. Each boy was graded for his recitation; at the end of the year there were oral examinations before the College Visitors. In Wendell's second year, written examinations began; teachers were permitted to lecture in their classes and substitute written examinations for a part of the recitation, but the older teachers disliked this innovation.

There were, however, lectures in science. Louis Agassiz, the Swiss naturalist who had come to Cambridge ten years before, disregarded much of the discipline, and lectured entertainingly on geology. But he was unusual:

> The competent and learned instructors did not give us of their best, but having listened to our stumbling recitations and inscribed an estimate of our blunders, would then withdraw to the congenial companionship of erudite neighbors, contented if collegiate discipline had been reasonably secured.[9]

There was a small contingent of Southerners at Harvard — three in Wendell's class — who left later, when civil war loomed. They had come from estates in slave-holding country, and spoke with the habit of command; they were gentlemen, had graceful manners, were charming and quick to quarrel. The code of the duel was part of their background; their coarse talk about adventures with slave women shocked Wendell. Beacon Hill's opinion was that Southerners had breeding but not brains; "strictly speaking, the Virginian had no intellect," Henry Adams said. But they shared with the New England boys a passion for chivalry.

Poetry reading was a gentlemanly entertainment, and Tennyson was a rising star. Emerson had arranged to have *The Lady of the Lake* published in Boston; in 1859, when *Idylls of the King* was published, young men and women were ravished by it, Wendell among them. King Arthur's court was fixed in their imaginations, as the spiritual ancestor of

Boston's aristocracy. Lord Byron was an idol, dissolute and glorious, thoroughly disapproved of by their elders.

It was curious that the revival of medieval chivalry came simultaneously with a flourishing of science. Just as Wendell came to Harvard, the new sciences swept over it. Boylston Hall was built in 1857–1858, to house the anatomical museum that Jeffries Wyman was assembling, where casts of the Venus de Milo, the Venus de Medici, and the discus thrower were added to the Anatomy Museum collection, beside the skeleton of a mastodon unearthed in New Jersey. A chemistry laboratory and lecture rooms were housed in this new building. In that same year, Francis Calley Gray left fifty thousand dollars, which Louis Agassiz captured and brought to Harvard, to establish a museum of natural history. These were immense enterprises for the little Unitarian college, still ruled by ordained ministers.

Science meant close observation and careful analysis. In the patterns of data, in the arrangement of species or the stratification of rocks, one could see the working of hidden principles and the progress of evolution. Wyman and Gray were already evolutionists and corresponded with Charles Darwin.

To Wendell, the new method was all-encompassing. "History should be the finest . . . the all comprehending study," Wendell exclaimed.[10] He meant that history should be the record of the movement of great submerged forces. The new science was sweeping away the religion and slavery of more primitive ages. Wendell began to write:

> And now some begin to say, Why is this so? Is it true that such ideas as this come from God? Do men own other men by God's law? And when these questions are asked around us, — when we, almost the first of young men who have been brought up in an atmosphere of investigation, instead of having every doubt answered, "It is written," — when we begin to enter the fight, can we help feeling it is a tragedy?[11]

In Wendell's first year, he was cautious. He was not punished, and did not distinguish himself. His rank at the end of the year was barely in the first third of a class whose lower ranks were all but illiterate.

He did make friends, above all with Norwood Penrose Hallowell — Pen — from Philadelphia, a savage Abolitionist, a fighting Quaker, who blushed at his own militancy, intolerant of criticism or opposition, but the most absolutely generously gallant spirit Wendell had ever met: "an inspirer of a man's ideals."[12] Mrs. Holmes welcomed Pen to their house. The Hallowells returned her hospitality, and Wendell visited them in Philadelphia during the holidays.[13]

After his first year, life was freer. Wendell began smoking a pipe and joined in the drinking parties. Classes, although long, were not difficult.

For the first time, Wendell was his own master for a large part of the day and night. Freedom was a tremendous novelty.

> College is [a] perfect delight, nothing to hold you down hardly, you can settle for yourself exactly what sort of a life you'll lead. And it's delightful — one night up till one at a fellow's room, the next cosy in your own. In the day, boating, etc. And not too hard (as a general thing) lessons.
>
> Today I've been out to row twice, this afternoon sacrificing History to the fowls [and] afterward reading my lesson over in the class clandestinely.[14]

He continued to draw and to experiment with wood engraving, and found that his skills as a draftsman were a social asset and a door to education. He read John Ruskin, whose first three volumes of *Modern Painters* were exciting the world of art, whose *Elements of Drawing* appeared that year and taught one to see with scientific accuracy and analysis of detail.

Louis Theis, who was assembling a collection of prints for Harvard, befriended Wendell and encouraged his interest in engraving. Theis and he smoked and talked late into the night, and Theis let the young man buy some inexpensive prints for a nascent collection of his own. There was a little print shop on Harrison Avenue, in the South End of Boston, that Wendell also began to haunt. The shop was crammed with all sorts of etchings and engravings, and the shopkeeper, who seemed an old man to seventeen-year-old Wendell, kept cats and wrote poetry.[15] The shopkeeper, too, sat up late with this eager, talkative youth. Wendell smoked his newly acquired pipe, and took away with him a book of the older man's poetry.[16]

Turning over numberless copies of old prints, and talking over his discoveries with Theiss and the shopkeeper, Wendell was pleased to discover that the remarkable images in a few great works that had so impressed him — Holbein's "Dance of Death," Dürer's engravings — "were the incarnations by genius of some great popular tradition."[17] Here was his first glimpse of the subterranean forces of history.

Wendell often visited his grandmother's house, where his Uncle John had taken up a permanent bachelor existence. John Holmes's conversation was milder and more congenial than the doctor's, but not less interesting. The younger brother, in his youth, had gone to sea as a sailor. Wendell sometimes visited late in the evening, after classes, when his grandmother had retired. Uncle and nephew sat up together late, smoked — John smoked vile five-cent cigars, Wendell was fond of recalling, to keep from developing refined tastes — drank, told stories, and enjoyed each other's company.

In his sophomore year, Wendell also found time for young women. To Lucy Hale, he wrote,

> After leaving you . . . I was not extremely voluble and for the next three days at home I am sorry to say was so cross that no one could come within a mile of me and they were glad to get rid of me when I went off to finish my vacation at Beverly. Why, I could do nothing but look at those *flowers* and growl.[18]

She was at a school for women in Hanover, and his flirtation with her, begun in the summer of his freshman year, was carried on by mail.

> Being of a slightly jealous disposition the regulations [of her school] about riding with young gentlemen afford me huge satisfaction. If you knew how the "artist (going-to-be) friend," the young gentleman who drives *fast horses* etc. stick in my memory it might perhaps afford you considerable satisfaction.[19]

In such flirtations, a conquest meant no more than getting the lady's photograph — and Wendell soon had a collection of these. But he delighted as well in breaking through the surface of convention, and he had learned to flatter young women for their intellects. To Lucy Hale he said:

> Now almost all my best friends are ladies and I admire and love ladies' society and like to be on intimate terms with as many as I can get. So long as I write to you like a donkey I never can hope you'll have any real confidence in me but if I write in other terms than those of a silly flirtation I know that you at least could have a good influence on me — When you honestly speak to yourself don't you feel that these flatterers are not those that you would ever speak to about what you really deeply felt? . . . In the little time I have seen you I tell you frankly that you seemed to me to have a good deal of capability as yet unaroused.[20]

Wendell often visited the Cambridge house of Epes Sargent Dixwell, the master of his old school, who had five daughters. The family lived an isolated life, far from the center of Cambridge, and were a little eccentric. There was talk that a nephew had married a Chinese woman.[21] Dixwell, a tall bony man, wore brightly colored clothes: a purple frock coat, green velvet waistcoat, and black and white checkered trousers, which were enough to mark him as artistic. A photograph of Dixwell from this time showed him sitting in a visibly uncomfortable pose, one elbow propped up, his hands clasped, looking a little warily into the camera's eye. He had dark, smoothly waving hair, a high forehead, a fringe of beard around and under his chin, leaving his full mouth bare. His eyes were small and close together, and the little round lenses of his eyeglasses made him seem to squint. His nose was long and thin; rather a plain man, but pleasant looking.

The eldest of the daughters, Fanny, had smooth, dark hair, and resembled her father in many ways. In repose she was a little plain, but her brown eyes were attractive, if closely set, and she was full of energy and sharp wit. She too had artistic inclinations, and talked of studying art. But she was obliged to help care for the younger, prettier daughters, and to share in the management of the house. When Dixwell was away he sent "My love to Fanny, whose works also praise her."

One imagines flurries in the household when the young Harvard student came to visit. Dixwell welcomed him with cheerful condescension and asked about his studies; perhaps about Professor E. A. Sophocles' Greek history class and their neighbor Agassiz's lectures. Mrs. Agassiz had begun a girls' school in the upper rooms of their house, which Clover Hooper was attending; the Emerson girls came by carriage from Concord. During his visits, the Dixwells chattered, and later the younger girls sang and played the piano.

Wendell was a social success. He dined with the Porcellian, which had been his father's club, and caroused with Hasty Pudding as his father had. He was elected poet of his class, and composed a poem for the supper at the end of their sophomore year:

> Two years have passed since fair Harvard received us, —
> Two years touched the face of our smiling young earth, —
> She, who with many a pang has conceived us,
> Two years from now will give some of us birth;
> And we shall love her,
> Our bountiful mother,
> We shall all love her, wherever we go;
> Both for her motherhood,
> And for our brotherhood,
> We shall all love her, wherever we go.[22]

Pen Hallowell was elected president of the Hasty Pudding, and Wendell, secretary and poet. The club ate dinners at Taft's in Boston, recited poetry, and sang songs of varying quality, and drank late into the evening. In the spring, there were boat races; in Wendell's junior year the Harvard crew first tied crimson handkerchiefs around their heads, to set themselves off from the Yale men. Wendell visited the mill girls in Lawrence: "I joined a picnic of the factory hands and on a visit to the factory next day with my classmate who was my host found that we were suspected to be responsible for the nonappearance of a girl that morning. I believe we convinced them of our innocence of any escapade."[23]

He was tall and very thin, not at all athletic, but cheerful, talkative, and self-confident to the point of arrogance, a young man devoted to words, talking when he was not reading. The doctor watched his progress with bemusement: "I am just going to Cambridge to an 'exhibition,' in which Oliver Wendell Holmes speaks a translation . . . of the Apology for Socrates: Master O. W. Holmes, Jr., being now a tall youth, almost six feet high, and a lover of Plato and of art."[24]

Wendell finished his junior year twelfth in his class, a higher rank than he had had before; he was again elected class poet, he was secretary of the Hasty Pudding Club, and one of the three editors of the *Harvard Magazine*. He performed in all of the Hasty Pudding farces in his senior year; he was Sergeant Damme in *The Lady of the Lions*, and Sam in *Raising the Wind*; he played the "respectable gentleman" Ludovico in the "Great Tragico-Comico-Melodramatico Burlesque Othello." He drew the illustrated "shingle" for "Mrs. Jarley's Waxworks," a skillful engraving that was much praised, showing the symbolic remains of a late-night party, presided over by a clown carrying the flag of the class of '61.[25]

The elderly Dr. Walker retired as president of Harvard in Wendell's junior year and was replaced by Cornelius C. Felton, a much-liked man, who was charmed by Wendell's manner and conversation and who made a favorite of him.[26]

That year, still eighteen years old, Wendell prepared to write two essays that would appear simultaneously in the fall. One was on Albrecht Dürer's wood engravings and was to be an essay on art, and one on Plato, which was to be on philosophy.

For the Dürer study, Wendell could draw on years of fascinated study, his own knowledge of the medium, his long hours of browsing among the prints in the South End of Boston, and his long talks with Theis. He knew Dürer from the inside and could reconstruct his engravings intuitively, from the first mark of Dürer's pencil on the wood block.

> ["Melancholy"] is hidden under the curiously crumpling folds of the enveloping garment . . . massive and imposing, but . . . hiding its naked strength under the thousand folds of a disguising fancy. That solitary woman is the true picture of [Dürer's] soul, in its strength and weakness; powerful, but half over come by the very objects of its universal study; crowned with the wreath of the elect, and beautiful with ideal genius, but grave with thought and marked with the care of the world; winged, yet resting sadly on the earth.[27]

For the Plato essay, much more was required, and Wendell began to take books out, one by one, from the Boston Athenaeum. He read Plato's works in English and in Greek, read Grote's *History of Greece* and all the works that he could find by modern followers of Plato.

He went to Emerson, who had first fired his interest in philosophy: "I said to him 'I am going to study Plato.' He said, 'You must hold him at arm's length. You must say, Plato, you have pleased the world for two thousand years; let us see if you can please me.'"[28]

Wendell had read Plato with the expectation that the secrets of life would be revealed. He had been puzzled, and disappointed, to find only a philosophy of ideas. Plato's Socrates seemed to him a big figure, a sort of sportsman of argument, and Plato's stories of Socrates were as evocative as Dürer's engravings. Plato seemed an artist of thought, expressing the philosophy of his age. But Wendell found nothing in Plato that seemed absolute.

On February 20, he borrowed from the Boston Athenaeum R. A. Vaughan's *Hours with the Mystics*. Wendell kept this book with him for a week, and it seemed to him to mark the end of his boyhood and the beginning of his life as a man.[29]

Vaughan talked of philosophy and religion in confident, modern scientific language. Emerson's oriental sages were lightly spoken of — the primitive "Hindoos" and early Yogis and the somewhat less savage Platonists — as steps in a steady progress of evolution. There was nothing fundamentally mysterious in religion, no more than in any subject of investigation. Even mysticism was only a mode of feeling; mystics, like other people, were driven by motives that could be understood and categorized. Religion, like all the organs of life, was evolving.

Wendell's two essays now crystallized into a single, faceted discourse. He saw that Plato and Dürer each expressed the spirit of a prescientific age. Dürer — like all artists of genius — expressed deep, perhaps unconscious, ideals of the human race; the artist's imagery was the voice through which humanity became articulate and conscious. But Dürer's religious imagery belonged to an earlier day and was being displaced by reason. Philosophy, too, had progressed. As Dürer's religion was giving way to a rational system of duty, Plato was being displaced and disproven by physical science. Even Emerson, the modern Plato, Wendell thought, was only an artist, giving voice to the spirit of his time, and not a philosopher, a scientific observer of its progress: "[Emerson] was a poet, and from my point of view, the poet and philosopher are two opposite poles of the conscious life."[30]

Wendell alone would reconcile the poles, would be both artist and philosopher, poet and scientist.

He gave the essay on Plato to Emerson. But Emerson only said, "When you strike at a king, you must kill him."[31]

PART II

THE
TWENTIETH
REGIMENT

4

SWIMMING

IN AIR

BRAHAM LINCOLN WAS ELECTED PRESIDENT OF THE UNITED
States on Tuesday, November 6, 1860, with forty percent of the
popular vote. He would not take office until March of the following year.

In the interval, delegates to Congress met in Washington, in the lobby
of the old Willard Hotel near the White House and in shabbier rooming
houses, searching for compromise. The unfinished dome of the Capitol
was a metaphor floating over the muddy fields.

In South Carolina, a popularly elected convention of white men declared the federal Constitution dissolved and offered to meet with other
seceding states to form a new national government.

In Boston, the talk was still of preserving the federal union. Dr.
Holmes wrote a condescending poem for *The Atlantic* addressed to the
secessionists, "Brother Jonathan's Lament for Sister Caroline":

> *She has gone, — she has left us in passion and pride, —*
> *Our stormy-browed sister, so long at our side!*[1]

At Harvard, the faculty and students were mildly Whiggish or
entirely detached from political affairs. The most active were the

quarter of the student body who were Know-Nothings — nativist bigots.

The term drew to its end, and the Hasty Pudding Club had its farewell dinner on January 11, at Porter's. The menu was goose, roast chicken, game birds, turkeys, oysters. Pen Hallowell presided and the young men sang Wendell's song:

> *So fill to the brim your glasses, my boys,*
> *And with hearts all joyous and free,*
> *Drink a health to the Club that we're leaving —*
> *Drink a health to our old H.P.C.*[2]

In Washington, conciliation was failing. Radicals on both sides called for secession or war. Wendell Phillips, Holmes's cousin, was a leading speaker for the Radical Abolitionists. He called for Abolition at all costs, for disunion, for war to abolish slavery. Respectable Boston shunned him. In December, 1860, on the anniversary of John Brown's rebellion, Wendell Phillips tried to address the Abolitionists' convention. A "broadcloth mob" of well-dressed men — merchants, bankers, tradesmen, the men whose livelihoods depended on the prosperity of railroads and cotton mills — occupied the hall, elbowed the Abolitionists off the platform, and conducted the meeting themselves. When they were done, the Abolitionist chairman returned to the platform, but he was shouted down, and when he tried to continue, police broke up the meeting.[3]

Two weeks later, the Abolitionists met again, in the Music Hall, and were better prepared for trouble. Wendell Phillips this time reached the platform. With Boston police keeping order, and protected by an armed bodyguard, Phillips gave a deliberately insulting speech — "Mobs and Education" — addressed to his opponents. Afterward there was a near riot. The police had difficulty getting Phillips out of the hall and through the shouting crowd in the streets. In the following days his life was repeatedly threatened.

For a third time, the Abolitionists announced a meeting at which Phillips was to give an address: on January 24, in Tremont Hall. Richard Hallowell, Pen's older brother, organized a new bodyguard. Wendell Holmes joined it, and carried a billy club.[4]

Emerson had agreed to address the meeting, to stand beside Phillips, and see that he was heard.

The meeting of the Anti-Slavery Society began on the morning of January 24. Volunteer guards were stationed at the ends of the speakers' platform, where stairs led up from the floor. The gallery opposite the platform was filled by the broadcloth rioters, who kept up a steady disorder. When the business of the society was concluded and the speeches began, the mob in the gallery drowned out every word by shouting.

Emerson tried to speak, but could not be heard. In his diary for the day he wrote:

> Do the duty of the day. Just now, the supreme public duty of all thinking men is to assert freedom. Go where it is threatened & say, "I am for it, & do not wish to live in the world a moment longer than it exists."
>
> [Wendell] Phillips has the supreme merit in this time, that he & he alone stands in the gap & breach against the assailants. Hold up his hands. He did me the honor to ask me to come to the meeting at Tremont Temple, &, esteeming such an invitation a command, though sorely against my inclination & habit, I went, and though I had nothing to say, showed myself. If I were dumb, yet I would have gone & mowed & muttered or made signs.[5]

At college, the Southern students went home for the winter vacation, and did not return. "It [is] sad to think we must break so many of our social ties and part with our best friends all on account of a lot of *damned Niggers*," Wendell's classmate William Bartlett wrote in his diary on January 10, shortly before he himself enlisted in the New England Guard.[6]

A few of the Massachusetts men at Harvard began putting in their names for this unit of militia, informally known as the "Fourth Battalion." Bill Bartlett joined early in 1861, as did Henry Abbott — "Little" Abbott — and his brother Edward. Little Abbott was a year ahead of Wendell and was studying law. By April, Pen Hallowell and Wendell had put in their names. William Putnam and James Jackson Lowell, in their first year at the law school, joined them.

From January through March, six more Southern states seceded. Massachusetts began to arm. Henry Adams's father, Congressman Charles Francis Adams, came home from Washington, all attempted compromises having foundered in bitterness. There would be war between the states — between what were now plainly two rival confederations — for power over the Western territories, and ultimately over the continent. "Whether we are called two confederacies or one, the question of slavery in the Territories has got to be settled by war, and so has the possession of the Mississippi and the Gulf of Mexico."[7]

The President took office and quickly ordered that the federal government's Fort Sumter, in South Carolina — now claiming to be an independent nation — be reprovisioned. On April 12, South Carolina fired on the fort. On April 14 it fell, and on April 17 Lincoln called for the loyal states to send 75,000 militia troops to the aid of the federal government.

Massachusetts militia regiments began assembling in Boston. Four regiments were ordered to Washington, fighting their way through crowds in Baltimore. The Sixth Massachusetts Regiment suffered casualties on the march. Fighting had begun, and Wendell's friends waited for the Fourth Battalion to be called.

"We believed in the principle that the Union is indissoluble," Wendell recalled. "Many of us, at least, also believed that the conflict was inevitable, and that slavery had lasted long enough."[8]

He had been a thin and fearful child, and his father was amused at the young intellectual's war fever:

> Even our poor "Brahmins" — . . . pallid, undervitalized, shy, sensitive creatures, whose only birthright is an aptitude for learning — even these poor New England Brahmins of ours . . . count as full men, if their courage is big enough for the uniform which hangs so loosely about their slender figures.[9]

Their friend John Lothrop Motley wrote when he heard that Wendell was enlisting:

> It is a noble and healthy symptom that brilliant, intellectual, poetical spirits like his spring to arms when a noble cause like ours inspires them. The race of Sir Philip Sidney is not yet extinct, and I honestly believe that as much genuine chivalry exists in our Free States at this moment as there is or ever was in any part of the world, from the Crusaders down.[10]

For the first time in eighty years, Beacon Hill felt its honor and its interests engaged in a war. But it was not prepared for fighting.

Wendell often referred in later years to their naive idea of a gentleman strolling, as if down the steps of the State House on a sunny afternoon, after a good dinner, pulling on his gloves, to ride into battle on the Common:

> When I went to war I thought that soldiers were old men. I remembered a picture of the revolutionary soldier . . . a white-haired man with his flintlock slung across his back. I remembered one or two living examples of revolutionary soldiers whom I had met, and I took no account of the lapse of time.[11]

But, however unsuited and unprepared they were, for Wendell Holmes like the others, "the war was of a character which left no choice to a man of his condition."[12]

If Southern gentlemen enlist, Northern gentlemen must also.[13]

He talked with his parents before enlisting. The doctor thought it would be better for Wendell to finish school before going into the army, but Wendell had little patience for such calculation, and his mother thought it right to go immediately.[14]

But the Fourth Battalion had not yet been called, and while Wendell waited he continued the routine of college life, impatiently. He and some friends had too much to drink in a college room, and one of them pitched a brick through a hall window.

Cornelius Felton, president of the college, wrote to his friend and dining club companion Dr. Holmes on April 23, as if Fort Sumter had not fallen, as if the boys were not now going to fight, as if the world were not convulsed:

> I regret to inform you that your son has incurred a censure for being engaged in breaking the windows of a member of the Freshman Class. Ordinarily this is regarded as a very high offense; but in this case the Faculty were happy that they were able to treat it as of a character less serious than usual. . . . I have to add that your son incurred an additional admonition for repeated and gross indecorum in the recitation room of Professor Bowen. I hope he will not persist in this inconsiderate conduct, now that he is near the end of his course. He is an excellent young man; but of late, under some influence to which he has not heretofore yielded, his conduct has been frequently the subject of complaint.[15]

Two days later, on Thursday, April 25, the men who had put their names in for the Fourth Battalion were told to report to the Boston Armory. Bill Bartlett went that morning to say good-bye to President Felton, but Wendell did not trouble himself to take leave from the college. Dr. Holmes went in his place to Felton's office that morning to explain and apologize.

Wendell went to the armory at noon, and with the other men volunteered for guard duty and training at Fort Independence, on Castle Island in Boston Harbor. At two, they left the armory and took a steamer to the fort.[16]

Tom Higginson described the feelings of the young men:

> Those of us whose fortunate lot it was to enlist in the army, during that magic epoch of adventure . . . will never again find in life such a strange excitement as that when they first put on uniform and went into camp. It was a day absolutely broken off from all that had gone before it. To say that it brought a sense of utter novelty, is nothing; the transformation seemed as perfect as if, by some suddenly revealed process, one had learned to swim in air, and were striking out for some new planet. The past was annihilated, the future was all.[17]

The fort was dirty and cold, and the men slept twelve to a room. Meals were monotonous — salt meat or ham, bread and coffee, served in basins from which the men fed with their hands — "rather disgusting," Bill Bartlett wrote in his diary. But Wendell was happy and did not complain. "Send me of the fat of the land," he wrote cheerfully to his mother. "Several *lbs.* of butter would be a good thing — also fresh meat, olives &c."[18]

Their main occupation was drilling. The twelve-man squads in their Zouave uniforms, copied from the French North African corps — dark blue tunics, red caps, and baggy pale blue pantaloons — drilled for two hours each day, and then the squads joined into companies to drill for four hours more; then dress parade again, supper, lights out, and turns at guard duty.

Infantry traveled in columns, but they would fight in "line" — in two ranks, shoulder to shoulder, the second rank firing over the shoulders of the first as they reloaded their muskets. Drilling taught the men to deploy in lines at various angles to the line of march, and then, still in line, to swing about, and to advance or retreat. They repeated these movements over and over, from marching column to double rank of muskets and bayonets. They drilled until the movements became natural and habitual.

On May 1, Wendell wrote to his mother, to say that he was well and enjoying himself. Two messmates had cut his hair short, and he enclosed a little sketch to show his bristling scalp and his faintly bristling new mustache. There was a cannonade at the fort, to salute Mr. Charles Francis Adams, sailing for England as the new United States ambassador and taking his son Henry with him.

Parties of visitors came to the fort in the evenings. Parents, Dr. Holmes among them, came with provisions, drinks, clothes, gossip. On Monday, May 20, a crowd of young women came over on the steamer and presented the battalion with a flag.

By Saturday, May 25, their drilling done, the Fourth Battalion cleaned their quarters, packed their knapsacks, and marched in good order onto the *Nelly Baker,* the steamer that had brought them, a disorderly mass of young men, and gave a cheer for their drillmaster, old Sergeant Pass, as they pulled away toward Boston.

At Long Wharf, the streets were lined with spectators, and the men marched to the Common to the sound of cheers and applause. The Fourth Battalion maneuvered on the Common, to more applause, marched back to the armory, and was dismissed.

The United States had no standing army. At the outbreak of war, there were only 12,000 federal troops, in a nation of thirty million. Ultimately, a million and a half men would serve the Union cause, but it took years of effort in the midst of war to make a national army. At first, the state militias had been called up, but their moment was already past;

the Fourth Battalion was disbanding, and the young men, Wendell among them — their military experience consisting of one month's drilling as privates — vied for officers' commissions in the new federal army.

Many of the Harvard men were going into the Twentieth Massachusetts Volunteer Infantry Regiment. The Twentieth was organized by William R. Lee, a civil engineer from Roxbury, a West Point graduate, who would be its colonel. He chose for his lieutenant colonel Francis Palfrey, known as Frank, a Harvard man.

Frank Palfrey brought the other Harvard men to the Twentieth. Bill Bartlett and John Putnam were to be captains. Pen Hallowell, Willy Putnam, and Little Abbott were to be lieutenants. But Wendell — who seemed frail and had not displayed any special aptitude as a soldier — heard nothing.

A cousin of Wendell's mother, Henry Lee — as an aide to the governor he bore the courtesy title of colonel — was called on to help. In May, Wendell met him walking across the Harvard campus and asked him to intervene; he said he would. Still, however, nothing happened.

The Fourth Battalion had broken up; the Harvard seniors who had enlisted returned to college to take their final examinations and to graduate. Wendell had been elected class poet for the Class Day exercises on June 21. Pen was elected orator, and Wendell delivered his poem, as he had trained in the Fourth Battalion, at the side of his friend Pen Hallowell.

Until late in July, Wendell waited for a commission. Father and son were together more in this month of waiting than they had been for some time.[19] Dr. Holmes gave his son a bottle of laudanum for pain, that he might take all at once to avoid a painful death. Wendell carried the bottle in his pocket in his first battle.[20]

Eventually, the doctor must have gone to see the governor, for on July 12, he went to Readville, where the Twentieth was in camp, carrying a letter from the governor's military secretary, A. J. Browne, saying that the governor would be pleased to see a commission granted.[21] Yet still Wendell heard nothing.

The war now began in earnest. On July 21, hastily organized Union forces attacked the Southern army in Virginia, hoping for a quick, decisive victory. But the battle of Bull Run was a disaster for the Union. Untrained federal troops panicked and were routed; there were 2,300 casualties.

The newly formed regiments were going south. Wendell at last learned that he would receive a commission in the Twentieth and had himself photographed in officer's uniform, sword across his knee, looking frail and thin. He was more than six feet tall and weighed 130 pounds.

But the waiting continued. When at last an order came, Wendell was sent to Pittsfield for about a month, to recruit volunteers for the regiment. Bill Bartlett, who had been promised a captaincy in the Twentieth, was in Pittsfield then as well, directing the recruitment. They were trying to fill up Bartlett's company.[22]

Wendell was very much at home in Pittsfield. He made his headquarters at the Kelloggs' elm-shaded house, with wisteria vines climbing the columns of their front porch. Carolyn Kellogg, little Carrie, who was then nine years old, remembered Wendell's arrival. The young officer, who seemed godlike to the little girl, brought his bags into the parlor and made his recruiting station there.[23]

Wendell took Carrie for drives in the Kelloggs' phaeton, along the familiar roads, and attended the school "tableaux" in which she appeared. On the Kelloggs' front porch, Wendell would smoke an evening cigar and talk to the little girl. She kept in her private box of treasures the last cigar Wendell smoked before leaving.[24]

In August, the short northern summer ending, Wendell was ordered to his regiment, which was in camp at Readville, less than ten miles from Beacon Hill. Recruits were gathering. Wendell was to be a first lieutenant. The other officers were familiar friends from Boston and Harvard: Lieutenant Colonel Frank Palfrey, Major Paul Revere, Captains John Putnam, Bill Bartlett, Tom Crowninshield, and Harry Tremlett, Lieutenants Pen Hallowell and Little Abbott, James Lowell, and Willy Putnam. Twenty-eight-year-old Harry Tremlett, who had commanded Wendell at Fort Independence, was now his captain in Company A, where Charles Whittier was second lieutenant.

The noncommissioned officers and soldiers were workmen from Boston and had Irish and German names. Two companies, both officers and men, were entirely made up of German-speaking immigrants; the officers of these companies had fought in Europe in 1848.

The Harvard officers cultivated luxuriant mustaches, in the English style, and had personal servants. The Germans complained that "the Regiment was officered by young men, belonging to a certain aristocratic clique." A fellow Massachusetts officer, Colonel Charles Devens of the Fifteenth Regiment, warned Frank Palfrey, "The sooner you get this blue-blooded notion out of your head, the better for yourself and the Regiment." Governor John Andrew wrote still more bluntly that the Twentieth had become "the private property of a few neighbors, or of a mere clique."[25]

The regiment acquired a flag and a motto: *Fide et constantia.* Mrs. Caleb Chase and other ladies who had come down from Boston presented a beautiful silk standard to the regiment, with that motto embroidered upon it. Men, horses, wagons, drummers, ambulances assembled, an organism stirring into life.

The Seventeenth, Eighteenth, and Nineteenth Massachusetts regiments had moved to the front, and the central recruiting office was now sending all its new men to the Twentieth. On August 12, there had been only 469 enlisted men in the camp; by September 4, the regiment had 750 men, and for the first time received British muzzle-loading Enfield rifles, purchased by a Massachusetts agent in London.[26]

On September 4, the Twentieth at last received its orders to leave for the front. And so hundreds of new recruits, Boston workingmen who had yet to handle rifles, commanded by untrained young men just out of college, boarded the trains and traveled by rail and steamship to Washington.

As an officer, Wendell lived comfortably — *en aristocrate*, he liked to say. He and Whittier shared a servant. They traveled with substantial baggage, and when the regiment stopped overnight in New York, the Harvard officers left the regiment in its barracks and had dinner at Delmonico's.

They arrived in Washington on September 7, tired from their trip. They had left New England in cool autumn, but it was still hot summer in Washington. The regiment marched up Pennsylvania Avenue to Georgetown, passing in review before General Winfield Scott, the general-in-chief of the Union armies, and pitched their tents at Camp Kalorama on the Georgetown heights — in what was then open countryside outside Washington. They had joined the Army of the Potomac, which stood between the federal capital at Washington, and the Confederate capital at Richmond — an army that had already suffered a terrible defeat at Bull Run. At Camp Kalorama, they found their "formidable train of wagons, consisting of twenty-five baggage wagons, two hospital wagons, and five ambulances, with one hundred and twenty-two horses, including those of field and staff [officers]." Wendell discovered that his trunk had been badly dented and his brandy flask smashed.[27]

A substantial part of the Army of the Potomac was assembling at Camp Kalorama. "In every direction were troops — hubbub and confusion — the whole country like one great camp."[28] Wendell wrote home reporting his safe arrival, and sent a poem to his mother that he had composed on the way. She was instructed to show it to his friends.[29]

Just when the regiment had its voluminous baggage sorted and stored, orders came to move again, closer to Washington, to Camp Burnside on Meridian Hill. From the new camp, they could see the broad avenues of Washington City, and the incomplete white dome of the Capitol rising above the trees — "the most beautiful place we have been."[30] The Twentieth joined the Nineteenth Massachusetts and a company of sharpshooters, armed with the new Enfield rifles, in a brigade of about 2,000 men under Brigadier General Frederick W. Lander.

On September 11, there were rumors that the regiment would be moved again, and Wendell heard cannon fire in the distance for much of the day. The next morning, orders came to break camp. The regiment loaded its wagons again, slung knapsacks over shoulders, and set off to cross the Potomac into the Confederacy; but General Lander's aide countermanded their orders when they reached the Potomac, and sent them instead up the near side of the river.

This was the regiment's first march in the field. They traveled with two wagons of baggage for each company, carrying Wendell's trunk, "iron bedsteads, mattresses, mess chests, bathtubs and many other absurdities."[31] They traveled with advance and rear guards, with guns loaded, because there were rumors that rebel cavalry had crossed the Potomac.[32]

After three days' march the regiment reached Poolesville, Maryland, on high ground about three miles east of the Potomac. The river was wide, shallow, and muddy there; it made a broad sweep to the east through open Maryland farming country. Poolesville was at the focus of the river's arc. The regiment again unloaded its wagons and built a camp. Wendell found that his bedstead had been lost.

Lander's brigade had joined a division commanded by General Charles B. Stone, whose headquarters were at Poolesville. Lander assembled his two regiments and his companies of sharpshooters there, on the high tableland in open country, with a view of the distant Blue Ridge Mountains of Virginia. The days were sunny and the nights were growing cold.

The Twentieth arrived on Saturday, September 14, and on the seventeenth, Harry Tremlett's and Bill Bartlett's companies (Wendell with them), were ordered to fall in.

General Lander addressed the two companies. He did not tell them where they were going, only that they had a post of honor and must do their duty.[33]

Wendell packed his carpetbag and marched with the others two miles south to Edwards Ferry — a ford on the Potomac at the bottom of the river's arc. From the ford, they went up the river on the Maryland side, but could not find their post. Solemnity gave way to confusion. They marched back to Edwards Ferry for further directions, and then went off again, at last finding their place above the ford between a battery of artillery and a Minnesota infantry regiment. Wendell wrote:

> In silence we settle in a grove and lie down to pass the night as best may be. I had carried my invaluable carpet bag, Whittier his blankets which we shared. A drizzle and brief rain increased the liveliness of this first experience as groundlings. . . . But we were very tired and slept pretty well.[34]

In the morning light they could see across the river to Virginia, and Wendell saw a Confederate soldier for the first time: "one man in a straw hat sitting unconcernedly on his tail, apparently a guard on duty for the seceshers."[35] They spent the day on picket duty, and in the evening, Wendell wrote to his mother:

It seems so queer to see an encampment & twig men through a glass & think they are our enemies & hear some of our pickets talking across & so on. But I must get some sleep tonight, to make up for last & it gets late. I long for letters — write all of you all the time. The mails are irregular and the last I got was the one containing C. Walton's letter. You ask me if I like letters like yours. I delight in 'em. They are my great pleasure. Remember once for all that all details like those I've written of our actual movements are strictly private as we are strongly forbidden to write of such things. Love to everyone. Bestest love to Dadkin. . .
                                        Goodnight my loveliest & sweetest[36]

The two companies remained on their post from Wednesday to Saturday, quietly encamped and waiting for an attack that did not come. Lookouts regularly climbed into trees and occasionally reported seeing men and horses on the opposite bank. On Friday night, the companies were ordered to sleep in their boots, but nothing happened. On Saturday morning, they were relieved by two new companies and returned to Poolesville.

At the camp they found that a third regiment, the Seventh Michigan, had joined General Lander's growing brigade. Recruits continued to arrive, and noncommissioned officers drilled the men: company drill in the mornings, battalion drill and dress parade in the afternoon. Platoons were taken aside and given practice in shooting their rifles. "Many of them, we found, shut their eyes when they pulled the trigger, and bang went the gun, southeast or northwest as accident determined."[37] There were ambulance drills; the twenty-three men of the regimental band and a man from each company were taught to make tourniquets and to carry men in litters. Some of the officers resigned and were replaced; those who remained began to learn their duties.

On October 2 and 3, fifty men from another brigade, commanded by Colonel Edward D. Baker, came up the river. They were wounded and tired after an unsuccessful foray into Virginia.[38] Baker himself soon followed.

Colonel Edward D. Baker was a political appointee. He had been United States Senator from the new state of Oregon, and was a close personal friend of the President, who had named a son for him. Baker was a theatrically handsome clean-shaven middle-aged man with a high forehead, whose campaign photographs showed him in Napoleonic pose, jaw set and hair blown forward as if by a tempest at his back. He was eager to distinguish himself, but had been sent to Poolesville, where no fighting was expected, and put under the command of regular army officers.

On the morning of October 21, 1861, seven companies, including Wendell's Company A, were detailed to Baker's command, and Wendell along with them was lifted by a wavelet of history and thrown against the Virginia bluffs.

5

SOMEONE HAD BLUNDERED

AFTER BULL RUN, THE PRESIDENT HAD CHARGED GENERAL George B. McClellan — whom the press was calling the "Young Napoleon" — with reorganizing the Army of the Potomac, and with defending the federal capital.

By October of 1861, McClellan had built an army and was beginning to probe across the river into Virginia near Leesburg, well north of the capital, expecting the Confederates to withdraw from this extended position.

Leesburg was a busy rail terminus, a center of freight and troop movements. But it was too far north to be held against renewed federal attack. To protect Leesburg there were only a brigade of infantry and three troops of cavalry under the command of Confederate Brigadier General Nathan D. Evans, a whiskey-drinking regular army officer known as Old Shanks.

On the Maryland side, Federal troops were gathering at Poolesville, where McClellan had sent a division of infantry, in which Wendell now served, under command of General Charles B. Stone. He, too, was a regular army officer, and veteran of the Mexican War. His division was designated a "Corps of Observation," and its principal duty was to observe the withdrawal of Evans's troops from Leesburg and to stand guard on the right flank of the capital city. To this relatively unexciting spot, Colonel — lately Senator — Baker had been assigned.

On October 19, General McClellan, planning to send some troops across the Potomac farther south, telegraphed General Stone at Poolesville to "make some slight demonstration" of his presence opposite Leesburg, hoping by these feints to hasten the Confederate withdrawal.

On October 20, Stone's artillery began shelling across the river, at Edwards Ferry south of Poolesville, as if preparing for a crossing of troops. The Confederate pickets on the opposite bank withdrew from the shelling, and Stone moved a brigade across the river, as if preparing to march on Leesburg from that direction.

Farther to the north, midway up the river's arc, Stone sent a small party across the river to reconnoiter. The Potomac was particularly broad and shallow there as it made its sweep to the east. The Virginia bank, cut away by the river's bend, was a steep bluff about one hundred feet high, known locally as Ball's Bluff. The bluff was rocky and wooded, and so steep that it could not be climbed straight up; a narrow track zigzagged back and forth up its face.

Taking the most direct path, the men rowed across the river and in single file followed the path up Ball's Bluff. They were now in Virginia, in the Confederacy, for the first time. At the top of the bluff they found an open field; ahead of them, below the field, was a wood. The men moved carefully across the field and down a road through the wood, to the crest of a ridge. Open fields fell away before them to Leesburg, clearly visible a mile to the west. They saw what seemed to be the tents of a Confederate encampment shadowed by the setting sun, and in accordance with their orders withdrew and reported.

At ten that night, a messenger reached General Stone at Edwards Ferry, reporting the supposed discovery of a Confederate camp near Ball's Bluff. Stone, in reply, ordered four companies from the Massachusetts Fifteenth to "march silently, under cover of night, to the position of the [Confederate] camp referred to, to attack and destroy it at daybreak."[1]

At 5 A.M. on October 21, the Massachusetts men moved across the river into Virginia, filed up the steep path to the top of Ball's Bluff, and silently camped in the field there until daybreak. Colonel Devens of the Fifteenth then led his men through the wood. Coming out of the wood with the rising sun behind them now, he saw the open fields, broken only by stacks of cornstalks as far as Leesburg. The "Confederate tents" were only the trees of an apple orchard.[2]

Colonel Baker, at this time, had gone to see General Stone, asking for something to do. Stone sent Baker back to take charge of the little band that had crossed at Ball's Bluff, telling him to reinforce the Massachusetts companies already in Virginia or to withdraw them, as he thought best. Stone gave Baker seven additional companies from the Twentieth Massachusetts — Company A among them.

Farther to the south, McClellan had withdrawn his troops from Virginia, but he neglected to tell Stone that the principal part of the feint had been abandoned. And at Ball's Bluff, Confederate cavalry pickets came upon the Massachusetts outpost. There was a brief skirmish; the tiny federal force had been discovered, isolated in enemy territory.

Riding up the Potomac, Colonel Baker met a lieutenant coming down from Ball's Bluff, who told him of the skirmish and the discovery. The lieutenant was excited, and said that the Massachusetts companies were in trouble. Baker hastened forward.

At Ball's Bluff, he found himself in command of a brigade of three regiments and a large part of a fourth — the Twentieth Massachusetts. Thinking that the small group already in Virginia were in trouble, Baker hastily ferried his brigade across the Potomac in rowboats and a scow, and sent them single file up the steep bluff opposite. Expecting a battle now that the advance companies under Devens had been discovered, Baker moved his troops into line.

He prepared his men for battle in the open field, and waited to be attacked there. As troops laboriously filed up the bluff behind them, carrying artillery in pieces up the steep path, the Twentieth Massachusetts took their place in reserve, in the open field at the edge of the bluff.

A mile to the west, outside Leesburg, Confederate General Evans — Old Shanks — had better information about his enemy's movements than they of his. Evans's cavalry had discovered the movement across the river at Ball's Bluff, and he knew that the feint farther south had been abandoned. At 12:30, Evans sent three troops of cavalry and an infantry regiment to attack Devens's little outpost, and Devens, outnumbered, withdrew to the bluff, where he met Baker.

For an hour or two, the wooded ground that Devens had held remained unoccupied; Baker waited with his brigade in the open field, the river at his back.

The Confederates now moved into the woods, and sent their entire force — a brigade of infantry and three troops of cavalry — to attack Baker's brigade. The attack began at 3 o'clock in the afternoon, and by 3:30 the firing was heavy.

The Twentieth Regiment, which was in reserve, lay in the open field at the edge of the bluff, with no cover, as the Confederates fired at them from the woods. Wendell's Company A was at the center of the line, Bill Bartlett's company to their right. Bartlett described that first hour of their first battle:

> Well the first volley came and the bullets flew like hail. . . . The men now began to drop around me; most of them were lying down in the first of it, being ordered to keep in reserve. Those

that were lying down, if they lifted their foot or head it was struck. One poor fellow near me was struck in the hip while lying flat, and rose to go to the rear, when another struck him on the head and knocked him over. I felt that if I was going to be hit, I should be, whether I stood up or lay down, so I stood up and walked around, stepping over them and talking to them in a joking way, to take their thoughts away from the bullets, and keep them more self possessed. I was surprised at first at my own coolness. I never felt better, although I expected of course that I should feel the lead every second, and I was wondering where it would take me. I kept speaking to Little [Abbott], surprised that he was not hit amongst this rain of bullets. I said two or three times *"Why Lit., aren't you hit yet?"* . . . Lit was as cool and brave as I knew he would be. The different companies began to wilt away under this terrible fire.[3]

After an hour of this suffering the Twentieth were ordered to advance, but they made no progress and were slowly driven back toward the river. The Confederates followed, firing.

By six in the evening, the federal troops had all been driven back to the edge of the bluff.

The field now began to look like my preconceived idea of a battle field. The ground was smoking and covered with blood, while the noise was perfectly deafening. Men were lying under foot, and here and there a horse was struggling in death. Coats and guns were strewn in all directions.[4]

Colonel Baker, wandering lost between the forces, was killed. Many of his officers were already dead. The Confederates continued to advance down into the field. A Virginia infantry regiment, at the center of the Confederate line, had exhausted their ammunition; the federal troops were huddled at the edge of the bluff. Old Shanks gave a terse order: "Fix bayonets and run 'em into the river!"

This bayonet charge resulted in fighting of a desperate kind. Many of the Union soldiers were killed by bayonets, "and others, crying for mercy, threw down their arms into the river, and were drowned trying to escape."[5]

A seventeen-year-old Virginia infantryman recalled this final charge:

A kind of shiver ran through the huddled mass upon the brow of the cliff; it gave way, rushed a few steps; then in one wild panic-stricken herd, rolled, leaped, tumbled over the precipice. The descent is nearly perpendicular, with ragged, jutting crags, and water-laved base. Screams of pain and terror filled the air. Men seemed suddenly bereft of reason, they leaped over the cliff with muskets still in their clutch, threw themselves into the river without divesting themselves of their heavy accoutrements, hence went to the bottom like lead. Others sprang down upon the heads and bayonets of those below. A gray-haired private of the 1st California was found with his head mashed between two rocks by the heavy boots of a ponderous "Tammany" man, who had broken his own neck by the fall! The side of the bluff was worn smooth by the number sliding down.

From the beginning of the battle a steady stream of wounded men had been trickling down the zig-zag path heading to the narrow beach, whence boats were to convey them to the island. As it happened the two larger bateaux were just starting with an overload when the torrent of terror-stricken fugitives rolled down the bluffs upon them. Both boats were instantly submerged, and their cargoes of helpless human beings (crippled by wounds) were swept away to un-known graves. The whole surface of the river seemed filled with heads, struggling, screaming, fighting, dying: Man clutched at man, and the strong who might have escaped were dragged down by the weaker. Voices that strove to shout for help were stifled by the turbid sullen waters of the swollen river and died away in gurgles.[6]

The federal soldiers who had scrambled and tumbled to the foot of the bluff rallied there for a while, to allow the wounded to be taken away, but the Confederates remained above, shooting down at the men on the bank and in the river. Someone in the Twentieth recalled the final hours of the battle:

The picture of a skirmish line halfway up the bluff, holding back for hours the victorious Confederates who had gained the crest, while heroic men were endeavoring to carry over in frail boats and skiffs the wounded to Harrison's Island, the coming on of night, the dark river pebbled into foam by a shower of bullets, through which hundreds of men were struggling for their lives to reach the further shore, presents one of the most tragic and thrilling events of the war.[7]

By eight o'clock, what remained of the federal force surrendered and was marched to Leesburg.

When the heavy firing began at 3:30, Wendell lay in the grassy field with his men, among the reserve companies, and listened to the bullets falling around him, the cries of men being struck. After an hour, Colonel Lee had ordered the Twentieth Regiment to join the attack. Wendell had risen.

A spent ball immediately struck him in the pit of the stomach, knocking him down and breathless. He staggered a few steps to the rear, and the colonel, who was passing, said, "That's right, Mr. Holmes — to the rear." But Wendell caught his breath and, finding that he was not wounded, turned and ran ahead to rejoin the attack. For a few moments he stood — waving his sword above his head and crying out, "Will no one follow me?" A second bullet then struck him in the chest and he fell.

He was carried down the bluff, ferried across the river, and laid in one of the rough log houses that men on picket duty had built, and which was now filled with wounded. It seemed to him that he was dying.

I was hit at 4½ p.m. [he wrote in his diary], the heavy firing having begun about an hour before, by the watch — I felt as if a horse had kicked me and went over — 1st Sergt Smith grabbed me and lugged me to the rear a little way & opened my shirt and ecce! the two holes in my breasts & the bullet, which he gave me — George [Captain Tremlett's servant boy] says he squeezed it from the right opening — Well — I remember the sickening feeling of water in my face — I was quite faint — and seeing poor Sergt Merchant lying near — shot through the head and covered with blood — and then the thinking began — (Meanwhile hardly able to speak, at least coherently) — Shot through the lungs? Lets see — and I spit — Yes — already the blood was in my mouth. At once my thoughts jumped to "Children of the New Forest" (by Marryat) which I was fond of reading as a little boy, and in which the father of one of the heroines is shot through the lungs by a robber — I remembered he died with terrible hemorrhages & great agony — What should I do? Just then I remembered and felt in my waist coat pocket — Yes there it was — a little bottle of laudanum which I had brought along — But I won't take it yet; no, see a doctor first — It may not be as bad as it looks — At any rate wait till the pain begins —

When I had got to the bottom of the Bluff the ferry boat, (the scow,) had just started with a load — but there was a small boat there — Then, still in this half-conscious state I heard someone groan — Then I thought "Now wouldn't Sir Philip Sidney have that other feller put into the boat first?" But the question, as the form in which it occurred shows, came from a *mind* still bent on a becoming and consistent carrying out of its ideals of conduct — not from an unhesitating instinct of a still predominant & heroic *will* — I am not sure whether I propounded the question [aloud] but I let myself be put aboard.

. . . Well, the next question was how to get me from the ferry to the [field] hospital — this I solved by another early recollection — the "Armchair" — Two men crossed their hands in such a way that I could sit on 'em and put my arms around their necks — & so they carried me — the little house was filled so I was taken into the large building which served as a general hospital; and I remember the coup d'oeil on which I closed my eyes with the same sickening feeling which I had felt on seeing poor old Merchant — Men lying round on the floor — the spectacle wasn't familiar then — a red blanket with an arm lying on it in a pool of blood — it seems as if instinct told me it was John Putnam's (then Capt. Comdg Co. H) — and near the entrance a surgeon calmly grasping a man's finger and cutting it off — both standing — while the victim contemplated the operation with a very grievous mug. Well presently old Hayward [the regimental surgeon] approached and inspected me — "How does it look, Doctor, shall I recover? Tell me the truth for I really want to know" — (It seemed then and does now as if I was perfectly rational but Whittier says that when he saw me later I was very light headed —) Hayward in his deliberate way — "We-ell, you *may* recover — . . ."

. . . we all thought that night that I had a couple of bullets in my lungs — & bled from them (at the mouth) very freely — "That means the chances are against me, doesn't it?" "Ye-es, the chances are against you" — Meanwhile he picked something from the left opening — I thought it was bone until he told me it was a bit of flannel — again I felt for the laudanum and again determined to wait till pain or sinking strength warned me of the end being near — I didn't feel sure there was no chance — and watching myself did not feel the hand of death upon me beyond a hope — my strength seemed to hold out too well.

After this my recollection of events is confused — I remember poor Willy Putnam's groans — and his refusing to let the Dr. operate on him, saying he knew the wound was mortal and it would only be more pain for nothing — I remember hobnobbing with the man who lay near me, and when to my astonishment John O'Sullivan (Whit's and my servt) appeared telling him to help my neighbor too, and feeling very heroic after that speech — (By the way Hayward had turned me on my breast & this may have helped a good deal of the wound to heal almost by first intention) — I remember being very sleepy — (some enlisted man has since told me he gave me some coffee and my face flushed and I went right off —) & presently a Doctor of (Baxter's?) Fire Zouaves coming in with much noise & bluster, and oh, troops were crossing to the Virginia side, and we were going to lick, and Heavens knows what not — I called him and gave him my address and told him (or meant & tried to) if I died to write home & tell 'em I'd done my duty — I was very anxious they should know that — and then I imparted to him my laudanum scheme — This he dissuaded me and gave me a dose of some opiate — he said it wasn't laudanum, but I guess that was a white lie — and when I slumbered I believe he prigged the bottle —

Pen before I was moved came in & kissed me and went away again — Whittier came & saw me too, though I'm not sure if I remember it — and Sturgis of whom anon — I think I remember the confusion when some bullets struck the house — and the story that the enemy would shell the island. But all these recollections are obscure and the order of their occurrence uncertain —

Much more vivid is my memory of my thoughts and state of mind for though I may have been light-headed my reason was working — even if through a cloud. Of course when I thought I was dying the reflection that the majority vote of the civilized world declared that with my opinions I was *en route* to Hell came up with painful distinctness — Perhaps the first impulse was tremulous — but then I said — by Jove, I die like a soldier anyhow — I was shot in the breast doing my duty up to the hub — afraid? No, I am proud — then I thought I couldn't be guilty of a deathbed recantation[8] — father and I had talked of that and we were agreed that it generally meant nothing but a cowardly giving way to fear — Besides, thought I, can I recant if I want to, has the approach of death changed my beliefs much? & to this I answered — No — Then came in my Philosophy — I am to take a leap in the dark — but now as ever I believe that whatever shall happen is best — for it is in accordance with a general law — and *good & universal* (or *general law*) are synonymous terms in the universe — (I can now add that our phrase *good* only means certain general truths seen through the heart & will instead of being merely contemplated intellectually — I doubt if the intellect accepts or recognizes that classification of good and bad). Would the complex forces that made a still more complex unit in *Me* resolve themselves into simpler forms or would my angel be still winging his way onward when eternities had passed? I could not tell — But all was doubtless well — and so with a "God forgive me if I'm wrong" I slept.

. . . Later I only can recall, in a general way, being carried across the Island in a blanket — lying on the bank comatose, being ferried across to the Md shore with some hitch (we came mighty near being upset) — swearing terrifically — and finally after being put in the hold of a canal boat [on the Chesapeake & Ohio canal] and the hatches or scuttle or whatever you call it tumbling in and nearly all but smashing me & one or two others into sudden death, that I muzzed away the time till we got to Edwards Ferry —

. . . I was taken from the Canal boat and put into one of the two-wheeled ambulances which were then in vogue as one form

of torture — . . . Fortunately I directed our driver to go to the
Regt instead of to Poolesville and we got to the Hospital at early
dawn —
     . . . The hospital steward — a cockeyed Dutchman who after-
ward stuck me certain sheckels for his services — looked at my
wound and conjectured the true state of affairs — bound me with
an infernal bandage (which Hayward cut as soon as he saw,) having first rammed plugs of lint into the holes, and then left me
uncomfortable but still exceedingly joyful, for he had told me I
should live — I could have hugged him for that — After this —
whiskey — lightheadedness — laudanum . . .[9]

Two days later, Wendell wrote to his mother from the regimental hospital to say that he was alive, but wounded. The letter was all but illegible,
a part of it written crosswise on the already filled page:

My dear Mother
Here I am flat on my back after our first engagement — wounded
but pretty comfortable — I can't write an account now but I felt
and acted very cool and did my duty I am sure —[10]

Wendell told his mother the story of his bravery in the battle, and then
of his wound.

     I hope only one ball struck me entering the left & coming out
behind the right breast in wh. case I shall probably recover and
this view is seconded by finding a ball in my clothes by the right
hand wound — I may be hit twice in which case the chance is not
so good — But I am now so well that I have good hopes — The
first night I made up my mind to die & was going to take that little
bottle of laudanum as soon as I was sure of dying with any pain
— but the doctors told me not to take it. And now seem to think
I have a fair chance and all my friends whatever happens I am
very happy in the conviction I did my duty handsomely.[11]

The Battle of Ball's Bluff was thoroughly reported in the newspapers.
Indeed, it had had a civilian audience: "Fifteen hundred or two thousand
[civilians] thronged the heights around Leesburg during the battle and
gazed listlessly on the bloody spectacle enacted before them."[12] Telegraph reports reached Boston newspapers the next day, and two days
later a detailed account appeared in the *Boston Journal*.
     The Northern losses were fearful — in proportion to the total men
engaged, perhaps the worst of the war. On the Northern side, of 1,800
engaged, 921 were killed, wounded, captured, or missing.
     It had been the first battle of any significance since Bull Run, and it

had been another disaster. Senator Baker had been killed. A joint Congressional committee was established to look into the matter. His former colleagues refused to blame the martyred Baker. Abolitionists from the Massachusetts regiments accused General Stone of having connived with the rebels. Stone consequently was arrested and imprisoned. General McClellan, who, if less deft, might have been blamed for the disaster, was promoted and became general of all the federal armies.

Boston regiments — the Fifteenth and Twentieth Massachusetts — had sustained particularly heavy losses. Ball's Bluff produced a shock in Boston greater than perhaps any other battle. The Twentieth sent twenty-two officers to Ball's Bluff, of whom only nine returned unhurt. The city read the newspapers and waited for telegrams. Colonel William Lee, Major Paul Revere, Adjutant C. L. Peirson, Assistant Surgeon Edward Revere, and dozens of others were prisoners.

Wendell Holmes and James Jackson Lowell were seriously wounded; Willy Putnam was dead; John Putnam's right arm was lost. Captain George Schmitt, who had complained about the Harvard officers, was dead, shot through the head; Lieutenant Reinholdt Wesselhoeft drowned; Sergeant Gustave Magnitzky wounded in the leg; Captain Ferdinand Dreher, four separate bullet wounds, disabled; Captain Alois Babo, killed; on and on the newspaper lists ran. As they descended to the enlisted men, the names turned Irish and German: privates Doherty, Noonan, Quinlan, O'Neil, Cogan, Derry, Kelley, Murphy, Torsey, Galligan, McCullough; Joseff, Kraft, Vogel, Reiss, Fuchs, Heim, Rank, Rohm, Rupert, Meuble, Zeuner; all dead.

The *Boston Journal* compared the battle to the Charge of the Light Brigade and quoted a part of Tennyson's poem. The heroism of the men seemed all the more sublime because of the hopelessness of the battle. *Harper's Weekly* wrote an account:

> In the front of the fearful fire, with no means of retreat, with every chance against them, these young men stood serene, each man a hero. . . . Lieutenant Holmes, said the first dispatch, "wounded in the breast"; not in the back; no, not in the back. In the breast is Massachusetts wounded, if she is struck. Forward she falls, if she falls dead.[13]

When Wendell returned to Boston, to recover from his wounds, he found himself a hero of a celebrated battle.

The Holmes family had moved to a new house on Charles Street, at the foot of Beacon Hill, with its rear windows looking over the Charles River toward Cambridge. For two or three weeks, Wendell held court in his sister's bedroom, recovering from his wound. It had not proven to be serious; a single ball had glanced along a rib and passed out again.

Visitors streamed down Beacon Hill to see him. Senator Charles Sumner came in twice to see the wounded hero; Cornelius Felton, Professor Agassiz, and Mr. Dixwell came in from Cambridge; as did the Dixwell daughters, Ida and Fanny. Ellen Hooper came, and the Shattuck girls. "Wendell is a great pet in his character of young hero with wounds in the heart," the doctor said, "and receives visits *en grand seigneur*. I envy my white Othello, with a semicircle of young Desdemonas about him listening to the often told story which they will have over again."[14]

When Wendell was on his feet, he received a stream of invitations, and he began keeping late nights. He paid calls in Cambridge and went to see Louis Theis: "He opened his arms and embraced and kissed me and produced a bottle of wine and cigars."[15]

In December and at the New Year, evenings were as gay as Boston ever became, and Wendell, talkative and cheerful, slender and pale, was a lion of the season.

The Twentieth Regiment remained in camp at Poolesville, rebuilding itself. Colonel Lee was a prisoner of war in Richmond, held hostage and threatened with hanging. Frank Palfrey was in command of the regiment, plunged in deepening difficulties with his German officers; Bill Bartlett was acting lieutenant colonel; Little Abbott and Pen Hallowell became captains. With half the officers and men gone, the first task was to recruit replacements. Harry Tremlett came to Boston to open a recruiting office at 7 Howard Street, but there were few volunteers. Not until March would he find the 200 men he sought.

As he recovered, Wendell grew restless. "The life he led here was a hard one," the doctor said, "late hours, excitement all the time, — and I really thought that he would be better back in camp."[16]

And Wendell was anxious to return to his regiment. By early January, he was fully recovered, and eager to get back to Poolesville,[17] but to his disgust he received orders instead to go to Pittsfield to recruit. Once more, he boarded the railroad cars for western Massachusetts and opened his recruiting office in the Kelloggs' parlor, flirted with the Pomeroy girls and little Carrie Kellogg, and corresponded impatiently with officers still in camp.

The regiment was filling up again. Pen was now a captain; Wendell, when he returned, would be Pen's first lieutenant, which pleased both of them.

The regiment was riven by the political struggles that were convulsing the country. Black slaves were rebelling in an unforeseen way, not rising violently against their masters, which had been feared or expected, but simply and eloquently taking up their freedom.[18]

The peaceful rising of slaves was unexpected and embarrassing to the government. Federal forces that had invaded the Confederacy in Virginia and Maryland and on the South Carolina coast found themselves asked to command a new force of black soldiers and laborers and to govern whole new communities. General Benjamin Butler, commanding the federal occupation of New Orleans, organized a regiment of black freemen. In South Carolina, where federal troops had pushed in from the coast, Tom Higginson commanded a regiment of freed slaves. The radical Abolitionists in Congress wanted to use the army to liberate slaves in the Confederate states, and Massachusetts governor John Andrew ordered the Massachusetts regiments to follow the radical program.

But the federal government and the army under McClellan were still committed to the Constitution and the Fugitive Slave Law. Slaves escaped from the South were officially called "contraband" and impounded with other seized property of the rebels. Slaves in Maryland and other states loyal to the Union were to be returned to their masters.

Frank Palfrey, with the support of most of his officers, followed General McClellan's direction and ignored the governor of Massachusetts. Most of the Harvard officers held Governor Andrew in contempt. Perhaps they disliked slavery, and were fighting a slave-holding nation, but the slaves themselves had no call on their passions.

Wendell was torn. Pen Hallowell would join one of Governor Andrew's newly organized black regiments, but despite Wendell's views on slavery he remained with the Twentieth. He found that in his one hour's battle and his approach to death, he had become a soldier in his loyalties and affections. Duty lay with his regiment and not with the Abolitionists.

The war news was increasingly good. A campaign had begun in the West, and federal troops were driving inward on the Confederacy from the Mississippi River. For a moment it seemed the war might be won before Wendell could return to camp. On February 16, the rebel stronghold of Fort Donelson, Tennessee, capitulated to General Ulysses S. Grant, whose name then was first heard. His note to the rebels said, "No terms except unconditional surrender."

> Never was such ecstasy, such delirium of excitement [Dr. Holmes wrote to Motley] as last Monday a week ago, when we got the news from Fort Donelson. Why, to give you an instance from my own experience, — when I, a grave college professor, went to my lecture-room, the class which had first got the news a little before, began clapping and clapping louder and louder, then cheering, until I gave in myself, and flourishing my wand in the air, joined with the boys in their rousing hurrahs. . . . The almost universal feeling is that the rebellion is knocked in the head.[19]

On March 8, as Dr. Holmes was writing, the Confederates withdrew from northern Virginia, abandoning Leesburg without a fight.

At last Wendell received his orders to return to camp, and set off by rail, hastening to be there before the end. He met Harry Tremlett on the train going down, and they arrived in Washington on March 25, to find their regiment ready to make its way south. Wendell took his place gladly as Pen Hallowell's first lieutenant.

Wendell, James Lowell, John Putnam, and the other returning officers still had little training. While in Boston, Wendell had read books of military history: Napier on the Peninsular campaigns, and Kinglake on the Crimean War; he had begun to take an interest in politics and government for the first time; but this was little to the purpose for a lieutenant of infantry. Little Abbott looked at the returning officers with bemusement: "most thoroughly and amazingly deficient in military knowledge," he wrote home.[20]

On March 27, 1862, the Twentieth Regiment left Washington and boarded steamers south to Hampton Roads, Virginia, to join General McClellan's army, which was forming there, at the foot of the long peninsula that led to the enemy's capital at Richmond.

On March 31, the Twentieth arrived at Hampton, midway between the mouths of the James and the York rivers. They came ashore and camped; in the harbor that afternoon they could see the federal armored ship the *Monitor,* "a most insignificant affair," as it then appeared to Wendell.[21] It was bright spring, the trees were budding, and a mist of pale green hung in their branches in the afternoon sun. The flag of a sunken sloop, the *Cumberland,* fluttered above the waters of the bay like a symbol of hope.[22]

As the army assembled, the Twentieth moved north and inland a mile or two at a time, the Confederates retreating ahead of them. The federal army moved slowly through cornfields and villages, and came to rest five miles below Yorktown, just short of the town's defenses. There, on the night of April 6, it began to rain, a cold drenching rain that quickly saturated the clay soil.

Days passed. General McClellan had little intelligence about the small Confederate force guarding the approach to their capital, and wrongly thought or feared it to be as large as his own. The federal army had few maps, and none that were accurate. An aide dredged up British maps from the siege of Yorktown during the Revolutionary War.[23] On April 7, Wendell and his regiment went on a reconnaissance and brought back drawings of the countryside.

They settled down for a siege and built batteries for heavy artillery out of range of the enemy's guns. McClellan pleaded with his superiors in Washington for reinforcements and naval support on the two rivers. Days stretched into weeks; the army waited, with only their field provisions and equipment. It rained often in the cool nights, and there was no fresh food. Wendell, to his astonishment, found that he stood the strain as well as most of the men, and wrote cheerful letters home about the state of his bowels. He proudly reported that his weight (in uniform) was up to 144 pounds.[24]

On April 16, the regiment broke camp and moved forward about a mile toward the enemy's fortifications. They pitched a new camp in a clearing, and from this time onward were constantly in sight and hearing of the enemy. There was continuous scattered firing from the pickets of the opposing forces. During the day, the Twentieth could see the enemy's outworks through the bare trees, just coming into leaf; and at night they could see the enemy's fires and hear their talk.[25] Still they waited, and began to grow puzzled. "The notion now seems to be that McClellan is trying to out-general [them —] catch 'em if poss. without a big fight," Wendell wrote home.[26] The patient army suffered the cold rain and the Confederate snipers.

Bill Bartlett was hit in the knee by a sharpshooter; his leg was amputated in the field, and he was borne away on a stretcher. Bartlett had taken over much of the work of commanding the regiment, and now Palfrey was on his own. But Wendell's company suffered no casualties, and he wrote a chatty letter home:

> We go on picket every third day and it would have made you smile to see Pen and me yesterday morning sitting on a stump smoking our pipes & reading old letters after a night of raining like blazes, out in the woods with a constant popping of guns where the rebs and our men were exchanging compliments & every now & then *bang — boom* — as a shell was fired & exploded on the one side or t'other — we fire most — Now and then a bullet would whiz high over our heads from the other side. . . . My cold seems to have finally departed and except that the two rainy days before & while on picket my bowels played the Devil with me owing to the cold & wet & want of sleep I have been very well. . . . In short, all is exceedingly well except for the fewness of letters & diminishing chance of a fight.[27]

To the regiment's great pleasure, Colonel William Lee returned from imprisonment, having been exchanged for a Confederate officer, and took command of the Twentieth. On May 4, as if to give the colonel an opportunity to lead his regiment into battle without delay, the Confederates began an artillery barrage. But there was no battle; the firing was only to conceal a retreat. That morning the Confederates abandoned Yorktown, just as McClellan was about to complete his battery of heavy siege guns. Several hours passed before the federals realized that the enemy was gone, and then the Twentieth was the first to mount the abandoned earthworks and plant their flag.

That evening when the regiment returned to camp, Wendell found waiting for him the official notice of his commission as a captain. Bartlett's wound had opened another captaincy, and Wendell, now the senior lieutenant, was next in line. In the battles that followed he commanded Company G.[28]

On the morning of May 5, it was drizzling. The Twentieth broke camp and joined the army slowly moving along the clogged, muddy roads to the York River, where they would take steamers upstream toward Richmond, hoping to race ahead of the retreating Confederates. They camped for the night on the bank of the river, as the drizzle turned to a steady rain. Not until the next morning did they board the steamer *Cornelius Vanderbilt* and churn up the river to West Point, which was crowded with boats, tugs, and barges. The Twentieth spent the night on board, waiting for a chance to disembark, and in the morning they were ferried to the shore — where they were greeted by Confederate firing.

The Army of the Potomac now gathering on the York above Richmond, despite the depredations of disease and sharpshooters, had swelled to more than 100,000 men. They spread their camps over ten miles of river bank, from White House — where George Washington had married Martha Custis — down to West Point.

Wendell accustomed himself to his new command. Pen Hallowell, Jim Lowell, Little Abbott, and he were now fellow captains. The intermittent rains continued and fresh food was scarce, but the army was cheerful. There were rumors that the Confederates would give up their rebellion, that they would surrender their capital without a fight. Colonel Lee asked to be made provost marshal of Richmond.[29]

General McClellan visited the camp on May 11, and was cheered by the men. On the same day, news came that federal troops had taken Newport News at the mouth of the James and had blown up the Confederate armored ram, the *Virginia,* freeing the water route to Richmond.

The Confederates gathered their army on the heights before their capital, as if for a final battle. Still the federal army waited. The Twentieth changed its position every few days, marching a few miles on the increasingly muddy roads, building new corduroy roads where the mud was impassable, camping in the wet and then moving on again, making constant reconnaissance to draw maps. Then they turned west toward Richmond, and came to rest on the bank of the Chickahominy, a stream that meandered through a low, flat, swampy plain below the rising ground on which Richmond stood. The stream branched and shifted and vanished periodically into swamps. Weeks of rain had saturated the soil; the river spilled out of its low banks and into the surrounding fields, freshly plowed for the spring planting.

The main body of the federal army began to cross the Chickahominy. The Third and Fourth Corps crossed the river and moved up the main road toward Richmond, the Third Corps in advance, and began to fortify a position at a place called Seven Pines. The advance on Richmond had begun, and the army of 126,000 officers and men — the largest army ever assembled in North America — was in good spirits. The Confederate army — inflated in McClellan's imagination to a still larger number — now faced them.

May 30 was a humid, hot summer day on the peninsula. That night it rained again, a heavy rain falling on the already saturated ground. The Chickahominy was rising and flooding the fields, sweeping away the little bridges on which the army would have to cross.

The rain ended on Saturday morning, May 31. The federal army still straddled the swollen river. Many bridges were down, and further passage was nearly impossible. The Confederate commander, General Joseph E. Johnston, seeing his opportunity, decided to attack the federal troops who had reached Seven Pines. He promptly marched with twenty-six divisions down the road straight at them.

At one that afternoon the two armies met. The Third and Fourth Corps of the federal army, cut off from the main body by the Chickahominy, were greatly outnumbered by the massed Confederate troops. Jefferson Davis, President of the Confederacy, and his military advisor, Robert E. Lee, came out of Richmond to watch the battle.

At the first sounds of firing, General McClellan, still on the far side of the Chickahominy, told General Sumner, who was commanding the Second Corps, of which the Twentieth Regiment was now a part, to be prepared to advance on a moment's notice. Sumner formed his columns and brought them to the very foot of a fragile remaining bridge, awash in the river. The Twentieth waited, without their knapsacks, carrying only sixty rounds of ammunition and one day's rations apiece. They could hear the firing of the battle ahead. At 2:30, after an impatient hour, they were given the order to advance and streamed across the river, the weight of the troops holding the bridge down on its pilings against the rushing stream.

They went forward, double-quick, through the low flooded ground on the river bank and then up a steep rise onto the higher ground approaching Richmond, of open fields and big houses, fruit trees and lawns.

At 5:45 the Twentieth came to the field of battle, a clearing on a low ridge. The federal line was along the crest of the ridge. At the command "On the right by file into line!" the infantry column joined the line of battle. On their right, about a hundred yards off, there were a big white house and a battery of guns firing steadily. There was a tremendous racket. They were firing into the wood at the foot of the meadow before them. The smoke of the guns rose into the late afternoon light.[30]

Volleys of fire now were returned from the wood, and two companies of Confederates broke from the trees and tried to storm the artillery battery. Bullets rattled like a hailstorm on the shingles of the white clapboard house, but the charge withered under the fire of the federal line.

The enemy then attacked directly at the center of the infantry line.
Confederates ran up the meadow at them, yelling and firing at close
range; Wendell's company stood in line and fired back. Wendell, commanding in battle for the first time, told his sergeant to shoot any man
who ran; he himself lustily buffeted every hesitating soldier: "I gave one
(who was cowering) a smart rap over the backsides with the [flat side] of
my sword."[31]

The Confederate line seemed to break up, and small groups of men
could be seen moving in twos or threes. The Twentieth advanced double-
quick. They came down the meadow in a controlled run — Wendell
flung away his haversack with his pipe and his dry socks — crossed a
road at the foot of the meadow, and entered the woods firing. A company of Confederates was caught and knocked to pieces by the fire; Wendell's company ran past the fallen men.

Abruptly, the battle was over. The Twentieth Regiment, seemingly
alone in the gathering dark, commanded the ground where the enemy
had stood.[32]

> Well, we licked 'em [Wendell wrote], and this time there was the
> maneuvering of a battle to be seen — splendid and awful to be-
> hold; especially as the dusk allowed us to see clearly the lines of
> flames from the different Regts as they fired —[33]

The Twentieth spent the night at the edge of the wood, sleepless and
cold and exhilarated, expecting the battle to resume in the morning. As
the sun rose they heard firing, but the battle had moved elsewhere. In
the afternoon came word to prepare for an attack by Confederate cavalry. The regiment formed itself into a square, Wendell's company in the
place of honor at the front. He unsheathed his sword and held his pistol
ready — a cavalry charge would come right on them, and the men would
have to stand. Wendell swore loudly that he would shoot the first man
who ran or fired against orders.[34]

But the Confederate cavalry did not come. Darkness fell, and the
men of Company G cheered their captain for his bravery. The regiment
slept again in the rain on the muddy ground. Wendell wrote a message
to be delivered in case of his death. He wrote a long letter to his parents
that he knew they would show to his friends, describing the victory, not
making too much of his own part.

That night it rained again, and the flooded rivers rose still further.
The army waited in the rain and dug entrenchments in the mud.

6

RAIN

THE RAIN CAME STEADILY DOWN, COLD AND DRENCHING. THE river rose behind them and submerged the remnants of the bridge they had crossed. The Twentieth camped for two days on the ground they had captured, with no provisions but those they had carried into battle and surrounded by corpses. The dead men and horses began to stink.

It is singular with what indifference one gets to look on the dead bodies in grey clothes wh. lie all around. . . . As you go through the woods you stumble constantly, and, if after dark, as last night on picket, perhaps tread on the swollen bodies already fly blown and decaying, of men shot in the head back or bowels — many of the wounds are terrible to look at — especially those fr. fragments of shell.[1]

The Twentieth buried the Confederate dead. While they did this work they were fired on by Confederate sharpshooters. The bullets had "a most villainous greasy slide through the air."[2]

The days stayed hot. The Twentieth pushed another half mile closer to Richmond. They had come without knapsacks; the body of the army with its provisions was behind them across a now-impassable river. There was little fresh water and no fresh food. They were facing the enemy and kept their guns in their hands, even at night.

The Twentieth was in the forward line beyond the battlefield of Fair Oaks, with short rations of hardtack and occasional salt meat, with no tents or blankets, standing in the mud by day and lying in it at night in the rain. So they remained for twelve days. Wendell, like the others, contracted body lice, bowel disorders, and scurvy.

Bridges were slowly rebuilt over the Chickahominy behind them, and on June 11 they were relieved by another regiment. The Twentieth withdrew about a mile to a camp near Fair Oaks Station, where there were dry clothes and fresh water. They bathed and changed their clothes. There still was no fresh food, but whiskey was handed around in the morning in tin pails.[3] The rain stopped and the weather grew pleasant. Tents were pitched on platforms to get out of the mud;[4] Wendell wrote proudly to his parents that he stood the hardships "better than many a stout fellow who looks more enduring than I."[5] A few lemons and potatoes turned up, and Hayward gave Wendell some lemonade for the scurvy.

The regiment turned out each morning at 3 A.M. and stood in line in case of attack at dawn. There were false alarms every few days that brought them out again in the afternoons. The men built earthworks and entrenchments. On June 26, they heard artillery and musket firing far to their right. Union troops moved past them, but they knew nothing more.

After a breakfast of hardtack and whiskey on Saturday, June 28, the men of the Twentieth went on a work detail under Captain Macy to build a magazine in the woods. The men were already at work when officers came up hastily and told them to leave the magazine and to dig trenches. But the ground was too muddy, and they stopped. There were rumors of a disastrous battle on their right. The regiment waited until nightfall and there were still no orders. Officers and men bivouacked where they were, in silence. Before dawn the next morning, an order came to fall back.

The Twentieth formed a column and marched in the darkness through the woods to camp. It had been deserted, obviously in haste: tents had been left standing empty; blankets, boxes, pots, and knapsacks were scattered about. The regiment continued its march to the rear down a railway line nearby. At dawn they came to Fair Oaks Station. This had been a supply depot for the advancing Union army the day before. Now it too had been deserted; stores left behind were burning.

Retreating eastward down the railway line, they came to an open field, in which they found General Sumner's Second Corps drawn up in a line of battle. They were told that the Confederate army was following close behind. The Twentieth were ordered into a copse of saplings on the western edge of the field, a quarter mile in advance of the main body of the corps. Here they were to meet the Confederates and hold them while the corps withdrew.

The Twentieth heard Confederate troops cheering as they came into the deserted camp at Fair Oaks Station. Soon the Confederates came nearer, and the Twentieth heard pickets firing; then artillery shells began to fall. The Second Corps filed off along the railroad line. Confederates came up to the wood and began firing into the trees, but they did not attack, and the Twentieth quietly joined the retreat.

Down the railway to the next station — Savage's Station — they came to another Union depot. The sun was high now and the day was hot. A mountainous pile of hardtack in wooden boxes was burning. Men were breaking open whiskey barrels and carrying ammunition to a swamp in the woods. Stragglers were getting drunk and trying on abandoned clothes. A hospital had been evacuated, and the wounded who could walk were trying to follow the troops. Railway cars loaded with rockets and ammunition had been set on fire and exploded with an immense detonation, sending a mushroom cloud of white smoke high into the air.[6]

Again the Second Corps massed in a great open field. The Twentieth took a place in the line of battle, on high open ground. Two Pennsylvania regiments met the advance. Storm clouds came over the horizon with lightning in them and made a dramatic backdrop for the battle being fought below.[7]

At dusk the fighting ceased. The Second Corps turned southward into White Oak Swamp. Rain fell all during the night as they marched. The regiment rested briefly at dawn, and then marched again. The sun came up hot and clear, and despite the rain there was no fresh water. They marched terribly thirsty, chewing twigs for the moisture until afternoon. Then again the Twentieth found the Second Corps drawn up in a line of battle, in a field outside the deserted hamlet of Glendale. This time the Twentieth was in the fight. Wendell commanded Company G in battle for the second time:

> [We] came up double quick onto the field of action (knapsacks on backs). . . . Forward in line (whole battalion front) better than the regt. generally does it on drill — *Whang* goes a shell two men drop in Co G. "Captain! Noonan's hit" "No matter, Forward Guide Right" We go forward passing a deserted battery the dead lying thick around it and then begins the deuce of a time the Mich. 7th on our left breaks & runs *disgracefully* . . . Not a waver in our Regt.[8]

Captain Lowell's company had trouble standing in line under fire. Then they quieted. Wendell looked to his right down the line, caught Lowell's eye, and saluted. When he looked again, Lowell was gone.[9]

They stood briefly under fire, the men falling, but the regiment had been flanked and nearly surrounded. Palfrey gave the order to retreat, double-quick.

The Confederate attack continued all afternoon, at terrible cost to both armies, but did not succeed. When night fell, the Union army resumed its retreat to Malvern Hill, a broad plateau just above the James River, where the army formed for another battle.

The Twentieth reached its position on the high ground just before dawn. They were in a clover field looking north. As the sun rose they saw the broad peninsula from which they had just climbed, broken in the distance by woods and hills. Left and right stretched "a splendid line of battle of the whole army."[10] As the morning brightened they could see enemy troops and artillery approaching from the distance and taking position. Soon shells began to fall and were answered.

Confederate infantry marched toward the Union artillery entrenched above them and were killed in great numbers. Repeated assaults were broken. When darkness fell, the federal army reformed its great columns and once again marched all night through mud and renewed rain. On July fourth, the Army of the Potomac reached its goal, Harrison's Landing, on the north bank of the James River. Here they were on high, well-defended ground, in a bend of the river that shielded their flanks and from which they could be resupplied. Wendell scribbled a hasty note to his mother:

> We have had hard work for several days — marched all night — lain on our arms every morn'g & fought every afternoon — eaten nothing — suffered the most intense anxiety and everything else possible — I'm safe though so far — But you can't conceive the wear & tear — Lowell is probably dead bowels cut —
> > Patten wounded leg
> > Abbott wounded arm
> > Muller[11]   "
> Our Co. had 9 or 10 wounded & some missing out of 37.
> Give my love to all my friends & remember me in y'r thoughts & prayers —[12]

The next day, after a blessed sleep and a change of clothes, he wrote at more length to both his parents:

> The anxiety has been more terrible than almost any past experience but through all I kept pretty lively only getting down when on the last day of our march I was told by cheerful birds like Tremlett & co that we *must* surrender or be cut to pieces within 36 hours.
> Poor Lowell was hit just as Willy Putnam was & had to be left behind — beyond doubt dead. Patten hit in the leg. Abbott flesh

w'd in the arm. Muller wounded & missing Palfrey bruised not hurt N.P. Hallowell cut on the side not hurt. I was awfully frightened about him. . . . It was the thought of you dear ones sustained me in terrible trials.[13]

The Peninsular Campaign was ended, and so was the federal advance on Richmond. The Union losses in the campaign were 20,000 men. Confederate losses had been equally terrible.

Whiskey was dispensed pretty freely at Harrison's Landing. Army slang for being drunk was "shot through the neck." Wendell wrote cheerful letters to his family. He perhaps learned in a letter from home that his grandmother Sarah Wendell Holmes had died in Cambridge.[14] This was the first death to touch his father's family in many years.

With the federal army south of Richmond, the Confederates sent an army quickly northward through the Shendandoah Valley and into Maryland. The first Southern invasion of the North had begun, threatening to take Maryland out of the Union, appearing to threaten the capital. After its brief rest at Harrison's Landing, the Army of the Potomac was hastily summoned north to defend Washington. If anything had been gained in the terrible campaign on the Peninsula it was heedlessly abandoned.

On August 16, 1862, the Twentieth began their march back to Newport News at the mouth of the James, where steamers carried them north to Alexandria. They crossed into Washington City on the Chain Bridge, and marched through the city to Georgetown. At perhaps the moment when Wendell's company passed on Pennsylvania Avenue, his fellow Bostonian Charles Francis Adams, Jr., sat in the lobby of the Willard Hotel writing a letter to his father, the Union's minister to Great Britain:

> Here I have access to certain means of information and I think I can give you a little more light than you now have. Do you know that just before leaving the Peninsula McClellan offered to march into Richmond on his own responsibility? Do you know that in the opinion of our leading military men Washington is in more danger than ever yet has been? Do you know that but for [Gen.] McDowell's jealousy we should have triumphantly marched into Richmond? . . .
>
> Our rulers seem to me to be crazy. The air of this city seems thick with treachery; our army seems in danger of utter demoralization and I have not since the war began felt such a tug on my nerves as today in Washington. Everything seems ripe for a terrible panic, the end of which I cannot even imagine.[15]

A few miles to the north, the Confederate invasion of Maryland was underway. The Twentieth marched northward to meet it. Colonel Lee,

Captains Tremlett and Peirson, and many others, debilitated by the Peninsular Campaign, had come down with dysentery or typhoid. Frank Palfrey was again in command as the Twentieth hastened up the Georgetown road. He joined them on the march, coming out hastily from leave in Washington. It was a beautiful September day, and suburban ladies were enjoying the fine weather.

> On foot, on horseback, in carriages, everyone seemed to be out of doors. . . . As the shadows lengthened in the golden afternoon, well-appointed carriages rolled along the charming drives, bearing fair women in cool and fresh costumes, and by their side the ragged, dusty, sunburnt regiments from the Peninsula trudged along.[16]

Just outside Rockville, Maryland, the Twentieth drew up in a line of battle and sent out pickets. But the enemy had not come this far. The regiment resumed its march, north through suburbs and then out into more open farming country. They moved slowly and once again joined Sumner's Second Corps, at Frederick City, and turned westward toward the Confederates at Antietam.

The Twentieth was filled with excitement, as was the whole army. They would now have their chance to meet the Confederate Army of Northern Virginia and beat it, the chance they thought McClellan's rivals had taken from them on the Peninsula. Frank Palfrey remembered the welcome they gave McClellan when he joined them:

> While the long columns of the Federal army were resting on the Boonsboro Road, General McClellan passed through them to the front, and had from them such a magnificent reception as was worth living for. Far from the rear the cheers were heard, faintly at first, and gradually the sound increased and grew to a roar as he approached. The weary men sprang to their feet and cheered and cheered, and as he went the cheers went before him and with him and after him, till the sound, receding in the distance, at last died away.[17]

On September 16, the federal army reached Antietam Creek. At three the next morning, awake and anxious, Wendell wrote a brief letter to his parents.

> . . . you know all my last words if I come to grief — You know my devoted love for you — those I care for know it — Why should I say more — It's rank folly pulling a long mug every time one may fight or be killed — Very likely we shall in a few days and if we do why I shall go into it not trying to shirk the responsibility

of my past life by a sort of death-bed abjuration — I have lived on
the track on which I expect to continue traveling if I get through
— hoping always that although it may wind it will bring me up
the hill once more. With the deepest love

love to A & N —
Your Son W.[18]

The battle began with morning light. Pickets fired as the two armies
touched; the artillery began, and then there was the long roll of the line,
firing by regiments. General Sumner's corps lay waiting as the most violent battle of the war was fought just ahead of them. Sumner, as he had
at the Chickahominy, impatiently marched his troops to the very farthest
point permitted by his orders, and waited for permission to advance.

The order came at nine, and the Twentieth Regiment bounded forward on the double, forded a creek, and passed through a grove of oaks.
They came out of the woods into a field under artillery fire, passed
through the field, and then through another wood. They went down a
steep slope to a road — the Hagerstown Pike — across the road and into
a cornfield. Enemy soldiers ahead of them fired from farmhouses and
the fields of drying cornstalks, and the advance stopped abruptly. The
troops in the lead formed a line of battle, and Sumner impatiently
pushed the Twentieth up just behind them.

The Twentieth could not yet fight. Some of the officers began smoking as they waited, watching the line of battle just ahead firing and taking
casualties.

Wendell was at ease when a soldier beside him dropped suddenly to
one knee and began firing to the rear as if into his own troops. Wendell
thought the man had panicked and knocked him over. But the enemy
were coming in from their flank and now the bullets seemed to come
from every direction. The order came — retreat double-quick — and the
regiment began running to the rear.

A bullet struck Wendell in the back of the neck, and he fell. Perhaps
he was unconscious for a time. When he woke he was alone on the abandoned field. He walked in the direction the regiment had gone, his
thoughts racing irrelevantly:

> I remembered . . . that *Harper's Weekly* was flamboyant on my
> first wound at Ball's Bluff — about Massachusetts hit in the breast,
> etc. I thought to myself this time I am hit in the back, and bolting
> as fast as I can — and its all right — but not so good for the
> newspapers.[19]

The bullet that had struck him in the back of the neck had come
through, emerging from his throat to the left of his windpipe, leaving a
gaping hole, but he could walk, breathe, speak.

The battle had passed over, and there were only wounded and dead men on the field. In a while Wendell came to a log house, where wounded men lay in the yard. Wendell walked inside, and found Pen Hallowell there, his left arm shattered by a bullet. Wendell lay down on the floor beside Pen, not knowing how bad his own wound was, thinking that perhaps he was dying.

The Confederate advance had washed over and past the log house, and they were behind the Confederate line. They lay waiting for what would come. Late in the afternoon, Confederate soldiers moved into the yard, looking for officers, taking prisoners. Wendell, afraid that he would fall unconscious or die, wrote his name and address in pencil on a scrap of paper, a page from his pocket notebook.[20]

A Confederate soldier put his head through the window:

"Yankee?"

"Yes," someone answered.

"Would you like some water?" He threw his canteen into the room. A few minutes later he was back at the window.

"Hurry up there! Hand me my canteen! I am on the double-quick myself now!" The Confederates were retreating in turn. Some one spun the canteen to him and he vanished.[21]

Shells fell about the house and the windows shattered. Then it was quiet again. Late in the afternoon, a Union surgeon entered. It was Dr. Haven of the Fifteenth Massachusetts. Wendell was now alert and excited. Haven glanced at his wound and said it was not fatal;[22] he passed on to Pen and searched for something to make into a splint for his shattered arm. Wendell, his thoughts racing, saw a grandfather clock in the corner that was like one he had seen in the Kelloggs' parlor in Pittsfield. "Behind the looking glass in that clock," Wendell told the surgeon, "you will find a thin piece of board."[23] The splint was made.

The horse-drawn ambulances came, and Wendell was taken to a hospital tent in Keedysville, a village near the battlefield, where he lay until night. The surgeons continued to ignore him. There were ten thousand wounded men on the federal side. Heaps of amputated limbs lay beside the hospital tents. Corpses of men and horses were put into mass graves.

Charles Lowell, a Cambridge friend and now a cavalry officer, saw Wendell in the hospital. The next morning he sent the news home: "Wendell Holmes shot through the neck, a narrow escape, but it is not dangerous now."[24]

That morning, Wendell wrote to his own parents:

Usual luck — ball entered at the rear passing straight through the central seam of coat & waistcoat collar coming out toward the front on the left hand side — yet it don't seem to have smashed my spine or I suppose I should be dead or paralyzed or something — It's more than 24 h'rs and I have remained pretty cocky, only of course feverish at times — & some sharp burning pain in left shoulder Pen & I singular to say are the hardest hit officers he I think will lose his left arm — bone smashed above the elbow.[25]

In the afternoon, Wendell climbed on a milk cart bound for Hagerstown, where he planned to take a train to Philadelphia. In Hagerstown, he walked languidly to the railroad station, the bandage around his neck. A young woman came out of a house as he passed, and invited him to come inside and rest. It was the house of William Kennedy, a Union supporter who was taking in wounded soldiers for care.

Four days later, on September 22, Wendell wrote to tell his parents where he was:

Tho unheard from I am not yet dead but on the contrary doing all that an unprincipled son could do to shock the prejudices of parents & doctors — smoking pipes partaking of the flesh pots of Egypt swelling round as if nothing had happened to me. . . . In a day or two however I shall start & I may remark I neither wish to meet any affectionate parent half way nor any shiny demonstrations when I reach the desired haven —[26]

This letter did not reach the doctor, however; he had started for Keedysville as soon as he learned of Wendell's injury.[27] In Keedysville, he found that Wendell had been moved, and spent the next two weeks in Maryland and Pennsylvania, trying to find his wounded son. Eventually, the doctor received the Kennedys' telegram and finally caught up with Wendell, who was changing trains in Harrisburg, Pennsylvania, on his way to Philadelphia.

The doctor and Wendell traveled on to Philadelphia together. Father and son arrived at 10 P.M. and separated; Wendell to the Hallowells', and the doctor to stay with a friend of Wendell's, Charley Walton,[28] for the Hallowells' house was filled with wounded officers. Pen was already at home. His wounded arm would be saved. Ned Hallowell, Pen's younger brother, was home with typhoid fever, and the Hallowells had taken in Frank Palfrey, who also had a wounded arm. Wendell briefly made a fourth invalid from the regiment. He was not bedridden and needed little care, but he had considerable pain in his left arm and shoulder.

The next day the doctor — in no hurry, now that he had found Wendell reasonably well — paid calls and saw the sights of Philadelphia. That evening, Wendell, the doctor, and Charley Walton went to a minstrel show.[29]

The minstrel show was the doctor's idea of a pleasant distraction. Wendell was grim as they watched the white comedians cavort in blackface. Afterward, the three men went out drinking together — "Had a little symposium at the Continental," Walton said. Wendell spoke with bitterness and gallows humor about the senseless battles and the mismanagement of the army. Walton was a little taken aback: "It is very well to shoulder your crutch and show how fields were won; but here was our young soldier with a bullet hole through his neck talking of 'disastrous choices; of moving accidents.'"[30]

The next morning, a Saturday, the three drove to Kensington Depot; the doctor had arranged a special car with a bed for Wendell. They traveled courtesy of the railroad to New York, and then to Boston.

There was a letter waiting for Wendell when he arrived, from his company.

> sir Captain Holmes i take the opportunity of writing these few lines to you hoping that this will find you recovering from your wound fast. Captain the company feels very sorry for you we had 12 men wounded one killed. . . .
>
> [Sgt.] Hayes in behalf of the Company
>
> Captain we would like to hear from you[31]

Little Abbott, who had remained behind in Frederick City, had now come home to Boston to recover from his typhoid. He and Wendell spent some time together, and became friends.

Abbott was a Democrat and sympathetic to the South, but he was a talented officer and had qualities of composure and self-control that Wendell admired. Abbott had waived promotion to remain Bill Bartlett's lieutenant. When Bartlett lost his leg and Abbott came to command the company, he managed it as if it were an extension of his own body. On parade and in battle he was relaxed, even languid, but entirely alert, observant. He had remained in camp the first winter to learn his craft, reading manuals and drilling his company in tactical movements. After he had mastered the routine movements, he invented new maneuvers. When later he commanded the regiment, he rehearsed them in these. The regiment learned to break ranks and then, on the run, reform into a square, or into a square of double lines. Abbott did not subordinate the regiment to his will; he only flexed it, as if moving his own arm.[32]

At first, Abbott had been a little scornful of Wendell's intellectualism, his lack of training or native ability for military work, but he came to love Wendell and to admire his courage and cheerful determination. The two men became close friends.

The Confederate army had been halted, if not beaten, at Antietam. The brief invasion was ended and the war would continue. McClellan was a hero.

On the morning after the battle, President Lincoln read to his cabinet a draft proclamation emancipating the slaves in states that were in rebellion. It was a lawyerly document. Slaves were property being used to support the rebellion; this property would be confiscated. A week later the proclamation was issued. Lincoln also suspended the writ of *habeas corpus,* apparently illegally. Any person could now be arrested and held without trial. In the election that November, Wendell was still at home, and he voted for the first time. Perhaps a little wryly, he voted the Republican ticket, doing his duty.

Leave was brief. Once again Wendell recovered completely from his near approach to death. There was no reason to delay his return. Abbott was now recovered as well, and in November, 1862, just after the election, the two men traveled south together to rejoin their regiment.

They went first to Washington, expecting to find the regiment nearby. Not finding it there, they went on into Virginia, onto frankly hostile ground.

It was cold as they traveled, and word spread through the army camped around them that General McClellan, so recently acclaimed a hero, had been relieved of his command. McClellan had made sufficiently clear his unwillingness to use the army to carry out a program of emancipation of black slaves, his contempt for President Lincoln, and perhaps his too Napoleonic ambition.

The new commander of the Army of the Potomac was Ambrose Burnside, whom the officers called a humbug and blamed for Bull Run.

Wendell and Abbott searched through the dispirited encampments of the Army of the Potomac in a cold mist, which was followed by a drenching rain.[33] They walked for two days through Confederate villages and farms, stopping at farmhouses where the men were away. The Virginia women laughed and told them to go home and grow stronger.

On November 19, in the afternoon, they found the Twentieth Regiment at Falmouth, Virginia, a hamlet on a hill above the Rappahannock River, where the Army of the Potomac was gathering. The regiment was dispirited. Through Sumner's rashness, of the 400 engaged at Antietam, 150 had been lost in the single day's fighting. Captain Dreher, who had complained bitterly of the Harvard officers, was now acting in command, and was resented in his turn.

Wendell, truly disheartened for the first time, wrote home that the regiment was going to hell under "crack-brained Dreher" and his lieutenant colonel, "the obstinate ignoramus Shepherd":

> I wouldn't trust [the regiment] under them for a brass tuppence in a fight — They'd send it to the devil quicker even than Gen Sumner. . . .
> The army is tired with its hard, with its terrible experience &

still more with its mismanagement & I think before long the majority will say that we are vainly working to effect what never happens — the subjugation (for that is what it is) of a great civilized nation. We shan't do it — at least the Army can't.[34]

They were among hills on the north bank of the Rappahannock River. To the south lay the town of Fredericksburg in a bend of the river. Broken stone footings of what had once been a bridge rose from the water.

The federal army assembled — and waited. They saw the town of Fredericksburg emptying. Confederate troops appeared and built earthworks on ridges behind the town. Still they waited. Burnside had his army, but lacked pontoons to bridge the deep, swift river.

The Twentieth, because it had distinguished itself on the Peninsula, was given a place of honor: it would lead the advance into Fredericksburg, which was being steadily fortified.[35]

The army waited, absurdly, for the pontoons, and winter came down on the camp. On December 5, it snowed. Sickness spread, and Wendell grew ill. "Never since the terrible exposures of Fair Oaks have I been myself," he had written earlier; "I can digest hardtack or shingle nails but one damp night recalling those dreary times plays the deuce with me."[36] Now the bowel sickness returned. He lay on his cot, unable to eat, and steadily lost fluids, lost weight, lost strength. Hayward told him that he had dysentery. He applied for leave to go to Philadelphia to recover. But his request was delayed in the various headquarters of the reorganized command.

Before dawn on the morning of December 11, the regiment broke camp and moved down to the river opposite Fredericksburg. Wendell was too ill to go with them, and remained behind in the regiment's hospital, a tent where a few enlisted men were dying of dysentery and typhoid. A corpse was carried out as Wendell entered.[37]

At 5 A.M., signal guns began firing at intervals. The morning dawned cold and misty. As the gray light brightened, artillery began firing. By noon, the sun had cleared the mist away and the crash of artillery was almost continuous; Wendell lay in his hospital tent and listened. The guns ceased at nightfall, and Wendell, in pain and high fever, no longer cared if he died.[38]

On the morning of December 12, a few of the regiment returned. There had been a battle; the Twentieth had been in it. Captain John Cabot was killed; Wendell's second lieutenant, Thomas McKay, was wounded. There were wild rumors of victory and defeat. Wendell tried to dress himself and to leave the hospital but found he was too weak. Cold fog lay about the whole day. He tried to distract himself by writing a letter home.

Another day of anxious waiting — of helpless hopelessness for myself, of weary unsatisfied questioning for the Regt. When I know more I will continue my letter — I have no books I can read I am going to try to calm myself by drawing.[39]

Men returning from Fredericksburg said that there would be a battle the next day, a grand advance against the Confederate position.

Artillery fire began again early in the morning of December 13; the sound rolled up the river valley to the hill above Falmouth. Wendell thought that this might be the decisive battle between the two nations, whose outcome would decide the war.[40] He lay helplessly sick, emaciated.

Later in the afternoon, with the help of a lieutenant, Wendell walked up to the crest of a hill. The fog had cleared, and it was a pleasant sunny afternoon. Fredericksburg lay before him on the floor of the river valley. In the town, shade trees rose above white wooden houses on a half-dozen dusty streets, and a square white steeple stood higher than all. In the distance the low ridge held by the Confederates swept in a long arc behind the town. Streaming through Fredericksburg and on to the road west was the dark mass of the Union Army. Farther in the distance another column moved toward the southern end of the ridge behind the town. Confederates on the hills fired at the advancing Union Army.

[We] saw the smoke of the musketry; the flash of the shells as they burst; & the rest — We couldn't see the men but saw the battle — a terrible sight when your Regt is in it but you are safe — Oh what self reproaches have I gone through for what I could not help.[41]

Union troops did not reach the hilltops, but fighting went on until after dark. The next morning, December 14, was a Sunday, and after an early rattle all was quiet. News came back to Wendell's hospital tent of the disasters of the day before. "The brigade went at an earthwork & got it with cannister."[42] In Fredericksburg, the surgeons had set up their tables in the houses, and everywhere through broken windows could be seen the work of amputations. "Hayward they say looked like a butcher, red up to chin and elbows."[43]

That afternoon Wendell sketched the view of Fredericksburg as he had seen it from the hill. He wrote a few words more in his long letter home.

Yesterday the fellow I spoke of as near death the day of my going to Hospital perished & there's another candidate now — Poor devils — there's little enough comfort dying in camp except it be that one gets accustomed to it (as an Irishman might say) and has plenty of company — But it's odd how indifferent one gets to the sight of death — perhaps, because one gets aristocratic and don't value much a common life — Then they are apt to be so dirty it seems natural — "Dust to dust" — I would do anything that lay in my power but it doesn't much affect my feelings — and so I'll stop at present.[44]

The regiment returned to camp the next day. The battle was not to be renewed. It had been a disaster. Union troops flung stubbornly against the fortified hills had been destroyed.

The Twentieth, first into the Fredericksburg streets, had borne itself bravely. The Confederates had left a rear guard that fired from shelter into the streets. In his report, Colonel Norman Hall, who commanded the brigade, said that he had ordered the Twentieth forward to clear the enfiladed streets.

I cannot presume to express all that is due to the officers and men of [the Twentieth] for the unflinching bravery and splendid discipline shown in the execution of the order. Platoon after platoon was swept away, but the head of the column did not falter. Ninety-seven officers and men were killed or wounded in the space of about fifty yards.[45]

The Twentieth was in the lead again the next day as the army struggled up a clear plain toward a brick wall at the crest of Marye's Heights, from which invisible Confederate muskets and artillery fired at them. At the end of the day's fighting about half the Twentieth's already depleted force had been killed or wounded. Macy and Abbott, almost alone among the officers, were unhurt. The Army of the Potomac had suffered 12,000 casualties.

In the days after the battle, Wendell heard stories of the regiment's bravery. His health returned and his spirits rose. He took a vicarious pleasure in the regiment's now famous bravery, and wrote home to ask for carte-de-visite pictures of himself to give to officers of the brigade, with his compliments.[46]

Colonel Lee was still too sick to return to duty; Dreher and Cabot were wounded or dead. Captain Macy was acting in command of the regiment, and Little Abbott was acting Major. Wendell was the senior remaining captain.

The shattered army regathered on the north bank of the Rappahannock. Desertions became common; sickness swept through those who remained. Inactive, the officers and men waited in their winter tents. When Burnside reviewed the troops, there was utter silence as he rode before the ranks. A colonel called out, "Three cheers for the General!" but not one voice answered, and Burnside rode on in the awful silence.

The Emancipation Proclamation took effect on January 1, 1863. Democratic newspapers circulating in camp said that the army was being used for political purposes and that mismanagement and defeat were the results. Many of the officers and men in the Twentieth agreed.

In January, Wendell's leave was belatedly granted, although he had recovered by then. He paid a brief visit to the Hallowells in Philadelphia, where Pen and Ned were still invalids. The doctor and Mrs. Holmes came down from Boston, and there was a gathering of the two families.[47] The elder Holmeses were full of patriotic war talk; Mrs. Holmes rejoiced that the destruction of slavery was at last an explicit aim of the war.

But Wendell said the army would be doing well simply to fight, and answered his parents a little angrily. When the brief visit had ended, the heated argument continued in letters.[48]

Late in January, after Burnside's spasmodic efforts to resume the offensive were mired in cold winter rains, he was removed from command and the army was given to General Joseph Hooker. Spirits revived, as the early Virginia spring began to blossom. Recruits came, drawn by cash bounties for enlistment; equipment was replaced or restored; the food improved; the days grew warmer; illness subsided.

For its honorable service at Fredericksburg, the Twentieth was rewarded with duty as "provost guard" of Falmouth, the village below their camp, and Wendell was selected provost marshal, head of the village's civil government and its military police. He and the officers of the regiment moved into one of the larger and better houses of the town, Mrs. Dunbar's, and lived comfortably.

There was a gristmill in the village, and men came down from camp on leave, to buy wheat or corn flour (at two dollars a bushel), to have a meal in one of the civilian houses, and to get drunk. The weather was dry and cold. On the heights behind Fredericksburg, in plain sight, the Confederates remained in command of the field.[49]

Brigade and division headquarters were in Falmouth, and so Wendell for the first time became well acquainted with the senior officers of the regular army. Charles Whittier, who had been Holmes's lieutenant, now was aide-de-camp to General John Sedgwick, their division commander. When Wendell called, he charmed Sedgwick with his conversation. "Tell Capt. Holmes he must come over again soon I want to hear him talk," Sedgwick told Whittier. Would Wendell be interested in a place on the general's staff? But Wendell, although he would be glad to have a temporary staff position, wanted to go back to the Twentieth when the fighting began again. "I wouldn't leave the Regt."[50]

Colonel Hall, their brigade commander, wounded at Fredericksburg, returned to Falmouth, and Wendell made a friend of him as well. Wendell admired Hall:

> What a joy it is to have a man thoroughly educated to his biz, well bred, knowing what's what & imparting his knowledge in place of one who tells you his Regt . . . has been in 42 battles & other unending blowing.[51]

Hall was a teacher. He went over the battles of Fair Oaks and Fredericksburg with Wendell, drawing careful and clear maps, marking them with his comments.[52] Wendell began to see his own battles from an observer's perspective. Hall praised the Twentieth, which deeply pleased Wendell: "He said, 'Yes your Regt is more like old times' (meaning thereby the Regular Army where Officers *were* Gentlemen)."[53]

Hall described the fight in the streets of Fredericksburg to Wendell, marking positions on the map as he spoke. Hall had given the order to Macy, in command of the Twentieth, to clear the street ahead.

> Macy says quietly "Mr Abbott you will take your first platoon forward" to wh. A. "1st Platoon forward — March" and walks quietly ahead — His 1st Platoon is knocked to pieces (He lost that day 30 out of 60 — 10 shot dead) instantly — "You'll have to put in the 2d says Col. H. "2d Platoon forward" and A. leads them into the storm with the same semi indifferent air that he has when drilling a Battn.[54]

The image of Abbott easily leading his men to death fixed itself vividly in Wendell's memory; twenty years later he would describe the scene as if he, and not Hall, had seen it.[55]

Wendell's enthusiasm for his regiment — "I really very much doubt whether there is any Regt wh. can compare with ours in the Army of the Potomac" — carried him forward under the burden of dislike for the war.

In Massachusetts, Governor Andrew was organizing regiments of black freedmen commanded by white officers. Serving in such regiments would be an honor. Pen and Ned Hallowell had both been offered commissions in the first black Massachusetts regiment, the Fifty-fourth Infantry Volunteers, under Robert Gould Shaw. Pen was to be lieutenant colonel, and he undertook the difficult work of finding officers and organizing the regiment. He wrote to Wendell in February:

> By a power as irresistible as fate I am drawn into the coloured regiment (54th) as Lt. Col. Would you take the majority? not that it would be offered to you certainly, but your name would command attention. Bob Shaw has accepted the Colonelcy.

Difficulties of every kind rise up. One by one they will be over-come. I retain my position in the 20th for the present.[56]

Wendell again refused. He would remain with his own regiment.

In April, the Army of the Potomac was preparing to resume its of-fensive. It was a novel experience for the regiment to remain behind at Falmouth as the army marched off to fight. On May 1, they heard the first shots, and on May 2, the distant sounds of a great battle rolled down the river valley to them.[57] They watched the Confederate army withdraw from the heights behind Fredericksburg, going northward toward Chancellorsville to meet the new attack. In the evening of May 2, the Twentieth received orders to cross the Rappahannock and catch the Con-federates from the rear.

7

THE REGIMENT

CEASÉS

T HE REGIMENT BROKE CAMP AT MIDNIGHT AND MARCHED INTO
the now-deserted town of Fredericksburg, into the streets they
had cleared at so much cost in December, through the town, and
out on the plank road to Marye's Heights. As before, artillery fire came
down; the Confederates had left a rear guard on the heights. The regiment moved to the right and were halted by a canal. They were still
under fire, and so withdrew behind a low rise of ground, and lay down
until the battery could be silenced.

The Confederate artillery began to fire spherical case — shells filled
with shot and fused to explode high over the ground. Wendell, prone
with his men, lifted his head and saw the Confederates bring a gun to
bear on his regiment. It fired. With the first puff of an exploding shell
above them, Wendell saw that the gunners had their range. With the
second puff, a ball struck his knapsack supporter, knocking it to pieces.
The gun fired again; a white puff overhead; the man in front of him was
struck; another puff, and a ball hit the back of Wendell's foot, striking
into the bone of his heel.[1]

The battle was over for Wendell. Carried from the field, he scribbled
a note to his mother on a sheet from his pocket notebook: "Pour moi I'm
already hit in the heel — bullet fr. spherical case."[2]

Dr. Nathan Hayward looked at the wound, not sure whether the foot should come off. He gave Wendell chloroform, probed the wound, and extracted the shrapnel. No amputation would be needed. Wendell added a postscript to his letter: "probably shan't lose foot." He was sorry that the foot was not to be cut off, as that would have excused him from further fighting.[3]

But he would be out of battle for a while, at least. He was carried back to Falmouth, and slowly made his way to Philadelphia, New York, and Boston again. For a few weeks he was bedridden, as the infected wound slowly healed.

Wendell no longer seemed "nervous," his father said. Indeed, he seemed detached. There was the usual parade of visitors. Each came with a little self-congratulatory smile and said something about Achilles. To Wendell's cold eye the visitors looked like mechanical men, unconsciously repeating the same words.[4]

News from the regiment was bad. The battle of Chancellorsville had been another defeat. Federal losses were 17,000 men. The Twentieth had joined the general retreat across the Rappahannock.

The Confederates had once again broken the Union advance, and once again they had shifted the battleground to Union territory. The news came that General Lee had swung his army to the north, around the federal flank into Maryland as before. The Confederates continued to march, unopposed, into Pennsylvania, perhaps searching for a dramatic victory that would demoralize their enemy and force the European powers to recognize the Confederacy.

The Army of the Potomac hastily gathered near the village of Gettysburg, Pennsylvania, in the path of the Southern advance.

On the Fourth of July, the result of the battle was not yet known in Boston. The town was preparing for riots: the Conscription Act had just taken effect, and there had been antidraft riots in New York. The federal government arrested and imprisoned opponents of the war and held them without trial, for the writ of *habeas corpus* had been suspended. It was a sadly discouraged time.

The doctor had become one of the most extreme supporters of war to complete victory. The purpose of the war, the doctor said now, was not preservation of the Union but destruction of the civilization founded on slavery.

On July fourth, the doctor delivered the oration at Boston's Independence Day celebration. Wendell undoubtedly sat in the audience and listened to his father's arguments once more: "There were Holy Wars of old. . . . This is our Holy War. . . . There is no neutrality for any single true-born American."

To Wendell's plea that such a war could not be won, Dr. Holmes answered bluntly that the North was stronger. Even if the Southern whites were indeed united and Confederate feeling were universal among them, why then, the doctor said coldly, "There is material power enough in the North, if there be will to use it, to overrun and by degrees to recolonize the South."[5]

The news from Gettysburg came in, confused like all battle reports. The outcome was not clear. The Twentieth had been in it. Macy, acting in command of the regiment, had been disabled. Major Paul Revere, succeeding him, was killed. Henry Ropes, who had been Abbott's dearest friend, was killed. Ned Paine, commanding Wendell's company in his absence, was killed. Wendell's sergeant and friend Gustave Magnitzky was badly wounded; his second lieutenant, wounded. Forty-four in the regiment had been killed or mortally wounded. Of thirteen officers who went into the battle, only three remained with the regiment.

The battle had continued for three days on the same ground. On the last day, the regiment's field officers all gone, Little Abbott had been in command when they met Pickett's Charge. Abbott led the regiment in a counterattack when this last Confederate thrust was broken. The men fought face-to-face, clubbing each other with muskets when they were too close to load and fire.[6]

Wendell read the reports and carefully cut them from the newspapers.[7] The wounded and the corpses came back to Boston. Wendell was a pallbearer for Henry Ropes.

A few days later, there was a report from South Carolina. The Fifty-fourth Massachusetts, Boston's black regiment, had stormed the Confederates' Fort Wagner. Ned Hallowell was wounded; Colonel Robert Shaw had been killed with many of his men. Ned went home to Philadelphia and wrote sadly to Wendell:

> Will you shed a silent tear with me? Then we will laugh and hurrah for the next that dies. What an awful month July has been for us. I mean you and me. I feel at least one year older since I left Boston [in June]. Do you ever see John Ropes? How completely broken he must be, he and Henry loved each other not like brothers but like friends. Can you for a moment imagine how I felt about Bob Shaw? We became very much attached to each other. How I wish you could have seen him lead us straight up to that fort under the most severe fire I ever experienced, we shook hands when we started. . . .
> My wounds are doing well.[8]

A few days later, Ned wrote to Wendell again, saying that he was looking for officers to refill the devastated Fifty-fourth, and asking for suggestions of Boston men.[9] Wendell thought very hard about this hint. The suggestion was an honor; he was not clear in his mind that it was a duty.

If he did not join the Fifty-fourth, he soon would return to his own regiment. That was hard, after three times being hit. It was no longer a matter of instinctive courage. Ball's Bluff was long past. Since then Wendell had been wounded in the back, while his regiment was running in retreat. He had been wounded again, lying face-down in the mud. He had been sick nearly to death with humiliating bowel disorders. More of this waited for him on the battle line. He would die in some ignominious way without having had a chance to achieve what was in him.

In his scrapbook there was a sad page of pictures he had cut from the newspapers, hideous drawings of men whose feet had been cut off.[10]

Wendell was now the senior officer of the regiment, after Macy. If he went back it would be as lieutenant colonel. He hesitated; he told Abbott he would waive promotion in Abbott's favor. But that would not do; Abbott would not agree. Reluctantly, Wendell wrote to the governor to say he would accept the commission — not in the black regiment, but in the Twentieth. Abbott, when he heard the news, wrote promptly: "I believe you have done . . . what is thoroughly right & proper, instead of absurdly wasting yourself before the shrine of the great nigger."[11]

Wendell prepared himself to serve as a field officer. During August, he learned to ride. There was another winter holiday season in Boston. Little Abbott came home briefly on leave. But Wendell's wound was healed, and after the New Year, it was time to go back to the regiment.[12]

In January, 1864, the Twentieth was in camp in northern Virginia, not far from where Wendell had found them more than a year before. The regiment had learned to spend winters in the field. There were fireplaces in the tents, with wooden chimneys, and pine-log houses whose chimneys were plastered with mud.

None of the Twentieth's original captains were still heading companies. Of the twenty lieutenants, only five were still with the regiment. The regiment's accumulated losses in two and one half years were greater than its original strength. One hundred and fifty-nine of the men had been killed, and four hundred and eighteen wounded. One hundred and twenty-four men had been taken prisoner, and there had been uncounted desertions, discharges, and invaliding illnesses.[13]

With Macy and Wendell both wounded and on leave, Abbott had been acting colonel since Gettysburg. He was liked and admired and was becoming well known to the generals of the army.

Wendell's position was a little awkward. He did not care to displace Abbott as acting colonel, nor could he formally assume his new rank. George Macy, when he returned, would become colonel, but Macy, while on leave, was still nominally the lieutenant colonel. Wendell accordingly continued to serve as a captain under Abbott's command.

Charles Whittier had been writing to Wendell all the past summer and fall urging him to take a staff appointment. Sedgwick, their old division commander at Fair Oaks, who had liked Wendell's conversation, was now a major general in command of the Sixth Corps, and Whittier was his aide-de-camp. Whittier urged Wendell to join him on Sedgwick's staff, and Wendell yielded. He agreed to go on detached duty to the Sixth Corps staff. He would be aide-de-camp to Sedgwick's subordinate, General Horatio W. Wright, commanding the first division of the corps. Wendell considered this a temporary assignment, until the campaign began again in warm weather, when he would return to his regiment.[14]

Sixth Corps headquarters were at the Welford mansion, where there were black servants, warm beds, and fresh food. Some of the officers were accompanied by wives or sisters. They exchanged visits. Dignitaries called and were entertained. Each corps held a ball for every other. There were horse races and occasional visits to Washington.[15]

In March, Ulysses S. Grant took command of the armies of the United States and brought his headquarters to the field with the Army of the Potomac.

Wendell read manuals of tactics and regulations, assisted in reviewing troops, carried messages, practiced his horsemanship. He now had leisure to keep a diary, which he did at some length, recording his experiences of battle and his philosophical speculations.[16] He was in good spirits, cheerfully talkative, and feeling himself in a more familiar element. He gained a renewed sense of his abilities, of the success in literature or philosophy that he might achieve. Among the staff officers, he quickly got the nickname "Chain-Pump" by being continuously talkative, as the chain on a pump was continuously rattling.[17] His talk spilled over into a long letter to his father full of philosophical speculations.[18] The coming campaign loomed up over the horizon. Wendell, "compelled unwillingly to the work by abstract conviction,"[19] dreaded its coming.

Abbott was flourishing in his command. He was a frequent visitor to headquarters, and became well known to Grant and Meade. Sedgwick praised him above all his officers.[20] The regiment was filling up, draftees arriving in large numbers. In mid-April, a hundred fifty German-speaking immigrants arrived at the Twentieth's camp. When Abbott found that they sang beautifully in unison, he took them about in the evenings to serenade the generals of the army.[21]

It was time for Wendell to return to his regiment. Macy was back from leave and had assumed command. Wendell could now be mustered as lieutenant colonel. But Wendell — whether consciously deciding or only allowing the drift of events to carry him — allowed the question of his return to remain open. The time of fighting drew very close. On May 3 he wrote to his parents: "I suppose we fight in a day or two — till then goodbye — I have no new words of affection now — I am well and in excellent spirits. . . . I shall see the fight on the Staff in all probability."[22]

The Army of the Potomac prepared to advance toward Richmond once more. Before dawn on the morning of May 4, the great beast of 120,000 men stirred and moved forward in long columns, a black mass of soldiers, artillery, and horses. Cavalry regiments moved over the countryside, feeling for the enemy's position; staff officers rode to and fro between the advancing columns and their commanders.

Wendell now spent his days on horseback, advancing with the army. The Sixth Corps marched westward, passing above Fredericksburg into a wooded region where there were few roads, the uncultivated ground choked with second-growth pine, shrubs, and marshes. The place was called, locally, the Wilderness.

On the morning of May 5, the Army of the Potomac halted and began to form its line of battle on this unpromising ground. The Confederate Army under General Lee had moved into their path. Artillery shells fell on the Sixth Corps headquarters as Sedgwick hastily sent his infantry to the right through the wooded countryside. Little could be seen. The enemy was invisible. A New Jersey infantry regiment came jogging past the corps headquarters. Tom Hyde, one of Sedgwick's aides-de-camp, was standing near Wendell, fiddling with his horse's bridle, when a shell took off the head of a New Jersey man. The head struck Hyde, bursting, and he was knocked down, covered with blood and brains; even his mouth, gaping in surprise, was filled.[23]

The day passed in a succession of charges and countercharges, shrill rebel yells alternating with the deep hurrahs of the Union troops. Toward evening, panicky infantry troops came running back through headquarters. The generals and staff rallied them and reestablished the line.[24]

In the dark early morning of the next day, the Union Army made a broad attack across their whole line. The Sixth Corps as it advanced found Confederate entrenchments, an artillery battery, and a swamp, all hidden in the tangled wood. Their troops became mired in the swamp and were left behind to be captured. Confederate artillery shelled the corps headquarters steadily throughout the day.

Late in the afternoon reports came in of terrible losses. The Twentieth had joined in the advance and had been caught in a thicket of woods for hours. Colonel Macy was wounded again, and Abbott had taken command. Abbott, too, had been shot; was very seriously wounded; was in the hospital.

Wendell was scribbling a letter home with this news when he heard firing and yells and saw soldiers running desperately from the right. The Confederates had flanked them and broken the Union line, and the federal troops were running away. Sedgwick and Wright sent their staff officers — Wendell among them — to rally these troops; briefly, once again, Wendell whipped men into battle.

The rout was stemmed. Reinforcements and artillery came up; all that night Wendell and other staff officers rode with orders reforming the line of battle. In the morning they held themselves ready for a renewed attack, which did not come.

Little Abbott died in the hospital of his wounds on the night of May 6.

The news of his death reached headquarters while the battle was in progress and General Meade spoke feelingly of it to General Grant. . . . General Webb [said] in his official report: "Major Henry L. Abbott, Twentieth Massachusetts Volunteers, died from his wounds received in the advance of his regiment. It will be difficult to replace him. No better soldier was in my command. His reputation as an officer stood far beyond the usual eulogies pronounced on dead officers. I feel that his merit was so peculiar and his worth so well known to all the officers of the corps and to the general commanding, that it is not necessary for me to attempt to do him justice. My brigade lost in him its best soldier."[25]

The news came as a blow to Wendell, but there was little time for sorrow. The army had been halted and defeated in its advance. About a fifth of its men had been lost in two days of fighting. General Grant, in appearance unperturbed, turned his army southward and marched all night to Spotsylvania Court House, hoping to outflank the Confederates — but Lee was there before them. "Discreditable to us," Wendell wrote in his diary.[26]

The blunt clash of the two armies resumed. They fought continuously. Grant was confident in his larger army and better supplies; Lee was unable to withdraw from the approach to Richmond. The fighting was relentless, continual, confused. Wendell saw the Sixth Corps make advances only to lose the ground again for lack of support from the other corps. The armies simply fought. The fighting continued every day, and at night the Union troops shifted their position steadily to the left, working south toward Richmond. They were once again on the Peninsula, and fought back toward the Chickahominy.

The devastation was terrible. Thousands of men were killed each day. General Sedgwick was killed by a sharpshooter, and General Wright assumed command of the Sixth Corps. He kept Wendell with him and retained all of Sedgwick's aides, so that Wendell and Charley Whittier and Tom Hyde became fellow aides to Wright.

The fighting went on relentlessly, the two armies moving together like partners in a dance, never out of contact. On May 12 it rained, a heavy soaking downpour. They were under fire all day. In a space of a dozen feet between two traverses — the "bloody angle" — there were 150 bodies. "The dead of both sides lay piled in the trenches 5 or 6 deep — wounded often writhing under the superincumbent dead — The trees were in slivers from the constant peppering of bullets."[27]

The firing was still going on when Wendell slept at 2 A.M. He was up again at dawn, when the fighting resumed. And so they went on, forced marches alternating with battles, day after day.

The Twentieth was almost without officers. Wendell heard that it was being commanded by a lieutenant. His parents asked in a letter whether he would return to command the regiment. On May 16 there was a brief lull, and Wendell answered:

> ... Before you get this you will know how immense the butcher's bill has been — And the labor has been incessant — I have not been & am not likely to be in the mood for writing details. I have kept some brief notes in my diary wh. I hope you may see some day — Enough that these nearly two weeks have contained all of fatigue & horror that war can furnish — The advantage has been on our side but nothing decisive has occurred & the enemy is in front of us strongly entrenched. ...
>
> nearly every Regimental officer I knew or cared for is dead or wounded —
>
> I have made up my mind to stay on the staff if possible till the end of the campaign & then if I am alive, I shall resign — I have felt for some time that I didn't any longer believe in this being a duty & so I mean to leave at the end of the campaign as I said if I'm not killed before.[28]

The Army of the Potomac continued to smash at Lee, circling slowly to the left to drive him out of his entrenchments, down into the old fields of the Peninsular Campaign, closer to Richmond.

There was a last reminder of chivalry for Wendell. On May 28, after three weeks of nearly continuous fighting, he had a complete night's rest. The morning was beautiful and clear, and Wendell was at leisure. They were near the Chickahominy again, with Richmond only five miles away, and there was a sense that a decisive battle would come soon. The weather was sunny and dry. Wendell paid a call on the Twentieth, and saw the surgeon Nathan Hayward, who had long been a friend. Wendell talked of coming back to command the regiment. Hayward told him he was maintaining himself solely on nervous energy, and that he might not stand the strain.

At the end of the day, with the sun falling close to the horizon, General Wright gave Wendell a dispatch to carry. It was important; Wendell was not to spare his horse.

Wendell set off at a gallop. After a mile, he came on a boy running toward him, shouting: there were rebel cavalry ahead. Wendell stopped to consider, then rounded up four federal cavalrymen who had been foraging, and set off down the road again.

There were thick woods on both sides of the narrow dirt road; the late sun was setting ahead of him. The road ahead bent sharply to the right, and on the far side of the turn there was a dark line of men on horseback.

"Halt!" one of them cried. Wendell pulled up and answered, "Friends," thinking the dark line were Union men, but they were shooting — Confederates. Two of Wendell's escort turned and fled. Wendell spurred his horse and galloped forward, across the line of cavalry and down the road to the right, the remnant of his little escort following.

There was a mounted man in the road, a line of cavalry in the woods to the right. More shooting. "Halt, surrender!" The man in the road unslung his carbine. Wendell rode straight at him; the man was having trouble unslinging his gun. Wendell's thoughts were racing — an image from a novel, of putting his saber into the man until the hilt struck his chest — but the rebels were better horsemen — Wendell took up his pistol — he was abreast of the cavalryman and raised the pistol — it misfired — Wendell crouched behind his horse's neck and galloped on.

The Confederates did not follow, and a few minutes later Wendell had delivered his dispatch to General David A. Russell and had returned to the Sixth Corps headquarters by another road. At the Sixth Corps, he found he had been given up for lost.

Wendell told Whittier and Hyde the tale, and they said it was a gallant thing, "to get the order through and not knock under or turn back."[29]

But the gallant ride was only a moment of phosphorescence, quickly submerged by the tide. The next day brought hard fighting. Letters came from home: his parents were distressed about his decision to resign. He sent a nearly incoherent reply:

> I wish you'd take the trouble to read my letters before answering — I am sure I cannot have conveyed the idea, rightfully, that I intended resigning before the campaign was over (i.e. next winter just near the end of my term of service) — then I probably shall for reasons satisfactory to myself — I must say I dislike such a misunderstanding so discreditable to my feeling of soldierly honor, when I don't believe there was a necessity for it — I shall stay on the staff and wish you'd notify the Governor to commission new field officers for the Twentieth I waive promotion — I am convinced from my late experience that if I can stand the wear & tear (body & mind) of regimental duty that it is a greater strain on both than I am called on to endure — If I am satisfied I don't really see that anyone else has a call to be otherwise — I talked with Hayward the mentor of the Regt & told him my views on the matter — I am not the same man (may not have the same ideas) & certainly am not so elastic as I was and I *will not acknowledge the same claims upon me under those circumstances* that existed formerly —[30]

But his term of enlistment would be up in July, in the middle of the campaign, and not the next winter.

The sun was baking hot and the roads were dry and dusty. They fought through the next day, May 5, and in the night the Sixth Corps made yet another forced march from their position on the right wing of the army, across behind it to the left wing. Tom Hyde rode on ahead, to a crossroads called Cold Harbor. The next day they fought, stupid with weariness, in the heat and dust. They held themselves ready to fight again at dawn, and waited through another hot day. A photographer took a picture of the Sixth Corps staff in this brief respite. The officers lined up outside the general's tent. General Wright stood at the center stiffly, in a clean uniform evidently put on for the occasion. The staff stood around him. Wendell and Whittier were side-by-side in the back row, grinning like schoolboys. The officers were all lean and sunburned, like a team of young athletes. They were wearing all sorts of hats, coats, and boots — straw boaters, slouch hats, a bowler, tall-crowned city hats.[31]

On June 3, the whole army was flung forward. A victory would be decisive, and 40,000 men were put into the first charge against the Confederate position.

They had not explored the ground. The Confederates were thoroughly entrenched, their men hidden in complex works, with brambles heaped in front and bogs breaking the ground. Artillery behind the Confederate lines fired into the attacking troops. Whole companies fell together. There were 7,000 casualties in the first half hour. The charge was halted, the attack broken. Still the fighting continued all day in the growing heat.

At night there was quiet, but not rest. The men dug entrenchments, buried the dead, carried away the wounded. The staff rode outward with orders, inward with news.

The two armies remained fighting there for two weeks. As always on a campaign, there was very little fresh food, but there was plenty of whiskey and rum. Wendell trained his orderly to wake him in the mornings with a drink of whiskey and a chew of tobacco. The army was growing disorganized, and there was a mob of stragglers and camp followers behind them.

Dr. Holmes continued to write Wendell letters full of war propaganda and talk of duty. Wendell answered sourly to his mother, "Father'd better not talk to me about opinions at home & here." Wendell wrote to Governor Andrew directly to answer the repeated question: he would not return to the Twentieth; he had waived promotion. And he wrote to his mother — perhaps it seemed pointless to talk with his father anymore — explaining in a calmer mood his resolution to resign. It was not a hasty decision caused by the difficulties of the moment, he said, but a considered conclusion that his duties lay elsewhere:

> The campaign has been most terrible yet believe me I was not demoralized when I announced my intention to leave the service next winter if I lived so long — I started in this thing a boy I am

now a man and I have been coming to the conclusion for the last
six months that my duty has changed —

I can do a disagreeable thing or face a great danger coolly
enough when I *know* it is a duty — but a doubt demoralizes me as
it does any nervous man — and now I honestly think the duty of
fighting has ceased for me — ceased because I have laboriously
and with much suffering of mind and body *earned* the right . . . to
decide for myself how I can best do my duty to myself, to the
country and, if you choose, to God —

I believe that Governor Andrew understands my determination
to waive promotion — please be sure he does so — The ostensible
and sufficient reason is my honest belief that I cannot now endure
the labors & hardship of the line — Nothing further need be told
abroad —

I hope that this will meet your approbation — you are so sure
to be right — at all events I have tried to decide conscientiously &
I have decided —[32]

Again the army moved, swinging once more toward their left, trying
to flank their enemy, circling below Richmond to the James River and
then across the James toward Petersburg. They were constantly in contact with the enemy. The fighting had been almost without interruption
for more than a month. The Union had lost 60,000 men.

Wendell drank pretty heavily at times now. One morning, when their
headquarters was being shelled and there was nothing to do and no shelter from the shells, he got thoroughly drunk.[33]

His three-year enlistment was nearly over. It was high summer. The
trees were in full leaf. There was "the finest bush of wild roses . . . I ever
saw — all in bloom."

The army, thwarted in its advance on Richmond, now laid siege to
Petersburg. Shells occasionally fell among them. Tom Hyde one morning was awakened by a shell falling nearby. He went outside his tent and
found his black servant had been killed. Looking up, he saw "the tall
form of Mr. Lincoln slowly walking away to a more sheltered place. He
had a long-tailed black coat on and a rather battered high hat, and he
was leading his son Tad by the hand, occasionally looking back toward
the rebel batteries to see if another shot was coming."[34]

On June 21, Wendell wrote to Agnes Pomeroy in Pittsfield:

This letter is written under difficulties. Staff Officers coming in
and talking, the enemy dropping shells round our headquarters,
everything conspiring to interrupt and disturb me. Do you know
I shall never wear the "20" again? Now since the muster has been
in my grasp I have written the Governor that I waived promotion.

I find myself too weak from previous campaigns to do the duties of an officer of the line properly. . . . I got a letter from my dear Carrie Kellogg last night, bless her, how often in these weary nights and days when the sun seemed to have stopped a second time to prolong the fighting, have I thought of those peaceful and most happy days at Pittsfield.[35]

On June 24 he wrote to his parents:

These last few days have been very bad — . . . I tell you many a man has gone crazy since this campaign began from the terrible pressure on mind & body — I hope for success strongly before summer — but at what cost & bye & bye the sickness will begin — I hope to pull through but don't know. . . .
Goodbye.[36]

Unexplained orders came abruptly for the Sixth Corps to withdraw to the James River. Out of the dust and heat and constant shelling they marched, onto clean white side-wheeler steamers, and up the Chesapeake Bay and the Potomac for a cool respite. They landed on the ruined terminal wharves of Washington and marched out on Seventh Street.

By noon of July 11, the 12,000 men of the Sixth Corps had reached Fort Stevens, low earthworks built in the Washington suburb of Silver Spring. Within the fort, nervous officers and men had gathered hastily from desks in Washington to hold the fort until the Sixth Corps arrived. They were there to face Jubal Early's seasoned corps of Confederate infantry, sent north in a final diversion to draw Union troops away from Richmond.

There was a brief battle the next day. The President came out from Washington with an entourage to watch Jubal Early's troops beaten off.

Tom Hyde sat on a rampart of Fort Stevens the afternoon before the battle and saw Lincoln again. The President was standing a little way off on a low parapet. An officer standing on the wall between Lincoln and Tom Hyde was struck by a bullet, "and then a lot of people persuaded Mr. Lincoln to get down out of range."[37]

In the midst of this bizarre diversion into suburban Washington, Wendell learned that the Twentieth had been dissolved. Its officers had been killed and its ranks reduced to a fraction of their original strength. Accordingly, the few remaining companies would be reassigned elsewhere. The post of lieutenant colonel of the Twentieth, to which Wendell had been commissioned, had ceased to exist.

Dear Mammy
    Prepare for a startler — Unless something unexpected happens I shall probably leave this army for home about the 17th! The

Regt. ceases to exist as a regiment and the few old men not reenlisted leave for home to be mustered out —

. . . I of course shall not go in for 3 yrs more as Capt. of Infty having given up promotion for the sake of leaving the line — I might, to be sure, stay longer if I were one of the aides allowed the Genls by law but as I'm not and am liable to go back to the Regt if any change sh'd take place I leave — If it should be necessary to go into the service again I should try for a commission from the Presdt but I shan't bother myself about that for the present. . . .

Yr loving O W H, Jr[38]

The Twentieth had ceased, and with it his duty. In a few hours, Wendell was on his way back to Boston.

PART III

THE
COMMON
LAW

8

POET, SOLDIER, GENTLEMAN

I N THE EVENING OF THE NINETEENTH OF JULY, HOLMES CAME BACK
to the narrow brick house at 21 Charles Street, where he found familiar household smells and city noises and the astonishing safety
and comfort of home. There was perhaps a late supper, and Holmes
went up two flights of stairs to bed. There were books at hand, and gas-
light to read by, and things were clean.

The days were quiet. Everyone of wealth or fashion was at the seashore, but the Holmeses had stayed in town. Rugs and draperies were
put away, woven straw mats were spread on the floors, and light summer
curtains were drawn against the sun. Mrs. Holmes did war work in the
mornings, and the doctor had his summer semester for the medical
school until the end of June. They had had no summer house since
Canoe Meadow was sold, but went often to the yellow clapboard house
in Cambridge, with its gables and hipped roof, where the doctor's
younger brother, John Holmes, now lived alone. Mrs. Holmes worked in
the garden there when it was not too hot, and the doctor worked upstairs
in his father's study.

Holmes's younger brother, Ned — frail, with his father's asthmatic
cough — was still at school in Cambridge, finishing his first year at Harvard College. Amelia, little and dark, plump and intensely talkative, was

three months short of her twenty-first birthday. She went often to visit friends in Nahant, Conway, or Newport. Emily Hallowell had given Amelia piano lessons the summer before, and she now practiced relentlessly.

The doctor played his violin for the family after tea. He played cheerful, sentimental songs — "Auld Robin Grey" was a favorite. Sometimes he and Amelia played together. He had collected stereoscopic views of the landmarks of Europe, which the family in the evenings in the parlor could see with the hand-held viewer he had invented.

Holmes was joyously welcomed by this little family, their two servants, and a few neighbors who had stayed in town. The doctor perhaps was a little reserved, keeping Holmes at a distance with his cheerful talk. The doctor was the leading Wide-Awake and propagandist of the war, and Holmes, with whatever justification, had left the army before the summer's campaign was ended, while Pen and Ned Hallowell were field officers in a black regiment, Tom Higginson commanded another, and Bill Bartlett was a brigadier general.

But Mrs. Holmes was simply glad, now that the decision was made, to have her son at home:

What does a woman of my age care as much for as her children — what they are, what they will be — I assure you that I give more thought to them than to anything else in this world — Yes dear Wendell, you will find me the same fond mother when you come home that I was when I bade you goodbye — I suppose I bother you sometimes — but I love you very much —[1]

Amelia called him "Favorite" and complained a little teasingly that the family and their friends gave all their attention to the elder son.[2] But while he was at the center of his family, Holmes remained solitary, absorbed in his own thoughts.

The war hovered on the horizon, like a distant thunderstorm oppressing the atmosphere. The summer campaign in Virginia had ended inconclusively, for all its horrible destructiveness. The siege of Petersburg had continued into the fall. The Twentieth no longer existed, and the Sixth Corps had traveled westward, but Holmes kept in touch with individual officers, followed reports of the army in the newspapers, and cultivated senior officers on leave in Boston. If the war continued in the spring he might have to enlist again, and the war seemed no closer to its end. But for the moment he was free of duty to the war, free to concern himself with himself.

There were few amusements for young people, even when the usual parties began that winter. The young women worked in sewing circles. One later recalled that for a young woman it was "knit, knit, knit, every possible moment of the waiting day; making bandages, scraping lint, etc., all through those dreadful years fearing to look at the lists in the paper."[3]

Holmes — still painfully thin, long-necked, awkward, cheerfully talkative, negligent of his own accomplishments but lightly telling the stories of his encounters with death — was in demand. There were frequent callers at 21 Charles Street, and Holmes busied himself with the amusements of Boston's polite society — teas, formal dancing parties called "assemblies," conversations, late suppers in the "German" style. He called on friends in Cambridge and Boston, drank and smoked with them until late hours, slept in the mornings, fell asleep in his parents' entryway one night when he had drunk too much, and discharged as well as he could the considerable energies of a twenty-three-year-old man who had nothing in particular to do.

There were a few new faces. The James family — Henry James, his wife, their children William, Henry, Jr., and Alice, and a maiden aunt — had rented a house in Boston that summer. Two younger sons were away in the army. But the oldest son, William — Holmes's age — had stayed home from the war at his father's insistence. He was enrolled among Dr. Holmes's students at the Harvard Medical School, and the whole James family had come to Boston to be with him.

The father was a balding little man with a snub Irish nose and a round red face with a fringe of dark beard. He had a wooden leg and walked with a cane. Gentle and affectionate, he had a violent way of talking.

William James was dark, slight, thin, and energetic. His younger brother Henry was quiet, watchful, a little more composed, a little more calculated. Henry, too, had stayed home from the war. He had a vaguely described ailment, perhaps back trouble.

Holmes and William James had long talks, and wrote letters to each other in courtly adolescent mock-Elizabethan. William addressed his notes to "Sweet Wendell," and signed himself, "Thine Till Death": "I much regret that the stern necessity I am under of accomp'g my Ma to a party at Mrs. Theophilus Parsons' on Friday Eve'g will prevent my appearing simultaneously at your house. Oh cursed spite!"[4]

The two young men sat up late together, talking and drinking. Neither had yet chosen a career; neither had yet begun to narrow himself; they were all possibility. James had studied painting with John La Farge and William Hunt, science at the Lawrence School, and now medicine, which did not much attract him. Holmes was poised between philosophy and law, and was writing war poems. His ode on Henry Abbott's death was published in the *Transcript* in October; it was the most genuine and feeling poem that he had written.[5] But he had to find some way of supporting himself, which neither poetry nor philosophy would do.

> I was kicked into the law by my Governor . . . my head was full of thoughts about philosophy and in a vague way I thought about the medical school. But my Governor would not hear of that, and put on the screws to have me go to the Law School — I mean he exerted the coercion of the authority of his judgment.[6]

In October of 1864, Holmes joined the entering class of the Harvard Law School, which was housed in a two-story Greek Revival structure with portentous columns, only a few hundred feet from the yellow clapboard house in Cambridge. He continued to live at 21 Charles Street and rode the horsecars or walked to the lectures.

After the brief respite of the summer, Holmes threw himself into this new campaign. But he also kept up his friendships, flirted with the many young women who were at home and alone, and in the back of his mind nursed the possibility that he would have to reenlist in the spring. Lincoln was reelected that fall, and the war dragged on inconclusively. Holmes made a scrapbook of his war mementos, adding to it sad letters and news clippings about casualties. When his ode for Little Abbott was published he sent a copy to Abbott's father, who had lost both his sons. Judge Abbott wrote a heartbroken note of thanks:

> I cannot express to you how much I feel your kindness — It is a sad pleasure to know that my boy was known and his worth realized by those whose opinion is most to be regarded. No one can know the loss to me. After the death of Ned, what before was divided was centered on Henry — He was both son and companion — so loving and gentle.[7]

Holmes's days were filled by lectures at the law school, which he at first attended dutifully. All of the instruction was given by three men: Joel Parker, Emory Washburne, and Theophilus Parsons. Parsons and Washburne had been judges, and all three maintained active law practices.[8] They were dry, technical men of respectable accomplishments, if not scholars.

Most of the students were much younger than Holmes. There were no requirements for admission to the law school, other than a good character. Fewer than half the students had attended college, and most were still in their teens.[9] The nominal course of study was two years, but students were required to be in residence at the law school only eighteen months.[10] There were no examinations.

In the last generation, few lawyers had attended school at all. A practicing lawyer's education had consisted of a thorough knowledge of Blackstone's treatise on the common law of England, perhaps a boyhood reading of the Latin classics for their style, and apprenticeship in a lawyer's office. The law they learned was still more English than American.

The English Constitution had impressed its order on the law, and many of the specialized forms and manners of speech developed in the English courts were preserved like fossils of an earlier time in American law.

Preserved also was the curious tradition that courts made their own law. The "common law" was the body of precedents observed by the courts of England, a chain of decisions reaching back into the twelfth century, when manor courts were presided over by the lord of the manor, and ecclesiastical, merchants' and guilds' courts were all autonomous, and when even the courts of the growing central government — the king's courts of law, the chancellor's court of equity, the courts of admiralty — were independent, followed their own precedents, and fought among themselves over jurisdiction.

The American colonies inherited the tradition of the courts' autonomy, along with the tangle of precedents and rules concerning jurisdiction it had spawned. Courts of law granted jury trials; courts of equity and admiralty did not. A court of law could impose fines; a court of equity could not. Unless the nice distinctions of form were followed, a lawsuit would be lost.

The world had changed, the practice of law had changed, and the study of law reflected its practice. Blackstone was no longer taught,[11] and there was no single compendium of law to take its place. Instead, there was a jumble of specialties. The intimate connections among fields of law had been shattered. There was a law of real property now, whose archaic forms reflected a feudal English system that no longer existed anywhere and had never existed in Massachusetts. But the law governing marriage had been reformed and no longer depended on feudal property rights. The law governing commercial activity had proliferated into unrelated specialties reflecting the vigorous new business world. The law of private wrongs was a miscellany of rules with no obvious order. The law of contracts was a jumble of particular customs.

Railroads, mills, and factories were growing into larger, more complex and powerful institutions than the common law had ever encompassed. A continent-spanning government linking the nation together with telegraph and rails had been born in the Civil War. The law in disjointed fashion had begun to reflect these changes.

Burdened by an unwieldy system of precedents and forms, the independent modern courts of America tried to deal with the proliferating specialization of the law. Mills and railroads were judged by the standards set for medieval landowners in nuisance cases. The law was slowly rationalized to fit modern circumstances, but it was accessible only through the technical language and forms of older centuries, and its meaning and purpose were obscure.

When Holmes began the study of law, therefore, it was a huge mass of disjointed particulars with no apparent relation to everyday affairs.

Separate chains of precedent stretched back almost a thousand years into medieval Britain. Feudal rules for deciding disputes over real estate were matched by similarly convoluted bodies of maritime law, commercial law, bailments, equity, pleadings, agency, wills, criminal law, arbitration, and so on, the very names smelling of decay.

The three professors of law lectured; the method of questioning and discussion had not yet been invented. There was a list of recommended reading for the students, textbooks on specialized topics, but no books of general introduction, no works of history or theory. Holmes's heart sank. "What is this to my soul?"

> [He was] plunged in a thick fog of details — in a black and frozen night, in which there were no flowers, no spring, no easy joys. Voices of authority warned that in the crush of that ice any craft might sink. . . . One heard Burke saying that law sharpens the mind by narrowing it. One heard in Thackeray of a lawyer bending all the powers of a great mind to a mean profession. One saw that artists and poets shrank from it as from an alien world.[12]

For a student in Boston, the law lacked even those attractions that it might have had in a capital city. London was still the world capital of English-speaking law. In Washington, great Constitutional questions were argued; in New York and Philadelphia, the railroad and steel magnates fought their wars. But Boston law practice was made up of ordinary transactions: real estate sales, personal injuries, divorces, bankruptcies, agreements between business people, squabbles over taxes, inheritance. These mundane and unromantic matters, encrusted with the customs of forgotten centuries, were the matter of the common law.

Holmes, who had hoped to make law a point of departure for philosophy, was discouraged, but he attacked the reading. He set himself daily assignments and grimly read through them.

His studies were somewhat enlivened by friendship and combat. The law students had informal clubs in which they tried cases, taking turns serving as lawyers or judges.[13] The law school also had a more formal "moot court" in which mock trials were held, where the senior faculty member, sixty-nine-year-old Joel Parker, lately chief justice of the New Hampshire Supreme Court, sat as judge. The students argued the sorts of cases that filled the courts: disputes between neighbors. A landowner had dug a ditch or built a fence, and the ditch had flooded his neighbor's cellar or muddied his well; the fence had blocked his light. There were centuries of precedent to search. When Holmes found an old decision to support his side, it was like grasping a rapier. When he stood before Judge Parker, excited and exhausted, he felt a sharp pain on the left side of his face and neck, as if from the wound received at Antietam.[14]

Argument gave life and excitement to the law, but did not yet give it meaning. Holmes, restless in the narrow boundaries of the school, ventured out into a wider landscape. After two semesters he had read the textbooks, heard the lectures. He began on his own to read the opinions of the courts, the precedents themselves, in a systematic way. At the same time he began to search for theoretical studies and explanations. Few had been written in the United States, but the work of English theorists was beginning to appear. Henry Sumner Maine's *Ancient Law* was published in the United States in 1864, and caused great excitement. Holmes's classmate John Fiske exclaimed when he read the book:

> I have passed through an era and entered upon a new Epoch of my life! . . . No novel I ever read enchained me more. . . . It has thrown all my ideas into definite shape. It has suggested many new and startling views of social progress. It has confirmed many new generalizations that were beginning to arise in my mind as faint suspicions. . . . it is perfectly GLORIOUS.[15]

Maine's great work was a slim volume, clearly and easily written. In it, Maine used classical Rome to illustrate his exciting theories about the evolution of law.

Ancient law began with family relationships. The father had been the head of the family, and the family had been the fundamental unit of society. The law had reflected family order, a fixed hierarchy of status, from father to child, from master to slave.

All ancient societies began with such laws, but "progressive societies" — those of western Europe — had freed themselves from the ancient bonds. Inheritance and slavery had given way to voluntary agreements; laws had insensibly changed, new rules growing like embryos within the shells of old forms; law based on status had become law based on contract.[16]

Here was order, meaning, and intellectual excitement. Here was an eye that saw, as from high above, the vast simple geological patterns of the landscape. Law was part of the natural order.

But neither Maine nor Roman law was taught in the Harvard Law School nor recognized in the courts of Massachusetts. If any theory at all was recognized it was the dry, puritanical thought of the Utilitarians and their founder, Jeremy Bentham. Prisons, Bentham thought, should be built in the shape of wheels, with cells for solitary confinement about the rim. Prisoners should read and be taught reasonable principles until they were sufficiently educated to return to society. Poetry, Bentham thought, was only printed matter with lines of irregular length. The vast untidiness of society should be corrected by rational legislation.

John Austin was Bentham's prophet among lawyers. His book *The Province of Jurisprudence Determined* seemed to explain all of law the way Euclid deduced his theorems. Law, said Austin, was not a species of morality or revelation.[17] Law was the command of the sovereign, backed by the force of the state. Public force had suppressed private violence, and its only justification was the greater happiness of the people.

The great mass of tradition, custom, religious principle, and common sense on which the law of the manor courts had risen, the fixed arrangement of society on which Blackstone had rested, were not law, *properly speaking*. Law was what the sovereign — in England, since the seventeenth century, Parliament — enacted. The autonomous local courts, the king's courts, and the ecclesiastical courts, made law only so far and as Parliament directed or allowed.

Implicit in this was the radical doctrine that what Parliament had thoughtlessly allowed it might now consciously revise. The common law, encrusted by obsolete purposes and merely historical survivals, might be replaced by orderly legislation for the common good. Reform, even radical reform, logically followed.

Austin ignored history. There was neither life nor movement, neither passion nor meaning in his law, only dry logic and relentless purpose.

In the spring of 1865, the war ended at last. In the early days of April, the siege of Petersburg was finally successful. The city was taken, the last barrier protecting Richmond fell, and the Confederate government fled their capital. General Robert E. Lee wearily surrendered to Grant. The killing, which had gone on so long, was over.

In Boston, the news came with the early flowers. Veterans and prisoners of war, wounded and ill, began to come home.

On April 15, President Lincoln was shot as he sat watching a play. Outrage and grief tainted the celebration.

But Boston was at peace. There was a literary flowering. Newspapers and magazines were filled with cheerful or solemn reminiscences of the war. Young Henry James published a story for the first time, in *The Atlantic Monthly*, a tale of a wounded soldier who came home to his mother — a woman strikingly like Mrs. Holmes.

Holmes himself particularly enjoyed and admired the war poems of Henry Brownell, a poet who had practiced law. The doctor said, "Colonel Holmes was buttonholing all his friends like the Ancient Mariner," to tell them of his enthusiasm for Brownell.[18] Holmes wrote to Brownell himself, "I bullied and snubbed my daddy at tea the other day with my acquaintance with the great poets of the country."[19]

Brownell's "Death of the Old Sergeant" was a sentimental favorite. Holmes memorized it and liked to recite it. He sent Brownell sketches of his own he thought of working up into finished poems. Philosophy and poetry continued to lure him away from his studies:

It is so easy and pleasant to go from day to day satisfying yourself for not having knocked off a hundred pages of Evidence or

Contracts with the thought that you have turned over a few stones in some new mind and seen all sorts of funny things wiggling, or have read some new poem or (worse) written one.[20]

To Henry James these were "the 'epoch-making' weeks of the spring of 1865 . . . of unforgettable gropings and findings."[21] Holmes, Bill and Henry James, Clover Hooper, Minny Temple, Eleanor Shattuck, the Shaws, John Gray — just returned from the army — made a circle of flirtations, saw one another often, wrote to each other when apart. Bill James and Holmes both flirted with Clover Hooper and Minny Temple, who was half in love with John Gray. They were intelligent, awkward, passionate friends.

Class Day at Harvard was festive that summer. There was a hot-air balloon, and Clover Hooper went up in it.[22] Just after the commencement exercises there was a commemoration to honor the college's war dead. The solemnities were mixed with rowdy celebrations. The undergraduates, for whom the war was already far in the past, drank too much. The old men and the businessmen and the politicians who had stayed at home said a great deal about chivalry. General Meade consented to be honored.

Holmes sat quietly in the audience, wearing his uniform. There was a touching moment when Bill Bartlett, crippled and ill since the war, spoke a few halting words and could not go on.

Emerson spoke; Emerson, who saw with a clear and disinterested eye, and whose chilling words sank into Holmes's soul. War, Emerson said, was good not in spite of, but because of, the killing.

> The old Greek Heraclitus said, "War is the Father of all things." . . . War passes the power of all chemical solvents, breaking up the old adhesions and allowing the atoms of society to take a new order. It is not the Government, but the War, that has appointed the good generals, sifted out the pedants, put in the new and vigorous blood. The War has lifted many other people beside Grant and Sherman into their true places. . . .

> You all know as well as I the story of these dedicated men, who knew well on what duty they went — whose fathers and mothers said of each slaughtered son, "We gave him up when he enlisted." One mother said, when her son was offered the command of the first negro regiment, "If he accepts it, I shall be as proud as if I had heard that he was shot." These men, thus tender, thus high-bred, thus peaceable, were always in the front and always employed. They might say, with their forefathers the old Norse Vikings, "We sung the mass of the lances from morning until evening.' . . .

We see — we thank you for it — a new era, worth to mankind all the treasure and all the lives it has cost; yes, worth to the world the lives of all this generation of American men, if they had been demanded.[23]

Then everyone went to the seashore; to Nahant, for instance — "Cold Roast Boston," as Tom Appleton called it — where the little doctor was lifted onto a table to sing his songs — or to Newport or the White Mountains. The Jameses took a house in Newport. Henry James, Jr., in the midst of his awakening, moved restlessly back and forth from Boston to Newport to New Hampshire. He invited Holmes to join him in a visit to North Conway, in the White Mountains, where Minny Temple was staying.

Holmes and Henry James had their own mild flirtation that summer. Holmes put into a scrapbook cuttings of Henry James's first reviews for *The Nation*, and wrote to him in praise. With Holmes making advances of friendship, Henry became a little coy about his invitation to North Conway, and when at last he made it definite, Holmes turned him down, pleading his constant excuse of illness and overwork.[24] The two men would repeat their dance of mutual advance and retreat into their old age.

Holmes was in his third term at the law school and, having exhausted the school's meager offerings, he did not trouble to finish his third semester's course of lectures.[25] He disliked listening passively to other people talk — "I used to say I wouldn't go to hear the Apostle Paul — or anybody but myself, which last I couldn't avoid."[26]

As winter began, Holmes went to work instead as a clerk in cousin Robert Morse's small law office, where he copied documents, ran errands, and did research: "In Bob Morse's office, I saw a real writ, acquired a practical conviction of the difference between assumpsit and trover, and marveled open-mouthed at the swift certainty with which a master of the business turned it off."[27]

With his first sight of a practicing lawyer's office came his first ventures into courtrooms. Judge William Endicott, descendant of the first Puritan governor of Massachusetts, was Holmes's image of a judge:

Distinguished in person, with the look of race in his countenance which . . . suggested a resemblance to that first Endicott to whom Massachusetts owes so much, he sat without a thought of self, without even the unconscious pride or aloofness which seemed, nay, was, his right, serenely absorbed in the matters at hand, impersonal yet human, the living image of justice, weighing as if the elements in the balance were dead matter, but discerning and collecting those elements by the help of a noble and tender heart.[28]

The circle of Holmes's friends grew closer. Fanny Dixwell and he drew closer still. Fanny was a year older than Holmes. They were cousins — Mrs. Holmes was Fanny's great-aunt, whom she had addressed as "Aunty" when a girl.[29] But Fanny was not part of the Boston and Cambridge circle in which Holmes moved. Her family were not in polite society, and she herself was a solitary woman. She was vivacious and filled with eccentric humor and a yearning for artistic expression. That summer Bill James fell in love with her, as he seemed often to do with Holmes's ladies:

> The only fellow I care anything about is Holmes, who is on the whole a first-rate article and one which improves by wear. He is perhaps too exclusively intellectual, but sees things so easily and clearly and talks so admirably that it is a great treat to be with him. . . . I made the acquaintance the other day of Miss Fanny Dixwell of Cambridge (the eldest); do you know her? She is decidedly A-1, and (so far) the best girl I have known.[30]

Sharing flirtations, drinks, and cigars, Holmes and Bill James spent late evenings talking and arguing philosophy. Henry James lingered a little behind, observant. When Holmes went abroad that summer, Bill James called on Fanny every day, morning and evening;[31] Henry James, with confused and tender feelings, called at 21 Charles Street for news of Holmes himself.[32]

The late-night talks with Bill James added to the strain of work. Holmes was reading philosophy, preparing for his trip abroad to finish his education, struggling to learn all of the law, clerking for Bob Morse, and beginning to practice law on his own,[33] all at once.

The Holmes family talked and planned Holmes's trip. He would go to London and be introduced in polite society and then go on for a tour of the Continent. Mrs. Holmes half-joked that her son would find out how bad her cooking and her coffee were. The doctor had not been abroad since his days as a medical student, and they exchanged curious stories they had heard of small differences in manners that might embarrass an American. One of them had heard there was a proper London way to knock on doors. Steamship tickets and a hotel in London had to be arranged. Holmes bought a pocket diary for the trip, like those he had carried in the war, and wrote: "John Gray wants cigar holder, pipe-shaped and not too long." The doctor asked Holmes to look out for stereoscope pictures. Holmes noted the name of a Bond Street tailor and a shop for gloves in Piccadilly.[34]

In the last week of April, 1866, Holmes left Bob Morse's office. His trunk and boxes were carried down to the railroad station, and he followed them to New York. At the foot of Manhattan, accompanied by a comfortable contingent of Bostonians, he boarded the Cunard side-wheel steamer *Persia* and, after two weeks of the featureless North Atlantic, came upon the black smoke of tugs in Liverpool harbor; the sight of green grass was startling.

Holmes had his first dinner in England at a hotel in Liverpool — "fried soles" — which he had not tasted before. Still surrounded by Boston travelers, he went up to London the next morning, found his hotel — "Beastly place" — and walked in the streets until evening. There were the Horse Guards, the Houses of Parliament, Westminster Abbey, Charing Cross, but "all seemed an old story after the stereoscopes."

A better lodging was needed, and the next morning he found a private apartment at a Mrs. Draper's, 23 Sackville Street. He went to the Baring Brothers bank, in which the Bostonian Russell Sturgis was then a partner, and to the American embassy, where Charles Francis Adams and his son Henry had been in residence since the beginning of the war.

Holmes was fitted for boots, bought dinner clothes, and stared at the crowds in the streets. London was immensely bigger than any city he had seen; he walked all afternoon and into the evening.

When he returned to his room, he found that Henry Adams had called. Before sleep, he made the first entries in his little pocket diary: "First impressions — common people like ours — swells finer — 2 types — saxon & dark — all dressed alike   Lavender gloves & sailor ties. [Evening:] whores stop you everywhere."

In the following days, Holmes did more shopping, had lunch with the Adamses, and after lunch a good talk with Henry Adams over cigars. Henry put Holmes's mind at ease about small differences in manner and speech.

With Henry Adams's help, he delivered his letters of introduction; one left the letter with a calling card at the door. He saw the sights — the Royal Academy ("much disappointed — Landseer pale and feeble"), Regent Street, Westminster Abbey again, St. James's Palace, the curious ecclesiastical courts, the lawyers' Temple Bar — walking about in new boots that left his feet sore. At the Chancery Court, the Lord Chancellor called him up beside him on the bench: "people looked at me and grinned."

Russell Sturgis had him out for a weekend — "regular English country place — heard nightingales." Holmes saw and heard a lark for the first time. But he was moving in a little cloud of Bostonians. Clover Hooper and her father were in London, as were the Caspar Crowninshields, young Sumner, Charley Grinnell. Bill Bartlett had brought over his new bride, Agnes Pomeroy, from Pittsfield. They all met at the Adamses' and the Sturgises'. Holmes flirted with Mary Adams and Clover Hooper.

In his first brief forays into English houses, Holmes felt that he was treated as a negligible quantity. The ladies, showing more bare shoulder than he was used to, let their eyes wander very freely past him as they spoke. The men condescended, and Holmes found the pervasive consciousness of class oppressive. He was a provincial, middle-class young man visiting the capital of the greatest empire in the world; his letters to his parents had a discouraged tone.

Holmes did have letters of introduction to a few of the titled gentry who had sympathized with the Union cause during the war, and to the leading radical writers and thinkers, most of whom were middle-class in English terms, but who formed a self-styled intellectual aristocracy a little like Boston's. Of the first group, Holmes particularly hoped to meet Sir John Kennaway and the Duke of Argyll. Of the second group, Holmes had letters to John Stuart Mill, whose work he had assiduously read in preparation for their meeting. Holmes hoped also to meet Herbert Spencer. But Henry Sumner Maine was in India.

Holmes slowly began to receive replies to his letters of introduction and to receive invitations from friends of the Adamses. Lady Belper invited Holmes to dinner. He left his letter for John Stuart Mill at the House of Commons, and Mill came out and was very civil. Although he seemed a dry, unimaginative man, Mill alone among the English people whom Holmes met seemed unaware of social class. The Adamses took him one evening in June to a party with the Liberal leader in the House of Commons, William Gladstone, who talked kindly and at length to this unknown young man, and asked about his war experiences: "Gladstone had a voice like Emerson and in '66 seemed to me the one man who was like an American. He came out to meet you and had gusto —"[35] At a dinner where they met again, Gladstone made much of Holmes, and insisted he sit down, "in consideration of [his] wounds."

Holmes began to feel more at ease. Tom Hughes, lawyer and author of *Tom Brown's School Days,* had him to dinner, and Holmes flirted with the twelve-year-old daughter of the house, who was helping to serve the guests. At dinner with Henry Cowper, younger son of the sixth Earl Cowper — "This is the way to see pictures — Van Dyke etc. etc. around the dining and drawing room" — he and Cowper became friends.

From the St. James's Club, where Henry Adams had given him a guest membership, Holmes was taken occasionally to late parties with the young men. At the Political Economy Club, there was the sort of talk he was used to in Boston, and after an evening there he had a long walk in the streets with James Fitzjames Stephen, a stout, energetic young criminal lawyer, one of the leaders of the new generation of Benthamite reformers. They walked and talked until 11:30, and the next morning Stephen sent to Holmes's rooms a copy of his *Essays by a Barrister.*

The Duchess of Argyll invited Holmes to dinner. A copy of *The Autocrat of the Breakfast-Table* was tactfully displayed. Holmes was given a place of distinction at the dinner table, but he was nervous and did not shine. The prettiest girl he had yet seen in London was there, a Miss Campbell of Stonefield, yet he did not succeed in talking to her.

It was June; the air was fresh; the days were sunny and seemingly endless, the London nights brief and bright. Holmes began to be known, and invitations started to crowd each other. "Breakfast Mrs Gladstone — 10. Mill dinner? Mr Stephen 77 Gloucester Place — dinner." He found that the young women came along on late-night visits to grog shops and dancing parties; in Boston mixed parties had never begun after dinner. He found that the ladies drank with the men and talked politics and literature. At an aristocratic dinner he quoted "The Traveller" and got the negligent reply from his partner, "Oh, one of our classics. We don't read them." He ventured a remark about poetry to a young woman, who answered, "Tennyson told me that others may have written better poetry, but none wrote poetry that sounded better."[36] Holmes began to adopt the same self-confident lightness of speech:

Dined at the Members [of Parliament] dining room with Mr. Mill with whom was Mr. Bain [the] psychologist — and we talked — I was struck with absence of imaginative impulse esp. in Mr. Bain — excellent for facts & criticism but not open to the infinite possibilities — Eh?[37]

The conversation was combative, but Holmes had been trained by talk with the doctor, who was a master, and as he gained confidence he began to hold his own. He prepared some responses beforehand. One incident particularly pleased him.

I read Kinglake's *Crimean War* when I was in the army. . . . [At a dinner] I met Kinglake who said he had a question to ask — I knew what it would be. Did our men fight in line? I grinned and said . . . of course our men fought in line, and that I believed you could make baboons do it, if you had the right sort of officers.[38]

Holmes met the painter Sir John Millais and Robert Browning, whose poetry had set him on fire. He was now very far from Boston indeed.

There were letters from home, to emphasize the distance he had traveled. His mother wrote often. Bill James was calling daily on Fanny Dixwell, and Mrs. Holmes had teased Fanny about it. Ellen Hooper and Minny Temple had called to ask for news of him; so had Henry James. Holmes answered cheerfully, or not at all; he was very busy:

Wednsday, June 6: The Chancellor asked me to dine today but I was engaged to the Att. Gen. So did Mr. Mill . . . Dinner at the Att. Gen.'s delightful — Lady Laura bluff & pleasant — took her down & sat on her left. Afterwards talked with her daughter about art. . . .

Thursday, June 7: I am just returning from breakfast wh. was uncommonly pleasant. The Duke of Argyll & Duchess Mr Adams — Ld Houghton — etc. etc. Mr. Gladstone seated himself on my right — Mr Adams said with hardly an exception it was the pleasantest thing of the sort he had seen since he'd been in London. . . .

To Lady Lyell's to lunch. . . . Called on Lady Herbert. Dined with Mr. Stephen & his brother [Leslie] — then walked down to St. James' Club & with Parker & Capt Campion to Cremorne [where there was music and dancing] — when we returned (2½) — dawn was breaking — a rare assemblage of virtue & fashion — as well as beauty — The ladies got a little tight late in the evening —

The dinner with Fitzjames Stephen and his younger brother Leslie marked a particular success in the intellectual circle, and opened a new friendship for Holmes.

Leslie Stephen was almost ten years older than Holmes. He was tall, thin, bony, energetic; his dark hair and full beard were long and unruly. A bachelor don, his passion and sensuality were invested in his intellectual life. He, too, had been raised on the novels of Sir Walter Scott and the love of chivalry; like Holmes he was a self-made aristocrat, a philosopher, a passionate skeptic. He was prone to bursts of resentment and helpless rage, which occasionally gave a bloodthirsty tone to his writing.[39] He was a great talker, a skilled draftsman, a solitary and intense thinker.

At dinner June 7 with Fitzjames Stephen, there was talk about the new sport of mountain climbing. Leslie was planning a mountaineering trip to Switzerland that summer and recommended to Holmes that he try the dangerous amusement. Before the evening was over Stephen had invited Holmes to a meeting of the Alpine Club, of which he was president, in a "pothouse in Leicester Square" the following week.

It would soon be time for Holmes to leave London. The people he had come to see would scatter to resorts and country houses. Holmes had planned to go on to the Continent, for the customary Bostonian's grand tour through France, Germany, and Italy. But a European war threatened. Prussia had grown belligerent over conquests in Denmark that she jointly administered with Austria; war between the two rivals for a German-speaking empire was likely that summer. Perhaps Holmes would be wiser to take an excursion into the Swiss Alps rather than Germany or Italy. Stephen suggested an itinerary.

It was a turbulent summer. Gladstone made his radical proposal to give workingmen the vote. The Whig gentry abandoned him, and the Liberal government fell. Britain was slipping into an economic smashup, and class warfare threatened.

On June 15, Bismarck precipitated his war with Austria, and the

Prussian army moved into neighboring German states; the violent birth of a new German empire had begun. Early the next day, Holmes left his hotel and began his trip to France and Switzerland.

In Paris, Holmes was simply a tourist. He breakfasted at cafés, dined with Bostonians, and trudged dutifully to see everything that his father had suggested. He feet troubled him badly after days of walking on pavements and marble floors. "I have hardly had a comfortable moment in Europe on acct. of my feet," he wrote irritably in his diary. He bought new shoes, shopped for gifts. He bought silver cuff buttons for his brother Ned.

But the food and music were revelations. At the cafés, *omelette aux champignons, omelette aux confitures*; at dinner, lobster mayonnaise; "the turbot was the best I ever tasted." "Mem. Sauce hollandaise for turbot." In the evenings he went to concerts and to plays. "Then to hear Ristori [sing] . . . Médée. There is nothing to say except that it was great."

Day after day, he systematically surveyed the Louvre. The statues and antiquities, familiar from reproductions, did not move him beyond a few exceptional moments: "Sensation when the Venus de Milo shone before me." He did not care for the French paintings. But when he at last came to the Renaissance masters, "for perhaps the first time [he] really gloated: J. Van Eyck — P. Veronese — Velasquez — Rembrandt . . . the little J. Van Eyck is absolutely perfect."

Color alone, the purely sensuous, did not move him; but the old portraits, nearly monochrome with age, spoke to him. The Van Eycks sank into his memory; he returned to see again the delicate portraits of noble young men; he would recall them years later.

The days passed slowly. Holmes often dined alone, walked aimlessly, stayed in his room and read. There were occasional excitements. John Hay was the American consul in Paris, and he, Holmes, and Colonel Charles Francis Adams, Jr., had some lively evenings. They went to the Théâtre Français — "devilish good." One night after dinner the three Americans went to the Prado — "a mad scene — It was crowded and hot and fermenting — And perhaps they didn't dance the Can-Can."

On July 2, Holmes said good-bye to Hay, left his trunk and his purchases to be sent on to England, and met Leslie Stephen at the Gare de l'Est.[40] They took an overnight train to Basel.

In their climbing, Stephen — Holmes still called him "Mr. Stephen" — made no allowance for Holmes's inexperience or sore feet. He kept an unrelenting pace, and Holmes limped after him, swearing quietly to himself all the profanities that he knew.[41] Stephen called him "Yank," and shouted at him from ahead, "Can you come up, Yank?" as Holmes, frightened, crawled up to him.[42] They sometimes slept on the mountain, rising at dawn for the next morning's climb.

Thursday, July 5: Oh — didn't sleep — That's all — After breakfast (mountain trout) started up the Gemmi pass. . . . There was a
stiffish drop — sheer down to the valley with one break from the
top — one saw the Mischabel — Weisshorn — Matterhorn — . . .
picked flowers from edge of yawning gulf — but I felt an unpleas-
ant creeping in my backbone —

Friday, July 6: Today have been up the Balme Horne. . . . Rose at
4. Weather uncertain and very windy — Started 5. At first stones
of the nastiest sort — the foot of Glacier — Then rope put on —
steep ascent — grub & rum — Then along the edge of such a
precipice as yesterday's except frozen over & you could tumble
either way . . . for an hour or two like going along the edge of an
oyster shell — Oh wasn't I scared? . . . When we were nearly up
the finest sight I ever saw burst upon us — beyond the precipice
— vast rolling masses of cloud & above & beyond that a panorama
of the greatest alpine peaks — Mischabel — Monte Rosa — Weisshorn — Rothhorn — Gabelhorn — Matterhorn — Dame Blanche
— Grand Cornier — Combin — Mont Blanc &c. Stephen said he'd
never seen the like — Mem. slide downhill sitting — bully —

Holmes was joyful, exhausted, his digestion out of order. After a thir-
teen-hour trek from Schwarenbach to Lauterbrunnen he had a rest, and
then they set off again. An avalanche poured roaring from the Jungfrau,
a sound that recalled the rolling fire of a line of battle. Holmes was limp-
ing and growing very badly sunburned; he did not sleep well. He bought
an alpenstock and they undertook a real climb, an ascent of the Monk
with guides and a porter, sleeping in a cave with "the glacier lying dark
& cold like a slain dragon" below them. In the morning of July 11 they
continued the climb:

Up steeps of snow & rock we went wh. were like the side of a
house until at about 6½ or 7 we reached the foot of the peak —
the Monk — wh. we were to ascend — grub, & then to work —
up a pull of rock then along interminable ridges of ice covered
with snow — a precipice on either side — guides cutting steps —
and at 10.10 the top — Saw a wilderness of mountain tops mostly
below us — and a vast meadows of clouds wh. we also looked
down upon. . . . Then after grub down the Aletsch Glacier wh.
was covered with snow in the nastiest manner to the very bottom
— We didn't leave the snow till 5½ p.m. 14 hours — and got to
Eggishorn at 8 — burned — stiff — exhausted — There is nothing
to say about that most horrible grind — it almost recalled an army
march.

After that trip Holmes never climbed again, but the exuberance of conquering the mountains was like a door opening, releasing an emotion whose memory he would repeatedly recall and that would color his speech ever afterward.

> I cannot describe the gradual lightening of the peaks by wh. we were surrounded while the valley was still dark below.[43]

> I came down from the Monch to the top of the Aletsch Glacier and felt as if we were committing a shuddery sacrilege, surprising Nature in her privacy before creation was complete.[44]

In that sacred moment as Holmes came onto the glacier he exultantly shouted an obscenity — to Stephen's amused surprise.[45]

There was a last week of hiking and climbing. Holmes, lame and sunburned almost beyond recognition, rode a mule and Stephen walked, as they worked their way toward Zermatt, talking comfortably of metaphysics.

At Zermatt a letter came for Stephen. It was addressed in a woman's handwriting, and Stephen was visibly excited, but he would not explain. He said only that he would have to leave the mountains.[46]

Holmes was briefly at a loss. London was deserted. Dr. Holmes had written to advise going back to tour museums and galleries, but Holmes wrote to Sir John Kennaway and the Duke of Argyll at their country houses. When Holmes returned to Paris, he found their invitations waiting, and set off quickly for Britain. He had a quiet night passage across the English Channel, but the ventilation was bad, and he had nightmares.

Kennaway's seat, Escot Hall, was in Devonshire. Holmes arrived in the rain, and by a later train than expected, so that there was no one to meet him. He walked up the road in a drizzle with an umbrella in one hand and a hatbox in the other. But the great old stone house was hospitable, his room was warm and dry, and, after a hot bath, he had dinner with Kennaway — a great brown-bearded man — and a walk around: "Ancestral acres — Devonshire cream — pheasants — stable — garden — beeches — Prayers — Bed — Dream."

It was Sunday morning. A dignified servant arranged Holmes's clothes. Outside his window there was a view of meadows and woods receding to gentle hills. After breakfast, he went with the family to church in the village, Ottery St. Mary's. The Kennaway family pew was fenced off in a little enclosure. The country people touched their hats or curtsied to Sir John and his lady.

For a week, Holmes settled comfortably into feudal life. In the mornings, Sir John read from the Bible to the family and assembled servants, and explained the day's lesson. The cook, butler, and housekeeper, who had been in the household since their childhood, stood respectfully.

Holmes and Kennaway hunted rabbits in the mornings. Holmes shot well, although he had not hunted since boyhood. In the afternoons, Sir John or Miss Kennaway took Holmes driving through the lanes to see a church or a ruin; once they went to Stratford-on-Avon. In the evening after dinner the men talked over drinks and cigars; Holmes occasionally smoked his pipe, and told anecdotes of war and mountain climbing.

On Friday, August 3, Holmes took the overnight train to Glasgow and then traveled by gradual stages to the Duke of Argyll's castle near Inveraray. It was Lord Lorne's, the Duke's eldest son's, coming-of-age, and a British man-of-war, gaily decorated with flags and firing guns in salute, was in the harbor to help in the celebration. There were forty to dinner at the castle. Holmes with great pleasure took in a very young ducal daughter, Lady Edith; it was her first dinner in company. There was a ball afterward, the guests danced reels, and to Holmes's delight Miss Campbell of Stonefield — the beautiful girl Holmes had seen at the Duchess of Argyll's dinner in London — was there. He met her father, and Stonefield itself was not far off. Perhaps Holmes would visit?

In the morning there were Scottish games to celebrate Lord Lorne's majority: throwing the hammer, tossing the caber, putting the stone. There were horse races. Holmes joined the duke and his guests fishing for Atlantic salmon in the duke's streams and shooting grouse — Holmes killed four brace of grouse, "and wasn't I proud." A tenant gave the hunting party bread and butter, milk and whiskey — "spice to keep out the cold." They hunted red deer and, to Holmes's great joy, after several missed shots, he killed a buck — "shot smack through the head — it was better than £10." On one rainy afternoon Holmes recited "Death of the Old Sergeant" and other sentimental Civil War poetry to the assembled family.

After a week, Holmes went on to Sir John Orde's for more shooting and wrote to the Campbells of Stonefield that he would accept their invitation. On Friday, August 17 — the time for returning to Boston was close — Stonefield's letter arrived — *Come* — but on the next morning, Stonefield abruptly fell ill, and the visit was delayed a week.

Holmes spent the week in a funk, and it rained. But on Sunday, going to church in the interminable drizzle, he found the Campbells there and was told, "Come on Monday — Stonefield is much better."

When Holmes arrived, he found Miss Campbell "playing battledore & shuttlecock in the hall with her brother & looking very pretty."

That evening he took Miss Campbell in to dinner. The other guests were Colonel and Mrs. Campbell of Skipness — with their daughter, another Miss Campbell, a handsome, dark, and strong-featured young woman. On Tuesday, a third Miss Campbell arrived, Miss Campbell of Auchindarroch.

Holmes's days were divided between flirtations with the three Misses Campbell and shooting with his host. To the ladies, Holmes recited poetry, talked charmingly of the war — they were all Southerners there, Miss Campbell of Auchindarroch warned him archly — and flirted with pale Miss Campbell of Stonefield, dark Miss Campbell of Skipness. In the evenings when the ladies retired, the men smoked and drank, talked and told stories until midnight. Then up at five, for shooting in the wet weather.

Holmes was happy, excited, and weary. The beautiful Miss Campbell of Stonefield seemed to return his interest. The pain in the left side of his neck returned, and his joints felt stiff. The trip was almost ended. It had been a success, and he was not the same man who had left Boston.

Near the end of his visit, Miss Campbell of Auchindarroch proposed a game. Each of the guests was to write a poem, answering a series of questions: What do you admire in men? in women? What are your own characteristics? What do you enjoy most? If you were not yourself, who would you be? Where would you live? What is your favorite flower, color, etc.? They were each to have their answers in verse the next day.

After the evening's smoking and talk, Holmes sat up a little later, composing his answer. The first rough sketch was tipsy, scrawled and blotted. "Poet — Soldier — Gentleman — Sir Walter Raleigh," he began. But it was too late to write, and he had had too much to drink. He scribbled notes to be polished in the morning. "Heroines — let him talk lots of love — Foil villains — save lives. . . ."

The next day he wrote a finished poem. The childish image of Sir Walter Raleigh was submerged, but in his place rose an artist, soldier, mountain-climber — gentleman.

> Give me a man who's simple, wise,
> Restrained in speech and brave to dare —
> A woman in whose candid eyes
> I read her true as she is fair —
> And faith I think my greatest bliss is
> To get his wisdom and her kisses —
>
> Characteristics? They're not one but many,
> Or (its the same thing) I don't think I've any —
>
> Demand not what might happiness appear
> But look around — for happiness is here
>
> Rise ere the lark — and in the dark —
> Walk o'er the roughest bits of land

And snow and rock — that men in mock-
Cry call the fun of Switzerland —

I like the little flower best
She gave me when we said goodbye —
And sure no hue of all the rest
Can match what sparkles in her eye —

If not myself I wouldn't be at all —
Why if you please I'd live at Escot Hall . . .

Favorites . . . again methinks a choice in vain is
Genius not Rome confines, nor Venice
But still as I've a taste Germanic
I'll name that charming aged John Van Eyck.[47]

On his last morning, Miss Campbell of Stonefield made eyes at him over the breakfast table, and with that trophy he set off for home.

9

THE FIRST
VENTURE

A TRIAL LAWYER, GEORGE O. SHATTUCK, HAD PROMISED HOLMES A
position. Shattuck looked like a farmer: he was big, square,
bearded, heavy-browed, quiet, and indeed he had grown up on
a farm and still owned land in Mattapoisett, near New Bedford, where
he did some farming in the summers. Holmes said of him: "I think he
had a sympathy with the great forces which he saw at work, and a sympathy with the animals of the farm; also the visible return which the
earth makes for labor, pleased him."[1]

He was a partner in the firm of Chandler, Shattuck and Thayer. Shattuck had joined old Peleg Chandler twelve years before, when he was
just out of Harvard Law School, and had brought his classmate James B.
Thayer with him. Chandler was now old and deaf, and Shattuck had
taken over the firm's trial work. He was thirty-seven years old when
Holmes went to work for him, in the fall of 1866,[2] and Holmes, twenty-
five, admired him:

> [George Shattuck] seemed to like to take great burdens upon
> himself — not merely when there was a corresponding reward,
> but when his feelings were touched, as well. He was a model in
> his bearing with clients. How often have I seen men come to him

borne down by troubles which they found too great to support, and depart with light step, having left their weight upon stronger shoulders. But while his calm manner made such things seem trifles, he took them a good deal on his nerves. I saw the ends of his fingers twitch as he quietly listened and advised. He never shunned anxiety, and anxiety is what kills.[3]

Shattuck fought for his clients with implacable determination. Once enlisted in a cause, he was relentless. He enjoyed battle and had a deep reluctance to accept defeat.[4]

He was a great man with the jury in every way. His addresses carried everything before them like a victorious cavalry charge, sometimes . . . sweeping the judge along with the rest in the rout.[5]

To Holmes, he was "all compelling force."[6]

Yet, there was something almost self-effacing about the man. Like the military officers Holmes had admired, Shattuck submerged himself in the battle.

On his return from Europe, Holmes had plunged back into literature, philosophy, courtships, law. Boston's social season was beginning, and he was an engaging and eligible dinner guest who had learned to talk to women.

It was an age that admired fat, taciturn men, with broad chests, heavy paunches, thick calves; yet Holmes was charming, and his light talk about serious matters, about war and philosophy, men and women, made him attractive. He had gained confidence and began to be a success among the ladies. He wrote poetry, read philosophy, and talked late into the nights.

Shattuck observed, however, and soon said to Holmes, still flushed with the excitement of London, that at least for a time a lawyer must give himself up wholly to his profession.[7]

Holmes wondered how a man like Shattuck, of such capacity, could devote himself wholly to work that was largely anonymous. Only a few judges could hope for a reputation beyond their own circle. Most lawyers would perish unknown. But Shattuck said to Holmes: "The attempt to do well what our hands find to do seems to me about the only thing open to us in this world."[8]

Holmes remained divided in mind. The devotion that law required would oblige him to sacrifice his hopes for success in literature and philosophy.[9] He did narrow the circle of his social activities; in the holiday season he visited only a few friends with whom he could talk, and he worked at the law with furious determination, but he did not quite succeed in forgetting himself in his work and did not entirely forget his larger ambitions.

The friends with whom he continued to spend evenings were prin-cipally William and Henry James, John Gray, his uncle John Holmes, a few friends of the college years, and the Dixwells.[10]

The Dixwells lived in a modest wooden house capped with a mansard roof like a bonnet pulled down over its brows. The house stood on Gar-den Street, an unpaved road in still rural Cambridge, behind a big elm.[11] Fanny, of the lively black eyes and fey wit, was often at home when Holmes called.

A little circle of scholarly lawyers also was forming. Closest to Holmes was John Gray. Holmes would meet Gray occasionally at a lecture in Cambridge, and walk or ride back to Boston with him in the crowded horsecar, their feet deep in the winter straw. Gray was two years Holmes's senior, had graduated from Harvard Law School just before the war, and had served on the judge advocate general's staff. Their mu-tual friend was John Ropes, brother of Henry Ropes, who had served and died in the Twentieth Regiment. Others in the circle were Nicholas St. John Green, Holmes's classmate at the law school, and Melville Bigelow, who was a little younger than the others, too young to have served in the army.

They were all ambitious to make their marks on the law by writing books and articles. There were few professional journals, and so Ropes and Gray began one, the *American Law Review*. Holmes and the others of their circle were contributors. Holmes began writing book reviews and was paid for his effort by being allowed to keep the books he reviewed.[12]

But Holmes had to make time for his scholarly work outside the hours taken by the practice. On December 6, 1866, he wrote in his diary: "Went to Woburn for [Bob] Morse. My first legal job — to get some information."[13] Three weeks later, Morse paid him three dollars: his first legal fee.

The office of Chandler, Shattuck and Thayer was at 4 Court Street, on Beacon Hill, a few paces from the courts and the State House. Holmes often walked home with Shattuck after work, around the shoul-der of Beacon Hill, as years before he had walked with his schoolmaster Mr. Dixwell, chatting. Some evenings Holmes and Shattuck walked out Beacon Street to the Mill Dam, where the city was beginning to fill in marshes for building.[14]

No great passion, as Henry Adams observed, replaced those roused in Boston by the war. But the fortunes accumulated by the war were being invested in new empires: the age of trusts and monopolies had begun, and a new organism, the industrial corporation, stretched its limbs across the continent.

It was an age of railroads, telegraphs, science. Engineers were its pop-ular heroes. Bridges and canals and railbeds fed the growing factories. Business people were learning to make and manage companies on a con-tinent-spanning scale.

In Washington, now so distant, the President and Congress fought for supremacy over the growing federal empire. The recolonization of the South that Dr. Holmes had foreseen was underway. In the West, a murderous new war against the Indian nations had begun.

In Massachusetts, cotton came in ample supply again to the mills of Lawrence and Lowell. The workers were no longer young women from the long-settled seacoast towns, working for their independence, but immigrants from Ireland and the German states. These workers took their places in the system of canals and hydraulic machinery. Boston was no longer an English town, but a center of the American empire. In the working-class neighborhoods, where so many of the children died of mingled disease and malnutrition, the first trade unions of immigrant Irish and German workers began to form.

The governing stratum of Boston remained diligent, reserved, prosperous, calm. The religious passions of the last generation were stilled, and a mildly rational Unitarianism permeated Cambridge and Beacon Hill. The years following the Civil War, Henry Adams said, "were marked by a steady decline of literary and artistic intensity, and especially of the feeling for poetry, which at best had never been the favorite form of Boston expression."[15]

Boston still ate dinner at two. Afternoons in a law office were commonly sleepy. Tea was at six, and the Holmes family still gathered for that meal. All three children, although now grown, were still at home. In winter, there were occasional evening dinner parties, assemblies, balls. At the Boston Theatre, a false wooden floor could be laid over the seats for dancing. One evening, Holmes escorted Clover Hooper, and John Gray brought Sarah Mason, to an assembly at the theater. Lorenzo Papanti, whose dancing school at 23 Tremont Street everyone had attended, presided.[16]

Sundays were as always dreary and quiet. On Christmas Day, which was otherwise not noticed, they exchanged modest presents. This year Holmes's gifts from his family were sedate: Edmund Burke's collected works; a Japanese lacquer glove box. As he had done each year since leaving the army, Holmes walked out with Clover Hooper after Christmas dinner.[17] On New Year's Eve, he walked to Cambridge to see Fanny Dixwell. She lent Holmes an embroidered picture for his room, which he would return the following New Year's Eve. Before midnight, as 1866 ended, Holmes was back in his room alone, hanging his new embroidery, morning glories on a gilt background, and making the year's final entry in his diary.

Holmes called often on the Jameses in Ashburton Place, where he sometimes found Minny Temple visiting from Connecticut. John Gray was likely to be calling as well when the Temples were in Boston. Minny was the center of the circle on these occasions, a slender, dark, animated, charming girl about whom Henry and William James, Holmes and Gray, revolved. Minny was attracted first to one and then another. Mrs. James, who was a partisan of John Gray's, retired early one January evening to write a letter:

> The Temples are in the parlor with Willy and Harry. Holmes has been spending the afternoon here and staid to tea, and has just left. John Gray was also here but left earlier. Minny I think is quite disenchanted, and evidently looks at Holmes with very different eyes from what she did; that is she sees him as others do, talks of his thinness and pinchedness, as well as of his beautiful eyes, and seems to see his egotism. Mr. Gray is as nice as ever.[18]

When Minny returned to Connecticut the men met and talked philosophy.[19] Holmes's late talks with Bill James were particularly satisfactory. They settled into a pattern, Holmes's materialism in combat with James's doubting idealism. When they were apart they continued their arguments and discussions in long letters.

Bill James, warm and fearful, took a step back from their intimacy. He explained, in a letter to Holmes:

> You have a far more logical and orderly mode of thinking than I . . . and when we have been together I have somehow been conscious of a reaction against the ascendancy of this over my ruder processes. I put myself involuntarily into a position of self-defense, as if you threatened to overrun my territory and injure my proprietorship.[20]

James grew depressed and was troubled by indistinct ailments. He went to Germany to study and to take the water cure, and perhaps also to protect his proprietorship from further invasion. Talks gave way to long letters, which became gradually less frequent.

Holmes was examined by two attorneys and admitted to the bar of Massachusetts on March 9, 1867. To mark the day, he bought a second chair for his office, presumably for clients to sit on. "My first day as a lawyer," he wrote in his diary. "The rush of clients postponed on account of weather."[21]

He made his first argument in a courtroom, before Judge Ebenezer Hoar, who thought young Holmes very promising; Hoar thought he had his grandfather Charles Jackson's manner, with the doctor's expression now and then flashing out.[22]

His sister Amelia entered Boston's polite society, but she and Wendell moved in different circles. Hers was her mother's realm, the wealthy descendants of ship captains and traders who had invested in banks and railroads and had grown stolid. The network of cousinship, of Lees, Jacksons, Higginsons, Curtises, Cabots, and Wigglesworths, enmeshed her.

Young Ned, asthmatic and thoughtful, puffing along behind his elder brother, began to attend the law school.

At the heart of this quiet existence Holmes lived in a frenzy of labor. He worked energetically for Shattuck, doing research on points of law, interviewing witnesses, preparing Shattuck for trial, seeing clients, writing briefs, appearing in court, dealing with other lawyers.

At the *American Law Review,* Holmes had progressed from writing occasional book reviews and had become a member of the staff. In 1868, he began writing for each quarterly number summaries — "digests" — of the more important decisions of state courts. For this work he read, or at least looked over, all the volumes of reported decisions of the supreme courts. This gave him a cosmopolitan view of the law, but at considerable cost. There were weary, exulting entries in his diary: "Finished 1st Quarter Digest, [reviewed] *13 vols.*"

He wrote curious little reviews of some of the volumes of state decisions, in which he recorded his dawning ideas. Reviewing a year's decisions of the Iowa Supreme Court, Holmes burst into philosophy and paradox: the Iowa court, unencumbered by tradition, had been able to arrive at sensible results more in accord with modern times than the decisions of more learned judges: "No branch of knowledge affords more instances than the law, of what a blessing to mankind it is that men begin life ignorant."[23] This paradox, of a kind that Holmes liked to drop into his conversation, remained in his mind.

Holmes also digested the opinions of the English courts, and reviewed new editions of law textbooks as they appeared, garnering a library of review copies as reward: Roscoe's *Criminal Evidence,* Story's *Equity,* Washburne's *Easements and Servitudes,* Byles's *Commercial Instruments.*

He somehow found time to read haphazardly in the history of law. He read again Maine's *Ancient Law,* which had first shown him the picture of law developing like a living thing.

Once a week, Holmes paid his calls in Cambridge, saw his uncle John, and visited the Dixwells. Fanny cared passionately about art but, like so many others in that climate, in badly lighted houses in dark northern winters, her health was uncertain and she had trouble with her eyes. Holmes told Bill James:

> She has suffered a good deal for some time past with her eyes — a sad disappointment as she was expecting to go into painting in good earnest. But she said yesterday that they were nearly well and that she thought she might begin her lessons before very long. I wish she may, if only for her own sake to find a voice for something within her.[24]

Nothing came of the painting lessons. Fanny labored on at her embroidery, and busied herself in Cambridge with amateur theatricals. She was not an intellectual, did not read for pleasure; she got what she could vicariously from the experiences of Holmes and Bill James.

In the summer of 1869, John Gray courted Minny Temple in New Hampshire. He sat in her parlor, bearded and solemn, discussing Trollope's novels, boring Minny to tears when they were in company, and charming her with his frankness when they were alone.[25] Minny was increasingly thin, coughed wretchedly, was feverish and lovely; she began to suspect that she was dying of tuberculosis. She wrote to Gray:

> But you mustn't think that I am in any special danger of dying just at present, or that I am in low spirits — for it is not so. The Dr. tells me that I am not in any danger, even if the hemorrhages should keep on. "But you can't fool a regular boarder," as Mr. Holmes would say.[26]

The City of Boston was filling in the land behind Charles Street; the Holmeses' rear windows would no longer look out on the river. The doctor testified vigorously against this deprivation of settled property rights, but to no avail. The Holmes family began to look for a new house farther out on Beacon Street.

Bill James returned from Europe, not much improved in health or spirits; he and Holmes and John Gray and Fanny Dixwell and Minny Temple became more intimately enmeshed. Bill James courted Fanny, Minny Temple and John Gray exchanged long letters about their feelings for each other and talked of their mutual affection for Bill. Holmes continued to flirt with Minny, whose interest in him revived.[27] In that summer of 1869, Holmes and John Gray stayed with the Jameses in Newport, where the Temples were also visiting. Minny and Fanny grew better acquainted, and Minny wrote to John Gray about it.

> I think she impresses me with a possibility — in her abandonment, devotion to an idea, a conviction, more than most people. She has what people call *self*-reliance very strongly, which seems to my mind reliance on God. . . . She gave me one of her embroideries — an extraordinary production for a young woman of the 19th Century, very beautiful in the workmanship, original in the design.[28]

Holmes was working harder than ever by the fall, and as always in times of stress his health troubled him. He made one of his periodic efforts to give up smoking, and this left him sleepless.[29] He had returned to a relentless round of social calls in Boston and kept up as well as he could by letter with his English friends. Leslie Stephen answered with interminable letters of his own addressed to "beloved Wendie." He was to be married; the mysterious letter that had ended their Swiss climbing expedition was from Stephen's fiancée.

There were momentous changes in Holmes's little world. His younger brother Ned finished the law school and went despite ill health to Washington, to serve as secretary to Senator Charles Sumner. Sister Amelia was engaged to a widower, Turner Sargent, and would soon leave home.

George Shattuck, too, was making changes. He planned to set up a firm of his own, and would leave Chandler, Shattuck and Thayer.

Holmes was obliged to consider his own career. Law practice did not seem to suit him very well. He did not have Shattuck's physical presence, his ease with juries, or his aptitude for command. After three years' enlistment in Chandler, Shattuck and Thayer, as a junior subaltern, Holmes rebelled against subordination and anonymity.

The scholarly work Holmes had begun doing for the *American Law Review* attracted him, however. It called on his intellectual and literary talents and led, more directly than did law practice, toward the goal of philosophy.

Thayer had a proposal for him. Chancellor James Kent's *Commentaries on American Law,* a widely used text, an old-fashioned, untheoretical, commonsensical work, was due for revision. A succession of editors had kept it up-to-date by adding footnotes every year or two for the twenty-five years since Kent's death. Thayer had been asked to add yet another routine round of notes to the already overburdened margins.

Thayer turned to Holmes to assist him, and Holmes seized the opportunity with a vigor that surprised the older man. Holmes proposed to expand the modest work he had been offered into something much more substantial.

Kent's *Commentaries,* after all those years of routine additions, Holmes said, were a chaos of citations, "collected with really faithful labor, but which lay in a tangled mass across the current of the text, and too often obstructed where they should have enlarged."[30] Instead of adding another layer, Holmes proposed that the whole accumulated mass of footnotes should be discarded. He would write a new set of notes summarizing in coherent form the law of the past twenty-five years.

This would be a much more ambitious undertaking than the publishers had planned; it would amount to writing a new "Commentary" on modern law in parallel to the old. Holmes persuaded Thayer, and through him James Kent, the chancellor's grandson and the owner of the copyright. In the fall of 1869, Holmes wrote a sample of the new essay-notes he proposed, and on November 18 he triumphantly wrote in his journal, "Began editing Kent's Comm[entaries]."[31]

Two years were allowed for the work. Holmes agreed to spend most of his time at it, and was to receive a modest stipend — $3,000 over two years, in quarterly installments.[32]

To supplement this income, Holmes obtained a post as lecturer at the Harvard Law School. The new young president of Harvard, Charles William Eliot, had begun to reorganize the professional schools, and was appointing "university" lecturers. Holmes taught Constitutional law. The lecture fees, with the modest stipend for editing Kent and occasional supplements from Shattuck for legal chores, were enough for Holmes, still living with his parents, to subsist on.

During his brief career as a scholar, Holmes's place of work was a table in the Social Law Library, the Boston bar's reference library, then housed in the county courthouse. There was a perpetual heap of books on his table. Other members of the little circle of scholarly lawyers might be found nearby. John Gray, Nicholas St. John Green, and Melville Bigelow, who all lectured at the Harvard Law School with Holmes, were also habitués of the library. Bigelow was working on a book of his own, and had a similar heap of volumes on his table next to Holmes. One of their students, Brooks Adams, younger brother of Henry, often dropped in to chat with his teachers.[33]

They were allied spirits, however different in temperament and thought. Progress and reform were in the air; they read Austin and were enflamed by his cold puritanical fires of reason. Few law books as yet had been written by Americans, and none had the spirit of the postwar scientific age. Everything lay before them to be done.

Austin was the mark for them to hit. Holmes, Bigelow, Gray, Brooks Adams, and Green all began to read history, searching for the origin and meaning of the logical order that Austin described.

10

TWO PILLARS

OF HIS LIFE

HOLMES AND HIS FRIENDS WERE NEARLY THIRTY YEARS OLD AND unmarried. Their younger brothers and sisters were marrying. Amelia Holmes was now Mrs. Sargent; Ned Holmes married a cousin, Henrietta Wigglesworth, from a prosperous and, to Holmes's eye, mediocre and complacent tribe. Fanny Dixwell's younger sisters and brothers were marrying — her sister Mary married George Wigglesworth, and Fanny and Holmes exchanged sour jokes about their common in-laws. Clover Hooper's younger sisters were marrying; the Shattuck sisters were marrying. The round of flirtations in a narrowing circle grew a little wearisome. Clover wrote to Eleanor Shattuck: "A pleasant little dinner at Brooks' [Adams's] with soup, fish, Sayles, & Gray — ditto at James' on New Years, with the variation which Boston affords of raw oysters, then soup Gray & Holmes that was quite different you see if only one thought so."[1]

Minny Temple's younger sister, Kitty, married. Minny herself and John Gray drew closer, but Minny was increasingly ill, her hemorrhages more frequent. She wrote to Gray:

If I am not dead before June, I am to go to Europe with my cousin Mrs. Post. . . . I feel tired out and hardly able to stir — but my spirits are good enough & I don't propose to lose them if I can help it, for I know it all depends on myself whether I get thro' this, or not. That is, if I begin to be indifferent to the result, I shall go down hill quickly. . . .

I feel the greatest longing for summer, or spring, I think I would like it to be always spring for the rest of my life, & to have all the people I care for always with me, & never even to speak of going away — but who wouldn't like it so? Good-bye. Write soon.[2]

Bill James was idle, having finished medical school with no plan for the future. He was alone at home with his parents, all of his siblings away: Henry was in Europe, Alice traveling for her health, the two youngest brothers searching for careers in the South and West. He was increasingly depressed, suffered from vague ailments and a painful back. He experimented with anesthetics, noting the effects in his journal. In January of 1870 he was experimenting with chloral hydrate and accidently took an overdose. He wrote to his brother Henry that he had taken this new "hypnotic remedy . . . for the fun of it, and as an experiment, but whose effects are already on the wane."[3] Soon afterward, he suffered a more serious depression, in which he had a terrifying hallucination of himself as a patient in an asylum, which left him in a state of dread from which he did not completely emerge for several months.[4] He and Holmes rarely met after that time.

On March 8, 1870, Minny Temple died of tuberculosis. "Her death affected me more than almost any I have had to lament," Holmes said.[5]

But he had seen too much death to linger over lost friends or friendships. He labored on at his law, and in the summer of 1870, became coeditor with Arthur Sedgwick of the *American Law Review*.

New friends, often younger than he, filled the gaps in Holmes's horizon. He had tutored Brooks Adams in preparation for law school, and Brooks was now among Holmes's students and his frequent visitor at the Social Law Library. Henry Adams, now teaching medieval history at Harvard, drifted toward Brooks and Holmes in their legal studies, and himself began to study the medieval history of legal institutions. Henry Cabot Lodge, another former student of Holmes's, was among Henry Adams's students. Ties were established that would draw Holmes to Washington thirty years later.

Holmes now had some general ideas about law, which he liked to talk over with the younger men. These ideas were somewhat abstract and academic, reactions to Austin and other books; they did not yet flower from his own experience. In the October, 1870, issue of the *American Law Review* Holmes published an article, "Codes, and the Arrangement of the Law." In it he spoke with learned and exquisite conservatism about the Benthamite program. On the whole, Holmes thought, the reformers would be disappointed. Codes of legislation would prove to be as complex as the common law, but less flexible and adaptive. In any case, a thorough understanding of legal principles would be needed before a code could be written. These Holmes condescended to explain.

The law, he said, was founded on duty. Holmes sketched out a logical categorization of duties. There were duties of sovereign powers to each other, duties of all persons to their sovereign, duties of each person to every other person, and of each to all, and so forth. It was the sort of abstract, lifeless scheme that Holmes would later ridicule.

In the midst of this otherwise inert discussion lay a nearly hidden jewel. What was law? The answer that had been repeated thoughtlessly for the past three hundred years by English-speaking lawyers was: Law is the command of the sovereign. Holmes thought this gave a political answer to a legal question. From the heart of his own experience sprang a new answer that in its simplicity would echo down the century.

The search for law ended at the judge's bench: "Courts . . . give rise to lawyers, whose only concern is with such rules as the courts enforce."[6] The student of law therefore looks to the decisions of the courts — and no farther — for the law. The courts in turn might look into many sources. Often, indeed, they enforced the commands of a political superior. But at other times, courts enforced the customs of their community. Sometimes — often — the judges themselves were unaware of the sources from which they drew their decisions:

> It is the merit of the common law that it decides the case first and determines the principle afterwards. Looking at the forms of logic it might be inferred that when you have [a] minor premise and a conclusion, there must be a major, which you are always prepared then and there to assert. But in fact lawyers, like other men, frequently see well enough how they ought to decide on a given state of facts without being very clear as to the [reason]. . . .
>
> It is only after a series of determinations on the same subject-matter, that it becomes necessary to "reconcile the cases," as it is called, that is, by a true induction to state the principle which has until then been obscurely felt.[7]

Commonplace as it later came to seem, this was an original, even a revolutionary, thought. It freed law from dependence on a particular political theory and gave the student of law a definition of his subject: the decisions of the courts. It seemed to promise that the study of law could be a science.

Still more novel and surprising, Holmes's idea pointed to unconscious wellsprings for judges' motives.[8] Holmes had taken a first step in a new direction, but it would be years before he saw where it led.

More immediately valuable to Holmes were the growing notebooks of cases, articles, and random data that he was collecting for the Kent edition. Holmes began arranging his materials under the conventional headings, but as the material accumulated it began to arrange itself in new ways. In these notebooks Holmes had begun his own original work.[9]

He had become extraordinarily busy, assimilating and arranging in little essays all of recent law, to bring Kent's *Commentaries* up to date, digesting the more important decisions of the courts for the *Law Review*, teaching a course in jurisprudence at the law school,[10] occasionally practicing law, reading omnivorously, and talking with friends until late hours about history, philosophy, and law, and still making the rounds of Boston's modest social scene.

In November, 1870, the much-diminished Holmes family moved — Amelia and Ned were established in households of their own — to 296 Beacon Street, well out along the fringe of newly filled land in the Back Bay. Tall, narrow brick houses stood stiffly along the water side of Beacon Street, each with its little flight of steps up to the front door. There were still many gaps among the houses, through which a passerby could see the river, and,

> where passing in sharp wintry weather it was prudent to turn up one's coat collar against the icy blast from the river; as also, for that matter, at every cross-street. On the opposite side there were struggling groups of houses running further west along the Mill Dam, under which, at some points, the tide flowed in and out from the Back Bay. . . . The water still came up to Dartmouth Street and . . . Copley Square.[11]

The front windows of the Holmeses' new house faced southward across Beacon Street and were flooded by sunlight. The rear windows looked out over the expanse of the Charles River. Holmes spent a large part of the next thirty years in this high, narrow house.

He was now a scientist, studying the decisions of the courts. From these facts he drew the principles of law. A law book, he thought, should be like a textbook of botany, with the legal principles explained and the cases neatly arranged according to genus and species. A lawyer-scientist would discover the table of the elements of law; like Linnaeus he would classify its species; but, more than this, like Darwin he would discover the underlying principles of the law.

The law-book writer was also the law giver, for whoever stated the principles of the law had set down the law itself in its most general form. Parliament, or the Massachusetts legislature, might enact those principles into a code of legislation, but in any case the book would be the source of the true principles of decision in the courts, and so of the law itself.[12]

It was no abstract inquiry in which Holmes was engaged, therefore, but a search for power, the solitary power that a thinker can exercise.

In Boston and Cambridge and London there were other such men. In the spring of 1871, Henry Maine brought out his second powerful work, *Village Communities,* tracing English legal institutions back to early Anglo-Saxon and Teutonic customs. The scholarship of this work was plainly thin, and it was far behind the historical work being done on the Continent, but it struck a chord in London and Boston alike.

Henry Adams seized Maine's work and tried to make it the beginning of a scientific theory of history: "The man who should solve the riddle of the Middle Ages and bring them into the line of evolution from past to present would be a greater man than Lamarck or Linnaeus."[13] The principles of law were the key to legislative power; the principles of history were the key to political power.

There were a half dozen students — Cabot Lodge among them — in Henry Adams's seminar on medieval institutions. They met in the evenings in the parlor of the college president's old house. The slight, dark teacher seated himself comfortably before the fire, sipping sherry and smoking a cigar, which his students were forbidden by college rules to share. He walked his seminar carefully through Maine's *Village Communities* and the texts of surviving Anglo-Saxon and Frankish laws.[14]

Adams thought he would find the source of democracy and the laws of its evolution in the Teutonic tribes of northern Europe. "By a happy chance he was in the full tide of fashion," he remarked sardonically. The brief Franco-Prussian War in 1870 had ended with a Prussian victory, and "the Germans were crowning their new Emperor at Versaille. . . . Germany had never been so powerful."[15]

In the South that year there were skirmishes that might lead to a new civil war. In North Carolina, a convention had met and had purported to dissolve the state government. A secret club of Confederate officers, the Ku Klux Klan, came into the open in renewed rebellion. Congress authorized the President to suspend again the right of *habeas corpus,* the Constitutional right against arbitrary arrest, and to use federal troops to put down the Klan. New Constitutional amendments forbidding slavery and race discrimination were fought over in the streets and in the courts; the recolonization of the South was being resisted bitterly.

Holmes was not very much moved by these distant events. He wrote about them in the *Law Review* with a detached tone and seemed to view them as a judge reviewing precedents might, as if they had no more intrinsic interest than the judicial opinions of the sixteenth century.

He had stopped even reading the newspapers. The practice of law had allowed him many distractions, but the study of law was consuming. He was entirely immersed in his work now, thoroughly concentrated on his single object, and determined to pursue his course: "The man of action has the present, but the thinker controls the future; his is the most subtle, the most far-reaching, power. His ambition is the vastest, as it is the most ideal."[16]

The Kent edition would not be finished on time. Only one volume of the four was complete, and the two years allotted were ending. More time and money would be needed, and Holmes, having committed so much of himself, argued that he alone and not Thayer should appear as editor of the new edition.[17] Thayer stepped aside, and the publishers agreed to give more time and money; Holmes was able to hire a young student to assist him.[18]

But he had run into other difficulties. The law was not revealing to him its principles or its line of evolution. His difficulties came to a head when he tried to answer one of the important legal questions that had arisen since Kent's death, the ownership of grain stored in public "elevators."

The proprietors of an elevator had possession of the grain and the right to sell it, but the farmers who had not yet been paid for their wheat nevertheless thought they still owned it. They had receipts for deposit of their grain and expected to be paid when it was sold. When elevators went bankrupt, who would get the grain — the creditors or the farmers?

Holmes struggled with "property" as an abstract proposition. The farmers, it seemed to him, owned the wheat, but what had they given to the elevator companies? Holmes built up an intricate imaginary contract between farmers and elevator companies for what the common law called a *bailment* — storage of another's goods. The farmers retained that mystical interest, ownership, and the elevators had only physical possession and control.[19] This gave a just result, but an elaborate fiction that begged the question was needed to arrive at it.

This was not very satisfactory. Struggling with his confusion, Holmes began to see dimly that there were difficulties and ambiguities in the abstract idea of property itself.

He was struggling through the woods without a guide. He plunged more deeply into the old common-law cases on bailment, on the duties and liabilities of warehousemen, and the continuing mystical *ownership* of property that had long since passed out of the possession or control of the owner. Neither history nor logic was taking him to the heart of the matter, and his conclusions seemed somewhat arbitrary, even to himself. But Holmes was too busy to stop and begin again.

It was a difficult time. He said in later years that he had sympathy for the young men he met, for he had had his own period of extended unhappiness. He spoke of the great fog banks that lay about a person in his twenties. He spoke of sailing for the North Pole alone in the Arctic night. Holmes was drifting alone with his scholarship and did not yet see where it was carrying him.

Clover Hooper and Henry Adams were engaged; Gray, Bigelow, and Green now were rarely seen in the Social Law Library. Henry James, after a brief return, had sailed again for Europe; William James and Holmes were no longer close. Fanny Dixwell, however, remained unmarried, and she and Holmes were both closer and more solitary than ever.

The doctor had begun writing a new series for *The Atlantic*, "The Poet at the Breakfast-Table." As always, he made free with his family, turning them into the population of a rooming house. There was a Young Astronomer at the table, who had a knack for mathematics — pretty soon this shaded into philosophy — that the Poet didn't share. And there was a new boarder, Scheherezade, a young woman of thwarted artistic aspirations.

One evening the boarders all visited the young Astronomer's observatory. Scheherezade looked through his telescope at the moon and chattered with an odd, off-center humor very like Fanny's:

> If there were any living creatures, what odd things they must be. They couldn't have any lungs, nor any hearts. What a pity! Did they ever die? How could they expire if they didn't breathe? Burn up? No air to burn in. Tumble into some of those horrid pits, perhaps, and break into bits. She wondered how the young people liked it, or whether there were any young people there; perhaps nobody was young and nobody was old, but they were mummies all of them — what an idea — two mummies making love to each other!

The Young Astronomer showed her a double star, one orange-red, the other emerald green. Two suns, the Young Astronomer said, each shining, but with a different light, for the other.

> How charming! [the girl replied.] It must be so much pleasanter than to be alone in such a great empty space! I should think one would hardly care to shine if its light wasted itself in the monstrous solitude of the sky. Does not a single star seem very lonely to you up there?

> — Not more lonely than I am myself, — answered the Young Astronomer.

Holmes had not entirely given up poetry. He had written a poem about his struggle to find meaning in the law, about the ambition that seemed to dominate his life to the exclusion of anything else. He showed this poem to the doctor.[20]

In the next installment of "The Poet at the Breakfast-Table," a poem appeared. The Poet claimed that the Astronomer had given it to him, but confessed that he had revised the poem pretty freely: "I will not attempt to say just how much of the diction of these lines belongs to him, and how much to me. He said he would never claim them, after I read them to him in my revision."

And so, the doctor published his own version of Holmes's poem. The doctor's share of the work gradually increased until, in the third install-ment, it was entirely his own. But for two months, Holmes seemed to speak through the Astronomer, torn between self-effacing duty and flaming ambition:

> *Another clouded night; the stars are hid,*
> *The orb that waits my search is hid with them.*
>   *Patience! Why grudge an hour, a month, a year,*
> *To plant my ladder and to gain the round*
>   *That leads my footsteps to the heaven of fame,*
> *Where waits the wreath my sleepless midnights won?*

The Astronomer imagined that his discovery of a new planet would make his name immortal, but he was troubled by his own ambition:

> *Must each coral insect leave his sign*
>   *On each poor grain he lent to build the reef,*
> *As Babel's builders stamped the sunburnt clay,*
>   *Or deem his patient service all in vain?*
> *What if another sit beneath the shade*
>   *Of the broad elm that I planted by the way, —*
> *The noblest service comes from nameless hands,*
>   *And the best servant does his work unseen.*
> *Who found the seeds of fire and made them shoot*
>   *Fed by his breath, in buds and flowers of flame?*
> *Who forged in roaring flames the ponderous stone*
>   *And shaped the moulded metal to his need?*
> *Who gave the dragging car its rolling wheel,*
>   *And tamed the steed that whirls its circle round?*
> *All these have left their work and not their name, —*
>   *Why should I murmur at a fate like theirs?*[21]

This glimpse of peace was short-lived. As the poem continued, the Astronomer was overwhelmed by false lights, false shadows, vague un-certain gleams. He became Prometheus, bound to the rock and prey to the vulture of a vast desire. When he struggled to escape, a false enchant-ress sang her song of solitary glory and bound him to the rock of ambi-tion again.

The Astronomer abruptly withdrew to the heavens. He saw time and space with the eye of God. The earth circled the sun, a burned-out cin-der, the race of humanity extinct:

I am as old as Egypt itself. . . .

I dwell in spaces vague, remote, unknown,
  Save to the silent few, who, leaving earth,
Quit all communion with their living time.
  I lose myself in that ethereal void,
Till I have my wings and long to fill
  My breast with denser air, to stand, to walk
With eyes not raised above my fellow men.
  Sick of my unwalled, solitary realm
I ask to change the myriad, lifeless worlds
  I visit as my own for one poor patch
Of this dull spheroid and a little breath
  To shape in word or deed to serve my kind.[22]

Holmes struggled, paradoxically, to be at peace. He did not, could not, give up his ambition for the solitary power of the thinker, but he turned nevertheless to work and to marriage, which would be the two pillars of his life.

March 11, 1872

My Dear Ann,

I have the pleasure of telling you of an engagement which is to be announced Wednesday next.

Oliver Wendell Holmes, Jr.

to

Miss Fanny Dixwell

daughter of his old instructor and friend Mr. Epes Dixwell — granddaughter of old Mr. Bowditch.

We know her thoroughly and value her and love her very much. She is a very superior and a charming woman and will make friends of all who meet her. The attachment is a very long and faithful one — very much as my Edward's was — both of them dating almost from childhood. When they are married they will come and be with us for a while, which will be a comfort as we should be lonely in the large house without any of the children.

I know you will be glad to hear all our children are so well mated . . . now Wendell has found the reward of his fidelity to a young lady of most remarkable gifts and qualities. . . .

Your affectionate brother,

O. W. Holmes[23]

Holmes was thirty and Fanny Dixwell thirty-one years old. His income was still very modest, perhaps $2,000 a year between the stipend for Kent's *Commentaries* and his lecture fees. Fanny would not bring anything substantial to the marriage. Holmes accordingly spoke to Shattuck about joining his new firm, which was prospering, and for the time being, Holmes and Fanny would live with the doctor and Mrs. Holmes.

Other young people were arriving in the Back Bay, on the newly filled land. At 302 Beacon Street, a few doors down from the Holmeses, Mrs. Augustín Ruíz Santayana — a Spanish-born widow of the Sturgis clan — moved in with her small children, giving the Back Bay an unaccustomed cosmopolitanism. Henry Adams and Clover were also looking for a house in the Back Bay. And a still more striking delegation arrived from the emperor of Japan.

It had been only five years since the shogun — Americans for some reason had called him the Tycoon, and had begun jocularly referring to each other as "tycoons" — had abdicated, and the fifteen-year-old emperor had been restored to rule. Civil war had subsided and the restored emperor had abolished feudalism. Young men and women of the nobility and the samurai class were sent to Europe and America, to learn Western languages, science, and systems of government. Four hundred students had already reached the United States. Among the first, in 1868, had been Enouye Yoshikadsu, who at sixteen years of age had come to Boston, learned English, and attended grammar school.

On January 15, 1872, the steamer *America* arrived in San Francisco, with a new delegation from the emperor. On board were 107 Japanese passengers, of whom 49 were officials of the embassy. The remainder were genteel young men and women (and their servants) who had come to stay for a time and study Western ways.

A part of the delegation came to Boston. The doctor was on the welcoming committee. He and Holmes met Enouye, whose English by now was good and who would serve as a guide for the newer arrivals. Enouye found boardinghouses for the three students who would remain in Boston. He himself planned to go to law school, for which Holmes would tutor him.

Fanny prepared for her wedding, which was to be in June. Holmes, too, was busy. At the *Law Review,* his coeditor, Arthur Sedgwick, was leaving, and Holmes would be sole editor, beginning with the July issue. This would be ready for the printers before the wedding, but afterward there would be the October issue and the seemingly interminable Kent.

The old yellow clapboard house in Cambridge was at last sold to Harvard, which eventually tore it down to make room for the expanding university campus. Before moving into new quarters on Appian Way, John Holmes planned to visit Europe that summer after the wedding, and arranged to sail on a Cunard liner from New York with Henry and Clover Adams, who were on their own wedding journey. The doctor and Mrs. Holmes would go to Newport for the summer, leaving Wendell and Fanny to get settled in the house at 296 Beacon Street. The young couple would take the third floor of the house, perhaps turning Ned's old bed-room into their sitting room.

On June 17, 1872, Wendell Holmes and Fanny Dixwell were married in the Old North Church in Boston, and Holmes wrote in his journal for that day: "Married. Sole editor of Law Rev."[24]

The doctor and Mrs. Holmes left for Newport, and very briefly Wen-dell and Fanny were alone in the brick house on Beacon Street, whose back windows looked out over the Charles River to Cambridge. "A man does but half live until he is married," Holmes wrote to Bill James.[25]

A woman servant had stayed in Boston to help them. In the July heat she became ill, and died. With frightening abruptness, Fanny too became ill. She was feverish; her joints were painful; she was almost unable to move. The doctor and Mrs. Holmes returned hastily from Newport. Mrs. Holmes herself was growing weak and ill in those years; the remaining servant gave notice; and the doctor, almost beside himself, took charge of the household.[26]

Fanny's illness was rheumatic fever. It would not be fatal, but it was protracted, and there was little treatment to give except rest.

The doctor and Mrs. Holmes now remained in Boston, and Fanny, although bedridden, slowly began to recover. Life resumed its orderly pattern. On August 2, the doctor and Waldo Emerson joined in saying good-bye to the departing Japanese delegation.[27] Holmes went on tutor-ing Enouye Yoshikadsu for admission to the law school, borrowing a room at Shattuck's office for the purpose. He began sending the notes for the first volumes of Kent to the printer in Cambridge.[28]

Fanny's recovery was slow, however, and Mrs. Holmes was little bet-ter. In October, the doctor noted the "severe and long-continued illness of my daughter-in-law and the consequent worry and exhaustion of my wife. . . . My daughter-in-law has not yet got downstairs."[29]

Ned Holmes and his new wife had been abroad, hoping to restore his health, and in the fall they returned, but Italy had not improved his asthma, and as always a return to Boston worsened it. He had symptoms now of heart disease as well.[30]

Holmes occupied himself with work. In a near frenzy he labored to finish the Kent. Sole editor of the *Law Review*, he was also one of its principal authors. He wrote essays in preparation for Kent, then con-densed them into long footnotes. The essays themselves appeared in the *American Law Review* as soon as they were written. His goal seemingly was to get his philosophical work on the law completed and into print before he retired to private practice.

In the October, 1872, number of the *Law Review*, Holmes published afresh his table of legal duties in all its mathematical nicety. But he had added a new dimension: time.

Duties were only a cross-section of the law, a static picture of hierarchy. How did the law accommodate *change* — the succession of one person to another's duties, the absorption of the wife into the married estate, the passage of ownership from one hand to another?

Holmes's answer was purely technical. The relation between owners of real estate and their successors, the relation between a person and his heirs, was governed by some of the oldest forms in law, as old as Roman jurisprudence. These forms had been imported into English law in the Middle Ages.

Holmes thought he saw the progenitor of all modern successions in Henry Maine's Rome, in the formalities of inheritance. In early Roman law, there had been few sales or successions, except on death. Inheritance itself was a peculiar process, and rested on a fiction that the heir became identical with the deceased, that the son became the father and somehow inhabited his persona.

When sales of property to unrelated persons came to be recognized, conservative lawyers and judges continued to pretend that the buyer had stepped into the skin of the seller. Sales of real estate followed the forms of inheritance, and the forms were carefully repeated generation after generation. The marks of the original fiction of identity between father and son remained visible over the centuries.[31] But legal "ownership" was not a mystical entity with its own existence; it was created by courts whenever particular sets of facts arose.[32]

Holmes tried to tumble down the boundaries between ancient categories of law — real property sales, inheritance, assignments, trusteeships — and to sweep all into a grand new category of "successions," which he analyzed with Benthamite logic into an orderly scheme. There were partial and complete successions, each category minutely subdivided.

In this article, Holmes succeeded as no one else yet had in linking Maine's historical method and John Austin's Benthamite logic into a single system. The scholarship of the effort was impressive. The result was brilliant, original — and useless. Holmes's system, although founded on both history and logic, remained disconnected from modern law. Its categories reflected meaningless survivals of form that had persisted despite their change in content. It was orderly, and empty. The content of the law, its meaning, remained elusive as ever.

In one last article for the *Law Review* before returning to practice, and his last theoretical effort for the Kent, Holmes conducted a thought experiment or dissection to show his theories at work.[33]

The law of torts — law Latin for "wrongs" — was the category of duties that each person had in his daily affairs. It was the set of rules of behavior that courts would observe and enforce.

A violation of such duties — a "tort" like negligence, say, or slander — therefore was not a failure of morals or of will. A tort was only a failure to follow the course of conduct that in the circumstances the court thought proper. A court might consult its own precedents, statutes, the custom of the community, or its own notions of public policy. On those and the facts of the case a court would rest its judgment.[34] The duty of a person charged with a tort, like the rights of a person claiming ownership, was a legal result arising from objective facts. The moral worth of the person, his subjective state and motives, were irrelevant.

Holmes's legal system had become a dry calculus of logical deductions from objective facts. At times, he diverged into talk about present realities: he spoke of the way courts and lawyers truly functioned as he had seen them. But the separate lines of his thought — history, logical order, and present function — lay inert and disconnected, fragments of a theory.

Holmes had done what he could, for the time. He sent copies of his last articles in the *Law Review* to his English friends. But Fitzjames Stephens failed to see that Holmes was trying to link the two great schools of English legal thought, Bentham's and Maine's, into a single system: "I am amused to find you so deep in the historical method, which my friend & neighbor Sir. H. Maine invented to a certain extent in this country — we are constantly together & he talks history & I talk Bentham — like Fielding's Thwackum and Square."[35]

If anyone understood and valued Holmes's scheme of duties based on facts, he made little sign. Indeed, Holmes himself had not yet seen the significance of his intuitions. For the time being, he would have to be satisfied to make the anonymous contribution of a coral animal to the structure of the law, insensibly advancing its growth.

Fanny was growing stronger, and Holmes's career as a scholar, as an Astronomer, was nearly ended. Work and marriage were about to begin.

11

THE

COMMON LAW

O N THE NIGHT OF NOVEMBER 9, 1872, A LARGE PART OF BOSTON burned. The fire began in the cellar of a new five-story building at the southeast corner of Summer and Kingston streets; a dry-goods store and a hoop-skirt factory were on the floors above.[1] The fire spread through rows of granite-faced wooden buildings newly built in the French provincial style, blocks of little factories, offices, apartments, and shops, each capped by ornate brick chimneys rising from its mansard roof like plumes.

The first alarm sounded at 7:24 in the evening. Most of Boston had finished the evening meal. Henry Cabot Lodge was reading, and when the first signal was followed by the pealing bells of a general alarm, he went out into the street:

> I crossed the Common and strolled down Summer Street. The fire had then made but little progress, comparatively speaking, and was raging in the lower part of the street. . . . I went from point to point and watched the fire spread, which it did with terrifying rapidity. I saw tall buildings catch in their roofs like huge matches and blaze up, I saw walls falling and stone crumbling in

the heat, and in a short time I realized the fire was beyond control.[2]

Holmes and the doctor went out to see the conflagration. Their house, well out on Beacon Street, was not threatened, but the doctor had begun to think of his railroad bonds on deposit in State Street. The fire was making its way toward the banks and brokerage houses.

By morning, a sixty-acre tract was burning. Crowds were in the streets trying to get into banks and shops that stood in the path of the fire. Troops were summoned. Henry Higginson and a crew of veterans brought up wagons and gunpowder, and blew up buildings on Milk Street (to their owners' horror) to make a firebreak. Holmes and the doctor stood among the crowd and watched as burning buildings collapsed silently as if falling into feather beds.[3] Engines sprayed water impotently into the fire storm.

On the third day the fire burned out, having reached the waterside, where wharves and vessels waiting to unload had burned. Inland the fire stopped, for no apparent reason, just short of the Merchants' Exchange on State Street. A huge rectangle of thirty streets from Washington Street to the inner harbor was leveled and black. Ruined chimneys rose here and there from the waste. Holmes was startled to see, close at hand, the ocean.

But he was only briefly diverted from his work. Proofs of the first volumes of Kent had arrived and needed correcting and revision to bring them up to date. He was still writing notes for the fourth and last volume, and he had the January number of the *American Law Review* to prepare. On New Year's Eve, quietly at home with Fanny, Holmes noted in his journal that he had finished revising[4] the proofs for volume I, that the revisions themselves had cost him much effort, and that he had reached page 382 of the proofs for the third volume.[5]

Shortly after the New Year, he wrote out his will, on a plain piece of blue-lined paper, and signed it in the presence of three witnesses:

I leave all my property of every kind to my wife Fanny B. Holmes.
O. W. Holmes, Jr.[6]

Fanny was better, but did not care to go out very much; Holmes sometimes went out alone, but he was too much absorbed in finishing the *Commentaries* to be very social. The notes for the fourth volume of Kent — a set of elegant little essays on modern law, condensed from longer versions already published in the *American Law Review* — were nearly finished, and Holmes carried them about with him in a frenzy of final work. Mrs. James described him to her son Henry, who was in England:

Wendell Holmes dined with us a few days ago. His whole life, soul and body, is utterly absorbed in his *last* work upon his Kent. He carries about his manuscript in his green bag and never loses sight of it for a moment. He started to go to Will's room to wash his hands, but came back for his bag, and when we went to dinner, Will said, "Don't you want to take your bag with you?" He said, "Yes, I always do so at home." His pallid face, and this fearful grip on his work, make him a melancholy sight.[7]

On February 7, 1873, Holmes wrote triumphantly in his journal, *"Finished notes to vol. IV of Kent."*[8]

Fanny was well enough now to help read the printers' proofs. She diligently compared the newly printed text with the last edition that had been published in the chancellor's lifetime,[9] while Holmes's student assistants, Henry Parkman and Joseph Warner, went over the footnotes and index, verifying citations.[10] By March 1, Holmes had finished his revisions. The twelfth edition of Kent's *Commentaries on American Law* was complete.

There was no respite. On March 3, he began work at Shattuck's firm, which became Shattuck, Holmes and Monroe.

The *Commentaries* went on sale, four volumes to the set, on December 13, 1873. Reviews were respectful but a little puzzled. Many of the citations Holmes had added were to English cases. Large parts of the treatise had been restored to the appearance of the last edition in Kent's lifetime, twenty-five years before, with few additions. Whole chapters stood as the chancellor had written them, with perhaps a single note or cross-reference added by Holmes. Here and there, however, below the line of the original work, Holmes had added dense essays on points of law that Kent had not addressed, or on topics and categories that he had not imagined. Some of the essays, instead of adding new law, added historical discussions. In the chapter on descent of real estate to heirs, Holmes had added no modern citations, but he had written a tight little essay on the new anthropological work of Fustel de Coulanges, *La Cité Antique,* tracing modern law to rituals of ancestor worship. Holmes ignored the whole great area of conveyancing — preparation of deeds — then still a staple of law practice. He instead wrote an essay on more modern questions connected with contracts for sale of real estate. Under "Bailments" there was more historical research and — startling in this setting — an essay on negligence, in which Holmes summarized his ideas on jurisprudence and his new theory of torts. The notes displayed coherence among themselves, however, and immense labor. He wrote in the preface:

I have devoted more than three years to the attempt to bring this work down through the quarter of a century which has elapsed since the author's death. While it has been in progress I have tried to keep the various subjects before my mind, so far as to see the bearing upon them of any new decision in this country or England. Almost all of my more important notes have been partially or wholly rewritten — many of them more than once — in the light of cases which have appeared since their first preparation; and every case cited has been carefully examined in the original report.[11]

The burden of the *Commentaries* was at last lifted; Holmes had resigned from the *American Law Review* and had given up his courses at the Law School. Law practice seemed a comparatively light burden. For the first time, he was mildly prosperous and at ease. He read novels. He and Fanny began to look for an apartment of their own. Fanny, who had shared in the labor, shared in the pleasure at its completion.[12]

His law practice was devoted to Shattuck's clients — combative businessmen, buccaneers. Holmes was combative enough in his own sphere and had an admiring respect for these pirates. There was not much moralizing in this work; it was just war without guns.

Holmes assisted Shattuck, drafted documents, argued appeals, and appeared in court when the judge sat without a jury, as in admiralty cases. His formal demeanor and erudition nicely complemented Shattuck's forceful ease. Shattuck himself handled jury trials.

> Mr. Shattuck rarely made a mistake. He saw the bearing of every answer on every part of the evidence. If by any chance he got an unexpected reply, he adjusted himself to it in a flash, and met it by a new approach from some remote side. He could bring out the prejudices that unfitted an [opposing] witness for just this case, and yet leave his general value and his personal feelings untouched, with a delicacy, clearness and force that left me simply astounded.[13]

They represented Joe Nickerson, "a fierce old Philistine," and his son Albert.[14] One of the Nickerson ships had gone aground off Nova Scotia, the cargo was lost, and the insurers thought it was the Nickersons' own fault. Richard Henry Dana, Jr., appearing for the insurance company, told Judge John Amory Lowell that the Nickersons were slippery characters, and then was indignant when Holmes "endorsed and made himself responsible for his clients"[15] — which was not proper. Holmes won, and then won again on appeal.

He was not too concerned about niceties. In later years, he liked to tell a story about a French trial:

> A duellist was tried on the ground that he had done a forbidden thing — grasped his adversary's weapon — and a lot of experts

testified that that couldn't be done. Then a lot of duellists went on
the stand and said that is a fencing school rule — when you go on
the ground you go there to kill the other man and you do what
you can.[16]

The combat was not only in the courtroom. Shattuck represented the
Atchison, Topeka and Santa Fe Railroad in the years when railroads
bought up legislatures in bulk and hired toughs to beat down the competition. The Santa Fe was having a private war with the Denver and Rio
Grande over Western routes. Holmes was present at a peace negotiation,
and when the two sides made their terms, he wrote out the agreement
on a sheet of writing paper.

As Holmes and Shattuck walked away from the meeting, Holmes said
what was in his mind: it was a big thing they had done, but it would be
quickly forgotten.[17]

At the tea table, Holmes and the doctor carried on their dialogue.
The doctor, to be sure, did most of the talking; Holmes was watchful,
guarded. The other children were gone, Mrs. Holmes was showing her
age, and she did less to deflect the doctor's monologues, but Fanny often
managed the doctor or diverted the flow of talk.

> She certainly looks innocent enough, but . . . there is nothing
> in all this world that can lie and cheat like the face and tongue of
> a young girl. Just give her a touch of hysteria, not enough to make
> her friends call the doctor in, but a slight hint of it in the nervous
> system, — and "Machiavel the waiting maid" will take lessons from
> her.[18]

The conversation certainly touched at times on human evolution, the
great topic of the time.[19] Eugenics — marriages and children planned to
improve the racial stock — was the new, progressive nostrum.[20] Francis
Galton had published *Hereditary Genius,* and the doctor himself had written about the inheritance of character. Darwin's *Descent of Man* had appeared the year before. Humanity had been firmly placed in the animal
kingdom; evolution seemed to have been placed on a scientific basis.

The doctor thought that Darwinism promised "the whole future of
human progress and destiny." In place of the Fall of Man, "science comes
to substitute the RISE of man," the doctor sang.[21] Yet the doctor was
tenderhearted, not liking to see suffering. Holmes took a harsher view.
There was class warfare on both sides of the Atlantic. Business was organizing itself into trusts, labor into unions, and the two sides were
drawn up into lines of battle. In London, gas stokers, whose work was
filthy and dangerous, went on strike, in the winter holiday season of
1872, illegally. London was plunged into darkness for several nights. The
ringleaders of the strike were convicted and sentenced to a year in jail.

"Class legislation," the progressives said, condemning the law under which the strikers were convicted.

"Certainly," Holmes replied, deriding the soft-mindedness of people who affirmed evolution as a progressive principle, perhaps the only principle of progress, and then shrank from its application.

Holmes, looking the thing in the face, said that natural selection depended on the death of men. Industrial development was a war, and there would be casualties. In the struggle between masters and men, race and race, class against class, the fittest ultimately would survive. In this way would the progress of humanity be secured.

> The struggle for life . . . is mitigated by sympathy, prudence and all the social and moral qualities. But in the last resort a man rightly prefers his own interest to that of his neighbors. And this is true in legislation as in any other form of corporate action. . . . The more powerful interests must be more or less reflected in legislation; which, like every other device of man or beast, must tend in the long run to aid the survival of the fittest.[22]

If Holmes had ever felt much empathy with strangers, he had lost those feelings in the war. He had accepted his own duty, which was to risk his life in the war, and felt no qualms about the sacrifices of others.

Nothing would alter Malthus's iron law: spawning population would always outgrow the means of subsistence. This, and not injustice, was the ultimate source of poverty and hunger. Race and class struggled for their shares of the inadequate wealth, and the fittest would prevail, and ultimately make a better world.

> By changing the law . . . you do not get rid of any burden, but only change the mode of bearing it. . . . [The] tacit assumption of the solidarity of the interests of society is very common, but seems to us to be false. . . . Why should the greatest *number* be preferred? Why not the greatest good of the most intelligent and most highly developed? The greatest good of a minority of our generation may be the greatest good of the greatest number in the long run.[23]

As in battle, it would be foolish and ultimately unkind to blur the boundaries of identity and take others' suffering too much as if it were one's own.[24]

Not long after these discussions, in the fall of 1873, there was a financial panic. An inflated market for railroad securities collapsed, brokerages and banks closed their doors, and bankruptcies of the railroads quickly followed. The country plunged abruptly into a severe depression. Millions of men and women and children — children who had

worked in the mines and factories — were unemployed, with no resources to fall back on beyond those that nature provided.

In Boston, Irish and German immigrants were seriously hurt. The
year before, the great fire had destroyed acres of tenements and factories, leaving thousands homeless and unemployed. Now many were
homeless again. It was winter, but families slept in doorways, under
bridges. A comet appeared in the sky; some thought it would strike the
earth.

The Holmeses were not seriously affected by the panic. The firm of
Shattuck, Holmes and Munroe prospered, as doctors may prosper in a
plague city. Fanny and Holmes bought a farm in Mattapoisett, near
George Shattuck's, where they could spend summers.

> I was glad to get a place in reach of [Shattuck's]. . . . I got a Mr.
> Boules (I think) to buy for me an old double house, the two halves
> separately inhabited and one half at least quite old with a noble
> old fireplace into which one could put half a tree. . . . The farmer
> who lived in the half facing the harbor continued to live there and
> my wife and I when we could came down for a weekend in the
> other half.[25]

Fanny's brother found an apartment for them in Boston, over a drugstore at 10 Beacon Street, on the crest of Beacon Hill, near the State
House and the courts. They began planning their long-deferred wedding journey. Henry and Clover Adams had returned from Egypt and a
long stay in London, and settled into their new house in the Back Bay,
at 91 Marlborough Street, not far from the Holmeses. Henry brought
home with him reports of long visits with Henry Maine, Leslie Stephen,
James Bryce, and Tom Hughes.

Holmes and Fanny made shopping lists, packed carefully. Holmes
wrote letters to old friends in England, and also wrote letters introducing
himself to illustrious men he had not yet met. He sent his edition of
Kent's *Commentaries* as a calling card, and received an astonished reply
from Henry Maine:

> I have to thank you for a valuable, indeed magnificent, present.
> Your four volumes reached me. . . . I have looked into portions of
> them which deal with parts of the law in which I happen to take
> an interest just at present and I can assure you without flattery
> that I thought your additions to the commentary most instructive
> and useful. The work is one which I shall not only prize but pretty
> constantly consult.[26]

In May, Holmes and Fanny sailed on the Cunard Line from New

York to Liverpool on their first and very nearly their last trip abroad together.

Having written to old friends, Holmes expected to receive invitations; he would not have to struggle up the approaches to a hostile capital again. He planned to visit the courts and to become better acquainted with judges and lawyers, and he hoped on this trip to cultivate an acquaintance with Sir Henry Maine.

Fanny, however, was on her first sea voyage, her first trip abroad, and her first venture into London's polite society. She was thirty-three, childless, and unsure of herself. Even in Cambridge, little more than a village, she had been solitary. In Boston, she was ill at ease in society and had grown accustomed to Holmes going out alone while she remained at home, embroidering, and talking with the doctor. She had no strong intellectual interests, knew contemporary affairs only from the Boston newspapers, and her conversation was limited and prone to fly into eccentric fantasies. She was not handsome, and by London standards she was badly dressed. She was, in short, a provincial woman with little to distinguish her except beautiful dark eyes, intelligence, and a sharp observant wit.

The trip did not begin well for her. She was seasick on a cramped steamer filled with Bostonians she did not like. "Never, never, never put myself in such a fix again," she wrote in her diary on their first day at sea; "14 days more of it perhaps."[27]

In London they took a private apartment at 9 Bolton Street and began their round of visits to bank, embassy, and shops; they left their cards at doors. There were a great many Americans in London, tourists like themselves as well as expatriates, the postwar wealthy who had come to live in the capitals of Europe. The Holmeses repeatedly met snobbish Charles Tuckerman, ambassador to Greece in Grant's first administration, now adrift in Europe. Tuckerman and his wife condescended to them, which infuriated Fanny: "I have seldom seen a man who combined in such small quarters such gigantic defects of manners, mind and heart. . . . That portable trunk of nuisances Mr. Tuckerman and his green-eyed monster of a wooden-mouthed wife."[28]

Breakfast, lunch, and dinner were social rituals, conducted for hours at a time over a profusion of meats. Fanny filled her diary with appalled notations about the heavy meals:

> *ordinary* breakfast: omelet Fish cutletes potted rabbit Mushrooms potato boiled eggs white and brown cold tarts Toast hot bread three kinds of Jam — Honey — Fruit Tea coffee & [pastry]
> ordinary lunch Mutton — hot lamb — cold a fish made dish clotted cream jelly tart trifle fruit claret cup sherry (cider in Devonshire)
> Ordinary dinner soup fish cutletes Hare 2 mutton 1 salad or

moulded jelly or both Tart whipped cream Goat cheese Ice Fruit
Sherry Port Hock Champ[agne].[29]

Fanny noted with mixed amazement and disapproval the dress, manners, and conversation of her hosts. At the Stanleys:

The Dean very disagreeable in black stockings, long coat, black
sash and ribbon around his neck. Overheard some joke between
him and two or three fat old ladies covered with feathers, lace and
chains about "St. Peter's daughter — and he, you know, was not a
married man" — at which point up went the fans and the Dean's
hand to conceal his face from his own joke — altogether the whole
impression not of a gospel of humility and simplicity. Fat old ladies with immense bosoms and larger stomachs both adorned with
gold and precious stones.[30]

Lady Belper, who had been among the first to accept Holmes on his
first visit, Fanny thought a "twinkling hippopotamus," and noted the excesses of dinner: soup, a fish course, chicken and quail, an entremet of
sherbert, a meat course (saddle of mutton), a profusion of vegetables,
desserts — tarts, cheeses, cakes, fruit — and a great deal to drink.[31] At
another dinner, the man beside her, learning that she was recently married, asked if she had children, and at her answer said laughingly, "*Le
bon temps viendra.*"[32]
Fanny began to stay behind when Holmes went out. She read the
newspapers and clipped out odd little personals from the front page of
The Times:

An Indian Gentleman wishes a pleasurable home.

Cherie — You shall have what you ask for.

An advertisement:

RECKLESS FREEDOM in eating causes influenza, heart disease,
tuberculosis. . . .

She saw some of the sights, made little sketches of architectural details and embroidery patterns. She drew clumsy little caricatures — this
perhaps for Holmes's amusement as much as her own — of the people
they met. Holmes looked over Fanny's diary entries and added a word
of his own: "I sat next to Mrs. Willoughby [at dinner] whom I love.
O.W.H. Jr." Fanny noted his flirtations in her sardonic way: "Wendell off
on the rampage. . . . Wendell off to see his charmer and return [her]
book. Brought the book back with him." Perhaps because Holmes was to

read them, Fanny's diary entries were girlish, clumsy, misspelled, sadly teasing.[33]

Holmes had written to Sir John Kennaway, perennial host of traveling Bostonians, whose estate in Scotland Holmes had visited in the fall of 1866. One evening in June, Kennaway came to the Holmes apartment in London, and found Fanny at home alone: "He staid an hour with me, and when he went off he said, 'Why, this is awfully lonely for you. If I were not going to dine from home myself I should take you with me now whether you liked it or not.'"[34] There were other bright moments. At Devonshire House there was a large crowd, which perhaps made it easier for Fanny: "It was delightful. I was called 'My Lady' by the servants and as I went up the great marble circular staircase step by step the blood of the Dixwells rose from a long sleep and was at home again."[35] But it would be thirty years more before Fanny had a social position in which she felt comfortable, and the rest of the trip was torture. She counted not only the days but the hours until their return; every night she subtracted 24 hours from the remaining total written in her diary.

Holmes was busy and cheerful, and Fanny perhaps did not begrudge him the pleasures of the trip. He succeeded in having dinner with Maine, who had been hard to nail down and who finally, with apologies, took Holmes to his club. Nothing came of their meeting.[36]

An encounter with Frederick Pollock was more promising. Pollock's grandfather — the "celebrated Sir J. Frederick Pollock, Bart." — had been attorney general and Lord Chief Baron of the Court of Exchequer, a fierce old judge who during the Civil War years had decided the famous case of the Confederate armored ship the *Alabama* against the United States.[37] Pollock's father, who succeeded to the baronetcy in 1870, became a judge in turn, senior master of the Supreme Court of Judicature. In June of 1874 Holmes visited his court and sat beside him. Sir Frederick was a linguist, a mild antiquarian, interested in the history of men's costume, and was at work on a translation of Dante.

The youngest Frederick, tall, thin, beak-nosed, reserved in manner, was four years younger than Holmes, and like Holmes was recently married. Again like Holmes, he was an attorney who had turned to scholarly work.

> Pollock is an extraordinarily accomplished man. Not many goods in his shop window but just when you think things are rather silent he spears out some shaft of wit or insight. . . . He learns all sorts of languages easily — has a mighty tough body — for a long pull at rowing . . . likes fencing — has written about the sword — the kindest and most generous of hearts. Only defect a little too all round. But so much more interesting — so much more a living soul than most of the lawyers who have succeeded at the bar.[38]

"There was no stage of acquaintance ripening into friendship," Holmes said later. "We understood one another and were friends without more ado."[39]

Pollock had been a student at Cambridge when Leslie Stephen was a mathematics don there. Holmes entered their circle — James Bryce, Albert Venn Dicey, the young mathematician William K. Clifford, whom they thought the brightest of all. Clifford's young fiancée, Lucy Lane, only twenty, was a little like Fanny: observant, quick-witted. Holmes and Fanny had dinner with Clifford and Lucy Lane.

Holmes was at ease among these young lawyers and teachers. They shared an interest in speculative philosophy, jurisprudence, and mathematics. Pollock had begun work on a book on Spinoza's philosophy, which their circle was doing much to revive. Leslie Stephen and his young wife Minny, Thackeray's daughter, were in London; Holmes and Fanny dined with them and had a pleasant evening.

Early in July, Holmes and Fanny left London to tour the Continent, and by August they were back in London, with an invitation to visit Kennaway in Scotland for the shooting. They made brief visits to Oxford, Cambridge, and Eton, where they were shown birch twigs used by the masters to beat the boys. Fanny was very much upset.[40] She had a horror of violence to children.

At Kennaway's, Holmes was up early and late, hunting rabbits in the mornings, talking over whiskey and cigars at night. Fanny was bored by the continual talk and was ill at ease in the feudal atmosphere. At dinner her neighbor asked, "What language does the peasantry of America talk?"[41] She was tired and unhappy: "Prayers breakfast — Minister looked through his fingers at me all through prayers — Walk [which] I didn't — talk Lunch talk drive — Dinner . . . stories after dinner."[42]

The visit to Scotland — twelve days, 288 hours — was at last over, and the Holmeses sailed for New York. As always, they were back among Bostonians as soon as they went on board the steamer — among them Henry James, returning for a brief visit home.[43]

The apartment above the drugstore at 10 Beacon Street had been prepared for them in their absence. They moved out of the doctor's house and at last were in their own quarters. They were next door to the Athenaeum, and their back windows looked out over the Old Granary Burying Ground sloping down toward Tremont Street, near the street where Holmes was born. Holmes was thirty-three and Fanny thirty-four. They were independent of their parents for the first time.

Their apartment had a gas ring but not a proper kitchen. A young woman came in to clean. They ate dinner at Parker's hotel, a short walk down the hill. Once a month Holmes dined at the recently formed Tavern Club, and less regularly with an informal group who called themselves simply "the Club";[44] after dinner Holmes's friends might come to his apartment for drinks, smokes, and talk. George Shattuck often came by in the evenings.

Holmes and Fanny did not go out very often. They did visit John Holmes in Cambridge, who wrote fond little notes to them, addressed to "Guendelus meus et Guendela mea," and signed himself "U.J."[45]

They were independent but not prosperous, and were careful about money. Fanny paid attention to details, and there were touches of charm: flowers, embroideries. She collected small ornaments for the apartment. Holmes said to her, "You even make roses bloom on a broomstick."[46]

And Fanny, who had surprised her uncle John Dixwell one Christmas with a three-foot caterpillar, played pranks. On April Fool's Day, she always had a rude surprise for Holmes — a false rat, perhaps — and on a sheet of plain paper, a stick-figure portrait of herself, round face grimacing or grinning: "April Fool" written in big childish capital letters.[47]

She made a scrapbook of their souvenirs: a note from T. R. Sullivan, ten-year-old Wendell's schoolmaster, recommending him to Mr. Dixwell; the Harvard College Class Day program for 1860, when Holmes had been the class poet; the flattering, not-to-be-repeated letter from Sir Henry Maine. She decorated the margins of the big scrapbook pages with heavily drawn flowers and bells, and clumsy sentimental watercolors.[48]

In December, Fanny was thirty-five. It was plain, after almost three years of marriage, that they would not have children.[49] But if there were no children, young people gathered around them and became lifelong friends. Louis Brandeis, Samuel Warren, Henry Cabot Lodge, and Owen Wister were on their ways through college or graduate schools and formed the habit of dropping in at 10 Beacon Street. After graduation from law school, Warren came to clerk at Holmes's firm, but Brandeis, a Kentuckian, said good-bye, and went west to Ohio to practice law.[50]

Japanese students were also callers. Holmes had tutored Enouye Yoshikadsu and Nawa Michkazu for the law school in the hot summer months of 1872 when Fanny was ill.[51] In February, 1876, Holmes began tutoring Kaneko Kentaro, who would be his lifelong friend.[52]

Kaneko, a twenty-four-year-old man of the samurai class, had hoped for a military career. His large handsome eyes, high-ridged nose, and long waxed mustache made him seem a slighter, more darkly colored version of Holmes. He was from Fukuoka, and his domain lord, Kuroda Nagahiro, had chosen him to accompany the mission to the United States in 1872. Kaneko had hoped to attend the American Naval Academy, but his health was not strong and he had decided instead to study law.

The Japanese civil war was contemporary with the American, but how strange it must have been for Holmes to hear stories of these men who had fought in armor. When Kaneko left home, samurai men had still worn swords as part of their ordinary dress. Bushido, their code of chivalry and their romanticism about the feudal age just passing, struck a chord in Holmes. The Japanese had a "gentlemanly air of incurious languor,"[53] and were privately a little scornful of the blunt practicality of most American life.[54]

Kaneko came to Holmes's apartment in the evenings for tutoring and often stayed until midnight, when the last horsecar would take him to a rooming house in Cambridge. He had seemingly inexhaustible energy, tact, and grace. After four years in Boston and Cambridge, his English was cultured, if not entirely idiomatic. He had organized a supper club among the Harvard undergraduates and joined in their activities. Alone among Holmes's visitors, he called on Fanny as well. He talked to her about Japanese art and found embroidery patterns for her. Fanny began to collect Japanese prints.[55]

Kaneko and Holmes talked about Japan.[56] Perhaps they also talked about bushido and chivalry. Inazo Nitobe, a little younger than Kaneko, recalled his training in swordsmanship in his grandfather's school, where it was held a true warrior needed no weapon: "A true warrior should by the sheer strength of his will, the force of his spirit, which flashing in his eye or revealing itself in his voice and in his whole demeanor, so strike terror into his opponent as to subdue him without striking a blow."[57] How must Holmes have felt at such tales, remembering the artillery at Malvern Hill, the blind slaughter in the thickets of the Wilderness. "Somehow," Nitobe remembered, "it did not strike me as honorable to slay an enemy at a distance."[58]

This was a happy and fruitful time for Holmes. At peace and unhurried, he had begun to work again at his theory of jurisprudence. After ten years of law practice he had gained a settled mastery. He had arrived at clear ideas and he began to write them down.

In April of 1876, the first of a leisurely new series of Holmes's essays appeared in the *American Law Review*. In this first essay, liberated from the extreme compression of his digests and notes for the *Commentaries*, he wrote at relaxed length, with a profusion of detail and illustration. Beneath the remarkable complexity of the common law — the complexity of conscious thought and social institutions — lay simplicity, as clear and orderly as anatomy.

The order lay in a system of elements or structures of unconscious thought.[59] In his first essay, "Primitive Notions in Modern Law,"[60] Holmes dissected one such element, the obscure thought or feeling that compelled an injured person to seek vengeance, the primitive impulse that led a person to kick the stone on which he had stumbled. This impulse, Holmes thought, was traceable to an instinctive animism, which endowed all things that moved with life.

In primitive cultures and in the oldest legal records that could be found, vengeance was taken on a weapon that had inflicted an injury, or an animal that had attacked a person. Holmes coolly cited Roman law, "the still older and more primitive customs of [Classical] Greece," and the Old Testament, as records of primitive cultures: "If an ox gore a man or a woman, that they die: then the ox shall be surely stoned, and his flesh shall not be eaten; but the owner of the ox shall be quit." The same animism could be traced up through medieval English law: "When a man killeth another with the sword of *John at Stile*, the sword shall be forfeit as deodand, and yet no fault is in the owner."

As law replaced combat, the owners of such accursed things were required to surrender them up to the injured person or his family. And as social systems became still more complex and notions of public policy more sophisticated, persons were held liable for injuries caused by their weapons, ships, cattle, servants, or slaves. A new element of culpability or blame, equally unconscious, began to replace the older impulse of vengeance. Forms of law survived by the force of precedent, but new reasons or rationalizations were given for them, and slowly the forms themselves began to alter under the pressure of the underlying structures.

Holmes believed that his discoveries were not merely academic. Once the process of evolution in the law was exposed to view — once scientific investigation had revealed what before had been unconscious and had brought it into awareness — lawyers and judges could frankly remake the law, removing anachronisms that no longer served its purpose or meaning, openly molding it to achieve the purposes of the modern state.[61]

Holmes was well pleased with this essay. The disparate streams of the history, logic, and function of law that had been so stubbornly divergent during his labor on the *Commentaries* merged into a single image of evolution. He wrote to Emerson:

I send by this mail the article of which I spoke. It is called "Primitive Notions in Modern Law." If the clothing of detail does not stand in the way I hope the ideas may not be uninteresting to you. It seems to me that I have learned, after a laborious and somewhat painful period of probation, that the law opens a way to philosophy as well as anything else, if pursued far enough, and I hope to prove it before I die. Accept this little piece as written in that faith, and as [a] slight mark of the gratitude and respect I feel for you who more than anyone else first started the philosophical ferment in my mind.[62]

Holmes also sent copies of this essay to his correspondents in England. The responses were cautious and respectful, but puzzled, not entirely sure — Holmes himself was not entirely sure — what had been accomplished. Pollock, with whom Holmes had established such immediate understanding, was perceptive. He saw very clearly that Holmes's article only illustrated and explained an intuition of a method, and that immense further labors would be needed for something that was plainly in Holmes's mind — an orderly restatement of the common law:

> Your position seems well made out by evidence and analogy, and I think it a good piece of work in itself, and of just the kind now wanted to clear the way for an adequate handling of the general body of the Common Law. Whether it would be at all possible, until much more has been done in this way, to produce a really good institutional book, [I question].[63]

Holmes had not written a history or even an orderly exposition of theory. His essay was an artist's aperçu. To build his intuition into a theory of evolution, to restate the law by tracing it to its unconscious elements, and finally to show how it should be revised to accord with modern ideas of policy were tasks for a lifetime of labor — perhaps for many such lifetimes.

"Primitive Notions in Modern Law" was also marred by an argumentative streak, a tendency to justify and explain Holmes's earlier writings and to attack the idols of jurisprudence, especially Austin. But the idols were unshaken. Outside Holmes's circle of correspondents his articles went largely unnoticed.

But Holmes refreshed himself in the salons and at the dinner tables of Beacon Hill and the Back Bay. He occupied himself in introducing Kaneko Kentaro into polite society. The Japanese had grown Bostonian enough to be pale and ill with overwork, and Holmes's recommended treatment was a course of feminine company.

Kaneko had no proper clothes for dinner parties, however, and the first step was to have a swallowtail coat made for him. This was a bold step for one of the closely constrained Japanese students. Another had remarked,

> A jacket becomes me better than a swallow-tail. After I have studied five or six years longer, I may be fitted for parties, for drinking and smoking, and dancing, but not yet. . . . I do not think these are the accomplishments in which my country is anxious to see me successful.[64]

But Kaneko was ready to assault the ramparts of polite society. In a new swallowtail coat, a serious expression, and light manner, he followed Holmes to teas and dinner parties, a medieval knight visiting nineteenth-century Boston.

Kaneko was a great success, which Holmes seems to have enjoyed as much as he. When both men were old they liked to reminisce about this time. Thirty-five years later, Kaneko wrote to Holmes:

> I am delighted to know that you feel young although advanced in age, and [are still] enjoying the "society of women," which is chronic in your nature since the Beacon Street days when I was often led into the circle of the fair sex by you, in spite of Mrs. Holmes' admonition. I am still as young as I was [when] introduced to Miss Mary Perkins of Boston by you at Mrs. Winter's ball at Marlborough Street. . . . P.S. Don't forget to tell Mrs. Holmes about Miss Perkins.[65]

Holmes and Kaneko called on Mrs. Gray — John Gray was newly married to the lovely Anna Lyman, called Nina. Holmes and Kaneko both fell in love with Nina Gray's delicate chin, small graceful mouth, big pale eyes. Nina wrote poetry, enjoyed their conversation, and was entirely affectionate and charming.

Undoubtedly, they also called on Mrs. Jack Gardner — Isabella Stewart Gardner — who received guests on most afternoons from five until seven, and who like Kaneko was studying art history with Professor Charles Eliot Norton. Belle Gardner was a tiny blonde woman with a fine athletic figure and a charming crooked smile, who had been the first to wear Worth's revealing gowns in Boston. She had begun to collect art and old books, and she exchanged presents with the Holmeses, senior and junior.

Fanny herself was not at home to callers, and did not go out. She remained at home, occupied with her embroideries and a growing menagerie of pets — birds, mice, squirrels. She read the newspapers, which Holmes did not, and in the evenings amused him with newspaper oddities, puns, and riddles she collected in her commonplace book.

In the summer, on Holmes's three-week vacations, they would go to their farm at Mattapoisett and sail with Shattuck or drive on the Cape Cod roads. Fanny liked to stop at the rural churchyards and collect curious inscriptions for her book.

Henry Adams, Frederick Pollock, Leslie Stephen, James Bryce, Albert Dicey all had books published. Adams and his students had done a study of medieval legal institutions that greatly interested Holmes. Stephen's book on eighteenth-century philosophy was a big accomplishment, although his young wife had died and it was ashes to him.[66] Bigelow and Green were teaching at the new Boston University Law School, and Bigelow had two books out. Holmes read their books and wrote them up for the *Law Review*. He practiced law and calmly pursued his course, conscious that he had not yet emerged from anonymity.

William James married, and brought his new wife, Alice, to Mattapoisett to meet the Holmeses. He and Holmes were far apart on

widely diverging paths, however, and Holmes, as always, threatened him
a little:

> [Holmes] is a powerful battery, formed like a planing machine
> to gauge a deep, self-beneficial groove through life; his virtues
> and faults were thrown into singular relief by the lonesomeness
> of the shore, which as it makes every object, rock or shrub, stand
> out so vividly, seemed also to put him and his wife under a sort of
> lens for you.[67]

Holmes continued to publish articles in the *American Law Review*, one
each summer. He had his method and had begun the immense effort of
applying it. He searched for traces of elementary structures, unconscious
elements that lay beneath the surface of the law, like bones within a
hand.

In his first article he had traced diverse forms of modern liability to
a common root in the primitive thirst for vengeance. The second essay,[68]
in the summer of 1877, returned to the curious ancient fiction that an
heir literally succeeded to the deceased's place. There was another intuition here, that, at a primitive level of the unconscious mind, perhaps
revealed in ancient and primitive societies, the son absorbed and became
his father.

The third essay[69] was still more wholehearted and passionate. Holmes
searched out the root of private property in English law, which he traced
to a primitive instinct of territoriality. Here, Holmes's method of argument was attack. He chose for his object the German empire. The Kaiser
had crowned himself successor of the Roman emperors; German scholars had revived Roman law.

Holmes happily waded into combat with the new imperial theories.
He did not read German, and had read very little of German philosophy,
even in translation. But he knew something of the Roman law, and he
knew enough German philosophy to set it up as a target. He tumbled
Hegel, Rousseau, and Kant together with the modern Roman-law scholars, and buried them under his contempt.

Rights of property, in the German theory, had a substantial reality of
their own, an existence independent of law and courts. Rights were an
expression of will. Legal rights accorded to an owner were "an objective
realization of free will."[70] Holmes cheerfully demolished this opponent.

In English law, rights were founded on simple force of arms. Holmes
gleefully cited the folk customs of their Teutonic forebears against the
modern Germans. The law of northern Europe, back to the time when
courts were principally occupied with cattle-stealing, was that the man
who had possession of cattle might keep them, and recover them by force
from any who tried to take them. A "right" meant physical possession
and the power to enforce it, which the courts would respect.

More refined notions of ownership and right came later, but at the core of modern law could still be found this primitive impulse. In England and in Massachusetts, one who had possession of a thing, the power to exclude others and the intent to exercise that power, had a *right* of possession that a court would enforce. But this "right" was no ideal entity or expression of disembodied will. A court was no more than a register of power, and a substitute for private violence:

> Law, being a practical thing, must found itself on actual forces. It is quite enough, therefore, for the law, that man, with an instinct which he shares with the domestic dog, and of which the seal gives a most striking example, will not allow himself to be dispossessed, either by force or fraud, of what he holds without trying to get it back again. Philosophy may find a hundred reasons to justify the instinct, but it is totally immaterial if it should condemn it and bid us surrender without a murmur. As long as the instinct remains, it will be more comfortable for the law to satisfy it in an orderly manner, than to leave people to themselves. If it should do otherwise, it would become a matter for pedagogues, wholly devoid of reality.[71]

With great care and learning, with unusual singlemindedness and thorough scholarship, Holmes set down his arguments and then, in a victorious peroration, announced that history, analysis, and theory — the three disparate lines of thought he had so long struggled to unite — all converged.[72] The German will was vanquished, and English matter-of-factness prevailed.

Holmes at nineteen years of age had pronounced that scientific observation and analysis would replace the philosophers's ideals; now it seemed that he himself as lawyer-scientist was proving his prophecy correct.

Holmes was very pleased and excited. He sent copies of "Possession" to Pollock and Sir Henry Maine. To Arthur Sedgwick, his old coeditor, he opened his heart: "I think the theory which I state and wh. is simply that wh. would occur to the unregenerate mind as the only natural one is much more advanced than Hegel's rot on the subject. But if I am right it makes a pretty big hole in his philosophy."[73] But the world did not yet catch fire from his flame. Maine did not answer. Pollock wrote, "Sir H. Maine tells me that he duly received your paper, and . . . has not yet been able to acknowledge it as he would like. I don't know that I have any comment to make myself, as I agree, with little or no exception."[74] This was rather flat, for a theory that knocked holes in Hegel. But Holmes was already back on the firing line.

For the first time, he had a reasonable chance of becoming a judge. When Judge George F. Shepley died on July 20, 1878, a vacancy appeared on the federal bench, and Holmes let his friends know that he would not refuse the place if it were offered to him:

> The place is not desirable for the money for the salary is only $4,000 — but it would enable me to work in the way I want & so I should like it — although it would give me a severe pang to leave my partners. . . . The way the bar have spoken about me has given me much pleasure, & I can't help feeling nervous about the result until the thing is settled, although if I were appointed I should hardly know whether to be glad or sorry.[75]

Nominations for the federal courts passed through the hands of United States senators and the attorney general to the President. The campaign for such an appointment was hard fought; federal judges were appointed for life, and vacancies were not frequent. John Gray apparently organized the campaign on Holmes's behalf.[76] He circulated a petition among members of the bar, but was not successful in obtaining the support of either the attorney general, Charles Devens, who had commanded the Fifteenth Massachusetts at Ball's Bluff, or of Senator George Hoar. Hoar, indeed, had his own candidate.

Horace Gray, John's half-brother, then chief justice of the Massachusetts Supreme Judicial Court, helped in the campaign. He extended himself thoroughly on Holmes's behalf, so much so that he was a little bruised by the effort.[77] Shattuck undoubtedly did what he could. But Hoar and Devens met with the President, and Hoar emerged with the appointment for his own man.[78]

This must have been a great disappointment, although Holmes said little about it afterward. Because vacancies on the federal district court were so rare, Holmes perhaps had missed his opportunity.

Amelia Holmes's husband, Turner Sargent, died in 1877, leaving her embroiled in a bitter dispute with her in-laws over an inheritance. Holmes represented his sister in this dreary matter.[79] Amelia returned to 296 Beacon Street, where her mother now needed care.

Ned, too, was seriously ill; his asthma and heart ailments had worsened, and he had begun another hopeless round of travels to resorts: "When shall we live in Boston again? Heaven only knows. The winters are so severe, or the changes so great, or for some reason unknown, I cannot breathe there, and we must leave the place."[80]

Fanny had become a little more noticeably eccentric. Her pet birds and small animals grew more numerous. Little ornaments and decorations seemed to fill the small apartment. She made no effort to appear attractive, and even seemed to choose unbecoming clothes, an unflattering manner of wearing her hair; she made an almost studied effort to be plain.[81]

She had few friends of her own generation, but was very fond of her numerous nieces and nephews. Fanny's solitary days were taken up in making amusements and gifts for the children and by her embroidery. She was an awkward draftsman, but she had good native taste and a critical eye. In her silk embroideries she was able to render others' designs and Japanese patterns. These monuments of effort she gave to relatives or kept for household decorations, or simply put away. Occasionally she lent some for shows of needlework at the new Museum of Fine Arts, and in 1880 the museum showed fourteen of her now locally famous embroideries. The *Daily Advertiser* gushed uncomfortably, "This is, probably, the most remarkable needlework ever done."[82] Her embroideries were also shown in a Ladies' Decorative Arts Exhibition in New York. Fanny perhaps cringed at the whole affair, and at the condescending praise that was politely lavished on the "ladies." But *The Nation* saw what was best in Fanny, without overpraising: "[Her] pictures are entirely free and individual, being in nothing more remarkable than in their avoidance of the semblance of conventionality, good or bad. In fine, she is an American artist of noticeable qualities."[83]

But Fanny, whether because she lacked skill, or lacked encouragement, did not fulfill her old ambition to paint. She remained at home with Holmes and her embroideries, increasingly reclusive.

Kaneko had finished his law studies and had departed with his swallowtail coat. He had translated a sentimental Japanese folktale for *The Atlantic,* in which the heroine committed suicide at the end, rather a shocking conclusion for a Christian audience, and he left Boston in a flurry of explanations and farewells to hostesses and professors. Enouye Yoshikadsu, who had left earlier, could not adjust to his native country after his long stay in Boston and killed himself.[84] Nawa died of typhus.

In that summer of 1879, Holmes was lonely, overworked, overtaxed by the need to make a living and to cut his path as a scholar at the same time. As a philosopher of law he had as yet accomplished little beyond a few essays in a provincial journal. Holmes wrote to Pollock, who had already published two books and was at work on his *Spinoza*:

> When I have accumulated enough material I shall hope to rewrite [my *American Law Review* articles] in the form of a book. But I can assure you it takes courage and perseverance to keep at a task that has to be performed at night and after making one's living by day. I have to thank you and other English friends for encouragement which has been very valuable to me.[85]

To James Bryce he wrote:

> I was extremely pleased to get your letter and to see that you hadn't forgotten me. . . . There are so few men as I was saying to Dicey who have any kind of idealism in their practice that I cling

pretty closely to those who have . . . the men who care more for a fruitful thought than for a practical success are few everywhere and I doubt if the fellowship is complete anywhere without going beyond national boundaries. . . . I have great contempt for the run of successful lawbooks and their authors on this side of the water anyhow. I wish the necessity of making a living didn't preclude any choice on my part — for I hate business and dislike practice apart from arguing cases.[86]

But gaps in the circle around Holmes were filled. Louis Brandeis came back to Boston and clerked for Horace Gray. He and Holmes's clerk, Samuel Warren, sometimes sat up late with Holmes, drinking and talking.[87] Brooks Adams and Henry Cabot Lodge remained in Boston, writing and campaigning for political reform. Adams ran unsuccessfully for the legislature, and Lodge organized a Mugwump club of reform-minded Republicans. These young men around Holmes were filled with progressive ideas, enthusiasm for reform, political ambition.

Holmes thought that the future would be with them. He interrupted his essays on the common law to write a defense of government regulation of grain elevators, recently upheld by the Supreme Court. State Street thought this decision a piece of communism. But Holmes wrote calmly, as if observing from London:

Cities have grown up whose existence depends on the railroad, and the products of millions of acres have to pass through the elevators of Chicago. If you cut the motor nerve, you paralyze the hand. If the railroads and elevators have a constitutional right to charge what they please, it is just as truly a right to destroy the property of others as a right to make noxious vapors would be.[88]

Holmes wrote a fourth long essay for the *American Law Review*,[89] and ended with his now customary appeal: change and reforms, for so many centuries made unconsciously and through ignorance, should be conscious and purposeful. Reforms should be openly confronted and discussed, and judges should "consider questions of policy with a freedom that was not possible before."[90]

This was radical talk, hardly calculated to advance Holmes's career at the bar or on the bench. But he saw, perhaps through the eyes of the younger men around him, how the world was changing. The law, willy-nilly, would reflect those changes. To Holmes it seemed that the change should be made consciously, even scientifically, to accommodate new purposes. He was willing to fight for his own class and nation on those terms.[91]

It was the doctor's seventieth-birthday year, and on Wednesday, December 3, 1879, *The Atlantic* held a "Reception and Breakfast" for him that began at noon and proceeded from sole, oysters, omelette with chicken livers, chicken cutlet with peas, filet of beef and potatoes, through woodcock, quail with truffles, to creams and ices, cake, fruit, and coffee.[92] Literary and publishing Boston was present; the President of the United States, Rutherford B. Hayes, sent a congratulatory message.

Holmes was offered a more modest honor. Would he give the Lowell Lectures the following winter? It would be a course of twelve talks in a public hall, on successive Tuesday and Friday evenings. The lectures would give Holmes a chance and an inducement to draw together his scattered articles on the common law into a single connected work.

Holmes hesitated. Shattuck was ill and planning to go abroad for his health, which would leave Holmes the senior member of the firm. Work would be more demanding than ever.

But Holmes had a superstition that a man must make his mark, if at all, before the age of forty. With the spur of the Lowell Lectures he might have his book on the common law published before his fortieth birthday, March 8, 1881.[93] This swung the balance.

He accepted and set to work on *The Common Law* much as he had worked on Kent's *Commentaries*. He wrote essays on topics of law and published them in the *American Law Review* as he went along.

The gaps remaining to be filled in his past work were tremendous. In the whole field of criminal law he had written nothing, and he had little experience in practice. On the subject of ordinary contracts he had done nothing, and even on the subject of torts, the law of harms, after two attempts he had no systematic treatment. Once more Holmes plunged into a solitary frenzy of work.

He began at the heart of his subject, the confused mass of decisions concerning everyday behavior that had come to be gathered together under the heading "torts." A tort, Holmes had written in the *Commentaries* and his earlier, unsuccessful, article on torts, was a violation of a rule of behavior. Holmes had not found any order or meaning in the rules themselves, nor had he found any underlying principle to explain their diversity.

There was a moment that summer when Holmes saw a simple principle that seemed to bring order into the jumble.

The organizing principle of the law was not found in the rules themselves, which were hopelessly diverse, as disparate and varied as the circumstances of human behavior. People came into court because they had been injured in some way and not because someone had violated a rule of behavior. Was the injury being complained of an accident — of which the law took no notice — or was it someone's fault? Under the skin of modern law lay not rules of behavior but a primitive impulse: blame. "Even a dog distinguishes between being stumbled over and being kicked."[94]

The law of torts was simply the line drawn between accidental and blameworthy injuries. The line had not been drawn all at once, but by inarticulate decisions in one case after another. The concept of blame had evolved from an instinctive impulse for retribution to a modern notion of fairness. People were now held accountable only for injuries they might have foreseen and forestalled. What a person of ordinary intelligence and foresight could not foresee was accidental and therefore blameless.[95]

It was the summer of 1880, and Holmes was filled with confidence and enthusiasm. He had the fundamental principles of law in his grasp.

On Tuesday evening, November 23, 1880, Holmes began his course of lectures at Huntington Hall, a short stroll from his apartment down Beacon Hill and along Tremont Street toward the Common. The hall was whitely lit by gas. Holmes stood a little stiffly, turning his brilliant pale eyes occasionally to the audience. He was tall, exquisitely thin, erect, his mustaches stiffly waxed. He spoke in a clear tenor, with the formality of an orator. His young circle were in attendance — Brooks Adams, Louis Brandeis, Cabot Lodge — as were his former colleagues and partners, many of them now law professors: Thayer, Gray, Bigelow, Green. Certainly Fanny was there, the doctor and Mrs. Holmes. There were members of the bar, judges, some of his Back Bay neighbors, for whom the lectures were an entertainment, and some of the working people for whom they were an education. He began:

The life of the law has not been logic; it has been experience. The felt necessities of the time, the prevalent moral and political theories, institutions of public policy, avowed or unconscious, even the prejudices which judges share with their fellow men, have had a good deal more to do than the syllogism in determining the rules by which men should be governed. The law embodies the story of a nation's development through many centuries, and it cannot be dealt with as if it contained only the axioms and corollaries of a book of mathematics.[96]

For twelve evenings, Holmes spoke steadily, a frail figure describing an extraordinary vision. The common law seemed to be spread out before him like an immense, forbidding landscape, its contours heaved and buckled by unconscious forces — the passions for vengeance and blame, the fierce instinct with which an animal defends what it has, the strange fantasy that an heir absorbs and becomes his father. Law began as a substitute for private violence and unrestrained passion. Its rules and explanations were only rationalizations for what judges felt obliged to decide. Unconscious motives lay behind their opinions. As civilization advanced and society became more complex, precedents were mechanically repeated, but new explanations were continuously invented, and eventually the outmoded form was reshaped by its new purpose.

In this landscape every person stood alone. Law had little to do with love, charity, or moral sentiment. Law was what courts did, and the courts only punished or shifted injuries from one pair of shoulders to another. The rules of law were patterns cut by these impositions of public force. A man must study these patterns to know what his legal duties were, at peril of suffering the public force on his own person.

There was a spectrum of duties. At one extreme stood the true duties, the obligations of criminal law. At an intermediate point were torts or civil wrongs, no longer questions of strict duty but only of prudence and foresight. Finally, there were voluntarily assumed duties: legally enforceable agreements. The courts were indifferent whether these were performed, so long as — once again — the party who broke the agreement bore the burden of damages.

The law imposed these solitary obligations on isolated people, determined solely by the circumstances in which they stood. Legal rights and duties passed from one person to another, not through the fabric of human relationships, but in a process of succession, founded on a fantasy that one person had replaced another.

The force that imposed these solitary duties was an invisible presence that lay behind the courts; it was the force of collective instinct, of the common passions and prejudices of those who ruled. This looming existence had evolved, as the race had evolved, through the struggle for life, the clash of nations and classes. Its evolution was like the maturation of a single person. Dim unconscious motives slowly became evident to self-awareness; the unconscious became conscious, the subjective gave way gradually to the objective. The primitive law of vengeance gave way to more refined impulses of blame, and finally to modern ideas of fairness.

With the discovery of this process, nations could take control of their own development. Law, which had been blind and inarticulate, could henceforth serve conscious, openly stated purposes.[97]

On March 3, 1881, just five days before his fortieth birthday, Holmes received from Little, Brown and Company the first copy of the book based on his lectures, *The Common Law*. The book had been hastily written and was difficult to follow. The essays of which it was made up had been written over a period of years and varied widely in tone and manner. Large areas of law had been neglected, or treated cursorily, while others were examined in exhausting depth. Flashes of insight were strung together by obscure and hasty argument, the contemptuous dismissal of rival views, or exaggerations.[98]

The force of the presentation overwhelmed all these defects. Beneath its immense burden of learning and its detailed expositions of history, *The Common Law* was a work of art more than it was a work of scholarship. It was a coldly passionate expression of intuitions. Holmes saw the landscape of the common law illuminated by his thought as by a beacon. The force of his certainty infused every word. Phrase after phrase sprang from the well of his intuition. *The Common Law* took on a life of its own; the author himself did not know fully what he had made.

PART IV

AN
OBSCURE
JUDGE

12

THE MOVING BANNERS OF A HIDDEN COLUMN

A T FIRST, THERE WAS ANTICLIMAX. HOLMES WAS FORTY YEARS old. A year of fighting at the limits of his ability to make a book out of his intellectual life, the heart of his being, had ended abruptly. *The Common Law* was printed and bound, and on sale to a largely indifferent public, for $3.75 a copy. Little, Brown and Company had offered Holmes their royalty for literary works — fifteen percent — but Holmes had insisted on the twenty percent traditionally paid for law books ("on account of the greater intellectual effort involved — we keep our smiles to ourselves").[1] Little, Brown sent Holmes the first copy from the press and he wrote on the flyleaf, "First copy of book, March 3, 1881." He and Fanny went to their farm in Mattapoisett for a quiet celebration. They opened a bottle of champagne, and Holmes set aside the cork — for the rest of his life he kept it in the right-hand drawer of his desk.[2] The weekend over, he was back in his law office and settled down to work with his junior partner and the clerk.

There was the important matter of reviews. Holmes sent copies of the book to friends in England.

My dear Pollock
I have failed in all correspondence & have abandoned pleasure

as well as a good deal of sleep for a year to accomplish a result which I now send you by mail in the form of a little book *The Common Law.* . . . I should like it very much if my book was noticed in England but I suppose there are few anywhere who interest themselves in such things. . . . I have been wont to look for companionship more to a few men on your side [of the Atlantic] — although I should be unjust and ungrateful not to add some Americans in the same line.[3]

To George Shattuck, still in Italy but soon to return, Holmes sent a copy of the book and a long letter in which he spoke still more strongly, more resentfully, of the burden of law practice, about the meanness of business-getting, the "suicidal race for fortune" that had broken down Shattuck's health and threatened his own.[4] Holmes had entered middle age. One morning, in the bathroom, he was frightened to find that he was bleeding, and briefly, as in the winters of his military service, he feared that he would die ignominiously of disease, without any notable accomplishment to mark his passing. But, after all it was not serious, and he cheered himself up by taking out of the Athenaeum the volumes of Casanova's memoirs that were kept in a locked safe.[5]

Work went on, and for a while there was only silence.

Dear Pollock

I hope you will read my book — it cost me many hours of sleep & the only reward I have promised myself is that a few men will say well done — I find it was sent to the *Saturday Review* & [the] *Spectator* but I fancy it is an accident whether it falls into hands of people who will realize that the work is at least a serious one.[6]

A vacancy had appeared on the Supreme Judicial Court of Massachusetts that winter, and James Thayer submitted Holmes's name on the strength of the Lowell Lectures, but he was again passed over.[7] His hopes now rested with his book and the reception it would receive; all depended on the reviews. But, despite Holmes's desperate impatience, the silence continued for a time.

With summer, reviews began to appear. *The Nation,* which had gone out of its way to pan his father's books, ran a sourly obtuse review, and said the philosophy might have been left out without harm to the book. There were more flattering but still uncomprehending reviews in American law journals. And then at last there was the reward Holmes had promised himself, praise from a few English friends. In June, Pollock's unsigned notice appeared in *The Saturday Review,* giving cool, intelligent appreciation.[8] And then, more generous and understanding, Albert Venn Dicey wrote in *The Spectator:*

Holmes' book is the most original work of legal speculation which has appeared in English since the publication of Sir Henry Maine's *Ancient Law*. The feature which gives this special original- ity to Mr. Holmes' *Common Law* is, that the treatise exhibits in com- bination two different methods of treating legal problems. One school, of whom Sir Henry Maine is the most brilliant English example, have examined legal institutions and conceptions exclu- sively with a view to their historical development. Another school, deriving their parentage from Bentham . . . have treated laws al- most entirely as a matter of logic and analysis . . . of this kind of one-sidedness Mr. Holmes' book does not exhibit a trace. His ob- ject, as we understand it, is to explain, and to justify, the *principles* which govern the different departments of the Common Law. . . .

Mr. Holmes is both a profound "case" lawyer, a student of history, and (what is no mean qualification for a jurist) a man immersed in the practice of the Courts. . . . Mr. Holmes' work [consequently] gains a kind of reality lacking, for example, to Austin's celebrated *Lectures on Jurisprudence*.[9]

But it was not all praise, even from Dicey; as Pollock had said years before, Holmes had found a method, but to apply it thoroughly, to re- state the common law fully, would be the work of a lifetime. And there were doubts about matters of detail. Holmes's English friends did not entirely understand his insistence on treating the decisions of courts as scientific data and thought he was perhaps provincial, immoderately re- spectful to English judges. But the praise! They had put Holmes above the great figures of the two English schools, and, even more than this, they said Holmes had fused those two schools into a single transcendent system of his own.

There were few tangible rewards, other than accolades from friends. George Shattuck wrote from Italy, fatherly, personal, and calmly earth- bound: "I congratulate you on the publication of your book. . . . I see from the papers that you have argued the will case. It would be well if we could look into that class of cases — ."[10]

The firm's office manager was Gustave Magnitzky, Holmes's sergeant in the Twentieth; he too was growing old. There was a new clerk, Glen- dower Evans, struggling as Holmes had with the troubles of youth. Holmes drew him into his circle of talk: "Now, Evans, if you will advance any proposition I will refute it for you."[11]

Ned Holmes returned to Boston, and then once more fled. He went to a resort among mountain lakes in New Jersey, where he seemed to drift, purposeless.

Holmes was back in the infantry line, where anonymous duty and ultimately death waited. He could not resign himself to this life, and when in the fall of 1881 President Eliot spoke to him about returning to the Harvard Law School, Holmes gave the proposition careful thought.

There were difficulties. Holmes still hoped for a judicial appointment some day, despite repeated disappointments, and his friends — perhaps Shattuck, who was back from Italy now — warned him that it would be more difficult to be appointed from the law school than from a practice before the court. And there was the question of salary. A law professor was paid only $4,500 per year, little more than Holmes had earned from writing and lecturing ten years earlier.

There were even more difficulties from the university's point of view. The law school had no funds for a new professor, and Eliot left these details to be worked out by others. An endowment for a new chair would have to be raised, but it was not clear who would do this. The existing faculty members — except Thayer, Holmes's former partner — were less than enthusiastic, and the talk dragged on.[12]

There was a new generation of fledgling lecturers at the law school drawn from Holmes's circle of young men. Brandeis was to teach evidence that fall, and Brooks Adams was to give lectures on Constitutional law, as Holmes himself had done ten years earlier.

A second vacancy appeared on the Supreme Judicial Court. The chief justice, Horace Gray, who had once worked hard but unsuccessfully to have Holmes appointed to the federal district court, was himself appointed to a seat on the United States Supreme Court, and Holmes's name with Gray's support was submitted to the governor to fill the vacancy Gray's promotion would leave. Once again, however, Holmes was passed over.

Discussions of the professorship resumed; difficulties, and Holmes's doubts, were resolved one after another. Brandeis undertook to raise the money to endow a new professorship, and with good luck raised the whole sum — approximately $100,000 — from a single contributor, a wealthy young former classmate, Samuel Weld.

Weary of law practice, with a great wrench Holmes tore himself away from his comrades, his partners, and left the line of combat.[13] On March 1, 1882, he joined the Harvard Law School, and began to attend faculty meetings. He was assigned to teach five courses; he would have the summer to prepare his lectures and would begin classes in the fall. For a while he returned to the library and wrote long memorandum-essays on new topics he would address, fitting them into the structure of *The Common Law*. Henry Adams, back from Washington for the summer, had a helpful suggestion for the lectures on equity, but otherwise Holmes's essays were elaborations of the ideas he had developed before. They were heavy, thorough, burdened as none of his earlier writings had been with exhaustive footnotes. Fanny noticed that his whole manner had become heavier.[14]

On April 27, 1882, Ralph Waldo Emerson died, in the evening, after a long withdrawal into silence and forgetfulness.

There was a last matter for Holmes to clear up for Shattuck, one with a special poignancy. For the last time, Holmes argued a case in the Supreme Court of the United States. He retraced the path to Washington, the Southern village that had now become a town. Streets were paved and the signs of war were long vanished; the Washington Monument and the Capitol dome were complete, and the Supreme Court had moved into the old Senate chamber ringed by marble columns, where the nine black-gowned justices now sat at their high bench like fates or Apostles.[15]

That summer he and Fanny went to Europe. A long vacation was one of the prerogatives of a law professor, and Fanny willingly agreed to submit to another summer in Great Britain.[16] They spent very little time in London, however, perhaps because Holmes did not care to appear there in the character of a professor. They went first to Oxford, and visited James Bryce — the Samuel Weld Professor of Law calling on the Regius Professor of Civil Law — saw Albert Venn Dicey and other academic friends. When they went on to London, it was all law and intellectual circles. They had a friendly second meeting with the Pollocks.

Leslie Stephen had married again, to a widow with three children of her own. When Holmes and Fanny called on them in London, the Stephens were newly settled in their house at 22 Hyde Park: a dark five-story house very much like the houses of Boston, with a large back garden. The Stephens had added rooms to make space for their nurseries. The unhappy daughter of Stephen's first marriage needed a nursery to herself; there were the three children of Julia's first marriage and the infant Virginia, born in January, the first of their children together. There was a dinner party at 22 Hyde Park at which the beautiful Julia presided.

But, for the most part, it was a round of sight-seeing and law talk. Kennaway took Holmes to a sitting of the court of the Privy Council. Holmes visited other courts and saw more thoroughly than on earlier visits the work of English judges:

> To an American lawyer . . . the speed of English courts appears unbelievable. We saw case after case disposed of by the Court of Appeal without the examination of any papers. The counsel would state the point of law involved, with a citation or two, if necessary. Occasionally one of the judges would look at the citation, and after a very brief argument, each of the judges in turn would give his opinion orally on the case.[17]

After three weeks in London, they went off for a sight-seeing tour on the Continent, and by early September, well in time for the beginning of classes in October, Holmes and Fanny were back in their apartment at 10 Beacon Street.

The faculty of the Harvard Law School was still small, but President Eliot had replaced the stolid practitioners of Holmes's student days with a group of scholars: James B. Thayer, Holmes's good friend John Chipman Gray, James Barr Ames, and the dean, Christopher Columbus Langdell, whose method of teaching by questions was transforming the school.

Able as these men were, their work and their ambitions did not excite Holmes. The insights yielded by his fifteen years of practice and study were in *The Common Law,* and he did not want to spend the rest of his life filling in details. He had begun to think that, as a philosopher-scientist, he would want other fields of study than the law.[18]

With his new leisure, Holmes paid more calls and visited the salons that young married women of fashion were beginning to keep in Boston. The principal meal was now in the evening, at seven or eight, and ladies were at home after five, until it was time to dress for dinner. Holmes called on Belle Gardner at 152 Beacon Street, where he sometimes met Henry James, lingering in Boston for a few months after his mother's death; James was growing stout, and more English in manner. He and Belle Gardner held a sort of court at teatimes, sitting side-by-side in the window seat — Henry barely taller than little Belle, both dressed in black. Holmes called once a week on Nina Gray and occasionally went to dinner parties alone.

In November, Holmes's diminishing chances for a judicial post seemed to vanish entirely. He had been a loyal and dutiful Republican, and his hopes depended on his party. But Republican Governor John Long, a square-jawed, thick-browed Boston lawyer, only a little older than Holmes, who had fought and won three difficult elections, announced that he would not run again. In November, the Democratic candidate, Ben Butler, who had been one of the despised political generals in the Civil War, was elected. Holmes resigned himself to what had begun to seem half a life as a teacher.

Soon after the election, on Friday, December 8, 1882, Holmes had lunch with his fellow professor James Barr Ames in Cambridge. As they were eating, George Shattuck appeared and asked Holmes to come with him. Fanny was waiting in a carriage outside, and all three set off immediately for Boston. Shattuck explained as they went. There was a last chance for a seat on the Massachusetts court. One of the justices, Otis Lord, was in poor health and had decided to resign in the closing days of Governor Long's term.

There was little time. The governor would serve for only three weeks longer; a judicial appointment must lie before the governor's council for a week, but the council was to adjourn that afternoon, with no date set for another meeting. Long, in deference to the election results, had thought of appointing a Democrat. But Shattuck had persuaded him to appoint Holmes — if Holmes would consent before three that afternoon. "It was a stroke of lightning."[19]

Within an hour, Holmes and Shattuck were with the governor, and it was done. That afternoon, Governor Long submitted Holmes's name to his council and, there being no objection, the appointment took effect one week later. Holmes had become the youngest member of the Supreme Judicial Court of Massachusetts. The chief justice, Marcus Morton, who graduated from the Harvard Law School a year before Holmes was born, welcomed him generously:

> You can hardly realize how great a satisfaction I feel by your appointment as the successor to Judge Lord. The Governor could not have made a selection more satisfactory to the court and I can assure you of a cordial welcome from all its members.[20]

At a meeting of the President and Fellows of Harvard College, January 8, 1883, the secretary coolly noted that "the resignation of Professor Oliver Wendell Holmes Jr. was accepted as of December 15, 1882, that being the date on which he took the oath of office as Associate Justice of the Supreme Judicial Court of Massachusetts." Holmes had taught his classes for just two months, and had resigned in the middle of the term. There was some heat over the resignation. President Eliot let it be known that Holmes had behaved badly; it was some years before his feelings subsided. The law school faculty were offended, not only because Holmes left so abruptly, but because he had not stopped to consult or even inform them. They learned about the appointment from the newspapers.[21]

But the young instructors were happy for him. Brandeis sent a note as soon as he read of Holmes's appointment: "As one of the bar I rejoice. As part of the Law School I mourn. As your friend I congratulate you."[22]

There were other kind words and letters from friends. The Boston Bar Association held a dinner in Holmes's honor. The doctor read a poem after dinner that jocularly embroidered on what he had been saying in conversation: "To think of it — my little boy a Judge, and able to send me to jail if I don't behave myself."[23]

After years of scrambling, Holmes had come out on high ground. He would be among men who welcomed him, doing honorable and satisfying work. Instead of struggling to impress his opinions on others, he would listen and decide. A whole era of his life was ended; his time for scholarly work was over, and a new profession had begun.

Holmes's life took on a new shape. He was assured a salary of at least $6,000 a year.[24] After seven years in their apartment at 10 Beacon Street, he and Fanny looked for a house of their own — or rather, Fanny did.

. . . after looking at one house and jointly condemning it, Mrs. Holmes suggested that I leave it to her, and the next thing I heard was an enquiry if I would dine that night at No. 9 Chestnut Street. After I gave my august consent to this house she . . . spent her summer in altering and getting it into shape, determining what should be my library and even the color of the shelves against the will of the architect and coming out clearly right.[25]

The new house was at the foot of Beacon Hill on filled land between the old house on Charles Street and the Charles River, where the doctor had once sculled his boats. Fanny brought family furniture and silver that had been kept in storage, filled and decorated the new house, and hired servants. They would need a cook and a man to help with the heavy work, as well as a maid. She bought two caged nightingales and a mockingbird to add to her collection of pets.

Holmes turned his own attention fully to his new career. The work of the court would be physically taxing. The supreme judicial court was not only the highest court of Massachusetts, but still carried on traditions from colonial times, when it was nearly the only court. The seven justices traveled together each fall to sit in rural county seats, beginning with Pittsfield. The justices, except the chief justice, then traveled two at a time to hold trial courts in county courthouses, while the remaining five sat together and heard appeals in the county seats or Boston.

When not traveling, presiding over trials, or hearing appeals, the judges studied briefs and voluminous records of trials, and wrote opinions. "Some of the older Judges affirm that no one can do all the work without breaking down," Holmes said;[26] his own grandfather had resigned from the court, unable to carry the burden, and Holmes was not sure of his own health or stamina.

Accordingly, there were to be no more dining out, no more late parties, drinking, or talk. Even aside from the constant worry over his health, the work was new and required alert attention; "I can't [dine out] and feel as well and fit for work the next day," Holmes conceded.[27] Fanny was the drill sergeant for this new discipline. In a house of their own, they could have servants and proper dinners together every night. At his doctor's suggestion, Fanny began reading novels and poems aloud to Holmes in the evenings, to spare his eyes; Holmes sometimes would play solitaire while Fanny read.

On January 3, 1883, the first Monday of the new year, the supreme judicial court began its hurried session in Boston as a court of appeals for the whole Commonwealth of Massachusetts. The seven members of the court sat together briefly, and then two justices went off to sit singly as trial judges in the western counties. In the spring, all the justices would scatter to the county seats to preside over trials, to sit in divorce cases and as judges in criminal trials where the sentence might be death.

It was a complex, exhausting, unreasonable, and highly cherished system.[28]

When the seven justices gathered in January, Holmes was distinctly noticeable. The other men were older, stouter, shorter, heavily whiskered. The court was a portrait of Boston manhood of the older generation: stolid, taciturn, heavy. Holmes, however, was tall, slender, youthful, talkative. His ample brown hair was barely growing gray. His luxuriant mustache, waxed out to sharp points, was too flamboyant to be military any longer.

The great Constitutional questions that Holmes would decide were still far in the future. The stuff of the court's work was adultery, greed, the private warfare of commerce, fights between neighbors and within families, wills, rapes, murders: the trivial, violent constants of human life, of the thousand-year-old common law. Holmes had the messenger bring him some quill pens, and he worked at his grandfather Charles Jackson's desk.

He loved the work, could not get enough of it, volunteered to take others' assignments, asked for the dreariest and most technical common-law cases, and wrote opinions with astonishing — British — speed.[29]

The cases were wildly varied. Lilly Ismahl had been convicted of keeping a house of ill fame, another woman of selling intoxicating liquors and causing injuries thereby. A man was killed while standing on the front platform of a railroad car, and the railroad company sought to avoid liability by saying that he had been negligent in standing there. A defendant convicted of manslaughter thought he should have been allowed to testify that his victim — who first attacked him with a knife and fork at dinner — was a big man, a former prizefighter. Another man sold some real estate on condition that the buyer build a cotton factory on it; the buyer had gone bankrupt and did not build; the seller wanted his land back, even though it had meanwhile gone for taxes. A contractor had failed to build houses in a workmanlike manner — but Holmes had to excuse himself, for George Shattuck argued the contractor's case. Two partners had gotten into financial trouble, and a lower court judgment for $1,154.71 had not been paid. The partners said their creditor had agreed to accept less, but centuries of English precedent were against them, and Holmes — writing his first opinion — disposed of this argument in a paragraph of technical language, not troubling to cite authorities.[30]

A Mrs. McDougall had slipped and fallen on an iron grating in the sidewalk of Porter Street, but the City of Boston would not pay for her injuries because ice on the street, and not the city's grating, had caused her fall. A man named Palmer sued to recover his losses at an illegal card game. A defendant was sued for the price of milk deliveries — six cans a day. An undertaker sued for the expenses of a funeral.

John Ropes and John Chipman Gray appeared for a landowner, and Holmes wrote the opinion denying their suit.[31] A man had killed a woman in the course of performing an illegal abortion; Holmes upheld the conviction.[32] Another defendant said his arrest was improper because he had not received sufficient notice of the proceeding. An English patent had proven invalid, but the men who sold it wanted to keep the money they had received. A man was convicted of having tried, unsuccessfully, to rape a ten-year-old girl.

The opinions of the court were brief, workmanlike, conservative. The judges wrote without any display of learning, without elaborate citations. The court reporter would state the facts, and the judge to whom the case had been assigned would write a brief explanation of the court's decision. It was a conservative, businessman's court. It held for creditors more often than for debtors. It gave solemn attention to financial affairs, but affirmed the convictions of criminal defendants, if the facts were not in dispute, with little discussion.

Holmes was fascinated as a schoolboy by this glimpse of vivid tumultuous life. The clashing, multifarious cases made a strange harmony, and from the violent symphony a new note sounded in Holmes's opinions that would echo through American law.

He had been given an ordinary, dreary dispute over a house built but not paid for. From this unpromising material, Holmes extracted an elegant, thoughtful opinion, longer than most the court had delivered that term, dense with citations of ancient authority and soaring suddenly into a triumphant statement of theory.[33] Holmes was fulfilling the ambition of his youthful essays on Dürer and Plato: he was at once an artist, expressing the spirit of the common law — and a scientist describing its slow evolution. Each of his opinions was a pencil stroke, marking the contours of *The Common Law* on the map of Massachusetts: "Since my appointment I have been sitting en banc and writing opinions all the time. Next month I hold equity alone and the next (May) sit in divorce cases. I enjoy the work so far extremely."[34]

In equity court, where Holmes presided in April, each day's work began with a prayer given by the chaplain. It was still a Puritan court, furnished with wooden benches. The judges did not wear robes; Holmes, like the others, wore a black frock coat and gray trousers, stiff white standing collar, and black silk tie. He sat erect, with a disconcerting direct gaze, alertly attentive to what was said and done before him, absorbed in the task.

> If you want to hit a bird on the wing, you must have all your will in a focus. You must not be thinking about yourself, and, equally, you must not be thinking about your neighbor; you must be living in your eye on that bird.[35]

The attorneys who appeared before Holmes felt his considerable energy focused on them.

> Nobody who sat on this court in my time had quite such a daunting personality — to a young lawyer, at least. Holmes was extremely courteous but his mind was so extraordinarily quick and incisive, he was such an alert and sharply attentive listener, his questions went so to the root of the case, that it was rather an ordeal to appear before him. In arguing a case you felt that when your sentence was half done he had seen the end of it, and before the argument was a third finished he had seen the whole course of reasoning and was wondering whether it was sound.[36]

Jewish immigrants from eastern Europe, newly arrived in Boston, had a tangled tale of persecution. Their landlord had aroused the neighbors to drive them out of their rented house and violate their lease, so that the owner might sell the property and still keep the rent money that had been paid in advance. Holmes listened to arguments, sent the matter to a special master for further hearings, and ultimately decided for the immigrants.[37]

In May, Holmes presided over the divorce court, and a door opened into yet another sphere of existence. Holmes heard a working-class woman testify that she would not sleep with her husband because he would not change his clothes or wash; another testified that her husband beat her. The suits were brought by women against their husbands, and the grounds were usually adultery, desertion, gross and continual habits of intoxication, or cruel and abusive treatment. The wives were the principal witnesses. Newspapers sometimes made entertaining stories of these cases, and Holmes did what he could to preserve the witnesses' privacy: "I remember saying that if reporters saw fit to withdraw out of hearing it would be a very proper and considerate thing, and I let the woman testify in a very low voice."[38]

In July, the court went into recess, except that a single justice kept the equity court open in Boston. (The assignment came around in order, once every six years, to each associate justice.) By August, most of the justices were in the country, working on opinions, but Holmes was finished and at rest. He had written his opinions in the evenings and on weekends while the court was still sitting.

> Well, I like the work more than I dreamed beforehand — the experience is most varied — very different from what one gets at the bar — and, I am satisfied, most valuable for an all-round view of the law — One sees too a good deal of human nature & I find that I am interested all the time.[39]

Holmes and Fanny took over both halves of their house at Matta-poisett that summer and for the first time had room for their servants and for guests. They hired a local man who cooked and carried for them, "a rough customer. Once he was arranging with my wife for dinner and went on in a perfectly level voice, 'Yes, madam, roast beef, potatoes, peas, God damn them flies I wish they was to Hell, carrots.'"[40]

Fanny, Holmes, and George Shattuck went sailing from the Matta-poisett shore, leisurely afternoon sails to nearby islands. On one clear day they sailed to Martha's Vineyard, and Holmes landed them at Gay Head, but there was a sign forbidding trespassing: "I hesitated to go ashore at the place. . . . I thought it unbecoming that a Judge of the Sup. Jud. Court should be had up before a Justice of the Peace."[41] John Holmes came out to visit and reported to the doctor that Fanny and Wendell were pleasant and bright.[42]

Holmes was a public figure in a modest way, and was talked of for political office. Henry Cabot Lodge was now state Republican party chairman, and it was natural for him to suggest that Holmes — who bore a famous name — run for governor. When Holmes demurred, Lodge tried to tempt him with the prospect that, after serving as governor, he could be senator. Holmes said, "I don't give a damn about being Senator."[43]

On Thursday, September 11, 1883, the leaves darkening and the air growing cool, the supreme judicial court began its session in Pittsfield, the Berkshire County seat, and at the opening of court there was a little ceremony of induction and welcome for Holmes. The *Pittsfield Sun* was proud to point out the new justice's early connections with Pittsfield, and said that Holmes looked much younger than his forty-two years.[44] After a two-day sitting, the other justices returned to Boston, and Holmes re-mained behind in Pittsfield to hold court alone. He arraigned James Bar-rett for the murder of Richard Savage, trial put over until a later date, heard eight divorce cases, a request for an annulment, and seven appeals from earlier divorce decrees.

Until the end of September, Holmes and the other justices traveled to the county seats of Massachusetts and presided over trials. Holmes's first jury trial was in Lowell, a mill town in Middlesex County.

He was a meticulous trial judge. At the close of a trial, he carefully and thoroughly instructed the jury — marshaling the evidence of both sides, and explaining the burden of proof that was to be met, carefully setting aside his own view of the matter.[45] It was solitary work. Holmes would sit all day in court, then have dinner alone in his hotel, read or play solitaire on the bed, and then sleep.

In October, the seven justices gathered in Boston for their confer-ence. Each judge read aloud the opinions he had written; the others attacked and he defended. Chief Justice Morton presided and brought them to agreement. The written opinions were then given to the reporter. There were no dissenting opinions; they came to a decision in each case and went on to the next matter.

In 1884, Holmes presided over murder trials for the first time. As a member of the full court he heard Mary Murphy, indicted for murder, plead guilty to the lesser charge of manslaughter. Sitting with Judge Charles Devens, who had commanded the Fifteenth Massachusetts Volunteers at Ball's Bluff, he presided while James Nicholson was tried for premeditated murder. Nicholson admitted shooting his estranged wife. He had eluded capture for months while the newspapers shrieked in outrage.

The defense was insanity. Nicholson had been drinking heavily, and there was evidence he suffered from delirium tremens when the murder was committed. He broke down and wept when he testified, but the attorney general pressed for conviction of murder in the first degree. A single juror held out for not-guilty and then gave in. Holmes and Devens heard the verdict, and sentenced Nicholson to be hanged.[46]

This was more cold-blooded than war; it required a detachment — perhaps not entirely healthy — like a surgeon's.

The Common Law and Holmes's solitary struggle for scholarly achievement were behind him; his views of the law were settled and were proving themselves in practice. His book had not done all that he had hoped; it had not become a source of the law itself, an authority to be cited by courts as Blackstone and Kent had been. He had only marked a method and an insight, and these were becoming the common property of the legal profession, as invisible as the air. But his opinions were being cited by younger scholars and through their books his thought was finding its way into the opinions of other courts: "When one begins to think sadly what does indicating a line of thought amount to — people will go to and fro over it without remembering you — It is well to recall that this is universal . . . the thing is to have done it."[47]

While occasionally melancholy, Holmes was happy in his work: "If a man gets a year's life out of a year he can ask no more."[48] And at times he was more than content; he was joyous:

> . . . what a profession the law is! . . . what other gives such scope to realize the spontaneous energy of ones soul? In what other does one plunge so deep in the stream of life — so share its passions, its battles, its despair, its triumphs?[49]

As the work grew more familiar, and consequently less demanding, Holmes again began to make calls at teatime and occasionally to dine out, to sit up late with cigars and talk. With a new self-confidence, he took pleasure in frankness, in talking lightly of his intimate thoughts and feelings. This was attractive, particularly to women.[50]

He began to receive invitations to speak publicly as well. In the speeches that he began to give, Holmes himself was the subject; he applied his philosophical method to his own experiences; the speeches were an extension of his dinner-table conversation.

On May 30, 1884, he gave his first important public address outside the law,[51] his debut in a literary form invented by Emerson. For this debut he accepted an invitation to give the Memorial Day address at Keene, New Hampshire, far from the critical eyes of Boston, but he had the speech printed and sent copies to the Boston newspapers.

He gave his carefully rehearsed speech in a white painted town hall on the village common, before the John Sedgwick Post No. 4 of the Grand Army of the Republic. Fanny rode up to Keene with him in a carriage through the late New England spring.

What was the meaning of Memorial Day? Holmes asked. There was one meaning for the soldiers themselves, gathered in that hall, and a second meaning for the nation that kept up this observance when other memories of the Civil War had faded. For the soldiers, there was a difficult lesson. Holmes and his fellows had fought and killed men from the South, to make a national government and to destroy slavery:

> But we equally believed that those who stood against us held just as sacred convictions that were the opposite of ours, and we respected them as every man with a heart must respect those who give all for their belief. The experience of battle soon taught its lesson even to those who came into the field more bitterly disposed. You could not stand up, day after day, in the indecisive contests where overwhelming victory was impossible because neither side would run as they ought when beaten, without getting at last something of the same brotherhood for the enemy that the north pole of a magnet has for the south — each working in the opposite sense to the other, but each unable to get along without the other.

The soldiers — Holmes spoke of himself — felt this mysterious harmony of opposites. But what meaning did Memorial Day have for the nation at large, the great organism of society made up of people who had not fought and perhaps would never fight?

For the answer, Holmes returned to poems he had written twenty years before that recalled in vivid, idealized images the deaths of his comrades Willy Putnam, James Lowell, and Little Abbott.

The meaning of Memorial Day was the meaning to be found in their courage:

> I think that, as life is action and passion, it is required of a man that he should share the passion and action of his time at peril of being judged not to have lived.

If this be so, the use of this day is obvious. . . . We can hardly share the emotions that make this day to us the most sacred day of the year, and embody them in ceremonial pomp, without in some degree imparting them to those who come after us. I believe from the bottom of my heart that our memorial halls and statues and tablets, the tattered flags of our regiments in the Statehouses, and this day with its funeral march and decorated graves, are worth more to our young men by way of chastening and inspiration than the monuments of another hundred years of peaceful life could be. . . .

I seem to hear the funeral march become a paean. I see beyond the forest the moving banners of a hidden column. Our dead brothers still live for us, and bid us think of life, not death — of life to which in their youth they lent the passion and glory of the spring. As I listen, the great chorus of life and joy begins again, and amid the awful orchestra of seen and unseen powers and destinies of good and evil our trumpets sound once more a note of daring, hope and will.[52]

13

———

COURTLY LOVE

THE DOCTOR AND MRS. HOLMES NOW SPENT THEIR SUMMERS IN Beverly, the village where Mrs. Holmes's mother was born, on the Atlantic shore north of Boston, where their widowed daughter, Amelia, owned a house.

Fanny and Wendell were in their own house at Mattapoisett. Ned had returned to Boston, had bought a house on Beacon Street just opposite the Public Garden, and was busy with amateur archeology and volunteer work in the arts. He was a member of the Committee to Examine the Boston Public Library and, having just finished writing the committee's report, suggesting certain improvements, he went with his wife and young son to their summer house in Milton.

During the night of July 17, 1884, Ned died in his sleep. Fanny and Wendell, the doctor and Mrs. Holmes came into town, and the little family gathered. The doctor and Mrs. Holmes were old; Wendell and Amelia were middle-aged. Ned's young son and namesake was the only child there would be in the Holmes family.

But Holmes's young friends opened windows to the future for him. Henry Cabot Lodge led the Massachusetts delegation to the Republican National Convention that year and befriended a still younger man, the speaker of the New York House, Theodore Roosevelt. Lodge and Roosevelt joined forces at the convention, to oppose the nomination of Senator James G. Blaine, "the plumed knight from Maine," as he was called in a nominating speech. Blaine was one of the founders of the Republican party, but he carried a lingering taint of the scandals of the Grant years. Blaine was nominated, and Lodge and Roosevelt went home in disgust, believing it their duty to support the party's nominee but certain that it would be political suicide to do so. Reform-minded Republicans, sick of corruption, decamped to the Democratic candidate, Grover Cleveland, who had nothing worse against him than an illegitimate child.

The campaign was a difficult one for Lodge. Old friends stopped speaking to him. He and Roosevelt drew closer to each other. In October, Lodge held a dinner in Boston for Roosevelt, who was visiting, and Holmes attended.[1] Holmes never thought much of the Republican nominees, but he was loyal to his friends and to his party. He remained one of the few Boston respectables who kept up friendly relations with Lodge, who would later remind Roosevelt of this loyalty.

At the October conference of his court, Holmes was particularly eager to persuade his colleagues to uphold the conviction of a doctor who had killed a woman by carelessly prescribing a fatal medicine. There was no evidence that the doctor intended any harm or that he realized his error, but Holmes was persuaded that the doctor should be held up to an objective standard of reasonable behavior. ("If my opinion goes through it will do much to confirm some theories in my book," he wrote to Pollock.)[2] The justices gave him his way — and the objective standard of *The Common Law* became the law of Massachusetts.[3]

Justice Waldo Colburn died that winter. The usual memorials were read in court and at the meetings of the bar, and then the governor appointed a new man, William Gardner, and the work went on as before. From October, 1884, until March, 1885, Holmes went on circuit with the court, sat as a single judge, wrote sixty-five opinions for the court, addressed bar association dinners in the county seats and in Boston.

In the humdrum of the courts Holmes was a puzzling figure. When lawyers gathered over drinks at John Ropes's, Holmes would let his conversation flow unchecked, trying out phrases and ideas. "Life consists of making the means the end; it is so impossible ever to reach the end that we have to make what we can of the means."[4] His colleagues of the bar were a little uncomfortable. They did not quite understand what he was driving at or where he would end.[5]

In the salons Holmes was less out of place. Belle Gardner's parlor was lively with men and women in their twenties — writers, musicians, friends of her young ward Joe Peabody, and her own protégés. Sarah Whitman made another such nucleus of literate talk, where young people might gather. Still thin and youthful, his hair only slightly touched with gray, his cheerful tenor rattling on in spirited talk, Holmes was at ease among the handsome, troubled young people. Jim Storrow and

some fellow students just beginning law school — Holmes's young friend
Owen Wister and John Jay Chapman, one of Joe Peabody's friends —
rented a house on Appian Way in Cambridge.[6] The young men had
dinner parties to which they often invited Judge Holmes. "There, over
our champagne, he would loaf and invite his soul with beguiling expa-
tiations," Wister recalled.[7]

> [Holmes] was lean as a racehorse . . . and had just finished mak-
> ing a cup with red wine for his three guests, informally asked to
> supper on the South Shore. The ice tinkled in the pitcher as he
> brought it in. Art had gone into this, as into all else that he
> [did]. . . . Two brilliant listeners — handsome ladies both — set his
> talk going. . . . His talk would always bubble and sparkle from
> him, a stream of seriousness and laughter, imagination and phi-
> losophy, in which enthusiasm was undying.[8]

Jack Chapman, tall, dark-haired, conscious of his brilliance, was in
love with Minna Timmins. These two put their dark heads together in
the deserted upper floor of the Athenaeum in the afternoons, reading
Dante. Holmes found them together at Mrs. Whitman's, at Belle Gardner's, or at the home of Minna's guardians, the Brimmers. He grew fond
of the young law student from the house on the Appian Way, and the
willful girl. The young people flirted inconclusively, as Holmes had done
twenty years before. But Chapman conceived bizarre fantasies. He imagined that young Percival Lowell was a seducer and that Minna was his
victim. At the end of a party one evening, Chapman followed Lowell
down the porch stairs and beat him with a heavy cane. Two days later,
Chapman, alone in the house on Appian Way, plunged his left hand into
the coal fire, and held it there with his right hand for two minutes.[9]
Chapman's injured hand was amputated at Massachusetts General
Hospital, where he remained for a time. His family were in New York,
and Minna was not permitted to see him. An "alienist" visited and told
Chapman that he did not need to be institutionalized, perhaps in part
because Holmes and Fanny had agreed to take him into their home.
Holmes visited him repeatedly in the hospital, and when Chapman was
ready he came to 9 Chestnut Street, where Fanny cared for him.
Through Holmes, Jack and Minna exchanged notes and messages.
When at last Chapman could travel he went home to New York. The
separation from Minna was painful, and Jack wrote to Holmes:

> All that Minna Timmins ever spoke and shall speak of me to
> anyone is a consecration & not a desecration — I take the dust
> her feet have touched & put it on my head.
> I have been near madness — Do not answer me, I shall write
> you how I am getting on. . . . I hope you are all right — I was

afraid you were going to break down — the strain you were under during these two months — was telling on you. Please give my love to Mrs. Holmes.[10]

Jack Chapman's friend Joe Peabody killed himself over an unhappy love affair, and news came from Washington that Clover Hooper, who had married Henry Adams, had committed suicide. When her father died, she drank cyanide.

At the two hundred fiftieth anniversary of the First Church in Cambridge, where Holmes's grandfather Abiel had been minister, he spoke of the need for faith even when belief was lost.[11] And he was given an opportunity to address young people more directly. Yale invited Holmes to their law school commencement in June, 1886, to receive an honorary degree.

Early in June, Fanny and Holmes took his mother to Beverly. The doctor was going abroad with Amelia, to rest from his labors and to have a little fun. It was his first return to Europe in fifty years, and he sailed for England on the *Cephalonia* in great excitement.

In London, Dr. Holmes was given a hero's welcome. Lady Granville held a reception for one thousand people in his honor; he visited 10 Downing Street at Mrs. Gladstone's invitation, went to the Derby with the Prince of Wales and his lovely, youthful princess — "The Prince has a lively temperament and a very cheerful aspect"[12] — saw Tennyson, Browning, and Wilde. The doctor and Amelia took rooms at Mackellar's Hotel, near Piccadilly, and were swamped with invitations; they hired a secretary to help write their replies. Oxford, Cambridge, and Edinburgh all invited him to speak and to receive honorary degrees. What a contrast, the doctor said to Amelia, from his first visit to London fifty years before, when he had two letters of introduction to obscure people, one of whom invited him to dinner and the other to tea.

Holmes continued in his comparative obscurity in Boston. But he took real pleasure in the prospect of the honorary degree at Yale.[13] The commencement exercises were held on June 30, 1886, and Holmes left Fanny in Beverly to care for Mrs. Holmes while he went down to New Haven. When he rose to address the students he looked happily at the young faces and spoke as if he were no older than they, as if he were a young knight entering on a life of combat. In his speech he entwined thoughts of chivalry and religion, of honor and duty:

> The power of honor to bind men's lives is not less now than it was in the Middle Ages. Now as then it is the breath of our nostrils; it is that for which we live, for which, if need be, we are willing to die. . . .
> One would sometimes think, from the speech of young men, that things had changed recently, and that indifference was now

the virtue to be cultivated. I never heard anyone profess indifference to a boat race. Why should you row a boat race? Why endure
long months of pain in preparation for a fierce half-hour that will
leave you all but dead? Is there anyone who would not go through
all its costs and more, for the moment when anguish breaks into
triumph — or even for the glory of having nobly lost? Is life less
than a boat race? If a man will give all the blood in his body to
win the one, will he not spend all the might of his soul to prevail
in the other?

I know, Mr. President, that there is a motive above even honor
which may govern men's lives. I know that there are some rare
spirits who find the inspiration of every moment, the aim of every
act, in holiness. I am enough of a Puritan, I think, to conceive the
exalted joy of those who look upon themselves only as instruments
in the hands of a higher power to work out its designs. But I think
that most men do and must reach the same result under the illusion of self seeking. If the love of honor is a form of illusion, it is
no ignoble one. If it does not lift a man on wings to the sky, at
least it carries him above the earth and teaches him those high
and secret pathways across the branches of the forest the travelers
on which are only less than winged.[14]

In August, Mrs. Holmes suddenly became very much worse. Her intellect seemed to fail her. Holmes cabled his father and sister from Beverly to return. The doctor cut their trip short; he and Amelia took Mrs.
Holmes back to their house at 296 Beacon Street and arranged for a
nurse to live with them.[15]

Since the first of September I have been on the stretch all the
time, & during the summer our life was sad & wearing. . . . Father
is very well but somehow seems much more distinctly an old man
than heretofore — this and my mother's breakdown & the fact
that I have started eyeglasses all make me realize what otherwise
I should often forget, that I have got into middle life — but I am
happy & I always think that when a man has had his chance —
has reached the table land above his difficulties — it does not matter so much whether he has more or less time allowed him in that
stage . . . the real anguish is never to have your opportunity — I
used to think of that a good deal during the war.[16]

Work allowed him few amusements, and late hours, cigars, or drink
made him ill. When he tried to step out in the evenings as of old, Fanny
threatened him with the specter of imminent death. He was elected to
the Saturday Club and dined with them one afternoon each month at
Horace Parker's hotel, recently renamed the Parker House — "some-

times pleasant and not infrequently dull"[17] — where his father often dominated the conversation.

When released at last from duty in the summer, Holmes gave himself a few days' vacation at Bar Harbor, Maine, almost desperately amusing himself — "immersed in society" at the Louisburg Hotel, Barrett Wendell observed disapprovingly[18] — but by September 3 he was on the bench in Boston again.

The doctor had decided to write another book. He had experimented with novels that were not well received. Now he returned to the triumph of the Autocrat, and began work on the first installment of a new series for *The Atlantic*: "I know it is a hazardous experiment to address myself to a public which in days long past has given me a generous welcome." The first number had gone to the printer, and Holmes was in Boston for the January sitting of his court, when on February 6, 1888, Mrs. Holmes died.

I have been a little slow in thanking you for your kind letter because having been somewhat upset & a little delayed in my work I had to make up for it & have been very busy. My mother's death was not to be regretted on her account but such an event when it happens must be a shock & gives one a tug that goes far down to the roots.

Father seems well & takes his loss as I would have him. My sister will live with him & he will be happy.[19]

There was still another loss. The house at Mattapoisett, which Holmes and Fanny loved, burned to the ground. A brushfire had spread across the dry stubble of a field and burned the house.[20]

Holmes plunged into the law, taking on more of the administrative work of the court, helping the aged chief justice. The court reporter retired, and Holmes interviewed candidates for the post: "Such occasions make you realize in a painful way how many clever agreeable men are on the verge of failure in the battle of life."[21]

One of the young historians at Harvard, Ernest Young, a protégé of Henry Adams, killed himself in March; Holmes told his friends that overwork was probably the cause, and that overwork was breaking down his colleagues on the court.

Holmes himself, whatever his worries as to his own health, continued to take more than his share of cases, and in the printed reports of the court the Holmes opinions — usually for a unanimous court — soared above the stolid, workmanlike decisions of his colleagues. His opinions were written as if from a pinnacle above time and place, as if by a man whose eye saw every intricacy of the common law spread over a thousand years as a single clear pattern.

In April, 1888, he undertook to write for the court in a tangled case of great moment, in which the judges were hotly divided. It would mark a point of departure for his future career, and ultimately for the law of the nation.

The question in the case did not seem important in itself: who would be reimbursed by a federal commission for war-risk insurance premiums paid during the Civil War? A federal statute of 1882 had provided that these reimbursements be paid, but did not say to whom they were due. Many shipping companies had paid such premiums because of Confederate privateers like the *Alabama*, but had gone bankrupt during the war and sold what assets they had. Now the former shipowners were in court asking reimbursement for premiums they had paid, but facing them were the buyers who had taken over their assets — including, they said, any right to reimbursement the shippers might have had.

To Holmes the case was an elegant experiment, in which elements of the complex idea of property were dissected out separately for inspection. It was plain to him that the shippers, whatever their moral rights might have been, had no legal right to be reimbursed until a right was created by the statute of 1882. Having nothing recognized by law, they could not have given anything to their creditors until after the statute was passed. In an elegant little essay, Holmes gave his reasons; at bottom, they were simply that property rights had no legal existence until created by law: "It is only tautologous to say that the law knows nothing of moral rights unless they are also legal rights."[22]

This brought on a rare, outraged dissent from Justice Walbridge Field, a stout old Vermonter who had learned law in a law office, not in a school. Field wrote firmly that the creditors' claims were founded on natural justice, not a statute; that they arose from *property*, and so were sensible things that could be passed from hand to hand, with or without a statute.[23]

This was the first serious division in the Massachusetts court since Holmes had joined it, and the first serious challenge to the theoretical system he had been writing into the law of Massachusetts. The vague disquiet that some of Holmes's friends had felt now found a voice in Field's dissent, for Holmes had persuaded a majority of the court that property rights were not sacred things above the law, but were made and could be unmade by the legislature.

For more than five years, Holmes had been under the relentless physical and intellectual pressure of the court's work. He and Fanny had suffered through Jack Chapman's terrible distress, the death of friends, Mrs. Holmes's long illness and death. But it was summer, and his opinions for the court were finished.

The Massachusetts legislature had finally lifted the burden of hearing divorce trials from the supreme judicial court and shifted it to the lower courts. It was not Holmes's year to be in the equity courtroom, and so he asked for a vacation. The chief justice excused him from the June conference, and Holmes and Fanny then joyously planned an escape, almost a second wedding journey — a trip across the country on the new transcontinental railroad lines, followed by a summer's rest together at Niagara Falls, without work or family worries.

On May 5, they boarded the railroad car on which they would remain for the next month, except for brief stops. They went first to Chicago, where they stayed overnight and where Holmes saw the courts and was introduced to Melville Fuller, who had just been nominated by President Grover Cleveland to serve as chief justice of the United States.

They continued on to southern California, and then went up the Pacific Coast into Canada, and back to Boston.[24] "Home again — 9,000 miles in one car! — everything an immense success."[25] They were at home only long enough to call on the doctor at Beverly ("Glad and thankful to see you back in good condition. . . . As soon as you get in order you must come and see us. . . . We dine at 2 p.m. / Your affectionate Papa") and to pack for Niagara Falls.

In June and July they lived in the Clifton House Hotel within hearing of the roar of the falls. "It was like living on intimate terms with the Prophet Isaiah," Holmes said. They were at leisure together and filled their days with reading, sight-seeing, and talk. Holmes set himself a task, as always: to read the Bible for the first time.

At the end of August, they were back at 9 Chestnut Street. The presidential election year had come around again, and Holmes, almost alone among his Cambridge and Back Bay friends, remained loyal to the Republican party, however tainted by corruption. The progressives — Mugwumps — were all for an end to the spoils system, but the Republican candidate, Senator Benjamin Harrison, declined to commit himself to civil service reform, and the Mugwumps were going to desert him: "Wendell Holmes is going to vote for Harrison, God knows why, except to show the seamy side of himself — he couldn't give an articulate reason the other night."[26]

Ethel Grenfell came to call in September, a luminous young visitor from another, half-forgotten world. In 1866, on his first visit to England, Holmes had met and befriended her uncle, Henry Cowper, by whom she had been raised and of whom she had been immensely fond. When Cowper died, Ethel traveled to Canada and America, and in September, 1888, came to Boston, calling at 9 Chestnut Street on her uncle's old friend.

She was slender, graceful, and fey. Her enormous eyes were delicately downcast, and she spoke in a hesitating, almost affected, drawl. Holmes and Fanny were charmed. Holmes brought her to his courtroom, and they talked in the parlor at 9 Chestnut Street, hung with Fanny's embroideries. Holmes spoke warmly of her late uncle; Fanny gave her a parting gift, a necklace of cameos — little carved cupids.[27]

Ethel Grenfell was drawn to Holmes. From London, she wrote in her neat schoolgirl hand:

> I can hardly bear to speak of him [her uncle], but to you who loved & sympathised with him so well it was no pain (after the first) to talk of what we remembered — how one misses him at every turn of life. . . . You were *so good* to me when we met, & I have a great wish that we may always be friends — in memory of that love, common to us both. I have since thought of so many things I should like some day to tell you.[28]

But duty bound Holmes to Boston, and Ethel Grenfell's downcast eyes soon were as distant as memories of London.

The doctor, although in good health, was approaching eighty, and took a certain pleasure merely in survival. He became interested in genealogy and began to answer the numerous letters from people with his own surname, who inquired about common ancestors. The doctor developed a theory that the American Holmeses were all descended from an English admiral. He took a skeptical interest in spiritualism, and began to collect odd coincidences and evidence of telepathy.

Amelia, distressingly, was ill, and in March it became plain that the illness was serious. Fanny took up residence at 296 Beacon Street to manage the household and to help in caring for her. Holmes called to see them, and dined out alone at the Parker House. For a time Amelia seemed to be growing better, and then on April 3, she had a convulsion, lapsed into a coma, and died during the night.[29]

Holmes and Fanny moved into the house at 296 Beacon Street, to care for the doctor. The burden of keeping him company fell to Fanny, who did not find him easy company. For Holmes, it was difficult to be back in his father's house, to sit politely at his father's table and hear the old man's talk, as egotistical as ever and now growing rather cold.

> It is settled now that we go to live with my father — the only practicable or possible thing.
>
> I have been rather under the weather. I suppose a sort of nervous reaction, but am better and am getting better. Mrs. Holmes wants me to go abroad this summer prophesying that it will make the first summer easier for my father.[30]

Hesitating until the final moment, Holmes at last did go abroad, his first trip alone in twenty-three years. The doctor again gave him letters of introduction, and Holmes reserved rooms at Mackellar's Hotel on Dover Street, where the doctor had stayed. Holmes made a new will, saw Fanny and the doctor off to Beverly for the summer, and went to New York alone.

On June 22, he boarded the Cunard *Cephalonia,* which had its usual complement of Bostonians. William James was there on his way to visit sister Alice and brother Henry in England and then to attend a conference of psychologists in Paris.

Passing in the other direction, Kaneko Kentaro was coming to Boston, bringing copies of the new Japanese constitution. From Boston he would continue on to Europe, to study the parliaments of England and Germany, the great models for the new Japanese government. Kaneko visited the Harvard Law School, where he had studied fifteen years before, and made a present to them of one copy of the Japanese constitution. He then went up to Beverly and visited Fanny and the doctor, reviving his warm friendship with Fanny, who declared that a room of the house was his henceforth.[31]

On the *Cephalonia,* Holmes had recovered from his fears about the trip and had immersed himself in the little society of shipboard. His intimacy with William James was long past and was not renewed. James watched Holmes's social triumphs from a distance. He, too, was traveling to relieve low spirits. But Holmes was in search of flirtation, James only of escape: "I confess I find myself caring more for landscapes than for men — strange to say, and doubtless shameful; so my stay in London will probably be short."[32]

When the *Cephalonia* made its first landfall at Queenstown, on the south coast of Ireland, James went ashore and toured the green devastated landscape from the harbor westward through the mountains toward Killarney. It was the time of rack rents and of the Land League. Ireland was governed from London, and when rents owed to English landlords were not paid, Irish tenants were evicted. James visited the family of his Boston servant, and found them in a pitiful house, all in a flurry at the visit of this grand person, their daughter's American employer: "It is the most extraordinary thing to see coming out from the midst of this filth, misery and squalor, this jovial, sociable, witty, intelligent race, supported by, and living *entirely* upon an ideal."[33]

The Land League had become the rival government of Catholic Ireland, and Charles Stewart Parnell, Member of Parliament for Ireland, its head. Against the organized force of English courts and police it marshaled the force of social organization. The Irish ostracized the agents of the landlords, refused to provide services, conducted protests, and abused them; there were implicit threats of violence. Captain Charles Boycott led an especially effective application of these methods against a County Mayo estate and lent his name to a new weapon of class war.

At Mackellar's Hotel, Holmes had a bedroom and parlor on the ground floor, chilly and damp like all of London even in July. He sent out a stream of notes, and invitations slowly came back. Soon, there were breakfast, lunch, and dinner invitations. London was at the height of its season. Holmes dutifully called on professional men of high position or accomplishment, but he attended more to the young women who were his dinner partners than to the old men who were his hosts:

> The common or garden judge didn't fizzle. . . . I would rather talk to a nice girl. Perhaps if I had been less interested in talking to nice girls it wd. have been better for my reputation, considered as an article to be helped or hurt by conduct; but I always have neglected it in that way.[34]

There was a weekend with Lord Davy when Holmes tried to talk shop about the common law:

> I was struck with the finality with which he said, "That is *not* the law of England." I replied that I was well aware of it, but was considering whether it should not be the law of Massachusetts. He did not go beyond his groove, although working very admirably and clearly within it.[35]

He saw the intellectual friends he had found on his first visit. The Pollocks had young boys and were comfortable and placid; Leslie and Julia Stephen were busy with their growing young family.

In this circle Holmes again met Lucy Clifford, the young widow of Stephen's Cambridge protégé, William K. Clifford. She had not remarried, but had supported herself and two small daughters by writing girls' stories and plays. She was independent, intelligent, and forthright, a strong-minded woman of the middle class, with a sharp eye and a louche sense of humor, rather like Fanny in her younger age.

With Lucy Clifford, Holmes began a flirtation that became something more. Courtship in the world of cold rooms and ever-present servants was necessarily difficult for a man visiting only briefly from another country, but there was a moment in a hansom cab and another in the chilly rooms at Mackellar's that Holmes liked to recall years later.

At a picture gallery, Holmes saw a striking young woman with curly hair, widely spaced eyes, and an athletic figure that caught his eye. He inquired; she was Lady Castletown, an English peeress in Catholic Ireland. He contrived to be introduced, but no more.

Ethel Grenfell was pleased to return Holmes's hospitality at 4 St. James's Square and at the Grenfells' country house, Taplow Court, in Maidenhead. Her husband, Willy, whom Holmes now met for the first time, was a model of taciturn English manhood, a handsome sportsman with a Guards mustache.

A circle of young women swirled around the Grenfells at Taplow Court, drawing friends and lovers into their orbit. They were young women of wit, charm, and energy who were making a great social success, the only success open to them. Ethel Grenfell's delicate beauty was at one center; the brilliant Tennant sisters at another. Margot Tennant — slight, dark, strong-featured, and impatient — and her lovely blonde sister Charlotte, known as Charty — were good friends of the Grenfells. The circle that grew around them was being noticed in the newspapers. They and their young men were being called "the Souls";[36] chivalry, Wordsworth, Thomas Love Peacock, and courtly flirtations were among their fashions. Holmes flirted with the young women, talked beautifully, with light self-confident frankness, and was taken into their circle. At Taplow Court he met Arthur Balfour, then serving a Tory government as First Secretary for Ireland.

The talk perhaps slid toward Ireland. A landlord had been murdered, and the Conservative government in London had charged Parnell with encouraging the violence. The London *Times* published letters that seemed to show Parnell in sympathy with the killings. But the letters had been forged. A young lawyer, Herbert Asquith, began a political career in the Liberal party by helping in Parnell's defense; the forgeries were proven, and Balfour was reduced to saying, in answer to questions in the House of Commons, that he really had not followed the matter very closely.

The Conservative policy in Ireland was coercion: relentless enforcement of property rights on the ground that any other policy would eventually lead to the loss of ownership. Balfour presided coolly over the coercion.

The men who called at Taplow Court held public positions, but it was the women whom Holmes found remarkable. Ethel Grenfell had "a kind of rainbow exquisiteness." Holmes felt that to some degree he had taken the place of her uncle. Margot Tennant was pleased with his talk; she, of them all, was perhaps the most ambitious, the most troubled:

> When I read of Parnell or Lassalle or smaller men who have arrested attention, I feel full of envy, and wish I had been a man. In a woman all this internal urging is a mistake; it leads to nothing, and breaks loose in sharp utterances and passionate overthrows of conventionality.[37]

She confided in Holmes:

> We have had a lovely summer & lots of people on & off. . . . Arthur Balfour was here & I went and stayed with him he is a perfect friend — I am not going to marry him he does not want to marry me & I can't imagine somehow or other being married.[38]

The married women had affairs, and the unmarried flirted mercilessly. They rode and hunted. Margot Tennant told Holmes of her pleasure in riding, where I forget all but God & the grass — you can imagine the emotions & pleasure I derive from the pace & the air & the thud of horses galloping with something live under one to control — the risk & devil of it all fills ones whole being with free joy.[39]

Holmes entered into the excitement with his whole heart:

You may say what you like about American women — and I won't be unpatriotic — but English women are brought up, it seems to me, to realize that it is an object to be charming, that man is a dangerous animal — or ought to be — and that a sexless *bonhomie* is not the ideal relation.[40]

In August, when London began to empty, Margot invited Holmes up to the Tennants' place in Scotland, the Glen, for a weekend. He visited Taplow Court as well. He and Ethel Grenfell exchanged portraits. (She lightly suggested that he have a photograph taken of his head only, as "modern clothes do not adapt.") He had no position in society, was not a sportsman or an athlete, and he knew little or nothing of current affairs or of the personalities that were talked of. But his conversation soared over all these social disabilities. He put himself, his open heart, into his talk and found to his joy that his talk was valued by these beautiful, powerful young women.[41] Ethel Grenfell said on parting:

Will you let me tell you then how I value your friendship? It is not insincere or affected or "modern," but the very true truth when I say that I owe you much happiness, much illumination, much encouragement, of the sort that comes from an assurance of the existence of what is true & strong. And all I can do in return is thank you from my heart & to send you — what I think you know you have — my wishes strong & earnest for your happiness.[42]

There was a last flirtation, and Holmes was on his way to Boston. That moment of parting, like one twenty-three years before, was with another young Campbell. At a country house weekend he met Nina Campbell, whom he had glimpsed before in London. It was his last day. They walked in a green late-summer lane.

She sat on a style, I below her, gazing into her eyes — then, "remember this lane" — "while memory holds its seat, etc." "Adieu" And I still do and ever shall remember her, & I rather think she does me a little bit.[43]

In America, the Republicans returned to national office after the most corrupt and brutal election campaign in the country's history. Irish and German immigrant workers were organizing for battle against Anglo-Saxon factory and mine owners. Holmes, revived in spirit, returned to duty.

14

ANOTHER

WAR

Fanny and Wendell lived upstairs at 296 Beacon Street as they had when they first married. Fanny cared for the doctor: "Mrs. Judge knows how to make comfortable and does it wonderfully well," he wrote complacently.[1]

Holmes dined at the doctor's table and listened to the doctor's conversation. He had returned tired and ill from London, and, as Fanny did not care for society, they refused all invitations to dine out and spent their evenings at home with the doctor. On Fridays, when the doctor went to symphony orchestra rehearsals, Fanny and Holmes went to the theater. On Sundays, to spare the servants, the three went out for dinner to the Parker House or Young's Hotel, and once a month Holmes and the doctor had dinner with the Saturday Club.[2] The routine was stultifying, and Holmes's only departures from duty were occasional teatime calls in the Back Bay or on Beacon Hill. On Tuesdays, he visited Nina Gray — with whom he spoke of his unhappiness, as he rarely did with men.[3] On other days, after court, he might call on Belle Gardner or Sarah Whitman, in whose parlors he sometimes found the doctor discoursing. Despite Holmes's caution, his health, never good since the war, continued to trouble him. "The doctor says it won't come to cutting me open — he thinks — and salts not the knife is my remedy."[4]

In December, 1889, Frank Palfrey died at Cannes. Holmes wrote a brief obituary for the newspapers, thinking of himself as well as of his fallen comrade:

> At last the shot which struck him at Antietam has done its work and he suffers no more. His name is added to the glorious list of those whom he loved and who loved him — Revere, Bartlett, Ropes, Putnam and so many more — who, like him and no more than he, fell in battle, although the end was delayed.[5]

Installments of *Over the Teacups* — the doctor's most recent sequel to *The Autocrat of the Breakfast-Table* — resumed in *The Atlantic*. In the new series, the doctor was a guest at a faintly disguised Back Bay tea table like one of those at which both he and Holmes were often found. The hostess was rather like Belle Gardner, a middle-aged woman of great personal attraction rather than beauty, with charming face and round arms.

The Astronomer was gone; in his place sat a newcomer, stolid and a trifle grim:

> He is a Counsellor and a Politician. Has a good war record. Is about forty-five years old, I conjecture. Is engaged in a great law case just now. Said to be very eloquent. Has an intellectual head, and the bearing of one who has commanded a regiment or perhaps a brigade.[6]

Holmes received occasional visitors from the larger world. Kaneko Kentaro, on his long return journey home from London and Berlin, stopped in Boston in April and refreshed their friendship. But for the most part Holmes depended on the mail to bring him glimpses of more distant horizons. He wrote courtly, passionate, and philosophical letters to the young Englishwomen of the Souls, and asked, insisted, that they answer and assure him of their affection. Ethel Grenfell replied with reassuring and tactful praise; Margot Tennant answered cheerfully:

> Your fidelity & affection deserved a letter sooner from me — Forgive me — I read with immense interest yr. Memorial day speech & think it beautiful, you must have enjoyed making it. Thanks also for the other speech wh. I did not care so much about (S. Bartlett) & yr. photograph wh. I like very much — Yes you shall have one of mine soon. . . . Good bye — dear friend — I don't forget you.[7]

But such replies were few. For the most part, Holmes moved between the doctor's household and his own court.

After seven years, there was little novelty in his work. The wild diversity of cases had become familiar through repetition. In case after case, someone had been injured at a railroad crossing. Holmes now always asked if the injured party had stopped and looked along the track before crossing; only if he had was it a case for the jury.[8] Workers were injured in the textile mills, and the question was usually whether they or their employers had been careless. Holmes listened impatiently to a tedious exposition of the design and workings of the machinery in which a boy had been hurt. It became a proverb with him that the only thing that mattered was the point of contact — the place where the boy had his fingers pinched.[9] Holmes leafed impatiently through court papers and listened restlessly to lawyers' arguments. He often interrupted with questions. "One citation will be enough, if it is in point," he said crisply to a lawyer who had heaped up thirty volumes of reports on the table beside him.[10]

> The cases which I have had this year have not been remarkable for universal interest — although there is always the pleasure of unraveling a difficulty.[11]

> One begins with a search for a general point of view. After a time he finds one, and then for a while he is absorbed in testing it, in trying to satisfy himself if it is true. But after many experiments or investigations have all come out one way, and his theory is confirmed and settled in his mind, he knows in advance the next one will be but another verification, and the stimulus of anxious curiosity is gone. He realizes that his branch of knowledge only presents more illustrations of the universal principle.[12]

Devens, the oldest member of the court, was visibly failing, and in August Chief Justice Morton resigned. Walbridge Field, the Vermonter who had dissented so strongly on behalf of the rights of property in the *Alabama Claims* case, became the new chief.

Still sick himself and carrying some extra burden because the court was shorthanded, Holmes was struggling through his routine. He was constantly reminded of old age and mortality. The bound volumes of decisions of the court, from its beginning in 1699 to the last term, stood in uneven rows on his shelves:

> It is strange to think of that monotonous series as a record of human lives. I have seen upon the section of an ancient tree the annual rings marked off which grew while the Black Prince was fighting the French, while Shakespeare wrote his plays, while England was a commonwealth, while a later republic arose over the Western waters, and grew so great as to shake the world. And so,

I often think, may all our histories be marked off upon the backs
of the unbroken series of our reports.[13]

William James brought out his big book *The Principles of Psychology*,
which made a national sensation and marked James as one of the important thinkers of his generation. Holmes sent him a generous note of
appreciation. Cabot Lodge was in Washington, elected to his second term
in Congress. Brooks Adams was writing theories of history and politics.
Louis Brandeis, with his partner, Holmes's former clerk Samuel Warren,
was making an extraordinary success of his little law firm and had begun
to interest himself in public affairs.

For Holmes, however, it seemed that no adventures remained. The
only advancement he could hope for depended on his surviving and
then replacing his new chief on the Massachusetts court or Horace Gray
on the Supreme Court. In his talks to the bar, he sounded again the now
somewhat weary note of duty, the honorable but anonymous duty of
judge and lawyer.[14]

Early in 1891, Marcus Morton and Holmes's old comrade Charles
Devens both died. Morton and Devens, with William Allen, had encouraged Holmes's enthusiasm and had helped him carry the more reluctant
members of the court for his opinions, allowing him to write his theories
into law. Holmes had been fond of these older men of a now vanishing
world and had depended on them. Of the three, only William Allen, now
growing very old and infirm, remained on the bench.

The new judges were younger; for the first time there were judges
younger than Holmes himself. And the work of the court was changing.
Criminal trials, divorce cases, and most lawsuits were now handled by
the lower courts. But there were more appeals to hear, and more opinions to write. These, too, were changing. There were many more statutes
now: laws for the regulation of labor and for the safety and health of the
public. There was a steady stream of challenges from the business community, fighting every inch of governmental encroachment.

Holmes's fiftieth birthday slipped past:

> Life grows more equable as one grows older; not less interest-
> ing, but I hope a little more impersonal. An old man ought to be
> sad. I don't know whether I shall be when the wind is west and
> the sky clear.[15]

With the spring, however, Holmes had another round of illness, and
in June, when the skies were clear, William Allen died suddenly. Four of
the six judges who had welcomed Holmes to the court were dead. The
new chief justice, Walbridge Field, was overwhelmed by the burden of
work on the shorthanded court, and himself became ill and had to withdraw for a time. Holmes struggled to pick up the slack.

In the summer, breaking into his rest, was the solemn business of preparing a talk on William Allen's death that Holmes would give in September. At a low ebb, he wrote as if composing his own obituary:

> He would have preferred not to be celebrated with guns and bells and pealing requiems, the flutter of flags and gleam of steel in the streets, and all the pomp which properly is spent on those who have held power in their right hand. . . .
> Such men are to be honored, not by regiments moving with high heads to martial music, but by a few others, lonely as themselves, walking apart in meditative silence, and dreaming in their turn the dream of spiritual reign.[16]

As if this were a conclusion, Holmes decided to collect his speeches into a book, beginning with his Memorial Day address in 1884 and ending with this obituary for William Allen — an extended self-portrait in thought. The slim volume of only fifty pages[17] he sent to friends: Bryce, to whom he had not written in years; John Holmes, whom he had long neglected; Ethel Grenfell, Margot Tennant, and Nina Campbell, who answered: "No, I have not forgotten the green lane — nor shall I forget — Goodbye — it would be *delightful* if you would write again."[18]

He sent a copy to Lady Castletown, whom he had met only once: "I was so much flattered to receive your little book of speeches & the letter which accompanied it & I felt quite flattered at your remembering my existence after all this time!"[19]

He sent a copy to Walt Whitman, whose poetry he admired. Whitman answered warmly: "When I came from the country yesterday, dear Judge Holmes, there greeted me that little white book with contents like the Puritan which it describes, . . . full of a high & mystical beauty."[20]

Brandeis wrote; as always he was brief, tactfully acute, gracefully encouraging: "When the Lawyer's Bible comes to be made up — the book of Holmes will be its Job, and your Hymn of Praise will be the Te Deum of their service."[21]

But there were no reviews, save a solitary notice by Simeon Baldwin of Yale, to whom Holmes had sent a copy. The book dropped without a trace.

Holmes felt increasingly isolated. His fellow judges, however pleasant, were narrow in their interests and unimaginative. Fanny long ago had ceased to share his work, and in any case was absorbed in domestic concerns and in caring for the doctor. Holmes wrote to James Bryce:

> I long to come to London. . . . Possibly I may get over next summer. But I find it very hard to leave my wife & she can't leave my father. You are a happy man to have a clear canon of duty. It is rather a bore to do one's duty & expect to regret on one's death-

bed that one hasn't allowed oneself more latitude. This last sentence does not refer to standing by my wife as it might seem to do from its place.[22]

A criminal case came before the court that fall. Josiah Perry, who owned a woolen mill in Dudley, had fined one of his weavers, a man named Fielding, forty cents for imperfect work and had withheld this fine from Fielding's wages. Like other mill owners, Perry made a practice of withholding such fines for imperfections in the cloth. But in the spring of 1891 the Massachusetts legislature had made this practice a criminal offense. Perry was purposely defying the law. He was convicted and he appealed, on the principal ground that the statute under which he had been charged was an unconstitutional interference with his property.

The Supreme Judicial Court, led by Charles Allen, emphatically agreed with him. The mill owner's right to make contracts with weavers free from interference by the legislature, Allen said, as if it were self-evident, was one of the rights of property and so was protected by the Massachusetts constitution.[23]

Holmes for the first time published a dissenting opinion:

I have the misfortune to disagree with my brethren. I have submitted my views to them at length, and, considering the importance of the question, feel bound to make public a brief statement, notwithstanding the respect and deference I feel for the judgment of those with whom I disagree. . . .

So far as it has been pointed out to me, I do not see that [the statute] interferes with the rights of . . . property any more than the laws against usury or gaming. In truth, I do not think that clause of the Bill of Rights has any application.

Perhaps, Holmes conceded, the legislature had power only to make "reasonable" laws. Was this law unreasonable because it compelled mill owners to pay for defective goods? For the first time, Holmes expressed a creed of deference — of judicial self-abnegation — that thirty years later would, paradoxically, make him a national hero:

I should not be willing or think myself authorized to overturn legislation on that ground [of unreasonableness], unless I thought that an honest difference of opinion was impossible, or pretty nearly so. . . .

I suppose that this act was passed because the operatives, or some of them, thought that they were often cheated out of a part of their wages under a false pretense that the work done by them was imperfect, and persuaded the legislature that their view was true. . . . I cannot doubt the legislature had the right to deprive the employers of an honest tool which they were using for a dishonest purpose, and I cannot pronounce the legislation void, as based on a false assumption, since I know nothing about the matter one way or the other.[24]

Holmes's solitary dissent was widely reported, and to his disgust the Democratic papers praised him as a friend of labor, while in other circles the dawning opinion that he might be a dangerous man was strengthened.

Beyond the borders of Massachusetts, the war for control of mines and mills was far more violent. The year of 1892 opened on a series of the most bitter labor conflicts the nation had yet seen. In New Orleans, there was a general strike. In Buffalo, switchmen struck against the railroads. In Idaho, there was a violent copper miners' strike. In the fields of east Tennessee, the coal miners struck.

In the Monongahela River valley of western Pennsylvania, Henry Frick, executive officer of the Carnegie Steel Company, had decided to break the steelworkers' union. He hired the Pinkerton agency, who had been General McClellan's Civil War intelligence arm, and fortified the Homestead works as if for a military campaign. Frick then told the Homestead workers that their wages would be cut. On July 1, 1892, a strike began, and the aging Bessemer furnaces were silent. Frick brought barges of armed Pinkerton guards up the river at night, and planned to bring new workers into the mill under guard.

A battle began at dawn. The union was less well armed, but they held the hills above the mill, where many had their homes. The Pinkertons were overwhelmed, and some were captured and beaten. There were deaths on both sides. The union briefly occupied the Homestead works; then the government intervened. There could be only one outcome, and after five months of struggle the union was broken and its leaders blacklisted.

This was an outbreak of civil war; more violence was promised to come. Louis Brandeis, reading of the Homestead strike, threw away the materials he had planned to use in a course on business law and began to think of what should be done.

Holmes, for his part, went quietly to see a man he did not know, Frank Foster — a labor union leader — in his small office at 595 Washington Street, Room 31.[25]

I made a pilgrimage to his very humble shrine & bid him sit & deliver his sentiments. . . . "Sir," I said, "I am Judge H. of the Supreme Judicial Court — I have no ulterior motives & no particular questions to ask or observations to make, but I thought in the recently published interviews you talked like a man of more sense than the rest & as a judge & as a good citizen I like to understand all phases of economic opinion — what would you like if you could have it?[26]

Foster was thirty-four years old, a printer, and president of the Typographers' Union. He was a soldier in his own way, and he got on easily with Holmes. Foster had learned to set type as an apprentice at *The Churchman* in Hartford, Connecticut. He was an educated man; he went to the theater, read books, attended lectures.

He was also editor, publisher, and principal reporter of *The Labor Leader*, a newspaper that sold for three cents. He had been through the Knights of Labor's disastrous strikes and had learned the lessons of their failures. Organization and unity were his first principle, he told Holmes: organization of working men and women to meet the united force of capital. His second aim was to reduce the work week from sixty to forty hours, without loss of pay. And the third was the referendum — popular votes on the laws — to counterbalance the influence of wealth in the legislature.[27]

After calling on Foster in his office, Holmes brought the union leader home to 9 Chestnut Street, where they talked at more leisure; Foster said, "You have changed my feeling: I used to see an enemy in every house."[28]

Holmes, for his part, despite his unswerving loyalty to his own class, listened sympathetically to Foster's plea for fairness. But his heart sank at the prospect of mass democracy triumphant. Foster's unions seemed to threaten an end for all time to aristocracy — and to the art, gentility, and aspirations that Holmes believed depended on the existence of a leisure class: "I see that you people have aims, but I don't see that you have *ideals*. . . . There is something in the world besides comfort, something worth loving and dying for."[29]

In London, in the summer of 1893, Baring Brothers bank failed, crushed by the collapse of American railroad bonds.

American railroads had become little more than prizes of war. A railroad line would be built parallel to the already existing track of a competitor; a rate war would follow, one line would fail or be swallowed by the other, and rates would then rise as high as the traffic would bear. The new and now profitable combine would be challenged by another, still larger, parallel system, rates would be slashed again and the cycle would be repeated. Bonds were issued to finance the purchase of competing lines, or only to fatten current profits and inflate stock prices. Earnings of the railroads were mortgaged for generations into the future by immense debt. By 1893, there were 200,000 miles of track, owned by hundreds of competing railroads, more than the nation would ever need, built redundantly and without plan. The structure of debt abruptly collapsed in the summer of 1893. One hundred fifty-six railroads, representing about half the nation's total trackage, slid into receivership. Security holders panicked, and sold into the falling market; thousands of businesses failed; creditors demanded gold; the commercial life of the country faltered.

The United States slipped into the deepest economic depression it had yet felt. Most working people — many of them now were recent immigrants — had no margin of savings. There was no insurance or state assistance to fall back on, and unemployment meant hunger. An army of unemployed men marched on Washington.

A few financial institutions began to buy up and consolidate hundreds of little competing railroad lines and steel mills. The most successful reorganizer, J. P. Morgan, said, "We do not want financial convulsions, and have one thing one day and another thing another day."[30]

On June 15, 1894, the doctor and Fanny went as usual to Beverly Farms, leaving Holmes in town, and in October they returned to Beacon Street. The doctor was rested and, although coughing asthmatically, apparently well. On Sunday, October 7, he attended services alone at King's Chapel. In the evening, the doctor, Fanny, and Holmes sat in the parlor, reading. The doctor's noisy breathing seemed to stop. When Holmes went to him, he was dead.[31]

The memorial service in King's Chapel was conducted by Edward Everett Hale. The doctor was buried beside his wife in Mt. Auburn cemetery in Cambridge, not far from the Charles River and the place where he was born.

From the moment of the doctor's death there was a great deal for Holmes to do. The newspapers had to be answered, the doctor's wide circle of friends written to. Letters and telegrams of condolence came from all over the United States and Great Britain; many required answers. Unauthorized editions of *The Autocrat of the Breakfast-Table* appeared with surprising speed. Holmes, as executor of the doctor's estate, arranged for law firms in New York and Chicago to bring suit for injunctions to halt the unauthorized printings.

Houghton Mifflin wanted to publish an authorized biography — and Holmes chose his cousin on his mother's side, John T. Morse, for that task. The doctor's papers had to be collected and turned over to Morse. The doctor's business affairs had to be taken in charge, the estate inventoried, the will probated, the various bequests carried out. Holmes, as the only surviving member of the doctor's immediate family, was the principal beneficiary, both of the doctor's own estate and of the trusts set up by Mrs. Holmes's and Amelia's wills.[32] Holmes and Fanny would be prosperous, even wealthy.

There was the question of where Fanny and Holmes now would live. Holmes was reluctant to sell the house at 296 Beacon Street. Practical considerations to the side, it was the place where his father, mother, and sister had lived and died. The houses in Cambridge and Montgomery Place had been torn down, the house in Pittsfield sold long ago. The house at 296 Beacon Street, where Holmes and Fanny had come when they were married, was all that remained of their family's past. Like the Roman heirs of whom he had written so many years before, Holmes stepped into his father's place:

> My father's death although of course a very great event in my life seems to me to have come at a fortunate moment. I was fearing many things for him & he painlessly avoided them — having had all that he could expect from life. My own life is — that of a recluse. I go nowhere, & keep well. I expect that we shall keep on living at 296 Beacon St.[33]

In the dreary autumn that followed the doctor's death, Fanny suffered a return of her rheumatic fever. She became terribly ill and, either through the illness or the treatment given, lost her hair.[34]

It was not a fatal illness, but it was persistent. She was confined to her room for months. In the spring, she was sitting up, haggard and suddenly very old. Her hair had begun to grow back, gray, and gave her an eccentric ill-shorn appearance.

Holmes went out alone, and occasionally took the train to New York on weekends for recreation. Fanny redecorated a parlor at 296 Beacon Street as her own, with her embroideries on the walls and over the mantel, and there she spent her days. Some of her birds were allowed to fly freely, marmosets and squirrels ran uncaged in the bedroom. Fanny spoke to the animals, and talked somewhat oddly to the servants.[35] There was a violent intensity in her eccentricities. She wrote angry, disordered messages to Holmes — "Put [your book] away with care lest the Binding Should be hurt by my terrible furnace heats," she said in one — scribbled grotesque caricatures, complained of his jaunts to New York to call on ladies: "I don't suppose you intend to go to New York after Miss Bradley's friend. . . . If the fancy has come into your mind banish it. You have a wife once a week —"[36]

Thirty-one years had passed since Holmes had mustered out of the federal army. His immediate family, but for Fanny, was dead; Fanny was ill and perhaps would never fully recover. The judges of his court who had been his closest companions had fallen away, and among the new judges he was more isolated than before.

Duty, however, remained. The conflict of labor and capital was the new problem for the common law. Holmes's work as judge required him to understand political economy more fully, and so he began a systematic course of reading, beginning in the seventeenth century with Hobbes's *Leviathan* and continuing with Hegel, Karl Marx, Herbert Spencer, and William Morris on socialism. He slogged glumly through *Das Kapital*: "I can't imagine a combination less to my taste than Hegel and political economy."[37]

Once thoroughly immersed in Marx's big book, however, he found it interesting: "With some misgivings I am inclined to believe K. Marx a great man — more or less perverted into bitterness by proscriptions but having worked out for himself under Hegelian inspiration a sort of evolutionary theory."[38]

But the socialism espoused by some trade unions and by their Beacon Hill friends as a formula for utopia seemed to Holmes a pious dogmatism on a par with the temperance agitation before the Civil War. Holmes had long ago decided that Malthus's doctrine was true — that population would naturally grow faster than the means of subsistence. Uncontrolled propagation would always breed poverty, and then war. Scarce resources were being exhausted, and the world could not support an uncontrolled population, so it mattered little whether goods were distributed evenly, by private owners or by public authorities; there would not be enough to go around unless population were controlled.[39]

This seemed so obvious to Holmes that he never could understand any disagreement: "When I read Malthus I thought he had ripped the guts out of some humbugs — but they are as alive as ever today. Humbugs have no guts — and live all the better without them."[40]

He was particularly roused by a new book that was making a sensation — Charles Pearson's *National Life and Character* — which predicted that England and America would be penned within their borders by the more rapidly growing brown and yellow races of the tropics. Denied resources or room for expansion, Anglo-Saxons would subside into a static socialism, perhaps without misery, but also without hope. "Life will be tolerable, though the sky above may be more gray," Pearson concluded.[41]

At home and abroad, it seemed to Holmes, every social improvement would immediately be absorbed by an increase of population unless propagation were placed under limits. Nor could he imagine any but brutal methods for controlling population.[42]

Holmes had seen death continually since his boyhood. He was deeply scarred by the memory of having been sent, as it then seemed, by his own parents to die in the Civil War. He would have no children of his own, bound as he was by duty to a childless marriage.

In the heart of his unhappiness Holmes evolved a logical, brutal Malthusianism. He imagined that science might advance so as to permit merciful euthanasia of the unfit, who otherwise would breed irresponsibly, and whose children would otherwise starve or come to the prisons or the gallows.[43] The survival of his nation, he believed, depended upon weeding out the unfit in this way and breeding a race of warriors.

Socialism without such measures was a fraud. The best the socialists could achieve — without taking life scientifically in hand — would be an evenly spread mediocrity.

Yet, deeply as he believed that the trade union movement and the socialists meant death to his people and to his ideals, perhaps death to European civilization; troubled as he was by his terrible private vision of the murder of children; it seemed to Holmes that his duty as a judge was to let the unions have their chance on an equal footing with capital. Law must take the place of violence. Humanity was evolving toward self-awareness, and the war of race against race, class against class, was becoming however slowly a peaceful clash of arguments. This, at least, seemed to Holmes to be the lesson of the common law.

He found it in trivial disputes. Women working in a buggy-whip factory, making silk snaps for the ends of the whips, had heard a rumor that the silk was poisoned with arsenic. A doctor named Fessenden started the rumor, by telling it to a patient. The women went on strike and the factory owner sued the doctor for defamation.[44] In another case, a man gave honest advice to a friend, a married woman, that led her to leave her husband. The husband sued.[45] In still another, the *Boston Advertiser* ran a series of articles on corruption in the New York customs house, naming a man as a principal figure in the bribery. He sued for libel.[46]

Holmes was tantalized by these cases. They seemed to contradict the fundamental principle of liability he had announced in *The Common Law*. Measured by that objective standard, the doctor, the friend who gave advice, and the newspaper that exposed corruption should all have been liable for the injuries they caused: each should have foreseen that his act might cause damage. And yet it was pretty plain that by the precedents none of these defendants would be held liable — unless they had acted on bad motives. The courts seemed to examine their subjective will, not their objective behavior. But this was contrary to the whole direction of development of the common law, as Holmes understood it.[47]

For the first time since he sent *The Common Law* to the printer, Holmes began a new work of legal theory.[48] Once again an Astronomer, from the timeless perspective of the common law he looked at the awesome collapse of the economy, the violent clashes of race and class, the growing consolidation of capital, and the defensive union of labor. He wove together in his mind, for the first time, private and public affairs, the disputes of individual parties and the war of classes.

The key was in those troubling, intricate defamation cases. Why was a man privileged to give honest advice, a newspaper to publish damaging reports, or a doctor to tell his patient that her employer was poisoning her? Injury to other people could be expected in each case, yet the courts did not impose liability for these foreseeable harms.

The courts were evidently defending freedom of speech. But why? Speech was said to be "privileged" at common law, but this was only a name for the conclusion, and not a reason.

In every case, beneath a surface of Latin maxims, Holmes saw, there was only a question of policy. Beneath the conscious complexities of the judges' opinions were the workings of simpler, unconscious forces. Judges *felt* it worth all the resulting harms to have honest advice given, to have newspapers report freely on official corruption. This might have been obvious, but, "questions of policy are legislative questions, and judges are shy of reasoning from such grounds. Therefore, decisions for or against the privilege [of free speech], which really can stand only upon such grounds, often are presented as hollow deductions from empty general propositions."[49]

In other cases, business people had been privileged to injure each other freely in competition. Steamship companies had even been allowed to combine and to conduct a boycott. The reason was again the same. The judges felt, if they did not precisely say, that the benefits of freedom justified the injuries it caused.

Yet these inarticulate grounds of policy had not been impartially applied. Businessmen were privileged to combine and to conduct boycotts, but the same behavior by workers in a union was punished by English courts.

Holmes questioned whether the economic sympathies of the judges, rather than any conscious policy, were the true ground for denying to working men the privilege of free peaceful competition extended to businessmen:

> I make these suggestions, not as criticisms of the decisions, but to call attention to the very serious legislative considerations which have to be weighed. The danger is that such considerations should have their weight in inarticulate form as unconscious prejudice or half conscious inclination. To measure them justly needs not only the highest powers of a judge and a training which the practice of law does not insure, but also a freedom from prepossessions which is very hard to attain. It seems to me desirable that the work should be done with express recognition of its nature. The time has gone by when law is only an unconscious embodiment of the common will. It has become a conscious reaction upon itself of organized society knowingly seeking to determine its own destinies.[50]

A judge's duty was to set aside his private loyalties of race and class, to decide fairly, and to allow disputes to be resolved by the clash of arguments in court, rather than by violence. Only in this way, through free speech and free association, would the evolution of humanity become peaceful, conscious, and self-directed.

Memorial Day came around again, and Holmes was asked to speak to Harvard's graduating class and to receive an honorary degree. Fred Pollock and John Gray were to receive degrees at the same time; it would be a meeting of friends. But Holmes took no pleasure in it: "The degree comes too late for me to care much for it except negatively. I take it as a mark the president [Charles Eliot] has buried the hatchet."[51]

The law school was celebrating the twenty-fifth anniversary of its now-famous dean, C. C. Langdell, but Holmes had no word for him. Instead, he gave a kind of obituary for the studies of the common law to which he and Langdell had devoted their lives and which now seemed to be completed. The past had its uses, but "the present has a right to govern itself so far as it can; and it ought always to remember that historic continuity with the past is not a duty, it is only a necessity."[52]

The law eventually would be entirely rewritten, Holmes said, discarding tradition and vague sentiment. Sociology and physiology would be its basis, for the foundations of the law ought to be scientifically designed to attain the goal of the social organism: survival. The law would be remade, "once for all, like a yacht, on lines of least resistance."[53]

He was more deeply moved by another part of the ceremonies, when he stood before the young men who were graduating. He spoke to them of the future, which to him appeared bleak. He struggled to find in the prospect of inevitable world war some source of faith in ideals. His speech to them had a chilling beauty:

> Any day in Washington Street, when the throng is greatest and busiest, you may see a blind man playing a flute. I suppose that someone hears him. Perhaps also my pipe may reach the heart of some passer in the crowd. . . .
>
> The society for which many philanthropists, labor reformers and men of fashion unite in longing is one in which they may be comfortable and may shine without much trouble or any danger. . . . But who of us could endure a world, although cut up into five-acre lots and having no man upon it who was not well fed and well housed, without the divine folly of honor, without the senseless passion for knowledge out-reaching the flaming bounds of the possible, without ideals the essence of which is that they never can be achieved? I do not know what is true. I do not know the meaning of the universe. But in the midst of doubt, in the collapse of creeds, there is one thing I do not doubt, that no man who lives in the same world with most of us can doubt, and that is that the faith is true and adorable which leads a soldier to throw away his life in obedience to a blindly accepted duty, in a cause which he little understands, in a plan of campaign of which he has no notion, under tactics of which he does not see the use.[54]

A visitor from imperial Germany called on Holmes to say how much he admired this speech, and spoke of his sons who would someday serve in the Kaiser's army. Copies of the speech — "The Soldier's Faith" — went to Holmes's friends in London and Tokyo and Washington.

"By Jove, that speech of Holmes's was fine," Theodore Roosevelt said to Cabot Lodge.[55] When he came to Boston later in the year, Roosevelt made a point of congratulating Holmes.[56]

The President of the United States, Grover Cleveland, who was then pondering the possibility of war with Britain over rival claims in the Caribbean, read the speech aloud to his secretary of state, and was stopped by emotion.[57]

15

LADY

CASTLETOWN

AFTER THE COMMENCEMENT ADDRESS, HOLMES JOINED FANNY AT Beverly Farms, and Holmes, fifty-four years old in that summer of 1895, learned to ride the bicycle:

> My routine has not changed much except for the, to me, astounding experience of learning the bicycle — I do not say I have learned — far from it — but I have got over the first general black & blue color of my person — my ankle & wrist are no longer twisted, to speak of, & after I have got on, which I do not do with infallible ease & grace I powder ahead at a comfortable judicial speed which gives me much pleasure. I take about five miles of an afternoon — get pretty warm over it & feel like a bird. It is no slight thing for an old gentleman to learn that he can tumble off & not break — I was pleased as a boy at the discovery.[1]

By the following summer Fanny thought he should go to London and have some fun. She was not well enough to go with him, and he was reluctant to leave her alone. But at last he was persuaded.

He was back in his bedroom-and-parlor at Mackellar's Hotel, 17 Dover Street, ticking off in his little memorandum book a list of shops and of people to notify of his arrival. Once there, he reveled in London; it was

> a wonderful romantic place to an outsider momentarily let inside. . . . The pace is tremendous. A lady said to me, "You Americans disconcert one by waiting for us to finish our sentences" & certainly some of them seem to know what is coming by the time one gets his head open — One is pretty sure that his neighbor at dinner will have a lot of psychologic small change at her command, enough to secure admission to the interior of the building. So an endless procession of possibilities streams before one's eyes which once in a while realizes itself & you swear eternal friendship & forthwith vanish.[2]

Holmes revisited old friendships, carefully nurtured by letters and gifts over the years, but not all were thriving. Leslie Stephen, that first friend of his youthful assault on London, was nearly inaccessible. Stephen's wife, Julia, and his brother, Fitzjames, had died. Leslie was cut off by deepening bitterness and by growing deafness; visitors were obliged to shout at him, and he groaned loudly to himself.[3] But Bryce, Dicey, and Pollock were all welcoming and cheerful: Holmes would have to come to Oxford for a visit.

From his first evening in town Holmes was often with Lucy Clifford, no longer quite so young a widow at forty-two. He and she slipped easily into their old friendship. They paid calls together, had dinner at the new Savoy Hotel, went to the Indian Exhibition and the theater, had tea with her two daughters.

Ethel Grenfell was warmly welcoming. Margot Tennant had married — not Arthur Balfour, indeed, but his political enemy, Herbert Asquith, the young Liberal counsel. She was less responsive now than Holmes liked. Lady Edward Cecil was cordial, and there was to be a weekend at her father, Admiral Maxse's, house. Nina Campbell invited him to her house at Windsor — and telegraphed "Delighted" that he could come. Holmes courted Nina Campbell — "at whose feet I somewhat vainly laid the devotion of an ever faithful heart"[4] — who did, yes, once more remember that green lane.

At Nina Campbell's he met, and carefully noted in his memorandum book, Lady Burghclere, Alice Stopford Green, the young actress Elizabeth Robbins, and Ethel James, who was in her twenties: "I shall always entertain a very warm recollection of you and your kindness. . . . I was most unwilling to let go. However I hope that it is by no means our last meeting."[5]

Lady Castletown was in his memorandum book and he left his card for her at 101 Eaton Place.

Dear Mr. Holmes:
I remember you well — I am so sorry to have missed you this
afternoon — but do come to luncheon one of these days? perhaps
Wed'y? We *may* be away on Monday & Tuesday —

Yours sincerely
Clare Castletown[6]

Holmes marked the tentative appointment for Wednesday, July 8, in
his memorandum book, but something interfered, and lunch was put off
until Saturday, when there was a crowd at Eaton Place. Holmes managed
to advance his acquaintance another step and to invite Lady Castletown
to see the Indian Exhibition, to which he had already taken Lucy Clifford, the following Wednesday.[7] This was a success, and Holmes was invited to dinner the following week, again in a large company, and then
again to lunch.

The London season was ending. Mrs. Clifford was leaving for Bayreuth;
Mrs. Green asked Holmes to stop to see her if he got over to Ireland. The
Castletowns would be at Granston Manor, near Abbey Leix; perhaps he
would visit them there or at Lady Castletown's family seat, Doneraile Court,
in the south of Ireland. Holmes copied out directions into his book.

He spent a week at Oxford with Pollock, whose two sons were at
school there. The four men went boating, and had a late festive dinner
— "at 11:00!" — with Lady Pollock in London. "I look back at that whole
expedition & the grand finale in town with a sort of enchantment."[8] He
saw Margot Asquith alone, for a moment, before she and her husband
went up to Scotland — a moment of intimacy in which neither said very
much, but that partly reestablished their friendship.[9] Ethel Grenfell, with
Willy and their two boys, went to Taplow Court, but she left graceful
reassuring words for Holmes:

Dearest friend — it is so difficult to put it all clean through the
veil of words — but I want you to know it is well that I know you
& prize the knowledge — for above & beyond the mere intimacies
& to & fro of the moment; they may or may not be there in our
friendship, it is delightful when they are, but always *alongside* only
of the true deeper sense of you that possesses my heart. Everything you have said to me this year has fenced round that knowledge more surely, & made it more certain & steadfast. . . . I am
your friend always in loyal truth —[10]

For a little while, Holmes remained in London. The late dinners, the
wine, the London chill and damp were always difficult for him, but he remained healthy, which pleased and relieved him. Still, he was tired, London
was winding up, and he was feeling left behind as his friends scattered to their
country houses. At loose ends, he suggested a weekend with Henry James,
who had rented a house at Rye. "Saturday to Monday will be delicious!"

James cabled. A long letter about train connections and clothes followed, and a second letter, the same day, enlarging on the directions, and, following all this, a cable Friday canceling the visit, and then still another letter:

> I was heartbroken & desolate at having, an hour ago, to send that monstrous telegram; but it was — it is — the only course that was open to me.[11]

There followed a mildly probable story of a deadline approaching, a story unwritten:

> It makes me sick makes me ill — & to have to write in this mood is tragic. Kick me! ever abjectly yours,
>
>   Henry James

Alone in London for the weekend, Holmes wrote a long letter to Fanny from his hotel. On Monday, there was another letter from James:

> I launch this into the void to reiterate my desolation of Friday & to try to catch hold of you somehow.

Holmes at last replied, accepting a suggestion of dinner in town, and Henry wrote excitedly, with many underlinings and corrections, to make exact arrangements. They had dinner in London the following Saturday. James stayed over in town that night, had tea with Holmes on Sunday, and saw him off. Later, James wrote:

> [Your portrait] makes me feel as if I were talking to you now & you were bearing with me patiently — in spite of your so handsome haughtiness — as you have often done before.[12]

It was Holmes's first trip to Ireland. After an overnight stay in Dublin, he followed Lady Castletown's careful directions for the train: "Go by Hollyhead to Kingston & on to Maryborough & then to Buttevant." He searched through the train for his name in a window, to find his sleeping berth. The next morning in Buttevant, he was driven in a yellow omnibus through the green countryside to Doneraile Court.

Doneraile was near the south coast of Ireland, in the Ballyhoura Hills, rolling green countryside at the western spur of the Galtee Mountains, in County Cork. Brooks fell through pools in the rocky hills above Doneraile and joined to make a little stream, the Awbeg, which tumbled through the village. The main street was lined by blocks of brick workingmen's houses. Beyond the village, there was a convent, boys' and girls' parish schools, the parish church; beyond these again was the old viscount's park and manor — Doneraile Court, where Lord and Lady Castletown now spent a portion of every summer. It was part of the great estate once given by Queen Elizabeth to Edmund Spenser. Not far off was the ruin of Kilcoman Castle, where Sir Francis Drake had come to call and where Spenser had written *The Faerie Queene.* The first steeple-chase had run from Buttevant to the church at Doneraile.

Lady Castletown — Ursula Emily Clare St. Leger, daughter of the Viscount Doneraile — was forty-three years old, intelligent, at ease with herself and her place in the world. She had married Barnaby Fitz-Patrick, Baron Castletown. They traveled, collected souvenirs, had no children. Lord Castletown was a good-humored sportsman who wore a Guards mustache like Holmes's. He spent much of his time at Granston Manor, his own family seat in Kilkenny County in central Ireland.

When Holmes arrived at Doneraile, Lord Castletown was away, per-haps at Granston. The other guests were the Godfrey Levingers and an-other man alone, Eustace Bechen ("pronounced *Beechen,*" Holmes care-fully wrote in his diary), invited, Holmes soon realized, in case the Yankee experiment should prove tedious.[13] They were five at dinner, and afterward looked at photographs from the Castletowns' travels in India. Perhaps there was some talk about Lady Gregory and her young protégé William Butler Yeats, who had been collecting folktales in the neighbor-hood, and had taken down a story told by a Doneraile shepherd.[14]

The next morning, Mr. Bechen was sent off to hunt rabbits and the Levingers to sight-see. Lady Castletown showed Holmes the conserva-tory, which in a chilly house filled with servants was a warm and private place. That evening Holmes entered in his diary the single word "Jas-mine."

He had planned to stay only three days, but his visit stretched to a week. He paid no other calls in Ireland and left at the last possible mo-ment to catch his ship, the *Etruria,* at Queenstown. He scribbled a hasty letter at the Queen's Hotel before embarking:

> My dear Lady,
> It is the stopping so sudden that hurts. . . . I forgot to steal some notepaper & I can't write with this pen — I can only cling to your hand for a moment until the earth puts its shoulder between us — which is more than the world can do I hope in twenty years. Goodbye dear friend goodbye, my heart aches to think of how long it may be.[15]

The next morning, August 23, he was at sea, and began writing another long letter, which could not be mailed until his arrival in New York.

> I sent you a line of farewell last night & now am well out to sea. But still I can't break off. There are so many things I should have said but only thought of too late. . . .
> 24th. Last night I talked with an old Catholic priest who united with me in the vice of smoking. I talked with him because he came on board with me from Queenstown & he seemed to keep me a

little nearer to Hibernia. It is a gray morning with a leaden sea &
I too am somewhat leaden — not from the sea — you are reading
my Queenstown letter. . . .

Nothing has touched the freshness of the impressions under
which I went off — Oh what a lot of things I want to say — but
hardly to write. *Evening.* The sun has set over a quiet sea. We shall
land early tomorrow a.m.

Goodbye — Do you still remember my existence?[16]

In Boston, he went first to the courthouse, where he had told Lady
Castletown to address her letters, but there was no telegram waiting for
him as he had hoped. He did find news that the chief justice was ill and
that there would be delays and added work. He found, too, that his
nephew, Ned, had announced his engagement to Miss Mary Beaman,
and a celebration was planned for that evening in Beverly Farms, where
he was expected. But the trip from New York had tired him, and perhaps
for other reasons Holmes was not yet ready for a family gathering. He
decided to stay in Boston that night. Fanny could not wait, however, and
after the party at Beverly Farms she went to a livery stable, hunted up
horses and a driver, and drove to Boston, arriving at 1:30 A.M. She did
not wake Holmes then, but in the morning she greeted him, cheerful
and talkative.[17]

The little white-painted house they had rented for the summer in
Beverly Farms, and his father's narrow dark brick house in Boston, rose
up around Holmes again, blocking the horizon. His court began its sittings in Boston and in a few days would go off to Pittsfield and then to
the other western county seats.

On Saturday, September 5, there was a letter at the courthouse from
Lady Castletown. Holmes devoured it, and a cloud of doubt and loneliness lifted:

I have this moment received your most adorable letter. It is what
I have been longing for & is water to my thirst. You say & do
everything exactly as I should have dreamed. I shall keep it &
when I am blue & you seem far away I shall take it out & read it
& be happy again. Do I often come back? I love your asking it. . . .
Oh yes indeed I do & shall. I do not forget easily, believe me — &
your letter was all that was wanting to assure me that we should
abide together. If you believe that, distance is easily, or at least
more easily, borne. I say your letter was all that was wanting to
assure me. Possibly one thing more — an assurance that you too
do not forget easily when the moment is past.

(*Later.* Tell me this for I have been thinking about it.) If you say
it I shall believe it. I still carry in my pocket a handkerchief (one
of my own) with a little infinitesmal dark smear upon it — with it

I once rubbed away a — Do you remember? isn't that a fool thing for a serious judge?

. . . well dear Lady I must stop for the moment. Write to me soon. I long every day to hear from you, & live Doneraile over — I picture you to myself in all sorts of ways. By & by we shall settle into some sort of rhythm in writing — but I have not yet learned patience in writing. The thing to believe & take comfort in, however, is that we are not going to part company — & I am very sure it will not be I who does it — I am only less confident that it will not be you.[18]

A stream of letters flowed from Holmes's courthouse, page after page written in one breath, without corrections.

My heart gave a jump when I saw the corner of your letter in my box 10 minutes ago, for I thought it was from you before I saw a letter of the handwriting. . . . This morning (& many others) at a little after 7 I was thinking she is perhaps now in the conservatory. It is 12 in their premature country — possibly she is remembering a party that once sat there with her. Oh my friend I don't want to uproot you — on the contrary — nor could I if I tried. (I wonder how one tries!)[19]

At first he addressed her as "My dear Lady," perhaps for fear the letters should be seen; then more familiarly as "dear Lady," and then "Hibernia," as if Ireland were her kingdom, and at last "Clare," but this was rash, and she answered:

Please — I don't advise this way of beginning your epistles — it gives me a shiver & chills I don't know why — I do like to be given my name by you but not in that bold sort of way! You will say it is dreadful foolery but I don't care et voilà comme je suis. So go back to the old "Hibernia" or to no name at all but keep Clare up your sleeve & only let it fall accidentally & tenderly & as if it meant more than just a formal approach to a letter — you know what I mean & I won't embark on trying to explain & you will be good & understand?[20]

Folded into the note was a sprig of leaves from the conservatory.[21]

Holmes wrote every day, at first, and then once or twice each week, sometimes from the bench, from his study, from Beverly Farms, or from a country town:

I find your writing adorable — You talk and that is what one should do. . . . How you would hate this town where I am spending a week. [He was on circuit in Worcester.] How dull and squalid the whole business and surroundings would seem — and yet when you put into them that they offer a chance to do part of one's work they don't trouble you and your spirit is as calm as great fatigue will let it be. I shall go back to my hotel in a moment — play a game of solitaire on my bed, read a little Hegel and turn in early.[22]

Oh my very dear friend how I do long to see you. I know your hands reach across the sea and I kiss them. I continually hunger and thirst for your letters. But oh if I could see you.[23]

Do you not exaggerate a little the part which whim plays in your life? It has an airy swaggering sound to say that one follows the fancies of the moment — but somehow that does not quite fully answer my conception of you — Does that sound like a clergyman? What charm is added to life, and to the person, by the experiences which make us subtle and untrustworthy.[24]

The illusion of freedom. A man says Now I am going to let myself slide and have my heart out — and he finds that, [while under] restraint he got an infinity by suggestion, which vanishes before the finite fact. . . . You must keep on at least one stocking if you want a figure to look undressed.[25]

Some years ago . . . at a dinner of men of weight in this community . . . the majority opinion condemned me as a very dangerous man (i.e. in my judicial tendencies). How few understand the intellectual indifference — the impartiality which is supposed to be a judge's business is understood to be an impartiality within the limits of the prejudices of his class — not more. I dare say I may have to pay for it practically before I die. So perhaps you'd better chuck me — Ah me, bitterness of heart is never far away.[26]

How hard you find it to get away from blague [banter] — don't you — and how you delight in form to put one on the outside and to hint at all manner of games to which he is not a party — at suggestions of expressed preference of the finite to the [unrealized] infinite à propos de toi. My friend I should be sad indeed if I believed you practiced that device. Yet there is something that sounds flat in my not blagging back. If it is always war between men and women and each to get as much as they can, I ought to do so — or if the distance gives it a different turn, I ought at least as I said the other day to hint that the Ewig Weibliche [eternal feminine] is to be found in most parts of the inhabited world, like the notary public and the domestic dog. Do not write hereupon that you are sorry I do not like your letters, as you know I love them. . . .

Oh hang it, I know very well as well as if you had told me that you are ready for adventures — and perhaps the only way is for me to give it back to you — and yet I don't feel so — Au revoir — dear friend. I like you still as you say.[27]

Ah my dear friend — a very little is enough to make me happy and you say in this "I remember you all the time" and you are a curly headed early Norman angel — . . . .[28]

You cut me to the heart with pleasure and with a little shame (not too deep, this last) that so far it always should be you who do the charming things and that I always seem to receive. No matter it's part of the confidence of affection to talk without hesitation — and I do and will wear your heart [an enamel tie pin] — not upon my sleeve. It is beautiful also, and you are a dear.[29]

I wish I knew more definitely why you were always sad. Women are more often sad than men, I think. . . . I have some things to feel sad about for one. My old partner [George Shattuck], with whom I studied, and to whom I am bound by a thousand ties, is very ill — a great head, a strong heart and a mighty energy — Yet I am such a damned egoist, I am so full of my work, so eager to prove my power — that I get the fundamental vital happiness out of life in spite of everything.[30]

I should like to decide every case — and write every judgment of the court, but I'm afraid the boys wouldn't see it.[31]

I do love the insouciance of real intellect that just chucks down an idea, wriggling, and takes it or leaves it — instead of rigging up an image with a bogus sword and masonic jewels.[32]

Usually I take a big sheet my dear lady when I have a line from you — but today I take a small one — partly because I too am hurried with many things, including another funeral this morning, partly because I am just the least bit chilled by yours (acknowledging receipt of photograph etc.) I have been longing to hear from you and probably got a little too tense, but I fancied you preoccupied, and all but bothered by the necessity of writing. But I make more of it than it is even by writing so much. . . .
Meantime I thank you for the useful lesson as to the proper place for the pin — the mistake is rectified and at this moment it no longer keeps me in mind of you by an occasional prick of my chin.[33]

I must send a line to catch the mail. You do enchanting things. Your telegram of a couple of days ago gave me a thrill of delight and a big lump of happiness which stays by and nourishes me. . . .

You do know how to come up to snuff and no mistake — and the manner of it makes me chuckle with inward glee. So my beloved Hibernia I kiss your hands.[34]

Nansen's book — (Farthest North) It is as beautiful as a Greek statue. . . . Nothing could be more enchanting than to see a man nearly killing himself for an end which derives its worth simply from his having affirmed it. You see the pure ideal in the concrete — Nonsensical and sublime.[35]

. . . if the universe is all of one piece, as it seems to me to be, personality merely means a particular kind of a knot tied in the tail of the infinite, or less hyperbolically, a point of intersection of certain forces, as the rays of the spectrum make white light if brought together at a point, and it is idle to draw the limits of personality at a man's hide. He is a nodus at a particular point — and the sum total of his position, wealth and all the rest is a part of *him* while it lasts as much as his tenor voice or his power of self-sacrifice. You can take anything away from him by a little effort — even if in one case you must remove half an inch of mucous membrane or a little gray matter under his skull — while in another you have only to imagine a commercial crisis or a change in the laws.[36]

Don't you like to get even a galloping word to say yes now now now I am thinking of you as well as so much other of the time? You can do the same however busy you may be. I kiss your dear hands. . . .

I am rather interested by my nephew — my only near relation. He is intelligent but although engaged hardly yet awakened to life — his grandfather — my father — was very slow in that way. Just now he is in the great fog bank that lies around 25 and thinking poorly of himself. I told him that there was philosophy in the substance of the Christian notion of losing oneself to find oneself. Although an old wife's tale in that form. The happiest or best gifted reach it emotionally in religion or in disinterested love of their kind — but I told him the result of salvation could be reached through the intellect — in the irony of Sunday afternoon.[37]

Time has only made our intimacy more settled, more certain. Is it not so? When I read between the lines I do not mistake do I? You have the gift of hints that may mean much or nothing. . . . I have your pin underneath my chin at the moment and in the right place.[38]

The nephew is still *sub judice* as to how much I shall care for him. If I decide, not much — my relation to the future of the world will become somewhat detached and speculative. But he is a good lad and if he has some children, which seems to be his function, and my father's race is not destined to extinction, I may find myself becoming more interested and optimistic. But I have a streak of gloom which babies will find it hard to eradicate. But — but — but — these buts are like always turning to the left and end by bringing one round in a circle.[39]

I grieve over your [riding] accidents. You seem to smash yourself up a good deal and you keep me in a worry for fear something has happened to you, whenever there is any long interval in your letters. . . .

Just now I am holding court . . . and am suffering from a take down in the hint that the younger men, — or I dare say the bar generally, think I talk too much on the bench and don't give 'em chance enough to develop their ideas. I will be a monument hereafter but I think it uncivilized to have to listen to speechifying instead of telling at once where my trouble is when I am the man they want to convince. However as I like to talk law I daresay I have talked too much — though I hate to admit it.[40]

Life is an art not a thing which one can work out successfully by abstract rules. It is like painting a picture. At every moment one has to use one's tact and pigments in getting the right proportions between inconsistent desirables — between reading and writing — saving and spending — work and play etc. The trouble with many moralists as with many men of business is that they give too absolute a right of way to some one interest — to the principle of telling the truth — to the game of affairs — in law, to property —[41]

I am in a pleasant little place by the sea [Beverly Farms] looking straight across to you — or more strictly to Spain, I suppose, unless I look a good deal North — as I do most of the time. Birds, no skylarks alas, but, still meritorious birds, sing inside and out of the house.[42]

I was just called to the window by a great piping of small voices — and saw our driver carrying a crowd of about fifteen small boys whom he has collected at Mrs. Holmes' request and is taking over with a couple of horses to the circus in a neighboring town — unlimited peanuts and a great lark.[43]

I looked into a new book by [Edward] Bellamy [*Looking Backward*] . . . — a socialist writer. . . . I think him a pretentious imbecile. . . . While I write in this abstract way I am thinking of you until you seem almost present — and I can hardly go on.[44]

Apropos of nothing it is said that we all are artificial and un-
natural in society. Do you think it true? Don't you think that one
of the great merits or deep damnations of society is that people
learn to talk straight and from their depths with ease.[45]

I observe you never speak of that other man — [a visitor at
Doneraile] — who was the dark horse earlier in our correspondence. Why? You will pass this question in silence and I shall remember and regret. I kiss your hands.

I have received word this morning that the people I spoke to
have received the pink and blue pond lily roots and also have got
the red gourd seed and that they would pack and send them off
at once. . . . There is a very handsome pink marsh mallow[46] that
grows wild on the South Shore of Mass. I wonder if you would
care for that if it can be got. I remember once when life seemed
at a low ebb driving over on a dreary sandy waste and suddenly
coming on a lonely pool — with woods on one side — a dead tree
hanging over it with the appropriate crow — and over on the
other side a wilderness of pink flowers — standing about as high
as my breast I shd think — and I felt that the romantic could be
found almost anywhere after that.[47]

I have just finished a history of Egypt by Flinders Petrie. How
fascinating it is to see authentic monuments standing on the very
edge of the black unknown — to see mummies — the actual tissue
of men who lived almost at the beginning of recorded time. It is
one of the things that comes nearest to making me accept the
miraculous view of the world — which I reject. The time of man's
articulate life has been so short.[48]

At times I could wish that you were not quite so constantly on
guard — and I hope and quaveringly believe that your confidence
in me hasn't diminished with longer acquaintance. I think if you
were not so constantly in the semi chaffing humor it would be
easier to write one's feelings and interests to you from week to
week but still I have talked pretty straight — and to me the
thought of you is full of intimate delight. So I kiss your hands and
bid you remember me still . . . I shall cut down to once a fortnight
if I don't hear from you once in six months — dear betrayer of
my innocence —[49]

You are an enchanting creature. I love your Christmas present
which enables me to carry you in my pocket as well as in my
heart. . . . You can't tell how touched and delighted I was by the
little memorandum with which my pocket book begins.[50]

I deny that I talk law tediously and I scorn your threat to let another take my place in the conservatory. I have some skepticism and cynicism but also a very quasi-simple article of faith.[51]

I suppose I *am* a little solemn at times.[52]

Two days ago — Tuesday — we had a wonderful snowstorm. I wish even now you could see us — all traffic was interrupted and my court was empty. So I fell to clearing out my front drawer. Among other things were some of your letters which I could not make up my mind to burn at once. Before committing them to the flames, as I did, I read them over — and seemed to get a further impression from taking them in that way. I realized their charm more than ever and they were less hard hearted than I had imagined when I first read them. I suppose my first impression was because I wanted so much. They made me quite wild to see you — but then I don't need a great deal of spurring for that.[53]

I begin to get a new set of impressions from nephews and nieces (mostly of my wife's) who are coming out esp. from one of her nieces — who is a bud and a belle and who puts up with us once in a while when she is going out, and brings in some little companion. I like to hear the twitter of these innocent little birds — and I like the unconscious tyranny of youth. . . . Then a little older lot of recently married persons occasionally looks in on us and do something to keep one's feelings young — also I generally have some incipient lawyer on the string to whom I prophecy from time to time.[54]

Oh I am tired. My mind is like a dead jellyfish on the beach. . . . Don't blame me for talking law. If my pen will shape any words it is as much as I can expect.[55]

I simply love your letters latterly. They do not seem to keep one on the outside — of course I know that was only a form, but it does give me a glow when the form and the fact agree. You are a dear and I kyh. You cant read that.[56]

You have no idea how nice you have been in your later letters or what a trump you are. I started to speak of your charms but I suspect that you suspect their existence and peculiarity. Your hands are being kissed now. Goodbye.[57]

And now do you think that you can meet time and distraction and still care for me as much? I believe you will. I firmly believe it will make no difference to me. Oh my dear what a joy it is to feel the inner chambers of one's soul open for the other to walk in and out at will.[58]

16

THE PATH
OF THE LAW

ALTHOUGH HE HAD PROMISED FANNY THAT HE WOULD LIVE VERY carefully, and made one of his spasmodic efforts to stop smoking, and did not rejoin the Law Club, and said that he would not dine out, still Holmes on his return to Boston in September, 1896, was busier in the evenings than he had been in many years. Fanny's illness had subsided into a chronic state and had become a sort of vocation, not uncommon among her contemporaries. As Fanny did not go out, Holmes went alone to dinner parties. Boston's hostesses took him up, and Holmes's light talk brightened winter tables.[1]

Fanny had few friends of her own generation, but she was fond of young people. There were her nieces and nephews and the young lawyers who hovered around Holmes. Ethel James, one of the young women Holmes had met in London that summer, came over with her new husband, the young barrister Leslie Scott, on their wedding journey, and befriended Fanny as well as Holmes.

The doctor's estate had been distributed. Holmes and Fanny now owned, in addition to their Mattapoisett property, the house at 296 Beacon Street and a small commercial property on State Street; there was about $200,000 in securities, largely railroad bonds, which Holmes valued at par, inherited from the doctor. A stream of royalties from the doctor's books continued to flow.

Holmes's work was as it had been, alternately tedious and vivid. He was more impatient than ever with long-winded arguments, and now, disciplining himself not to interrupt, he wrote letters to Lady Castletown while listening with half his attention ("you throw in an attentive manner calculated to make counsel think you are taking notes of the argument").[2]

Conferences of the judges were always contentious now. Holmes called them the "ratpack."

> We are in a long consultation in which every man's hand is more or less against everyone else. I walk into my neighbors and intimate in more or less polite language that they are talking what Brooks Adams delicately calls hogwash — and when they go for me ... I am ready to maintain every word is better than the 10 commandments. We make tolerably long days and there isn't much left at the end.[3]

On circuit, Holmes was among country people, whom he liked, and he enjoyed sitting alone as a trial judge, sole master of the proceedings.

> I feel in these days that I would pay a dollar & a half & go across the street to see a good stiff prejudice of any kind. They have them in [Worcester] which is uncommonly strong in local feeling & I find it pleasant for a change — I like to hear of the various great men of the neighborhood who are believed in without too much pallid cosmopolitanism & they have some strong chaps here.[4]

William Jennings Bryan was running for president on a radical ticket, Populist and Democrat. He promised relief from the depression of 1893 by inflating the currency. In Boston, where fortunes rested on gold bonds, there was an uneasy apprehension that uncontrollable forces were being unleashed. There were no Mugwumps now. Owners and creditors, bankers and business people, united behind the Republican candidate, William McKinley.

Holmes was sitting alone as the equity judge in Boston, when Frederick O. Vegehlan came into his courtroom. Vegehlan owned a furniture factory on North Street. The skilled upholsterers who worked there — most of them were German-speaking immigrants — had asked for higher pay and shorter hours.

Your upholsterers do hereby kindly submit the enclosed Price-
list for your earnest consideration, the object is to ensure a more
equal competition this we would ask to go into effect on and after
Oct. 29, 1894, and we kindly request that after that date Nine
hours constitute a day's work.

Vegehlan refused, and fired the union's business agent, George Guntner. The union went on strike, and organized a "boycott"; they tried to
persuade tradesmen not to deal with Vegehlan, and insurance companies to cancel his policies. Vegehlan advertised for new workers, and the
union in response put pickets on a patrol outside the factory to discourage anyone from taking a job there. Some of the new workers left and
joined the strike; others remained. There were threats, a fistfight, and
Vegehlan came into court to ask for an injunction halting picketing and
the boycott.

Holmes gave Vegehlan half of what he asked. He ordered the union
not to obstruct the factory door and to refrain from violence or threats
of violence. But he declined to prohibit peaceful picketing, and he allowed a peaceful boycott to continue.[5]

When the full court came to review this case in the fall, they were
divided. At the October conference, Walbridge Field, whose Vermont
independence seized him unpredictably, said irritably that Vegehlan
should be given nothing, not even the limited injunction Holmes had
issued.

But the majority of the court planted itself on the rights of property
and contract. Charles Allen wrote their complacent opinion, dissolved
Holmes's order, and put a stop to the picketing and the boycott entirely.

An employer has a right to engage all persons who are willing
to work for him, at such prices as may be mutually agreed upon;
and persons employed or seeking employment have a corresponding right to enter into or remain in the employment of any
person or corporation willing to employ them. These rights are
secured by the Constitution itself.[6]

Holmes, unable to join Field in simply brushing the whole matter
aside, wrote a solitary dissent. He set out in compressed form his understanding of the common law. Violence, of course, was forbidden. But
peaceful competition was life itself. The law and his duty as a judge
obliged him, Holmes thought, to decide on grounds of objective social
policy whether the union should be privileged to conduct a peaceful boycott.

It was true, Holmes conceded, that working men had combined for
the purpose of injuring their employer. He did not deny that the strike

and boycott were a struggle between owner and workers, in which one would be hurt if the other prevailed.

But, Holmes said, the law would recognize a privilege to carry on peaceful competition, if a legitimate social purpose were the motive. Organizing a union and striking for higher wages, Holmes thought, was a legitimate social purpose, and a privilege should be recognized.

> I have seen the suggestion made that conflict between employers and employed is not competition. But I venture to assume that none of my brethren would rely on that suggestion. If the policy on which our law is founded is too narrowly expressed in the term free competition, we may substitute free struggle for life. . . . Combination on the one side is potent and powerful. Combination on the other is the necessary and desirable counterpart, if the battle is to be carried on in a fair and equal way.[7]

The Democratic newspapers again praised Holmes as a friend of the proletariat, State Street and the bar shook their heads, and Holmes reveled in his indifference to both. He cheerfully told young Arthur Hill, a neighbor on Beacon Street, "I have just handed down an opinion that shuts me off forever from judicial promotion."[8]

This was putting it a little too strongly. Holmes had remained loyal to the Republican party year after year, and Cabot Lodge, now a senator and leader of the progressive wing of the party in Massachusetts, was not distressed by Holmes's views. On the contrary, Holmes would give the party added strength among the new immigrants. In November, Holmes had the governor to dinner to meet a visiting Englishman. But in what Holmes had done, there was enough risk for him to take some pleasure in it.

Filled with self-confidence and pleasure in his work, he gladly accepted an invitation to talk to the law students at Boston University, where Melville Bigelow, once his companion in the Social Law Library, was now dean. Holmes painted in rapid uncorrected brushstrokes his vision of law as a science. Law study began with what seemed sordid and unpromising materials. But when pursued with scientific, even religious, devotion, it became a way to wisdom. He called this speech, "The Path of the Law."[9]

And yet, when this subordination of oneself to the facts of the law was complete, when the lawyer had expunged his subjectivity and thoroughly submitted himself to his calling, then, paradoxically, ideals reappeared:

> Happiness, I am sure from having known many successful men, cannot be won simply by being counsel for great corporations and having an income of fifty thousand dollars. An intellect great

enough to win the prize needs other food beside success. The re-
moter and more general aspects of the law are those which give it
universal interest. It is through them that you not only become a
master in your calling, but connect your subject with the universe
and catch an echo of the infinite, a glimpse of its unfathomable
process, a hint of universal law.[10]

McKinley was elected President, at which Holmes was relieved — he
had viewed the election with real trepidation. Fanny, still frail, was in
better health than she had been since the rheumatic fever, and so when
Ned Holmes was married the following summer to Mary Beaman in
Windsor, Vermont, Holmes and Fanny decided to make a holiday of it,
driving up slowly by carriage, stopping along the way, through southern
New Hampshire across the broad Connecticut River valley and into Vermont. They drove through the soft summer mornings, resting in the hot
afternoons, reading and talking. Ahead of them was the beginning of
new lives, perhaps the beginning of a new generation.

> [The drive] was perhaps the most delightful of my life. We . . .
> saw lots of charming scenery & interesting old New Hampshire
> landlords including a number of old soldiers with whom I ex-
> changed recollections & hobnobbed much to my pleasure.[11]

> We had a Yankee driver who has driven us for years. . . . There
> was also room for a lunch basket out of which Mrs. Holmes (who
> bossed the whole show with a foresight that never went wrong)
> produced at psychologic moments all manner of comforting
> things — from pâté de foie gras to chewing gum! . . . We . . . dined
> & snoozed & read about polar regions & played solitaire during
> the midday hours.[12]

> [I] married off my young man — & came back by a different &
> even more pleasing route than we went.[13]

Fanny was happy and animated again, "wonderful in resources of imaginative humor & forethought & seemed to awaken to a life & joy which
she has not known for a good while."[14]

At Beverly Farms, when they returned, Holmes bought a bicycle —
an American-model Humber — and in the mornings rode confidently
over the unpaved roads, sometimes going fifteen or twenty miles, "sometimes getting tipped off by a rut or loose gravel but no harm done."[15] In
the afternoons, he and Fanny took a carriage and rode out together,
Fanny swathed in white, her face curtained from the sun by veils, their
one-horse carriage stopping occasionally at cemeteries while they looked
for wildflowers and inscriptions.

They kept to themselves. Brooks Adams sometimes joined Holmes on his bicycle jaunts; on other days he talked philosophy with old Eliot Cabot, who was a student and admirer of Hegel. A newspaper reporter asked Holmes about the possibility that he would be appointed to the Supreme Court by the new Republican administration, but Holmes turned the suggestion aside. Horace Gray was still on the Court, and it was unlikely two Boston men would be appointed; there were so many political considerations it did not pay to speculate.[16]

When work resumed, Holmes seemed to have a renewed taste for it: "I am tired all the time, but the work is an excitement and a joy."[17]

There was talk that England would go to war in China, that the United States would go to war against Spain. Lodge and Roosevelt led the chorus of belligerence: Cuba must be freed. Holmes's talk to Harvard students in 1895, "The Soldier's Faith," was often quoted by the war hawks, but Holmes was very reluctant to see another war. It was one thing to extract an ideal from an unavoidable duty; it was another to wish for the horrors to return:

> I suppose there is a body of humanitarian feeling [for Cuban freedom] here & I conjecture without knowing that private inter- ests wd. be glad to make a row. But I hope devoutly that cool sense will prevail with the Cubans to get out of their difficulties as best they can.[18]

When the American battleship *Maine* was blown up in a Cuban har- bor, Holmes thought that would justify a fight, but he still hoped it would "pass off in resolutions, etc."[19] The secretary of the navy was John Long, who had appointed Holmes to the bench; he was a Temperance man and president of the Pacifist League. But his assistant was Theodore Roosevelt, who ordered a fleet to the Pacific, to prepare for war.

By the end of April, President McKinley, pressed by Roosevelt, Lodge, the other young Jingos in the Senate, and by the Hearst news- papers, asked for a declaration of war. Roosevelt was immensely pleased, and resigned from the Navy Department to organize a volunteer cavalry regiment. Holmes regretted the decision.

> If I had bossed the job with my present lights I should have kept the peace if the country would have let me — but war having begun I back it with my heart. There is a chance they [the Spanish navy] will try to shoot at us here [in Boston,] in which case the place where I sit would be the center of their aim. A good deal of my property is in Boston but I have made no change, regarding that as what one means by having a stake in the country.[20]

But Holmes fretted over the war, and over the chances of getting back to Ireland that summer. Fanny was urging him to go abroad, but he disliked leaving her, and disliked leaving the country when it was at war.[21] Week after week he wrote of his uncertainty to Lady Castletown, asking for encouragement, for assurances that they would have an extended time together, asking whether they would have some privacy, whether he should stay at Mackellar's Hotel or some other place that she would suggest. All of this she ignored, as he knew she would.

He reserved a steamship ticket, but continued to vacillate. He asked the chief justice to move up the date of the June conference, so that if he went to London Holmes would not have to leave his opinions to fend for themselves. The chief declined.

The war with Spain was proving a one-sided affair, and there was no danger to Boston that Holmes need stay to face. And so, on June 18, he telegraphed Lady Castletown at the last possible moment that he was coming, and boarded the *Umbria* in New York.

He stayed at Mackellar's again. For four weeks in July, he had breakfasts, lunches, and dinners, walks in the park, and visits at tea time. He saw Lucy Clifford almost daily, and they were like an old married couple going about together. They paid calls on Miss Montague, Miss Chamberlain, and Lady Burghclere. They had dinner at the Savoy and went to the theater. At Miss Chamberlain's, Lucy Clifford read her new play, *The Likeness of the Night,* the story of a barrister whose marriage was no longer happy and who renewed an old love affair.[22]

There was little time for lawyer friends. "We are sadly disappointed that you can't find a day or two to come to us," Bryce wrote from Sussex.[23] Holmes was unable to accept an invitation from young Winston Churchill, who had lent him a book.[24] He did find time for dinner with the new American ambassador, John Hay, who was celebrating the victory over Spain. Henry Adams and Henry James were both in town, and there was news of Roosevelt, who had returned in triumph from Cuba to announce his campaign for governor of New York.

On July 11, Holmes perhaps was surprised to receive an invitation from Lord Castletown to have dinner at the Traveller's Club. After this ritual meeting, Holmes was invited to Castletown's seat, Granston Manor, where Lord and Lady Castletown would be in August.

From Dublin, Holmes took the train to Maryborough Junction, changed to the train for Kilkenny, and was met at Abbey Leix station. There was a five-mile journey to Granston Manor, where a mile-long private drive wound between high ivy-covered stone walls. The manor itself was a big, much-added-to house begun in the sixteenth century, and now crowded with Lord Castletown's hunting trophies, Lady Castletown's antiques, and their souvenirs of travel. In the forty-foot front hall, Castletown had hung a military trophy — arms taken in the Fenian rising in 1865.[25]

Holmes stayed at Granston Manor for a week. There were other guests, and Holmes paid calls at other houses: he called on a general who had been at Balaclava, had dinner with Miss Curry and Lady Fingall. There were only brief moments alone with Lady Castletown, but she would soon go on to Doneraile, and Holmes was to join her there.

Perhaps it was the stress; Holmes began to suffer sharp pains in the left side of his face and neck, and then in his arm and shoulder; something odd seemed to be happening to his skin; he had difficulty sleeping. It was a painful case of shingles. He returned briefly to London and then went on to Doneraile, in pain and excitement.

There were other guests at Doneraile. Holmes went sight-seeing with them in the yellow omnibus, and out on the moors to see shooting, which he did not join. In the evening there was an Irish jig or a walk to the tavern. But there were also walks with Lady Castletown, and long visits in the conservatory.

On August 22, Holmes and Clare Castletown walked in the gardens together in the morning, wandered on the lime walk, and spent an hour and a half together in the conservatory. Holmes drew a little plan of the conservatory in his memorandum book, and marked the place. On the next day, they drove around the lake, and for the next two days they were alone together at Doneraile. The yellow omnibus took him to Queenstown on August 26, at the last possible moment to catch his ship.

17

CHIEF JUSTICE

WAITING FOR HOLMES IN BOSTON WAS THE NEWS THAT Charles Allen, too old and ill to carry on, had resigned from the court, leaving Holmes the senior associate justice. Within the space of a few weeks, John Holmes, almost ninety, and Fanny's father both died, cutting the last ties to Cambridge for Wendell and Fanny.

Holmes's friends of the younger generation were rising, as if to step into the vacant places. John Hay was called home to serve as secretary of state; Henry Cabot Lodge was gaining influence in the Senate; Theodore Roosevelt was elected governor of New York. An invitation came to Holmes to address a New York Bar Association dinner in honor of the new governor. He delivered a paean to Science and to the future of law rewritten on scientific principles.[1]

Chief Justice Walbridge Field, who was only sixty-six years old, suffered a stroke the following year and could no longer carry his share of the work, but he was not yet ready to resign. Holmes, as senior justice, stepped in to assume the burden of administrative work, of arranging the justices' complex schedule of sittings and conferences, assigning cases, negotiating a consensus on opinions. Already shorthanded, they were now down to five members. Holmes picked up most of the slack.

I am bossing the show. . . . It looks as if the [Chief] wd. not resign before Autumn — one side of his face is paralyzed though I
believe this is not publicly known & what I fear is that he may
become imbecile before he has resigned and then there may be
trouble. He ought to resign now in my opinion but as the interested I can't say.[2]

Field, who was not wealthy, was reluctant to give up the salary of an
active judge, and after venting his impatience, Holmes said, "Poor soul
— poverty is hard."

In April, Clare Castletown wrote in a sad humor: "It is impossible to
keep in touch." Holmes answered, "Oh my dear it is possible to be un-
changed after 20 years — I care for you as much as when we were together."[3] But there was no further letter from Ireland for weeks, and
Holmes grew alarmed. He wrote and at last telegraphed to mutual
friends and learned that Lady Castletown had had a bad riding accident.
She was at Doneraile with her husband, too ill to read or write. Holmes
wrote hesitantly to Lord Castletown. There was a reply:

I am grateful for your kind letter. I quite reciprocate your view
of our friendship. I am pleased to say my wife is a little better but
it is a very slow recovery. . . .
I read her your letter received last night — I hope ere the next
comes she will be able to read herself.[4]

They were preparing for war in South Africa, Lord Castletown wrote.
Lord Roberts was planning maneuvers of 10,000 men near Doneraile.
Germans were arming and training the Boers.

In Boston, Field was spared having to resign. The news came to
Holmes first by telegram:

July 17th, 1899
Chief Justice Field died last night funeral Wednesday one o'clock
from Dr. Hale's church.

A few days later, the governor of Massachusetts nominated Holmes
to succeed Field as chief justice, and on August 2, 1899, the judicial
council not objecting, the nomination was confirmed. "It seems to have
been generally expected," Holmes wrote to Pollock:

I am idling [at Beverly Farms] playing solitaire & sleeping —
not much even of belles lettres. I suppose it is a sort of automatic
insistence of one's mind upon rest. . . . I am sad with the sense of

the transitoriness of things brought home to me by the C.J.'s death & my appointment.[5]

There were a great many letters of congratulation to answer. Only a few touched him. Nina Gray wrote:

Once in a while, in some tired moment, I know you have had a little the feeling that every man's hand was against you, but in the general satisfaction expressed at your appointment, you see dear friend how far that is from being the case. I congratulate you with all my heart.[6]

The news from abroad was distressing. The war in South Africa had begun very badly for the British. Castletown decided to join his regiment, and Lady Castletown, recovered well enough to travel, went to South Africa with him. For Holmes, whatever would happen, this was a more profound separation from her than ever before.

Holmes presided for the first time as chief justice at a sitting of the court in Pittsfield, and there was a little ceremony. The court reporter noted the proceedings:

At the coming of the Court, the commission of Oliver Wendell Holmes as Chief Justice . . . [was] read by the Clerk. . . . Marshall Wilcox, Esq., of Pittsfield, requested permission of the Court, to make a few remarks, which being granted, he spoke of his service as an attorney at the Berkshire Bar for fifty-two years, and mentioned judges of the court whom he had known and honored, and closed with a welcome to Chief Justice Holmes to the office he had assumed, and of the honor in which he was held by the Berkshire Bar and the pride which the bar took in his appointment because of his early residence in the County.[7]

Holmes saw that in the audience, Mrs. Bartlett — the Agnes Pomeroy whom he and Bill Bartlett both had courted more than thirty years before — smiled from among the lawyers and judges.

Judge Holmes said that . . . on returning to this section he was touched by the same feeling and sympathy, and he was by no means sorry that Mr. Wilcox had spoken in the way he did although it was a bit out of the ordinary. Judge Holmes, in a way, belongs to this region, and in the honors that have been heaped upon him, Pittsfield and Berkshire have a share.[8]

The seven justices had their picture taken seated together behind the high bench of their courtroom in Boston, hot white gas mantles flaring above the oak wainscoting behind them. Holmes, as chief justice, sat at the center of the row, leaning forward on his elbows and looking up at the camera, to conceal his height and his long neck; his left eyebrow was cocked as if he were staring through a monocle. There was a book open in his hands, and he was smiling under his mustache, alert and happy. He looked younger than the other justices, slender and modern. His careful pose seemed more natural and more comfortable than their uncalculated, awkward postures.

At the first conference of his court, Holmes assigned the lion's share of cases to himself and undertook to help young Caleb Loring, appointed to the newest vacancy, to find his way. Loring's grandfather and Holmes's own had been justices of the court together, more than sixty years before.

The work of a chief justice was not entirely edifying. The docket of cases had to be kept moving, and each of the justices therefore had to do his part. But William Barker was not carrying his share of the burden, and his cases were piling up undecided. Holmes himself took over a part of the backlog of opinions, and Barker thanked him, but said pretty plainly that he would not work any harder than he had. Marcus Knowlton, on the other hand, was establishing himself as Holmes's rival in divided cases, perhaps hoping to be his successor. There were strained exchanges between the two men as Holmes tried to bring the court his way; Knowlton lobbied the justices and complained of Holmes's quick and occasionally high-handed manner of settling decisions.

Holmes gave careful attention to the mechanical details of command, as he had been trained to do long ago. He suggested that the judges should wear robes once again, in the British manner, and wrote to Horace Gray about it. Justices of the Supreme Court of the United States had always worn robes and Gray offered to lend his as a pattern.[9]

New York's court of appeals had recently resumed wearing robes, abandoned since the Revolution, and there had been much criticism in the newspapers of this aristocratic fashion. But Holmes thought that if he began quietly, it might pass off without much notice.

On the morning when the judges donned their robes for the first time, they were surprised to find they did not know how to put them on. When the chaplain arrived, he found them still in the conference room:

> I found a room full of dignified gentlemen wandering about in a bewildered fashion, some of them with their gowns still in their hands, one or two with their gowns put on askew. On my offering to help them, they were most grateful. I remember Judge Holmes saying, "Ah, an expert." Anyhow, I showed him and his confreres how to carry the ribbons across their chests and tie them behind, under the gown, so that they were able to march into court properly adorned.[10]

Holmes, despite his new authority, remained a minority of one on Constitutional questions and in labor cases.[11] But these did not seem to him the most important questions. He did not think of his court as a political branch of government. It was a common-law court, part of the world system of English-speaking courts in which the common law was slowly being evolved. His opinions in common-law cases, written with mastery, still swept his court along with him. As he told a Beverly neighbor, Mrs. Curtis: "We are smashing through the docket & everything is going with a whiz. . . . At such times I feel like Dr. Somebody who said that pure surgery was the highest pleasure of which the human mind was capable."[12]

When the Boston bar held a dinner in his honor, attended by the leaders of government and the bar, and by the justices of neighboring states, they stood and applauded him; and he spoke with moving frankness:

> I look into my book in which I keep a docket of the decisions of the full court which fall to me to write, and find about a thousand cases. A thousand cases, many of them on trifling or transitory matters, to represent nearly half a lifetime! A thousand cases, when one would have liked to study to the bottom and say his say on every question which the law has presented, and then go on and invent new problems which should be the test of doctrine, and then to generalize it all and write it in continuous, logical, philosophic exposition, setting forth the whole corpus with its roots in history and its justifications of expedience real or supposed! . . .

> The joy of life is to put out one's power in some natural or useful or harmless way. . . . The rule of joy and the law of duty seem to me all one.[13]

He and Fanny continued in the habits they had formed during the doctor's life, of going to the theater on Fridays, and dining out at the Parker House on Sundays. In June, they still moved their household to Beverly Farms for the summer. On their first wedding anniversary of the new century, Fanny left a note on Holmes's pillow:

> *My dearest Wendell*

> *All the things.*

> *Your loving wife*
> *Fanny*[14]

   In the afternoons at Beverly they went for drives in a carriage rented
from Wyatt & Trout's livery stable, driven as they had been for years by
George Larcom. On other days Holmes rode his bicycle or walked down
to the beach, or paid a call on old Cabot to talk philosophy. Once a week
he would visit Mrs. Curtis, or Mrs. Codman across the road, carrying a
bunch of roses from Fanny's garden.
   On Sundays there were often family visitors for early dinner. Two of
Fanny's sisters, and numerous cousins, nephews, and nieces, were
nearby. One Sunday afternoon, Fanny's sister Mary, her husband,
George Wigglesworth, Justice Horace Gray and his wife were there.
Holmes frowned when the dessert was carried in. He looked at Fanny
and said, "Dickie, is this stick-jaw?" Fanny admitted that it was. Holmes
nodded, picked up the dish of pudding, walked to the window, and
hurled it through the screen.[15]

   Life seems short — one's remaining friends few & solitude near
   — but I shall catch some new ones if necessary & generally I feel
   about as keen as I did at 20 & have a damned sight better time.[16]

Horace Gray, after twenty years on the Supreme Court, was plainly
close to retirement, and by tradition his replacement would be another
New Englander. President McKinley was certain to be reelected in November; Theodore Roosevelt, after only two years as governor of New
York, would be his vice president. If Holmes were ever to join the Supreme Court, it would be now.
   Overtures were made on behalf of various candidates for the seat,
perhaps including Holmes. But McKinley promised to appoint a Boston
lawyer, Alfred Hemenway, when Gray retired. If Holmes knew of this or
was distressed over it, he made no sign.
   It seemed that Holmes, not yet sixty, was settled in his place for life.
It was not likely there would be a second opening for a New Englander
on the Supreme Court while he was young enough to take it.
   Early in 1901, the war in South Africa was ending, and the Castletowns returned to Ireland, unhurt. Fanny encouraged Holmes to go
abroad that summer, as she knew he longed to do, and by June 30, he
was back in Mackellar's Hotel on Dover Street. Arthur Balfour was again
in a Conservative government; Holmes's Liberal friends — Bryce, Asquith — were in the opposition. But Holmes was not concerned with
politics. He saw his old law friends, long neglected, as well as Lucy Clifford, Ethel Grenfell, Margot Asquith. He saw Edna Bradley, whose
friend he had once proposed to follow to New York; Lady Burghclere,
Alice Stopford Green, and Nina Campbell.
   There was his customary dithering with Henry James over a weekend
visit. Since Holmes's last visit to England James had bought a house in

the village of Rye, seventy miles from London; he sent Holmes a telegram and three long letters about the visit.

> I greatly rejoice that your note, received this a.m., brings the
> question of your coming down here to a point. . . . Saturday 23d
> will do beautifully, as I wired you this a.m. — subject, as you say,
> to the other constant quantity, which, I trust, will not this time
> intervene. Let me meantime nourish you in the clear knowledge
> that you will find me utterly alone and unadorned. The 4.38 from
> Charing Cross is *the* train & you change for Rye at *Ashford*.[17]

Holmes spent three weeks at Doneraile.

It was raining when he arrived, and the damp and strain combined
to bring on a return of illness. He kept to his room and read a good deal
at first, but then there were walks with Lady Castletown and visits to the
conservatory. They were old friends, and now perhaps no more than
that.

By August 31, Holmes was back in Boston, and six days later, a senseless blow turned his world over. A man named Leon Czolgosz, an
anarchist, shot President McKinley as he visited an Exposition of
Pan-American Trade in Buffalo, New York. McKinley suffered for a
week and then died. Theodore Roosevelt, who was forty-three years old,
was summoned from a camping trip in the Adirondacks to become President of the United States.

For Holmes, it was another stroke of lightning. He saw immediately
that he might now expect appointment to the Supreme Court. Within
days, on October 14, 1901, he wrote to his cousin William Upham, with-
drawing from a business venture: "Reasons have arisen which I am not
at liberty to disclose." Holmes wrote to friends in London what he could
not say to anyone at home, that he might soon be called to Washington;
he spoke of his fear that his health would not stand the strain.[18] Cabot
Lodge turned down other aspirants by telling them that Holmes was his
candidate for Gray's seat. Lodge then wrote to the President, formally
proposing Holmes.[19]

The President answered that he was favorably disposed toward
Holmes, whom of course he knew well.[20]

Roosevelt liked to keep the management of all his affairs under his
own hat. This Supreme Court appointment was unusually important,
but when Horace Grace resigned in July the President consulted neither
George Hoar, the senior Massachusetts senator, chairman of the Judiciary Committee, nor the attorney general inherited from McKinley.

It was an important appointment because the Supreme Court, with
Gray gone, was evenly divided on the greatest issue facing it: the new
American colonies. Roosevelt had fought in Cuba and did not intend to
see legal niceties keep the United States from governing its empire.

The brown-skinned peoples of Puerto Rico and the Philippines, acquired in the Spanish War and now under American military government, had not been made citizens of the United States, could not vote in federal elections — and yet were subject to American taxes, most notably a tariff on sugar and tobacco. This open imperialism — so uncomfortably like British policy toward the American colonies — deeply offended many Americans and was bitterly attacked by William Jennings Bryan, who was again the Democratic candidate for President in 1900. Congress moved to extend the Bill of Rights to the new colonial subjects, but the power of protectionist senators from the South and Midwest was such that no legislation to govern the colonies could be passed unless it included tariffs on sugar and tobacco.

The constitutionality of these tariffs was challenged, and the question quickly went to the Supreme Court, where an adverse decision threatened to bring down the whole structure of empire.

In January, 1901, while McKinley was still alive and Horace Gray still sat on the Court, the justices heard four full days of argument on the question of the tariffs, and on May 27 delivered themselves of ten different opinions in four separate cases. Five justices voted to sustain the tariffs, but for different reasons, and four voted to strike them down. Finley Peter Dunne's Mr. Dooley remarked, "Mr. Justice Brown gave the opinion of the Court, and only eight other justices disagreed with him."

A stubborn minority of four justices, led by Chief Justice Fuller, said the Constitution applied to new territories as soon as they were acquired. A faction of three, led by Justice White, a former senator from Louisiana, who had led the fight in the Senate for the Sugar Tariff of 1894, said that the Constitution did not apply to the territories until Congress should act to bring them into the Union — which it had not done. Brown and Gray, the two remaining justices, struggled to find intermediate positions, but voted with White, to let the tariffs stand.[21]

Tangled and confused as the matter had become, Justice Brown was at least plain about its importance: "A false step at this time might be fatal to the development of what Chief Justice Marshall called the American Empire."[22]

The question was not finally settled; more challenges were heading toward the Court, and with Gray gone it stood evenly divided. The new justice would cast the deciding vote on imperialism.

Roosevelt was inclined toward Holmes, principally because Holmes's speech "The Soldier's Faith" had reassured him on this question. He liked Holmes's "mental attitude" as shown in that address, but he wanted to be certain, he told Lodge. Before filling this most important place on "the highest court of the entire civilized world," he wanted to know that Holmes would be a man of sound Republican principles:

[A] minority so large as to lack just one vote of being a majority
— have stood for such reactionary folly as would have hampered
well-nigh hopelessly this people in doing efficient and honorable
work for the national welfare, and for the welfare of the islands
themselves, in Porto Rico and the Philippines. . . .

Now I should like to know that Judge Holmes was in entire
sympathy with our views, that is with your views and mine and
Judge Gray's.[23]

Lodge called on Holmes, and verified that he was a good party man.
"I told the President you had always been a Republican," Lodge said
afterward, somewhat amused, "and never a Mugwump." Lodge then
assured the President that Holmes was safe on imperialism. "I would
not appoint my best beloved — unless he held the position you
describe."[24]

Holmes was at Beverly Farms, awaiting the outcome of these conversations. It had been some years since he had done any systematic reading. He idled, and rested. He read his friends' books. Owen Wister's
novel *The Virginian* was a best-seller that season. Brooks Adams sent him
The New Empire, gloomily prophesying state socialism and war. William
James sent *The Varieties of Religious Experience,* which Holmes read without much pleasure. There was the new sociology to keep up with. But
for his own satisfaction Holmes turned to Spinoza.[25]

At last came the invitation to Oyster Bay to see the President. On the
morning of July 25, Roosevelt and Holmes sat down together, the stocky
young President with his famous toothy grin, and the tall, slender judge
twenty years his senior. Roosevelt exerted himself to be flattering and
charming, and Holmes was flattered and charmed; Roosevelt offered the
Supreme Court appointment, and Holmes accepted.[26]

Only then did Roosevelt inform George Hoar. Senator Hoar was unhappy; he had a candidate of his own — his nephew Ebenezer Hoar —
and in any case it was a slight not to have been consulted, but the thing
was done, and Hoar made no open protest.[27] On August 11, Roosevelt
announced the nomination of Oliver Wendell Holmes, chief justice of
the Massachusetts Supreme Judicial Court, to the Supreme Court of the
United States.

There was no great stir in the country. The Senate was in recess. The
newspapers did not think Holmes would disturb the Puerto Rican decisions; the Democratic papers, which might have been critical on that
score, thought Holmes would be a friend of labor and so did not oppose
him. Outside Massachusetts, the editorial writers knew very little about
him and filled up their columns with amused remarks on his supposed
resemblance to his father. *The Nation* and the *New York Evening Post* commented sourly that Holmes was too literary, more brilliant than sound,[28]
a remark that stung.

There was blunt talk as to whether, at sixty-one, he was not too old for the post and might die before having served an adequate term, which indeed was Holmes's own fear. *McClure's* said that he was of long-lived stock and might be good for another fifteen years or more.[29] The *Boston Evening Transcript* was complacent and condescending. On balance, the *Transcript* thought, Holmes could not be so fine a judge as Horace Gray, but they were content to see him succeed Gray. As to Holmes's twenty years as a judge, they said only, "His striking originality of mind will help him when it does not hinder."[30] The memory of this condescension smarted for years.

His reward again came from friends. There were congratulatory letters from England, and Brandeis had written: "I trust that years enough may be given you to make the deep impression which you can upon Federal jurisprudence."[31]

Holmes answered gratefully: "For many years you have, from time to time, at critical moments, said things that have given me courage, which probably I remember better than you do. You do it again now, with the same effect and always with the same pleasure to me. I thank you."[32]

There were farewell addresses to give, in which Holmes was irresistibly reminded of his Civil War days, somewhat to the amusement of the younger members of the bar:

> We will not falter, we will not fail. We will reach the earthworks
> if we live, and if we fall we will leave our spirit in those who follow,
> and they will not turn back. All is ready. Bugler, blow the charge.[33]

Dixon Weston, a young nephew of Melville Fuller's, wrote to the chief justice the next day, "There is about to be a charge on your Court."[34]

Holmes and Fanny, at sixty-one, were moving away from Boston for the first time. Holmes began cleaning out desks, drawers, and closets of old letters, drafts of articles begun but abandoned. The process gave him a strange feeling of lightness:

> Burning old papers which have cumbered and annoyed one for
> thirty years, while it gives one for a moment a sigh of freedom,
> makes one feel a little later that it is the freedom of a cut flower
> — one little root in the past is gone.[35]

Fanny burned most of her embroideries, keeping only a few of her favorites. It was pointless to preserve them just so that nieces someday would store them in attics. Like Holmes, she was putting one life behind her and beginning another.

PART V

THE
MASTER
OF HIS ART

18

WASHINGTON, D.C.

THE CHIEF JUSTICE OF THE UNITED STATES, MELVILLE W. FULLER, was barely five feet tall. He used a footstool to keep his feet from dangling from his chair and wore his hair long and full on top. He had drooping mustaches and alert dark eyes.

Theodore Roosevelt, impatient and self-willed, wanted to offer Fuller's seat to William Howard Taft, the genial, well-liked viceroy of the Philippines. Taft was a potential rival for the presidential nomination in 1904, and the crucial Ohio state Republican convention was to be in June, 1903, only six months ahead. Taft, an Ohioan, might be endorsed by that convention. Roosevelt tried to persuade, and then to order, Taft to take a seat on the Supreme Court, without success. But Taft did want to be chief justice, and so Roosevelt tried with increasing impatience to open that place for him. Anonymous stories appeared in the newspapers that Melville Fuller was too old and would soon retire. After this had gone on for a while, Fuller said, "I am not going to be paragraphed out of my place."[1]

He had grown up in Maine, but had settled in Chicago. When Holmes gave an address at the Northwestern Law School, Fuller quietly saw that he would receive a warm reception and had even taken the trouble to write to a legal newspaper to suggest an item: "A Compliment to Chief Justice Holmes."[2]

Fuller now planned for Holmes's arrival in Washington. The Court was shorthanded and had been falling behind its docket since Horace Gray's resignation. Justice George Shiras, who had reached the age of seventy — with ten years' service, a justice could retire on full pay at seventy — announced that he, too, would leave the Court in a few weeks. The Court would be reduced to seven members, but Senator Hoar's Judiciary Committee had not yet acted on Holmes's nomination. Hoar was still annoyed and, though he could not oppose, he might delay, Senate confirmation. Fuller asked Hoar for prompt action, and then announced a dinner party at his own house in Holmes's honor on December 9, 1902, to which Fuller invited the President, the other justices, and leading members of the Senate. (The President, amused but not caring to worsen things with Hoar, declined.) Hoar, peppered from all sides, reported Holmes's nomination to the Senate, and on December 4, it was unanimously confirmed. But Hoar could not restrain a malicious note to Fuller:

> We have contributed from New England some very tough oak timbers to the bench, State and National. Our lawyers in general, especially those in the country, do not think carved ivory is likely to be as strong or enduring, although it may seem more ornamental.
>
> I trust you will not think me guilty of indecency, in telling you, in strict confidence, what is on my mind.[3]

And so the capital city prepared in characteristic fashion for Holmes's arrival, with maneuverings of which he knew nothing.

On Thursday, December 4, as soon as word of the Senate's confirmation arrived, Fanny went to Washington and rented a furnished house at 10 Lafayette Place, just across Pennsylvania Avenue from the White House. Holmes remained in Boston, finishing his work at the Supreme Judicial Court, and spent Thursday night at the Grays'. On Friday, he said good-bye at the court, gave to Nina Gray the manuscript of his last address, and tore himself away from Boston. Accompanied by his messenger, James Doherty, Holmes went to Washington.[4]

While Boston had been moderate, cool, brick and gray stone, Washington was tropical, brilliant, and complex. Holmes stepped from the railroad station onto broad Pennsylvania Avenue, which lay extended before him. Far to the left was the White House, freshly repainted by Roosevelt; far to the right, on the crest of a low hill, was the Capitol. The crowds on Pennsylvania Avenue were black and white and brown and yellow. Holmes had not seen black faces in numbers since the war.

Washington was still a Southern city, under Northern occupation. It was the capital of an empire, and yet it was quiet, almost rural. The houses were low and graceful, with French and Palladian fronts. The side streets were broad and shaded by trees: "The whole place is like a large country town from the absence of large business and manufactories. One sees and hears crows (which I adore) and wild birds light and sing."[5]

Holmes was met at the Pennsylvania Station by John Craig, who had been Horace Gray's messenger and would now be his. Craig politely suggested that it was customary for newly appointed justices to call on the President as soon as they arrived. Holmes sent Doherty to the New Willard Hotel with his bags — the old white-painted Willard Hotel near the White House, where Holmes had been refused a room during the war, had been replaced by a grand New Willard, an immense pile of brick in the French provincial style, capped with mansard roofs — while Holmes went to leave his card at the White House.[6] The house Fanny had rented was still being put in order; they would stay at the New Willard until it was ready.

On Monday morning, December 8, 1902, just before noon, Holmes rode up to the Capitol and mounted the broad stairs to the entrance.

A corridor ran along the axis of the Capitol building. At the south end, it was filled with men hurrying among the bustling offices of the House of Representatives. The north corridor led to the relative calm and dignity of the Senate. Where the freestone walls that marked the old part of the building ended, an undistinguished door led to the courtroom in the old Senate chamber. Across the hallway was the clerk of the Court's cramped office and the robing room.

Holmes went to the robing room, where the justices were gathered. Chief Justice Fuller administered the first of the two oaths Holmes would take. Here in privacy he took the loyalty oath required of federal office-holders since the Civil War, swearing that he had not taken up arms against the United States government. This done, the nine justices in their voluminous black robes walked across the hallway to their courtroom. A policeman in the corridor said, "Stand back! Stand back!" Passersby stood against the walls, waiting, as the justices went by.

They were an oddly assorted procession, led by an elderly marshal of the Court in a frock coat, followed by the chief justice. Behind him strode John Marshall Harlan of Kentucky, bald, clean-shaven, jut-jawed, broad-shouldered, and irascible, a foot taller than the chief justice. Then followed David Brewer and Henry Brown, genteel New Englanders who had been friends at Yale, had gone west in their youth, and had served on courts in Kansas and Michigan. Behind them, a great bear of a man, Edward D. White of the Catholic aristocracy of New Orleans, who had joined in the rebellion, and who had fought also against Reconstruction; he had served in the Senate and had been a commanding presence there as on the Court.

Then followed George Shiras, the Pennsylvanian who was waiting to retire, and Joseph McKenna, wiry, intense, the son of Irish immigrants who had followed the gold rush to California. Behind him was white-haired Rufus Peckham, whose family had lived in Albany, New York, since the seventeenth century.

Last in order of seniority, and one of the youngest members of the Court, Holmes walked rather stiffly, looking over the heads before him. He stood very straight. His hair was still dark, just beginning to turn white; his mustache was white and bristling; a stiff standing collar rose almost to his chin. He followed the justices across the corridor and into the courtroom.

The chamber was a reminder of an earlier age. It was not very large by the standards of the new empire, but the high domed ceiling gave it a spacious air. It was painted pale gray and pale blue. The justices sat behind a long bench on a dais, and behind them stood a row of marble columns. A red velvet canopy topped by a golden eagle with outspread wings hung over the center of the bench, where the chief justice took his seat. There were tables for counsel, the clerk, the reporter of the Court, and the news services; reporters for the daily newspapers had to take seats among the spectators, of whom there were rarely very many.

At noon, when the justices entered, Holmes stood in front of the bench, while the others took their places behind it. The marshal called the room to order: "Oyez! Oyez! Oyez! God save the United States and this Honorable Court!"

The chief justice announced that Holmes had been nominated by the President and confirmed by the Senate, and asked the clerk to read the commission. He then administered the second oath, the oath of judicial office. Holmes solemnly swore that he would faithfully and impartially perform all of his duties.

The marshal then escorted him to the vacant seat at the left end of the bench, but first, Holmes reached beneath his gown and took out a sheet of paper, and handed it to the court reporter. It was the text of a telegram to the governor of Massachusetts, resigning as chief justice.[7]

The Court held its session from noon until two, and then adjourned for half an hour, while the justices ate a hurried lunch brought to them by their messengers in their conference room, the old courtroom down-stairs. The conference room was windowless and overheated, furnished with spittoons and perpetually filled with cigar smoke. A few tattered volumes announced that the room served also as the Court's library. The justices returned to the bench at 2:30 and heard arguments until 4:00. The courtroom, too, was close and overheated, and the only windows were hidden by the draperies behind the bench. The older justices drowsed.

Each party in a case was given two hours for oral argument, and more time was given for important cases, so that a single matter might be argued for two or three days. The long arguments were difficult to attend to, especially in the drowsy afternoons. The justices occasionally enlivened the arguments by interrupting or asking questions. In a case of less than compelling interest, one of the justices might be correcting proof sheets, another writing a letter, another whispering to one of his colleagues, while still another had the habit of walking back and forth in the space behind the seats of his associates.[8]

The lawyers read portions of the record aloud, and read extended passages from cases they cited as precedent. The justices rarely took notes at oral argument, however, and relied on their memories and the lawyers' written briefs. White and Harlan had particularly acute memories, and White had difficulty writing. He could write only in a contorted posture, with his right index finger beside his nose, the pen clasped in the remaining fingers of his right hand, his head bent almost to the paper.[9]

On the afternoon of the day that Holmes took his seat, the Court heard arguments in the case of Louisville and Jefferson Ferry Company against the State of Kentucky.[10] Alexander Pope Humphrey, counsel for the ferry company, wearing the customary swallowtail coat and striped gray trousers, stood before the bench and explained that his client's ferries ran across the Ohio River from Louisville, Kentucky, to Jeffersonville, Indiana. The State of Kentucky had levied a tax on the ferry company's assets, including a tax on the franchise for ferry service that Indiana had given it. This Kentucky tax on property in Indiana was unreasonable and unjust: it followed that Kentucky had taken the ferry company's property without the due process of law guaranteed by the Fourteenth Amendment to the Constitution of the United States.

Holmes took careful written notes of the argument, as he had for many years.

At 4 P.M., as usual, the Court adjourned and Holmes walked down Capitol Hill to Pennsylvania Avenue, and north in the winter twilight to the New Willard. He had not rested since adjourning his court in Boston, and he was tired from his journey to Washington. He suffered from his old pains in neck and shoulder, and had come down with a bad cold.[11] But John Craig brought to his hotel room the printed briefs and records of proceedings in the lower courts for the cases that were being heard by the Supreme Court, and Holmes plunged into them excitedly. "Egotism vanishes in the great business to be done. I hope I may do my share nobly, but It not I is the thing one thinks of."[12]

The justices had no chambers; Congress had not troubled to leave room for them in the Capitol but instead had given each justice an allowance to buy books and furniture and to keep an office in his house. Until the rented house on Lafayette Square was ready, Holmes would have to work in his hotel room. He read records and briefs in the morning, and then at 11:30 he walked up to the Capitol, joined the other justices in the robing room, and took his seat with them at noon. All afternoon, they heard arguments; then they returned to their homes for more briefs and records, motion papers, and petitions. The Court held conferences on Saturdays, and on Monday mornings announced its decisions and heard motions.

Holmes was stretched to his limit. The cases involved new questions and the procedures were unfamiliar. "I feel like asking my omniscient black [the messenger, Craig] what a writ of error brings up in the case before me."[13] The lawyers here were the leading counsel of New York and Philadelphia, at home in this courtroom and accustomed to great national affairs. Large sums of money, great political questions, and new principles of law were often at issue. The justices' questions and the casual talk in the conference room showed a quick apprehension of questions that Holmes arrived at only with difficulty. At first, he felt as if he were among demigods with huge heads and big faces, who understood everything with diabolic swiftness.[14]

Each Saturday, the Court held its conference in the windowless old courtroom downstairs. The chief justice presided tactfully, sitting between the great bulks of Harlan of Kentucky and White of Louisiana, who did not get on with each other very well. The Chief brought up each case that had been argued in the past week, gave a brief summary, and added his thoughts. The associate justices, beginning with Harlan and continuing in declining order of seniority, commented in turn, Holmes speaking last. Holmes brought with him and relied upon for these discussions his detailed notes of the oral arguments. If there was disagreement, they would talk further, and the Chief would try to draw them into consensus. When they had all formed an opinion, they voted, beginning with Holmes and progressing in reverse order back to the chief justice. Each justice kept a docket book in which he recorded the votes of all the justices on every case, and on Saturday night the chief justice would send around a slip by messenger, showing which justice he had assigned to write the opinion in each.[15]

In most of the cases there was little discussion or disagreement. The larger number were appeals from lower courts, which the Supreme Court was obliged to hear[16] but of which they had no trouble disposing in routine opinions. But there was a steady stream of important and difficult cases on which the justices might differ. They were strong-willed men accustomed to rule in their own spheres, and "they were from a generation which regarded a difference of opinion as a cockfight and often left a good deal to be desired in point of manners."[17]

The house on Lafayette Place at last was ready. Across Lafayette Square were the houses that Henry Adams and John Hay had built when Clover Adams was still alive and where Adams now lived on alone. No. 10 was small and there was not enough room for formal entertaining, nor for most of their books and furniture, but Holmes now had at least a working library and a place to read.

To his mind's eye a wide landscape had opened, a new geography stretching from the Caribbean island colonies across the continent, across older territories and Indian lands, to the Pacific Ocean and thousands of miles still farther to Hawaii, Alaska and the Philippines. The Supreme Court heard cases from every state and territory and colony. The diversity of this vast realm and the wild variety of cases coming to his new court astonished Holmes. There were ordinary commercial disputes, of a familiar kind, and the relentless, ubiquitous suits against railroads for personal injuries. From the Western territories and the District of Columbia, from Alaska and Hawaii and the Philippines came appeals from criminal defendants convicted in federal courts. There were suits and claims against the federal government itself, each of which was entitled to an appeal to the Supreme Court. The Court heard argument in a suit for $310.37 against the Interstate Commerce Commission. From the lower federal courts rose up a cloud of appeals and writs of error from bankrupts and their creditors. There was a suit by an Indian tribe to keep the Department of the Interior from granting oil drilling rights on their land, and a suit from Alaska over territorial fees. Patents and copyrights were challenged, trademarks were defended. The postmaster general impounded the mail of the Magnetic Healing Society on the ground that it was perpetrating a fraud. The superintendent of a federal mint was found to have a deficit in his accounts of $25,000.

> The variety and novelty to me of the questions, the remote spaces from which they come, the amount of work they require, all help the effect. . . . I have heard conflicting mining claims in Arizona and whether a granite quarry is "Minerals" . . . and fifty other things as remote from each other as these.[18]

> Great affairs are so absorbing — they so swallow your personality that everything seems different. . . . All my interest and energy have been taken up in this mighty panorama of cases from every part of our great empire involving great interests, raising questions I never have heard of, argued by the strongest men the country can show.[19]

Rising above the jumble of ordinary disputes were the cases on Constitutional law. These were not the intellectual puzzles in which Holmes had gloried in the past, but great practical questions of government. Over and over again, indeed, a single great question was asked, the terrible question that he had once offered his life to answer, the question of the federal government's power over the states.

The broad commands of the federal Constitution were easily invoked. In many criminal cases in state courts, and in many civil trials, the losing party could claim that proper procedures had not been followed, or that the state's laws themselves were unreasonable, and that due process of law — guaranteed by the Fourteenth Amendment — therefore had not been observed. Everywhere state governments were adopting laws to regulate banks and railroads, grain elevators, and public utilities. It was nearly always possible for these companies to find, with sufficient ingenuity, some argument claiming that the federal Constitution had been violated, and so to gain a series of appeals in federal courts. The Supreme Court was therefore obliged to hear — and the states often were obliged to delay the enforcement of their laws during the appeal — dozens of cases every term, hundreds in recent years,[20] in which the most serious possible question was repeatedly raised.

> Since I have been here the novelty solemnity and augustness of the work has made my past labors seem a closed volume locked up in a distant safe. Thoughts of self are almost forgotten and it is just a concentrated effort to do one's part as a wheel in a tremendous machine.[21]

Dozens of times in each term, convicted criminals, not denying the fact of their crime — most often murder — filed appeals claiming that the trials in which they had been convicted were so badly conducted, or questions of law so arbitrarily decided, evidence favorable to them so unfairly excluded, that "due process of law" had been denied. Despite the gravity of the issues involved, and although lives often depended on the outcome, the legal arguments were repetitious and often frivolous. In dozens more cases, railroads and banks fought every trivial state tax and regulation to the last Court, and when all else had failed made the same claim — that the tax or regulation was so unfair or so arbitrary as to have denied them due process of law. As other grounds failed, the Constitutional claims were urged with growing passion and self-righteousness.

These Constitutional claims were usually based on the Fourteenth Amendment, passed and ratified in 1868, which had authorized the Reconstruction of the South. The Fourteenth Amendment said, "nor shall any State deprive any person of life, liberty or property without due process of law; nor deny to any person within its jurisdiction the equal protection of the laws."

Federal power was exercised in gingerly fashion by a generation for whom talk of civil war was not empty bluster. The Supreme Court steadily held that the Fourteenth Amendment gave only modest and limited protection to claims of civil rights or property rights. State laws and state proceedings, although harsh and discriminatory, would pass review under the Fourteenth Amendment unless they were grossly unreasonable.

A minority of the Court did cling to a radical view of the Fourteenth Amendment. David Brewer, occasionally joined by Henry Brown (his fellow at Yale), Rufus Peckham, or John Harlan, dissented repeatedly, saying that the federal government was charged by the Fourteenth Amendment with defending the most expansive claims of liberty and property. But Melville Fuller and Edward White held a steady majority for moderation. They gave the federal government its due for victory in the war, but they did not think the Constitution therefore enshrined all the rights claimed by the victors.

Despite this strong majority view, hopeful petitioners continued to stream into the Court with their claims of liberty and property. They were entitled to an appeal so long as they could find a Constitutional claim, and the attorneys for railroads and banks and many criminal defendants felt entitled to use every appeal available. And so the cases came. The Missouri, Kansas and Tennessee Railroad complained that its constitutional right to due process and equal protection of the laws had been violated by a twenty-five-dollar penalty in Texas for allowing weeds — Johnson grass — to go to seed on its railbed.[22]

It was easier to dismiss such cases than to explain why. The justices had been accustomed to develop elaborate procedural arguments, especially in criminal cases, to bar such trivial or baseless suits. When all the procedural hurdles had nevertheless been overcome, the Court would deliver rationales that somehow failed to persuade.

To such cases, Holmes brought his magnificent gift of frank expression: "Great Constitutional provisions must be administered with caution. Some play must be allowed for the joints of the machine."[23]

Chief Justice Fuller eagerly seized on Holmes's facility in writing opinions, and made Holmes the spokesman for the majority,[24] as he would remain for twenty years:

My way of writing a case is to get into a spasm over it.[25]

At the end of each week a case is assigned to me and by Monday morning I am in a delirium, if as is often true the case is important and interesting, and work until I go to Court and then walk back and work again until dinner time. It is dyspeptic but thrilling.[26]

There were legitimate principles on both sides in every Constitutional case, even if the principles sometimes had been stretched beyond reason. On one side, liberty or property; on the other, the state's power to govern. It decided nothing to call the principles on one side "rights." Holmes had long been fond of saying that general propositions did not decide concrete cases. "You can't carry out constitutional provisions to their logical extremes."[27] Constitutional rights, like the rights and duties of the common law, had no independent existence. They were created by a system of law that recognized conflicting rights and obligations. In each case it was the judges' job to say where the boundary between conflicting claims would fall, and these judgments would eventually mark out a line. It was the task of the judge to find objective grounds in precedent and social policy by which to choose between competing principles — and, above all, to make his choice consciously and to express the true reasons for his decision.

Where were objective principles to be found? For Holmes, the answer lay in the common law.

The power of the states to enact laws was as limitless as that of Britain's Parliament, except where it encountered specific prohibitions in the Constitution. These prohibitions were few and general. "Due process of law" had to be observed — among other things, this meant that laws must in some fundamental sense be reasonable. This limitation was to be understood more fully by looking not at the bare words themselves, nor at what the authors of the Constitution may have thought, but at principles established by the decisions of the courts.

Due process of law, Holmes said in his first opinion for the Court, embodied "only fundamental rules of right, as generally understood by all English-speaking communities."[28]

The federal government would interpose its power on behalf of individuals in their struggles with state power — but only when fundamental rules of right were touched. The Court would consult, not its members' private ideas of justice and right, but the decisions of the courts of the English-speaking world, to determine what was fundamental. Constitutional law was part of the system of judge-made common law to which Holmes had devoted his life.[29]

He had written his first opinion, but the Court did not pause in its work. Briefs and petitions streamed into the justices' hands; arguments continued day after day. Cattle were driven through Wyoming to Nebraska, grazing en route; were they, while grazing, still in interstate commerce and so exempt from Wyoming's tax? An Illinois statute taxed inheritances of lineal descendants but not those passing to collateral heirs; had the state deprived the lineal heirs of equal protection of the laws? Could Iowa punish a banker's crime, despite federal regulation of the nationally chartered bank? The cases grew in complexity and profusion.

At the close of arguments on Friday, December 18, 1902, the Court adjourned for two weeks, to give the justices time to write opinions. Holmes happily reported to the chief justice that he had already written his first opinion, and was ready for more assignments. After their conference on Saturday, the Chief assigned to him two more opinions.[30] He paused for a moment to write to Mrs. Curtis:

[Sunday,] December 21, 1902

Now I am in our temporary house — looking out on Lafayette Square — the White House just across the road — wonderfully convenient and sufficiently comfortable. I have begun to get the hang of the work. I think I can do my share all right. I am in better health — and I begin to be cheerful. I wrote my first decision this last week and yesterday at 11 sent it to the printer. When I got home the proofs were waiting. I shall have nine copies of the corrected thing tomorrow and give them to the other gents to pick at. For the first time in my life I have had flashes of a sense of responsibility. You know that I always said one should not have — One should think about the question — to feel responsibility is to let steam out of the boiler — egotism in disguise — but things here are so solemn and tremendous that the thought will break in at times.[31]

The chief justice, White, Brown, and McKenna all told him promptly and with flattering words that they approved what he had written in his first opinion, and would not ask for changes, so that he was assured of a majority.[32] And then the President of the United States invited him to dinner. Holmes was as excited as a boy.

Dear Chief Justice

Or ought I have said Mr. Chief Justice? I enclose another opinion and have my third nearly ready. I have not heard from Harlan, Brewer, Shiras or Peckham JJ as to 41, Otis v. Parker. I suppose I am to do nothing until the next conference? Mr. J. Harlan to be sure said on the day that he received it that he had read it and I understood him to agree — I also want to consult you as to what we are to do on New Year's Day as to the President. But perhaps I shall hear from him on Tuesday as I believe we are to dine and go to the play with him on that day. I cannot tell you how much I am impressed by and enjoy the work here.

With much respect,
Sincerely yours,
O.W. Holmes[33]

Two more of his opinions were approved by his brethren, this time unanimously, and again with praise.

I am beginning to gain confidence. The brethren seem to like what I have written so far and I feel as if it should count for more than merely one vote. . . . But I tell you this is a center of great forces and with all the obvious shortcomings of this country you must be powerful on a world scale to weigh here.[34]

The work is hard and absorbing — oh how absorbing. It is more filling to the imagination than I dreamed. The men here may not be very strong on the philosophy or history of the law, but the abler ones administer it as statesmen governing an empire. The variety of great questions, the diversity, even geographical, the tremendous importance of what we do, everything, makes it seem the beginning of a new life on a different plane —[35]

The work of the past seems a finished book — locked up far away, and a new and solemn volume opens.[36]

19

SMILES
AND LIES

W HEN THE COURT RETURNED FROM ITS HOLIDAY RECESS, THE
attorney general, Philander Knox, presented resolutions on
the recent death of Horace Gray. The chief justice responded movingly. Fanny was in the audience, as was the First Lady,
Edith Kermit Roosevelt.

Holmes was to make his debut that morning. When the remem-
brances of Gray were completed, he read aloud the three Constitutional
opinions he had written for the Court.[1] They were short enough to be
read in their entirety, and he read them well in his practiced tenor.

That afternoon, Fanny for the first time was "at home" in the rented
house on Lafayette Square and found herself nearly swamped by callers,
including, she thought, two female newspaper reporters who did not
identify themselves.[2] Her debut, like Holmes's, was handled modestly
and well.

Holmes was writing swiftly and easily, and asked the chief justice to
assign still more opinions to him. He got them, and he began to be embroiled in the disputes among the justices, where tempers were hot.

They disagreed violently about a case from Kentucky. A traveling circus had copied an advertising poster, added their name, and distributed
thousands of the posters without paying the copyright owners for the

privilege. The copyright holders, Donaldson Lithographing Company, sued.

The circus owners cheerfully took advantage of their bad reputation, and argued that the posters — outline drawings of circus animals and young women in tights — had no artistic merit, and therefore were not protected by the copyright laws.

Holmes, who had drawn advertising cards for the Hasty Pudding Club, wrote the opinion in a single breath:

> I fired off a decision upholding the cause of low art and decid- ing that a poster for a circus representing décolletés and fat legged ballet girls could by copyrighted. Harlan, that stout old Kentuck- ian, not exactly an esthete, dissented for high art.[3]

When Harlan disagreed with Holmes, he sometimes lost his temper, but Holmes never lost his. Holmes called him "My lion-hearted friend." When Harlan was haranguing, Holmes coolly interrupted, "That won't wash." In the silence that followed, as Harlan grew apoplectic, the chief justice interposed himself gently, making a gesture as if at a washboard, and said, "Still I keep scrubbing and scrubbing."

Holmes invited Mrs. Roosevelt to the court to hear his opinion in the copyright case, of which he was quite proud. The next day, the *Chicago Herald-Record* had a cartoon of Holmes in his judicial robes, pointing with a stick to one of numerous sketches of high-kicking women on the wall, with the legend "The Supreme Court says they are all right."[4] Fanny began a new scrapbook, in which she pasted the cartoon, the first of many.

In February, the Court was again hotly divided, over the power of Congress to make lotteries a crime. There was a craze for lotteries. The Pan American Lottery Company sold twenty-five-cent tickets for monthly drawings supposedly held in Asunción, Paraguay; the company itself was in Fresno, California. The Louisiana Lottery Company, driven out of that state after it had corrupted its governments for a generation — Justice White had first come to prominence in the state by leading the struggle against the lottery — was now calling itself the Honduras Lot- tery and doing business through the mails, from Chicago, in the very states from which it had been barred. Many states forbade gambling, but the interstate lotteries had escaped their reach. Congress accordingly passed a statute making it a federal crime to send lottery tickets across state lines. Lottery companies were prosecuted, and promptly challenged the constitutionality of the law.

This was a new venture for the federal government into regulation of public morality. The Constitution gave Congress power to regulate "commerce" among the states, and the framers of the Constitution per- haps thought of nothing more than keeping the channels of trade open.

But the language of the Constitution and the traditions of the Supreme Court had given Congress broad authority over the flow of goods across state lines. Perhaps none of the drafters of the Constitution imagined that Congress would eventually use its power to prohibit, rather than to free, commerce between the states, or that copies of lottery tickets would be found to be goods in commerce at all. But the Court so held.

Not without difficulty. A minority — led by Brewer and Peckham — saw that the power to prohibit lotteries would allow the federal government to meddle almost without limit in the life of the country. The conference at which the Lottery case was discussed was more than usually violent: "[Peckham's] major premise was God damn it. . . . a good man, faithful, of real feeling — and a master of Anglo-Saxon monosyllabic interjections."[5]

To Brewer and Peckham, the law against lotteries promised a cataclysm, a revolution against economic liberty, a revolution in the form of government,[6] as perhaps it did.

Harlan, championing the cause of morality, was equally violent on the other side. White, more courtly but no less decided, brought two other justices with him in support of federal power — and Holmes quietly made the deciding vote. He thought the law foolish but did not doubt that Congress had power to enact it.

As the dissenters had warned, a stream of federal regulatory statutes quickly began to flow: pure food and drug laws, meat inspection laws, a plant quarantine act, the White Slave Act — prohibiting travel across state lines for immoral purposes — the Warehouse Act, the Grain Standards Act, the Serums and Toxins Act, labor legislation, and eventually, a statute prohibiting commerce in the products of child labor. By this decision, a new federal police power was unleashed, whose limits had not yet been glimpsed, limits that Holmes would try to set twenty-five years later.

When the Court adjourned at 4:00, Holmes and Edward White walked home together, past the railroad station, the public market, and the famous political saloons on Pennsylvania Avenue, to Lafayette Square. White then went on alone to his comfortable brick Victorian house on Rhode Island Avenue.

"White and I are getting to be pals," Holmes said.[7] He and the big Southerner talked freely and cordially as they walked. White was a scholar of the civil law — the Napoleonic Code having been to Louisiana what the English common law was to Massachusetts — and was at ease in Latin, Frènch, and Spanish, fluent also in political stories of Washington and Louisiana. It was of White as well as Fuller that Holmes had spoken when he said that the abler of his colleagues were statesmen.

When the Court recessed for two weeks in February to write opinions, Holmes clamored to be assigned more cases. The case assigned to him on Saturday he had usually written by Monday or Tuesday, and he sent corrected copies to his brethren by Wednesday, even when the Court was hearing oral arguments. A few days into their recess he was free for more work, and peppered Fuller with impatient little notes:

> I am on my last case barring the one you told me not to write until further notice . . . if you will give me some of yours I shall be grateful. . . .
> P.S. I shall finish the last tomorrow. If there are two more weeks — I can write almost any old thing that anyone will give me. A case doesn't generally take more than two days if it does that.[8]

Despite the great distance he had traveled, Holmes found that he was again a member of what was fundamentally a common-law court; he brought to the work the accumulated knowledge and skills of forty years:

> I don't believe in the long opinions which have been almost the rule here. I think that to state the case shortly and the ground of decision as concisely and delicately as you can is the real way. That is the English fashion and I think it civilized. Then I try each week when we are sitting to turn off my case, and to announce it the following Monday. I think it pleases the chief who as Executive Officer likes to get the work done.[9]

Fuller, indeed, was immensely pleased, both with the quality of Holmes's work — whenever the messenger brought one of Holmes's opinions, Fuller set down what he was doing to read it, and would exclaim with pleasure as he read — and with the sheer number of cases Holmes handled.

> We shall dispose of more than fifty cases at our next meeting — more than ever before I believe. . . . The Nimble Holmes has got out his last — I delayed his progress for about a week but he . . . I suppose [is] eager for more work.[10]

If the Chief was pleased, he was also troubled by criticisms of Holmes's style. Holmes's opinions had always been easy to read but difficult to understand. They flowed on in a conversational way, but distinct points were difficult to isolate and questions were presented in a kind of mosaic that one took in as a whole. It was an art form peculiar to Holmes. Fuller had begun to make marginal criticisms on Holmes's opinions and to speak to him privately about the need to give more ample explanations. Holmes took the criticisms in good humor, but he could not do otherwise than to pursue his craft as he understood it. He had a new edition of his speeches printed up that summer, and he sent a copy to Fuller, with a little note that said he could drool on at length when the occasion suited. Fuller answered this with his usual tact: "I shall endeavor to take the lesson to heart that what is elevating and appropriate in the one case may be 'drooling' in the other."[11]

And indeed Fuller admired Holmes's literary talents. He often consulted Holmes on questions of style or asked for Holmes's criticisms.

On February 24, when the Court returned from its recess, briefs were submitted in the case of *Giles v. Harris,* in which a group of black men demanded that they be added to the voter registration lists of Alabama.

Giles and his fellow plaintiffs had tried to register to vote in the last Congressional election, in November, 1902. The Alabama county registrars had refused to put their names down; all over the state, blacks were being refused. On January 1, 1903, a new state constitution went into effect and imposed stringent new qualifications for voters — unless they had previously been registered.

Alabama was joining a wave of reaction sweeping through the South. The Reconstruction constitutions had guaranteed freed slaves the right to vote, and they had voted in large numbers, although the voting procedures and the governments were often deeply corrupt. In 1890, Mississippi adopted a new constitution in which a series of tests and qualifications were imposed that the former slaves could not meet. Congress, dominated by white Southern delegations, in 1894 removed the last vestige of federal presence in the former Confederacy by repealing the statute that required federal oversight of elections. Other Southern states then followed Mississippi's lead, and the black electorate shrank almost to zero. Forty years after the Civil War the federal army at last withdrew in defeat from the South.

But surely the federal Constitution prohibited racial discrimination in voting. Wilfrid Smith, counsel for the black Alabamians, wrote in his brief to the Court:

> The purpose the [Alabama constitutional] convention had in view in framing the provisions on suffrage and elections was to invent a scheme by which to disenfranchise the Negroes without disenfranchising a single white man.[12]

Smith asked the Court to issue an injunction ordering the state registrars to enter the plaintiffs' names on the voter registration lists.

The state of Alabama's attorney general, in his brief, did not deny that under the old state constitution blacks had been prevented from registering for no better reason than that they were black. That was past. Under the new constitution, tests were equally applied: anyone descended from a veteran of American wars, or who could pass literacy tests and tests of good character — or who had voted in previous elections — was eligible to register: "The constitution of Alabama applies, it is admitted, a test which will exclude with many whites, the mass of the negro population from the privilege of voting."[13]

But there was no discrimination by race now. And in any case, whatever the facts of the matter, Alabama said, the case was beyond the power of the Court to decide; for no federal court could issue orders to a state government in political matters.

> The object of this suit is to restrain the operations of the state government for the assertion and vindication of a political right to be an elector. . . . it is wholly beyond the province of a court of equity by its decrees to interfere with the ordinary operations of government, as here proposed.[14]

This last was a proposition for which the state could cite substantial authority, including previous decisions of the Supreme Court of the United States. At their next conference, it appeared that a majority of the Court accepted this argument. Holmes was among them.

The chief justice assigned the opinion to Holmes, perhaps to ensure its prompt issue, and perhaps also to show that even the Massachusetts justice agreed.

Holmes wrote, as usual, briefly and to the point. The Constitution did not allow federal suits against state governments by their citizens, and even if the suit could be heard, the relief that was asked would require not a judgment but an army.

> This is alleged to be a conspiracy of a State, although the State is not and could not be made a party. . . . The circuit court has no constitutional power to control [the state's] action by any direct means. And if we leave the State out of consideration, the court has as little practical power to deal with the people of the State in a body. The [plaintiffs charge] that the great mass of the white population intends to keep the blacks from voting. To meet such an intent something more than ordering the plaintiffs' name to be inscribed upon the lists of 1902 will be needed. If the conspiracy and the intent exist, a name on a piece of paper will not defeat them. Unless we are prepared to supervise the voting in the state by officers of the Court, it seems to us that all the plaintiff could get from equity would be an empty form. . . . [R]elief from a great political wrong, if done as alleged, by the people of a State and the State itself, must be given by them or by the legislative and political departments of the government of the United States.[15]

Holmes's opinion drew angry dissents from Harlan and Brewer. Indeed, Holmes seemed to have departed from his own usual standard of duty and had allowed his own bitter experience of war to color his judgment.

A few years before, David Brewer had written an opinion for the Court concerning an injunction issued against a labor union to end a Pullman strike:

> The strong arm of the National Government may be put forth to brush away all obstructions. . . . If the emergency arises, the army of the Nation and all of its militia, are at the service of the Nation to compel obedience to its laws.[16]

Holmes himself had written, time and again, that all law ultimately rested on the power of courts to summon the armed force of the state. Yet, his opinion seemed to say, so far as black suffrage was concerned, there was no federal law and no national government. George Hoar was openly contemptuous, and told the newspapers that this opinion was worse than the Dred Scott Case.

Holmes did not agonize, but neither, for once, was he entirely open.

> The importance of the things we have to deal with makes me shudder from time to time but I don't lie awake over them — and try to think of them merely as problems to be handled in just the same way whether they involve $25 — or the welfare of a state or a people.[17]

Fanny found a house for sale, at 1720 I Street. They had looked at Horace Gray's former house, now for sale by his widow, but she was asking too much. The house on I Street, just west of Lafayette Square, suited them, and they decided to buy it. Fanny immediately plunged into the renovation of the house and preparations for their move. There were an architect and contractors to arrange for, renovations to design, decorations to choose: "I hope my wife will have more amusement in making it charming than in going out to dinner or rushing about madly returning calls on people she doesn't know."[18]

Fanny indeed had been consumed by social duties. Although her inclination was always to remain solitary, and she avoided being photographed or interviewed, she threw herself as duty required into the elaborate formalities of Washington society. Holmes watched with bemusement: "The women have got up a good deal of formalism as to calling, etc.," he remarked.[19]

Fanny's Monday afternoons at home were well attended. The stream of more or less official callers continued unabated, and Fanny with cheerful energy returned them. Dinner invitations followed. There were regular invitations from the White House, and after dinner with the President and First Lady, Holmes and Fanny often accompanied

Mrs. Roosevelt to the theater; the President did not care for it as a general rule. The Holmeses became known as intimates of the President — Holmes sensed a degree of resentment from those less favored — which helped Fanny in her efforts to establish a social position. It was a task that required not only energy, but patience, which Holmes sometimes lacked:

> Rum stickling of timid meticulosity — I hear of one Senator's wife who was offended that I didn't ask to be presented to her —[20]

> A dinner is a terror to the host if there are a lot of officials present. If anybody is not put in his or her precise place he or she sulks.[21]

One evening, Attorney General and Mrs. Knox invited the Holmeses to a dinner for the President, knowing them to be friends. The President, who liked Fanny, took her in to dinner — which upset the ladies of the cabinet, who thought it their occasion. But Fanny was at ease and amused the young President as she did her nephews and nieces. She had found that the women who were her social rivals were not often people of ability: "My wife has seen tragedies — wives of men whom they had helped to arrive — and when they get here with their clothes they realize that now they are an encumbrance."[22] Fanny herself put it more succinctly: "Washington is full of famous men and the women they married when they were young."[23]

A position in society required other skills than those Holmes had developed as a cavalier of London flirtations.

> It seems as if everybody smiled and lied. I don't do that sort of thing — but am as my wife says a child of nature — so don't twig unless she puts me on.[24]

> One realizes the possibility of having enemies — which one rather thought a romantic fiction in Boston. But here rivalries — envies — ambitions — grow fierce. I believe Hoar regards my appointment as a chronic grievance.[25]

Holmes had a moment of disquiet even about his new friend Edward White. There had been a reception at the White House for the judges:

> It is said that Southerners bolted because there was a negro present. I noticed that one of my colleagues [White] . . . left for some reason at once and he is a Southerner. He is a pal of mine — but to me he played the naif.[26]

The thought that White's friendliness toward him might be calculated rose in his mind, but Holmes brushed it away.

At formal dinners, Holmes, who in London had so often been paired with amusing young women, now often took precedence over the other guests and so sat beside the elderly wives of senior senators, not the young married women alert for adventure. He and Fanny were obliged to leave dinners early so that other guests could depart, and this cut off chances for flirtation in the drawing rooms:

> Perhaps it is just as well in this center of gossip — I made one call of politeness of a Sunday afternoon and heard of it at once — The graves would echo if one tried a tune on the flageolet.[27]

> I think I will close out that department, and be a kindly cynic of eld for a space and then a survivor (if I succeed in surviving) — [28]

But if Holmes often was out of his element, Fanny quickly mastered the intricacies and the deceptions, enjoying her position and the friendship of the Roosevelts, who alone seemed above the maneuverings: "[Fanny] has been a great success although she won't believe it. Mrs. Lodge said she wrote to Boston the other day that my wife was It. . . . We are on top of the wave."[29]

Spring came softly and Fanny and Holmes went out together in a rented horse-drawn carriage as they had done in Beverly. They drove into the countryside, and stopped to look at wildflowers or to read the inscriptions in the country cemeteries.

They were enveloped in the Roosevelts' affection, and Holmes was amused and flattered by the President's attention. At White House dinners, Roosevelt talked well. One evening, he described the Mongol invasion of Europe in a way that set Holmes's imagination aflame. The President's masculine forcefulness, amplified by the power of his office, was compelling, seductive: "He makes every man he talks to feel as if that man was one of the 10,000 women on whose bosom Chopin expired (as Tourgenieff says). I do."[30] When the two men were alone they exchanged war stories. Roosevelt sent Holmes a copy of a letter from an old Rough Rider, addressed to "Colonel Theodore Roosevelt, Washington, D.C.":

> I have the honor to report that comrade Ritchie of Troop G is in jail at Trinidad, Colo., on a charge of murder. . . . Ritchie was one of the boys in Troop G and was a splendid soldier and I am going to see that he has a first class defense.
> Also have to report that comrade Webb late of Troop D has just killed two men at Bisbee, Ariz. . . .
> Was out at the Penitentiary yesterday, and had a very pleasant

visit with comrade Frank Bito whom you will remember was sent to the Penitentiary from Silver City for killing his sister-in-law. The sentiment in Grant County is very strongly in his favor. You will doubtless recall that he was shooting at his wife at the time he killed his sister-in-law. Since he has been in the Penitentiary his wife has run off with Comrade Coyne of Troop H, going to Mexico. This incident has tended to turn popular sentiment strongly in Bito's favor.[31]

Roosevelt sent Holmes an annotated newspaper clipping, which reported that the emperor of Korea had abolished his supreme court — "Respectfully referred to Mr. Justice Holmes. . . . The merit of the suggestion is obvious."[32]

The demands of their social position left Fanny little time to attend to the new house until June, when Washington began to empty for the summer. The Court was in recess from June until October, and Fanny told Holmes to go abroad while she made their new house ready.

The President, when he learned of Holmes's planned trip to London, gave him a letter to carry, concerning a dispute with Canada and Great Britain over the Alaskan boundary near the gold strikes in the Yukon. Roosevelt had no patience with an arbitration of the dispute that was going on. His letter said that he would ignore the decision if it were adverse to the United States. Troops were quietly put in readiness.[33] Cabot Lodge was already in Europe with a similar letter, and the President had sent several other such messages in a campaign of threats.

Holmes was not sorry to be away from Washington for the summer. His opinions were written and he was at leisure. Before leaving he went to see Clover Adams's monument in Rock Creek Cemetery: "A figure that is more despair than hope — hardly more woman than man — defying epithets as the universe defies them — it is silence and the end."[34]

Holmes was sixty-two years old; it was forty years since he had taken Clover Hooper to a dance in Boston. He and Henry Adams were neighbors now, living at the capital of the empire. "This is the Götterdämmerung," Holmes said bemusedly in his letters, [35] but whether he referred to the climax of his own career, or to the coming death of empires, was not clear:

> For the first time in my life I am up against a greatness that comes from outside. Hitherto I have constructed from within what seemed like lines of the infinite. Now it is the simple grandiose — the external fact of feeling a vast world vibrate to one's determinations. . . . At bottom I am profoundly happy.[36]

Before the Court adjourned for the summer there was a last important matter, the matter for which Holmes had been chosen. A man named Mankichi was found guilty of manslaughter in a Hawaiian court by a jury voting nine to three for conviction. In any federal court within the continental United States, the Fifth Amendment to the Constitution as then interpreted would have required a unanimous verdict of twelve jurors. Mankichi said that his constitutional rights had been violated. The Supreme Court accordingly was again obliged to consider whether the Constitution extended in all its terms to the colonies of the American empire, or whether the whole structure of political compromises that supported the empire would be undone.

The Court was still divided. Chief Justice Fuller, Harlan, and Brewer, each for his own reasons, still believed that the Constitution applied in all its terms to the colonies. Justice White led four justices who, also for different reasons, believed Congress could apply the Constitution to the colonies selectively.

Brown, alone in his view until then, continued to hold a middle ground. He wrote a separate opinion, saying that only the most fundamental principles of due process applied to the colonies — as they did to the states — and that the requirement of a unanimous jury was not fundamental. Holmes concurred in Brown's opinion — and the rule of the empire was sustained.[37]

The President was pleased. He continued to beam upon Holmes, who sailed for England with Roosevelt's letter in his pocket.

London was in its summer season. The war in South Africa had been won, at terrible cost, and London was still the center of the world. Holmes filled a memorandum book with the names and addresses of London friends: Lucy Clifford, the Pollocks, Mrs. Joseph Chamberlain, Lady Castletown, Ethel Scott, Lady Burghclere, Nina Campbell, Alice Green. In the evenings there was the theater — Réjane in *The Doll's House*. A brief visit with Henry James:

> Wendell Holmes was also lately with us for a couple of days, in his usual flash of enjoyment of the London hurly-burly; a wonder of wonders to me for being more exactly his "old self" always, after no matter what intervals, than anyone I see. . . . I have never seen anyone so unmodified, through the years, who had equally *lived*. . . . Wendell has moved and moved like a full glass carried without spilling a drop.[38]

After a winter of seven-day work weeks and of evenings spent with senators' wives, Holmes enjoyed himself:

> London I filled as full as it would hold. . . .
> There are many Londons, but mine is the enemy of the *banal*
> — makes you fire snap-shots, talk short, be casual, and take your chances of missing when you say your best thing — It helps a lot

to write better decisions when we get back — no padding in mine, if I can help it.[39]

I have had some fun — all the fun there was I think. I saw most of my old friends and was more careful to see much of them than to make new ones, although one can't help making a new one once in a while and I brought back one new scarf pin.[40]

After six weeks in London he went with the Castletowns to Granston Manor, then, as an old friend, going on with them to Doneraile Court. As an old friend, Lord Castletown could now bring him to meet Canon Sheehan, priest of the parish. This was a compliment to Holmes, as only "visitors of distinction in the literary or educational world" were brought to meet the canon at his rectory.[41]

Holmes and Sheehan, both lonely and talkative, enjoyed each other's conversation, and Holmes walked down to the rectory most mornings during his stay.[42]

Afternoons at Doneraile were quiet, interrupted occasionally by a garden party or an excursion with other guests to a horse show: "I might shoot or fish if I liked while here — but I prefer the role of Samson in the lap of Delilah so far as permitted."[43]

There was bridge in the evenings, to which Holmes preferred a book.

The house in Washington was not quite ready when Holmes returned — and so he and Fanny had a brief rest in Beverly and then once again camped in rented quarters in Washington, dining at the New Willard. Holmes had not yet been inside the new house — "Mrs. Holmes is bossing it and I don't want to interfere."[44]

He was refreshed by his trip. The bloom of London and Doneraile clung to his fingertips. The work of the Court was inviting, and Fanny, who was happy and well, arranged everything for his comfort. "Things in general are so pleasant with me nowadays that I shudder."[45]

The Court convened, and the work was beginning to seem familiar and less taxing. A heap of briefs and petitions for certiorari had arrived in his absence and were to be discussed at the first conference after Holmes's return — "but we turned them off, and for the first few days the arguments seemed to deal with easy points." The round of formal entertainments had not yet begun. The President was back in Washington, however, and Holmes and Fanny dined at the White House every week or two, often finding Owen Wister or the Lodges there.[46]

The new house was to have a little apartment for young Dorothy Upham, who had spent summers with Fanny and Holmes in Beverly Farms and who was coming now to live with them. She was the daughter of Holmes's cousin William Upham. Young Dorothy was now alone, and Holmes and Fanny had taken her in.[47]

Nephew Ned Holmes and his wife, it was now plain, would have no children. The Holmes line was running out. Dorothy would bring youth to Holmes's house, but the Holmes name — and the doctor's line — would end with Ned. Holmes's premonition that this would be so, and his cold thought that the future would mean less to him, had been confirmed.

But, for the moment, all was happy beginnings. The house on I Street was nearly ready, and Holmes was impatient to get into it: "I long for the day when I shall be in a house of my own. I expect to feel a good deal more at home there than I ever did in Beacon Street. That was my father's house — not mine!"[48]

It was a four-story brick house in a solid row like those on Beacon Street. One entered a narrow hallway that ran through to the rear of the house. On the left, there was a white-painted staircase with a mahogany banister; on the right, doors opened into two connecting parlors and a good-sized dining room. The front parlor was carpeted red, and one of Fanny's embroideries hung over the mantel. (When guests admired it, she would say that it was done by Holmes's first wife.) In the dining room, Fanny hung Copley's portraits of James Fenimore Cooper and of Holmes's great-grandfather Jonathan Jackson. The kitchen and pantry were below-stairs.

On the second floor, in front, were the master bedroom and dressing room. At the rear of the second floor, two connecting rooms had become Holmes's library.

There was a little apartment for Dorothy on the third floor, and a room for overnight guests. On the fourth floor were rooms for the cook and the maid.

Holmes was particularly pleased with his library. There were fireplaces in both rooms, floor-to-ceiling painted bookshelves, and in the rear room where he would work, the tall windows looked south. His grandfather Charles Jackson's old-fashioned upright writing desk was at the window, and Holmes would stand there to write letters or brief opinions, dipping a rusty steel-nibbed pen into the inkwell. He could look out over the low housetops and see the white chiseled obelisk of the Washington Monument: "The sun streams in the back — and I feel that I am settled for good in a place which is mine."[49] He spent a weekend putting books on his shelves:

> Oh the heavenly joy — for the first time in one's life to see what he has — it is fecundissimus — I have a family shrine over one of the fireplaces in the two rooms which make my library, where I have put all the works of my two grandfathers and my father and myself — [50]

Over the mantel in the rear library, which would be his workroom, he hung his great-grandfather David Holmes's sword, powder horn, and a tomahawk trophy from the French and Indian War. Crossed with David Holmes's sword was his own. On the mantel were framed photographs of Clara Stevens, Ellen Curtis, Ethel Grenfell — the young women who were both his and Fanny's friends — and an etching he had made in his youth, of a kitten.

His grandfather Charles Jackson's cherrywood desk, at which Holmes worked when sitting down, was before the fireplace, and there Holmes would spend most of his working hours.

An Irish cook and maid from Boston lived upstairs and Holmes's messenger, a manservant, and two local girls came in each day, and a hired carriage and driver were always ready for their call.

Dorothy arrived, the social season opened, and Fanny began to entertain. Holmes expanded:

> We had a sort of housewarming tea . . . which pleased me as I thought the house seemed to hold the guests with a kind of spacious embrace that was not devoid of elegance. In fact I love it and am happy to wake up in it every day.[51]

Every weekday morning at 11:30 when the Court was in session, Holmes descended his front steps, walked a few paces down I Street to Lafayette Square, where Fanny had amused him by finding dandelions blossoming in November, walked briskly with long-legged strides past the brick houses and gentlemen's clubs to Pennsylvania Avenue, and then up that broad boulevard to Capitol Hill. Craig followed later with Holmes's lunch in a metal box, and at 4:00 Holmes walked home again over the same route with Edward White.

White was stout and walked slowly. Holmes would get chilled and suggest they go more quickly; White would say he had walked slowly on Holmes's account, and for a while they would step along, but soon they would be going as slowly as before.[52]

One afternoon they were talking of the government's new effort to deport anarchists. Holmes said, perhaps to provoke White, that he thought persecution was perfectly logical, if you believed in the truth of your own ideas. White agreed, but what he said stuck in Holmes's memory: "None of us live logically. You profess skepticism, but act on dogma. Those who profess dogma do not and could not carry it out dogmatically — the spirit of the times is too strong for us."[53]

Once Washington's season began, Holmes and Fanny went everywhere together, although of course they played their separate parts in the dinner parties. "Look at him," the President said to Fanny one evening, watching Holmes charm his elderly dinner partner, "the sex instinct is so strong in him as to make him talk to Mrs. ——— . I wish I could do that. Do you suppose it is real or is he putting it on?"[54]

Dr. Oliver Wendell
Holmes at about the time
of his first son's birth
in 1841.

Dr. and Mrs. Holmes and
their three children,
Edward (Ned), Amelia,
and Oliver Wendell, Jr.,
about 1860.

Mrs. Holmes and her elder son, Wendell, probably photographed by
Dr. Holmes at the family house in Cambridge about 1860.

Wendell Holmes in uniform,
probably during the summer
of 1861.

Holmes as a law student
in 1865.

Holmes as "the Astronomer" — philosopher and legal scholar — shortly before his marriage to Fanny B. Dixwell and his return to law practice in 1872.

Fanny B. Dixwell in 1860.

A cartoon of Dr. Holmes, "The Autocrat of the Breakfast Table," by "Spy." The doctor kept the framed original in his library.

Holmes's mother, Amelia Lee Holmes, about 1870.

Holmes's brother, Edward
Jackson (Ned) Holmes,
in 1864.

Holmes's sister, Amelia Jackson
(Mrs. Turner Sargent), in 1881.

John Holmes, Dr. Oliver
Wendell Holmes's brother, in
an undated photograph
possibly taken by the doctor
at Beverly Farms.

Kaneko Kentaro in the 1870s, at about the time when Holmes was tutoring him for the Harvard Law School and introducing him to Boston society.

Holmes in May, 1883, just after his appointment to the Massachusetts Supreme Judicial Court.

Holmes in the 1890s, at about the time of his friendship with Lady Castletown. The awkwardly placed tiepin may be one that she gave him.

Holmes in the 1880s. This picture might have been taken by Clover (Marian) Adams in 1884, shortly before her death.

The Massachusetts Supreme Judicial
Court in 1900, when Holmes became
its chief justice. From left to right,
John W. Hammond, John Lathrop,
Marcus P. Knowlton, Holmes,
James M. Morton, James M. Barker,
and William C. Loring.

Holmes at the time of his appointment to the United States Supreme Court in 1902.

The Supreme Court of the United States in
March, 1903, the first photograph of the Court
in which Holmes was included. Back row, left
to right: Holmes, Rufus W. Peckham, Joseph P.
McKenna, George Shiras; seated, left to right:
Henry B. Brown, John M. Harlan, Chief
Justice Melville W. Fuller, David J. Brewer,
Edward D. White. (Supreme Court Historical
Society.)

Holmes on a visit to Great Britain,
possibly at Leslie and Ethel Scott's
country house in Ireland in the
early 1900s.

Ethel Grenfell, later Lady Desborough, in an undated photograph among Holmes's papers.

Nina (Anna Lyman) Gray, in 1922.

Holmes's nephew, Edward J. (Ned) Holmes, Jr., and his wife, Mary Beaman Holmes, on a trip to Italy in 1907.

Chief Justice Edward D. White. White served as chief justice from 1911 until 1921. (Supreme Court Historical Society.)

J.C. McReynolds   O.W. Holmes
Edward T. Sanford

The Taft Court in 1925. Standing from left to right: Edward T. Sanford, George Sutherland, Pierce Butler, Harlan F. Stone. Seated from left to right: James C. McReynolds, Holmes, Chief Justice William H. Taft, Willis Van Devanter, Louis D. Brandeis. (Supreme Court Historical Society.)

Holmes with his legal secretary Alger Hiss at Beverly Farms in the summer of 1930. (John Knox)

Holmes with Justices Harlan F. Stone and Louis D. Brandeis on the steps of the Capitol at about the time of Holmes's ninetieth birthday.

The President and Mrs. Roosevelt bathed them in hospitality and friendship as before, but Holmes was faintly uneasy; at the back of his mind was the thought that he was writing an opinion that would distress Roosevelt and, as he could not discuss the case, he was obliged to dissemble.[55]

The case had been argued for two full days in December. The President had personally directed that the suit be filed and Attorney General Knox himself had argued for the government. The defendants were James J. Hill, the great railroad entrepreneur of the Northwest, J. P. Morgan, his banker, and their allies and corporate enterprises.

Hill was a railroad man, not just a speculator in railroad stocks, president of the Great Northern Railroad, which ran from Lake Superior to the Pacific Coast. His road had survived the crash of 1893 and had run at a profit. J. P. Morgan had helped Hill absorb bankrupt railroads into the Great Northern, making it into a great system linking the cities of the Midwest farm states to the Pacific coast.

Morgan and Hill together had tried to buy a small line, the Chicago, Burlington and Quincy Railroad, which would have joined the eastern ends of their transcontinental roads into a single system running from Chicago to Portland and Seattle and would have linked the nation's mining and manufacturing center on the shores of the Great Lakes, the great cattle and wheat regions, and the Pacific.

Another such transcontinental system was being assembled by E. H. Harriman and his banker, Jacob Schiff, along a southern route. It would run parallel with Hill's system and threaten it with competition, but with Hill's acquisition of the Chicago, Burlington and Quincy, the Hill system would reach past the northern flank of the Harriman system and cut it off from Chicago and the Great Lakes.

Harriman, threatening all-out war, asked to be let into the Chicago, Burlington and Quincy purchase. When Morgan and Hill refused, he launched a raid on the stock of one key component of their system, the Northern Pacific. Harriman first tried to buy a controlling interest in the Northern Pacific on the open market, but found himself forestalled — Hill and Morgan increased their own holdings to an absolute majority of the common stock.

On May 1, Harriman then launched a "bear raid" on the entrenched owners of the Northern Pacific common, selling the stock for later delivery in massive quantities, driving down the price. Speculators joined Harriman in selling short. But Morgan's group responded by buying every share of stock they could reach, and by May 9, there were too few shares of Great Northern common stock remaining on the market for Harriman and the speculators to meet their contracts. There was a desperate scramble to buy stock at any price. The price of Northern Pacific common suddenly shot up from a few dollars to $1,000 a share. As the government's lawyers later put it: "The markets of the world were convulsed, the equilibrium of the financial world shaken, and many speculative interests were in a critical condition."[56]

But the bankers were not willing to see another plunge into chaos like the panic and depression of 1893. J. P. Morgan presided over a treaty of peace. With Hill, he organized a holding company in New Jersey — the Northern Securities Company — to take ownership of the Hill and Morgan lines, exchanging its stock for theirs. Harriman was given a minority interest in the holding company and a seat on its board of directors — presumably to ensure not only that he would share in the profits of the competing line, but that the new combine would not turn to attack his Southern Pacific system.

Morgan announced the terms of the treaty on June 1. As he later testified, the Harriman and Hill groups had agreed, "that they were acting under what we know as a community of interest principle, and that we were not going to have that battle in Wall Street. There were not going to be people standing up fighting each other."[57]

Hill became president of the Northern Securities Company, and began to take over operations of all the Hill and Morgan lines. The company was modeled on the United States Steel Corporation, which Morgan had put together that same year to consolidate the nation's iron and steel industry, and the Standard Oil Company, in which John D. Rockefeller had consolidated most of the nation's oil business. Industry after industry was being consolidated in this way by groups of bankers and industrialists. In a few years, it appeared, much of the nation's economy might be under the control of a few cartels.

In Japan and Germany, such great cartels were favored. In the United States, many Progressives favored them, and looked forward to the end of panics and turmoil and a coming of more efficient management. It seemed that the United States would need the largest possible organizations to compete on a world scale.

Holmes, who years before had written out on a scrap of paper a similar peace treaty for the Atchison, Topeka and Santa Fe Railroad, watched the gathering wave of consolidations with some trepidation: "It seemed to me that the trades unions and the trusts pointed to a more despotic regime. . . . I am not particularly in love with it."[58] But, as he had often said and written, such consolidations were the natural and inevitable outcome of competition.

Perhaps it was the open arrogance of Morgan's exercise of power, but the Northern Securities Company became a public symbol of unrestrained monopoly. Shortly after Roosevelt became President — on February 19, 1902 — apparently without consulting or warning anyone, except the attorney general, he announced that he was directing Mr. Knox to file suit to break up the Northern Securities Company.[59] It would be the first significant antitrust suit since the Cleveland administration. The stock market shuddered, and Washington was consumed with speculations. Henry Adams was gleeful:

> Suddenly, this week without warning, [Roosevelt] has hit Pierpont Morgan, the whole railway interest, and the whole Wall Street connection, a tremendous whack square on the nose. . . . I doubt whether he spoke even to Cabot [Lodge]. Root [the secretary of war, a former railroad lawyer] was much upset by it. The Wall Street people are in an ulcerated state of inflammation.[60]

J. P. Morgan called on the President, to inquire whether this was a general attack on his interests, but apparently was reassured; and indeed no further suits followed.[61]

By the time this symbolic case had reached the Supreme Court, it had accumulated more than 8,000 printed pages of transcripts of trial, printed briefs, and arguments, the delivery of which at his doorstep Holmes observed glumly.

The government's case rested on the Sherman Antitrust Act of 1890, a very brief and general declaration that had proven to be — and perhaps was intended to be — of little practical use. The Sherman Act declared to be illegal every contract or combination "in restraint of trade," and every monopoly or attempt to monopolize was equally made a crime.

This apparently powerful language was crippled from the outset in two ways. It applied only — could apply only — to interstate commerce, which the Supreme Court had said in the past was only the flow of goods across state lines. The Supreme Court had drawn a line between factories and mines, which lay within the states' power, and the flow of goods across state lines — which was subject to federal control.[62] The purpose of the line originally had been to protect state power to regulate the mines and factories.

Chief Justice Fuller himself had written the opinion applying this doctrine to antitrust cases. The Sherman Act, limited as it was by the Constitution to interstate commerce, did not apply to industrial facilities. The federal government, therefore, seemed to have no power to interfere with the ownership of railroads; the Northern Securities Company apparently was beyond federal reach, the President's suit no more than a gesture.

The attorney general therefore had a difficult task. He had to show not only that his case was within federal power, but that, even if it were, the joining of several railroads into a single system would be a "monopoly" or "restraint of trade."

His argument was simple and forceful. The combination of railroads, simply because it was large and powerful, lay like an obstruction in the channel of commerce, restraining the free flow of goods. While not in itself commerce, it was an obstruction to commerce, and should be broken up.[63]

That was enough for Harlan. He had dissented in favor of the federal government in earlier cases, and needed little argument now to persuade him. It was enough also for William Day, Roosevelt's new appointee, and for McKenna and Brown. At the first conference, four justices were for the government.

But Fuller had not changed his mind. Ownership was one thing and commerce another. Holmes stood with him, as did White and Peckham. Only David Brewer was undecided, leaving the Court divided four to four.

Brewer evidently was torn. He had consistently opposed the power of government to meddle in economic affairs. Yet he thought it a real question whether a single business enterprise should be allowed to control the whole transportation system of the country.

Harlan, as the senior justice favoring the government, began writing an opinion that would be either a majority opinion or a dissent, depending on how Brewer voted. Harlan's opinion seemed to roar with indignation: of course, the federal government had the *power* to stop this combination in restraint of trade. The question did not need analysis. This opinion did not persuade Brewer.

Fuller asked both White and Holmes to write opinions on the other side, and to circulate their opinions to Brewer and the other justices. White wrote with slow concentration, piling irresistible authority upon irresistible authority: the power claimed by the government was forbidden to it by the Constitution and reserved to the states.

Holmes wrote an elegant and brief opinion, saying that, even if the Constitution permitted this suit to proceed, the antitrust law did not. The Sherman Act did not forbid a partnership or corporation from forming.

The statute, read as it must be in the light of the common law, did not forbid agreements among former competitors. It did not require them to continue their struggle even after one was exhausted and the other victorious. It forbade only the excesses of competition — the violent overreaching of power, the destruction of competitors by improper means. The statute required only, and the federal government's power was adequate only, to punish excess and ensure a civilized restraint.[64]

The chief justice hoped that White's and Holmes's opinions would persuade Brewer — he had particular hopes for Holmes's opinion — "Yours will hit him between wind and water," he jotted on a note to Holmes.[65] But, in the end, Brewer, despite his qualms, voted with Harlan — and Holmes's opinion became his first dissent.

It was an election year for the President, and he was preoccupied by political affairs. He demanded loyalty; accusations of unfaithfulness fell frequently from his lips. At a White House dinner on March 9, when the *Northern Securities* decision had not yet been announced, the President meditated aloud and bitterly on former friends who had proven faithless.[66]

Holmes listened uneasily to the President's complaints. He was acutely aware that he had already written an opinion that would appear to the President to be disloyal.

On Monday, March 14, the Supreme Court announced its decision, and Holmes, for the first time, read a dissent in open court. Melville Fuller listened in admiration: "When [Holmes's] voice, refined and clear, rose in the Court Room you could hear a pin drop & his sentences were as incisive as the edge of a knife."[67]

It was a new voice, speaking words that had a claim to be read as literature. Holmes wrote in a modern style, freed from heavy Latinate formations. It was a conversational style that had the rhythms of modern American speech, as different from Harlan's oratorical bombast as if it were written in another language entirely.

I am unable to agree with the judgment of the majority of the Court, and although I think it useless and undesirable, as a rule, to express dissent, I feel bound to do so in this case and to give my reasons for it.

Great cases like hard cases make bad law. For great cases are called great not by reason of their real importance in shaping the law of the future but because of some accident of immediate overwhelming interest which appeals to the feelings and distorts the judgment. These immediate interests exert a kind of hydraulic pressure which makes what previously was clear seem doubtful, and before which even well-settled principles of law will bend. What we have to do in this case is to find the meaning of some not very difficult words. We must try, as I have tried, to do it with the same freedom of natural and spontaneous interpretation that one would be sure of if the same question . . . excited no public attention and was of importance only to a prisoner before the court. . . . I say we must read the words before us as if the question were whether two small exporting grocers shall go to jail. . . .

There is a natural feeling that somehow or other the statute meant to strike at combinations great enough to cause just anxiety on the part of those who love their country more than money, while it viewed such little ones as I have mentioned with just indifference. This notion, it may be said, somehow breathes from the pores of the act, although it seems to be contradicted in every way by the words in detail. . . .

I am happy to know that only a minority of my brethren adopt an interpretation of the law which in my opinion would make eternal the *bellum omnium contra omnes* and disintegrate society so far as it could into individual atoms. If that were its intent I should regard calling such a law a regulation of commerce as a mere pretense. It would be an attempt to reconstruct society. I am not concerned with the wisdom of such an attempt but I believe that Congress was not entrusted by the Constitution with the power to make it and I am deeply persuaded that it has not tried.[68]

Once more Holmes had stated his conviction that the Supreme Court, independent and equal with the other branches of government — supreme over them in constitutional disputes — was not a *political* branch of government and would not hear of political aims or political rights. The Supreme Court was only a neutral arbiter, reading documents in a dry light, tying itself as closely to precedent as changing circumstances would permit. Holmes asserted the objectivity, the independence of an artist or a scientist.

The President was furious, or said he was. Stories of his anger appeared in the newspapers. Henry Adams reported, "Theodore went wild about it."[69] There was a malicious edge to the gossip — "Theodore" had brought Holmes to Washington to do his dirty work, and now was angry at Holmes's insubordination. Yet Roosevelt said nothing to Holmes. On April 3, Holmes and Fanny were invited to dinner at the White House, where all was bland and nothing was said about the Northern Securities Case: "If the President has been angry he seems to be getting over it. I don't quite know how it has been. Of course the newspaper stories of stormy interviews are not true."[70] But Holmes was reminded how often people smiled and lied. He began again to feel the distance separating him from the men in Washington, for whom not intellect but friendship was the medium of power. The rumors and newspaper stories continued.

I have had no communication of any kind with [the President] upon the matter. If he should take my action with anger I should be disappointed in him and add one more to my list of cynicisms where before was belief. But I have such confidence in his great heartedness that I don't expect for a moment that after he has had time to cool down it will affect our relations. If however his seeming personal regard for us was based on the idea that he had a tool the sooner it is ended the better — we shall see.[71]

Harlan had begun to criticize Holmes's terse, conversational opinions more openly, and Brewer now regularly dissented from them, generally bringing one or two others with him, arguing for the supremacy of rights:

I have been rather lonely at moments in a legal way — although I always get great comfort from my brother White and the Chief. . . .

When the newspapers begin to drivel, while they say nothing worth hearing, they reduce one to confusion so far as to wonder whether everything he did was done in vain and whether some other kind of man is wanted.[72]

20

SOLITUDE

K
ANEKO KENTARO — HE WAS NOW BARON KANEKO — CAME TO
the United States again in 1904. Japan and Russia were at war
in Manchuria, and Kaneko, who once had wished to be a naval
officer, now served as a diplomat. In March, when he came to Washington, he called on Holmes and Fanny, bringing small gifts, among which
was a new book on bushido, the Way of the Warrior. The book recalled
to Holmes long talks he and Kaneko had had thirty years before.

> [Bushido] is not a written code — at best it consists of a few
> maxims handed down from mouth to mouth or coming from the
> pen of some well-known warrior or savant. . . . It was an organic
> growth of decades and centuries of military career. It, perhaps,
> fills the same position in the history of ethics that the English Con-
> stitution does in political history. . . .
> Fair play in fight! What fertile germs of morality lie in this prim-
> itive sense of savagery and childhood. Is it not the root of all mil-
> itary and civic virtue?[1]

Rectitude, valor, benevolence, truthfulness, courtesy, honor, and the duty of loyalty were bushido's virtues; the institution of ceremonial suicide its ultimate expression.

Kaneko remained in Washington through the war and the long peace talks, over which President Roosevelt presided. Holmes and Fanny welcomed him, helped him with introductions, and gave a dinner in his honor. Holmes offered suggestions and advice for securing American support, and after the peace talks were over, Kaneko returned to Japan, well pleased.

"You got the swag," Holmes told him.

"I cannot help thinking of a shrewd Scotchman," Kaneko answered; "therefore I confess we came out . . . with all the booty we could carry and cast a discreet smile on our 'wily Oriental faces.'"[2]

After he was gone, the Japanese ambassador presented Fanny with a set of golden cups, bestowed upon her by the emperor. A neatly typewritten letter in excellent English explained that the presentation of gold, silver, and wooden teacups was a "time-honored custom."[3]

Holmes's work was growing familiar, and no longer absorbed him with religious intensity:

I . . . vainly urged my wife to introduce me to a being in pink of possibly bad form but certainly good shape. . . .[4]

We gave each other notice of hostile intentions and that we were out for scalps & she told me that I might play in her backyard if I didn't play with other girls — and jabbered French tutoying me at once — But I fear the tragedy ends there — I don't have time to play in backyards, and for other reasons too numerous to mention.[5]

In the adjournments of the Court, he began going up to New York for weekends, however. He shopped, went to the theater, and called at houses where he thought money was too much in evidence — and revived old flirtations.[6]

Nina and John Gray urged him to hire a secretary each year from the graduating class of the Harvard Law School, as Horace Gray had done for twenty years. This Supreme Court clerkship had become a tradition and a kind of prize for the better students. But Holmes hesitated — working as he did, firing off opinions so quickly after hearing arguments, he did not see how a young lawyer would help him.

In the summer of 1904, Holmes had three months of leisure and rest at Beverly Farms with Fanny and Dorothy. Dorothy was growing up; she visited friends and had callers. Fanny insisted that she be chaperoned when young men were in the house, but one afternoon Fanny, returning home, met a young man coming down the steps. That night Fanny spoke to Holmes, and the next morning, at breakfast, he addressed the subject of a niece's duties. He and she had grown close and had an intimacy that Fanny envied.[7]

Beverly Farms was solitary and peaceful, but the summer was marked with reminders of gathering old age. Leslie Stephen, the first friend of Holmes's assault on London so many years before, died that spring, leaving his daughter Virginia terribly distraught. Young Frederick Maitland was collecting Stephen's letters for a life, and Holmes, who had carefully kept all of Stephen's letters, sent them along. At Beverly, Eliot Cabot was dead. In July, Mrs. Whitman died, and Holmes spoke a few words for her at a quiet country meeting. "My old friends are dead," Holmes said to Nina Gray.[8]

There were new neighbors in Beverly, however. William Howard Taft was summering nearby. He had at last joined Roosevelt in Washington, as secretary of war, his potential rivalry for the presidential nomination smothered under Roosevelt's friendship. Senator Albert Beveridge, another friend of Roosevelt's, was nearby at work on his biography of John Marshall. But Holmes kept largely to himself. He read light novels aloud to Fanny, and they rode out together in the afternoons again. He read Aristotle and reread the Gospels. For the first time since his appointment to the Supreme Court, Holmes allowed himself to slip off into the landscape of intellect. He filled up a page of his journal with his book list, writing in a very small hand to make room for dozens of titles.

Melville Fuller and his wife were summering at their house in Sorrento, Maine, when Mrs. Fuller, just sixty years old, suddenly and inexplicably died.

> My dear Chief:
> We were grieved by your telegram. It is the fall of a great town and we shall feel that a large space has been left empty. . . . I know your courage and that you will rise to your duties in the same heroic way you always have and if it is any pleasure to you to hear that I think of you always with the same affection and faith I like to tell it to you and hope that you know it beyond a doubt.[9]

War and death were always just over the horizon, but Holmes rested and recovered his energy. He was growing stout — he noted with pleasure that his weight on the railroad scale was now up to 178 pounds — and his older clothes no longer fit him. His hair was turning white.

> I have been meditating in a melancholy way how much of one's life is wasted in getting to the firing line (the place where your thought carries forward the world's thought,) how little comparatively is spent on what really are the problems of mankind in one's business.[10]

The justices were subdued when they gathered again in the fall. Brown was ill, and they were all, it seemed, old men. There was more talk in the newspapers that Fuller would resign and that Taft would succeed him. But Fuller went on as before. He and Holmes drew closer. Holmes called on the Chief every Sunday morning now, and helped him with the administrative work of the Court.

Roosevelt's campaign to be elected President in his own right was at its peak. Taft helped to organize the Constitution Club, a network of Republican lawyers dedicated to reestablishing a government of law — by which they meant that state regulatory legislation should be struck down and the courts given greater power over labor organizations.

The Supreme Court itself continued to brush aside such Constitutional claims, which streamed in without abatement. Three men convicted of running a false gold-brick confidence game in North Carolina complained that sentences of seven and ten years in prison were unconstitutional: "The sentence is not due process because the people are opposed to judge-made crimes and only tolerate them when followed by the mildest punishment."[11]

A privately owned power company claimed that it was unconstitutional for the City of Joplin, Missouri, to compete with it for electric power business;[12] building contractors in Kansas said that it was unconstitutional for the state to set a limit of eight hours' work each day for laborers on state contracts.[13]

Aliens were being arrested and deported in large numbers as suspected anarchists, in a campaign that had begun after the assassination of President McKinley. They petitioned federal courts for hearings, and attacked the immigration laws as unconstitutional, although the Court had repeatedly held that aliens in the United States without permission had no Constitutional protections whatever. Clarence Darrow appeared before the Court and argued for a British trade union organizer who had entered the country illegally, presumably from Canada, and who had been giving talks on anarchism in New York when he was arrested. Darrow reached for every conceivable argument founded on the Constitution, quoting even the works and theories of the Southern secessionists.[14]

With patience and courtesy, the Court turned all these claims aside. Holmes or Fuller usually wrote the opinion of the Court in these cases; Brewer dissented over and over, sometimes taking Brown or Peckham or McKenna with him.

In November, Roosevelt was elected, and Taft was the heir apparent.

The night before last a dinner at the White House. . . . The President was happy, of course, and showed it with an ingenuousness which had my entire sympathy. He is a good man, and, incidentally, all right to me. . . . he talks with a freedom at the White House that would turn your hair gray.[15]

The swarm of cases at the Supreme Court grew denser and more biting each year:

A few minutes ago I laid down the last record after about as fierce a ten days as ever I had. . . . I had written 3 cases in that time while sitting constantly — examined all my own records without using a secretary, and made various hostile memoranda touching opinions of my brethren.[16]

By writing opinions that denied both property rights and civil rights claims, Holmes attracted criticism, and very little praise, from outside the Court. He then wrote an opinion that profoundly offended the leaders of the Republican party, and perhaps ended his chances of becoming Chief Justice.

A new round of cases had come up from the Philippines, Alaska, and Hawaii, testing yet again whether the Constitution protected the inhabitants of these colonies. Ten million Filipinos had been subjected to U.S. military rule for a decade. Taft had presided over the suppression of their rebellion and had governed the colony: an enormous man in white clothes and a topee holding court, he was an image fixed in the national imagination.

The legality of Taft's reign in the Philippines was challenged indirectly, in an attack on the tariffs he had imposed. The President and the Congress had approved Taft's tariffs, after the fact, and it seemed likely that the Supreme Court would do so as well. But the members of the Court were still bitterly divided into opposing factions led by Fuller and White. The disagreement within the Court encouraged further challenges by lawyers hoping to shift a single vote. Fuller did not want these divisions to continue.

Nearly all the justices now would have upheld Taft's tariff against Constitutional challenge, but they could not agree on a rationale. They at last agreed that the Philippine case need not be met squarely. There were defects in both President McKinley's and the Congress's acts of ratification, apparent carelessness in wording, that seemed to leave Taft's actions without any precise authorization. Unable to agree on a way to uphold the Philippine tariff, the Court abruptly — and unanimously — struck it down.

Holmes wrote the opinion. Unlike Fuller and White, he refused to take into account the political importance of the case, and, as was his usual practice, he wrote the opinion as if it had none. The tariff was authorized by neither the President nor Congress, he said briefly. McKinley's order was issued in wartime and expired at the end of the war.

Congress ratified only actions taken under McKinley's order; tariffs imposed after the war accordingly were not authorized and were invalid. Millions of dollars were to be refunded. Holmes's opinion was terse, almost insulting in its brevity, as if he disdained to soften the blow only because it fell on important men.[17]

Taft, now a member of the cabinet and heir apparent to the presidency, was furious — and let his anger be known. He complained furiously to members of the Court; he demanded that the solicitor general immediately request a reargument of the case, which was done, and suggested retaining Elihu Root, who had returned to private practice, to handle the reargument. He went to the length of asking that the secretary of the treasury ignore the decision and refuse to refund the tariff payments until the case had been reargued. He was, in short, beside himself. He unburdened his heart to Root:

> If there ever was a fool decision, this is it, and turned off as flippantly, though it involves $7,000,000 and the legality of transactions of the government extending over two years, as if it involved a bill at the corner grocer's. . . . I think the rest of the Court have merely passed it off without fully examining the foolishness of Holmes.[18]

Taft then personally began to draft new legislation ratifying his tariffs, determined to win in the end, regardless of what the Supreme Court should now say.

There was pending in the Court at this time an appeal from the Territory of Alaska. A woman named Rasmussen had been charged with keeping a house of prostitution and was convicted by a six-man jury. Such juries, a great convenience in the sparsely settled territory, had been authorized by Congress. Rasmussen appealed, claiming that she had been denied her constitutional right to a twelve-man jury. The case was not argued in person; Rasmussen's lawyer submitted a brief, and the whole of the case was contained in perhaps one hundred pages.

With the Philippine tariffs invalidated on other grounds, there was no need to decide whether the Constitution protected the native peoples of the Philippines and Hawaii. The Court could agree that Alaska, at least, had been incorporated into the union and that the Bill of Rights applied there in all its terms. Rasmussen's conviction was quietly reversed.[19]

The attacks on Holmes were still growing in volume when White announced the decision in the Rasmussen case. In his opinion he said that the Court had now adopted his view, hammered at in case after case for five years, on all such questions. Holmes had given him his opportunity, and Harlan alone dissented.

When White had finished reading his opinion from the bench, he called Charles Butler, the court reporter, up to him and stepped behind the curtain. Butler remembering going to join him:

> My approach back of the screen was from one side and Justice White's from the other. As he came towards me, the breeze from the open window blowing out his gown, he was flourishing the proof sheets of his opinion in one hand and shaking the fist of the other at me, it seemed. Then he exclaimed in a voice that was probably heard by all those who were on the other side of the screen:
> "Butler, now [my view] . . . is the opinion of the Court and I want you to make it so appear in your report of this case."
> To Justice White it was as great a victory as winning his first case in the Supreme Court would be for a youthful attorney.[20]

White took fierce pride in what he had done, having drawn the Chief Justice and the other members of the Court behind him. "Why, sir, if we had not decided as we did," he told Charles Warren, "the country would have been less than a Nation!"[21] He had taken a long stride toward the chief justice's chair, stepping over Holmes.

The chief justice announced that requests to reargue the Philippine Tariff case had been granted. Two full days were given to an attack on Holmes's opinion, and when Fuller reaffirmed it, White joined in the attack and dissented.[22]

Congress promptly passed Taft's statute expressly authorizing the Philippine tariffs, and White then had the added pleasure of upholding them under the new law in a solemn, cautious, and ponderously irrefutable opinion — for a unanimous Court.[23]

In the midst of this turmoil, Holmes had written a strong dissenting opinion in a Constitutional case that drew more ire down on him. New York's rowdy legislature had adopted a law protecting bakery workers. It was made a crime for any employer to require his workers to labor more than ten hours per day or sixty hours per week in a bakery. The stated reason for this law was to protect the health of the workers. A baker, Lochner, was convicted of violations of the law, and appealed, challenging its constitutionality.

Two days of argument were given to the case in February, 1905. At first, it seemed to be just another of the Constitutional claims that the Court had so often turned aside. At the first conference, a majority voted to uphold the law and Lochner's conviction.[24] Under the Court's precedents, many of them written by Holmes, there was no question that a state constitutionally could adopt reasonable measures to protect the health of its working people. Harlan promptly wrote an opinion for the Court, expecting the usual dissents from Brewer, perhaps from Peckham or McKenna or Brown. But the case touched some spring of feeling, and Rufus Peckham, rarely heard in these cases, wrote a violently worded dissent, which carried the other usual dissenters — and Fuller himself.

A vote changed, and there was suddenly a majority to strike down the statute. Peckham's dissent became the opinion of the Court. The New York law purported to protect the health of workers, but this was a sham, Peckham said. The law was something else entirely, an interference in the relations between workers and their employers, a blatant measure to change the bargains between private parties. This law was a violation, not necessarily of property rights, but of liberty — the liberty of the worker to labor for longer hours and more pay, the liberty of the employer to run his business profitably, the liberty of all to make voluntary agreements. The Fourteenth Amendment's promise of liberty had been breached unreasonably, without due process of law.[25]

Harlan's ill-tempered opinion became a dissent in which White and Day concurred. This was a health measure, Harlan said, figuratively pounding the table, and that was that.

Holmes felt obliged to write an opinion of his own. The Court had abruptly, if only briefly, abandoned the rules of decision that he had repeatedly announced since his first opinion for the Court.

To Holmes alone of the justices it seemed plain that if they dealt frankly with their past decisions, this New York law must be upheld, whether as a health measure or as a law to favor the worker against his employer. Holmes reminded the Court of his own opinions on their behalf, reminded them that in the Northern Securities case they had freely interfered with the supposed liberty to make voluntary agreements. In truth, liberty had nothing to do with the majority's decision.

This case is decided on an economic theory which a large part of the country docs not entertain. If it were a question whether I agreed with that theory, I should desire to study it further and long before making up my mind. But I do not conceive that to be my duty, because I strongly believe that my agreement or disagreement has nothing to do with the right of a majority to embody their opinions in law. It is settled by various opinions of this Court that State constitutions and State laws may regulate life in many ways which we as legislators might think as injudicious, or, if you like, as tyrannical as this, and which equally interfere with the liberty to contract. Sunday laws and usury laws are ancient examples. A more modern one is the prohibition of lotteries. The liberty of the citizen to do as he likes so long as he does not interfere with the liberty of others to do the same, which has been a shibboleth of some well-known writers, is interfered with by school laws, by the Post Office, by every State or municipal insti-

tution which takes his money for purposes thought desirable,
whether he likes it or not. The Fourteenth Amendment does not
enact Mr. Herbert Spencer's *Social Statics.* . . .

[A] constitution is not intended to embody a particular economic theory. . . . It is made for people of fundamentally differing
views, and the accident of our finding certain opinions natural
and familiar or novel and even shocking ought not to conclude
our judgment upon the question whether statutes embodying
them conflict with the Constitution of the United States . . . unless
it can be said that a rational and fair man necessarily would admit
that the statute proposed would infringe fundamental principles
as they have been understood by the traditions of our people and
our law. It does not need research to show that no such sweeping
condemnation can be passed upon the statute before us. A reasonable man might think it a proper measure on the score of
health. Men whom I certainly could not pronounce unreasonable
would uphold it as a first installment of a general regulation of
the hours of work.[26]

The majority's decision was widely criticized in the press and by political leaders. Harlan's pugnacious dissent was widely praised. Holmes's
solitary dissent was not much noticed, except by those whom it offended.[27]

I am beginning to feel the fatigue of the business a little and I
shall not be sorry when the time comes to shut up shop for a
while.[28]

Holmes decided to hire a secretary now, and to begin he hired
Charles K. Poe, a recent graduate of a Washington law school who was
on the spot, but for the future he asked John Gray to send a new Harvard graduate each year. Poe sat at Dr. Holmes's old desk in the front
library, and Holmes worked at his grandfather's desk in the rear library,
with the sliding doors open between the two rooms.

Summer in Beverly Farms revived Holmes. Philosophy was part of
the refreshment. He read Hegel — the reading itself was a chore — but:

[In Hegel's] *Philosophy of History* you see the great man revealed.
Old as it is and behind the times in detail I know of no such picture of the movement of intellect to completed self-conscious-
ness.[29]

Holmes chatted about Hegel and metaphysics in long letters to John
Gray; perhaps he also spoke in imagination with the absent figure of
William James. Holmes renewed in his own mind the debates he had

had with James in the whitely lit upstairs bedroom on Charles Street forty years before. As he had then, Holmes ended with Chauncey Wright's dictum, a lesson of humility in the face of ultimate facts. The cosmos was not bound to follow a merely logical argument; one could not say, *necessary*, to the cosmos:

> As I probably have said many times before, all I mean by truth is what I can't help believing — I don't know why I should assume except for practical purposes of conduct that that *can't help* has more cosmic worth than any others — I can't help preferring port to ditch-water, but I see no ground for supposing that the cosmos shares my weakness. I *guess* that man is not so important as the philosopher would make him out, and I resign myself to the conjecture that I don't know all about it with composure — demanding of my philosophy simply to show that I am not a fool for putting my heart into my job.[30]

The Grays' daughter Eleanor married a man named Tudor, but something kept Holmes from acknowledging the invitation to the wedding. Nina Gray would soon be a grandmother. Years were passing, moving like a glacier, with something always toppling off in front. "It is not only that grandmothers are younger and bottles smaller than once, but years are oh so much shorter."[31]

In October, the tide of cases rose a little higher. Holmes plunged into the work: "I have been at it very hard, more almost than usual — and having a bully time in consequence."[32] He fired his opinions from the bench still flaming with the intensity of his effort.

> It may be that I am growing less self-exacting with age but it seems to me at least as if I turned off my work with a certain precision of expression and thought on which once in a while in happy moments I plume myself.[33]

But he labored still largely in solitude, without any public acclaim.

> The vulgar hardly will believe an opinion important unless it is padded like a militia brigadier general. You know my view on that theme. The little snakes are the poisonous ones.[34]

> One cannot be perfectly clear until the struggle of thought is over and you have got so far past the idea that it is almost a bore to state it; but decisions can't wait for that, and writers usually *won't*. Therefore I do not regard perfect luminosity as the highest praise. An original mind at work is hardly likely to attain it. Those who are perfectly clear are apt to be nearer the commonplace.[35]

Holmes was immersed in his solitary art when Frederick Maitland's *Life and Letters of Leslie Stephen* arrived in the mail. The book told the story of Holmes's and Stephen's friendship, of their youthful climb in the Alps. Their long affectionate letters to each other were quoted. Holmes read the biography with deep feeling for his lost friend, and a curious sense of chastisement.

There was something great and impressive in Stephen's modesty and reverence for others. It stings me with self-criticism when I see some of those Englishmen who have done noble work never making themselves the center — thinking of what they do only as humble work for the Empire or their fellow men and treating it as much on a level with cricket. I feel genuine cosmic modesty — modesty for my race, which I surmise not to be the repository of final secrets. But when it comes to the purely human basis I can't help feeling in a personal way and wanting to beat the whole crowd — thinking about my work as *my* work and not simply as work which I hope may be useful. I fail too in regarding my work as simply part of my life — on a par with the rest of what one does. . . . But, . . . I don't worry too much.[36]

John Hay died. Henry Adams was alone in the twin houses on Lafayette Square. Adams, like Holmes, had few remaining friends of his own generation. They met cordially enough on the streets or in Lafayette Park, but rarely called on each other. Holmes, for his part, thought Adams too inclined to play the Old Cardinal meditating on ashes. But Adams sent him a copy of *Mont Saint Michel and Chartres*, his final effort to fix a point in the Middle Ages from which lines of development could be drawn through the present. Holmes read the work with great pleasure and admiration, but he and Adams exchanged only brief notes.

Henry James, too, was in Washington on a lecture tour, and dined with Holmes and Fanny. Holmes attended one of James's lectures:

He discoursed, mainly to ladies, yesterday afternoon, on the lesson of Balzac & said some good things — but one felt his consciousness in the artificial tones of his voice (the quality of which was fine) and somewhat in his discourse — which seemed to me to have an oblique eye to himself. He says, "Poor Wendell" and "Poor William" have chosen success — hum —[37]

Holmes's sixty-fifth birthday passed. His principal companions outside the Court were diplomats and hostesses on whom he occasionally called, and the young people who came to his house. He wrote avuncular letters to young women in London and played solitaire while he listened to Fanny read aloud in the evenings.

A young English author, H. G. Wells, came to call on the Holmeses in Washington, with letters of introduction from mutual friends in England. Wells was filled with excited talk about the new movement toward conscious, scientific management of society, talk of a "new republic" managed by "intellectual samurai,"[38] a movement that in England counted Holmes among its founders.

But, in the United States, the vistas of philosophy that Holmes tried to open went unremarked:

> I was amused yesterday. Having heard that Lester Ward — author of "Dynamic Sociology" and patriarch of the theme in this country — was about to leave Washington, I called, simply to express my homage. He seemed pleased and asked me what court I was judge of.[39]

> [He] expressed a polite surprise that any member of our Court should read his books.[40]

To Edward Ross, whose books on the new sociology Holmes also had read and admired, he wrote:

> I cannot refrain from writing a word of appreciation of the two books. . . . I have said to myself what vanity to think of intellectual solitude when such adequate thinking is going on. . . . "I could have painted like that youth you praise so" one thinks. But I do not repine.[41]

Holmes and Fanny continued in their joint and very busy solitude, dining with the President and Mrs. Roosevelt, receiving callers, dining out, working.

In June, there was a two-week recess, in which Holmes had only two opinions in minor cases, and then another summer of leisure opened before him. He began to pack for another trip to London: "I sail for England without gaiety of heart. As I grow older the notion of leaving my wife weighs on me more, and I do not believe I ever shall do it again."[42]

Fanny went with him as far as New York. It was a difficult parting. There was a crush of leave-takers; a newspaper photographer insisted on getting Holmes's picture.

At Beverly Farms, Fanny found the Boston newspapers waiting for her, with Holmes's picture in them:

> My dearest dearest Dearest —
> Please — please — You did not think I did not care. I was in a maze and I shall be till heavenly September comes — I wanted to

throw myself away when you went out of sight — Why could my wings not have sprouted and carried me into your stateroom for five minutes — I am so glad those men had their way and took the shot for when I got down here your poor face all filled with love and grief as I saw it last made me almost faint — Yet the Blessed Herald had another last look for me when I opened it and saw you again I almost shouted He did know his loving wife his other half left here to love and long for him —

It is cold and Apple Blossom here Pretty enough for those who like it — Everything that the servants can do to make me comfortable they are doing Even Ruthie made some Biscuits for my tea. . . . But Fanny without her husband finds the joyless house mournful tonight.

Don't ever think I am rough or cold or anything but your —
Adoring Wife

11 June 1907
How did you dare weep when I could not reach out to comfort you — Don't — don't again Please please don't[43]

In London, Holmes went through his rounds of entertainment a little mechanically. The newspapers talked of a new fast set in society, the "Coterie," who were the children of the Souls. Ethel Grenfell's boys and Lucy Clifford's girls were teenagers.

My ladies for the most part are growing older (along with me).[44]

I pose here more or less as an old fellow who remembers what no one else does.[45]

In Washington, the Roosevelt presidency was waning. Holmes's thoughts turned to his own retirement. He had set ten years on the Court as a kind of goal, or term of enlistment; he would then be eligible to retire on a pension, if he chose. But he began to say to friends that he would be pleased merely to survive to the age of seventy.

Among Holmes's own generation there was a sense of time running out, of their age ending. Henry Adams sent his *Education*; Holmes was touched by the sadness and sense of failure of the book, and wrote an encouraging note to Adams, who answered:

My dear Wendell
Your letter is a noble New Year's gift. . . . At seventy, it is hard not to take one's helplessness seriously. Just now I am desperately struggling to understand the new electric-aether which has been injected into chemistry and physics as the ultimate substance or deity of the new dispensation. . . .

I am driven to the conclusion that the law of mind in motion follows the same formula as the law of electric mass. . . .

This law is well enough for past history, but brings us into infinite speed, and contradictions in terms, within no time at all. We must be there now.[46]

This seemed to mean some vast cataclysm was impending, some gigantic discontinuity in history. Holmes did not believe in Adams's wild scientism, but he shared the sense that their age was ending. Brooks Adams, too, prophesied a kind of exponential world crash. There would be a vast consolidation of industry into state enterprises, and then war among the empires over exhausted natural resources. Holmes received long letters from a man in New York, Franklin Ford, who said the old order of governments based on arms was passing. The true powers and rulers were the financial exchanges and the news bureaus. Holmes puzzled over these letters, tantalized by hints of forces beneath appearances.[47]

On Sunday mornings, Holmes walked with Dorothy. In good weather they might walk up to Georgetown on the old towpath of the C & O Canal, down which Holmes had been carried from the battlefield at Ball's Bluff. After the walk, he would call on the chief justice. In the afternoon, he would write letters, if there were no opinions waiting for him, and would drop in on friends — perhaps Baroness Moncheur, wife of the Belgian ambassador, with whom he liked to venture an occasional flirtation, knowing that it would be calmly rebuffed, or the Brazilian ambassador, who encouraged him to read Portuguese literature. His friend James Bryce was now the British ambassador, and Holmes often called on him and his lady at the British embassy on Massachusetts Avenue. Holmes was more at ease among the diplomatic corps, aristocratic outsiders, than at occasional dinners for the powerful:

Last night I went to a dinner of men (I hate men's dinners) where I felt the pulse of the country with a vengeance. A gentleman high among the political powers — high even among the potentates present — when he had got or seemed to have got a little warmed up — took possession of the table. And proceeded (my host professed, to his astonishment, although I suspected a put up job,) to call up about 2/3 of those present — and there seemed to be joy at getting some of those present committed about the District of Columbia which wants an appropriation (the host is a power in the District). He even proposed my health — adverting unfavorably to my drinking only water. And later he disported himself with profanity and humor over various personalities — calling most of them by their first names. . . . In calling up one of the older Judges he took the occasion to remark that though he didn't care a damn for later comers he loved Harlan and White. . . . I was kept late and went away with an irritation that has grown.[48]

At White House dinners there was an air of imminent parting. One evening, Holmes sat beside Charles Evans Hughes, governor of New York, whom he liked and who told him that *The Common Law* had first inspired his interest in the law. After dinner on the White House terrace, the President called Holmes over to make a foursome with the chief justice — and William Jennings Bryan. Holmes cheerfully and with secret malice lectured Bryan about the folly of trying to break up railroads. Bryan was not persuaded. Holmes ended by saying, amiably, "You are stiff-necked," to which Bryan answered, "You are weak-kneed."[49]

The *Northern Securities* matter was at last in the open; Roosevelt joined in the conversation, and then invited Holmes to return for a tête-à-tête dinner the next night. "We said one last word about the old No. Securities Case & that matter is finished."[50]

Charles Poe had gone on to Seattle to pursue his law career, sending back friendly reports to Dorothy of his work and marriage, and was succeeded each year by a new secretary from Harvard, chosen by John Gray. The secretaries kept up-to-date the red-leather-bound docket book, and summarized for Holmes, in a single page of handwriting — there was no typewriter in Holmes's house — the documents that accompanied the growing numbers of requests for Supreme Court review that the messenger brought almost daily. The secretary was also expected to help Fanny serve tea and entertain guests on her at-home days, to pay bills, keep Holmes's checkbook up to date, and accompany Holmes on afternoon walks.

Some of the secretaries did not rise above the status of members of the domestic staff. Holmes would try their ability with an innocently given assignment. What was the origin of negligence in tort law? he would ask; if the secretary understood that the question tested his familiarity with Holmes's own writings, he might get further assignments. But even then, only rarely. At most, Holmes would occasionally ask the secretary to find a pertinent case.

When Tom Corcoran, one of the secretaries of whom Holmes grew fond, was finally given permission to look up a case, he went to the Library of Congress and found a decision of the House of Lords, exactly on the point wanted. He rushed back to I Street and burst into the library exclaiming, "I've got a case, I've got a case." Holmes told him to quiet down and then, after a pause:

"Is it a case of absolutely prime authority? Is it an opinion of Holmes for the Supreme Court of the United States?"

"No, sir."

"Is it the next best thing, a Holmes opinion of the Supreme Judicial Court of Massachusetts?"

"No, sir."

"Then why are you so excited?"[51]

For the favored secretaries, there would be serious talks; some became near-worshipful admirers of the old man, whose courtly manners and cheerful good humor never seemed to fail.

Holmes's colleagues were growing feeble. Justice Brown was too ill and weak to continue serving and was obliged to leave the Supreme Court; his replacement, Attorney General William Moody, too, was soon in ill health. Peckham was having trouble with his eyes, and Brewer was going deaf. White bent ever more deeply over his papers, index finger beside his nose. They were old men, and it was plain that Fuller, now nearly eighty, could not much longer lead them.

If Holmes thought of being chief justice, he said nothing about it. Certainly he knew that his only real chance for the post would come if Fuller resigned while Roosevelt was still President. But Holmes encouraged Fuller to stay on and remarked occasionally that he had learned not to rely on the President's friendship.

Progressive legislation continued to come before the Court for review, and generally passed muster; but occasionally, when a statute seemed to take the labor side in a struggle between workers and employers, the Court struck it down, repeating its new formula: Liberty of Contract. Holmes dissented in these cases, mildly repeating what he had said twenty years before in Massachusetts:

> I quite agree that the question what and how much good labor unions do is one on which intelligent people may differ — I think that laboring men sometimes attribute to them advantages, as many attribute to the combinations of capital disadvantages, that are really due to economic conditions of a far wider and deeper kind — but I could not pronounce it unwarranted if Congress should decide that to foster a strong union was for the best interest, not only of the men, but of . . . the country at large.[52]

Holmes's old friend Louis Brandeis appeared before the Court on January 15, 1908, as one of the counsel for the state of Oregon, defending a law limiting women's labor in factories and laundries to ten hours per day. The Grand Laundry in Portland had required one of its workers, Mrs. E. Gotcher, to work more than ten hours on a Saturday; the owner of the laundry, Joe Haselbock, was fined ten dollars and appealed.

Brandeis did not ask the Court to rise above its prejudices or to uphold the law as a measure favoring labor. He instead cut his case sharply away from disputes between labor and capital, and with inexorable illustrations proved to the Court that a limit on the hours of women's work was a hygienic, a eugenic, measure. He cited to the Court similar laws of Germany, Switzerland, and England; he detailed research that had shown women's health and morals depended on their working conditions and that the fitness of children depended on their mothers' welfare.

Justice Brewer, of them all the most likely to be hostile to measures favoring labor, wrote the opinion upholding the law for a unanimous Court. He approvingly summarized Brandeis's brief — which thereby became famous — and quoted from German sources:

> As healthy mothers are essential to vigorous offspring, the physical well-being of woman becomes an object of public interest and care in order to preserve the strength and vigor of the race.[53]

The Bakery Workers case seemed forgotten; but if Holmes had played some role in the Court's new affirmation of progressive principle, it was unremarked.

> My friend and colleague White, pitching into me as usual for under brevity and obscurity, told me the other day that there was no man in the U.S. whose reputation so little corresponded to what he had done. If I could accept the implication of good as well as the rest I should be content. Anyhow, I am doing the best I can.[54]

Holmes and Fanny bought the house in Beverly Farms they had rented for many summers, a big house with verandas and bay windows like the one Holmes fondly remembered at Canoe Meadow, and in 1908 they went about the property happily, planning plantings that would not come to maturity for many years, considering seriously how a tree might alter the landscape, how blue flowers would look under the pine.

The presidential election came and passed. Taft was nominated and easily elected, as had been expected, with Roosevelt's active support. The social season in Washington began, with past and future Presidents both on the scene:

> We have been dining out all this week, once with Taft and afterwards to the White House to see moving pictures of a wolf hunt — where the man caught the wolf by grabbing him in the mouth behind the big teeth and the Presdt. [Roosevelt] had the man there. But I own as I grow older I dislike the cruelties of sport and in this case my sympathies were all with the wolf — when I saw a crowd of men, horses and dogs all after this poor little creature in his native home. Last night we dined at the White House and had

some pleasant talk with the Presdt. He repeated to me at more length than heretofore how he had been warned against me by the respectable men of weight in Boston etc. as a partial anarchist and generally dangerous person.[55]

Holmes would miss Roosevelt. The new President struck him as a man of ordinary abilities, remarkable mainly for a certain impression of frankness:

I am conscious of contradictory feelings within — sadness of sympathy with the departing [Roosevelts] and a feeling that as persons they are irreplaceable and on the other hand relief from a continued row and rumpus that to my Philistine mind hasn't seemed to amount to much.[56]

On March 4, a Thursday, a miserable cold rain fell, and the inauguration of the new President consequently was held indoors in the Senate Chamber. On the following Monday, March 8, Holmes was sixty-eight, close to the mark of seventy he had set for himself:

Praise be to Allah I am a merry bard — or at least life feels to me so like a job or a race that as yet I don't repine as I draw toward the post — I have not had as much recognition as I should like.[57]

21

JEU SUI ARNAUT

WHEN THE SUPREME COURT GATHERED FOR THE OPENING OF its term on the first Monday in October, 1909, four of the justices were past seventy years old. Chief Justice Fuller, who was seventy-six, presided and was still alert, but he was no longer able to write his share of the opinions. White and Holmes carried between them a large part of the burden of the Court's work. McKenna, always erratic and never, in Holmes's view, a substantial figure, could not be counted upon. William Moody, who had served only two years and was comparatively young, was disabled and bedridden with rheumatism.[1] Brewer was deaf and growing confused. Harlan, the senior justice, had always found the work difficult, and wrote very few opinions now. President Taft was impatient:

> The condition of the Supreme Court is pitiable, and yet these old fools hold on with a tenacity that is most discouraging. Really the Chief Justice is almost senile; Harlan does no work; Brewer is so deaf that he cannot hear and has got beyond the point of the commonest accuracy in writing his opinions; Brewer and Harlan sleep almost through all the arguments. I don't know what can be done.[2]

The President did not yet know that Peckham, too, had fallen gravely ill during the summer and that when the Court convened in October there would be two vacant chairs.

Holmes, however, was refreshed by his summer, and full of energy. He welcomed the chance to write a bigger share of the Court's opinions and prepared himself for a steady siege of work with few diversions.

During the summer, he and Fanny had gone to England together, for the first time in almost thirty years. Holmes had been invited to receive an honorary doctorate at Oxford — the invitation had arrived without warning in May:

> a fine old-fashioned document requesting the hono*u*r of the presence of The Honourable etc. at the Encaenia on Wed. June 23, the Hebdomadal Council having resolved to propose to the Convocation of the University that the degree of Doctor of the Civil Law, honoris causa, be conferred upon him, etc.[3]

Fanny had insisted that he should go, difficult as their last separation had been, but Holmes would not leave Fanny behind. Dorothy was married now, and Fanny would be alone. So they went together to accept the honor. It was an easier journey for Fanny than earlier visits to Great Britain had been. In London, they stayed with Leslie and Ethel Scott, who were like niece and nephew to Fanny. Holmes went out in society, and Fanny, who remained behind, was entertained and cared for. The Scotts' house was a gem:

> You go down by the Houses of Parliament and turn into a little street to your right. You pull out your passkey and go through a little door in a wall of the 10th Century (St. Dunstan's) and within is the house. My bedroom window looked out on a spacious garden with trees lawn and flowers — to the left the wall of the Westminster School — opposite my windows the Deanery with Abbey rising behind — to my right the towers of Parliament. All the traffic of London was round the corner and the only sounds were the cooing of ring doves and the chiming of the hours.[4]

At Oxford, the ceremony was gratifyingly medieval. Holmes was given a scarlet gown with crimson silk sleeves, and a black velvet Holbein cap trimmed with gold thread. There was a carriage ride with Fellows of All Souls College and a procession in gowns up the aisle of the Sheldonian Theatre. The gallery was crowded with young men in black and white and ladies in brightly colored summer dresses. William Holdsworth, historian of law, gave an address in Latin, and Holmes was too preoccupied to attend to what was being said. An undergraduate sang out from the balcony, "Can you translate, sir?" and Holmes looked up with a grin.

He was honored, not for his work as a judge but for *The Common Law*. Holdsworth and the scholars of a still newer generation of legal historians had recognized Holmes as a forebear. Holmes said, "I don't care for it as much as I should have twenty-five years ago,"[5] but he was immensely pleased. The vice chancellor spoke; Holmes mounted steps to the pulpit, shook hands, and took his seat in a row of red-gowned doctors.[6]

In the evening, he dined at Christ Church, and was called on to make a speech for which he had had little chance to prepare; but, the dinner "was so harmonious and charming that when it came to be done I felt at home and at ease and said my few words without anxiety."[7]

In London, Holmes saw old friends. Willy Grenfell had been ennobled by Arthur Balfour's government, now out of office; he and Ethel were Lord and Lady Desborough. Herbert Asquith was now prime minister in a new Liberal government, and Margot sent characteristic scribbled notes from 10 Downing Street: "Do look in at the [Foreign Office] party not later than 10:30 & see us all with our Royalties."[8] Lord and Lady Castletown were in town, and Holmes saw them there. But Holmes and Fanny did not linger in London. When the Scotts went to their Irish country house, the Holmeses went with them: "A remote old house with a scrap of lovely Norman church built on to an earlier tower of refuge, with an effigy of an old boy in armor. . . . A nightingale sang in the afternoon."[9]

In September, Beverly Farms, where they rested until it was time to return to Washington, was in its own way like the cloistered houses of Ireland and London. Servants cared for them. The landscape, familiar and harsh, was strewn with personal memories and the history of three centuries. Holmes rented a carriage, as usual, from Wyatt & Trout, and their driver, as always, was George Larcom, the talkative old Yankee. "We toddle round behind a single horse — jawing with the driver," Holmes said. He liked to think of himself and Larcom as the last Yankees.

> This country has my earliest associations and they largely affect if they don't control our deepest loves and reverences. Among the foundations of my soul are granite rocks and barberry bushes, and the steps in Boston leading down from Montgomery Place.[10]

Fanny had insisted that they install a telephone — their number was "Beverly Farms 14" and the telephone was listed under Fanny's name to keep off strangers — but Fanny would not use the telephone at all, and Holmes would not talk if he could avoid doing it. He would tell people to leave messages and not ask to speak to him. When he was obliged to speak, he would announce very loudly into the mouthpiece, "This is Mr. Justice Holmes," and would complain that he could not hear.[11]

He turned to books again that summer. With great pleasure he read the newest volumes in Holdsworth's magisterial history of the common law, and was pleased to feel the influence of his own work. Holmes's ideas had changed very little in twenty-five years, and he liked to see the younger men confirming them. The human race was evolving toward greater consciousness, self-awareness, and self-direction. Law someday would be an instrument for conscious shaping of human evolution itself. But he thought now that day might be far in the future. He had grown more skeptical of scientific knowledge, yet he still clung to the idea that mankind someday might "take its own destiny consciously and intelligently in hand."[12]

His own original scholarly work was far in the past. He chatted benignly with the younger men and made epigrams: "I . . . have to turn my old ideas and try to pass them off for new on strangers, with the help of a swagger — "[13] He was content with the law as he found it, and was more concerned to preserve its fabric than to make it new. He jumped when he heard someone say, "The boys liked Roosevelt because he didn't give a damn for the law." To young Clara Stevens, Holmes scolded:

> In your last [letter] you spoke somewhat contemptuously of the law-abiding attitude. I don't agree with you in your feeling. . . . I think we have too little of it. . . . And this is not because of my job, but because the instinct is the foundation upon which society coheres.[14]

In September, there was a dinner in Boston for the new President, who was summering in Beverly. Holmes and Fanny stayed at a hotel in Boston that night, and after the long dinner they walked through familiar darkened streets to their hotel. As they passed two men, Holmes overheard snatches of conversation: "A good judge — we thought him a trifle erratic — Chief Justice."[15]

There was a parade of Civil War veterans in Essex County, and the President reviewed the parade. Holmes rode in the procession as a guest.[16]

> I was moved as I always am when I see a lot of [veterans] together and could but think that every year now the line would grow shorter a good deal. I began to realize what when I was a boy I used to think it would be a fine thing — to be carried in a civic procession as a survivor. I little thought what it was to be a survivor, then.[17]

The summer ended, and the cautious journey to Washington began. The servants went ahead, while Holmes and Fanny stopped in New York City to see a friend off on the Cunard line.[18] At the foot of Manhattan, where the ships sailed, an old soot-blackened church was overshadowed by new office buildings. Fanny said, "The churches used to reach nearest heaven but now business looks down on the steeples," a remark that Holmes liked to repeat.[19]

In Washington, the seven members of the Court who could still attend its sittings gathered. Chief Justice Fuller's face had the slackness of great age. He seemed still more tiny and frail between Harlan and White. The absent Moody, crippled by rheumatism, was still bedridden at his home in Haverhill, Massachusetts, and unlikely to recover, but he was not yet eligible for a pension and therefore was reluctant to resign. There would be an effort to have Congress authorize a pension for him, but that would take months, and meanwhile his chair would remain vacant. The severity of Peckham's illness was not yet apparent, but he, too, would be absent for some time.

President Taft had already decided on Moody's replacement. The new man was to be Horace Lurton, an old and close personal friend.[20] There were difficulties — the President had been publicly complaining about the age of the present members, but Lurton was sixty-two, older than any man yet appointed to the Court. And Lurton was a Democrat, while the President and Senate were Republican. But Taft had set his heart on his friend's appointment, and he found inducements to persuade the Senators to accept his choice. There were rumors of what was offered and what was taken, but before the Court convened in October the thing was accomplished. White — who kept up his friendships in the Senate — wrote sadly to Holmes:

> Yes, Lurton seems to be the man. He was here some days since. Many things which have been said to me, which I hope are not true, as to supplying the place, bode ill for the country and point to degenerate times.[21]

It would be months before Lurton could replace Moody, however, and Peckham was still ill; Holmes prepared himself for the work.

> I am not likely to be idle. With two judges ill and at best no immediate prospect of their return and the Chief and two seniors pretty old, I think the working oars are likely to be White, Day and myself. . . . I have served notice on the two or three people I oftenest call upon down here that they must not expect much and have pretty well got my decks cleared for action.[22]

There were few distractions, in any case. Baroness Moncheur was gone; the baron had somehow displeased his government and was transferred that summer to Constantinople; Holmes could no longer call on the baroness every Friday, as had been his habit. He could only write

long affectionate letters to her. The Brazilian ambassador, Joaquín Nabuco de Araujo, another close friend, fell ill that fall, and by January
would be dead. To his widow Holmes wrote, "Let me add a word of private grief to the public expressions that we all hear. . . . I loved him and
I feel what the loss must be to those who were nearest to him."[23]

Peckham died on October 24, and the justices went up to Albany for
his funeral, in accordance with tradition, although this took a week out
of their sittings and further exhausted them. Horace Lurton, already
chosen for Moody's seat, was appointed to Peckham's.

Illnesses and death among Holmes's colleagues prompted uncomfortable thoughts.[24] Perhaps the most difficult thing of all for Holmes
was the chief justice's slow failing. Fuller was often absent from Court
that winter. Aside from his fondness for the Chief, Holmes's work depended so much on what the chief justice assigned to him, and Fuller
had been so uniquely generous, taking more pleasure in Holmes's opinions than his own, that his resignation would be a great personal loss.

Holmes himself fell ill that fall, suffering the deep wrenching cough
that he remembered so well from his brother's and his father's last years.
The cough kept him awake at night. He wondered whether he should
keep on; perhaps he would retire at seventy-two, when he would have
the ten years' service required for a full pension.[25] But he went on cheerfully, talking and writing. To the baroness, he wrote lightly about etchings he had bought, and a reception at the grand new house on Dupont
Circle that spoiled Mrs. Hubbard's charming garden. There had been an
exhibition of the much-talked-of modern dance, "without the hoped-for
improprieties."[26] At times his talk became too relentlessly cheerful, for
which he mildly apologized:

> Charley Whittier in the Army used to say to me you are such a
> cheerful nut. The transitoriness of things is felt more as one grows
> older — and I have my reflections — but I think it the part of a
> good soldier to keep them to oneself for the most part — and
> regard people who are eternally prophesying evil or drumming
> on the void, like Brooks and Henry Adams, as showing their fear
> and not doing the gallant thing. . . . I never despair about the uni-
> verse — as H. A. does in a little book [*The Education of Henry Ad-
> ams*] recently printed — the foundation of that kind of despair is
> arrogance.[27]

He settled into a determined regime. He rose at 8:30 each morning,
and at 9:30, seven days a week, he was at his grandfather's big desk in
the rear library, occasionally rising to write at the standing desk at the
rear window, where he could look out over the garden and the housetops. If there was no opinion to write, he wrote letters. At 11:30, when
the Court was in session, he walked to the Capitol. On his return at five,

he was at his desk again, until seven. After dinner, if they had dined at home, he would return to the library for an hour and then would come down to the parlor, listen to Fanny, play solitaire or read to himself until 1:30 in the morning, and then sleep. Opinions for the Court flowed in a steady stream from his desk:

> [W]e must be cautious about pressing the broad words of the Fourteenth Amendment to a drily logical extreme. Many laws which it would be vain to ask the Court to overthrow could be shown, easily enough, to transgress a scholastic interpretation of one or another of the great guarantees in the Bill of Rights. They more or less limit the liberty of the individual or they diminish property to a certain extent. We have few scientifically certain criteria of legislation, and . . . it often is difficult to mark the line where what is called the police power of the States is limited by the Constitution of the United States. . . .
>
> It is asked . . . where we are going to draw the line. But the last is a futile question. . . . With regard to the police power, as elsewhere in the law, lines are pricked out by the gradual approach and contact of decisions on the opposing sides.[28]

His occasional dissents slid through the air like bullets:

> I cannot believe that in the long run the public will profit by this Court permitting knaves to cut reasonable prices for some ulterior purpose of their own and thus to impair, if not to destroy, the production and sale of articles which it is assumed to be desirable that the public should be able to get.
>
> The conduct of the defendant falls within a general prohibition of the law. It is fraudulent and has no merits of its own to recommend it to the favor of the Court.[29]

His letters, and his now rare speeches, flowed with a powerfully assured spontaneity:

> Do you remember a generalization on which I used to pride myself, that friendship, truth and property have a common root — time? That the human plant shapes its roots to the crevices where it grows, and after they have gradually adjusted themselves, cannot be torn out without assailing life . . . ?[30]

> I have been reading a golden book, or rather books, for there are ten volumes of it: Fabre's *Souvenirs Entomologiques*. . . . It is simply the exquisitely told tale of a life-long watch of beetles and wasps, but from it we learn the faith I spoke of. . . . Fabre tells us

of grubs born and having passed their whole lives in the heart of
an oak that when, after three years, the time for metamorphosis
comes, build a chamber that as grubs they do not need with a
broad passage for the beetle that is to be. They obey their destiny
without any sight of the promised land. The law of the grub . . .
is the law also for man.[31]

When Lurton came on to the Court in January, the pressure on
Holmes eased a little. In the quiet mornings he began to read Dante's
Divine Comedy with an English prose translation lying beside the Italian.

A single passage in the *Purgatory* pierced his marrow. Among those
guilty of the sin of lust Dante found his old Master of Song bathed in
flames. The Master pointed to another who he said was a still greater
poet. This great troubadour spoke to Dante out of the flames, in an old
French like that of the law books:

Jeu sui Arnaut, qui plor e vau cantan

I am Arnaut, who weeps and goes singing.[32]

Holmes closed the book and rushed outside. For a week afterward the
line echoed in his thoughts.[33]

There were bizarre rumors circulating in Washington. Theodore
Roosevelt and President Taft were said to have an agreement that Roosevelt would return to the presidency in 1912. In exchange for turning
back the presidency, Taft would be made chief justice.

You hear fears that we shall live the rest of our lives under a
benevolent despotism, that [Roosevelt] will come in and stay with
a subservient Congress, that 500,000 armed men would come to
New York on his call, etc., etc., all of which I don't believe.[34]

Halley's comet hung in the sky, seemingly motionless, growing
brighter. On May 19, 1910, the earth passed through the comet's tail,
and there was uneasy talk of catastrophes. Holmes and Fanny went to
the Naval Observatory on Massachusetts Avenue that night, where there
was a party, and saw the comet with a strange exhilaration. They were
separated by the crowd and were carried off to different suppers and did
not meet again until two in the morning.[35]

Justice David Brewer died suddenly that month. Holmes confided to
the baroness, "I think it was a good thing for him and (between our-
selves) the Court. He had grown very deaf, his energies seemed to me to
be failing."[36] Only four justices remained who had been on the bench
when Holmes joined it.

Charles Evans Hughes, the governor of New York, who had spoken flatteringly to Holmes at a White House dinner two years before, was appointed to Brewer's place. Taft told Hughes — who was a potential rival for the presidency in 1912 — that he meant to make him chief justice when Fuller retired.[37]

The Court, reduced again to seven members while it waited for Hughes, adjourned early. Holmes wearily helped Fanny to pack for the summer in Beverly Farms:

> The term has left me somewhat tired. Just think — it is the Eighth — 8th ! that I have been here . . . years tick by like seconds to me. Last night I dreamed that I was to be executed — a sort of unpleasant premonition of the approach of *finis*. One begins to sum up — a vain attempt.[38]

On the Fourth of July, Melville Fuller died quietly at his house among the trees in Sorrento, Maine. His daughter Jane was alone in the house with him, and heard him call, "I am very ill," but when she came to his room he was dead. Holmes received a telegram that day, and the next night he spent on the train.[39]

> The services at Sorrento moved me through and through. It was touching enough to see the place where the Chief had sat and tamed the squirrels so that they came and sat on his shoulder. And all the details of the ceremony were free from a single false note. The sun shone, the birds sang, the coffin was put on a buckboard and spread with a coverlet of flowers . . . the parson read the service extremely well, which is rare, the church built by Richardson was charming, and a choir of four young villagers sang sweetly and movingly. "It was not death the avenger but death the friend." . . . He died in the same place and with the same quiet as his wife a few years before. And so ends a great career. . . . He loved me and I shall miss him as long as I sit on the Bench.[40]

Holmes went with the family to Chicago, where the other justices joined them. There was a seventeen-gun salute over the lake, followed by grand solemnities and bombast at Graceland Cemetery. Then another long journey by train, finishing a wrenching week of travel, and Holmes was back in Beverly Farms. The Chief's death had stirred hardly a ripple in the life of the nation:

> How can one care for the average interests of one's fellow men — The newspapers gave much more attention to the movements of [Jack] Johnson the black pugilist after his battle than to a great man dead.[41]

And still more bitterly, "I think the public will not realize what a great man it has lost."[42]

> He was true not only to the duties but to the dignity of [his] office and he never would see it impaired even in the slightest detail. He was brave and good and wise. He did great service to the state and he made life happier to one who would call him friend.[43]

On August 26, 1910, William James died of heart disease at his summer house in Chocorua, New Hampshire. Holmes and Fanny and the few remaining survivors of the circle of friends who had flirted and fallen in love in those summers more than forty years past gathered again. They seemed old to each other's eyes. Henry James and Holmes were pallbearers.

Holmes said little about it. He was saddened, and obscurely angry. The *Boston Evening Transcript* said that William James had been the greatest of contemporary Americans.

> Wm James's death cuts a root for me that went far into the past, but of late, indeed for many years, we had seen little of each other and had little communication except as he occasionally sent me a book. Distance, other circumstances, and latterly my little sympathy with his spiritualism and pragmatism were sufficient cause. His reason made him skeptical [but] his wishes led him to turn down the lights so as to give miracle a chance.[44]

Two more deaths affected Holmes that summer. His Civil War sergeant, Gustave Magnitzky, who had been office manager for Shattuck, Holmes and Munroe and who had continued to keep Amelia's trust accounts for Holmes, died in September: "I was expecting to stop and see Captain Magnitzky on going to town this week, when the telephone told me that he was dead. Our friendship had lasted for nearly fifty years."[45]

For a last time that summer Holmes was a pallbearer: for Lloyd Bowers, the solicitor general of the United States, of whom Holmes had become very fond and whom he had hoped to see appointed to one of the vacancies on the Court.[46]

It was sadly like wartime. During Holmes's tenure Shiras, Brown, Moody, Peckham, Brewer, and Fuller all had died or been disabled. Holmes was now third in seniority on a diminished Court, and Harlan, who was visibly too old for the work, was presiding.

Before Holmes returned to Washington in October, he had an interview with Taft in Beverly Farms, and the President came to dinner one evening. They talked about the need for a new chief justice. Holmes himself, of course, was one of the possible candidates. It would certainly be the last opportunity, if it was an opportunity: "I have always assumed absolutely that I should not be regarded as possible."[47] If anything was said about the Philippine tariff case, neither man mentioned it afterward. Holmes was not distressed. He confided to Nina Gray:

> If I ever put my ambition in office, I perhaps should note that everyone on the bench except McKenna and me has been suggested for Chief Justice. But as the possibility of my appointment never has entered my head I confine my aspirations to being the greatest legal thinker in the world — or as near as I can get — which I am sure you will think modest.[48]
>
> I wouldn't do much more than walk across the street to be called Chief Justice instead of Justice.[49]

A kind of peace descended over Holmes after the season of deaths and the passing of perhaps his only opportunity to be Chief Justice. Holmes found himself, a little to his own surprise, quite happy. He was alive; it was early autumn in Beverly Farms.

> Well, I believe that a good digestion and a hard heart are the conditions of a green old age.[50]
>
> The Virginia creeper on the fence in front of the house is brilliant, the asters make a fat purple wreath on this side, and it is crowned with clematis in bloom.[51]

Washington, when Holmes and Fanny returned in October, was filled with rumors about the new chief justice. Holmes, with most others, supposed that it would be Hughes, who had given up his governorship and a chance for the presidential nomination. The newspapers reported this, and Hughes himself thought so.[52] But White was lobbying for the post through his friends in the Senate. And Harlan had let it be known that he, too, would like the position, as a capstone for his career, on the understanding that it would soon be available again for a younger man.

When the Court met on October 10, Harlan presided, and White was uncharacteristically moody.

Holmes, quite certain by then that he, at least, would not be chief justice, was more calm and at ease than he had been since coming on the Court. He was no longer overburdened with opinions to write, but Harlan gave him his share, including some of the interesting little ones of which he was so fond:

The time is going on busily but peacefully. It may be simply that now I take 8 instead of 7 hours in bed and mostly in sleep but at all events for some reason I don't worry — either over my work . . . or over consequences — I think of the future with the sadness of the old, but I enjoy my part in helping to bring it about as much as ever.[53]

Time passed, and still there was no announcement of a chief justice. The newspapers continued to speculate that Hughes would be nominated; he was growing embarrassed and wished that the matter would be settled promptly. One Sunday evening in December, he received a telephone call from the White House; half an hour later, while he was still dressing to see the President, another call came and canceled the invitation. He heard nothing further that night.

That afternoon and evening a group of senators had met with the President, and lobbied him very strongly to promote Justice White. Perhaps they changed Taft's mind; afterward, however, he liked to say genially that it was the Philippine tariff cases that first called White's abilities to his attention.[54]

The next morning, December 11, while the Court was sitting, a messenger handed Justice White a note, and he left the bench; outside the courtroom a group of senators, led by Henry Cabot Lodge, waited to tell him that the President had nominated him for chief justice.[55] The Senate approved the nomination by acclamation that same morning. The next day, White was sworn in by Harlan, and moved one seat to his right. Holmes said afterward, "Hughes' dignity was magnificent, he didn't turn a hair but just went on with his work as if nothing had happened."[56]

Holmes was pleased at the appointment, and for his friend Edward White he was both pleased and concerned, for he thought the new Chief would worry too much over his work: "He thinks like a legislator of consequences, all the time — and sees the ruin of the republic in a wrong decision — which makes it harder for him, but is valuable for the Court."[57]

Holmes's seventieth birthday passed. He had achieved the first milestone of survival that he had set for himself. He and Fanny celebrated quietly; there was no public notice of the event. But Harlan, his lionhearted friend, put a bunch of violets at his place on the bench that morning.[58]

In June, Holmes and Fanny closed up the house on I Street as usual, but with a modern flourish, to which Holmes halfheartedly objected — "Fanny has got one of those dust-devourers that swallows everything into a bag and men are doing my library. I suffer — [but] it must needs be."[59]

At Harvard's commencement that summer, Holmes said a few words, for it was the fiftieth anniversary of the graduation of his class. He spoke as he always did when addressing the young, with pleasure, and ended with an image that Fanny had suggested to him:

> One learns from time an amiable latitude with regard to beliefs and tastes. Life is painting a picture, not doing a sum. . . . I [have] learned . . . what I think the best service that we can do for our country and for ourselves: To see as far as one may, and to feel, the great forces that are behind every detail — for that makes all the difference between philosophy and gossip, between great action and small: the least wavelet of the Atlantic Ocean is mightier than one of Buzzards Bay — to hammer out as compact and solid a piece of work as one can, to try to make it first rate, and to leave it unadvertised. . . .
>
> When one listens from above to the roar of a great city, there comes to one's ears — almost indistinguishable, but there — the sound of church bells, chiming the hours, or offering a pause in the rush, a moment for withdrawal and prayer. Commerce has outsoared the steeples that once looked down upon the marts, but still their note makes music of the din. For those of us who are not churchmen the symbol still lives. Life is a roar of bargain and battle, but in the very heart of it there rises a mystic spiritual tone that gives meaning to the whole. It transmutes the dull details into romance. It reminds that our only but wholly adequate significance is as parts of the unimaginable whole. It suggests that even while we think that we are egotists we are living to ends outside ourselves.[60]

Dorothy came to Beverly Farms that summer once more, to have her baby and to be cared for by Fanny in what had become her home.[61]

In September the Holmeses returned to Washington, and when the Court convened in October, Harlan seemed feeble and complained of stomachache. He had trouble walking when he left the bench, and did not return. He seemed to fail quickly after that; at times, he seemed delirious, and on October 14, he died.

A little more than a year remained until Holmes would have served the ten years required to retire with a pension:

> The time is drawing near when if I live I shall be master of my fate. I don't know in the least what I shall do when my time is up, a year from next December. If I keep in my present condition I flatter myself that the brethren will want me to keep on, but I have seen the evils and I shall leave the decision till nearer the time. It would be very nice, in any event, to feel that one was free to do as one chose.[62]

From his place in Washington he could see waves of change sweeping over the world, but had no intimation of the part he had yet to play.

The managers of business enterprises, fifty years after the Civil War, had learned to operate continent-spanning industrial corporations. The big companies assembled by the bankers — United States Steel, Standard Oil, American Tobacco — had become enterprises of great power. President Taft dutifully brought suits under the antitrust laws to break up these great corporations.

The justices of the Supreme Court had been deeply divided over these suits, but Chief Justice White wrought them into harmony. The growing organization of industry would be allowed to proceed, but unreasonable or unfair practices would be punished. Once again, the law would permit deep changes in society so long as they proceeded peacefully, and fairly.

Holmes, his more serious concerns satisfied, now for the most part concurred instead of dissenting in the antitrust cases, although he continued to denounce the laws privately as foolish. The antitrust laws said you must fight, but you may not win.[63] "If Harlan had had his way, he would have cut all these concerns into inch bits."

The world was being organized into a half-dozen empires, each arming as if for war. England, preparing for conflict, allied itself with America and Japan. The newly risen German empire allied itself with its old rival, the Austrian. France and Russia agreed to defend each other. Continent-spanning railways, great steel works, and munitions companies prepared for war. Long-range cannon and high explosives seemed to make war too destructive to be fought, but the arming continued, for no state would be a nation without weapons.

James Bryce, as British ambassador, labored to create a system of agreements among the empires that would allow arbitration of international disputes — a system of law in place of violence.

In the spring of 1912, when Holmes wrote to John Gray approving his choice of secretary for that year, he added with evident relish that he now reserved the right to die or resign, for on December 8, he would have served ten years on the Court and would be free by his own reckoning to leave it.[64] It was spring again:

> The hyacinths and tulips are fat and splendid, and the park is full of misty blurs of bliss, red of maple and green of willow and a thousand tender grays and browns, and the birds sing, and the brooks and the young frogs (until you come too near and try to see them) and on Saturday we found a bank alive with bloodroot, and windflowers, and the other flowers whose names I forget, and all the trumpets blow another charge, I hope not yet the last.[65]

New honors came to Holmes that summer, as if to mark the conclusion of his term of service. *The Common Law* was translated into German
and was well received by a new generation of German scholars for whom
evolution was the guiding principle of history. A French historian of the
Roman law paid Holmes a graceful compliment. The Massachusetts Bar
Association commissioned his portrait, Williams College gave him an
honorary degree, and, at Harvard, an undergraduates' club of which he
had been a member fifty years before gave him a dinner:

> Just now I have been receiving several pats of a friendly
> kind. . . . The last was last night when they gave me a dinner at a
> College Club at Cambridge where were the Presdt. of Harvard
> Coll., the Dean of the Law School et al. and a lot of clear eyed
> lads. They really did what they could to make me think myself a
> great man.[66]

He spoke to the undergraduates of his trust in the forces that carried
them together into the future.[67]

While the machinery of the modern state and of modern warfare rose
around him, Holmes read Alfred Zimmern's *Greek Commonwealth* with
great pleasure, and all summer long he said in letters that the collapse
of empires and exhaustion of resources might not be without compen-
sations, if only it meant a return to communities like Athens.[68]

Roosevelt and Taft fought each other for the Republican nomination
in 1912, but the Republican regulars gave it to Taft. At the party's convention in Chicago, Taft asked a political clubman from his native Ohio,
Warren G. Harding, to give his nominating address. The handsome
Harding, with a performer's presence and geniality, stood on the national stage for the first time. Roosevelt, who so many years before had
remained loyal to James G. Blaine and the party regulars, now rebelled
and took his insurgents out of the convention into a radical new Progressive party, loudly complaining that he had been denied the Republican nomination through corruption and fraud. There were threats of
violence and new rumors of armed revolt. Roosevelt said that nothing in
the Constitution should be allowed to thwart the power of the majority.
He called himself "Colonel," and campaigned at times in the sombrero
that was a reminder of his service in the Spanish War. He attacked the
courts — they were out of reach of the majority's power — and called
the judges corrupt:

> Behind the ostensible government sits enthroned an invisible
> government owing no allegiance and acknowledging no respon-
> sibility to the people. To destroy this invisible government . . . the
> people [have forged] a new instrument of government [the Pro-
> gressive Party] to give effect to their will.[69]

In October, a man fired a pistol into Roosevelt's body as he walked to give a speech in Milwaukee, but Roosevelt was not gravely injured, and gave his speech before letting the doctors see him.

The courts, the Supreme Court in particular, were vilified from every side. Gustavus Myers, a socialist, published a popular "History of the Supreme Court," in which its present members were said to be connected with "predatory" business and "fraudulent ventures." The Socialist party's candidate, Norman Thomas, attacked the corruption of the courts. The Democratic candidate, Woodrow Wilson — whom Holmes despised as a demagogue[70] — bowed to the radical sentiment without precisely endorsing it.

To all this William Howard Taft replied with only a weary caution, for which the country no longer had any patience. In November, the vote was divided among the four parties, none achieving a majority. Wilson became President with a narrow plurality, and for the first time in almost twenty years the Democratic party was in power.

On December 8, 1912, Holmes became eligible for a pension, and he talked of retirement: "This date my ten years are up and if I chose I could notify the President tomorrow and retire on a pension — Ha — doesn't that make one free?"[71]

But, from all sides, Holmes was urged to remain on the Court past retirement age, to deny the Democrats a seat. Taft wrote to him:

> I beg of you in the interest of everything that you and I think worthy of preservation in what our fathers handed down to us, don't think of giving up when you are doing such great work and when you can not know what manner of man your successor would be.[72]

White, too, urged him in strong terms to remain; and Holmes, not sorry to have the call of duty renewed, silently agreed.

The world that he had known seemed to be disintegrating with unnerving speed, an unfamiliar landscape rising in its place. The federal government had begun to spawn regulatory agencies: a central banking system, a Federal Reserve Board, a Federal Trade Commission with broad and vaguely defined powers, national labor legislation, a new antitrust law — all of which Holmes viewed with disquiet.

The new President's first appointment to the Supreme Court was James McReynolds, perhaps the worst such appointment in living memory. McReynolds quickly proved himself a bigoted reactionary, incapable of getting on with his colleagues, and it seemed the President had shunted him onto the Court only to remove him from the cabinet.

News from abroad was still more disquieting. Germany was building a navy in the North Sea; Britain was arming to meet its threat. Bryce left

Washington in defeat, his arbitration treaties spurned by Senate jingoes
led by Henry Cabot Lodge.

There was appalling personal news from Holmes's friends in England. Ethel and Leslie Scott had separated and were miserable. Lady Castletown wrote in a calm enough tone to say that she had had surgery, but
was discouraged about recovering the sight of one eye, and then added
without emphasis that she would like Holmes to speak to an art dealer
in New York, for the Castletowns were reduced to poverty and must sell
what they could.

Holmes wrote anxiously to Canon Sheehan:

I know that they have had reverses and I gather that he has
collapsed, but I can't ask Lady Castletown questions, and I don't
know exactly what it means.[73]

Sheehan answered promptly:

They had just returned here [to Doneraile], and then the crash
came. So unconscious was Lady C. that any danger impended, she
had spent £ 400 in erecting a new Hall in the village. Her grief
was pitiable; and so was Lord C.'s remorse. He had sold out all
the *purchased* estates; and had speculated wildly (so it was said) in
foreign investments, which proved useless. Receivers were at once
sent down to take charge of everything. Lord C. is at Granston;
Lady C. in London. I understood they are allowed £ 2,000 each
per annum; and the latest news is that the estate was not so involved as was first supposed; and that possibly, they may be able
to return [to Doneraile] at no very distant date. . . . One of the sad
things connected with the affair was the destruction of the entire
herd of deer in the Park. During the autumn, all day long we
heard the crack of rifles in the park. They wrapped the venison
in the hides and sent all along to the London market.[74]

That summer Holmes made his last trip abroad. Fanny would not go
with him, but insisted that he go, and so he went alone to London and
to Ireland, to give comfort where he could. "I have been spectator of
misery after misery," he reported.[75] In London, Leslie Scott was adamant
that the separation was irrevocable, and Ethel was distraught.

At Doneraile, Lady Castletown was old and ill, and complained bitterly of the violent unrest in Ireland. Lord Castletown was not yet recovered from the nervous collapse that had followed his financial crash,
and saw everything darkly, although he and Lady Castletown were again
at Doneraile Court. Holmes called on the canon in the mornings once
more, and found him dying: "though we had a cheerful daily talk, *that*

was in the background. Before I left he asked me to choose a book from his library."[76]

It was a relief to go home. As usual, he sailed on a Cunarder — the *Lusitania:*

> . . . as I grow older I grow calm. If I feel what are perhaps an old man's apprehensions, that competition from new races will cut deeper than working men's disputes and will test whether we can hang together and fight; if I fear that we may be running through the world's resources at a pace that we cannot keep; I do not lose my hopes. I do not pin my dreams for the future to my country or even to my race. I think it probable that civilization somehow will last as long as I care to look ahead — perhaps with smaller numbers, but perhaps also bred to greatness and splendor by science. I think it not improbable that man, like the grub that prepares a chamber for the winged thing it never has seen but is to be — that man may have cosmic destinies that he does not understand. And so beyond the vision of battling races and an impoverished earth I catch a dreaming glimpse of peace.
>
> The other day my dream was pictured to my mind. It was evening. I was walking homeward on Pennsylvania Avenue near the Treasury, and as I looked beyond Sherman's statue to the west the sky was aflame with scarlet and crimson from the setting sun. But, like the note of downfall in Wagner's opera, below the sky line there came from little globes the pallid discord of the electric lights. And I thought to myself the Götterdämmerung will end, and from those globes clustered like evil eggs will come the new masters of the sky. It is like the time in which we live. But then I remembered the faith that I partly have expressed, faith in a universe not measured by our fears, a universe that has thought and more than thought inside of it, and as I gazed, after the sunset and above the electric lights there shone the stars.[77]

22

THE SKY
AFLAME

HOLMES HAD GROWN HANDSOME IN OLD AGE. HIS HAIR WAS
thick and white, and he had thickened and solidified throughout, gaining gravity, even grandeur. His eyes were clear and attentive; the wings of his mustache swept up exuberantly. His dress and
manner were old-fashioned, and this too suited him. He still wore a tall
hat and a stiff collar, a morning coat and striped trousers. He wore a
boutonniere in his lapel, and on his birthdays it was a rose that Mrs.
Butler, the court reporter's wife, gave him, saying, "An American Beauty
for an American beauty."

He had gained a powerful physical presence that entered a room with
him, and left with him, too, like a strong light put out, as Brandeis's clerk,
Dean Acheson, observed.[1] He was abstemious, frugal, cautious. He
smoked cheap cigars — Between the Acts Little Cigars — while working
in his library, and allowed himself two good Cuban cigars in the evenings. He drank a single glass of wine with his dinner and was rather
close, in a Yankee way, with money. As their principal amusements, he
and Fanny went to the theater on Friday evenings, and on the weekends
rode into the countryside in their rented horse-drawn carriage, looking
for wildflowers and tombstones. Occasionally, Holmes would go alone to
the vaudeville shows at the Gayety Burlesque, whose offerings did not

yet include striptease, and enjoyed the broad jokes and buxom women. "I thank God I have low tastes," he liked to observe.[2]

He saw few of his contemporaries. The young were Holmes's principal companions. He had a new secretary each year to whom he would repeat his anecdotes, polished with long use, and his philosophical musings on vanity, faith, and the limitations of intellect.[3] As the Holmeses had fallen out of fashion, Fanny's Monday afternoons at home had gradually become a gathering of these young men and women — lawyers who had come to work in the new regulatory agencies, journalists, Holmes's former secretaries and their friends. Frances Noyes, the young journalist, was often the life of their afternoons. A young protégé of Louis Brandeis, Felix Frankfurter, came with a letter of introduction from John Gray. This slight, intense young Viennese Jew with thoughtful dark eyes flattered and pleased Holmes greatly. Frankfurter soon brought friends of his own — Herbert Croly and Walter Lippmann, whose books on politics Holmes admired, and eventually, Frankfurter's fiancée, Marion Denman, whose delicate oval face reminded Holmes of Bernardino Luini's Renaissance Madonnas; Holmes called her "Luina." He flourished under their affection: "These younger men (lawyers from the Departments, etc.) and women (some of them making their own living and good looking and intelligent) are very good to the old fellow and keep him young."[4]

On July 24, 1914, the armies of Europe were in movement; reserves were being called to duty. The complex timetables of mobilization had begun to run. Orders prepared carefully in advance were transmitted through chains of command; trains moved toward frontiers with their terrible burdens; tanks and guns were put in readiness. The machinery of war, millions of men and women, vehicles and weapons, stirred into life.

On that afternoon, in Beverly Farms, a neighbor, Henry Dalton, called on Holmes with a motor car. This was still a novelty. Holmes and Fanny motored with Dalton to nearby Topsfield, to see the unveiling of a bronze memorial to the Civil War dead.

The scene was one of those charming old New England town greens. The neighbors gathered and seated themselves on the stand — the old veterans in their Grand Army dress — a really impressive little band of old Yankees that made one proud. Mr. Dalton and I were requested to come upon the platform and soon, at just the impressive moment, two old soldiers hauled up the great flag on the staff in the green, to reveille. Then the band played and then a lot of little school children sang the old songs of the War till they made the tears roll down my cheeks — it was such a strange thing to think that those were realities fifty years ago.[5]

When the Great War began in August, at first Holmes did not grasp how destructive war had become: "I think the improved weapons mean smaller losses. The great [losses] used to come when troops stood within a few paces letting into each other."[6]

The continent-spanning machinery for killing, already assembled, was quickly put into motion. There had been great technical improvements in communications, transport, high explosives, poison gas, and armored tanks. There were machine guns and submarines. The British at first trusted to their navy and their courage. They had no conscription to begin with, and the young men who volunteered went off like the young men of Boston fifty-three years before, with flags embroidered by well-brought-up young ladies, but without adequate training and lacking shells for their rifles.

Holmes read anguished letters. The Baroness Moncheur was distraught at the invasion of her home and the enlistment of her son. Ethel Grenfell — now Lady Desborough — had two sons, and each obtained a commission.

From Germany as well, where Holmes was admired, letters came:

Dear Sir,
These days of terrible warfare have brought back to me memories of many a pleasant hour we spent together. . . . I reread your speeches . . . and felt again and again and was deeply touched by your fine address on Memorial Day 1895, "The Soldier's Faith."

Neither of us could have believed in those days that the peril of the greatest war in the world's history was so near to us. . . . My sons whose "sword-slashed faces" awoke your "sincere respect," as you wrote — are on the battlefield in France. . . .

Never in the world's history did 70 million people stand up like one man. How I regret that with your deep feeling for the poetic value of history you did not see this with your own eyes. . . . The faces of the men going to the front were radiant with joy. . . .

The blind obedience which you praise as the virtue of the warrior, characterizes this war more than any other. . . . The single man, however great his exertions mentally and physically, however heroic he may be, is only the blind instrument of an organized central power. . . . Every man is feeling that he is taking part in imperishable achievements and is aware that the necessity of sacrificing his own interests for the benefit of the entire community is not only his duty, but that his self-absorption and even his work of destruction will surely receive divine sanction. . . .

Never will [England] be able to free herself of the moral crime of having drawn Japan into the battle, and leading colored men of all shades against the white race.

Our government is keeping careful count of all these acts. The day of reckoning will come. . . .

With hearty greetings and compliments to you and Mrs. Holmes, in which Frau v. Gierke joins,

> I am,
> Yours very sincerely,
> Dr. Otto v. Gierke,
> Professor
> in the University of Berlin[7]

Men on foot, carrying rifles, ran against entrenched guns. On the eastern front, Russian cavalry armed with sabers rode against machine guns. But soon everyone understood, if such a thing can be understood, that the killing would be not in thousands, but in millions. A terrible anxiety descended.

Ethel Grenfell's elder son, Julian, wrote letters from the battlefield in France:

> I went out to the right of our lines, where the Germans were the nearest. It took about thirty minutes to do thirty yards. Then I saw the Hun trench and waited for a long time. . . . I peered through the loophole and saw nobody in the trench, then the German behind put up his head again, he was laughing and talking. I saw his teeth glisten against my foresight and I pulled the trigger.[8]

Six months later, both of Lady Desborough's sons were dead. She sent Holmes a clipping from the London *Times* and a poem Julian had written before his death. The poem and the newspaper memorial were like those sad notices that had appeared in the *Boston Transcript* fifty years before, which Holmes himself had so often written.[9]

Chief Justice White, in the summer of 1915, was physically distressed by anxiety over the war news. Holmes advised him to seek detachment, and he agreed that, not having the whole world in charge, it was useless to worry about it, but did not succeed in putting this belief into practice.[10]

Holmes himself was in a kind of frenzy of detachment, chattering ceaselessly about philosophy to everyone about him and in long letters abroad. He refused to read the newspapers, and plunged himself into work. When that did not suffice, he read Plato, Spinoza, French novels. He burst out regularly in spasms of impatience with the American pacifists and socialists who opposed entry into the war,[11] and with President Wilson, who seemed to do nothing. He was oddly cold to the women who sent their sons to war, as if he concealed some irrational anger toward them.

When his nephew, Ned, suggested enlisting in the army, "as an example," before there was any duty to serve, Holmes flared out in anger: "I told him if any son of mine talked about doing anything as an example I would boot him out of my house."[12]

America was preparing, however, if haltingly, to enter the war. Theodore Roosevelt and Henry Cabot Lodge were once again leading the militant faction, but the President, to Holmes's deep disgust, only suggested that everyone pray.

In that anxious winter, John Gray slipped into his last illness, and Nina sent word — "I write you thinking you would prefer to know of it from me. . . . It is heartbreaking to watch and be able to do nothing — except read aloud now and then."[13] Holmes, confined to Washington, sent brief comradely notes to his old friend: "I am somewhat lonely here in the intimate and ultimate regions of thought, and would give much if I could have one of our old time talks with you."[14]

A few days later, Gray died in his sleep. The Court was sitting, and Holmes could not leave Washington. He wrote to Nina and prepared a memorial for the Massachusetts Historical Society that stirred old memories and feelings.[15]

In the weary summer that followed, Holmes's messenger, John Craig, was burned to death trying to extinguish a burning curtain in his own house.[16] Ezra Thayer, dean of the Harvard Law School, who had been Holmes's friend, and who after Gray's death had agreed to send Holmes a secretary each year, fell into a deep depression, and drowned himself in the Charles River. Holmes's colleagues on the Court, too, were unwell. White, himself growing blind and deaf, sent a note from an Adirondack resort, written in a shaky hand: "I greatly fear *our brother Lamar* is seriously, yes, very seriously *ill* and if he rallies will in all probability never again be able to do our work *with safety to himself.*"[17]

Lamar died on January 2, 1916.

Henry James died, cutting almost the last tie to their circle of young friends. A few doors from Holmes, Henry Adams mourned their friend and thought of Clover — "how I have clung to all that belonged to my wife" – but he and Wendell did not speak.[18]

To Holmes is seemed that Gray, Thayer, Lamar, and others around him had buckled under the pressure of their work.[19] He himself was seventy-four and could not expect to continue at his post for many more years. He thought aloud to his friends about his approaching seventy-fifth birthday, and half-jokingly complained about America's neglect of her great men. In Germany, he began to remark to Frankfurter, every successful butcher or baker could expect to receive official recognition and in due course to receive appointment as purveyor to royalty, or whatnot. But in America, the public cared only to tear down, and the newspapers carried every ignorant criticism.

The war in Europe broadened, intensified. The German attack had been halted deep in France, at incomprehensible cost. Hundreds of thousands of men had died to fix a line on which to dig trenches. Month after month the two sides bombarded each other with heavy guns, gas, and high explosives, flung their infantry into spasmodic attacks, and returned to the trenches and the shelling.

A German submarine sank the *Lusitania* on its way from New York to Liverpool, just off the Irish coast. More than 1,000 passengers and crewmen died, of whom 128 were Americans. The newspapers clamored for immediate American entry into the war, but the United States had little more army than it had had at the outbreak of the Civil War. The President negotiated with the Germans and began building a fleet of ships, manufacturing arms, building a modern army under central control.

There was opposition to these preparations. Millions of recent immigrants from Europe had thought to escape its hatreds and wars. Millions of Irish- and German-Americans did not care to fight for the British. The Socialist party and unions of unskilled workers, Midwestern farmers of German descent, Communists, anarchists, and pacifists opposed the war. Americans of Irish descent sent money and arms to Ireland, where there was an uprising against the British on Easter Sunday, 1916. In the United States, "preparedness" became a struggle itself, which trembled on the edge of race and class war. Bombs exploded during strikes; at a "Preparedness Day" rally in San Francisco a bomb exploded in the crowd, killing ten people and wounding forty more.

Holmes, hating the war, still had no doubts:

> I believe in "my country right or wrong," and next to my country my crowd, and England is my crowd. I earnestly long to see her keep on top, and yet I shall grieve if, as I hope, Germany is crushed. I suppose the war was inevitable, and yet whatever the event, it fills me with sorrow. . . . But it shows us that classes as well as nations that mean to be in the saddle have got to be ready to kill to keep their seat.[20]

The late Justice Lamar's empty place on the Court now had to be filled, and the usual campaign was conducted in the newspapers and in private. One of the principal contestants was Louis Brandeis, who had advised Wilson during the 1912 campaign, had helped to raise money for him, and who had now asked for a place on the Court rather than a seat in the cabinet. The other candidate was the former President, William Howard Taft, whose friends put him forward.[21]

Brandeis and Taft were old antagonists. Early in Taft's administration, Brandeis had hurt him very badly. There had been a scandal — a junior employee of the Department of the Interior named Louis R. Glavis charged that coal-mining leases in Alaska were being given to friends of the administration. Taft's secretary of the interior, Richard Ballinger, tried awkwardly to hush the complaints. He fired Glavis and manufactured exonerating documents. Conservationists attacked in the press; a congressional committee investigated; and Brandeis, as special counsel to the Committee, in weeks of hearings, succeeded in embarrassing the secretary of the interior so badly that he was forced to resign and the President himself was made to appear either foolish or corrupt. The original charges seemed to lack foundation, but efforts to hush them up had crippled the administration.

It had been a costly victory for Brandeis. Many people — including Holmes, who was his friend — did not care for his relentless manner of conducting the Ballinger inquiry.[22] Woodrow Wilson, knowing what opposition Brandeis would face in the Senate, where old grievances were long remembered, was reluctant to nominate him to the Court; he knew also that the nomination would divide the public and would stir anti-Semitism as a cabinet appointment would not. But Brandeis pressed his case, campaigning indirectly through friends, senators, and contributors to Wilson's campaign, and on January 24, 1916, he was offered the nomination.

When Taft heard the news, he sourly mimicked Brandeis's German: "When you . . . think that men were pressing me for the place, *es ist zum lachen.*"[23]

The nomination was bitterly opposed. The protracted confirmation hearings revealed a depth of hostile feeling against Brandeis among lawyers who knew him and from people who had worked with him at Harvard,[24] that puzzled Holmes and seemed to go beyond conventional prejudice: "Long before the more public exertions of his I was made aware of an adversely critical attitude on the part of others whose opinions I respected while at the same time I never have understood it."[25]

Boston's dislike for Brandeis was like its shunning of Wendell Phillips; perhaps it was Brandeis's disloyalty to his class, his moral zeal, that accounted for this feeling among his old opponents, who said he was not a gentleman, and attributed this to his being a Jew. Brandeis, for his part, called his critics anti-Semitic.[26] Holmes watched in dismay, disgusted at the President's willingness to use the Court to pay his political debts: "The nomination was a misfortune for the Court because whichever way it went half the world would think less of the Court thereafter — but I expect [Brandeis] will make a good judge."[27]

The long-standing personal affection between the two men remained undiminished. When Brandeis's nomination was at last confirmed by the Senate, Holmes sent a brief telegram: "Welcome."

Brandeis and his wife came to Washington and rented a frugal apartment on Connecticut Avenue. The Brandeises were abstemious and made do with cramped quarters and old furniture. There were no works of art in the Brandeises' apartment; their visitors were often working people, and they did not go into society. Brandeis seemed to live with the sole purpose of improving his fellows, but, if ascetic, he was also apparently at peace. He and Holmes rarely met outside the Court, and Fanny did not encourage Brandeis to call at I Street nor did she extend herself to Alice Brandeis.[28] But, when Justice Brandeis did call, he cheered Holmes.

For a time, there was much to cheer him. As his seventy-fifth birthday approached, he was aware of preparations to honor him. Fanny arranged a dinner for March 7 — Holmes's birthday on March 8 would fall on Ash Wednesday — a small gathering of people of accomplishment. Holmes was disappointed only that the young people in whom he delighted were not present.

Just after the dinner guests had departed, and Holmes had gone up to his library, the house seemed to come alive with the sound of birds. He went down again to see what it was. There was a dim light in the middle parlor — and out burst a crowd of young people, the whole Monday afternoon club, tooting away on bird calls.

> They were all the group, and just as I realized who they were and began to think with dismay that I had no preparation for them the other doors opened [into the dining room] and there was a supper laid out with a bowl of very judicious punch. So there was much laughter and jaw until after midnight, and on my plate at dinner were some very pretty verses that one of them had written. Altogether it was very charming.[29]

Of course, Fanny had engineered the whole business, had bought the bird calls long before from a street peddler.[30]

Some of Holmes's young friends had prepared gifts that pleased him even more. Felix Frankfurter, now a professor at the Harvard Law School but a frequent visitor to Washington, organized an issue of the *Harvard Law Review* to honor Holmes, a Festschrift in the German style.[31] Frankfurter himself, Frederick Pollock, Dean Roscoe Pound, Eugen Ehrlich in Vienna, Dean John Wigmore, Judge Learned Hand, and the philosopher Morris R. Cohen all wrote essays that were perceptively flattering, and, for the first time, Holmes's work as a judge was publicly honored:

> [Holmes's] opinions form a coherent body of constitutional law, and their effect upon the development of the law is the outstanding characteristic of constitutional history in our decade.[32]

> The short and the long of it is that these opinions are literature, not merely law; classics, not merely technics.[33]

Others in the circle of young admirers, Herbert Croly and Walter Lippmann, were editors of a new magazine, *The New Republic,* which had quickly reached a wide audience. Lippmann published a birthday tribute to Holmes.

There was a steady stream of congratulatory letters and telegrams, prompted in part by these admiring tributes, and the newspapers took notice — although, as Holmes noted sourly, mostly to speculate that he would retire soon. He issued no denials, but he bought a new robe, which he called to everyone's attention, "as indicating a present intention to hang on."[34]

We'll call it a good job, but what of it? The question now is of 76 and so on. As long as a man is alive he can't just rest on his past.[35]

As an old fellow in a novel . . . says, Courage is never proved, but always to be proved. And so of other things.[36]

It was a curious thing about the circle of young friends: "I seem to be in with a considerable number of Jews," Holmes mused,[37] mildly surprised. His cousin John Morse asked archly what it was like to have Brandeis's company on the Court; Owen Wister sneered openly. Baroness Moncheur refused to receive Jews, and Mrs. Curtis gibed at Holmes mildly about Oriental influences.

Fanny, too, would twit Holmes and would tease him with old gossip that the Wendells were Dutch Jews. Holmes answered cheerfully that he would rather have the brilliance of the Jewish lads — and of his own Jewish side — than a God-damned Anglo-Saxon gang like Fanny's.[38]

Holmes was untroubled about other people's prejudices, but only wondered idly how there came to be so many Jews among his friends.

Part of the answer was Felix Frankfurter, who for several years had been bringing people to see Holmes: Lippmann and Croly of *The New Republic,* Morris Cohen, Judge Benjamin Cardozo, and Harold Laski. Frankfurter ensured that Holmes's admirers met the old man and that Holmes knew of their admiration.[39]

Walter Lippmann probably spoke for all of the young intellectuals who came to Washington with the Wilson administration and who came to call on Holmes:

The country's business at Washington is conducted in the odor of dead and dying cigars suspended in steam heat . . . in the halls of Congress, in the committee rooms, the air is warm and foul. It drags upon you till you wilt and your head swims, and the faces of the men testifying grow hazy. In that mean atmosphere, so like the corridor of a cheap hotel, there is an invitation to relax and grow bored and cease to care. You slouch in your seat, you dawdle through your business, compressed and dull and discouraged. Thick, tepid, tired air it is, in which vision dies.

But there is at least one place in Washington where things have an altogether different quality, and no one I think comes away from it unmoved. It is the home of Justice Holmes. When you enter, it is as if you had come into the living stream of high romance. You meet the gay soldier who can talk of Falstaff and eternity in one breath, and tease the universe with a quip. . . . A sage with the bearing of a cavalier; his presence is an incitement to high risks. . . . He wears wisdom like a gorgeous plume, and likes to tickle the sanctities between the ribs.[40]

Holmes felt that young people were drawn to him, and wondered about the reason: "These relatively young fellows . . . think I have some secret fountain of faith. I have none, except . . . the belief that I am in the universe, not it in me — and temperament."[41]

He didn't think much of the young people's political ideas, but he was willing to let the lads and lassies have their chance. They reminded him of the Abolitionists of his own youth, perhaps of young Wendell Holmes himself, these radical young Jews with aristocratic manners, with their socialism and eugenics and central planning and votes for women. "They catch postulates like the influenza," Holmes said, but they brought with them, "an atmosphere of intellectual freedom in which one can breathe."[42]

"You are a splendid young enthusiast and make me feel more alive," he said to Laski.[43] The young people in return flattered him so wildly that at moments he had doubts, "whether you young fellows were ironically trying how much the old man could stand in the way of flattering things,"[44] but he knew their affection was genuine, and he had a large appetite for it. After receiving his birthday tribute, he wrote to Frankfurter:

The Law Review has come, and I cannot tell you how touched and charmed I am. Very few things in my life have given me so much pleasure. I well know that I owe it to your constant kindness that I receive such a crowning reward, and I thank you from my heart.[45]

And a few days later: "Goodbye, dear lad. . . . Spring has broken loose, today the birds sing and I was the happier for just reading your letter."[46]

With these admiring young men and women, Holmes flirted as he had with the young matrons of London society, opening his heart and his mind:

Did I ever tell you of Corot — the painter — that I heard once that he began as a most careful draughtsman working out every detail and came to magisterial summaries at the end? I have thought of that in writing opinions latterly. Whether the brethren like it, I don't know. Of course — the eternal effort of art even the art of writing legal decisions is to omit all but the essentials — "The point of contact" is the formula — the place where the boy got his fingers pinched — the rest of the machinery doesn't matter. So the Jap. master puts five dots for a hand — knowing they are in the right place.[47]

Of them all, Harold Laski came closest to Holmes's heart. This thin, grave English Jew had a photographic memory and a creative intelligence. He seemed to have read everything. He gobbled a whole page with a single glance and plucked priceless old books out of bins the way Fanny found wildflowers in a bank. He was a socialist, an enthusiast of eugenics, and an expert on ecclesiastical history. He was twenty-four years old, and entirely astonishing: an instructor in history at Harvard and simultaneously a student in the law school, one of the editors of the *Law Review,* a regular contributor to *The New Republic,* and about to publish his first book on political theory. Frankfurter had brought him to Harvard and arranged that he and Holmes would meet.

Holmes was thoroughly charmed when Laski called at 1720 I Street with an introduction from Frankfurter:

I have just had here a wonderful young chap from Oxford — then lecturing at McGill and now at Harvard — Harold Laski — an unbelieving Jew with a specialité of Church History — who also beat our champion at tennis — in his 20s and is one of the most learned men I know.[48]

Holmes and Laski corresponded, and Laski visited Beverly Farms often in the summer. They talked late into the night, like courting lovers. Holmes's talk was inspired; Laski met him with confidence and with flattery. Laski recommended books for Holmes to read, gave him gossip of the political and literary worlds, and praised Holmes profoundly and sincerely.

Disqualified from military service by his frail health and slight stature, Harold Laski was a reminder of the stalemated war. In Europe, his generation was dying. The western front stretched for 470 miles, from Switzerland to the English Channel, and there the opposing armies continued to shell each other and fling themselves into futile attacks. Casualties had risen into the millions. A new virulent form of influenza swept through the trenches and hospitals, killing more men than the fighting, and swept into the civilian population, where it particularly ravaged the young.

As the war grew more horrible, and the United States drew closer to the fighting, Holmes took increasing delight in the young people who had been spared; he fretted over them, worried about their health, complained to Frankfurter and Laski that they were straining their machinery by overwork:

> How hard it is to believe that something is irrevocable — when I was young and a fool dentist pulled out teeth that he ought not have, I used to think, oh I will grow some more when I want them. And so one or at least I, got through life. When a vivid figure dies, one still expects to meet him somewhere. . . . One cannot realize the final blight that has been put upon the world by the Germans.[49]

In 1917, hoping to gain a decisive advantage before the United States could join the war, Germany began unrestricted submarine warfare against ships bound for England and France. In March, three American ships were sunk by German submarines, and on April 2, Woodrow Wilson, guarded by a troop of cavalry, rode in the warm rain up Pennsylvania Avenue to the Capitol, and addressed a joint session of Congress. He asked for a declaration of war. Four days later, on April 6, the declaration was given.

Formal entertaining in Washington largely stopped, and the ritual of the "at home" was suspended, but Fanny and Holmes encouraged their young people to come in quietly on Thursdays. The war dominated thought and conversation. Three of the justices of the Supreme Court had sons in the service; the others were caught up in one way or another.

An army was quickly drafted. The federal government moved hastily to forestall interference with the draft. On May 18, Congress passed the Selective Service Act, requiring every man of eligible age to register. There were still criminal statutes from the Civil War era to punish those who resisted, but on June 15, 1917, a new Espionage Act passed into law, forbidding even an attempt to cause insubordination, disloyalty, mutiny, or refusal of duty. The Justice Department's recently formed Intelligence Division, headed by young J. Edgar Hoover, and teams of prosecutors turned to the task of quelling opposition to the war. With assistance from the military, they conducted sweeps in the streets of major cities, stopping every man of draft age and demanding to see his registration card. On a single day in New York City, 20,000 men were taken into custody. The attorney general said, "Loyal citizens will cheerfully submit to the minor inconvenience."

The postmaster general impounded the mail of radical organizations and refused to grant permits for mailing their publications. Magazines and newspapers opposed to the war were closed. Local police, with help from Hoover's Intelligence Division, raided radical organizations and arrested their leaders.

The trade union movement was bitterly divided, like the country at large. Some unions enthusiastically supported the war; unions of immigrant laborers, the Irish and German-speaking, the newer immigrants from Italy and eastern Europe, opposed the war and the draft. A railroad strike threatened to cripple the country and the war effort. Holmes wrote to Laski in Boston:

> I hear rumors that we came near universal anarchy if the strike had gone on. I don't know that it is getting time to find out what is/ who are the governing power in this country. . . .
> The lad here [Holmes's secretary] calls himself a pacifist as well as a socialist — and exhibits a thin and stubborn rationality. I find myself very fond of him and even liking his society above the average of secretaries — but getting devilish little juice or promise out of his asms for isms — when he talks of more rational methods [of resolving international disputes] I get the blood in my eye and say that war is the ultimate rationality.[50]

Eugene Debs, trade union leader and the Socialist party's candidate for president, was arrested after saying in a speech that the draft was unconstitutional and urging workers to assert their constitutional rights against the draft.

Russia, which had kept the German forces fighting on the eastern front, was undergoing violent revolution; by October, 1917, a Communist party had taken control of the government. The Bolsheviks quickly withdrew from the war. Just as American troops were beginning to arrive in Europe, German armies, which had been immobilized in the east, wheeled toward the west. Germany launched an offensive that overwhelmed the static defenses of the Allies. The German army advanced toward Paris.

"Preparedness" at home in the United States gave way to full-scale mobilization. Fanny and Holmes rarely went out at all. Holmes, unable to participate directly, distracted himself by writing a steady stream of cheerful letters, chatting about philosophy and gossip when he was not occupied by work. When the baroness or Ethel Scott or Lady Pollock complained about his seeming lack of feeling, he would say, "How could I give you any pleasure by uttering a cry of anguish — you know how I feel."[51]

Holmes took refuge in the world of engravings and prints, as he had when on leave from his war and old Theis had welcomed him. He browsed in a print shop near the White House and in the Library of Congress collection. But the war consistently intruded, and when Paul

Warburg criticized the waste of money that otherwise might have gone into war bonds, Holmes gave up buying prints, and only browsed:

> The world here has had a bad time — an unusually cold winter and a dreadful shortage of fuel, freezing of gas, etc. The well-to-do have been at least uncomfortable and the poor, I fear, have had much misery.[52]

And finally, as he had fifty years before, he anxiously read the newspapers for reports of the German advance.[53]

> It is hard to write at this moment with the frightful anxiety hanging over us all. . . . in spite of detachment and the effort to preserve it, so much of all one loves depends on the event that one's happiness is bound up in it, unless indeed one should speak of happiness no more.[54]

> The first bad news about the German drive . . . made me lie awake, have the dyspepsia and get a violent cold now pretty much gone and, except when I have work to do, there is a dreadful ache underneath that even the spring does not make me forget — indeed, rather it becomes an expression of the inexorable.[55]

That spring of 1918 marked his seventy-seventh birthday; and he learned that Henry Adams was dead. Brooks wrote:

> Although our close relations naturally ceased several years ago, when Henry had his first stroke, I never realized the full loss until his death the other day. It is to me very great, nothing can ever make it good. From my boyhood he filled a place in my life which was all his own and now, I frankly admit that, reason with myself as I may, I cannot pull myself together at all — I do not suppose I shall ever be able to.[56]

Holmes thought of his own approaching mortality, of "eating dandelions by the roots" at Mt. Auburn Cemetery, where his father was buried. He cheered himself with the thought that, at any rate, "like the great artists, [he might] have succeeded in writing the definite and exact with a vista toward the infinite."[57]

He made a new will that spring, giving his estate to Fanny but with large bequests to Harvard and to various charities. To his nephew, Ned, who had no need of money, he left the best of his books; the rest of his library, prints, and engravings would go to the Library of Congress.[58]

In the spring and summer of 1918, mobilization reached a peak: 1,600,000 American men crossed the Atlantic to the battlefields.

The railroad system of the country had been placed under central federal control, as were the shipbuilders and the merchant marine. Agriculture and nutrition came under federal supervision. War propaganda filled the schools and all the media of communication; theaters performed patriotic plays and interrupted them with appeals for the purchase of war bonds.

Dissent and opposition had been suppressed. Tom Mooney, a radical labor leader, in a lynch-mob atmosphere was sentenced to death for his part in the San Francisco Preparedness Day bombing. Felix Frankfurter publicly recommended clemency, and so he himself — a German, a Jew, and a radical — was vilified. Hundreds of thousands had been arrested; many thousands remained in jail. In the Western states there were lynchings of German-speaking Americans. War fever and influenza seemed to rise together, as if to mark a generation of youth for destruction.

Prohibition became a patriotic cause. Grain was in short supply, and beer drinking an imported German custom. The Anti-Saloon League and the Women's Christian Temperance Union swelled with patriotic feeling. A federal wartime prohibition statute was passed, purportedly to conserve grain; more than twenty states went dry. When the federal statute was challenged, an irresistible movement to amend the Constitution gathered force.

Across the nation, courts and judges were caught up in the general confusion. Holmes said that some of the judges of the lower courts had become hysterical. The Justice Department's campaign against draft resisters insensibly broadened to include anyone who spoke against the war. When some judges declined to convict merely for an expression of opinion, Congress amended the previous year's Espionage Act to make it a crime to criticize the form of government of the United States or to speak in favor of its enemies.[59]

The Communist revolution in Russia was widely believed to have been engineered by Germany, to take Russia out of the war. Thousands of Communists, anarchists, and socialists in America, including recent immigrants from Russia and Poland, many of whom looked to the new Soviet state with hope, were rounded up as suspected agents of Germany. Succumbing to the pressure of opinion, the President sent a nominal military force into Russia, whose mission was not entirely clear. Japan invaded Russia through Manchuria in larger force, however, and Britain sent troops; it seemed that the allies were trying to reverse the Russian revolution.

Trade unions were suspect, and the Supreme Court, seized by the general patriotic fervor, struck down union-sponsored legislation, including a federal statute that prohibited interstate commerce in the products of child labor. Holmes dissented, and Brandeis alone joined him. The other justices thought it a poor time to express disagreement; Holmes told Pollock that the majority of the Court, led by his comrade

Edward White, thought his dissent as ill-timed and regrettable as he thought their decision.[60] But, for all his loyalty to the war effort, Holmes was quite clear where his duty lay:

> [I]f there is any matter upon which civilized nations have agreed — far more unanimously than they have with regard to intoxicants and some other matters over which this country is now emotionally aroused — it is the evil of premature and excessive child labor. I should have thought that if we were to introduce our own moral conceptions where in my opinion they do not belong, this was preeminently a case for upholding the exercise of all its powers by the United States.
>
> But I thought that . . . this Court always had disavowed the right to intrude its judgment upon questions of policy or morals. It is not for this Court to pronounce when prohibition is necessary to regulation [of interstate commerce] if it ever may be necessary — to say that it is permissible as against strong drink but not as against the product of ruined lives.[61]

He dissented again when the Court upheld the conviction for contempt of a newspaper that had criticized a judge.[62] In yet another prosecution by the government, Holmes circulated to the Court a memorandum in defense of free speech, but the government withdrew its case, and Holmes's memorandum was never published.[63]

The chill of repression deepened that summer. Holmes's young friends increasingly came under attack and were accused of disloyalty. William Howard Taft, whose son was in France, privately repeated the conventional prejudices of his class: Brandeis, Bernard Baruch, Walter Lippmann, and Frankfurter, he said, "surrounded" Wilson with a sort of cabal; "not one believes in his heart in fighting the war through."[64]

> [Woodrow Wilson] has really been in sympathy with the Bolsheviki. . . . There is a yellow layer in our social and political community, which includes Wilson and Brandeis and the editors of *The New Republic*.[65]

Frankfurter was the object of particularly virulent public attacks. Theodore Roosevelt publicly denounced him:

> You are engaged in excusing men precisely like the Bolsheviki in Russia, who are murderers and encouragers of murder, who are traitors to their allies, to democracy and to civilization as well as to the United States.[66]

And then, abruptly it seemed, the German drive collapsed, the German emperor was deposed, and the war was over.

> How differently the recent events make one feel about life. The horrible nightmare that has ridden us for so long seems driven off.[67]

As the term drew to a close in the spring, Holmes was joyous:

> I took the time yesterday morning and this to drive with Fanny down by the Potomac Basin and to walk by it to see the wonderful flowering of the double-blossomed cherry trees — pink and white and the blue sky above — and as you looked ahead mist on mist of yellow and tender green and pink again — and song sparrows and redbirds and a kingfisher faint cawings of more distant crows. Last week I saw the first bloodroot in Rock Creek Park. In spite of continuing anxieties I can enjoy nature now — I hardly could during the War. I found myself doing so one day and said to myself, How is this? And then I answered myself — why the Armistice.[68]

Yet if the war in Europe had ended, the war at home grew worse. In 1919, four million workers went on strike. The year began with a general strike in Seattle. A national coal strike soon followed. Another desperate effort to organize unions in the steel mills produced a nationwide steel strike that would be violently broken.

The Justice Department's campaign against subversives and aliens continued and was amplified. Holmes found that the government was pressing its cases against draft resisters. He thought that many of the cases were ill founded[69] and that it would have been better to drop all the draft-resistance cases and pardon the defendants, now that the war was past. But the President insisted on jail terms for the radicals who had opposed the war, and once the appeals came to the Supreme Court, they had to be decided.

During the war, Charles Schenck, general secretary of the Socialist party in Philadelphia, had mailed leaflets to men who were about to be inducted, calling the draft unconstitutional and saying, "A conscript is little better than a convict . . . ASSERT YOUR RIGHTS!" Fifteen thousand of the leaflets were printed. A jury in Philadelphia convicted Schenck of violating the Espionage Act of 1917, by mailing the leaflet with intent to obstruct the draft. He was sentenced to six months in prison.

When Schenck's appeal was argued before the Supreme Court, the justices were unanimous that the conviction should be upheld. Chief Justice White assigned the opinion to Holmes — in part, Holmes thought, because he was the strongest among them for free speech.

Holmes said there was no doubt that the government could punish speech that intentionally interfered with conscription during wartime, the Constitutional guarantee of free speech notwithstanding:

> We admit that in many places and in ordinary times the defendants in saying all that was said in the circular would have been within their constitutional rights. But the character of every act depends upon the circumstances in which it is done. . . . The most stringent protection of free speech would not protect a man in falsely shouting fire in a crowded theater and causing a panic. . . . The question in every case is whether the words are used in such circumstances and are of such a nature as to create a clear and present danger that they will bring about the substantive evils that Congress has a right to prevent. It is a question of proximity and degree. When a nation is at war, many things that might be said in time of peace are such a hindrance to its efforts that they will not be endured so long as men fight and that no court could regard them as protected by any Constitutional right.[70]

Five such cases of draft resistance were decided unanimously by the Court in the spring of 1919, Holmes writing the opinions.[71]

The most distasteful of the government's cases, to Holmes, was the continued prosecution of Eugene Debs, leader of the Socialist party of America, who had addressed an open meeting in much the same terms that Schenck had used in his leaflet for draftees. Debs had been sentenced to ten years in prison, a shocking sentence that could only be understood as a punishment for his political views, and to Holmes's disgust, President Wilson pursued the prosecution up to the Supreme Court and refused to pardon Debs or commute the harsh sentence. Distasteful as it was, however, at least to Holmes, the Court could neither pardon nor commute; it could only review the lawfulness of the government's prosecution. And however ill advised, the Supreme Court was unanimous that the prosecution was not illegal.[72] Debs went to prison, with great dignity, and the next year, while still in prison, he ran for President of the United States on the Socialist ticket and received one million votes.

> I had a disagreeable task in writing a decision against Debs the agitator, for obstructing recruiting by a speech — found by a jury to have been made with that intent. There was no doubt in my mind about the law but I wondered that the Government should have pressed the case to a hearing — as it enables knaves, fools

and the ignorant to say that he was really condemned as a dangerous agitator.[73]

Some of the newspapers, and an article by Ernst Freund in *The New Republic,* accused Holmes and the Supreme Court of exactly that. Anonymous threats against Holmes's life were made, and the post office intercepted a bomb in a package addressed to him. Another bomb went off on the doorstep of the attorney general a few blocks away. But all those closest to Holmes, including Laski, who was a socialist, accepted his opinion as regrettable but correct and hoped with him that the President would pardon the defendants.

The summer was filled with unrest, widening strikes, and continuing repression. A campaign was launched by Harvard alumni to oust Frankfurter from his post at the law school, and the criticism engulfed Dean Pound as well, who considered resigning.[74]

"I am filled with helpless anxiety," Holmes wrote to Laski. He wrote to President A. Lawrence Lowell of Harvard in warm support of the beleaguered faculty.[75]

Fanny fell ill that summer and was hospitalized. Holmes fled into books, and found them, for once, unsatisfying. He took comfort again among women. Wyatt & Trout's livery stable had been converted to a garage, and he could no longer rent a carriage to make his calls, but Ellen Curtis sent her own carriage and driver once a week, and his visits to her deepened into something more than flirtation. One visit was "the chief event of the summer . . . I hardly see how it could have been bettered."[76] At the age of seventy-eight, he loved more gently than in the past; he now said, "My beloved friend," "My loved and long-lost friend."[77]

> A platitude has come home to me with *quasi*-religious force. I was repining at the thought of my slow progress — how few new ideas I had or picked up — when it occurred to me to think of the total of life and how the greater part was wholly absorbed in living and continuing life — victuals — procreation — rest and eternal terror. And I bid myself accept the common lot; an adequate vitality would say daily, "God, what a good sleep I've had," "My eye, that was dinner," "Now for a fine rattling walk" — in short, life as an end in itself.[78]

The police force of Boston had organized a union, and when the chief of police refused to recognize or negotiate with them, the union went on strike in September. Looting and riots followed until the governor, Calvin Coolidge, called up the militia.

Harold Laski spoke to a meeting of wives of striking policemen, and a storm of violent criticism broke over his head. A Harvard undergraduate magazine, the *Lampoon,* called Laski "scum" and devoted a whole issue, ornamented with an anti-Semitic cartoon, to insulting him. Respectable Boston and Cambridge joined in the condemnation, and President Lowell, while publicly defending Laski, told him privately that he could not expect promotion at Harvard. Before the end of the year, Laski had accepted an offer to return to London.

Holmes observed all this with anguish:

It is disgusting that so serious a scholar and thinker as [Laski] should be subject to the trampling of swine.[79]

I fear we have less freedom of speech here than in England. Little as I believe in it as a theory I hope I would die for it. . . . All of which apart from its banalité I fear seems cold talk if you have been made to feel popular displeasure. I should not be cold about that.[80]

I received the paper [the *Lampoon* defaming Laski] and thought it such a childish and rotten little show as hardly to merit a second thought. . . . I do hope it hasn't cost you any worry.[81]

I shall miss you dreadfully if you go away.[82]

A year before, on August 23, 1918, which was a Friday, Hyman Rosansky left his apartment in East Harlem earlier than usual on his way to work at a hat-maker's shop at 610 Broadway, traveling almost the whole length of Manhattan Island. He belonged to a small group of about twenty anarchists, recent immigrants from Russia, who for a while had printed a newspaper in Yiddish. They had all fled from the persecution of the tsar's government and, like many such immigrants, at first they had welcomed the news of the revolution in their homeland. When the United States sent troops to Russia in 1918, this little group had joined in protests on behalf of the Revolution. Hyman Rosansky, at the group's request — as anarchists they had no leader, conducting their affairs by consensus — on that August morning in 1918, threw leaflets out of an open window from his third-floor hat-maker's shop on Broadway. Some were in English and some in Yiddish. The Yiddish leaflets were more militant. They condemned President Wilson for sending troops into Russia, and called upon American workers to resist.

WORKERS — WAKE UP!!

. . . .

Workers, our reply to the barbaric intervention has to be a general strike! An open challenge only will let the government know that not only the Russian worker fights for freedom, but also here in America lives the spirit of Revolution. Do not let the government scare you with their wild punishment in prisons, hanging and shooting. We must not and will not betray the splendid fighters of Russia. Workers, up to fight. . . .

The Rebels

They were all very young. Mollie Steimer, who was just past twenty, had rented an apartment on East 104th Street for their meetings and a basement shop on East 107th Street for the printing press. She worked in a shirtwaist factory, was as small as a girl, round-faced and radiant with outrage at injustice. Jacob Abrams, thirty-one, was slight, dark-haired, a bookbinder. When their leaflets fluttered down on Broadway that summer morning during the war, a shopkeeper brought one to the police, and Hyman Rosansky was quickly arrested. Within a few hours, five more of the group were in New York City jails, where beatings were still a common method of interrogation.

The five were tried, and convicted of violating the new Sedition Act by making false and derogatory statements about the form of government of the United States and by their leaflets attempting to obstruct the war effort. They were sentenced, in an atmosphere of war hysteria, to terms of twenty years in prison.[83]

When the Supreme Court convened in October, 1919, the appeal of Jacob Abrams, Mollie Steimer, and their comrades lay before the Court. As Holmes read through the record and listened to the arguments, it seemed plain to him that the anarchists had opposed the intervention in Russia, not the war against Germany, and that no reasonable person could believe their leaflets were likely to interfere with the war effort. These young people had been arrested and convicted for their beliefs; nothing else would explain the barbaric sentences given them.

Sixty years before, he had stood in Tremont Hall when Emerson and Wendell Phillips were shouted down by a respectable mob. Twenty-five years before, he had written a solitary dissent on behalf of the right of Socialist trade unions to organize and persuade.[84] Now once more it seemed that he would register a helpless dissent. For certain as he was that the convictions of Abrams, Steimer, and their friends should be reversed, Holmes found that he could not persuade his brother justices and that he would be in a minority on this matter, with only Brandeis likely to join him:

> I am stirred up about a case I can't mention yet to which I have sent round a dissent. . . . I feel sure that the majority will very highly disapprove of my saying what I think, but as yet it seems to me my duty. No doubt I shall hear about it on Saturday at our conference, and perhaps be persuaded to shut up, but I don't expect [to be].[85]

The majority did very highly disapprove of Holmes's dissent, and White tried to persuade him to be silent. When Holmes clung to what he thought his duty, three of the justices came to call on him in his library, and Fanny joined them in trying to dissuade him from publishing his dissent.[86]

But Holmes was not persuaded. He had written the opinions for a unanimous Court in the *Schenck* and *Debs* cases, announcing the principles under which Abrams and Mollie Steimer had now been convicted, and he felt it was his duty to say that his words did not extend so far as this.

When Holmes read his dissent in open court he spoke as if to the prosecutors, to the President who had directed the prosecutions, and to his colleagues who had upheld the convictions with their brutal sentences. He spoke to them of their own duty, and of the courage and humility that was required of them, their duty to deal fairly with dissent:

> In this case sentences of twenty years imprisonment have been imposed for the publishing of two leaflets that I believe the defendants had as much right to publish as the Government has to publish the Constitution of the United States now vainly invoked by them. Even if I am technically wrong and enough can be squeezed from these poor and puny anonymities to turn the color of legal litmus paper — I will add, even if what I think the necessary intent were shown — the most nominal punishment seems to me all that possibly could be inflicted, unless the defendants are to be made to suffer not for what the indictment alleges but for the creed that they avow — a creed that I believe to be the creed of ignorance and immaturity when honestly held, as I see no reason to doubt it was held here, but which, although made the subject of examination at the trial, no one has a right even to consider in dealing with the charges before the Court.
>
> Persecution for the expression of opinion seems to me perfectly logical. If you have no doubt of your premises or your power and want a certain result with all your heart you naturally express your wishes in law and sweep away all opposition. To allow opposition by speech seems to indicate that you think the speech impotent, as when a man says that he has squared the circle, or that you do not care wholeheartedly for the result, or that you doubt your power or your premises. But when men have realized that time has upset many fighting faiths, they may come to believe even more than they believe the very foundations of their own conduct that the ultimate good desired is better reached by free trade in ideas — that the best test of truth is the power of the thought to get itself accepted in the competition of the market, and that truth

is the only ground upon which their wishes safely can be carried out. That, at any rate, is the theory of our Constitution. It is an experiment, as all life is an experiment. Every year if not every day we have to wager our salvation upon some prophecy based upon imperfect knowledge. While that experiment is a part of our system I think that we should be eternally vigilant against attempts to check the expression of opinions that we loathe and believe to be fraught with death, unless they so imminently threaten immediate interference with the lawful and pressing purposes of the law that an immediate check is required to save the country.[87]

A great noise of vilification and praise went up all over the country. "I am told that my opinion led to my being cursed out by some of the respectable citizens of Boston," Holmes said to Ellen Curtis. His old friend John Wigmore attacked him publicly. But Herbert Croly wrote to him from *The New Republic*:

I have just seen the complete text — I was so moved by it that I cannot forbear to write you and tell you what a luminous and profound piece of legal and political reasoning it seemed to me to be. I feel sure that when the history of our time comes to be written it will be ranked among our greatest and most influential political documents.[88]

Holmes's dissent was all the more powerful, as coming from the author of the Court's previously unanimous decisions, a Civil War veteran, a man who seemed to embody American tradition. His dissent became a rallying point for resistance to the Red Scare. For the first time, Holmes stepped onto the national stage as a public figure.

23

OLYMPUS

WARREN GAMALIEL HARDING, A HANDSOME MAN FROM Blooming Grove, Ohio, was elected President of the United States on his fifty-fifth birthday, November 2, 1920. The President-elect had striking pale, widely spaced eyes, heavy dark brows, and the profile of a Roman senator. He was stout and solemn in repose, but when stirred to activity he was cheerful and had an attractive, boyish optimism. He radiated a confident, impersonal warmth, delivered a speech well, photographed beautifully, had an actor's self-awareness and control in public appearances, and got on well with newspaper reporters. For thirty years, he had been a faithful Republican. As editor and publisher of the Marion, Ohio, *Star,* he had loyally supported the party regulars — whom opponents at election time called the Machine — and when his time came he had dutifully served allotted single terms as state senator and lieutenant governor.

In 1908, and again in 1912, Harding had helped William Howard Taft to keep the Ohio Republican party loyal to his candidacy and out of the camp of the insurgent Rooseveltians. He had been rewarded. At the national convention in 1912 Harding gave the speech nominating Taft. He gave an assured and compelling performance, and in the hopeless campaign that followed he showed himself an able and loyal campaigner.

In 1914, when a United States Senate seat for Ohio was to be filled by popular election for the first time, he made a convincing candidate. He ran a popular, successful, openly anti-Catholic campaign against an Irishman named Hogan. The campaign was managed by a jowly Scots-Irish lawyer, Harry L. Daugherty.

Great upheavals were disturbing the political empire over which Republicans had presided since the Civil War. The Constitution, which had not been amended since the aftermath of that war, was amended four times in the brief space from 1913 to 1920. There were now an income tax, direct election of senators, and Prohibition; women had gained the right to vote. Other Progressive reforms were changing the political landscape. By 1920, the Republican party was obliged to hold primary elections to choose its nominees in twenty states.

The old lions of the Senate, the party bosses, were not popular candidates; they did not look or sound like tribunes of the republic. Party leaders tried to choose attractive candidates who also were loyal to themselves, but in the presidential campaign of 1920, for the first time independent candidates appeared and fought openly in primary elections for delegates to the Republican party convention. Hiram Johnson from California and Governor Frank Lowden of Illinois had enough money from their own backers to run national advertising campaigns, and fought from state to state for delegates. But no candidate came to Chicago that summer with enough delegates to assure his nomination, and so the old lions, bosses of the state party machines, met in a hotel room — in the "smoke-filled room" of political legend — and chose Warren G. Harding, the handsome, loyal publicist and speech-maker, who looked like a statesman, as their candidate for President of the United States.

The country was weary of war and influenza, weary of Wilson's sickly sanctimony, of twenty years of doing good and faring ill. A virulent post-war inflation ravaged the country, even as wartime factories began to close down. Farms sank into depression, and millions of demobilized soldiers found themselves out of work. A terrifying flood of immigrants was streaming into the United States from Europe, among them criminals, revolutionaries, many of the most adventurous and lawless people in the world.

The national addiction to alcohol — worsened by the returning soldiers and the flood of immigrants — was under attack. Prohibition had closed the breweries and saloons; Americans thereupon turned to hard liquor smuggled from abroad. The war on alcohol spawned a vast international criminal enterprise. The metaphorical war soon became a literal one, fought among armed gangs and Treasury Department agents.

Harding was optimistic and reassuring. Amid the turmoil, his campaign talks were addressed to his own people, threatened by the onslaught of change:

Call it the selfishness of nationality if you will, I think it an in-
spiration to patriotic devotion —
  To safeguard America first.
  To stabilize America first.
  To prosper America first.
  To think of America first.
  To exalt America first.[1]

Harry Daugherty became attorney general of the United States and
brought to Washington with him from Marion, Ohio, a large, sad-eyed
man, Jess Smith, to whom he seemed devoted. Smith and he rented a
house on H Street, near the White House, and Daugherty gave Smith
an office near his own at the Department of Justice.

A Marion County bank president became comptroller of the currency, and then governor of the Federal Reserve System; a chance acquaintance of Harding's became superintendent of the Mint. The vast
new Veterans' Bureau was headed by "Colonel" Charlie Forbes, who
proved later to have been a deserter from the army. The commissioner
of prohibition, the head of the Customs Service, and, more slowly, the
heads of the new regulatory agencies — all were soon political friends.
Many of them were small businessmen, or the self-made wealthy, who
knew little or nothing of government, to whom government jobs were
financial rewards for loyalty, and whose only guidance from the President was a program of cutting the government down.

"I don't like to seem ungrateful," the President said, and streams of
place-seekers flowed through the little house on H Street. People who
had trouble with the Justice Department now began to come there, to
talk with Jess Smith.

Soon after the election, Harding asked Taft to see him in Marion.
The two men talked over breakfast about cabinet posts.

"By the way," Harding said, "I want to ask, would you accept a position on the Supreme Bench, because if you would, I'll put you on the
Court."[2]

Taft thought about that a little, and the next day he answered that he
would like to be chief justice. White was getting old, and must soon retire; perhaps, as Taft had appointed him, he would return the seat to his
benefactor. Taft went hopefully to call on White, who complained of his
failing sight, illness, and overwork, but said nothing about retiring.

On March 4, 1921, Harding became the first President of the United
States born after the Civil War, and the first to have his inaugural address
electronically amplified. He seemed a little larger than life, and he spoke
of an indistinct but happy future. The grassy hilltop on which the Capitol stood was covered with a huge crowd, standing to hear him.

As Harding gave his address, Holmes let his eyes wander over the
crowd. It was a pleasant day, promising spring:

A heather of human faces filled full the whole space from the capitol to the Library [of Congress] and up the street beyond and to the Representatives Building and I should think to the Senate Building — There were bands of color, and a medley of tints from the women near to.[3]

The President's platitudes left Holmes unmoved — "I fear that he is a pumpkin and not a cantaloupe"[4] — but Holmes was relieved to see Wilson out of office and the Republican party in power again. The war was only a memory, the day was warm and brilliant, he was feeling well, and in four days he would be eighty years old.

He and Fanny were somewhat out of fashion in Washington society, and now entertained and dined out less often, to their relief. Holmes made teatime calls every Friday on Mrs. Rodgers, wife of the naval aviator Commander John Rodgers, and on Sundays called on Mrs. Beveridge or another friend. But he and Fanny lived in relative seclusion, as they had in Boston.

Fanny had few companions of her own generation. Dorothy, her nieces, nephews, and grandnephews occupied her affections. A Wigglesworth nephew was a congressman from Massachusetts, and his wife became a frequent caller. Holmes's secretary kept Fanny company, when Holmes was in court:

> Mrs. Holmes was a delight to talk with. She used to sit very straight, on the edge of a chair — not slumped back in the corner. She was bright, alert, quick — like some little bird. "Dickie" was a perfect name for her.
>
> She must have had the same irrelevant, diverse charm as a girl in Boston, before the War. . . . [She] told little amusing inconsequential stories. "The proletariat" was a phrase she fancied. One day we went out to see some apple blossoms. The farmer said that if we'd only been there a day or two before they'd have been really worth seeing. . . . "The proletariat," she said, "always loves to diminish one's pleasures."[5]

Fanny filled the house with little odds and ends that she bought from street vendors. At an oriental shop called the Pagoda, kept by a Mrs. Osgood, Fanny found artificial butterflies to hang on the fringes of lampshades in the living room, other little ornaments, and a porcelain figure to have made into an electric lamp for the middle parlor. She found a little red devil, and hung it by an elastic band from the chandelier in Holmes's library. She, like Holmes, was in better health and spirits than she had been for years,[6] and she presided over a large, smoothly running household, finely adjusted to Holmes's comfort. Annie Gough, who had come to them as cook, was now the chief housekeeper, with her own bedroom on the third floor; there were a cook, a parlor maid, and two local girls to assist her. A butler — Holmes called him "the inside man" — a chauffeur, and the Court messenger waited on Holmes.[7]

His young friends, too, ministered to him. Harold Laski, to Holmes's deep pleasure, arranged to have Holmes's articles and addresses on the law collected into a book.

Holmes fussed over the preparation of the *Collected Legal Papers,* peppering Laski with suggestions and doubts, hesitating whether this piece or that should be included, complaining at Laski's failure to include others. When he read over the proofs, Holmes was discouraged; it did not seem much to show for forty years. He waited with trembling apprehension for the reaction:

> I am glad to gather up this little basketful before my 80th birthday, as I was glad to get out *The Common Law* before my 40th.[8]

> I feel a mild excitement at the rather old little boy going out in a new jacket and trousers.[9]

When the book came out, he was pleased by its appearance; it seemed an important point to him that the book was printed on good paper. He sent only a frugal half-dozen copies to England — to Pollock, Bryce, Lord Haldane, and the British Academy, of which he was a corresponding member. As it was a law book, he did not send it to ladies, but he hugged himself with the thought that Baroness Moncheur had promised to buy a copy.

The reviews, when they came, treated it as a summing-up, and spoke of Holmes as well as of his book; they must have seemed like advance notices of his obituaries. The tone of the reviews was colored by the role he had taken, or been given, as a dissenter. The young reviewers praised him. In *The Nation,* Thomas Reed Powell, one of the new young scholars of the Constitution, admired him. The *Boston Transcript* had a gracious little puff. *The New Republic* carried a brief notice and then a long review by Morris R. Cohen. Holmes's *Collected Legal Papers,* he said, was "an extraordinary book of thoroughly matured human wisdom . . . the rich insight into the ever-recurrent issues of life is clothed in rare nobility of language."[10]

On Sunday, March 6, as Holmes was still savoring the reviews, Fanny suggested that they dine at home. They had kept up the habit of dining at the Willard or the Powhatan on Sundays, but Fanny said that it would help the servants if they ate lunch out and dined at home. Dinner would be a little late, and as the evening drew on, Fanny lightly suggested that they dress for dinner, in honor of their last Sunday in the seventies. Holmes had a moment of suspicion, but Fanny was entirely natural. They went down to dinner together a little after eight.

When the folding doors were opened there were 16 or 18 strapping chaps standing around the table for a dinner party. She had got my Ex-secretaries from far and near — one came from Chattanooga and went back at 12. Of course I was flabbergasted. And she says I yelled with joy when they began to pour out the champagne of which we had a case or two left. The alternative of grape juice was offered in case of conscientious objections but I saw none. She made them all come in the back door to conceal everything from me. We and I think all had a ripping time — and they were so affectionate and kind that it went to my heart.[11]

On his birthday, Tuesday, March 8, there were further celebrations, touching letters, telegrams, and gifts. John Wigmore, Learned Hand, Morris Cohen, and Felix Frankfurter wrote; there were other telegrams and flowers from Boston and London. Among the gifts was an issue of the *Harvard Law Review* dedicated to Holmes, with his photograph as the frontispiece, which opened with a wonderful essay by Dean Roscoe Pound of Harvard Law School saying that indeed the world now moved to the measure of Holmes's thought.[12] In *The New Republic* Lord Haldane, the former Lord Chancellor, gave a magnificent tribute.[13]

Holmes's deepest ambition was touched by this praise. Perhaps the most moving of all came from his colleagues — Chief Justice White and Justice Brandeis — who encouraged him to go on.

The spring is here in a rapture of flowers. A magnolia in the back yard fills my eye with pink when I look up — there are magnolias of all kinds everywhere — the cherry trees around the Potomac basin — the earlier single-flowering ones are just coming out — the robins have their spring note — I get a glimpse every morning by driving through the Smithsonian and walking across the botanic gardens at the foot of Capitol Hill. . . . In spite of 80 I am still on deck.[14]

He had lost very little of his physical presence: he was an alert, princely white-haired man, dressed impeccably in prewar English clothes. If he had become a little more careful of small sums of money, and was pleased to save a postage stamp or the price of a book, his eyes and his voice were as beautiful and seductive as ever.

To be sure, he had his ailments. A cough settled on him, apparently to stay, and often woke him at night. Then he would take Argyrol and read a book, but the next day he would be drowsy. He puffed and panted more, and was relieved when the doctor told him that while he suffered from asthma, as his father and brother had, there was nothing wrong with his heart.

He tried to keep from talking too much, which made him cough, but was easily tempted. He liked to rattle off his "old chestnuts" to any new visitor. He strung these stories and aphorisms into a sort of courting speech, which flashed with wit and passion, and addressed it to a steady stream of new secretaries and Monday callers. After an evening of talk he would worry that he had been a tiresome old man, dealing out egotisms.[15] Yet old age gave him license, and despite his occasional misgiving that he had become a little foolish, he continued to fire at every target:

> I have been chuckling since Monday with some devil talk I let off to an unknown female at our At Home. I told her abuses were the parents of the exquisite — which disappeared from this country with wine — that you couldn't have a society like that of Greece except on some sort of slavery — and that I loathed most of the things I decided in favor of.
> If she had been a newspaper reporter who for all I know or knew she might have been what headlines were possible as to cynicism in high places. But as I said to Wigmore yesterday, a paradox takes the scum off your mind.[16]

Fanny, too, was a prominent and somewhat eccentric figure in Washington, despite her passion for privacy and her refusal to be photographed or interviewed. She, too, had the license of great age for her eccentric habits of dress — hair pulled up tight at the back of her head, and the guimpes and ruffles of a much earlier age: "The [British] Ambassadress, whether she knew that she was speaking of my wife or not I was not quite sure, said I like to see an old lady like that with her white hair, still dining out. It is sporting."[17]

Harold Laski sent news and gossip from London, where he was now teaching, about old friends or the children and grandchildren of old friends, and Holmes would ask wistfully if the women he once courted, now growing old themselves, remembered him at all. Holmes seemed to remember everyone when they were boys: General Pershing when he was an understrapper at the White House, Lord Haldane when he was a clerk in Leslie Scott's office. He would meet the middle-aged children of women he had flirted with when they were still unmarried, and was startled when Margot Asquith's daughter Elizabeth, Princess Antoine Bibesco, helped him on with his coat.[18]

On a cold winter afternoon, leaving the Capitol, two justices insisted that Holmes take a taxi and not walk even part of the way home: "I saw them (in my mind) saying, 'the old gentleman ought not to take the risk of a tumble.'"[19]

He drew joy as always from the young, and now the whole country seemed to him to be young, struggling through its adolescence toward the future, and he took great pleasure in helping to ease its struggles. He never tired of lecturing his colleagues on their duty in this regard:

> Judges are apt to be naif, simple-minded men, and they need something of Mephistopheles. We too need education in the obvious — to learn to transcend our own convictions and to leave room for much that we hold dear to be done away with short of revolution by the orderly change of law.[20]

Of all the great hopes of the young in that season, the greatest was the hope of doing away with war. The genial President of the United States shared these youthful hopes. He convened a disarmament conference in Washington, in the first winter of his administration. The Asquiths came to Washington, and James Bryce, with his hopes for international law. Kaneko came with the Japanese delegation. Holmes saw his old friends briefly, and if he was not optimistic about the results of their conference, he was moved by it, and by the ceremonies that surrounded the meeting:

> First came the [burial of the Unknown Soldier]. I had been disgusted by the vulgarities of the bogus sentiment, the odious emptiness of reporters' talk that seems an echo of the popular mind. But when I saw the coffin borne into the great rotunda of the Capitol, which became beautiful and impressive in the dim twilight, and afterwards saw the miles of people marching through, three abreast, from early morning into the next day, I realized that a feeling may be great notwithstanding its inability to get itself expressed. . . .
>
> I couldn't help thinking how on the one side was a little life, probably like thousands of others, and on the other the passion of a people, striving to meet, and stretching away into the infinite, eternally drawing nearer, but like parabola and asymptote never quite meeting — for he will never know and we shall never know.[21]

On the morning after his eightieth birthday, Holmes was in court as usual, listening to "false intonations and bogus enthusiasms of counsel," wondering whether the justices would pick a hole in the last opinion he had submitted to them.

The chief justice was younger than he, but not as well. Cataracts in both White's eyes were slowly making him blind, and he had grown rather deaf. He could read only with great difficulty and had to be helped across streets. He had a painful bladder ailment that would require surgery, but he struggled to keep his seat on the bench. He had kept on for fear Wilson would appoint his successor, but now, Holmes supposed, he kept on for love of the place itself.

At the end of the term, the long-deferred surgery could not be further postponed, and White took a leave of absence. He sent a note to Holmes:

> I got to worrying about some of the work here and so came back to my library for a few days in order to get things straight and then go back and face the music, which I propose to do tomorrow. It is not dance music by any means, but all the same I am going to try to step out with hope and confidence in the outcome, which I know I will do if I can only fix my mind on the young fellow lying face down in the lines of Fredericksburg and fearful only of one thing — that he might be hit in the back.[22]

Holmes took over one of the Chief's cases and immersed himself in it with pleasure; it was one of three he had at once, and when he sent the opinions around he was pleased as a boy that the judges all agreed and seemed to like what he had written.[23]

On May 19, Chief Justice Edward White died.[24] That same day, hearing the news, William Howard Taft wrote to friends, hinting that his cause might now be moved forward, although the newspapers had been saying he was too old.[25]

The President, however, despite his offer to Taft, had promised the first vacant seat on the Court to another friend, George Sutherland, who had been chairman of the Senate Judiciary Committee and still had friends there. But fellow Ohioan Harry Daugherty sided with Taft, as did Taft's allies and friends in the Senate. The question remained at stalemate for some time.

Holmes was a little disturbed at Taft's candidacy, but did not think of the place for himself,[26] and when at last the President announced that William Howard Taft would be the new chief justice of the United States, Holmes sent a note of welcome, pledging his help and cooperation.

There was the summer to rest, and to think about the question whether he would continue under the new chief justice, who aside from personal considerations he thought indolent and undistinguished. Holmes's neighbor at Beverly, Senator Beveridge, told him a story of a Japanese who had been ambassador everywhere, a high official of his government, and who had resigned at the age of sixty — to meditate. This brought Holmes up short for a moment; but, he said: "I don't yield to the impression, because if meditating means thinking about the meaning of life I don't think I should add much to what I think now."[27]

Holmes read, drove with Fanny, and was read to, and decided, somewhat hesitatingly, to continue on the Court. He could not expect to add much to what he had already done. But work was life:

> I am thinking of starting a new ideal — to live to 90 . . . call the old job finished, and start this as a new one (continuing however to work on the bench, if only as a means of survival). It seems as if a man must reach 90 to be really old. But I guess it is pretty hard sledding to get there.[28]

> This last year has had such a series of notices as I never could have expected and seems to mark a windup. But there is a chance to figure as a survivor.[29]

> I feel my life has had its reward . . . I so tremble at the thought that I wish I could be declared Emeritus — my job finished . . . but alas there is no pause possible — "Does the road lead uphill all the way? Yes — to the very end." And one must still take one's chances.[30]

The October, 1921, term was a new beginning in many ways. Harding had brought with him a new Republican majority in Congress, and a new Republican chief justice. Washington was filling up with people hunting for houses and for jobs.

Justice Joseph McKenna — the last of the judges remaining from the Court that Holmes had joined almost twenty years before — administered the oath of office of chief justice to Taft. McKenna was seventy-nine, and was now shrunken and frail. His nearly bald head seemed too large for his tiny body. Beside him, Taft was an immense figure, over six feet tall, obese, his hair still dark, his eyes half-closed, a hint of a smile beneath his mustache. He answered McKenna's piping in a deep, confident baritone.

After the opening of court there was the customary reception at the White House. Harding was good-humored and at ease as he greeted the justices; he and Taft stood briefly side-by-side, two big Ohioans radiating masculine assurance. Holmes was cheered by their strength and confidence.

Brandeis, too, was making a new beginning. He was aware that he had helped to wreck Taft's presidency and that he had shouldered onto the bench ahead of Taft. They were now to spend their working lives together in the narrow confines of the Court. Brandeis determined to establish cordial relations.

In recent years, the conferences of the Court had grown bitterly acrimonious and emotionally exhausting. White had no longer been able to manage their work, and they had fallen farther and farther behind their docket. McKenna was embittered and would strike out at random. Justice McReynolds, a difficult and irascible man, had taken a violent personal dislike to the other Wilson appointees, Brandeis and John H. Clarke, and did not try to conceal his dislike. He wrapped his animosity toward Brandeis in anti-Semitic barbs, refused to visit houses where Brandeis had been invited — "I do not dine with the Orient" — and was bitterly contemptuous of Brandeis's opinions. In conference he would rise and leave the room while Brandeis spoke. Holmes, his courtesy for once failing him, called McReynolds a "savage."

Fewer cases were decided, and more dissenting opinions were issued. Important matters were determined by narrow votes, statutes were struck down by votes of five to four, with bitter dissents, and no single view commanded a majority. When Holmes, for five members of the Court, upheld the constitutionality of a rent-control law, McKenna dissented in such violent terms, for a minority of four, that it was difficult to remain civil afterward.[31]

The Court's inability to agree left its decisions weak and unpersuasive, and it came under wide attack. The American Federation of Labor proposed amending the Constitution, to limit the Court's power to decide the constitutionality of statutes. Senator Robert LaFollette proposed an amendment that would have allowed Congress to override Constitutional decisions of the Court. The *New York Times* and the *Wall Street Journal* both endorsed Senator William Borah's relatively mild proposal, which would have required a seven-to-two vote of the Court to overturn any legislation. Still other measures were proposed to strip the Court of part of its jurisdiction and force it to catch up with the growing docket of undecided cases.

Brandeis's presence on the Court, as Holmes had feared, put added strain on the relations among the justices, and added to the heat of public criticism. That tall, gaunt figure with deeply shadowed eyes, utterly unlike Taft, seemed to have had every excess stripped away from him:

> The bed he slept in looked like a camp bed, and the furniture showed distinct signs of wear.[32]

> One wondered at times, whether like some Eastern sage the body's grosser part had not been burnt quite away and mere spirit remained.[33]

To Holmes, Brandeis's optimism and moral certainty, so unlike his own skepticism, were cheering; Brandeis moved him, as only a few philosophers had, to hope. Brandeis was a comfort, and when Brandeis left their house, Holmes was likely to say to an unsympathetic Fanny, "There goes a really good man,"[34]

> though I am not sure that he wouldn't burn me at a slow fire if it were in the interest of some very possibly disinterested aim.[35]

Holmes was amused when he heard the Boston gossip that Brandeis held him in thrall. In some circles Holmes had been given up for lost, an aged dupe of Semitic Bolshevism. When Nina Gray hinted at such thoughts, Holmes laughed, "I am tickled by your, 'If only you stay thoroughly Anglo-Saxon. . . .'"[36]

For Brandeis, it was a time to retrench and to cultivate his remaining friends.[37] On the afternoon of the opening of the October term, Brandeis called on Holmes and Fanny at 1720 I Street and, with his usual quick understanding, encouraged Holmes to continue on the Court. Brandeis easily picked up the threads of a lifelong friendship.[38]

In the afternoons, Holmes now gave Brandeis a lift as far as I Street in his rented horse-drawn victoria, and often Brandeis would come in to continue their talk in the library. One afternoon, on the drive home, Brandeis

> grew really eloquent on the evils of the present organization of society. When I repeated my oft-repeated views as to the economic elements he told me they were superficial and didn't deal with the real evil, which was not a question of luxuries or victuals but of power. He was fierce and fine as [to] the men he knew who didn't dare say what they thought because of the power to which they were subject. He compared the Scotsmen who eat oatmeal, but stood up — men. Then said I hadn't seen and knew nothing about the evils that one who had been much in affairs had seen and known. He bullies me a little on that from time to time.[39]

But Holmes declined to feel resentment or indignation over facts. He liked to say that the inevitable was not wicked. He did not share Brandeis's sense that someone was to blame, but he was perfectly willing to see Brandeis's reformers have their day in the sun. So far as their everyday work was concerned, the two men usually agreed, so much so that Holmes grew testy at the charges of influence. But when Holmes was under the weather, felt stupid or muddleheaded while listening to the interminable arguments of counsel, "The dear Brandeis helps me to understand what the question is."[40]

Taft, too, was courting Holmes. The triumphant chief justice was determined to heal the divisions in the court and to quiet the dissents that were destroying its authority.

More than this, Taft wished to take control and to manage the whole judicial branch of government. As president and then as leader of his party, Taft had passed upon the appointments of perhaps one third of the whole federal judiciary. The new President and attorney general were political friends and allies; Taft expected to continue influencing appointments to all of the federal courts. He was impatient to see these appointments be made, especially on the Supreme Court itself, where at

least three places would be vacant soon. Two of the justices were chron-
ically ill and could not write opinions. McKenna, Taft thought, was worst
of all. He would be humble and deprecatory in the conference room, but
when criticized he would flare out in violent anger. He lost his temper
and his self-control entirely at Holmes one Saturday, but Holmes remained cheerful, and it passed over.[41]

Taft could not assign to McKenna any but the simplest cases and even
in those, Taft complained,

> he will write an opinion, and bring it to conference and it will meet
> objection because he has missed a point . . . or, as in one instance,
> he wrote an opinion deciding the case one way when there had
> been a unanimous vote the other, including his own. . . . He is
> jealous of Holmes, and tries to write as rapid opinions. He does
> not get the record straight and altogether it makes a difficult sit-
> uation.[42]

The new chief justice spoke to McKenna and hinted that it was time
to retire, but the older man refused: "He said that when a man retires,
he disappears and nobody cares for him."[43]

But if McKenna clung to his place, three younger justices resigned in
Taft's first year, and there were three seats to fill.

The President had already promised the first vacancy to George Sutherland, and Harry Daugherty had a candidate of his own, Edward Terry
Sanford, a district judge from Tennessee, for the second. Taft approved
these choices and was able to persuade the President to appoint his own
good friend Pierce Butler, a wealthy Minnesota railroad lawyer, to the
third seat. These new men, along with the present justices Willis Van
Devanter, whom Taft had appointed himself, and McReynolds, gave him
a solid majority of like-minded men, who shared his belief that Bolshevik
subversion threatened the nation and that the seeds of foreign revolution
must be found and destroyed.

More than just naming federal judges, Taft wanted to rebuild the
antiquated common-law courts. Each of the federal courts was an autonomous barony; there was no coordination among them and little sharing
of work. Worst of all, the Supreme Court had little control over its own
workload. Most of its time was still taken up by cases that it was obliged
to hear regardless of their importance. The Court, steadily falling behind
its schedule, seemed to spend great energies on numerous minor or frivolous appeals in which the attorneys insisted on their right to talk to the
bored justices for two hours each.

Taft's plan was to secure legislation reorganizing the whole court system under the chief justice's control, and rewriting the rules of jurisdiction so that the Court could choose among its cases, focusing its attention
on major questions of national policy. Taft also lobbied for funds to give

the Supreme Court its own building, with offices and a staff. The Court would become an equal, and in some ways the supreme, political branch of government, operating under the direction of the chief justice. To accomplish these aims, Taft wanted the support and harmony of the members of his Court.

A necessary first step was to soothe the personal animosities among them. He was cordial to Brandeis, and to Holmes he extended all the forceful charm of which he was capable. Holmes reciprocated; he would help to restore good feeling, and would help to bring the Court's work up to date.

> Association with Justice Holmes is a delight. He is feeble physically, but I cannot see that the acuteness of his mind has been affected at all. . . . In many ways he is the life of the Court, and it is a great comfort to have such a well of pure common law undefiled immediately next one so that one can drink and be sure one is getting the pure article.[44]
>
> His power of rapid work is still marvelous.[45]

The chief justice bought a house on Wyoming Avenue at Twenty-third Street and walked to the Capitol every morning. His course took him past I Street, and so he walked with Holmes for the last part of the way up Pennsylvania Avenue to the Capitol. They talked with growing ease and cordiality on these walks.

And so they began, Taft and Holmes walking in the mornings, Brandeis and Holmes riding in the afternoons. On Saturdays, after the conference, Taft gave both Holmes and Brandeis a lift in his car, and the three big men rode home together.

The conferences of the Court were no longer acrimonious. Taft presided as if over a seminar, carefully eliciting everyone's views of every case, and Van Devanter, who rarely wrote opinions but whose views were respected by his colleagues, served as Taft's deputy, mediating among the justices and negotiating changes in opinions to secure agreement. McReynolds occasionally flew off on his own, and Brandeis occasionally wrote a dissent, but these were not important defections, and even Brandeis was struggling to find a middle ground upon which to join his colleagues.

Holmes, having quickly overcome his first misgivings, was greatly pleased with Taft and with the new temper of the Court: "The conferences are long and tiring, but amiable. No one gets angry nowadays."[46]

In the first term of court over which Taft presided, the number of cases decided by the Court rose by half, but the number of dissenting opinions declined sharply; by the October term of 1924, the Court issued 232 opinions, most of them unanimous, and only 10 dissenting opinions.[47]

Taft succeeded also in driving through Congress the legislation he wanted, putting the chief justice in charge of a national judicial conference, with authority to harmonize the circuit court operations and to shift judicial resources where they were needed. Most dramatically, he secured legislation — drafted by a committee of the justices — fundamentally reforming the jurisdiction of the Supreme Court. Henceforth, in most cases, the Court would have discretion to grant or deny a hearing. Holmes had not favored this reform; he would have preferred to see the Supreme Court remain a common-law court, available to most appellants, and he did not care to see it taking a larger political role. But Holmes did not openly oppose Taft, and the historic change was made. The Court henceforth would be able to write its own agenda.

President Harding had not taken control of the executive branch in the same way that Taft had of the judicial. Rather, the President announced policies so general as to amount almost to platitudes, and turned the running of the government over to political appointees.

Rumors began to spread that friends of the administration were involved in alcohol traffic and that permits for alcohol could be obtained, and prosecutions quashed, by seeing Jess Smith at the little house on H Street.

But to the President and his men, it seemed that the threat to America came from abroad. In the Western states, Japan was feared and disliked. Elsewhere, Prohibition seemed threatened by Italian and German immigrants, who had brought with them their habits of wine and beer drinking. Organized criminal gangs of recent immigrants smuggled alcohol into the country and murdered each other on city streets. Immigrant labor was depressing wages, and immigrants from eastern Europe were bringing the viruses of Bolshevism and anarchy.

In 1921, at the administration's request, Congress enthusiastically passed the country's first general system of controls on immigration, forbidding immigration from Asia or Africa and limiting immigration from Europe by a system of quotas designed to preserve the ethnic balance of the United States as it had been in 1910. Soon the quotas were cut, and the benchmark was moved back to 1890. The war against Bolshevism, the struggle to restore prosperity, the war against alcohol, all merged into an instinctive defense of white Protestant America against the onslaught of foreign peoples and ideas: America First.

By January, 1922, when there was unusually cold weather and heavy snowfall in Washington, inflation had collapsed, prices and wages were falling, wages more quickly than prices. Five million were unemployed; there was a new wave of strikes in the coal fields and on the railroads. Harry Daugherty appeared personally in a federal district court seeking to enjoin an illegal railroad workers' strike, hoping to break the union as well as the strike.

It was the winter of Holmes's eighty-first year. On his birthday, he was up half the night coughing, perhaps because he had talked too much, and by April, an attack of asthma kept him for the first time from attending a conference of the Court. "The conference seemed dreary without him," Brandeis remarked.[48]

But June came around again, with its promise of rest. Brandeis gave him some reports on conditions in the textile mills to read during the summer; Holmes had dutifully trudged through such recommended reading from Brandeis in the past. But now Laski too recommended something similarly dull, and this was too much:

> You mention for Beverly Farms, good God! Webb on this and that — and *Clothing Workers of Chicago*. My boy I mean to enjoy myself if I can — to get the unexpurgated Pepys — even . . . John Dewey's last in a philosophical way or Pound on Law but if you think that I am going to bother myself again before I die about social improvement or read any of those stinking onward and up-warders — you err. I mean to have some good out of being old.[49]

Holmes and Fanny were looking forward to celebrating their fiftieth wedding anniversary that summer, and Holmes was to receive an honorary degree at Amherst College. But they had a hard journey up to Boston; the train jolted along and was an hour late, and then the motor ride to Beverly Farms was trying. At Beverly Farms, the dairyman had not delivered the buttermilk on which Holmes felt his digestion depended. A doctor was appealed to, who issued his fiat, and the buttermilk came. But there was worse trouble than buttermilk could fix. A few days after his arrival in Massachusetts, Holmes was in the Corey Hill Hospital in Brookline, awaiting prostate surgery. This was a grave matter, potentially fatal.

The surgery was performed on July 12, and on August 17, Holmes went home to Beverly Farms, after almost two months in the hospital:

> I tell you what, it is easier to get into one of these things than it is to get out. The operation was most successful and I recovered without hitch to the point of being discharged. Now comes the time for recuperation and more doctors.[50]

He had lost a great deal of blood, his face was pale, and he was weak to the point of helplessness. Encouraging letters came from friends and colleagues, and a particularly touching letter from the irascible Justice McReynolds: "I am much distressed by your illness . . . everybody wants to keep you many, many years. There are no more like you and we need you all the time."[51]

I lollup round upon my lounge — try to rejoice in irresponsibility and having nothing to do, read a little Shakespeare and snooze. Everything is encouraging but at this moment the fact is that I am rather a feeble old man — who however is going in for 90 if he can get it.[52]

While Holmes lolluped, Fanny planned their return to Washington. They stopped in New York to rest on the way down, and in Washington, at the railroad station, Holmes — to his indignation — was disgracefully wheeled in a chair to a taxi. They were to stay at the Powhatan for some time, for Fanny had arranged for an elevator to be installed between the first and second floors at 1720 I Street, obliterating a closet and ranks of bookshelves; the front library was a disaster of dustcloths and rubble.

On October 22, Holmes climbed the short flight of steps to his front door very slowly, putting both feet on each stair. He rode to the second floor in the elevator, which Fanny would not enter — she was sure she would put it out of order in some way. The workmen were gone, but there was still the job of doing something with the books and papers dislodged by the elevator. Many of the papers were consigned to the fireplace:

> What a divine gift is fire. In the clearing up that I have nearly finished I have cut short a thousand hesitations and shut out many fool vistas of possible interest by burning odds and ends. Civilization is the process of reducing the infinite to the finite.[53]

Some of the books that were not needed Holmes gave to the Pittsfield library, where his father's unwanted books had also come to rest.

He made some preparations for his demise. If he should die at Beverly, he would be buried with his family at Mt. Auburn Cemetery, but if he should die in Washington, Holmes decided to exercise the privilege accorded to former officers to be buried at Arlington National Cemetery. He and Fanny rode out to Arlington one afternoon, looked over the huge grounds, and found a plot that they liked in an undeveloped section.

Holmes now kept his will in his desk drawer, and at the beginning of each term of the Court, he showed the new secretary where it was, in an envelope along with a little pamphlet that explained the procedure for arranging burial at Arlington.[54]

Since his illness, there had been talk in the newspapers that he would resign. Holmes gave the possibility the formal consideration that it required.[55] He had reached the top, and perhaps it was only downhill ahead. But his mind was clear, and he decided to go on: "The work so far doesn't hurt me at all — but I don't go about, dine out or give dinners — I think that we shall drop out of society."[56]

To encourage him further, there were warm letters and an editorial in *The New Republic* organized by Frankfurter; it was the twentieth anniversary of Holmes's coming on the Supreme Court, and forty years — forty years! — since he had first taken his seat as a judge in Massachusetts.

> The soldier's faith, the faith he lived in war and lives in peace, he has described as "having known great things, to be content with silence." But for us, for whom the "great things" are still being wrought by the Justice — we cannot be content with silence. And so the *New Republic* also wishes to mark the anniversary of forty years of judicial service, and twenty years of Mr. Justice Holmes, with rejoicing and gratitude.[57]

There was a note from Brandeis — "Still the dash of a D'Artagnan"[58] — and a remarkable letter from Benjamin Cardozo, brilliant young judge of New York's highest court.

> I am taking advantage . . . of the approaching anniversary to ask you to enter me on the long and growing roll of your admirers and disciples.
> I cannot tell you what a help and inspiration you have been to me. It would be presumptuous of me to praise. Where praise would be out of place, it may be permissible to offer homage.[59]

McKenna resigned, and Holmes was now the senior justice. He sat beside the chief justice on the bench and presided in his absence. He assigned the opinion for the Court when Taft was not in the majority. But Taft was almost always in the majority.

The chief justice was in command of his Court. If Fuller's genius had been a self-effacing tact, if White had remained a politician, a senator, Taft was presidential. He was at the head of a federal court system that stretched from the Philippines to Puerto Rico. He had organized the Supreme Court into committees to work on legislation, and on plans for a new Court building. In big cases, justices in the majority worked together under his supervision, circulating drafts and meeting together. When he assigned cases, he often wrote out suggestions for points to be covered, to ensure a unanimous Court, and when there was disagreement he often took over the opinion himself and hammered out the offending passages. Even in one of their most difficult cases concerning labor relations, Chief Justice Taft wrote an opinion for a nearly unanimous Court, accepting the legitimacy of peaceful picketing and boycotts, adopting in his opinion the reasoning of Holmes's article "Privilege, Malice and Intent." Brandeis joined in this opinion with Taft and Holmes.[60]

Holmes joined Taft's majority on most matters. Soon after his illness,

Holmes was speaking for the Court on the greatest issue of the time, Prohibition: "The Eighteenth Amendment meant a great revolution in the policy of this country, and presumably and obviously meant to upset a good many things on as well as off the statute book."[61]

Holmes continued to speak for the Court when it tried to ensure that Prohibition was carried out peacefully and fairly. They unanimously struck down the administration's efforts to seize the property of accused persons without a hearing and to make the criminal laws retroactive.[62]

In the other great national upheaval, the vast warlike effort to preserve the supposed racial character of the nation, the Court was again unanimous, and Holmes again was often its spokesman.

The Constitution did not require, and the Court therefore could not extend, elementary fairness to aliens. Chinese had been excluded from entry into the United States for many years, and members of the Chinese "race" would be deported unless they could prove that they were citizens. The Supreme Court did not intervene. Asians could not become naturalized citizens, even when their entry into the country was legal, and the erudite George Sutherland from Utah wrote dryly intellectual opinions for a unanimous Court, holding that upper-class Indian Hindus and cultured Japanese were not "white," and therefore could not be citizens. California, by popular referendum, and other Western states by statute, forbade Japanese residents from owning land. The Court unanimously upheld these laws. Justice Brandeis, writing for a unanimous Court, upheld the deportation of one Bilokumsky, who had been arrested and imprisoned and was to be deported on the charge that he was an alien distributing seditious leaflets; the evidence was that he had failed to prove his citizenship.[63]

Holmes wrote rather sadly to Kaneko, saying that he hoped the tensions between their countries would not affect their friendship, but it had seemed to Holmes for many years that conflict among the races was inevitable.

Among other measures for racial hygiene were the laws adopted by many states to require sterilization of mental defectives. Virginia's statute came before the Court. A woman named Carrie Buck, said to be a mentally defective person, whose mother and daughters were also said to be mentally defective, was to be sterilized against her will. She was given a hearing and an apparently fair opportunity to contest the determination, before the surgery was to be performed.

The Court voted to uphold the Virginia law. The chief justice assigned the opinion to Holmes and sent a note along with it, with some suggestions:

> Some of the brethren are troubled about the case, especially
> Butler. May I suggest that you make a little full [your discussion
> of] the care Virginia has taken in guarding against undue or hasty

action, the proven absence of danger to the patient, and other circumstances tending to lessen the shock that many feel over the remedy? The strength of the facts in three generations of course is the strongest argument.[64]

Holmes accepted these suggestions, but he did not soften the Court's decision or mask the reasons for it. He spoke in frank and harsh terms, as he did whenever the ideas expressed in an opinion ran against natural feeling. He spoke in the hard language that sends children to be killed in war. Only Justice Butler dissented.

> We have seen more than once that the public welfare may call upon the best citizens for their lives. It would be strange if it could not call upon those who already sap the strength of the state for these lesser sacrifices, often not felt to be such by those concerned, in order to prevent our being swamped with incompetence. It is better for all the world, if instead of waiting to execute degenerate offspring for crime, or to let them starve for their imbecility, society can prevent those who are manifestly unfit from continuing their kind. The principle that sustains vaccination is broad enough to cover cutting the Fallopian tubes. . . . Three generations of imbeciles are enough.[65]

And so the Court did its duty and allowed social experiments to proceed, the immense and violent experiments in Prohibition and racial improvement, so long as Constitutional guarantees of fairness were observed.

Of course, they could not always agree among themselves, and when Holmes thought the disagreement touched fundamental principles of law, he continued to dissent.

He did so when the Taft majority united to strike down the District of Columbia's minimum wage law for women workers. Frankfurter had argued the case for the District of Columbia, lecturing the justices as if they were students. He said minimum wage laws were needed to protect the health and morals of women, and so ultimately the quality of their children. This was the argument with which Brandeis had succeeded as counsel for Oregon a decade earlier.

But Justice Sutherland, the Court's expert on racial hygiene, wrote the opinion for the majority. He brushed aside as a sham Frankfurter's argument that the law was designed to protect the health of mothers and their children. To Sutherland and his majority, the statute — like New York's law to protect bakery workers — was simply an intervention into the bargain between worker and employer, an unconstitutional restriction of liberty.

Holmes indignantly dissented:

To me, notwithstanding the deference due to the prevailing judgment of the Court, the power of Congress seems absolutely free from doubt. The end, to remove conditions leading to ill health, immorality and the deterioration of the race, no one would deny to be within the scope of constitutional legislation. The means are means that have the approval of Congress, of many states, and of those governments from which we have learned our greatest lessons.[66]

A New Yorker named Benjamin Gitlow was convicted of being an officer of the nascent Communist party, which taught the necessity of violent revolution. When a majority of his colleagues affirmed the conviction,[67] Holmes said:

If in the long run the beliefs expressed in proletarian dictatorship are destined to be accepted by the dominant forces of the community, the only meaning of free speech is that they should be given their chance and have their way.[68]

An immigrant woman, Rosika Schwimmer, was denied citizenship because she was a pacifist. Congress might have made a law denying citizenship to pacifists, but it had not, and it seemed plain to Holmes that Schwimmer was denied citizenship only because the judges disliked her opinions:

. . . if there is any principle of the Constitution that more imperatively calls for attachment than any other it is the principle of free thought — not free thought for those who agree with us but freedom for the thought we hate.[69]

Brandeis urged him to write dissenting opinions in these cases, and played on his sense of duty. In response to Brandeis's urging, Holmes wrote a dissenting opinion in a case about censorship of the mails, which for twenty years he had allowed to pass without objection.[70] With each dissent, he became more celebrated, but he did not look back with much interest at the parade of strangers who were carrying him at the head of their march.

For all the passion in his dissents, Holmes's work was no longer burdensome. Taft assigned to him for the most part small cases concerning technical questions of the common law, which Holmes enjoyed, and he wrote one such opinion on the average each week during the term. Assigned to him on Saturday night, the opinion usually was finished and sent around by Tuesday. Petitions for certiorari — requests for discretionary review under Taft's reform — streamed in in large numbers, but Holmes's secretary read "the bloody certs" and summarized each on a single page; Holmes only looked at the petitions themselves to ensure the accuracy of the secretary's report.

Except for the certioraris, mornings were quiet after the weekly opinion was done. The messenger, Thomas, came in with the mail as soon as Holmes sat down in the library armchair after breakfast. It was a minor household mystery how Thomas knew when to enter — Holmes's theory was that Thomas waited until he heard the armchair squeak. Thomas would wait quietly in the background while Holmes attended to the letters; the secretary for that year would be at work in the adjoining room beyond the ever-open double doors. After answering his letters, Holmes would read, or doze. He needed the help of the secretary and the messenger to help him out of the armchair to stand at the writing desk at the window, smoking his little cigars, his big stooped figure visible to the clerk in the other room, bulky and dark against the bright window, an aureole of smoke hanging over his head.[71]

Occasionally, Fanny would come in, sometimes to speak to the secretary, sometimes hailing her husband in the depths of his reading: "Holmes! Holmes, J.!" He would talk awhile, and then — "Now, Dickie, see here, you run along, I've got to work." Fanny, not at all disconcerted, would walk through the open double doors to the secretary's desk and talk with him, while Holmes fidgeted.

Since his surgery, Holmes no longer walked to the Capitol. The secretary would help him down the front steps when it was time for Charles Buckley, the coachman turned chauffeur, to drive him to the Court in a rented motorcar.

On spring afternoons, Fanny would come along with Buckley to fetch Holmes from the Court and they would drive out together to see the cherry blossoms. Fanny might linger in talk with Buckley while Holmes waited impatiently to get into the car, and then there would be an exchange: "Woman, less jaw and more git"; Fanny would turn and say cheerfully, "Holmes, you be damned."[72] Once in the open-topped car, they would kick each other under the lap robe like adolescents.[73]

One afternoon, on their way home together, they stopped to see the opening of the Freer Gallery, and then went on along the road beside the Potomac basin:

> At just a picturesque distance was a long bed of tulips — embowered with avenues of trees through which shone the declining sun — while maidens cantered by the side of it and three mockingbirds sang the poetry of the moment.[74]

Holmes fretted mildly that the business district was encroaching on his quiet street. His cough recurred and remained. But a doctor told him

again that his heart was a good pump, and that there were very few men
of his age as well off as he — to which Holmes answered that most of
them were dead. As his eighty-fifth birthday approached, he worried
whether it was not time to resign from the Court. He spoke to Taft of
his "ever-weighing misgiving" whether he ought not to quit,[75] but Taft,
his other colleagues, and friends continued to praise him and to urge
him to continue; and he had set his course for ninety.

Holmes received the newly dedicated Roosevelt Medal. Standing in
the White House, he said to the President: "For five minutes you make
the dreams of a lifetime seem true."[76]

As he approached eighty-five, the chorus of praises swelled. *The New
Republic* commissioned a portrait in prose by Elizabeth Shepley Sergeant,
a brilliant and charming young journalist, who managed to get Holmes's
cooperation after strong initial doubts. Fanny disliked her from the start;
to Tom Corcoran, Holmes's secretary that year, she whispered, "Ugh —
Slimey cat!"[77] When Sergeant sent a draft of the article, Fanny asked to
have all references to herself removed, which was done.

The article, when it was finished, however, was a beautiful portrait of
Holmes, an icon to carry in processions:

> Here is a Yankee, strayed from Olympus. Olympians are re-
> puted at ease in the universe; they know truth in flashes of fire,
> and reveal its immortal essence in cryptic phrase. . . .
> Oliver Wendell Holmes's tall and erect figure, which a ripe and
> white old age has scarcely stooped; his grand manner, at once no-
> ble and dazzling — those have never asked for quarter of time.
> Watch his snowy head for a moment among his younger peers on
> the bench. Note the set of his shoulders in the gown. . . . The eyes,
> the most striking feature, give off sparkles of scintillating gray-
> blue, and have more scepticism and gentle malice than mercy in
> their depths.[78]

Roosevelt and Lodge were dead; William and Henry James, Henry
and Brooks and Clover Adams, James Bryce, and Leslie Stephen, all
dead. Few were left from Holmes's earliest years. Letters still came from
Pollock, regular and dull as clockwork. Cousin John Morse called occasionally when he was in Washington, listened to Holmes's talk, and went
back to Boston shaking his head over Holmes's Jewish friends.

One afternoon, a year after the Sergeant article appeared, Fanny
came into the front library where the secretary of that year was working.
She carried a little white silk dress, all made of a countless number of
ruffles. It was the dress Holmes's mother had made for him before
he was born, brittle with age, and Fanny was going to burn it in the

fireplace. The secretary protested, and she paused, looking at the fine sewing.

"Think of her," Fanny said, "putting in all those little stitches." Then she crumpled the little dress in the grate and touched it with a match flame; it flared like tissue paper.[79]

24

FINAL DUTY

Three years before, in May of 1923, when Holmes and Fanny had gone to the opening of the Freer Gallery and had driven along the Potomac afterward, Washington was decked in red, yellow, and green bunting, and a yellow crescent-and-sword symbol was everywhere. Groups of men in tasseled red fezzes crowded the streets and public places; there were brass bands and parades. The Ancient Order of the Mystic Shrine was in convention, and the most prominent Shriner, Warren G. Harding, was playing host in his capital city.

The Shriners were like a visible manifestation of the President's optimism and his gregarious, impersonal affection. A time of peace and prosperity seemed to have begun, but there were odd, discordant notes. Charlie Forbes, head of the Veterans Bureau, had left abruptly for Europe; a congressional committee was looking into charges that he had been selling off the veterans' hospital medical stores. Charles Cramer, the Veterans Bureau general counsel, retired from his post and shortly afterward committed suicide. The secretary of the interior, Albert Fall, resigned after only two years in office and went back to his ranch in New Mexico, saying that his work was finished, but conservationists were raising questions about leases granted for the oil reserves at Teapot Dome. There were vague, disquieting rumors of corruption in the Prohibition

Bureau and in the Department of Justice. A congressional investigation of Attorney General Harry Daugherty had begun, and on Decoration Day, when Daugherty was staying as a guest at the White House, word came to him that his companion Jess Smith had been found dead of a pistol wound, an apparent suicide, at the little house on H Street they had shared for a time.

The President, in apparent good humor despite the upheavals in his cabinet, left Washington for a summer's journey to Alaska and the West Coast with his wife and an entourage of reporters and officials of the Department of the Interior. In Alaska, the President seemed to receive bad news, but he said nothing about it.

As the presidential party began the long journey home, Harding became ill. The First Lady's homeopathic physician, brought from Marion, Ohio, and commissioned a brigadier general, was with them, and issued a statement that the President had eaten tainted seafood but was recovering. When they reached San Francisco, the President seemed to be better, and then he abruptly grew ill again and died within hours. There was disquieting uncertainty at first about the cause, but the physicians who joined the party in San Francisco attributed the death to heart failure.

On the night of August 2, 1923, a messenger brought the news of Harding's death to Vice President Coolidge at his father's farm in Plymouth Notch, Vermont, where Coolidge was helping with the haying. There was no telephone. The older Coolidge, who was a notary, administered the oath of office to his son in the family parlor, standing before the carefully blacked stove with its gleaming nickel ornaments, by the light of a kerosene lamp. The slight, taciturn Calvin Coolidge, who as vice president had sometimes been left to lunch alone in a corner of the Senate dining room, was President of the United States.

A few weeks later, the Senate Committee on Public Lands opened hearings into the Teapot Dome oil leases, and in October Albert Fall appeared — an aggressive, angry witness. He had bartered the navy's oil reserves in a set of complex and secret transactions to obtain military facilities in the Pacific, to prepare for a possible war with Japan. He was not ashamed of the transactions; they had been conducted in secrecy and concealed from the Congress, only in the interest of national security. He denied having done anything wrong or having taken anything for himself.

Coolidge called on Chief Justice Taft to ask his advice about these scandals, but Taft advised him to do nothing. To Taft, it seemed only a repeat of the Ballinger affair, in which his political enemies had tried to bring down his administration. Harry Daugherty, himself under increasing investigation, said the same and launched an investigation of the Senators who led the attack.

Rumors circulated in Washington that the entire Harding cabinet, perhaps Coolidge himself, was involved in the oil leases. There were calls for the impeachment of the attorney general for failure to prosecute the wrongdoing within the administration. Coolidge, by then a candidate for election in his own right, felt obliged to announce that he had no recollection of Teapot Dome being discussed at cabinet meetings.

Early in the new year, the proliferating Senate hearings turned theatrical. Witnesses from oil companies testified that Albert Fall had received $400,000 for the oil leases. Jess Smith's attractive blonde widow, Roxy Stinson, appeared at open hearings and for days recounted what Jess Smith had told her: that he had dispensed patronage and offered to quash prosecutions, had accepted hundreds of thousands of dollars in bribes at the little house on H Street and a green house on K Street, where bootleg liquor was delivered to parties in Wells Fargo vans guarded by Treasury agents and where the President had been known to play poker.

For months, Daugherty refused to resign. The President appointed special prosecutors to look into the scandals, pointedly bypassing the Justice Department. He sent Taft to talk with Daugherty, but the attorney general continued to insist that the attacks on him were political, until at last Coolidge was obliged to order him in writing to resign.

Indictments and trials followed. Fall was convicted of taking bribes, but Daugherty, with the dead Jess Smith the principal witness against him, could not be convicted, and after two trials ended in hung juries, the prosecution was abandoned.

A few months after these scandals became known, a young woman from Marion, Ohio, Nan Britton, whose curly blonde hair and charming smile quickly became famous, published a book in which she asserted in convincing detail that she had been Warren Harding's mistress, had visited the White House and made love to the President in a cloakroom, and had borne his illegitimate daughter.

Against this gaudy background, Calvin Coolidge ran for President in 1924, saying and doing little, a mild and seemingly unadventurous man. Holmes, as a resident of the District of Columbia, could not vote in the presidential election, but he would have voted for Coolidge: "While I don't expect anything very astonishing from him, I don't want anything very astonishing."[1]

When the justices called at the White House, on the opening of the October, 1924, term, Coolidge engaged Holmes briefly in talk. He asked if Holmes had enjoyed the summer. Yes, the justice answered, he had seen towns celebrating their three hundredth year, and young ladies on the beach in the new bathing dress with bare legs. "Perhaps when I am your age I shall notice the legs," the President answered, and Holmes dutifully repeated this example of the President's wit to Nina Gray, who admired him.

To Holmes's Chief, William Howard Taft, it seemed as if the forces of order — the executive branch and the courts — were under siege. Taft's friends had vanished from an embattled White House. When McKenna at length resigned, Coolidge filled the vacancy without consulting Taft. He appointed Harlan F. Stone, who had come in as attorney general behind Daugherty to clean up the Justice Department, and perhaps did not fully understand the Bolshevik threat. McReynolds, who spoke more bluntly than Taft, said he was afraid that Stone would help Brandeis, "consciously boring from within."[2]

A mistrustful Congress tried to restrict the President's freedom of action. Congress forbade the President to remove postmasters without the Senate's consent. Harding had openly challenged the law, and when the case came to the Supreme Court, Taft, a former President and leader of an embattled party, wanted his court to hold that the President's power over his own employees was absolute and could not be withdrawn by Congress. The case was *Myers v. United States*.[3]

In conference, it appeared Taft would have a majority for his and the President's position. Holmes would not be with him. Holmes never doubted the power of Congress to legislate, absent some clear prohibition in the Constitution. Nor would Brandeis join Taft. McReynolds, too, defected, for reasons of his own, and Stone gradually drifted away. Taft gathered his loyal remaining forces around him, a bare majority of the Court, and they began to meet separately on Sundays, as a kind of second conference.

Taft had grown testy about Holmes's occasional dissents, which he blamed on Brandeis. He knew that Brandeis often urged Holmes to dissent, when Holmes might otherwise have remained silent: "I think perhaps [Holmes's] age makes him a little more subordinate or yielding to Brandeis, who is his constant companion, than he would have been in his prime."[4] And Taft was growing irritable at the steady praise for Holmes's dissents, and the continual attacks on himself, in the law reviews: "I shall continue to be worried by attacks from all the academic lawyers who write college law journals, but I suppose it is not a basis for impeachment."[5]

The *Myers* case, to Taft, was a test of Americanism. Holmes's and McReynolds's disloyalty infuriated Taft, but he reserved his greatest venom for Brandeis:

> Brandeis puts himself where he naturally belongs. He is in favor of the group system. He is opposed to a strong Executive. He loves the veto of the group upon effective legislation or effective administration. He loves the kicker, and therefore is in sympathy with the power of the Senate to prevent the Executive from removing obnoxious persons, because he always sympathizes with the obnoxious person. His ideals do not include effective and uniform administration unless he is the head. That of course is the

attitude of the socialist till he and his fellow socialists of small number acquire absolute power, and then he believes in a unit administration with a vengeance.[6]

The Court's brief harmony broke up. Taft had drawn a line that excluded Brandeis, and the two men struggled over Holmes's loyalty and prestige.

Holmes was not greatly disturbed by these events. He had been turning to Greek authors in his reading, and to Spinoza again, whom he liked to quote to the young lads. He reread *Moby-Dick,* and thought no other book better realized the terrors of the world or the abysses of the human spirit.[7]

There were fewer old friends to whom to write letters. Margot Asquith sent an occasional note, signing herself Margot Oxford, as Herbert had become Earl of Oxford and Asquith. But Lady Castletown was dead:

And yesterday a letter giving me my first news of the death of Lady Castletown. . . . [She] had had a stroke coming on top of other trouble so that her death seemed possibly a release, but it makes a great gap in my horizon.[8]

The young people filled the gap somewhat, although they did not know it was there. Felix and Marion Frankfurter came often, and Holmes welcomed their visits. "Kindly remain alive," he told Frankfurter. "Even my haircutter has died."[9]

Holmes was eighty-seven, and another spring had come around. He noted in his journal the dates on which the cherry trees blossomed, when he and Fanny saw the first bloodroot and first heard the frogs peeping in the canal. On occasion, he would have his secretary drive them out to Arlington to look at their grave site: "Life has been so much better than I ever dreamed it could be . . . and yet I don't know whether I should care to live it over again."[10] But it was spring, with magnolias everywhere, flowers in the woods and on the hillsides. Holmes and Fanny and Holmes's secretary drove into Rock Creek Park, where the tulip trees were just beginning to bloom, and Holmes got out of the car to look at the flowers.

In the State of Washington, four Seattle rumrunners were caught and convicted of Prohibition violations. Federal agents had tapped their telephones without a warrant and against the law of Washington that made wiretapping a crime. The convictions were based on evidence from the illegal wiretaps, and the rumrunners appealed. In the spring of 1928 their case came before the Supreme Court.

Taft's majority voted to uphold the convictions. To the chief justice, it was a simple question of choosing between the forces of crime and the forces of order. He fumed at Brandeis: "[Telephones] are most useful to criminals in their war against society, and the idealist gentlemen urge a conclusion which facilitates the crime by their use and furnishes immunity from conviction."[11]

Brandeis, for his part, went to work on a dissenting opinion, in which he argued that the Constitution forbade government wiretapping without a warrant.

No single provision of the Constitution might prohibit government eavesdropping, or even the use of evidence obtained by violating state laws. However, Brandeis argued, taken together, the provisions of the Bill of Rights revealed a more fundamental principle — the right of privacy.

Holmes was not persuaded by Brandeis's dissent, and at first was inclined to vote with Taft. He was reluctant as ever to rest his decision on vaguely embodied rights. But he was deeply troubled that the prosecutors' wiretapping itself had been a crime.

On the Monday morning in spring when the Court announced its decision, Taft spoke for a majority of five. The convictions would be upheld. Taft spoke calmly. His was the voice of the governing class of the American empire. State laws prohibiting wiretapping were only cobwebs, barely law at all.

> [To] forbid the reception of evidence if obtained by other than nice ethical conduct by government officials would make society suffer and give criminals greater immunity than has been known heretofore.[12]

Holmes sat beside Taft, and after the chief justice had spoken for the Court, Holmes read his own dissent, in which for a moment his life, too, drew to a focus. He sat leaning forward on his elbows, his head lifted, his eyebrow cocked. He seemed to empty himself of anything merely personal, and to personify an Olympian disdain, when describing the dirty business of government crime. He spoke briefly:

> Apart from the Constitution the government ought not to use evidence obtained, and only obtainable, by a criminal act. There is no body of precedents by which we are bound, and which confines us to logical deduction from established rules. Therefore, we must consider the two objects of desire both of which we cannot have and make up our minds which to choose. It is desirable that criminals should be detected, and to that end all available evidence should be used. It also is desirable that the government should not itself foster and pay for other crimes, when they are the means by which evidence is to be obtained. If it pays its officers for having got evidence by crime I do not see why it may not as well pay them for getting it in the same way, and I can attach no

importance to protestations of disapproval if it knowingly accepts and pays and announces in the future it will pay for the fruits. We have to choose, and for my part I think it a less evil that some criminals should escape than that the government should play an ignoble part.[13]

25

A GHOST ON
THE BATTLEFIELD

OLD AGE, HOLMES SAID, WAS LIKE A FIERCE DOG THAT CAME into the room with you and grew and grew until it filled the whole room. He who had been so erect and thin was now stooped, stout, no longer tall. His face was thickened and fleshy, in repose fell into lines of sadness, and in moments of uncertainty seemed angry. His secretary helped him on with his galoshes, giving the side of the shoe a professional slap that he liked, helped him up from the armchair and down the front steps to his car.

He rarely spoke of religion, except jokingly. To one of the young men who called on Mondays, he said, "If that ceiling should open, and through the opening should come the voice of God saying, 'Wendell, you have five minutes to live,' I should reply, 'Very well, Boss, but I wish it were ten.'"[1] To his secretary he said, "I am a little swirl of electrons in the Cosmos, and some day the swirl will dissolve." The secretary was a little frightened of this bleak old man looking composedly at his own extinction.[2]

Aloofness — calm — unsentimental clarity — words like these come to my mind when I try to describe the Justice's mental processes. His thought was a little cruel, it was so exact and so lacking in human prejudices.[3]

Holmes's cheerful manner had not deserted him, however. He composed little doggerel rhymes, and made puns like his father's. When two visitors from the Harvard Law School called — Austin Wakeman Scott and Sayre McNeil — Holmes came down from his library fingering their cards, saying gaily, "First you shuffle and then you deal. Which is Scott and which McNeil?"[4] He liked to turn English slang into purposefully dreadful Latin. "That won't wash," a favorite expression, became "Non lavabit." Chief Justice Taft was portentous; "Non lavetur," he corrected solemnly.[5]

Holmes's graceful manners, like his conversation, had achieved a childlike transparency through which his affection shone on his young friends.[6] He was touched and nourished by their praise. The adulation of Benjamin Cardozo, now the chief judge of New York's court of appeals, he regarded as one of the superlative successes of his life, so much so that he didn't like to talk about it.[7]

The letters he still wrote at his standing desk, looking out at the magnolia in the little yard, were filled with anecdotes recalled from London dinner parties or conversations with Emerson sixty or seventy years past. He liked to reach even farther back, into his father's anecdotes about Thomas Carlyle and Margaret Fuller, told and retold for a century. But be began to be uncomfortable about these letters, particularly those to Frankfurter and to Laski:

> I hope you burn my letters. I hate the notion of anything concerning me becoming public except what I write for publication.[8]

> If you have not burned them I should feel easier if you would assure me that none of them should be published after my death. I print what I want printed and write to you with a feeling of absolute freedom which could not be if there were such a possibility. Also I am not proud of my epistolary performances. They often come from a languid pen and are written so to speak in dressing gown and slippers.[9]

He spent his days seated at his grandfather's big desk, or in the leather easy chair that now stood beside it, which had a footrest that he could raise with a lever. When he had heavy volumes of printed records to get through, the secretary would help him into the chair, stack the books on the floor beside him, cover his legs with a shawl, and turn on an electric heater.

His principal exercise was a short stroll in the afternoon. He would say to his secretary, "Shall we creep an inch?" and away they would go, for a few blocks, chatting cheerfully as they went. In the evenings, in the parlor, Fanny would read to Holmes — a novel or a mystery story — while he played solitaire, or he would read with a sense of duty accomplished one of the big dead classic works. He carefully entered in his journal the title of every book completed, or, if he gave it up, the number of pages he had read. He liked to tell his secretaries that he expected to be examined on the Day of Judgment. He was sure that somewhere in heaven a great book of records was kept, where he got credit for dull but worthy books. These he was able to identify very easily by noticing whether he glanced ahead at the thickness of unread pages.[10]

By and large, Holmes said, when Brandeis urged him to write another dissenting opinion, he had had his say. The wonderful phrases still echoed in his mind; if he *were* going to write a dissent in one case, he would say, "it is for the authority that established the precedents to say how far the violet rays of the Fourteenth Amendment reach."[11] But despite Brandeis's blandishments he dissented without opinion. The opening paragraph of a new book on jurisprudence framed itself in his mind, but he did not think he would ever write the book.

Despite their differences on the Court, he and Taft had settled into the friendship of old men, and they worked together easily. Holmes presided over the Court whenever Taft was absent, and when Taft summered in Canada, Holmes was acting chief justice. They exchanged comradely notes about the business of the Court, and Holmes liked to play the young cavalier, calling Taft "My Lord" or "Emperor," and signing himself, "Your obedient servant."[12]

Holmes, who wished above all to be recognized for the contributions he made to the law when speaking for the Court, had become famous instead as the Great Dissenter. When a publisher proposed to bring out a volume of his dissenting opinions, Holmes said he could not stop publication, but he was distressed to see only dissents included in the book.

He told his friends that he had a last ambition, which was to write an opinion for the Court when he was past ninety; one had to be at least ninety, it seemed, to accomplish anything in the way of longevity.

The presidential election in 1928 caused him some anxiety. Aside from his usual apprehension over the possibility of a Democratic President, if Al Smith were to be elected Holmes would feel obliged to resign to allow Coolidge to appoint his successor. There were frequent suggestions in the newspapers that he was too old, and Holmes was aware that the chief justice of the Massachusetts Supreme Judicial Court, Arthur Rigg, who was a friend of Coolidge's, wanted his place. But Herbert Hoover was elected in November, and Holmes decided to try for another year.

Taft, too, was growing old, and his health was worse than Holmes's. Taft had been apprehensive over the election, but he had no more faith in Hoover than he had in Coolidge. He was sure that Hoover would appoint "extreme destroyers of the Constitution" like Brandeis:

> I am old and slow and less acute and more confused. However, as long as things continue as they are, and I am able to answer in my place, I must stay on the Court in order to prevent the Bolsheviki from getting control.[13]

Perhaps fearing someone worse, and with the fraternal feeling of their last years, Taft encouraged Holmes to stay on. Holmes reached eighty-seven, the age achieved by Chief Justice Roger B. Taney in the previous century; until then, Taney had been the oldest man to have served on the Supreme Court. On October 4, 1928, a date duly noted by the newspapers — for once to Holmes's pleasure — he became the oldest man to sit as a justice. Moreover, as Taft said, Taney had done little work in his last years: "not like our champion, doing his regular share of work and as Harlan used to say, 'a leetle to the rise.'"[14]

Holmes was often weary, and sometimes dozed during the Saturday conferences, but more than forty-five years as a judge had left him with instincts and reflexes that still astonished the younger men. When he had tired of a long wrangle among the justices, he would settle back for his nap, and after the arguments had run down, he would suddenly open his eyes and launch into their midst a summary of the issues so lucid and persuasive as to carry the whole Court with him.[15]

In February, 1929, just before the new President was inaugurated, Fanny slipped and fell in the bath. "My wife had a tumble on Saturday and aches, but no serious harm was done,"[16] Holmes wrote to their friends, perhaps concealing his worry. The ache did not dissipate, however, and the doctors pronounced that Fanny's hip was broken. This was a serious matter for a woman of eighty-eight. She was kept in bed, in considerable pain. But the fracture did not knit, and Fanny remained immobile, troubled by the large and small distresses of the aged bedridden, for three months, losing health and vigor, until one evening in the spring, she died.

Holmes went to the library and, seated at his desk, made an entry in his journal. On the flyleaf, he had written the dates of their births and marriage; beside Fanny's name he now wrote,

d. April 30, 1929. 9.30 pm.

He sent his messenger, Arthur Thomas, to tell the chief justice of Fanny's death, and within the hour Thomas returned a handwritten note from Taft: ". . . the hearts of all your friends, and of your colleagues go out to you in your deep sorrow. May your strength bear up under the heavy burden of your loneliness."[17]

In the morning, Taft came in person to offer help with the funeral arrangements. Fanny had called herself a Unitarian — "In Boston one had to be something, and Unitarian was the least one could be" — but she had not wanted any funeral service, and Holmes was inclined to respect her wishes. Taft thought something should be done, however, and after consulting the solicitor general, Charles Evans Hughes, Jr., he persuaded Holmes that there should be a simple observance for propriety's sake. Taft offered to make the arrangements himself — "One thing I know how to do is run a Unitarian funeral" — and quietly attended to the rites and the burial at Arlington.[18] Two weeks later, there was a brief memorial service at 1720 I Street, where Holmes read a sonnet, "To Night," a favorite of Fanny's:

> *Who could have thought such darkness lay concealed*
> *Within thy beams, O Sun!*[19]

There were letters to write to friends, the stream of condolences to answer. The funeral home provided a long list of senders of flowers and cards to acknowledge. Holmes gave most of them to the secretary, but he stood at his desk and answered those from old friends, saying to each the familiar comforting formulas:

> I am reconciled by the certainty that a continuance of life would have meant only a continuance of pain and suffering. . . . We have had our share. For sixty years she made life poetry for me and at 88 one must be ready for the end. I shall keep at work and interested while it lasts — though not caring very much for how long.[20]

> If I last a year or more longer I shall hope to die in harness, but all that remains of these side activities seem to me like a man's beard growing after he is dead.[21]

There was the business of wills to attend to, accounts to wind up. Holmes revised his own will. He had come to disapprove of private charity, as a kind of egotism, and in his will, after small bequests to the domestic staff and his former servants in Boston, he now returned to his remaining family — to Ned, to Dorothy, to other cousins on his father's side, and to Fanny's sister Mary — to Harvard University and to the United States government, roughly what he had received from each;[22] as if tidying up all traces of his presence.

The chief justice's health grew worse, and he asked Holmes to take over some cases that remained to be written before the end of the term. Taft, genuinely in need of help, also thought that Holmes would be glad to be kept busy, as perhaps he was. His secretary, John Lockwood, watched in awe as Holmes adjusted himself to Fanny's death: "one could see all of his experience coordinated and distilled by him and relied upon in the adjustment."[23]

That summer Holmes went to Beverly Farms, for the first time without Fanny. He was attended by widows. Ellen Curtis came often. Mrs. Codman came for lunch, as did Mrs. Beveridge. But Nina Gray thought it improper to be alone with Holmes in his house — he protested that it would be like visiting the Bunker Hill Monument — which precipitated a quarrel.[24]

Holmes and Taft exchanged frequent notes during the summer. Taft was briefly hospitalized, and wrote at length of his own bad health, thanking Holmes for help in managing the work of the Court. He wrote of his plans for the new Supreme Court building, which had been authorized by Congress, and by September he was out of bed and planning to return to the Court in October.

Yet the chief justice knew that he could not continue much longer. He hoped to preserve the majority he had built and the reforms that he brought into being; but the most that he could hope for, as he wrote to Justice Butler, was

> continued life of enough of the present membership . . . to prevent disastrous reversals of our present attitude. With Van [Devanter], and Mac [McReynolds] and Sutherland and you and Sanford . . . there will be five to steady the Court.[25]

Brandeis is, of course, hopeless, as Holmes is, as Stone is.[26]

When the Court met again, the chief justice was visibly ill, but despite his own bad health, when his brother Charles died that December, Taft made the long railroad journey to Cincinnati for the funeral, leaving Holmes to preside over the Court.

The trip exhausted Taft, and he wrote to Holmes on his return, saying that his doctors insisted he rest. He wrote again in January, from Grove Park Inn, in North Carolina, where his room had a good view of the Smoky Mountains, saying that he would soon return, but by the end of the month Taft was very ill indeed and suffering from hallucinations. He was carried home to Washington. It was plain he would not return to the Court.

> By an unspeakable brutality there was in one or more of the leading papers a photograph of him caught between the train and his house — with every spark of intelligence gone from his face.[27]

On February 3, 1930, Taft signed a letter of resignation and

Holmes formally became acting chief justice of the United States. He plunged for the last time into a new task and new duties. He reviewed with great care the orders of the Court and the brief, unsigned decisions prepared by the clerk's office. On Saturday mornings, he sat at the head of the table and conducted the conferences, as he had in Massachusetts, expeditiously. For the many cases and petitions that seemed to pose no difficulty, Holmes gave a succinct statement of the matter, said what he thought the disposition should be, and paused only for disagreement. This was a sharp departure from Taft's practice. Taft's summaries of the cases had been long and rambling, and his conferences were long, seminarlike affairs; Holmes said little, and only on doubtful matters or where disagreement was voiced did he invite comment.[28]

"Conferences are a joy, and we are dispatching business with great rapidity," Justice Stone reported to Frankfurter.[29]

When assigning cases, Holmes did not spare himself, taking a difficult patent case that no one else wanted. He wrote a letter on behalf of all the justices — this was perhaps most difficult — to the retired and now insensate Chief Justice Taft. He assigned to himself an endless dispute between Wisconsin and Illinois over Chicago's drainage canal, in which there was the record of a long trial before a Special Master.[30] Holmes spent days in the easy chair with volumes of transcript heaped around him, grunting with the effort of lifting them onto his lap. After he had mastered the record in the drainage canal case, the numerous counsel came to his library to argue their motions, and Holmes was once again, at the age of eighty-nine, a trial judge, insisting on speed and accuracy and managing the lawyers with the penetrating exactitude of his youth.[31]

Taft's majority survived him, as he had hoped, and continued to vote together as a bloc. Released from Taft's restraining courtesy, however, their opinions became more belligerent, more doctrinaire. McReynolds, speaking for the five, bitterly overruled a constitutional decision that Holmes had written for the Court, a precedent of twenty-five years' standing, angrily denouncing Holmes's decision as Holmes sat calmly beside him.[32]

Nor was McReynolds content to let the matter rest, but led the majority in a second attack. It was not a matter important in itself. The question was whether the Constitution forbade Missouri from taxing bonds legally situated in that state, although the same bonds had already been taxed as the property of their owner in Illinois. For thirty years, counsel had been arguing that "double taxation" was unconstitutional, but Holmes had brushed this aside for the Court along with all the other inventive objections that were raised to every tax. But now McReynolds spoke angrily for a new majority, and Holmes listened while his own opinions were denounced.

When McReynolds had finished, Holmes spoke in dissent, in words that penetrated the national awareness, that became embedded in its language:

> Although the decision can hardly be called a surprise . . . still as the term is not over I think it legitimate to add one or two reflections to what I have said before. I have not yet adequately expressed the more than anxiety that I feel at the ever increasing scope given to the Fourteenth Amendment in cutting down what I believe to be the Constitutional rights of the States. As the decisions stand, I can hardly see any limit but the sky to the invalidating of those rights if they happen to strike a majority of this Court as for any reason undesirable.[33]

There could be no question of Holmes continuing as chief justice, of course. President Hoover called former Justice Charles Evan Hughes to the White House. Hughes was not eager to leave the seat on the World Court that he now held, nor his New York law practice; his son had just become solicitor general and would have to resign if his father were put on the Court. But the President said he would find another place for the son, he would not be refused, and so Charles Evans Hughes, sixty-eight years of age, who twenty years before had confided to Holmes at a White House dinner that *The Common Law* had inspired him, who had been Holmes's colleague and friend, was now to be his Chief:

> This passing affair that I expect to turn over to you very soon has delayed a little my telling you what I hope you know without my telling you, that I shall welcome you with a double delight — that I am to have my friend near me again and that we are to have such an able and competent head for our work. It is most satisfactory and once again I can sleep in peace at home or by your side.[34]

On February 24, 1930, Holmes formally announced Taft's resignation, administered the oath of office to Hughes, and took a seat beside him. And there, as Holmes had cheerfully warned the new chief justice, he occasionally dozed.

When he returned to I Street, Holmes settled in the easy chair in his library, and his slender dark-haired secretary, Alger Hiss, brought a book to read aloud. Hiss was "a marvel of attentiveness," Holmes told Frankfurter,[35] and had gradually taken over Fanny's job of reading aloud in the evenings. Holmes at first had balked, but Hiss inquired and found out that the British ambassador allowed his secretary to read aloud to him, and so there was a precedent to follow. The reading aloud cheered Holmes, and now that the burden of the chief justice's duties had passed to Hughes, it kept him alert. At teatime, if there were no callers, he would say to Hiss, "Shall we have murder — or shall we improve our minds?"[36]

There were frequent callers: Holmes's former secretaries, Frankfurter on visits to Washington, the justices, the hostesses for whom he had become a lion once more. The widowed Mrs. Beveridge came once a week to lunch — "sweet, sad, lonely creature" — but Mrs. Rodgers, his good friend, too, had died.

> The servants are angelic — the little parlor girl lurks behind the door when I go up in the elevator at 11 p.m. so that if I get stuck, or anything goes wrong, she can call the electricity man.[37]

A sculptor said to be patronized by Mussolini asked to do Holmes's portrait. The Russian sculptor Sergei Konenkov, whose attractive wife kept the sitter entertained, did a bust for the Columbia Law School.

In January, the First Lady, Mrs. Hoover, came alone to lunch; she and Holmes were both charmed. He took her on his visitor's tour to Fort Stevens to see the place where Lincoln stood under fire and Jubal Early's troops were driven back.[38] Soon after, Holmes went to the White House, although he never went out now, for lunch with the President and Mrs. Hoover.

Holmes began to take an interest in genealogy, particularly in his Dutch ancestors,[39] and he startled Morris Cohen with the ancient gossip that the Wendells were descended from Dutch Jews named Von Dell.[40]

Charles Hopkinson painted Holmes's portrait for the Harvard Law School, full-length and larger than life. The portrait was hung in a place of honor in the five-hundred-foot reading room of the new library — Holmes thought it was perhaps the greatest law library in the world — opposite the portrait of Chief Justice John Marshall. Holmes's former secretaries banded together and had Hopkinson paint another portrait, seated this time, for the new Supreme Court building.

On Saturday, March 8, 1930, Holmes's eighty-ninth birthday, he was photographed walking up the steps of the Capitol, intent on the task before him and taking no notice of the photographer. Two policemen stood behind him, smiling with the condescension of youth. The photograph ran in a number of papers with the caption "Alert Justice Holmes." There were no birthday celebrations that day, however.

> On Saturday, just as we were expecting him at a conference of the Justices, we were informed that our brother, Mr. Justice Sanford, had become unconscious pending a slight operation. Five minutes later we received word that he was dead. Thus suddenly the light of a faithful worker, who was born also to charm, went out. Afterwards came the news that the late Chief Justice had

found relief from his hopeless illness in death. Such events must be accepted with silent awe.[41]

Spring came early that year, so early that Holmes feared a frost would blight the blossoms. On March 20, the magnolia at the end of his garden was in full blossom, and the next day he thought the double-flowering apple tree, which never blossomed before April, was showing pink buds: "Everywhere the air is full of promise — the promise that is better than any performance — and I should like to lie back and give way to enchantment."[42]

The stock market, inflated by debt, had collapsed in October, and there was a general running down of the economy. Workers were being laid off, but as yet there was no warning of how deep the depression would be, and Holmes observed this new panic calmly, as he had so many before. His own investments were little affected, for he had not invested in stocks but had stubbornly clung to the railroad bonds that had served his family so well. He continued to go down to the Riggs Bank with his secretary to "fish in the pool" — look through the bonds in his safe deposit box for coupons ready to be clipped.

He was conscious of constant attention from the press and of the preparations for his ninetieth birthday. The student editors of the Harvard, Yale, and Columbia law reviews were arranging a national radio program — one of the first coast-to-coast hookups — and the dean of the Yale Law School, Charles E. Clark, called to talk with Holmes about it. To Clark's pleased surprise, Holmes agreed to say a few words at the close of the program.

The three law journals were all dedicated to him in March, 1931. Frankfurter brought out a book of articles praising Holmes by John Dewey, Morris Cohen, Learned Hand, Harold Laski, Walter Lippmann, and himself, with an admiring introduction by Benjamin Cardozo.

Frederick Pollock arranged to have Holmes elected an Honorary Bencher of Lincoln's Inn, the first time that anyone outside Great Britain had been so honored; the Lord Chancellor and the attorney general of Great Britain wrote encomia. In the *Harvard Graduates' Magazine,* Arthur Hill wrote: "There is growing up around [Holmes] an increasing circle of younger men who feel toward him an affection and respect impossible to put into mere words."[43]

The American Bar Association gave him a gold medal, ornamented with a bare-bosomed figure of Justice that amused him. The President of the United States sent his greetings, and Nina Gray sent a huge bunch of yellow roses with a card written in a shaky hand, "Golden Roses for Golden Years."[44]

In the evening, radio technicians brought their equipment to his library and set the big clumsy microphone on his desk. Holmes had never spoken into a microphone before.

Chief Justice Hughes, the president of the American Bar Association, and the dean of the Yale Law School made flattering remarks from their respective cities. The chief justice said:

> We bring to Mr. Justice Holmes our tribute of admiration and gratitude. We place upon his brow the laurel crown of the highest distinction. But this will not suffice us or him. We honor him, but, what is more, we love him. We give him tonight the homage of our hearts.

Holmes had written out his reply on a single sheet of paper, making as always only a single draft. When Hughes was finished and the technician signaled that he was to speak, Holmes cleared his throat and read, and his voice was still fluid and transparent:

> In this symposium my part is only to sit in silence. To express one's feelings as the end draws near is too intimate a task. But I may mention one thought that comes to me as a listener-in. The riders in a race do not stop short when they reach the goal. There is a little finishing canter before coming to a standstill. There is time to hear the kind voice of friends and to say to one's self: "The work is done." But just as one says that, the answer comes: "The race is over, but the work is never done while the power to work remains." The canter that brings you to a standstill need not be only coming to rest. It cannot be, while you still live. For to live is to function. That is all there is in living.
> And so I end with a line from a Latin poet who uttered the message more than fifteen hundred years ago:
> "Death plucks my ear and says, 'Live — I am coming.'"[45]

On Monday morning, Holmes was in his place on the bench as usual, taking notes of the arguments as he had for almost fifty years. But it was to be his last full term of court. In the summer of 1932, in August, he suffered what he called a "pull-down." He felt as if some part of him had dropped out. It was difficult for him to write, and the letters on the page inexplicably became tiny and illegible.

He had not recovered when the Court resumed in the fall, but he continued on for a time, hoping that this disability would pass. On Friday, January 9, he wrote Ellen Curtis a New Year's greeting, one of the few that he did not turn over to his secretary.

> My beloved friend
> All my best wishes for 1932. As you rightly understand, it comes hard to me to write — I don't know why, but the act is difficult. The letters don't come right in the words — and everything is

hard. I hope it will change for the better — but have no great confidence.[46]

On Sunday, Chief Justice Hughes came to call. When they were alone in the library, Hughes explained the purpose of his visit: a majority of the Court had asked him to suggest that Holmes resign. Holmes received the suggestion without resentment or opposition. He called his secretary and asked to see the statute concerning retirements, and then wrote out his letter of resignation to the President with difficulty, but without hesitating.[47]

> The condition of my health makes it a duty to break off connections that I cannot leave without deep regret after the affectionate relations of many years and the absorbing interests that have filled my life. But the time has come and I bow to the inevitable. I have nothing but kindness to remember from you and from my brethren. My last word should be one of grateful thanks.[48]

Hughes went downstairs, with tears on his cheeks, leaving the justice wearing his customary expression of tranquil sadness. The parlor maid, Mary Donellan, came into the room weeping, and knelt at Holmes's feet, the secretary came in, and a few minutes later, Brandeis came and sent the others away.[49]

The next morning, Holmes sat beside Hughes on the bench for the last time. Hughes delivered a letter he had written on behalf of the justices — how often Holmes himself had written such letters — and Holmes answered gracefully:

> My dear Brethren:
> You must let me call you so once more. Your more than kind, your generous, letter, touches me to the bottom of my heart.[50]

There was no delay in naming a successor. The President appointed Benjamin Cardozo to Holmes's seat, and the Court remained divided much as before.

The stock-market panic of 1929 had deepened into a persistent worldwide depression; a new President, another Roosevelt, was elected. But Holmes regarded these events without curiosity or passion. Everything personal seemed to have slipped away. He did not seem to regret leaving the Court. Frankfurter continued to send a secretary each year, who filled Holmes's hours by reading to him, and Holmes continued diligently recording in his journal the title of every book they read.

"I am dead," Holmes would remark to his young visitors, who would cluck in concern or denial. But Holmes was only saying bluntly what seemed obvious to him. "I am dead, and glad of it."[51] When Frankfurter tried to interest him in affairs, Holmes said, "It's all very remote to me. . . . I'm like a ghost on the battlefield with bullets flying through me."[52]

When someone mentioned John Ruskin, Holmes remembered with dislike Ruskin's having written about his childhood: "Why he should think it important to the world whether something about him happened at seven or nine is beyond me; that he should think his puny personality mattered."[53]

A telegram from her daughter Eleanor told him that Nina Gray was dead.

On Holmes's ninety-first birthday the newly inaugurated President, Franklin Delano Roosevelt, came to call. It was a surprise arranged by Felix Frankfurter. The President and Mrs. Roosevelt waited downstairs while Holmes took off the old alpaca coat he liked to lounge in. Then the President came up alone in the elevator. After a brief conversation, he politely asked if Holmes had any advice for him, and Holmes replied, equally polite, "Form your battalions, and fight, sir."[54]

To Ellen Curtis, December 19, 1933:

> Belovedest of friends,
> You know that I have been unable to write. . . . So I just send you my love and prayer for a word — to assure me that all is well. If we meet I still can talk a little and keep a pretty long list of books. Not *only* murders but a little touch of improvement. But I have pretty well finished. This brings my love and my longing to say more.[55]

Annie Gough and Mary Donellan cared for Holmes, and his former secretaries, many of whom Frankfurter had summoned to the New Deal, called often, as did Cardozo, Brandeis, and Hughes. Ellen Curtis came to Washington for a week's visit, and at other times there was a circle of women with whom Holmes lunched and had tea, or took for an occasional drive. Eating and sleeping and listening to a book filled his days.

Justice Cardozo called one afternoon late in February, 1935, and found Holmes suffering from a cold. The secretary that year, James Rowe, said that the doctors looked on the ailment as trivial. But Holmes's cough deepened, and the cold became pneumonia. Some of the former secretaries gathered; Ned Holmes came down from Boston. Outside the house, newspaper reporters and photographers waited. At 3:30 in the morning of March 6, 1935, one of Holmes's former secretaries, Mark DeWolfe Howe, came downstairs and went to the door to tell the reporters that Holmes was dead.

Appendixes

APPENDIX A

Chronology of Holmes's Life

March 8, 1841	Born in Boston, Massachusetts, to Dr. Oliver Wendell Holmes and Amelia Lee (Jackson) Holmes.
October 20, 1843	A sister, Amelia Jackson Holmes, is born.
October 17, 1846	A brother, Edward Jackson ("Ned") Holmes, is born.
October, 1857– June, 1861	Attends Harvard College.
April 25, 1861	Enlists in Fourth Battalion, Massachusetts Militia.
July 23, 1861	Commissioned first lieutenant, Twentieth Regiment of Massachusetts Volunteer Infantry.
October 21, 1861	Wounded at Ball's Bluff, Virginia.
September 17, 1862	Wounded at Antietam Creek, Maryland.
May 3, 1863	Wounded at Chancellorsville, Virginia.
July 17, 1864	End of military service.

October, 1864	Enters Harvard Law School.
Summer, 1866	Receives law degree; first visit to Europe.
October 18, 1866	Begins work for Boston law firm, Chandler, Shattuck and Thayer.
January, 1867	First publication in the *American Law Review*.
March 4, 1867	Admitted to Massachusetts Bar.
December, 1869	Begins editing *Kent's Commentaries*.
1870	Leaves Chandler, Shattuck and Thayer, enters sole practice. Becomes coeditor of the *American Law Review*, begins lecturing at Harvard College.
June 17, 1872	Marries Fanny Bowditch Dixwell. Becomes sole editor of *American Law Review*.
July, 1872	Fanny Holmes suffers serious attack of rheumatic fever.
March, 1873	Joins George Shattuck's new firm, which becomes Shattuck, Holmes and Munroe.
December, 1873	Twelfth Edition of *Kent's Commentaries* is published; Holmes is sole editor.
Summer, 1874	Holmes and Fanny visit Europe together.
1876	Publishes first statement of mature theory, "Primitive Notions in Modern Law."
November–December, 1880	Delivers Lowell Lectures on "The Common Law."
1881	*The Common Law* is published.
January, 1882	Leaves law practice, becomes professor at Harvard Law School.
Summer, 1882	Tours Europe with Fanny.
December, 1882	Accepts appointment to Massachusetts Supreme Judicial Court; leaves Harvard Law School.
May 30, 1884	Delivers "Memorial Day Address" at Keene, New Hampshire.
July 17, 1884	Holmes's brother Ned dies, leaving a son, Edward J. Holmes, Jr., also known as Ned.
February 6, 1888	Holmes's mother dies.

April 3, 1889	Holmes's widowed sister, Amelia, dies childless.
Summer, 1889	Travels alone to United Kingdom, is taken up by "the Souls." Fanny cares for Dr. Holmes.
1892	Dissent in *Commonwealth v. Perry* gives theory of judicial review; judge's duty is to accept reasonable legislation.
1894	Holmes extends his theories to public law in article, "Privilege, Malice and Intent."
October 7, 1894	Holmes's father dies. Soon afterward, Fanny suffers another attack of rheumatic fever, remains physically and emotionally disturbed for three years afterward.
May 30, 1895	Delivers address, "The Soldier's Faith," at Harvard Memorial Day exercises.
Summer, 1896	Travels to London and Ireland without Fanny, forms friendship with Lady Castletown.
October, 1896	Dissents in *Vegehlan v. Guntner,* following reasoning of "Privilege, Malice and Intent."
January, 1897	Delivers address, "The Path of the Law," at Boston University School of Law.
Summer, 1897	Nephew Ned Holmes, Jr., marries; Fanny's health is greatly improved.
Summer, 1898	Travels alone to London and Ireland; visits Lady Castletown.
1899	Becomes chief justice, Massachusetts Supreme Judicial Court, August 2, 1899. Lady Castletown has riding accident, then accompanies Lord Castletown to South African war.
December 8, 1902	Takes seat as associate justice, Supreme Court of the United States. Holmes and Fanny move to Washington, D.C.
January, 1903	Delivers first opinion for Supreme Court in *Otis v. Parker,* stating principles of "due process of law." Becomes spokesman of Court in constitutional cases. Fanny begins career as Washington hostess.
Summer, 1903	Travels to London and Ireland while Fanny prepares house at 1720 I Street. Young cousin, Dorothy Upham, comes to live with Holmes and Fanny.
March 14, 1904	First dissenting opinion, in *Northern Securities Case,* offends President Roosevelt.

1905	Delivers opinion striking down Philippine tariffs, angering future president William H. Taft. Dissents in *Lochner v. New York* when Court departs from principles stated by Holmes in *Otis v. Parker*.
Summer, 1907	Travels to London alone.
Summer, 1909	Receives honorary doctorate from University of Oxford; Fanny accompanies him.
July 4, 1911	Chief Justice Fuller dies. President Taft chooses Edward White to succeed him.
1912	Forms friendship with Felix Frankfurter.
1913	Last visit to London; Castletowns are in distress.
1916	Holmes's seventy-fifth birthday celebrated by *Harvard Law Review*. Forms friendship with Harold Laski. Louis D. Brandeis appointed to Supreme Court.
1919	Opinions in Free Speech cases; Holmes becomes a public figure.
May 19, 1921	Chief Justice White dies; President Harding appoints former President William H. Taft to succeed him.
1925–1932	Taft's Court attempts to reverse direction of Constitutional decisions; Holmes dissents repeatedly.
April 30, 1929	Fanny Holmes dies.
February 3, 1930	Chief Justice Taft resigns. Holmes is acting chief justice of the United States, presides over Court dominated by Taft majority.
February 24, 1930	Charles Evans Hughes becomes chief justice.
March 8, 1931	Ninetieth birthday radio address, "Death Plucks My Ear."
January 11, 1932	Resigns from Supreme Court.
March 6, 1935	Holmes dies of pneumonia at his house in Washington.

APPENDIX B

A Note on Sources

As noted in the preface, this is the first full biography of Justice Holmes. Silas Bent's *Justice Oliver Wendell Holmes* (1932) was little more than a pastiche of published materials and is no longer useful. Catherine Drinker Bowen's *Yankee from Olympus* (1944) was a fictionalized account of Holmes's family. As noted in the preface, the late Mark DeWolfe Howe's authorized biography was interrupted by his death, and a number of important materials — including Holmes's letters to Lady Castletown, an important series of letters to Leslie Scott, letters revealing Fanny Holmes's serious illness in 1872, and additional letters and a diary of Fanny Holmes — were uncovered by Mark Howe and by me after his last published work had appeared.

My principal sources accordingly were Holmes's published and unpublished writings, listed in the bibliography that follows. This is the first complete bibliography of Holmes's writings and includes dozens of unsigned articles in *The American Law Review* that have not been previously identified and that are helpful in tracing the course of his reading and his thought. Most of the letters and photographs published here are appearing for the first time in print, and many of them were not known to previous scholars.

Elsewhere I have expressed my debt to Mark Howe, whose work provided an indispensable guide to Holmes's works. Holmes had a retentive memory and a respect for facts honed by years as a combat officer and a lawyer. With rare exceptions, Holmes's accounts of events can be verified from other sources. The few exceptions that I have found — as in the story he told about his supposed encounter with Lincoln at Fort Stevens — are described in the notes. In his letters, Holmes spoke freely of his thoughts and feelings; whenever in the text I attribute thoughts or feelings to Holmes, it is on the basis of his own accounts.

For the historical background — a century of European, American, and Japanese history — I have necessarily relied on secondary sources, which I have not cited except when quoting directly. For Oliver Wendell Holmes, Sr.'s life, each of the half-dozen published biographies was helpful, but Mark Antony DeWolfe Howe's *Holmes of the Breakfast-Table* (1939) gives the most vivid picture of the man, and Eleanor Tilton's *Amiable Autocrat* a good account of his career in medicine. Saul Touster kindly shared with me his unpublished work on the relationship of Holmes Senior and Junior, and the very helpfully indexed Holmes Papers at the Houghton Library, Harvard University, were invaluable.

Ernest Samuels's *Young Henry Adams* (1948) and Samuel E. Morison's *Three Centuries of Harvard* (1936) were principal sources for the background of Holmes's college years. For the military history of the Civil War, Bruce Catton's books on the Army of the Potomac were helpful. When my Civil War chapters were already written, I read Gerald F. Linderman's moving study, *Embattled Courage* (1987), and was pleased to find there that Holmes's experiences were widely shared. For the years after the Civil War, I found helpful Kenneth Stampp's *Reconstruction Era,* and Robert G. McCloskey's classic, *The American Supreme Court.*

Of the cultural and intellectual histories of the nineteenth century that I consulted, none were more helpful than John Fraser's *America and the Patterns of Chivalry* (1982), J. W. Burrow's *Evolution and Society: A Study in Victorian Social Theory* (1966), and Leslie Stephen's *English Utilitarians* (1900).

There is unfortunately no authoritative history of the Supreme Court during Holmes's tenure; indeed, for the crucial Taft Court of the 1920s there is no proper history at all. The incomplete volume of the Holmes Devise History for the White Court, Alexander Bickel and Benno Schmidt, Jr., *The Judiciary and Responsible Government 1910–1921* (1984), was interrupted by Alexander Bickel's death and unfortunately does not discuss Holmes's principal contribution during those years, his First Amendment opinions.

A word must be said about Catherine Drinker Bowen's *Yankee from Olympus: Justice Holmes and His Family* (1944), which I found helpful when used with caution. Bowen acknowledges the assistance of Dorothy Upham Vaughan, Holmes's young cousin, who lived with Holmes and Fanny in Washington for several years (although Bowen does not mention that fact, presumably to protect the Vaughans' privacy). Bowen visited houses that have since been torn down and spoke to people who remembered the Boston of Holmes's childhood. She collected material concerning Fanny Holmes that seemed reliable and illuminating. As to Holmes himself, however, she was limited principally to published sources and unreliable family gossip, which she supplemented with a mass of avowedly invented details. The result was not so much a biography of Holmes as a book about a set of Boston traditions that it seemed important to reaffirm during the Second World War.

The published and unpublished recollections of Holmes's secretaries were very helpful, as were the interviews collected by John S. Monagan, portions of which have been published in his *Grand Panjandrum* (1988). A good deal of caution must be exercised in using these materials, often recalled fifty or more years after the event. By far the most helpful was Arthur Sutherland's unpublished memorandum prepared for Felix Frankfurter shortly after Holmes's death and now among Sutherland's papers at the Harvard Law School. Finally, the numerous publications of Holmes's young friends Felix Frankfurter, Harold Laski, and the editors of *The New Republic* must be used with caution. These men were actively engaged in the political battles of their day, and even those articles published during Holmes's life were distorted by the purposes to which they were put.

In the end we have principally Holmes's own self-portrait, a final paradox in the story of a man who struggled all his life to transcend the merely personal and in the process left a deep impression of his personality on the law and history of his country.

BIBLIOGRAPHY
of Principal Works Cited

———

The following are the principal published works cited or referred to in the text.
   Also included are all of Holmes's published works (except individual judicial opinions, for which see below), even those not specifically cited.
   Unpublished works, and published materials that I have found helpful but have not specifically cited, are discussed in the "Note on Sources," above. A more complete bibliography of Holmesiana, as of 1976, was published by Judge Harry C. Shriver; see below.

BOOKS

Acheson, Dean, *Morning and Noon*. Boston: Houghton Mifflin, 1965.
Adams, Charles Francis, *Charles Francis Adams*. Boston: Houghton Mifflin, 1900.
Adams, Henry, *The Education of Henry Adams*. Boston: Houghton Mifflin, 1918.
———, *Letters of Henry Adams 1892–1918* (W. C. Ford, ed.). Boston: Houghton Mifflin, 1938.
———, *The Life of George Cabot Lodge* (1911), quoted in Edmund Wilson, *The Shock of Recognition*, 2nd ed. New York: Farrar, Straus and Cudahy, 1955.
———, *The Selected Letters of Henry Adams* (Newton Arvin, ed.). New York: Farrar, Straus and Young, 1951.
Allen, Gay Wilson, *Waldo Emerson*. Baltimore: Penguin, 1982 (1st ed., New York: Viking, 1981).
———, *William James: A Biography*. New York: Viking, 1967.

Amory, Cleveland, *The Proper Bostonians*. Orleans, Miss.: Parnassus Imprints, 1984 (1st ed., New York: Dutton, 1947).

Annan, Noel, *Leslie Stephen: The Godless Victorian*. New York: Random House, 1984.

Asbury, Herbert, *The Great Illusion: An Informal History of Prohibition*. New York: Doubleday, 1950.

Austin, John, *The Province of Jurisprudence Determined and the Uses of the Study of Jurisprudence*. London: Weidenfeld and Nicolson, 1954 (1st ed., 1832).

Baker, Leonard, *Brandeis and Frankfurter: A Dual Biography*. New York: Harper & Row, 1984.

Bander, Edward J., *Justice Holmes ex Cathedra*. Charlottesville: University of Virginia Press, 1966.

Barzun, Jacques, *A Stroll with Henry James*. New York: Harper & Row, 1983.

Beer, Thomas, *The Mauve Decade: American Life at the End of the Nineteenth Century*. New York: Knopf, 1926.

Bell, Quentin, *Virginia Woolf: A Biography*. New York: Harcourt Brace, 1972.

Bent, Silas, *Justice Oliver Wendell Holmes*. Garden City, N. Y.: Garden City, 1932.

Berger, Raoul, *Government by Judiciary: The Transformation of the Fourteenth Amendment*. Cambridge, Mass.: Harvard University Press, 1977.

Beringause, Arthur F., *Brooks Adams: A Biography*. New York: Knopf, 1955.

Berman, Harold J., *Law and Revolution: The Formation of the Western Legal Tradition*. Cambridge, Mass.: Harvard University Press, 1983.

Bickel, Alexander M., *The Least Dangerous Branch: The Supreme Court at the Bar of Politics*. Indianapolis: Bobbs-Merrill, 1962.

————, *The Unpublished Opinions of Mr. Justice Brandeis*. Cambridge, Mass.: Harvard University Press, 1957.

————, and Benno C. Schmidt, Jr., *The Judiciary and Responsible Government, 1910–1921*. Vol. 9 of the *Oliver Wendell Holmes Devise History of the Supreme Court of the United States*. New York: Macmillan, 1984.

Biddle, Francis, *Justice Holmes, Natural Law, and the Supreme Court*. New York: Macmillan, 1961.

————, *Mr. Justice Holmes*. New York: Charles Scribner's Sons, 1942.

Blair, John M., *Economic Concentration: Structure, Behavior and Public Policy*. New York: Harcourt Brace Jovanovich, 1972.

Blaustein, Albert P., and Roy M. Mersky, *The First One Hundred Justices, Statistical Studies on the Supreme Court of the United States*. Hamden, Conn.: The Shoe String Press, 1978.

Boorstin, Daniel J., *The Mysterious Science of the Law: An Essay on Blackstone's Commentaries*. Cambridge, Mass.: Harvard University Press, 1941.

Bowen, Catherine Drinker, *Yankee from Olympus: Justice Holmes and His Family*. Boston: Atlantic/Little, Brown, 1944.

Brandeis, Louis D., *Letters of Louis D. Brandeis*. 5 vols. (M. I. Urofsky and D. W. Levy, eds.) Albany: SUNY Press, 1971–1978.

Britton, Nan, *The President's Daughter: The Love Story of President Harding*. London: Lourse, 1927.

Brooks, Van Wyck, *The Flowering of New England: 1815–1865*. New York: Dutton, 1936.

————, *New England: Indian Summer*. New York: Dutton, 1940.

Bruce, George A., *The Twentieth Regiment of Massachusetts Volunteer Infantry 1861–1865*. Boston: Houghton Mifflin, 1906.

Bryce, James, *The American Commonwealth*. London: Macmillan, 1889.

Buckley, Thomas H., *The United States and the Washington Conference, 1921–1922*. Knoxville: University of Tennessee Press, 1970.

Buell, Francis Dwight, *Saturday Morning Club of Boston: Its History, Program, and Membership.* Boston: privately printed, 1971.

Burrow, J. W., *Evolution and Society: A Study in Victorian Social Theory.* Cambridge: Cambridge University Press, 1966.

Butler, Charles Henry, *A Century at the Bar of the Supreme Court of the United States.* New York: Putnam's Sons, 1942.

Campbell, Charles S., Jr., *Anglo-American Understanding, 1898–1903.* Baltimore: Johns Hopkins Press, 1957.

Chafee, Zechariah, Jr., *Freedom of Speech.* New York: Harcourt Brace, 1920.

Chapple, Joe Mitchell, *The Life and Times of Warren G. Harding: Our After-War President.* Boston: Chapple Pub. Co., 1924.

Chatto, William Andrew, *A Treatise on Wood Engraving. . . .* London: Bohn, 1861.

Clifford, Lucy ("Mrs. W. K. Clifford"), *The Likeness of the Night: A Modern Play in Four Acts.* London: Adam and Charles Black, 1900.

———, *A Long Duel: A Serious Comedy in Four Acts.* London: Jolen Lane, 1902.

———, *Proposals to Kathleen.* New York: Barnes, 1908.

Cohen, Morris R., *The Faith of a Liberal: Selected Essays.* New York: Henry Holt, 1946 (reprint ed., 1970).

Commager, Henry Steele, *The American Mind.* New Haven: Yale University Press, 1951.

Cooley, Thomas M., *A Treatise on the Constitutional Limitations Which Rest upon the Legislative Power of the States of the American Union.* Boston: Little, Brown, 1868.

Coolidge, Calvin, *The Autobiography of Calvin Coolidge.* New York: Cosmopolitan, 1929.

Corwin, Edward S., *The Constitution and What It Means Today,* 14th ed., rev. by Harold W. Chase and George R. Ducat. Princeton: Princeton University Press, 1978 (1st ed., 1920).

Cramer, John Henry, *Lincoln under Enemy Fire: The Complete Account of His Experiences During Early's Attack on Washington.* Baton Rouge: Louisiana State University Press, 1948.

Dicey, A. V., *Introduction to the Study of the Law of the Constitution.* London: Macmillan, 1897.

———, *Lectures on the Relation Between Law and Public Opinion in England During the Nineteenth Century.* London: Macmillan, 1948 (1st ed., 1905).

Dinnerstein, Leonard, *The Leo Frank Case.* Athens, Ga.: University of Georgia Press, 1987.

Donald, David, *Charles Sumner and the Coming of the Civil War.* New York: Knopf, 1960.

Donelski, David J., *A Supreme Court Justice Is Appointed.* New York: Random House, 1964.

Dyer, Thomas G., *Theodore Roosevelt and the Idea of Race.* Baton Rouge: Louisiana State University Press, 1980.

Eastwood, Granville, *Harold Laski.* London: Mowbrays, 1977.

Edel, Leon, *Henry James.* 5 vols. New York: Lippincott, 1953–1963 (revised 1 vol. edition, 1985).

Emerson, Edward Waldo, *The Early Years of the Saturday Club: 1855–1870.* Boston: Houghton Mifflin, 1918 (reprint, 1967).

———, *Life and Letters of Charles Russell Lowell, Captain Sixth United States Cavalry . . . .* Boston: Houghton Mifflin, 1907.

Emerson, Ralph Waldo, *The Complete Writings of Ralph Waldo Emerson.* New York: Wm. H. Wise, 1929.

———, *The Conduct of Life.* Boston: Ticknor & Fields, 1860.

Everett, Edward, *The Address of Mr. Everett and the Poem of Dr. O. W. Holmes, at the*

Dinner Given to H.I.H. Monseigneur the Prince Napoléon, Sept. 25, 1861. Boston: privately printed, 1861.

Feaver, George, *From Status to Contract: A Biography of Sir Henry Maine 1822–1888.* London: Longmans, Green, 1969.

Ford, Worthington Chauncy, ed., *A Cycle of Adams Letters 1861–1865.* Boston: Houghton Mifflin, 1920.

Frankfurter, Felix, *From the Diaries of Felix Frankfurter,* ed. Joseph P. Lash. New York: Norton, 1975.

———, *Mr. Justice Holmes and the Supreme Court,* 2d ed. Cambridge, Mass.: Harvard University Press, 1961.

———, ed., *Mr. Justice Brandeis: Essays . . . With an Introduction by Oliver Wendell Holmes.* New Haven, Yale University Press, 1932.

Frankfurter, Felix, and J. M. Landis, *The Business of the Supreme Court: A Study in the Federal Judicial System.* New York: Macmillan, 1927.

Franklin, Julian H., *Jean Bodin and the Sixteenth-Century Revolution in Methodology of Law and History.* New York: Columbia University Press, 1963.

Fraser, John, *America and the Patterns of Chivalry.* Cambridge: Cambridge University Press, 1982.

Freund, Ernst, *Standards of American Legislation: An Estimate of Restrictive and Constructive Factors.* Chicago: University of Chicago Press, 1917.

Friedman, Leon, and Fred L. Israel, eds., *The Justices of the United States Supreme Court 1789–1978: Their Lives and Major Opinions.* 5 vols. New York: Chelsea House, 1980.

Friedrich, Otto, *Clover.* New York: Simon and Schuster, 1979.

Fuller, Lon L., *The Law in Quest of Itself.* Chicago: Foundation Press, 1940.

———, *The Morality of Law,* rev. ed. New Haven: Yale University Press, 1969.

Garrison, Lloyd McKim, *An Illustrated History of Hasty Pudding Club Theatricals.* Cambridge, Mass.: Printed by University Press, 1892.

Gilmore, Grant, *The Ages of American Law.* New Haven: Yale University Press, 1977.

———, *The Death of Contract.* Columbus: Ohio State University Press, 1974.

Girouard, Mark, *The Return to Camelot: Chivalry and the English Gentleman.* New Haven: Yale University Press, 1981.

Gould, Stephen Jay, *The Mismeasure of Man.* New York: Norton, 1981.

[Grant, J. W.], *My First Campaign.* Boston: Wright & Potter, 1863.

Gratton, C. Hartley, *The Three Jameses: A Family of Minds.* New York: Longmans, Green, 1932.

Gray, John Chipman, *The Nature and Sources of the Law,* 2nd ed. New York: Macmillan, 1921.

Greenslet, Ferris, *The Lowells and Their Seven Worlds.* Boston: Houghton Mifflin, 1946.

Guinness, Desmond, and William Ryan, *Irish Houses and Castles.* New York: Crescent, 1971.

Guthrie, William D., *Lectures on the Fourteenth Article of Amendment to the Constitution of the United States.* Boston: Little, Brown, 1898.

Haldane, Elizabeth S., *From One Century to Another.* London: Alexander MacLehose, 1937.

Hale, Edward Everett, *A New England Boyhood.* Boston: Little, Brown, 1964 (1st ed., 1893).

Hart, H. L. A., *The Concept of Law,* 2nd ed. Oxford: Oxford University Press, 1963.

———, *Essays in Jurisprudence and Philosophy.* Oxford: Oxford University Press, 1983.

Hasty Pudding Club, 1846–1871: Catalogue of the Officers and Members of the Hasty-Pudding Club of Harvard College. Boston: privately printed, 1867.

Heuser, Herman J., *Canon Sheehan of Doneraile: The Story of an Irish Parish Priest as Told Chiefly by Himself in Books, Personal Memoirs and Letters*. New York: Longmans, Green, 1923.

Higginson, Thomas Wentworth, *Army Life in a Black Regiment*. New York: Norton, 1984. ("Originally published 1869.")

———, ed., *Harvard Memorial Biographies*, vols. 1 and 2. Cambridge, Mass.: Sever and Francis, 1866.

Highsaw, Robert B., *Edward Douglass White: Defender of the Conservative Faith*. Baton Rouge: Louisiana State University Press,1981.

Hirsch, H. N., *The Enigma of Felix Frankfurter*. New York: Basic Books, 1981.

Hiss, Alger, *Recollections of a Life*. New York: Seaver Books, 1988.

Hoar, George, *Autobiography of Seventy Years*. New York: Scribner's Sons, 1903.

Holmes and the Common Law: A Century Later, The Holmes Lectures 1981. Occasional Pamphlet 10. Cambridge, Mass.: Harvard Law School, 1983.

Holmes, Oliver Wendell, [Sr.], *The Collected Works of Oliver Wendell Holmes*. Boston: Houghton Mifflin, 1891.

Hovey, Richard B., *John Jay Chapman: An American Mind*. New York: Columbia University Press, 1959.

Howe, Helen, *The Gentle Americans: 1864–1960, Biography of a Breed*. New York: Harper & Row, 1965.

Howe, Mark Antony DeWolfe, *Holmes of the Breakfast-Table*. Boston: Houghton Mifflin, 1939.

———, *John Jay Chapman and His Letters*. Boston: Houghton Mifflin, 1937.

———, *Later Years of the Saturday Club, 1870–1920*. Boston: Houghton Mifflin, 1927.

Howe, Mark DeWolfe, *Justice Oliver Wendell Holmes: The Shaping Years, 1841–1870*. Cambridge, Mass.: Harvard University Press, 1957.

———, *Justice Oliver Wendell Holmes: The Proving Years, 1870–1882*. Cambridge, Mass.: Harvard University Press, 1963.

Hoyt, Edwin P., *The Improper Bostonian, Dr. Oliver Wendell Holmes*. New York: Morrow, 1979.

Hughes, Charles Evans, *The Autobiographical Notes of Charles Evans Hughes* (David J. Danelski and Joseph S. Tulchin, eds.). Cambridge, Mass.: Harvard University Press, 1973.

———, *The Supreme Court of the United States: Its Foundation, Methods and Achievements. An Interpretation*. Garden City, N.Y.: Garden City, 1936.

Hurst, James Willard, *Justice Holmes on Legal History*. New York: Macmillan, 1964.

Hyde, Thomas W., *Following the Greek Cross, or, Memories of the Sixth Army Corps*. Boston: Houghton Mifflin, 1894.

Ions, Edmund, *James Bryce and American Democracy, 1870–1922*. London: Macmillan, 1968.

Jackson, Charles, *A Treatise on the Pleadings and Practice in Real Actions: With Precedents of Pleadings*. Boston: Wells & Lilly, 1828.

———, A. Sterns, and John Pickering, *Report of the Commissioners Appointed to Revise the General Statutes of the Commonwealth*. Boston: Dutton and Wentworth, 1835.

James, Alice, *Diary of Alice James* (L. Edel, ed.). New York: Penguin, 1964.

James, Henry, *Autobiography: A Small Boy and Others, Notes of a Son and Brother, The Middle Years* (Frederick W. Dupee, ed.). Princeton: Princeton University Press, 1983.

———, *The Bostonians*. New York: Signet, 1980.

———, *The Notebooks of Henry James* (F. O. Matthiessen and Kenneth B. Murdock, eds.). New York: Oxford University Press, 1947.

James, William, *The Letters of William James* (ed. Henry James). Boston: Little, Brown, 1926 (one-volume ed.).

———, *The Principles of Psychology.* 2 vols. New York: Henry Holt, 1890.

———, *The Varieties of Religious Experience: A Study in Human Nature.* New York: Modern Library, 1936 (1st ed., 1902).

Johnson, Donald Bruce, and Kirk H. Porter, *National Party Platforms: 1840–1972,* 5th ed. Urbana, Ill.: University of Illinois Press, 1975.

Josephson, Matthew, *The Robber Barons.* New York: Harcourt Brace, 1962 (1st ed., 1934).

Kalven, Harry, Jr., *A Worthy Tradition: Freedom of Speech in America* (ed. Jamie Kalven). New York: Harper & Row, 1988.

Kammen, Michael, *A Machine That Would Go of Itself: The Constitution in American Culture.* New York: Random House, 1986.

Karl, Barry D., *The Uneasy State: The United States from 1915 to 1945.* Chicago: University of Chicago Press, 1983.

Karlen, Delmar, *Appellate Courts in the United States and England.* Westport, Conn.: Greenwood Press, 1963.

Kay, Jane Holtz, *Lost Boston.* Boston: Houghton Mifflin, 1980.

Kazin, Alfred, *An American Procession.* New York: Knopf, 1984.

Kellogg, Frederic Rogers, *The Formative Essays of Justice Holmes: The Making of American Legal Philosophy.* Westport, Conn.: Greenwood Press, 1984.

Kelsen, Hans, *General Theory of Law and State.* Cambridge, Mass.: Harvard University Press, 1949 (Anders Wedberg., trans.).

Kennedy, William Sloane, *Oliver Wendell Holmes: Poet, Littérateur, Scientist.* Boston: Cassino, 1883.

Kevles, Daniel J., *In the Name of Eugenics: Genetics and the Uses of Human Heredity.* New York: Knopf, 1985.

King, Willard, *Melville Weston Fuller, Chief Justice of the United States 1888–1920.* New York: Macmillan, 1950.

Konefsky, Samuel J., *The Legacy of Holmes and Brandeis: A Study in the Influence of Ideas.* New York: Macmillan, 1956.

Lambert, Angela, *Unquiet Souls: The Indian Summer of the British Aristocracy, 1880–1918.* London: Macmillan, 1984.

Langdell, C. C., *A Selection of Cases on the Law of Contracts.* Boston: Little, Brown, 1871.

Lanman, Charles, *The Japanese in America.* Washington, D.C.: privately printed, 1871.

———, *Leading Men of Japan.* Boston: Lothrop, 1886.

Larcom, Lucy, *A New England Girlhood.* Gloucester, Mass.: Peter Smith, 1973 (reprint; 1st ed., Boston: Houghton Mifflin, 1889).

Leech, Margaret, *In the Days of McKinley.* New York: Harper & Row, 1959.

Lerner, Max, ed., *The Mind and Faith of Justice Holmes; His Speeches, Essays, Letters and Judicial Opinions.* Boston: Little, Brown, 1943.

Levy, David W., *Herbert Croly of The New Republic: The Life and Thought of an American Progressive.* Princeton: Princeton University Press, 1985.

Levy, Leonard W., *Judgments: Essays on American Constitutional History.* Chicago: Quadrangle, 1972.

———, *The Law of the Commonwealth and Chief Justice Shaw.* Cambridge, Mass.: Harvard University Press, 1957.

Linderman, Gerald F., *Embattled Courage: The Experience of Combat in the American Civil War.* New York: Free Press, 1987.

Llewellyn, Karl N., *On Legal Realism.* Birmingham, Ala.: Legal Classics, 1986.

Lund, Thomas A., *American Wildlife Law*. Berkeley: University of California Press, 1980.

Maine, Sir Henry J. S., *Ancient Law: Its Connection with the Early History of Society, and Its Relation to Modern Ideas* (3rd American ed., from 5th London ed.). New York: Henry Holt & Co., 1885.

Maitland, Frederick William, *The Letters of Frederick William Maitland*. Cambridge, Mass.: Harvard University Press, 1965.

———, *The Life and Letters of Leslie Stephen*. London: Duckworth, 1906.

Maryatt, Capt. D. N., *The Children of the New Forest*. New York: Hayes & Bros., 1858.

Mason, Alpheus Thomas, *Brandeis: A Free Man's Life*. New York: Viking, 1946.

———, *Harlan Fiske Stone: Pillar of the Law*. New York: Viking, 1956.

———, *William Howard Taft: Chief Justice*. New York: Viking, 1965.

Matthiessen, F. O., *The James Family, Including Selections from the Writings of Henry James, Senior, William, Henry and Alice James*. New York: Vantage, 1980 (1st ed., 1947).

McAleer, John, *Ralph Waldo Emerson: Days of Encounter*. Boston: Little, Brown, 1984.

McBain, Howard Lee, *Prohibition Legal and Illegal*. New York: Macmillan, 1928.

McCloskey, Robert G., *The American Supreme Court*. Chicago: University of Chicago Press, 1960.

McCoy, Donald R., *Calvin Coolidge: The Quiet President*. New York: Macmillan, 1967.

McNeill, Frank, *The Labor Movement Today*. Boston, 1887.

McWhiney, G., and P. D. Jamieson, *Attack and Die: Civil War Military Tactics and the Southern Heritage*. Tuscaloosa: University of Alabama Press, 1982.

Meyer, Balthazar H., *A History of the Northern Securities Case*, Bulletin of the University of Wisconsin No. 142, Madison: 1906 (reprint, Da Capo Press, 1972).

Miller, Loren, *The Petitioners: The Story of the Supreme Court of the United States and the Negro*. New York: Pantheon, 1966.

Miller, Perry, ed., *American Thought: The Civil War to World War I*. New York: Rinehart, Inc., 1957.

Monagan, John S., *The Grand Panjandrum: Mellow Years of Justice Holmes*. Lanham, Md.: University Press of America, 1988.

Morris, Edward, *The Rise of Theodore Roosevelt*. New York: Coward, McCann & Geoghegan, 1979.

Morris, Lloyd, *William James: The Message of a Modern Mind*. New York: Charles Scribner's Sons, 1950.

Morison, Samuel Eliot, *Three Centuries of Harvard: 1636–1936*, Cambridge, Mass.: Harvard University Press, 1936.

Morse, Frances Rollins, ed., *Henry and Mary Lee, Letters and Journals, with other Family Letters 1802–1860*. Boston: privately printed, 1926.

Morse, John T., *Life and Letters of Oliver Wendell Holmes*. Cambridge, Mass.: Houghton Mifflin, 1896.

Motley, John Lothrop, *The Correspondence of John Lothrop Motley, D.C.L.*, ed. George William Curtis. 3 vols. New York: Hayes & Bros., 1900 (facsimile ed. 1973, by AMS Press, New York).

Musmanno, Michael A., *After Twelve Years*. New York: Knopf, 1939.

Napier, Sir Alfred, *History of the War on the Peninsula and in the South of France, from A.D. 1807 to A.D. 1814*. 5 vols. New York: Middleton, 1863.

Newmyer, R. Kent, *Supreme Court Justice Joseph Story: Statesman of the Old Republic*. Chapel Hill: University of North Carolina Press, 1985.

Nitobe, Inazo, *Bushido: The Soul of Japan* (intro. by William Elliot Griffiths). Rutland, Vt.: Tuttle, 1969 (first published, 1905).

Oberndorf, Clarence P., ed., *The Psychiatric Novels of Oliver Wendell Holmes*. New

York: Columbia University Press, 1946 (2nd ed., Westport, Conn.: Greenwood Press reprint, 1971).

O'Connor, Ulick, *All the Olympians: A Biographical Portrait of the Irish Literary Renaissance*. New York: Atheneum, 1984.

Palfrey, Francis Winthrop, *The Antietam and Fredericksburg*. New York: Charles Scribner's Sons, 1882.

———, *Memoir of William Francis Bartlett*. Boston: Houghton, Osgood & Co., 1878.

Palmer, George Herbert, *The Life of Alice Freeman Palmer*. Boston: Houghton Mifflin, 1909.

Paper, Lewis J., *Brandeis*. Englewood Cliffs, N.J.: Prentice-Hall, 1983.

Parrish, Michael E., *Felix Frankfurter and His Times: The Reform Years*. New York: American Free Press, 1982.

Patch, Joseph Dorst, *The Battle of Ball's Bluff*. Leesburg: Potomac Press, 1958.

Paul, Arnold M., *Conservative Crisis and the Rule of Law: Attitudes of Bar and Bench, 1887–1895*. Gloucester, Mass.: Peter Smith, 1976.

Pearson, Charles H., *National Life and Character: A Forecast*. London: Macmillan, 1893.

Pearson, Henry Greenleaf, *Son of New England: James Jackson Storrow 1864–1926*. Boston: privately printed, 1932.

Peirce, Charles Sanders, *Collected Papers*. 8 vols. (Charles Hartshorne and Paul Weiss eds. vols. 1–6; A. W. Burks ed. vols. 7–8). Cambridge, Mass.: Belknap Press of Harvard University Press, 1931–1935.

———, *Philosophical Writings of Peirce*, ed. Justus Buchler. New York: Dover, 1955.

Perry, Lewis, and Michael Fellman, *Antislavery Reconsidered: New Perspectives on the Abolitionists*. Baton Rouge: Louisiana State University Press, 1979.

Perry, Ralph Barton, *The Thought and Character of William James*. New York: Braziller, 1948 (1st ed., 1935).

Persons, Stow, ed., *Evolutionary Thought in America*. New Haven: Yale University Press, 1950.

Phillips, Harlan B., *Felix Frankfurter Reminisces*. New York: Reynal, 1960.

Pohlman, Harold L., *Justice Oliver Wendell Holmes and Utilitarian Jurisprudence*. Cambridge, Mass.: Harvard University Press, 1984.

Polenberg, Richard, *Fighting Faiths: The Abrams Case, The Supreme Court, and Free Speech*. New York: Viking, 1987.

Pollock, Sir Frederick, *For My Grandson*. London: Murray, 1933.

———, *Outside the Law: Diversions Partly Serious*. London: Cayme, 1927.

Porte, Joel, ed., *Emerson in His Journals*. Cambridge, Mass.: Belknap Press of Harvard University Press, 1982.

Posner, Richard A., *The Economics of Justice*. Cambridge, Mass.: Harvard University Press, 1981.

Pound, Roscoe, *Interpretations of Legal History*. New York: Macmillan, 1923.

———, *The Spirit of the Common Law*. Boston: Marshall Jones, 1921.

Pringle, Henry F., *The Life and Times of William Howard Taft*. New York: Farrar & Rinehart, 1939.

———, *Theodore Roosevelt: A Biography*. New York: Harcourt Brace, 1956 (1st ed., 1931).

Purcell, Edward A., Jr., *The Crisis of Democratic Theory: Scientific Naturalism and the Problem of Value*. Lexington: University of Kentucky Press, 1973.

Pusey, Merlo J., *Charles Evans Hughes*. New York: Macmillan, 1951.

Rehnquist, William H., *The Supreme Court: How It Was, How It Is*. New York: Morrow, 1987.

Rodell, Fred, *Nine Men: A Political History of the Supreme Court from 1790 to 1955*. New York: Random House, 1955.

Roosevelt, Theodore, *The Autobiography of Theodore Roosevelt*. New York: Macmillan, 1913.

———, *Selections from the Correspondence of Theodore Roosevelt and Henry Cabot Lodge, 1884–1918*. New York: Charles Scribner's Sons, 1925.

Rosenfield, Leonora Cohen, *Portrait of a Philosopher: Morris R. Cohen in Life and Letters*. New York: Harcourt, Brace & World, 1962.

Ruskin, John, *The Elements of Drawing* (intro. by Lawrence Campbell). New York: Dover, 1971 (1st ed., 1857).

Russell, Francis, *The Shadow of Blooming Grove: Warren G. Harding in His Times*. New York: McGraw-Hill, 1968.

Samuels, Ernest, *The Young Henry Adams*. Cambridge, Mass.: Harvard University Press, 1948.

Santayana, George, *Character and Opinion in the United States*. New York: Charles Scribner's Sons, 1920 (reprinted New York: Norton, 1967).

———, *The Last Puritan: A Memoir In the Form of a Novel*. New York: Charles Scribner's Sons, 1936.

———, *Persons and Places: The Background of My Life*. New York: Charles Scribner's Sons, 1944.

Sears, Stephen W., *Landscape Turned Red: The Battle of Antietam*. New Haven: Ticknor & Fields, 1983.

Sennett, Richard, *The Fall of Public Man*. New York: Knopf, 1977.

Sergeant, Elizabeth Shepley, *Fire under the Andes: A Group of Northern American Portraits*. New York: Knopf, 1927.

Shaku, Soyen, *Zen for Americans*, trans. Daizetz Teitaro Suzuki. La Salle, Ill.: Open Court Press, 1974 (first pub. in 1906 as "Summons of a Buddhist Abbot"; reprint of 1913 clothbound edition).

Sherman, Edgar Jay, *Some Recollections of a Long Life*. Boston: privately printed, 1908.

Shriver, Harry C., *What Justice Holmes Wrote, and What Has Been Written about Him: A Bibliography, 1866–1976*. Potomac, Md.: Fox Hills, 1978.

———, *The Government Lawyer: Essays on Men, Books, and the Law*. Potomac, Md.: Fox Hills, 1975.

———, *What Gusto: Stories and Anecdotes About Justice Oliver Wendell Holmes*. Potomac, Md.: Fox Hills, 1970.

Sidney, Sir Philip, *The Countess of Pembroke's Arcadia*, ed. Maurice Evans. New York: Penguin, 1977 (based on 1593 ed., with modernized spelling and punctuation).

Siemas, Johannes, *Hermann Roesler and the Making of the Meiji State*. Tokyo: Sophia University and Charles Tuttle & Co., 1968.

Smalley, George M., *Anglo-American Memories*. New York: G. P. Putnam's Sons, 1911.

Stampp, Kenneth M., *The Era of Reconstruction, 1865–1877*. New York: Knopf, 1965.

Stephen, Leslie, *The English Utilitarians*. New York: Peter Smith, 1950 (1st ed., London: Duckworth, 1900).

Strouse, Jean, *Alice James: A Biography*. Boston: Houghton Mifflin, 1980.

Strum, Philippa, *Louis D. Brandeis: Justice for the People*. Cambridge, Mass.: Harvard University Press, 1984.

Surrency, Edwin C., *History of the Federal Courts*. Dobbs Ferry, N.Y.: Oceana, 1987.

Sutherland, Arthur E., *The Law at Harvard: A History of Ideas and Men: 1817–1967*. Cambridge, Mass.: Harvard University Press, 1967.

Taft, William Howard, *Our Chief Magistrate*. New York: Columbia University Press, 1916.

Taylor, William R., *Cavalier and Yankee: The Old South and American National Character.* New York: Harper, 1969.

Tharp, Louise Hall, *Mrs. Jack: A Biography of Isabella Stewart Gardner.* Boston: Little, Brown, 1965.

Thayer, William R., ed., *Letters of John Holmes to James Russell Lowell and Others.* Boston: Houghton Mifflin, 1917.

Thayer, William Roscoe, *The Life and Letters of John Hay.* Boston: Houghton Mifflin, 1915.

——, *Theodore Roosevelt: An Intimate Biography.* New York: Grosset & Dunlap, 1919.

Ticknor, Caroline, ed., *Dr. Holmes's Boston.* Boston: Houghton Mifflin, 1915.

Tilton, Eleanor M., *Amiable Autocrat: A Biography of Dr. Oliver Wendell Holmes.* New York: Schuman, 1947.

Tocqueville, Alexis de, *Democracy in America* (trans. Henry Reeve), 8th ed. New York: Pratt, Woodland & Co., 1848.

Tribe, Laurence H., *American Constitutional Law,* 2nd ed. Mineola, N. Y.: Foundation Press, 1988.

Twiss, Benjamin R., *Lawyers and the Constitution: How Laissez Faire Came to the Supreme Court.* Princeton: Princeton University Press, 1942 (reprint, Greenwood Press, 1973).

Urofsky, Melvin I., *Louis D. Brandeis and the Progressive Tradition.* Boston: Little, Brown, 1981.

Vaughan, Robert Alfred, *Hours with the Mystics.* London: Strahan, 1856.

Vidal, Gore, *Lincoln: A Novel.* New York: Random House, 1984.

Waddell, Helen, *Mediaeval Latin Lyrics.* London: Constable, 1929, 1930.

Walker, Timothy, *Introduction to American Law: Designed as a First Book for Students,* 5th ed. Boston: Little, Brown, 1869 (1st ed., 1837).

Warren, Charles, *Congress, the Constitution and the Supreme Court.* Boston: Little, Brown, 1935 (1st ed., 1925).

——, *The Supreme Court in United States History.* Boston: Little, Brown, 1935 (1st ed., 1921).

Watson, Alan, *The Evolution of Law.* Baltimore: Johns Hopkins University Press, 1985.

Webb, Alexander S., *The Peninsula: McClellan's Campaign of 1862.* New York: Charles Scribner's Sons, 1882.

Welch, Richard E., Jr., *George Frisbie Hoar and the Half-Breed Republicans.* Cambridge, Mass.: Harvard University Press, 1971.

White, G. Edward, *The American Judicial Tradition: Profiles of Leading American Judges.* New York: Oxford University Press, 1976.

——, *Tort Law in America: An Intellectual History.* New York: Oxford University Press, 1980.

White, Morton, *Social Thought in America: The Revolt Against Formalism.* New York: Oxford University Press, 1976 (1st ed., 1947).

Wilson, Edmund, *Patriotic Gore: Studies on the Literature of the American Civil War.* New York: Oxford University Press, 1962.

——, ed., *The Shock of Recognition: The Development of Literature in the United States Recorded by the Men Who Made It,* 2nd ed. New York: Farrar, Straus and Cudahy, 1955 (1st ed., New York: Doubleday, Doran, 1943).

Wister, Owen, *Roosevelt: The Story of a Friendship 1880–1919.* New York: Macmillan, 1930.

Yeazell, Ruth B., *The Death and Letters of Alice James.* Berkeley: University of California Press, 1981.

Zimmern, Alfred, *The Greek Commonwealth: Politics & Economics in Fifth-Century Athens,* 5th ed. London: Oxford University Press (1st ed., 1911).

ARTICLES

Acheson, Dean, "Recollections of Service with the Federal Supreme Court," 18 *Alabama Lawyer* 355 (1957).

Aitchison, Clyde B., "Justice Holmes and the Development of Administrative Law," 1 *George Wash. L. Rev.* 165 (1933).

Allen, Francis A., "Criminal Law," 31 *U. Chi. L. Rev.* 257 (1964) (paper in a symposium, "Mr. Justice Holmes: Some Modern Views").

Atiyah, P. S., "The Legacy of Holmes through English Eyes," 63 *B.U.L. Rev.* 341 (1983), reprinted in *Holmes and the Common Law: A Century Later* (1983).

Bail, Hamilton Vaughan, "Harvard's Commemoration Day, July 21, 1865," 15 *New England Quarterly* 256 (June 1942).

Bailey, Thomas A., "Theodore Roosevelt and the Alaska Boundary Settlement," 18 *Canadian Hist. Rev.* 123 (1937).

Barbour, Walter, "Some Aspects of Fifteenth-Century Chancery," 31 *Harv. L. Rev.* 834 (1918).

Belknap, Chauncey, "A Retrospective Note," 28 *U. Fla. L. Rev.* 392 (1976).

Biddle, Francis, "Mr. Justice Holmes," 72 *New Republic* 105 (September 7, 1932).

Birmingham, Robert L., "Holmes on 'Peerless': *Raffles v. Wichelhaus* and the Objective Theory of Contract," 47 *U. Pitts. L. Rev.* 183 (1985).

Brewer, David J., "Working of the United States Supreme Court," 60 *Albany L.J.* 44 (1899).

Burgdorf, Robert L., and Marcia P. Burgdorf, "The Wicked Witch Is Almost Dead: *Buck v. Bell* and The Sterilization of Handicapped Persons," 50 *Temple L.Q.* 995 (1977).

Chagnon, Napoleon A., "Life Histories, Blood Revenge, and Warfare in a Tribal Population," 239 *Science* 985 (1988).

Cohen, Felix S., "The Holmes–Cohen Correspondence," *Journal of the History of Ideas* (1948), reprinted L. Rosenfield, *Portrait of a Philosopher: Morris R. Cohen in Life and Letters* (1962).

Cohen, Morris R., "Justice Holmes," 25 *New Republic* 294 (1921).

———, "Justice Holmes," 82 *New Republic* 206 (1935), reprinted (with some additions) in M. Cohen, *The Faith of a Liberal* (1946), p. 20.

———, "Justice Holmes," 82 *New Republic* 206 (April 3, 1935).

———, "Justice Holmes, Collected Papers," 25 *New Republic* 294 (Feb. 2, 1921).

———, "The Place of Logic in The Law," 29 *Harv. L. Rev.* 622 (1916).

Corwin, Edward S., "The Impact of the Idea of Evolution on The American Political and Constitutional Tradition," in S. Persons, *Evolutionary Thought in America* (1950), p. 182.

Currie, David, "The Constitution in the Supreme Court: 1910–1921," 1985 *Duke L. J.* 1111 (1985).

Cynkar, Robert J., "Buck v. Bell: 'Felt Necessities' v. Fundamental Values?," 81 *Colum. L. Rev.* 1418 (1981).

Dalton, Clare, "An Essay in the Deconstruction of Contract Doctrine," 94 *Yale L. J.* 997 (1989).

Darasz, Kathy A., "A Review of the Personal Correspondence of Justice Oliver Wendell Holmes, Jr.," 15 *Rutgers L. J.* 1141 (1984).

Denby, Charles, "An Extraordinary Man," 28 *U. Fla. L. Rev.* 393 (1976).

Dewey, John, "Justice Holmes and the Liberal Mind," 53 *New Republic* 210 (1928).

Dicey, Albert Venn, "The Combination Laws as Illustrating the Relation Between Law and Opinion in England During the Nineteenth Century," 17 *Harv. L. Rev.* 511 (1904).

——, "Holmes's *Common Law,*" *The Spectator,* Library Supplement June 3, 1882, pp. 745–747, published anonymously, reprinted as appendix to Touster, "Holmes A Hundred Years Ago: *The Common Law* and Legal Theory," 10 *Hofstra L. Rev.* 673, 712 (1982).

Donoghue, Denis, "Portrait of a Critic," *New Republic,* April 1, 1985, p. 29.

Dudziak, Mary L., "Oliver Wendell Holmes as a Eugenic Reformer: Rhetoric in the Writing of Constitutional Law," 71 *Iowa L. Rev.* 833 (1986).

Editorial, *Boston Evening Transcript,* August 12, 1902, p. 6.

——, "Justice Holmes and the Schwimmer Case," 59 *New Republic* 92 (1929).

——, "Mr. Justice Holmes," 33 *New Republic* 84 (1922).

——, "Mr. Justice Holmes," 46 *New Republic* 88 (1926).

——, "Mr. Justice Holmes at Ninety," *New Republic,* March 11, 1931.

——, *New York Times,* August 13, 1902, p. 8.

——, *New York Daily Tribune,* August 13, 1902, p. 6.

——, *The [Chicago] Tribune,* August 13, 1902, p. 12.

——, "Views of Justice Holmes," *New York Daily Tribune,* August 13, 1902, p. 1.

Elliott, E. Donald, "Holmes and Evolution: Legal Process as Artificial Intelligence," 13 *J. Legal Studies* 113 (1984).

Emerson, Edward W., "William James, 1842–1910," in M. A. DeWolfe Howe, ed., *Later Years of the Saturday Club, 1870–1920,* p. 192 (1927).

Farnsworth, E. Allan, "Legal Remedies for Breach of Contract," 70 *Colum. L. Rev.* 1145 (1970).

Fessenden, Franklin G., "The Rebirth of the Harvard Law School," 33 *Harv. L. Rev.* 493 (1920).

Frankfurter, Felix, "The Constitutional Opinions of Justice Holmes," 29 *Harv. L. Rev.* 683 (1916).

——, "The Early Writings of Oliver Wendell Holmes, Jr.," 44 *Harv. L. Rev.* 717 (1931).

——, "The Supreme Court and the Public," *Forum,* June 1930, p. 333.

Freund, Paul A., "Holmes and Brandeis in Retrospect," *Boston Bar J.,* September–October 1984, p. 7.

——, "Oliver Wendell Holmes," in 3 L. Friedman and F. L. Israel, *The Justices of the United States Supreme Court* 1755 (1980).

——, "Oliver Wendell Holmes, Jr.," *Yale Review* 178 (1987).

Fuller, Lon L., "Positivism and Fidelity to Law — A Reply to Professor Hart," 71 *Harv. L. Rev.* 630 (1958).

——, and William Perdue, Jr., "The Reliance Interest in Contract Damages:" 1. 46 *Yale L. J.* 52 (1936); 2. 46 *Yale L. J.* 373 (1937). Reprinted in R. C. Berring, ed., *Great American Law Reviews* 293 (1984).

Garraty, J. A., "Henry Cabot Lodge and the Alaskan Boundary Tribunal," 24 *New England Quarterly* 469 (1951).

——, "Holmes' Appointment to the Supreme Court," 22 *New England Quarterly* 291 (1949).

Gengarelly, W. Anthony, "The Abrams Case: Social Aspects of a Judicial Controversy," *Boston Bar J.,* part 1, March, 1981, pp. 19–24; part 2, April, 1981, pp. 9–15.

Gerard, Jules, "Capacity to Govern," 12 *Harv. J. of Law & Public Policy* 501 (1989).

Gordon, Robert W., "Holmes' *Common Law* As Legal and Social Science," 10 *Hofstra L. Rev.* 719 (1982).

Gunther, Gerald, "Learned Hand and the Origins of Modern First Amendment Doctrine: Some Fragments of History," 27 *Stanford L. Rev.* 719 (1975).

Hahn, Roger, "Keeping an Eye on America," *Washington Univ. Mag.,* Fall 1987, p. 24.

Haldane, Viscount, "Mr. Justice Holmes," 26 *New Republic* 34 (1921).

Hamilton, Walton H., "The Legal Philosophy of Justices Holmes and Brandeis," *Current History* 654 (1931).

——, "On Dating Mr. Justice Holmes," 9 *U. Chi. L. Rev.* 1 (1941).

Hart, Henry M., "Holmes' Positivism — An Addendum," 64 *Harv. L. Rev.* 929 (1951).

Hart, H. L. A., "Positivism and the Separation of Law and Morals," 71 *Harv. L. Rev.* 593 (1958).

Hill, Arthur Dehon, "Oliver Wendell Holmes, Justice of the Supreme Court of the United States," 39 *Harvard Graduates' Magazine* 265 (1931).

Hough, Charles M., "Due Process of Law Today," 32 *Harv. L. Rev.* 218 (1919).

Howe, Mark DeWolfe, "Holmes' Positivism — A Brief Rejoinder," 64 *Harv. L. Rev.* 937 (1951).

——, "The Letters of Henry James to Mr. Justice Holmes," *Yale Review*, Spring 1949, p. 410.

——, "The Positivism of Mr. Justice Holmes," 64 *Harv. L. Rev.* 529 (1951).

Howells, William Dean, "A Sennight of the Centennial," *Atlantic Monthly*, July 1876, p. 97.

Hunter, H. D., "Problems in Search of Principles: The First Amendment in the Supreme Court 1791–1930," 35 *Emory L. J.* 59 (1986).

Jackson, Charles, "Real Actions" (remarks on review of *Jackson on Real Actions*, in the second number of the *American Jurist*), 2 *American Jurist* 65 (1829). (Review is at 1 *Am. Jurist* 24 [1829]).

Kalven, Harry, "Professor Ernst Freund and Debs v. United States," 40 *U. Chi. L. Rev.* 235 (1973).

——, "Torts," 31 *U. Ariz. L. Rev.* 263 (1961).

Kanda, James, and William A. Gifford, "The Kaneko Correspondence," 37 *Monumenta Nipponica: Studies in Japanese Culture* nos. 1–4 (1982).

Kaplan, Benjamin, "Encounter with Oliver Wendell Holmes, Jr.," 96 *Harv. L. Rev.* 1828 (1983).

Kelley, Patrick J., "A Critical Analysis of Holmes's Theory of Torts," 61 *Wash. U. L. Q.* 681 (1983).

——, "Oliver Wendell Holmes, Utilitarian Jurisprudence and the Positivism of John Stuart Mill," 30 *Am. J. Jurisprudence* 189 (1985).

Kellogg, Frederic R., "Common Law and Constitutional Theory: The Common Law Origins of Holmes's Constitutional Restraint," 7 *George Mason L. Rev.* 177 (1984).

——, "Law, Morals and Justice Holmes," 69 *Judicature* 214 (1986).

Kevles, Sturchio and Carroll, "The Sciences in America, circa 1880," 209 *Science* 27 (1980).

[Kimball, Day], Note, "The Espionage Act and the Limits of Legal Toleration," 33 *Harv. L. Rev.* 442 (1920).

Landis, James M., "Mr. Justice Brandeis and the Harvard Law School," 55 *Harv. L. Rev.* 184.

Langdell, C. C., "The Northern Securities Case and the Sherman Anti-Trust Act," 16 *Harv. L. Rev.* 539 (1903).

LeDuc, Alice Sumner, "The Man Who Rescued 'The Captain,'" *Atlantic Monthly*, August 1947, p. 80.

Lerner, Max, "The Social Thought of Mr. Justice Brandeis," in F. Frankfurter, ed., *Mr. Justice Brandeis, Essays* 7 (1932).

[Lippmann, Walter], "To Justice Holmes," 6 *New Republic* 156 (1916).

Little, Eleanor N., "The Early Reading of Justice Oliver Wendell Holmes," 8 *Harv. Library Bull.* 163 (1954).

Llewellyn, K. N., "The Bramble Bush: Some Lectures on Law and Its Study," Columbia University School of Law, New York, 1930 ("Tentative printing for the Use of Students"), reprinted in K. Llewellyn, *On Legal Realism* (1986).

Lockwood, John E., "'I Always Prefer the Original,'" 28 *U. Fla. L. Rev.* 394 (1976).

Lombardo, Paul A., "Three Generations, No Imbeciles: New Light on *Buck v. Bell*," 60 *N.Y.U. L. Rev.* 30 (1985).

Loring, William Caleb, "Ought the Full Bench to Be Required to Go Circuit?" 5 *Mass. L. Q.* 65 (1919).

McLaughlin, Charles, "Historic Houses: Melville's Country Years: Literary Efforts and Modest Farming at Arrowhead," *Architectural Digest,* December, 1983, p. 168.

Murlin, Lemuel H., "Melville M. Bigelow," 1 *B. U. L. Rev.* 153 (1921).

Note, "Holmes, Peirce and Legal Pragmatism," 84 *Yale L. J.* 1123 (1975).

Note, "The Origin of the Modern Standard of Due Care in Negligence," 1976 *Wash. U. L. Q.* 447 (1977).

Phillips, Matthew, "Bungled River Crossing," *America's Civil War,* September, 1988, p. 42.

Pollock, Sir Frederick, "The Merger Case and Restraint of Trade," 17 *Harv. L. Rev.* 151 (1904).

Post, A. C., "Judge Oliver Wendell Holmes," *McClure's Magazine,* October, 1902.

Pound, Roscoe, "Judge Holmes' Contributions to the Science of Law," 35 *Harv. L. Rev.* 449 (1921).

————, "Liberty of Contract," 18 *Yale L. J.* 454 (1909).

Powell, H. Jefferson, "Joseph Story's Commentaries on Our Constitution: A Belated View," 94 *Yale L. J.* 1285 (1985).

Powell, Thomas Reed, "The Judiciality of Minimum-Wage Legislation," 37 *Harv. L. Rev.* 545 (1924).

Rabban, David M., "The Emergence of Modern First Amendment Doctrine," 50 *U. Chi. L. Rev.* 1205 (1984).

————, "The First Amendment In Its Forgotten Years," 90 *Yale L. J.* 514 (1981).

Ragan, Fred D., "Justice Oliver Wendell Holmes, Jr., Zechariah Chafee, Jr., and The Clear and Present Danger Test for Free Speech: The First Year, 1919," 58 *J. Am. Hist.* 24 (1971).

Roberts, E. F., "Mining With Justice Holmes," 39 *Vanderbilt L. Rev.* 287 (1986).

Rogat, Yosal, "The Judge as Spectator," 31 *U. Chi. L. Rev.* 213 (1964).

————, "Mr. Justice Holmes: A Dissenting Opinion," 15 *Stan. L. Rev.* 3, 254 (1962–1963).

————, and James M. O'Fallon, "Mr. Justice Holmes: A Dissenting Opinion — The Speech Cases," 36 *Stan. L. Rev.* 1349 (1984).

Rovere, R., "Sage" (book review), *The New Yorker,* Apr. 6, 1957, p. 146.

Schwartz, Warren F., Keith Baxter, and David Ryan, "The Duel: Can These Gentlemen Be Acting Efficiently?" 13 *J. of L. Studies* 321 (1984).

Schwarz, Joan I., "Oliver Wendell Holmes's 'The Path of the Law': Conflicting Views of the Legal World," 29 *American J. L. History* 235 (1985).

Seagle, William, "Oliver Wendell Holmes: Law and the Future," in *Men of Law, from Hammurabi to Holmes,* New York: Macmillan, 1947.

Sergeant, Elizabeth Shepley, "Oliver Wendell Holmes, Justice Touched With Fire," 49 *New Republic* 59 (1926), reprinted in *Fire under the Andes: A Group of North American Portraits* (1927), p. 305.

Sharp, Malcolm P., "Contracts," 31 *U. Chi. L. Rev.* 268 (1964).

Speziale, Marcia J., "Oliver Wendell Holmes, Jr., William James, Theodore Roosevelt, and the Strenuous Life," 13 *Conn. L. Rev.* 663 (1981).

Taft, William Howard, "The Jurisdiction of the Supreme Court under the Act of February 13, 1925," 35 *Yale L. J.* 1 (1925).

Thayer, James B., "The Origin and Scope of the American Doctrine of Constitutional Law," 7 *Harv. L. Rev.* 129 (1893), reprinted in R. Berring, ed., *Great American Law Reviews* (1984), p. 57.

Touster, Saul, "Book Review (*Patriotic Gore*)," 76 *Harv. L. Rev.* 434 (1962).

———, "Holmes A Hundred Years Ago: *The Common Law* and Legal Theory," 10 *Hofstra L. Rev.* 673 (1982).

———, "In Search of Holmes from Within," 18 *Vanderbilt L. Rev.* 437 (1965).

Tushnet, Mark, "The Logic of Experience: Oliver Wendell Holmes on the Supreme Judicial Court," 63 *Va. L. Rev.* 975 (1977).

Updike, John, "Reflections: Melville's Withdrawal," *The New Yorker*, April 10, 1982, p. 120.

Utz, Stephen G., "Maine's *Ancient Law* and Legal Theory," 16 *Conn. L. Rev.* 821 (1984).

Vetter, Jan, "The Evolution of Holmes: Holmes and Evolution," 72 *Calif. L. Rev.* 343 (1984). Reprinted in *Holmes and The Common Law: A Century Later*, occasional paper number 10, Harvard Law School (1983), p. 75.

Wales, Robert W., "Some Aspects of Life with Mr. Justice Holmes in His 90th Year," 28 *U. Fla. L. Rev.* 395 (1976).

Warren, Charles, "The Progressiveness of the United States Supreme Court," 13 *Colum. L. Rev.* 294 (1913).

Warren, Samuel, and L. Brandeis, "The Right to Privacy," 4 *Harv. L. Rev.* 193 (1890).

Wechsler, Herbert, "Toward Neutral Principles of Constitutional Law," 73 *Harv. L. Rev.* 1 (1959).

White, G. Edward, "From Realism to Critical Legal Studies: A Truncated Intellectual History," 40 *S. W. L. J.* 819 (1986).

———, "From Sociological Jurisprudence to Realism: Jurisprudence and Social Change in Early Twentieth-Century America," 58 *Va. L. Rev.* 999 (1972).

———, "The Integrity of Holmes' Jurisprudence," 10 *Hofstra L. Rev.* 633 (1982), excerpts reprinted in *Boston Bar J.*, December, 1982, p. 24.

———, "Looking at Holmes in the Mirror," 4 *Law and History Review* 440 (1986).

———, "The Rise and Fall of Justice Holmes," 39 *U. Chi. L. Rev.* 51 (1971), reprinted (without notes) in D. Burton, *Oliver Wendell Holmes, Jr.: What Manner of Liberal?* (1979), p. 135.

Wigmore, John, "Justice Holmes and the Law of Torts," 29 *Harv. L. Rev.* 601 (1916).

Zobel, Hiller B., "Enlisted For Life," *American Heritage*, June–July 1986, p. 57.

HOLMES'S PUBLISHED WORKS — BOOKS

Holmes, Oliver Wendell, *Collected Legal Papers*. New York: Harcourt, Brace and Howe, 1920.

———, *The Common Law*. Boston: Little, Brown, 1881.

———, *The Common Law*. Cambridge, Mass.: Harvard University Press, 1963 (ed. and with an introduction by Mark DeWolfe Howe); paperback ed., Boston: Little, Brown, 1963 (1st ed., 1881).

———, *The Common Law and Other Writings*. Birmingham, Ala.: Legal Classics Library, 1982 (includes facsimiles of *The Common Law*, *Collected Legal Papers*, and *Speeches*).

———, *Memoir of George Otis Shattuck*. Cambridge, Mass.: John Wilson & Son, 1900.

————, *The Occasional Speeches of Justice Oliver Wendell Holmes; Compiled by Mark DeWolfe Howe*. Cambridge, Mass.: Harvard University Press, 1962. (Based on 1913 edition of *Speeches*, with additions from Holmes Papers.)

————, *Speeches*. Boston: Little, Brown, 1891 (revised eds. 1895, 1896, 1900, 1913).

Kellogg, Frederic R., ed., *The Formative Essays of Justice Holmes: The Making of an American Legal Philosophy*. Westport, Conn.: Greenwood Press, 1984. (Selected law articles published before 1881.)

Kent, James, *Commentaries on American Law* (Oliver Wendell Holmes, Jr., ed.), 12th ed. Boston: Little, Brown, 1873.

Shriver, Harry C., ed., *Justice Oliver Wendell Holmes: His Book Notices and Uncollected Letters and Papers*. New York: Central Book, 1936. (Selected early miscellany.)

HOLMES'S PUBLISHED WORKS — ARTICLES

Of more than 100 articles and book notices Holmes published before 1881, only a half dozen have been reprinted and are widely available; dozens of his brief, unsigned articles and book notices have not before been identified in print.

Most of Holmes's speeches were published in newspapers during his lifetime, but I have listed separately only those that he published in law journals. All of his speeches are conveniently available in Mark Howe's excellent edition of the *Speeches*; see above.

UNDERGRADUATE PUBLICATIONS

"Alma Mater," 7 *Harv. Mag.* 49 (1860). (Unsigned; attributed to Holmes by Mark Howe, on basis of Frank Warren Hackett's index to the *Harvard Magazine*, in the Harvard University Archives.)

"Book Notices," 7 *Harv. Mag.* 111 (November, 1860). (Attribution by Mark Howe, as above.)

"Books," 4 *Harv. Mag.* 408 (December, 1858).

"Editors' Table," 7 *Harv. Mag.* 26 (September, 1860). (Attribution by Mark Howe, as above.)

Editorial, 7 *Harv. Mag.* 37 (September, 1860) (attribution as above).

"'Marion Graham; or, Higher than Happiness,' by Meta Lander" (book review), 7 *Harv. Mag.* 235 (March, 1861). (Attribution as above.)

"Notes on Albert Durer," 7 *Harv. Mag.* 41 (October, 1860).

"Plato," 2 *The University Quarterly* 205 (October, 1860).

THE AMERICAN LAW REVIEW

Holmes wrote for most numbers of the quarterly *American Law Review*, founded by his friends John Ropes and John C. Gray, from January, 1867, until January, 1880. Most of his contributions were unsigned. From October, 1868, until June, 1870, he wrote digests of recent American and English cases for each issue (which I have not listed separately; for these items, see M. Howe, *The Shaping Years* (1956), p. 315; H. Shriver, *What Justice Holmes Wrote . . .*). From October, 1870, he was coeditor of the *American Law Review* with his friend Arthur Sedgwick, and from July, 1872, to June, 1873, he was sole editor. As noted in the text, the longer articles he wrote for the *Law Review* were revised for his edition of Kent's *Commentaries* or for *The Common Law*. Notes in Holmes's copies of the bound volumes in the Library of Congress show that some of the brief unsigned reviews and articles were written with coauthors — often with John Gray or Arthur Sedgwick. Attributions are based on Mark Howe's notes, from Holmes's and John Chipman Gray's bound copies.

Thirty of the shorter articles and book reviews, with some letters and miscellanea, were reprinted in H. Shriver, ed., *Justice Oliver Wendell Holmes, His Book Notices and Uncollected Letters and Papers* (1936). Felix Frankfurter collected and reprinted a few of the longer pieces in volume 44 of the *Harvard Law Review* (March, 1931), and those same articles have been reprinted in book form: F. Kellogg, *The Formative Essays of Justice Holmes* (1986). A partial bibliography of Holmes's *American Law Review* pieces was given by F. Frankfurter, 44 *Harv. L. Rev.* 797 (1931), and reprinted by H. Shriver, *Justice Oliver Wendell Holmes — Uncollected Papers* . . . , p. 251.

"'The Academical Study of the Civil Law . . . ,' by James Bryce," 5 *Am. L. Rev.* 715 (1871).

"'American Leading Cases,' Hare & Wallace ed., 1871," 6 *Am. L. Rev.* 550 (1872).

"'The American Reports,' by Isaac Grant Thompson," 5 *Am. L. Rev.* 549 (1871).

"'American Trade-Mark Cases,' Rowland Cox, ed.," 6 *Am. L. Rev.* 553 (1872).

"The Arrangement of the Law — Privity," 7 *Am. L. Rev.* 46 (1872).

"'Cases Decided in the District and Circuit Courts of the United States for the Pennsylvania District . . . ,'" 5 *Am. L. Rev.* 725 (1871).

"'The Code of Iowa . . . ,' 'Codification in India and England, A Speech by Mr. Fitzjames Stephen,'" 7 *Am. L. Rev.* 318 (1873) (all but the first fifteen lines).

"'The Code of Procedure of the State of New York, as Amended to 1870, With Notes on Pleading . . . ,' by John Townshend," 5 *Am. L. Rev.* 359 (1871).

"Codes, and the Arrangement of the Law," 5 *Am. L. Rev.* 1 (1870).

"'Commentaries on Equity Jurisprudence, as Administered in England and America,' by Joseph Story, LL.D. (Redfield ed., 1866)," 1 *Am. L. Rev.* 554 (1867).

"'Commentaries on Equity Jurisprudence, as Administered in England and America,' by Joseph Story," 5 *Am. L. Rev.* 115 (1870).

"Common Carriers and the Common Law," 13 *Am. L. Rev.* 609 (1879).

"Correspondence," 6 *Am. L. Rev.* 392 (1872).

"'Curiosities of the Law Reporters,' by Franklin Fiske Heard," 5 *Am. L. Rev.* 717 (1871).

"'A Digest of All the Reported Cases Decided in the Supreme Court of Errors and the Superior Court of the State of Connecticut,' by Simon E. Baldwin," 5 *Am. L. Rev.* 542 (1871).

"'A Digest of the . . . Criminal Law . . . ,' by R. A. Fisher (American Edition)," 6 *Am. L. Rev.* 737 (1872).

"'A Digest of the Decisions of the Federal Courts,' by Frederick C. Brightly," 5 *Am. L. Rev.* 539 (1871).

"'English Chancery Reports . . . ,' Volumes I–III," 6 *Am. L. Rev.* 349 (1871).

"'An Epitome and Analysis of Savigny's Treatise on Obligations in Roman Law,' by Archibald Brown," 7 *Am. L. Rev.* 320 (1873).

"'Essays in Anglo-Saxon Law,'" 11 *Am. L. Rev.* 327 (1877).

"'Essays upon the Form of the Law,' by Thomas Erskine (London, 1870)," 5 *Am. L. Rev.* 114 (1870).

"'Fire Insurance Cases,' by Edward H. Bennett," 6 *Am. L. Rev.* 731 (1872).

"The Gas Stokers' Strike," 7 *Am. L. Rev.* 582 (1873) (the first three paragraphs were written by J. T. Morse).

"Grain Elevators: On the Title to Grain in Public Elevators," 6 *Am. L. Rev.* 450 (1872).

"'The History of the Law of Tenures of Land in England and Ireland . . . ,' by W. F. Finlason," 4 *Am. L. Rev.* 752 (1870).

"'The House of Lords Cases: On Appeals and Writs of Error, and Claims of Peerage, During the Sessions 1852, 1853 and 1854 . . . ,'" 5 *Am. L. Rev.* 116 (1870).

"'The House of Lords Cases . . . Volumes V and VI,'" 5 *Am. L. Rev.* 346 (1871).

"'The House of Lords Cases . . . 1858–1864,'" 5 *Am. L. Rev.* 544 (1871).

"Impeachment [of President Johnson]," 2 *Am. L. Rev.* 547 (1868).

"'An Index of Cases Overruled, Reversed, Denied . . . ,' by Melville M. Bigelow . . . ," 7 *Am. L. Rev.* 716 (1873).

"'An Index to Precedents in Conveyancing . . . ,' by Walter A. Copinger (London 1872)," 6 *Am. L. Rev.* 732 (1872).

"'The Journal of Psychological Medicine,' for April, 1871," 5 *Am. L. Rev.* 742 (1871).

"'Judgments Delivered in the Courts of the United States for the District of Massachusetts,' by John Lowell, LL.D., District Judge . . . ," 6 *Am. L. Rev.* 743 (1872).

"'The Legal Tender Cases of 1871 . . . ,'" 7 *Am. L. Rev.* 146 (1872).

"The Ku Klux Klan Bill," 5 *Am. L. Rev.* 749 (1871).

"'Law and Practice in Bankruptcy . . . ,' by Orlando F. Bump," 5 *Am. L. Rev.* 540 (1871).

"'Law and Practice in Bankruptcy . . . ,' by Orlando F. Bump" (4th ed., 1871), 6 *Am. L. Rev.* 137 (1871).

"'The Law Magazine and Review; or, Quarterly Journal of Jurisprudence,' September, 1870, to February, 1871 . . . ," 5 *Am. L. Rev.* 541 (1871).

"'The Law Magazine and Review,' . . . April 1, 1872," 6 *Am. L. Rev.* 723 (1872).

"'The Law of Contracts . . . ,' by Francis Hilliard," 6 *Am. L. Rev.* 558 (1872).

"'The Law of Domicile as a Branch of the Law of England, Stated in the Form of Rules,' by A. V. Dicey . . . ," 14 *Am. L. Rev.* 67 (1880).

"'The Law of Negligence,' by Robert Campbell," 5 *Am. L. Rev.* 536 (1871).

"'The Law of Torts,' by C. G. Addison," 5 *Am. L. Rev.* 341 (1871).

"'The Law of Wills,' by Isaac F. Redfield," 5 *Am. L. Rev.* 546 (1871).

"'Leading and Select American Cases on the Law of Bills of Exchange, Promissory Notes, and Checks . . . ,' by Isaac F. Redfield and Melville Bigelow," 5 *Am. L. Rev.* 720 (1871).

"Letter on the Legal Tender Cases," 4 *Am. L. Rev.* 768 (1870).

"'A Manual of Medical Jurisprudence,' by Alfred Swaine Taylor," 1 *Am. L. Rev.* 377 (1867).

"'The Massachusetts Digest . . . 1857 to 1869,' by Edmund H. Bennett and Henry W. Holland," 6 *Am. L. Rev.* 733 (1872).

"'Massachusetts Reports 103 . . . ,' Albert G. Browne, Jr., Reporter," 6 *Am. L. Rev.* 350 (1871).

"'Massachusetts Reports — 104 — . . . ,'" 6 *Am. L. Rev.* 556 (1872).

"'Michigan Reports . . . from April 28, 1868, to January 11, 1869,'" 3 *Am. L. Rev.* 357 (1869).

"Misunderstandings of the Civil Law," 6 *Am. L. Rev.* 37 (1871).

"'Notes on Common Forms: A Book of Massachusetts Law,' by Uriel H. Crocker . . . ," 6 *Am. L. Rev.* 732 (1872).

"'Outlines of the Roman Law,' by T. Whitcombe Greene," 7 *Am. L. Rev.* 320 (1873).

"'. . . Palmer v. DeWitt,'" 5 *Am. L. Rev.* 567 (1871).

"Possession," 12 *Am. L. Rev.* 688 (1878).

"Primitive Notions in Modern Law," 10 *Am. L. Rev.* 422 (1876).

"Primitive Notions in Modern Law — No. II," 11 *Am. L. Rev.* 641 (1877).
"'Principles of the Law of Real Property . . . ,' by Joshua Williams . . . ," 6 *Am. L. Rev.* 549 (1872).
"Reply to Correspondent on 'The Rights of Chinamen,'" 5 *Am. L. Rev.* 750 (1871).
"'Reports of Cases Argued and Determined in the Courts of Queen's Bench and the Court of Exchequer Chamber on Appeal from the Courts of Queen's Bench,'" 3 *Am. L. Rev.* 150 (1868).
"'Reports of Cases at Law and in Chancery Argued and Determined in the Supreme Court of Illinois, Vol. XLI,'" 3 *Am. L. Rev.* 556 (1869).
"'Reports of Cases Determined in the Supreme Court of the State of Nevada During the Year 1867,'" 3 *Am. L. Rev.* 148 (1868).
"'Reports of Cases Heard and Decided in the Supreme Court of Michigan, from July 11, 1867 to April 28, 1868,'" 3 *Am. L. Rev.* 141 (1868).
"'Reports of Cases Argued and Determined in the Supreme Court of the State of Wisconsin . . . ,'" 3 *Am. L. Rev.* 147 (1868).
"'Reports of Cases on Law and Equity, Determined in the Supreme Court of the State of Iowa,'" 3 *Am. L. Rev.* 357 (1867).
"'Reports of . . . Life and Accident Insurance Cases . . . ,' by Melville M. Bigelow," 6 *Am. L. Rev.* 554 (1872).
"'Roscoe's Digest of the Law of Evidence in Criminal Cases . . . (Power, ed., 1866),'" 1 *Am. L. Rev.* 375 (1867).
"'The Science of Legal Judgment . . . ,' by John Townshend," 6 *Am. L. Rev.* 134 (1871).
"'A Selection of Cases on the Law of Contracts,' by C. C. Langdell . . . ," 5 *Am. L. Rev.* 539 (1871).
"'A Selection of Cases on the Law of Contracts,' by C. C. Langdell . . . ," 6 *Am. L. Rev.* 353 (1871).
"'A Selection of Cases on the Law of Contracts,' by C. C. Langdell . . . , 'Principles of the English Law of Contracts,' by Sir William R. Anson," 14 *Am. L. Rev.* 233 (1880).
"The Theory of Torts," 7 *Am. L. Rev.* 652 (1873).
"'A Treatise on the American Law of Easements and Servitudes,' by Emory Washburne, LL.D.," 2 *Am. L. Rev.* 159 (1867).
"'A Treatise on the Constitutional Limitations . . . ,' by Thomas M. Cooley," 6 *Am. L. Rev.* 140 (1871).
"'A Treatise on the Law and Practice as to Receivers . . . ,' by William W. Kerr," 6 *Am. L. Rev.* 729 (1872) (third paragraph).
"'A Treatise on the Law of Bills of Exchange, Promissory Notes, Bank Notes, and Checks,' by Sir Edward Byles . . . ," 2 *Am. L. Rev.* 328 (1868).
"'A Treatise on the Law of Domestic Relations,' by James Schouler," 5 *Am. L. Rev.* 113 (1870).
"'A Treatise on the Law of Fraud and Mistake . . . ,' by William W. Kerr," 6 *Am. L. Rev.* 729 (1872).
"'A Treatise on the Law of Negligence,' by Thomas G. Shearman and Amasa A. Redfield," 5 *Am. L. Rev.* 343 (1871).
"'Treatise on the Law of Private Corporations Aggregate . . . ,' by Joseph K. Angell and Samuel Ames . . . ," 5 *Am. L. Rev.* 542 (1871).
"'A Treatise on the Law of Sale of Personal Property . . . ,' by J. P. Benjamin," 3 *Am. L. Rev.* 541 (1869).
"'A Treatise on the Rules for the Selection of Parties to an Action,' by A. V. Dicey," 5 *Am. L. Rev.* 534 (1871).
"'A Treatise on the Statutes of Elizabeth Against Fraudulent Conveyances . . . ,' by Henry W. May," 5 *Am. L. Rev.* 543 (1871).

"'A Treatise upon the United States Courts, and their Practice . . . ,' by Benjamin Vaughan Abbott," 6 *Am. L. Rev.* 149 (1871).

"Trespass and Negligence," 14 *Am. L. Rev.* 1 (1880).

"'United States Reports, Supreme Court, Vol. 94 . . . ,'" 12 *Am. L. Rev.* 354 (1878).

"Ultra Vires: How Far Are Corporations Liable for Acts Not Authorized by Their Charters?" 5 *Am. L. Rev.* 272 (1871).

LATER ARTICLES

Those marked with an asterisk were reprinted in Holmes's *Collected Legal Papers* (1920); the remainder, except "Just the Boy Wanted," were collected in H. Shriver, *Justice Oliver Wendell Holmes — His Book Notices, and Uncollected Letters and Papers* (1936).

"Agency; I," 4 *Harv. L. Rev.* 345 (1891).*

"Agency; II," 5 *Harv. L. Rev.* 1 (1891).*

"Are Great Fortunes Great Dangers?" *Cosmopolitan*, February, 1906; reprinted as "Economic Elements" in *Collected Legal Papers* (1920).

"Arthur Dehon," in T. W. Higginson, ed., *Harvard Memorial Biographies*. Cambridge, Mass., 1866.

"The Bar as a Profession," 70 *Youth's Companion* 92 (1896).*

"*Bracton de Legibus et Consuetudinibus Angliae*, George E. Woodbine, ed. . . ." (book review), 5 *Yale L. Rev.* 223 (1915).*

"Early English Equity," 1 *Law Quarterly Review* 162 (1885).*

"Executors," 9 *Harv. L. Rev.* 42 (1895).*

"John Chipman Gray," in *John Chipman Gray*. Boston: privately printed, 1917; reprinted, H. Shriver, *Justice Oliver Wendell Holmes — His Book Notices* (1936), p. 133.

"'A History of English Law,' by W. S. Holdsworth . . . vols. II and III," 25 *Law Quarterly Review* 412 (1909).*

"Ideals and Doubts," 10 *Illinois Law Review* 1 (1915).

"In Memoriam: F. W. Maitland," 23 *Law Quarterly Review* 137 (1907).*

Introduction, in F. Frankfurter, ed., *Mr. Justice Brandeis*. New Haven: Yale University Press, 1932.

Introduction, in Continental Legal Historical Series, vol. 1: *General Survey*. Boston: Little, Brown, 1913.*

Introduction, in J. H. Wigmore and A. Kocourek, eds., *Rational Basis of Legal Institutions*. New York: Macmillan, 1923.

Introduction, in Baron de Montesquieu, *The Spirit of the Laws*, reprint ed. Thomas Nugent, trans.; revised by J. V. Prichard. 2 vols. New York: D. Appleton and Co., 1900.

"Just the Boy Wanted: II, In the Law," *Youth's Companion*, February 7, 1889, p. 73.

"Law in Science and Science in Law," 12 *Harv. L. Rev.* 443 (1899).*

Letter, *New Republic*, January 2, 1920, p. 250.

Letter, 2 *Federal Bar Journal* 177 (1935).

Letter, 51 *Law Quarterly Review* 4 (1935).

Letter, 22 *Green Bag* 528 (1910).

"Natural Law," 32 *Harv. L. Rev.* 40 (1918).

"The Path of the Law," 10 *Harv. L. Rev.* 457 (1897),* published simultaneously as "Law and the Study of Law," 9 *Juridical Review* 105 (1897).

"Privilege, Malice, and Intent," 8 *Harv. L. Rev.* 1 (1894).*

"The Theory of Legal Interpretation," 12 *Harv. L. Rev.* 417 (1899).*

HOLMES'S PUBLISHED WORKS — LETTERS

IN BOOKS

Burton, David H., ed., *Holmes–Sheehan Correspondence: The Letters of Justice Oliver Wendell Holmes and Canon Patrick Sheehan.* Port Washington, N.Y.: Kennikat Press, 1976.

———, *Progressive Masks: Letters of Oliver Wendell Holmes, Jr., and Franklin Ford.* Newark, Del.: University of Delaware Press, 1982.

Howe, Mark DeWolfe, *Holmes–Laski Letters: The Correspondence of Mr. Justice Holmes and Harold J. Laski 1916–1935,* 2 vols. Cambridge, Mass.: Harvard University Press, 1953.

———, *Holmes–Pollock Letters: The Correspondence of Mr. Justice Holmes and Sir Frederick Pollock 1874–1932,* 2 vols. Cambridge, Mass.: Harvard University Press, 1941.

———, *Touched with Fire: Civil War Letters and Diary of Oliver Wendell Holmes, Jr., 1861–1864.* Cambridge, Mass.: Harvard University Press, 1946.

Peabody, James Bishop, *The Holmes–Einstein Letters: Correspondence of Mr. Justice Holmes and Lewis Einstein 1903–1935.* London: Macmillan, 1964.

IN PERIODICALS

Kanda, James and William A. Gifford, "The Kaneko Correspondence," 37 *Monumenta Nipponica* Nos. 1–4 (1982). Contains selections from the Holmes–Kaneko Kentaro correspondence.

Cohen, Felix S., "The Holmes–Cohen Correspondence," 9 *Journal of the History of Ideas* 1 (1948), (Holmes–Morris R. Cohen correspondence); reprinted in L. C. Rosenfield, *Portrait of a Philosopher* (1962).

Wu, John C. H., "Some Recent Letters of Justice Holmes," *T'ien Hsia Monthly,* October, 1935, p. 251 (Holmes–Wu correspondence); reprinted in H. Shriver, *Justice Oliver Wendell Holmes: His Book Notices and Uncollected Letters and Papers* (1936), p. 151.

HOLMES'S PUBLISHED WORKS — OPINIONS

Holmes's published opinions appear in the reports of the Massachusetts Supreme Judicial Court and the United States Supreme Court, from 1883 to 1932. He published more than 2,000 signed opinions (and an uncounted number of unsigned memorandum opinions), perhaps more than any other judge writing for courts of last resort. On the United States Supreme Court, he published 975 opinions; 873 for the full Court (more than any other justice), 30 concurring opinions and 72 dissenting opinions (at least ten other justices have published more dissents). See P. Blaustein and R. Mersky, *The First One Hundred Justices* (1978), p. 102. The Massachusetts opinions are listed in chronological order by Harry Shriver in *Judicial Opinions of Oliver Wendell Holmes* (1940), and listed topically by Felix Frankfurter, 44 *Harv. L. Rev.* 799 (1931). The United States Supreme Court opinions are listed chronologically in an appendix to Edward J. Bander, *Justice Holmes ex Cathedra* (1966), and the opinions through February 24, 1931, are arranged topically by Frankfurter, above. There are several useful collections of the better known opinions, as follows.

Lerner, Max, ed., *The Mind and Faith of Justice Holmes; His Speeches, Essays, Letters and Judicial Opinions.* Boston: Little, Brown, 1943 (selected Massachusetts and

United States Supreme Court opinions). This is by far the best annotated and most useful collection.

Lief, Alfred, ed., *The Dissenting Opinions of Mr. Justice Holmes.* New York: Vanguard, 1931 (United States Supreme Court dissents to October term, 1930).

————, ed., *Representative Opinions of Mr. Justice Holmes.* New York: Vanguard, 1931 (selected United States Supreme Court opinions).

Shriver, Harry C., *Judicial Opinions of Oliver Wendell Holmes.* Buffalo: Dennis, 1940 (selected Massachusetts opinions).

Manuscript Collections

In addition to the following specific collections, references are made to records kept in the Harvard University Archives, the Boston Athenaeum, and the Berkshire Athenaeum in Pittsfield, Massachusetts. The originals of Holmes's letters to Lewis Einstein are in the Library of Congress with Einstein's papers, but I have cited to the published versions; see above. Holmes's correspondence with Rosika Schwimmer, not cited here, is among the Schwimmer–Lloyd papers in the New York Public Library. The originals of Holmes's letters to Lady Castletown are in private collections; photocopies and typescripts are among the Holmes Papers at Harvard.

Felix Frankfurter Papers, Library of Congress, Washington, D.C., and Harvard Law School Library, Cambridge, Massachusetts.

Grant Gilmore Papers, Harvard Law School Library, Cambridge, Massachusetts.

Isabella Stewart Gardner Papers, Gardner Museum, Boston.

James Family Papers, Houghton Library, Harvard University, Cambridge, Massachusetts.

Learned Hand Papers, Harvard Law School Library, Cambridge, Massachusetts.

Oliver Wendell Holmes Papers, Houghton Library, Harvard University, Cambridge, Massachusetts.

Oliver Wendell Holmes, Jr., Papers, Harvard Law School Library, Cambridge, Massachusetts.

Thornton Hunt Papers, Keats House, Hampstead, London.

James Family Papers, Houghton Library, Harvard University, Cambridge, Massachusetts.

Leslie Scott Papers, University of Warwick Library, Modern Records Centre, Coventry.

Shattuck Family Papers, Massachusetts Historical Society, Boston, Massachusetts.

Arthur E. Sutherland Papers, Harvard Law School Library, Cambridge, Massachusetts.

William Howard Taft Papers, Library of Congress, Washington, D.C.

Notes

Names have been abbreviated as follows:

OWH — Oliver Wendell Holmes (1841–1935).
OWH Sr. — Oliver Wendell Holmes (1809–1894).
ALH — Amelia Lee (Jackson) Holmes, OWH's mother.
AJH — Amelia Jackson Holmes, OWH's sister.
EJH — Edward Jackson ("Ned") Holmes, OWH's brother.
EJH Jr. — Edward Jackson Holmes, Jr., OWH's nephew.
FBH — Fanny B. (Dixwell) Holmes, OWH's wife.

Manuscript collections are referred to as follows (see also the Bibliography, above):

HLS — Harvard Law School Library
LOC — Library of Congress
MHS — Massachusetts Historical Society

Thus, "OWH Papers, HLS," refers to the Oliver Wendell Holmes, Jr., Papers, at the Harvard Law School Library, Cambridge, Massachusetts. In citations to manuscript collections, manuscript box and folder numbers are indicated: B1 F1.

A few frequently cited books are referred to by abbreviated titles, as follows:

BOWEN — Catherine Drinker Bowen, *Yankee from Olympus: Justice Holmes and His Family* (Boston: Atlantic/Little, Brown, 1944).

BRUCE — Col. George A. Bruce, *The Twentieth Regiment of Massachusetts Volunteer Infantry 1861–1865* (Boston: Houghton Mifflin, 1906).

1 HOWE — Mark DeWolfe Howe, *Justice Oliver Wendell Holmes: The Shaping Years, 1841–1870* (Cambridge, Mass.: Harvard University Press, 1957).

2 HOWE — Mark DeWolfe Howe, *Justice Oliver Wendell Holmes: The Proving Years, 1870–1882* (Cambridge, Mass.: Harvard University Press, 1963).

OWH SR. WORKS — Oliver Wendell Holmes, *The Collected Works of Oliver Wendell Holmes* (Boston: Houghton Mifflin, 1891).

SPEECHES — Mark DeWolfe Howe, comp., *The Occasional Speeches of Justice Oliver Wendell Holmes* (Cambridge, Mass.: Harvard University Press, 1962).

TWF — Mark DeWolfe Howe, ed., *Touched with Fire: Civil War Letters and Diary of Oliver Wendell Holmes, Jr., 1861–1864* (Cambridge, Mass.: Harvard University Press, 1946).

The letters of OWH that have been published are listed in the bibliography, above, and are cited uniformly as HOLMES–LASKI LETTERS, HOLMES–POLLOCK LETTERS, etc. Citations are given to published works whenever possible, but the text has been verified against the originals in most cases. In a few of Holmes's published letters the original punctuation has been restored.

Mark Antony DeWolfe Howe, biographer of OWH, Sr., is referred to throughout as M. A. DeW. Howe. His son, Mark DeWolfe Howe, OWH's authorized biographer, is referred to by his full name or simply as Mark Howe.

CHAPTER 1. FATHERS AND SONS

1. OWH Sr. to John L. Motley, quoted M. A. DEW. HOWE, HOLMES OF THE BREAKFAST-TABLE 126–127 (1939).

2. V. BROOKS, THE FLOWERING OF NEW ENGLAND 29 (1936). The site of the house, which is not marked, is now covered by Harvard's Littauer Center.

3. OWH Sr. to Rev. William Jenks, February 21, 1839, quoted E. TILTON, AMIABLE AUTOCRAT 147 (1947).

4. "Old Ironsides," in 12 OWH SR. WORKS 2 (1891). See also from this time "The Last Leaf," 12 OWH SR. WORKS 3.

5. OWH Sr. to Phinehas Barnes, March, 1831, quoted 1 J. T. MORSE, LIFE AND LETTERS OF OLIVER WENDELL HOLMES 69 (1896).

6. The treatise was C. JACKSON, A TREATISE ON THE PLEADINGS AND PRACTICE IN REAL ACTIONS (1828). In Holmes's library at his death were two copies of this book, one of which was inscribed by Judge Jackson to Chancellor Kent, possibly purchased by John Chipman Gray, inscribed by him, and then inherited by Holmes when Gray died in 1910. See OWH Papers, HLS, Paige Box 25. Kent's flattering letter, the published review and Jackson's reply are in the inscribed copy.

7. Bedford Place ran part of the way between Bedford Street and Summer Street; it was later absorbed into the present Chauncy Street.

8. Montgomery Place is now Bosworth Street. The house in which Wendell Holmes was born was torn down after the Civil War and nothing now marks its place, but a bronze plaque nearby says, "Birthplace of Francis Amasa Walker 1840–1897." Walker was the third president of M.I.T., who apparently lived next door.

9. See the letters, "privately held," quoted by E. TILTON, AMIABLE AUTOCRAT (1947), and the interview notes collected by Mark Howe from those still surviving who remembered Amelia Holmes, OWH Papers, HLS, B53 F13. One

contemporary referred to her as "dull and stupid, though very affectionate" (OWH Papers, HLS, B53 F13).

10. ALH to OWH, May 21, 1866, OWH Papers, HLS, B44 F9.

11. OWH Sr. to Ann [Upham], March 9, 1841, OWH Sr. Papers, Houghton. This letter is often quoted, see, *e.g.*, BOWEN 86 (misidentifying Ann Upham as a younger sister).

CHAPTER 2. IN THE DOCTOR'S HOUSE

1. For descriptions of Montgomery Place in the 1840s, see W. S. KENNEDY, OLIVER WENDELL HOLMES: POET, LITTÉRATEUR, SCIENTIST 115 (1883); the trellis over the door is found in BOWEN 97. See also J. KAY, LOST BOSTON 92 (1980); E. HALE, A NEW ENGLAND BOYHOOD 3–4 (1964, first ed. 1893), describing Boston just before Holmes was born. As to the antiquity of the steps down to Providence Street, see OWH to William F. Barry, April 1, 1930, OWH Papers, HLS, B36 F27.

2. *Reflections on the Past and Future,* SPEECHES 163, 164; see also OWH to Harold Laski, May 8, 1918, 1 HOLMES-LASKI LETTERS 152, 154.

3. See, e.g., Sutherland, "Recollections of Justice Holmes," Arthur E. Sutherland Papers, HLS, B24 F7.

4. *A Provisional Adieu,* SPEECHES 150, 151. As to the whale-oil lamps, see A. E. Sutherland, "Reflections on the Past and Future," Arthur E. Sutherland Papers, HLS, B24 F7, and *Over the Teacups,* 4 OWH SR. WORKS 32. As to Sunday dinners and "stick-jaw," see Mark Howe, memorandum of interview with Austin W. Clarke, May, 1948, OWH Papers, HLS, B54 F6.

5. OWH to Harold Laski, July 16, 1918, 1 HOLMES–LASKI LETTERS 161, 162.

6. OWH to Alice S. Green, October 14, 1911, OWH Papers, HLS, B43.

7. Holmes told this story repeatedly in his old age; see, *e.g.*, F. BIDDLE, MR. JUSTICE HOLMES 20 (1942).

8. OWH Papers, HLS, B69 F1.

9. See Holmes's copybook, OWH Papers, HLS, B69 F1.

10. For a contemporary engraving of the celebration, see J. KAY, LOST BOSTON 138–139 (1980).

11. *Reflections on the Past and Future,* SPEECHES 163, recalling the Cochituate celebration, the funeral of John Quincy Adams, or "I know not what." Holmes often recalled this image — see for instance OWH to Frederick Pollock, April 27, 1919, 1 HOLMES-POLLOCK LETTERS 10, 11 — but Revolutionary War veterans apparently were not carried in either parade. See the Boston Post for March 11, 1848, p. 2, *Reception of the Remains of Mr. Adams in Boston,* and October 27, 1848, p. 2, *The Water Celebration.* It seems most likely that Holmes combined the memory of a Fourth of July parade with that of the Water Celebration; I have given the memory, rather than the event, in the text.

12. The town was named Boston Plantation at that time, and was renamed Pittsfield when the Civil War began.

13. *The Autocrat of the Breakfast-Table,* 1 OWH SR. WORKS 230–234.

14. OWH to Epes S. Dixwell, "July 11," probably 1853, OWH Papers, HLS, B21 F2.

15. Among the Holmes papers, there are nine sheets of pencil sketches of a curiously shaped stone, spotted with moss, perhaps suggesting the head of a lion, and drawn from slightly different angles. On one sheet is written, "From left of door." Pinned to the sketches is an envelope on which is written "Mrs. O.W. Holmes" in pencil. The connection with Holmes is conjectural, but seems likely.

16. OWH, Sr., 1854, quoted E. TILTON, AMIABLE AUTOCRAT 219 (1947).

17. Mrs. Kellogg's reminiscences of Dr. Holmes's visits are in a paper she read on June 10, 1895, to a church gathering shortly after the doctor's death; see the Springfield Republican March 5, 1945, Berkshire Athenaeum, "Berkshire Authors Room."

18. OWH to Harold Laski, March 27, 1921, 1 HOLMES–LASKI LETTERS 322, 323. John Updike suggested that Melville came to the doctor to be examined for insanity, in the difficult time after the failure of PIERRE, around 1852. Updike, *Reflections: Melville's Withdrawal*, THE NEW YORKER, April 10, 1982, p. 120.

19. H. ADAMS, THE EDUCATION OF HENRY ADAMS 38 (1918). Holmes said, "H.A. in his Education seems to me to drool about science and all his damned education [but] to talk about Boston and our boyhood with almost genius." OWH to Baroness Moncheur, December 24, 1920, OWH Papers, HLS.

20. OWH to Nina Gray, July 21, 1891, OWH Papers, HLS; see also 1 HOWE 32; Epes Sargent Dixwell to OWH, December 10, 1882, and the report card from Mr. Dixwell's school, OWH Papers, HLS, B42 F11.

21. Mark Howe, memorandum of interview with Austin W. Clarke, May, 1948, OWH Papers, HLS, B54 F6.

22. See, e.g., E. W. EMERSON, *Oliver Wendell Holmes,* in EARLY YEARS OF THE SATURDAY CLUB 143, 156 (1918); M. A. DEW. HOWE, HOLMES OF THE BREAKFAST-TABLE 96 (1939).

23. M. A. DEW. HOWE, HOLMES OF THE BREAKFAST-TABLE 95 (1939), quoting N. P. Willis in the HOME JOURNAL.

24. 1 HOWE 19.

25. *The Autocrat of the Breakfast-Table,* 1 OWH SR. WORKS 1, 7.

26. *The Professor at the Breakfast-Table,* 2 OWH SR. WORKS 94–95; OWH to Felix Frankfurter, May 21, 1926, OWH Papers, HLS; see also 1 HOWE 27, and sources cited there.

27. ALH to OWH, May 21, 1866, OWH Papers, HLS, B44 F9.

28. ALH to OWH, July 22, 1866, OWH Papers, HLS, B44 F9.

29. ALH to OWH, June 11, 1866, OWH Papers, HLS, B44 F9.

30. See, among other similar remarks, OWH on Charles Sumner: "His judgment like his speech to me, seemed to me formal and priggish — not that of real sympathy and insight." OWH to Harold Laski, January 14, 1920, 1 HOLMES–LASKI LETTERS 232.

31. OWH to Frederick Pollock, August 16, 1929, 2 HOLMES–POLLOCK LETTERS 251, 253.

32. ALH to Emily Hallowell, February 1, 1863, OWH Papers, HLS, B44 F7.

33. New York Daily Tribune, quoted 61 CALIF. L. REV. 165 (1973).

34. Richard Henry Dana, Jr.'s diary, quoted 61 CALIF. L. REV. 165 (1973).

35. OWH to Canon Sheehan, October 27, 1912, HOLMES–SHEEHAN LETTERS 51.

CHAPTER 3. EDUCATION

1. See E. TILTON, AMIABLE AUTOCRAT 231 (1947). The New York lecture is quoted in M. A. DEW. HOWE, HOLMES OF THE BREAKFAST-TABLE 88–91 (1939).

2. OWH, Sr., letter quoted in the Pittsfield Eagle, April 6, 1961.

3. Ralph Waldo Emerson, quoted in E. W. EMERSON, *Oliver Wendell Holmes,* in THE EARLY YEARS OF THE SATURDAY CLUB 141, 151 (1918).

4. *The Autocrat of the Breakfast-Table,* 1 OWH SR. WORKS 1, 83.

5. T. W. HIGGINSON, ARMY LIFE IN A BLACK REGIMENT 15 (1984; first ed. 1869).

6. G. SANTAYANA, PERSONS AND PLACES 192–193 (1944). Santayana attended Harvard after the Civil War.

7. BOWEN 119.

8. See S. E. MORISON, THREE CENTURIES OF HARVARD 301 (1936); E. SAMUELS, THE YOUNG HENRY ADAMS 24 (1948).

9. S. E. MORISON, THREE CENTURIES OF HARVARD 307 (1936), quoting an unnamed graduate of about this time. See also H. ADAMS, EDUCATION (1908); G. SANTAYANA, PERSONS AND PLACES (1944).

10. OWH, *Books,* 4 HARV. MAG. 408 (1858). Copies of Holmes's early publications are in the OWH Papers, HLS, Paige Box 22.

11. OWH, *Books,* 4 HARV. MAG. 408 (1858). As much as he was attacking orthodoxy Holmes was also reacting against the vague mysticism of his father's generation, pungently described by James Russell Lowell:

> Bran had its prophets, and the presartorial simplicity of Adam its martyrs. . . . Plainness of speech was carried to a pitch that would have taken away the breath of George Fox; and even swearing had its evangelists. . . . Communities were established where everything was to be common. . . . Men renounced their old gods, and hesitated whether to bestow their furloughed allegiance on Thor or Budh.

J. R. Lowell, *Thoreau,* reprinted in E. WILSON, THE SHOCK OF RECOGNITION 229–230 (1955). The similarity of the Transcendentalists to the generation that grew up in the 1960s has been remarked before; I suppose there is also a similarity in the rebellions of their hard-minded, greedy, and romantic children. Wendell, at any rate, adopted a hard-minded scientism in opposition to the soft unfocused religiosity of his father's circle.

See, for instance, Holmes's well-known letter to Morris Cohen:

> My father was brought up scientifically — i.e. he studied medicine in France — and I was not. Yet there was with him as with the rest of his generation a certain softness of attitude toward the interstitial miracle — the phenomenon without phenomenal antecedents — that I did not feel. The difference was in the air, although perhaps only a few of my time felt it. The Origin of Species I think came out while I was in college — H. Spencer had announced his intention to put the universe into our pockets — I hadn't read either of them, to be sure, but as I say it was in the air. . . . Emerson and Ruskin were the men who set me on fire. Probably a skeptical temperament I got from my mother had something to do with my way of thinking. Then I was in with the abolitionists, some of whom were skeptics as well as dogmatists. But I think science was at the bottom. Of course my father was by no means orthodox, but like other even lax Unitarians there were questions that he didn't like to have asked — and he always spoke of keeping his mind open on matters like spiritualism or whether Bacon wrote Shakespeare — so that when I wanted to be disagreeable I told him that he straddled, in order to be able to say, whatever might be accepted, well I have always recognized, etc., which was not just on my part.

OWH to Morris R. Cohen, February 5, 1919, HOLMES–COHEN LETTERS 313, 321. Holmes seemed to be saying here that among the sources of his scientific inspiration were Emerson and Ruskin. His "science" seems to have been a kind of pre-Darwinian evolutionism that was in the air — see J. W. BURROW, EVOLUTION AND SOCIETY (1966) — but that does not look very scientific to a modern eye.

12. See OWH to "l.b." (Clara Stevens), April 16, 1914, OWH Papers, HLS; OWH to Lewis Einstein April 17, 1914, HOLMES–EINSTEIN LETTERS 89.

13. Emily Hallowell to Mark Howe, May 24, 1942, OWH Papers, HLS, B43 F27.

14. OWH to Miss [Lucy] Hale, April 24, 1858, OWH Papers, HLS, B52, "Miscellany."

15. OWH to Harold Laski, February 27, 1917, 1 HOLMES–LASKI LETTERS 63.

16. *Id.*

17. OWH to Clara Stevens, February 9, 1916, OWH Papers, HLS (Holmes is speaking of the discovery made in his college years).

18. OWH to Miss [Lucy] Hale, April 24, 1858, OWH Papers, HLS, B52, "Miscellany."

19. *Id.*

20. OWH to Lucy [Hale], May 24, 1858, OWH Papers, HLS, B52, "Miscellany."

21. BOWEN 99; Mark Howe interview notes, OWH Papers, HLS. Howe's informant asked not to be quoted by name, and Bowen gives no source.

22. OWH, *Alma Mater,* 7 HARV. MAG. 49 (1860). In the OWH Papers, HLS, Paige Box 22, are Mark Howe's notes, apparently prepared for a contemplated edition of Holmes's published writings, in which he says:

> Holmes is identified as the author of [several minor publications including "Alma Mater"] in an index of *The Harvard Magazine,* prepared by his classmate Frank Warren Hackett, and preserved in the Harvard University Archives.

23. OWH to Harold Laski, May 18, 1919, 1 HOLMES–LASKI LETTERS 204, 205.

24. OWH Sr. to John L. Motley, April 29, 1860, in 2 THE CORRESPONDENCE OF JOHN LOTHROP MOTLEY 87, 90 (G. W. Curtis ed., 1900).

25. The Hasty Pudding Club programs are in the Harvard University Archives. For Holmes's shingle, see L. GARRISON, AN ILLUSTRATED HISTORY OF HASTY PUDDING CLUB THEATRICALS 20–21 (1892). Forty-two years later, in a memorable opinion, Holmes held for the Supreme Court that posters advertising a circus were entitled to copyright protection because they displayed the individual authorship required by the statute. See *Bleistein v. Donaldson Lithographing Co.,* 188 U.S. 239 (1903), discussed below.

26. See Cornelius Felton to OWH, Sr., July, 1861, quoted in M. A. DEW. HOWE, HOLMES OF THE BREAKFAST-TABLE 104 (1939): ("your son, who is to an unusual degree a favorite of mine . . .").

27. OWH, *Albert Durer,* 7 HARV. MAG. 58 (1860).

28. Chauncey Belknap's stenographic notes of OWH's conversation on March 30, 1916, OWH Papers, HLS, B54 F5. Belknap was Holmes's secretary at the time, and this was one of Holmes's chestnuts. See, *e.g.,* E. SERGEANT, *Oliver Wendell Holmes,* in FIRE UNDER THE ANDES 307, 315 (1927), giving the same account almost verbatim, ten years later.

29. "The book that I remember as marking my transit from boy to young man, before I went to college, is *Hours with the Mystics.*" OWH to Frederick Pollock, December 7, 1927, 2 HOLMES–POLLOCK LETTERS 207. R. A. VAUGHAN, HOURS WITH THE MYSTICS, was first published in London in 1856, and according to the Boston Athenaeum records, it was charged out to the Holmes family for a week on February 20, 1860, in the midst of Wendell's readings on Plato. See also OWH to Baroness Moncheur, November 22, 1918, OWH Papers, HLS, B36 F3 ("the first serious book I remember reading as a boy"): 1 HOWE 34.

30. Chauncey Belknap's stenographic notes of Holmes's conversation on

March 30, 1916, OWH Papers, HLS, B54 F5. The two essays were published as *Notes on Albert Durer*, 7 HARV. MAG. 6 (Oct., 1860), and *Plato*, 2 UNIV. Q. 205 (Oct., 1860), in each case as the lead article in the issue.

The Dürer article is an elegant and mature appreciation, of which scholars still think well; see 1 HOWE 57 and sources cited there; it is also an homage to Emerson, and accordingly drew sharp criticism from a member of the Christian Brotherhood, who viewed Emerson as a dangerous atheist, *A Review*, 7 HARV. MAG. 143 (1880); see also 1 HOWE 59.

Wendell describes Dürer as expressing an unconscious ideal spirit, and compares him to Plato, whom Wendell calls an "artist among thinkers." This much of his essay seems to draw on the idealism of his father's generation.

The essay on Plato takes the other side of the coin, and argues that science has shown idealism to be factually wrong, to be an early stage of primitive thought.

Taken together, the two essays give in embryo Holmes's mature philosophy. The judge, like the artist, expresses unconscious ideals, while the scientist (or lawyer) studies the work of the judges or the artists, to find the laws of their development.

Still lacking, however, was the rigorous materialism that Wendell would later profess and that would give his thought its distinctive character. In the Plato essay, like the doctor's somewhat later *Mechanism in Thought and Morals*, Wendell still preserved a dualism, so as to maintain a sort of enclave within the material world for a subjective spirit of self, a disembodied will. He surrendered this enclave after his experience of combat in the Civil War, and thereafter maintained that self-awareness was simply a material function, and that the "self" was only an illusion produced by evolving organisms to further their survival.

31. Chauncey Belknap's stenographic notes of Holmes's conversation on March 30, 1916, OWH Papers, HLS, B54 F5. See also E. SERGEANT, OLIVER WENDELL HOLMES, in FIRE UNDER THE ANDES 307, 315 (1927).

CHAPTER 4. SWIMMING IN AIR

1. 12 OWH SR. WORKS 284.

2. The bill of fare for the dinner at Porter's on January 11, 1861, and the ode sung at the dinner are in the Hasty Pudding Club records, in the Harvard Archives.

3. G. SMALLEY, ANGLO-AMERICAN MEMORIES 84–87 (1911).

4. This letter is in Holmes's Civil War Scrapbook, OWH Papers, HLS, Paige Box 4; quoted 1 HOWE 66.

5. 9 Emerson's Journal 305, quoted J. PORTE, EMERSON IN HIS JOURNALS 492–493 (1982); G. W. ALLEN, WALDO EMERSON 606–607 (1981).

6. Mark Howe's copy of passages from William Bartlett's diary, shown to him by Edith Bartlett, OWH Papers, HLS, B65 F12.

7. To his wife, July 20, 1861, 2 THE CORRESPONDENCE OF JOHN LOTHROP MOTLEY 191, 194 (G. W. Curtis ed. 1900).

8. *Memorial Day Address*, SPEECHES 4–5.

9. OWH SR., *Bread and the Newspapers*, 8 OWH SR. WORKS, 1, 9.

10. J. L. Motley to OWH, Sr., quoted in H. COMMAGER, THE AMERICAN MIND 52 (1951); J. FRASER, AMERICA AND THE PATTERNS OF CHIVALRY 14 (1982).

11. SPEECHES 78–79. This was a common illusion. Gen. Thomas Hyde recalled that at the time of his enlistment in 1861, "It [was] hard to imagine our forefathers of the Revolution as other than men gray and grave in homespun garb of the Continental cut; but they were boys like these, ruddy and of cheerful countenance." T. HYDE, FOLLOWING THE GREEK CROSS 15 (1894).

Doctor Holmes had the same fancy: "The young fellows who fell in our earlier struggle seemed like old men to us until within these last few months; now we remember they were like these fiery youth." *Bread and the Newspaper,* 8 OWH SR. WORKS 1, 13.

12. E. EMERSON, LIFE AND LETTERS OF CHARLES RUSSELL LOWELL v (1907). This must be understood in a narrow sense, of course. Few Harvard students left school. The small group who considered themselves aristocrats, however, who felt themselves knights of a Massachusetts gentry, had no choice and wanted none.

13. Charles Russell Lowell, Jr., to his brother James Jackson Lowell, April 29, 1861, E. EMERSON, LIFE AND LETTERS OF CHARLES RUSSELL LOWELL 204 (1907).

14. ALH to Emily Hallowell, February 1, 1863, HLS, B44 F7. This was written after two years of war, and after Holmes, on whom she doted, had been seriously wounded twice.

15. Cornelius Felton to OWH, Sr., OWH Papers, HLS, B65 F4 (copy).

16. Bartlett's Diary, OWH Papers, HLS, B65 F12 (copy).

17. T. HIGGINSON, *Preface,* 1 HARVARD MEMORIAL BIOGRAPHIES ii (1866).

18. OWH to ALH, May 1, 1861, in TWF 3, 4.

19. Dr. Holmes had delivered his first novel — *Elsie Venner* — to the press, and there was no *Autocrat* in preparation. The two men probably now had the conversations about the risk of painful death and the unreality of deathbed conversions, to which Wendell referred in his diary account of the Battle of Ball's Bluff. See below.

20. Holmes later told his clerks that his father had given him the laudanum. See *The Great Span,* THE NEW YORKER, April 5, 1970, pp. 29, 30.

21. E. TILTON, AMIABLE AUTOCRAT 265 (1947), citing "manuscript letter A. J. Browne to Lee." The date on which Wendell actually was commissioned is uncertain, and he might have had news of the decision at almost any time in July. The official notice of the commission to him is dated July 23, 1861. Civil War Scrapbook, OWH Papers, HLS, Paige Box 4. The commission, when it was granted, was back-dated to July 10, to coincide with all the Twentieth officers' commissions. It seems likely that despite the doctor's intervention, Holmes did not receive a commission in the Twentieth until the urgent reorganization of the army following the Battle of Bull Run created vacancies in the Twentieth.

22. BRUCE.

23. Typewritten memoirs of Carolyn (Kellogg) Cushing, courtesy of Dr. Franklin Paddock. A version of these memoirs was published as *The Gallant Captain and the Little Girl,* 155 ATLANTIC MONTHLY 545 (1935).

24. More than fifty years later, when Holmes was a justice of the Supreme Court, Carolyn Kellogg, then Mrs. Cushing, visited him in Washington and his wife introduced her to other guests as Wendell's "first love." Springfield Republican, March 5, 1945.

25. See 1 HOWE 84, 296–297, citing correspondence in Massachusetts archives.

26. Unless otherwise noted, the history of the Twentieth is taken from BRUCE.

27. OWH to ALH, September 11, 1861, TWF 6–7; BRUCE 9–10.

28. OWH to ALH, September 8, 1861, TWF 4–6. The sonnet describes the poet as in a dark wooded valley, crying out, "Is there no hope?" He gives no hint of the reason for his despair. His cry is answered:

> *Hearken — A soft melodious rapture thrills*
> *As from the forest's deepest heart replied*
> *Their hermit — and the music multiplied*

And rose echoing upward far and wide
From the dark valley to the sunlit hills —

Mark Howe twice gives the poem in full — TWF 6; 1 HOWE 89. The principal image in this poem is one Wendell would use often — an image of sunlight striking hilltops, leaving the valleys between in shadow. In this poem, for perhaps the first and last time, he puts himself in the shrouded valley, and looks up to the hills. After the war, he always placed himself on the heights, looking from peak to sunlit peak.

29. OWH to ALH, September 8, 1861, in TWF 4, 5.
30. OWH to ALH, September 1, 1861, TWF 6.
31. 1 HOWE 91, quoting Charles Whittier's memoir in the Boston Public Library, Twentieth Regiment collection.
32. BRUCE 15.
33. OWH to ALH, September 23, 1861, TWF 8; 1 HOWE 92.
34. *Id.*
35. OWH to ALH, September 23, 1861, TWF at 9, 1 HOWE 93.
36. OWH to ALH, September 23, 1861, TWF at 12.
37. BRUCE 20–21.
38. *Id.*

CHAPTER 5. SOMEONE HAD BLUNDERED

1. From General Stone's official report of the battle, quoted in J. PATCH, THE BATTLE OF BALL'S BLUFF 27 (1958). The account of the battle that follows is drawn from Patch and the sources he cites, HOWE, BRUCE, TWF, and William Bartlett's letters and diary. As might be expected, the accounts differ, and I have tried to extract the common elements.
2. BRUCE 30–31; see also M. Phillips, *Bungled River Crossing*, AMERICA'S CIVIL WAR, September, 1988, pp. 42, 45.
3. William Bartlett to his mother, October 25, 1861, in F. PALFREY, MEMOIR OF WILLIAM FRANCIS BARTLETT 19, 23–24 (1878); see also 1 HOWE 96.
4. F. PALFREY, MEMOIR OF WILLIAM FRANCIS BARTLETT 25 (1878).
5. J. PATCH, THE BATTLE OF BALL'S BLUFF 16 (1958).
6. Quoted in J. PATCH, THE BATTLE OF BALL'S BLUFF 18–19 (1958).
7. BRUCE vii.
8. Holmes was an atheist, engaged like many of his generation in constructing a rationalist substitute for religious belief; see, e.g., his undergraduate essay on Dürer, above.
9. This account is on loose sheets torn from an earlier memorandum book and inserted into the war diary Holmes preserved, now in the OWH Papers, HLS. Mark Howe speculated that the loose sheets were written late in the war, or after Holmes left the army. This is probably correct. The quoted passage may have been written in the spring of 1864, when Holmes was detailed to the Sixth Corps and had considerable leisure. When the fighting started he sent some diaries home for safekeeping, and this passage is probably all he kept of those. The text given here is from TWF 23–29. See also 1 HOWE 102–108. An emphasis in the second sentence of the original has been deleted.
10. TWF 13.
11. *Id.* 13–14.
12. Leesburg Democratic Mirror, Nov. 27, 1861, reprinted J. PATCH, THE BATTLE OF BALL'S BLUFF (1957).
13. *The Lounger,* 5 HARPER'S WEEKLY 706 (1861).

14. 2 THE CORRESPONDENCE OF JOHN LOTHROP MOTLEY 216–217 (G. W. Curtis ed. 1900).

15. OWH to Frederick Pollock, January 24, 1881, 1 HOLMES–POLLOCK LETTERS 257, 258.

16. OWH Sr. to John L. Motley, January 27, 1862, 2 THE CORRESPONDENCE OF JOHN LOTHROP MOTLEY 252, 254–255 (G. W. Curtis ed. 1900).

17. J. L. Motley to OWH Sr., February 26, 1862, 2 THE CORRESPONDENCE OF JOHN LOTHROP MOTLEY 239, 240 (G. W. Curtis ed. 1900).

18. See FREEDOM: A DOCUMENTARY HISTORY OF EMANCIPATION (I. Berlin *et al.* eds. 1986).

19. OWH Sr. to J. L. Motley, March 8, 1862, 2 THE CORRESPONDENCE OF JOHN LOTHROP MOTLEY 246, 247–248 (G. W. Curtis ed. 1900). This is perhaps exaggerated, since Dr. Holmes's letters were often meant to serve Motley's diplomatic purposes.

20. Quoted 1 HOWE 115.

21. BRUCE 80. The following account of the Twentieth Regiment on the Peninsula is taken from Bruce except where otherwise indicated.

22. Zobel, *Enlisted for Life,* AMERICAN HERITAGE, June–July 1986, pp. 57, 58.

23. A. WEBB, THE PENINSULA 51 (1882).

24. OWH to his parents, April 27, 1862, TWF 38, 42; to ALH, April 17, 1862, TWF 43; to parents, April 23, 1862, TWF 43, 45.

25. BRUCE 84–85.

26. OWH to his parents, April 23, 1862, TWF 43, 44.

27. *Id.* at 43–44.

28. According to Mark Howe, the commission was dated March 25, but was received May 4, citing Holmes's notation in his Civil War Scrapbook, 1 HOWE 299–300, n. 90. Neither commission nor notation is now in the scrapbook, OWH Papers, HLS, Paige Box 4. A copy of the commission is in the OWH Papers, HLS, B18 F15, with no indication of when received.

There was some criticism of Wendell within the regiment for accepting the commission, and as late as September, 1863, Little Abbott defended Wendell in a letter to his parents, saying that Wendell had done nothing himself to obtain the commission. 1 HOWE 300, note 92. Howe concluded that the matter of the commission was resolved "over Wendell's head," but Wendell was free to reject the commission, as he had promised to do. According to the "Muster Roll," which Holmes preserved, he was mustered in as captain "vice A. W. Beckwith, resigned" on May 1, 1863. This last date does not seem possible, but what the right date should be is not clear.

29. BRUCE at 88.

30. BRUCE 95–98.

31. OWH to his parents, June 2, 1862, TWF 47, 51.

32. *Id.* 48–50.

33. *Id.* 51.

34. *Id.*

CHAPTER 6. RAIN

1. OWH to his parents, June 2, 1862, TWF 47, 50–51.

2. *Id.*, TWF 50.

3. T. HYDE, FOLLOWING THE GREEK CROSS 63–64 (1894). The accounts given in this chapter are drawn from Holmes's letters, the memoirs of Hyde and J. S. Grant, who were near Holmes during these events, F. W. PALFREY, THE ANTIETAM AND FREDERICKSBURG (1882), Bruce's official history of the regiment,

the sources cited in Mark Howe's account, and Bruce Catton's volumes on the Army of the Potomac, where other sources are not specifically cited.

4. BRUCE 102–107.

5. OWH to OWH Sr., June 13, 1862, TWF 52, 54.

6. T. HYDE, FOLLOWING THE GREEK CROSS (1894); BRUCE 116.

7. BRUCE 117–118.

8. OWH to his parents, July 5, 1862, TWF 58–59.

9. OWH, *Memorial Day Address*, SPEECHES 9; *cf.* F. GREENSLET, THE LOWELLS AND THEIR SEVEN WORLDS 282 (1946).

10. OWH to his parents, July 5, 1862, TWF 58, 60.

11. TWF 57 has "Miller."

12. OWH to ALH, July 4, 1862, TWF 56.

13. OWH to his parents, July 5, 1862, TWF 58, 60.

14. BOWEN 14.

15. Charles Francis Adams, Jr., to his father, August 27, 1862, in 1 A CYCLE OF ADAMS LETTERS 176, 177–178 (C. W. Ford ed. 1920).

16. Quoted BRUCE 149–150.

17. BRUCE 158.

18. OWH to his parents, September 17, 1862, TWF 62, 64.

19. OWH to Frederick Pollock, June 28, 1930, 2 HOLMES–POLLOCK LETTERS 269, 270. Holmes blamed Sumner's impatience for this disaster: "Sumner who was an old cavalry officer I believe shoved our second line (I am talking of *lines*, not ranks), a *quasi* reserve, up so close to the front line that we could have touched them with our bayonets, and we got hit about as much as they did, but of course could do nothing, and when the enemy broke through on our left we were surrounded with the front. Whereas had we been a little farther back they would have got a volley." OWH to Frederick Pollock, June 28, 1930, 2 HOLMES–POLLOCK LETTERS 269, 270.

20. He kept this memento in his Civil War Scrapbook, OWH Papers, HLS, Paige Box 4.

21. N. P. HALLOWELL, REMINISCENCES 16–17 (1897), quoted TWF 65, n.1.

22. OWH to his parents, September 18, 1862, TWF 64, 66. Howe identifies the surgeon as S. Foster Haven, Jr. Holmes said that Haven had glanced at his wound on the day of the battle, and Pen Hallowell and Holmes both recalled a surgeon, who I assume was Haven, visiting them in the log house and splinting Pen's arm.

23. OWH to Lady Askwith, April 17, 1919, OWH Papers, HLS; quoted TWF 128 note p. See also BOWEN 169–170, 436. Bowen has the detail, repeated to her by a member of the family, that the clock resembled one in Pittsfield.

24. E. EMERSON, LIFE AND LETTERS OF CHARLES RUSSELL LOWELL (1907). A captain from a Western regiment, William LeDuc — an admirer of Dr. Holmes's writings — also came on Wendell in the hospital that night, and, recognizing the famous name, took Wendell in charge. (Bowen says that LeDuc claimed to have found Wendell abandoned on the battlefield, and took credit for saving his life.) LeDuc apparently did take Wendell out of the hospital, and they walked to a house in the village which LeDuc commandeered, ordering the family living there to spread a feather bed on their parlor floor. Captain LeDuc then went off to send a telegram to the famous father, saying that Wendell was in Keedysville, wounded — "thought not mortal." Alice Sumner LeDuc, *The Man Who Rescued "The Captain,"* THE ATLANTIC MONTHLY, August 1947, p. 80. In 1910, according to this article, LeDuc remembered the surgeon giving Wendell up for hopeless. LeDuc said that he had taken Holmes under his care despite the surgeon's verdict. This is not consistent with either Wendell's letter home reporting Haven's comment, nor with Charles Lowell's letter the next day reporting that Wendell's

wound was not thought to be serious. LeDuc, to judge by his later correspondence with father and son, shamelessly cultivated the connection with the famous Autocrat of the Breakfast-Table, and perhaps over time exaggerated his role in the "rescue." His version was not published until everyone involved was dead. See OWH Papers, HLS, B18 F18. The telegram to Dr. Holmes was quoted in *My Hunt after "The Captain,"* 8 OWH SR. WORKS 16.

25. OWH to parents, September 18, 1862, TWF 64–65.

26. OWH to parents, September 22, 1862, TWF 67.

27. See *My Hunt after "The Captain,"* 8 OWH SR. WORKS 16. In this celebrated article the doctor tells the story of the telegram that brought the news of Wendell's wound and of his setting out on a frantic search through Pennsylvania and Maryland for his son. It is curious, however, that among the doctor's papers are letters of introduction to the federal director of hospitals and to the surgeon general in Washington — dated a day or two *before* he learned of his son's injury. Also among his papers are the doctor's train ticket stubs and his receipts for purchases made during the trip. During his search for his son, he managed to tour hospitals and the Antietam battlefield, and to interview prisoners of war; his written account of the trip appeared with remarkable promptness in *The Atlantic*. It seems likely that the doctor had already planned a trip to Washington or to the front, that *The Atlantic* was already expecting an article from him when he received the news that his son had been wounded, and that the thrifty doctor combined two errands in a single trip.

28. Charles Walton to OWH Sr., October 1, 1862, OWH Papers, HLS, B18 F12. The doctor had asked Walton to write out his recollections of the visit for the doctor's use in his planned article for *The Atlantic*; this letter is Walton's response, and contains much of the detail the doctor used.

29. *Id.* The doctor mentioned the minstrel show in *My Hunt after "The Captain,"* but failed to mention that he brought his wounded son to see it, and omitted the drinking party afterward.

30. *Id.*

31. Civil War Scrapbook, OWH Papers, HLS, Paige Box 4. The letter is dated September 24, 1862, and in Holmes's hand is marked, "From my company."

32. See Palfrey, *Henry L. Abbott,* in 1 HARVARD MEMORIAL BIOGRAPHIES (T. W. Higginson ed. 1866). There is a similar description in BRUCE, presumably from the same source.

33. J. W. GRANT, MY FIRST CAMPAIGN 32–37 (1863).

34. OWH to AJH, November 11, 1862, TWF 70, 73. It is apparent from later letters that he wrote in a similar vein to his parents at this time, but that letter has been destroyed, by them or by him. See OWH to OWH Sr., December 20, 1862, TWF 79, answering his father's objections to an earlier letter, which has not been preserved. Since Wendell kept several war letters in which he expressed discouragement or doubt, sometimes in pretty strong terms, including the letter to Amelia, it is likely that the missing letter was destroyed, not because it was similar in content, but because it was disrespectful to the doctor, who had become a loudly enthusiastic partisan of the war. The December 20 letter to his father is probably a more temperate statement of Wendell's missing November letter.

35. BRUCE 200.

36. OWH to his parents, September 17, 1862, TWF 62–63.

37. OWH to ALH, December 12, 1862, TWF 74.

38. See G. H. Boker's poem "The Crossing at Fredericksburg," reprinted in 1 HOWE 147–148; as Howe notes, Holmes or the doctor was probably the source for this poem.

39. OWH to ALH, December 12, 1862, TWF 74, 75.

40. *Id.,* TWF at 75.

41. In Mark Howe's detailed account of this experience, he pointed out that Little Abbott was acting major during the battle. Howe assumed that Wendell, if he had not been ill, would have taken Abbott's place, since Wendell was senior to Abbott. He described the story of Abbott's bravery in leading a platoon into Water Street on December 11, a story that Wendell later wove into his speeches as a model of chivalric courage. Describing Wendell's agony in the hospital tent, Howe concluded:

> For Holmes who would have filled Abbott's post had not illness stood in the way [Abbott's courage] had a special significance. Accident had made this test another's when it should have been his. . . .
> Holmes, who had entered the war a radical and had clung to his convictions despite accumulating doubts realized that had he been called upon to perform Abbott's duties at Fredericksburg he might have failed.

1 HOWE 145. This is unlike Mark Howe's usual caution. First, Wendell probably did not know of the incident on Water Street until long after the battle. Howe says Abbott's courage was legendary in the regiment, which was true, but this particular incident was not well known and was not mentioned in the regimental history or any other account, including Frank Palfrey's detailed history of the battles of Fredericksburg and Antietam. Wendell did not mention it until March, 1863, when Colonel Hall told him the story.

Conceivably Holmes had the feelings Howe described even months after the battle when he first learned of Abbott's bravery, but in any case there were other captains in the Twentieth Regiment senior to Wendell. The regimental history, BRUCE, shows that captains Dreher and Cabot, who were present at the battle, were senior to Holmes. And even if Wendell had been acting major, as Abbott was, it does not follow — and there is not a word in the Holmes papers to suggest that Wendell thought — that he would have been chosen to lead a platoon in the particular incident that prompted the tale.

Wendell's hospital diary-letter shows him despondent about the course of the war and depressed by his serious illness. He was distressed to miss the potentially decisive battle, and his own feelings of the time seem to be reflected in a poem, for which he was the source and that Howe quotes, in which the protagonist fears that he will die ingloriously in a hospital tent instead of at his comrades' side. There is really no evidence, and Howe gives none, for the suggestion that Wendell's dominant feelings were guilt and self-doubt, then or at any other time.

This would not be worth belaboring, except that Howe's suggestion, to which perhaps he did not attribute great importance, led Saul Touster and Hiller Zobel into giving this incident a central place in their accounts of the war's effect on Holmes's thinking. See Touster, *In Search of Holmes from Within*, 18 VAND. L. REV. 437 (1965); Zobel, *Enlisted for Life*, AM. HERITAGE, June–July 1986, p. 57.

42. OWH to ALH, December 12, 1862, TWF 74, 76.

43. *Id.*

44. *Id.*, TWF at 77. A view of Fredericksburg similar to Wendell's sketch is given in BRUCE, facing p. 194.

45. F. W. PALFREY, THE ANTIETAM AND FREDERICKSBURG 147 (1882).

46. OWH to OWH Sr., December 20, 1862, TWF 79, 80.

47. ALH to Emily Hallowell, February 1, 1863, OWH Papers, HLS, B44 F37.

48. Wendell's March 29, 1863, letter to his father begins, "I had my blowoff in one of my last and now let bygones be bygones — if *you* will — for I fear I was somewhat in the mood wh. would have led to sass had I been at home —." TWF 86. The intervening letter, in which Wendell apparently was disrespectful to his father, has not been preserved.

49. J. W. GRANT, MY FIRST CAMPAIGN 59–71 (1863).

50. OWH to his parents, March 18, 1863, TWF 85, 86.
51. *Id.* at 85.
52. *Id.* at 90. Holmes enclosed Hall's maps with this letter.
53. *Id.*
54. *Id.*
55. *Memorial Day Address*, SPEECHES 9.
56. Civil War Scrapbook, OWH Papers, HLS, Paige Box 4.
57. BRUCE 249–250.

CHAPTER 7. THE REGIMENT CEASES

1. OWH to ALH, May 3, 1863, TWF 92.
2. *Id.*
3. See 1 HOWE pp. 15, 302, n.43.
4. This was a favorite anecdote. See, e.g., OWH to Harold Laski, July 15, 1906, 1 HOLMES–LASKI LETTERS 5, 6; 1 HOWE 156, quoting letter to Baroness Moncheur.
5. The text of the speech, which was widely reprinted at the time, is at 8 OWH SR. WORKS 78–120.
6. BRUCE 294–296. Details of the Twentieth Regiment, unless otherwise noted, are from this source.
7. Civil War Scrapbook, OWH Papers, HLS, Paige Box 4.
8. *Id.*
9. *Id.*
10. *Id.* There are no dates on the pictures, and it is only speculation, however likely it seems, that Holmes collected these pictures after the wound at Chancellorsville. There is nothing else like them in his papers.
11. H. L. Abbott to OWH, October 8, 1863, Abbott Papers, Houghton; see also 1 HOWE 159. Abbott is referring to the likelihood that Wendell would be killed if he accepted a commission in a black regiment.
12. See TWF 94, n.1.
13. BRUCE 324–335.
14. OWH to C. E. Norton, April 17, 1864, Houghton; quoted TWF 122, n.1.
15. T. HYDE, FOLLOWING THE GREEK CROSS 172–173, 178–179 (1894).
16. OWH to his parents, May 3, 1864, TWF 102. This diary is not in the Holmes Papers. Howe suggests that the diary account of Ball's Bluff, now found on loose sheets inserted into a later diary, was taken from this one, and the bulk of the book was destroyed.
17. Sutherland, "Reminiscences of Justice Holmes," Arthur E. Sutherland Papers, HLS, B24 F7 at p. 14.
18. OWH to OWH Sr., April 18, 1864, TWF 95, 96.
19. OWH to C. E. Norton, April 17, 1864, Houghton; quoted TWF 122, n.1.
20. BRUCE 217.
21. *Id.*
22. TWF 102, 103.
23. See T. HYDE, FOLLOWING THE GREEK CROSS 184–185 (1894). From Wendell's diary entry of May 5, 1864, it is plain that he was nearby, but he does not mention the hideous business of the infantryman's head.
24. T. HYDE, FOLLOWING THE GREEK CROSS 185 (1894).
25. This passage, quoted in BRUCE, probably was written by John Ropes, historian of the war, whose brother Henry had been Abbott's close friend.
26. OWH, Civil War Diary, May 7, 1864, TWF 108.
27. *Id.* May 12–13, TWF 116–117.

28. OWH to his parents, May 16, 1864, TWF 122–123.

29. OWH to ALH, June 7, 1864, TWF 141, 142. I have interpolated a few details from other letters describing this encounter, which also was one of the staple images of his later speeches.

30. OWH to his parents, May 30, 1864, TWF 135.

31. The photograph was published in T. HYDE, FOLLOWING THE GREEK CROSS (1894), and reproduced in TWF facing p. 135, where the officers are not identified. Holmes is sixth from the left, and Charles Whittier is to the right of him.

32. OWH to ALH, June 7, 1864, TWF 141, 142–143.

33. OWH, Civil War Diary, June 20, 1864, TWF 146.

34. See T. HYDE, FOLLOWING THE GREEK CROSS 215 (1894).

35. OWH Papers, HLS, B35, F2.

36. TWF 148.

37. T. HYDE, FOLLOWING THE GREEK CROSS 223 (1894). This incident has been much described. John Hay recorded in his diary for July 11 the President's story of a soldier who had ordered him roughly to get down. Sixty years later, Holmes, who liked to take guests on a tour to see Fort Stevens, often told them of having seen the President there. He usually said nothing about having spoken to the President. On a very few occasions, however, he added that he was the one who told the President to "Get down, you damned fool!" See John Cramer to Mark Howe, February 28, 1944, OWH Papers, HLS, B65 F13; J. H. CRAMER, LINCOLN UNDER ENEMY FIRE 101–124 (1948). After Holmes's death, Harold Laski published the story of Holmes's command to Lincoln with embellishments, and it was picked up and further embroidered by Alexander Wolcott. Most recently, Gore Vidal included a fictional version in his novel LINCOLN.

Mark Howe, who had the story directly from Holmes, plainly doubted its truth, but dutifully published it as given by Holmes. 1 HOWE 175–177. Howe collated the various accounts, and thought Holmes probably had not yet arrived at Fort Stevens when Lincoln visited on July 11. There was a similar incident during the battle the following day, when Lincoln returned with a large entourage to see the fighting, and General Wright and others urged him to get down out of sight. Howe thinks Holmes may have spoken to the President on this second occasion, but that seems unlikely. General Wright and Tom Hyde, who was serving with Wendell as an aide to General Wright, both describe the July 12 incident, and neither mentions Wendell's presence. There was a large entourage of senior officers around the President on July 12, and it seems unlikely that Wendell would have mistaken the identity of the visitor or shouted thoughtlessly to him. Holmes most likely heard the "Get down, you fool!" story, perhaps from Hay, and added it to his repertoire, uncharacteristically inserting himself into it on some occasions — most often when speaking to young women or very young men of whom he was fond.

38. OWH to ALH, June 8, 1864, TWF 151–152.

CHAPTER 8. POET, SOLDIER, GENTLEMAN

1. ALH to OWH, July 22, 1866, OWH Papers, HLS, B44 F10.

2. ALH to OWH, May 8, 1866, OWH Papers, HLS, B44 F9.

3. Mary Dixwell (FBH's sister, Mrs. George Wigglesworth), "Only Glimpses, Nothing More," undated typescript; copy OWH Papers, HLS, B54 F14.

4. Undated letters, William James to OWH, James Papers, Houghton; copies in OWH Papers, HLS, B45 F12. These are scribbled notes in a childish handwriting, evidently the earliest of the James letters to Holmes.

5. Reprinted 1 Howe 165.

6. Quoted by Felix Frankfurter, memorandum September 28, 1932, OWH Papers, HLS, B54 F5. See also 1 Howe 176. In fact, there was little choice. Of the professions, medicine was largely humbug, as his father and Bill James would both have told him, and the ministry was out of the question. Compare Henry Adams:

> Convinced that the clue of religion led to nothing, and that politics led to chaos, one had turned to the law, as ones scholars returned to the Law School, because one could see no other path to a profession.

H. Adams, The Education of Henry Adams 368 (1918).

7. OWH, Civil War Scrapbook, OWH Papers, HLS, Paige Box 4.

8. See S. E. Morison, Three Centuries of Harvard 336 (1936).

9. *Id.* See also Fessenden, *The Rebirth of the Harvard Law School*, 33 Harv. L. Rev. 493 (1920).

10. S. E. Morison, Three Centuries of Harvard 337 (1936).

11. Blackstone had seemed to be one of the Natural Law thinkers of the eighteenth century; see D. Boorstin, The Mysterious Science of the Law (1941), and Holmes was a famous critic of Natural Law. But in an important recent book, Richard A. Posner assimilates Blackstone to the modern view that law serves social purposes and so is fundamentally "functional," rather than moralistic. On this reading, Blackstone, "anticipat[ed] Holmes." R. Posner, The Economics of Justice 19–20 (1981). A similar case is made for the modernity of Chief Justice Shaw in L. Levy, The Law of the Commonwealth and Chief Justice Shaw (1957). However this may be, and I have doubts, it seems plain that Holmes read Blackstone (and Shaw) much as Boorstin did, and thought of himself as making a sharp break with their tradition.

12. *Commencement Address, Brown University,* Speeches 97, 98; Collected Legal Papers 164, 165 (1920).

13. Speeches 122.

14. See OWH to Harold Laski, November 22, 1917, 1 Holmes–Laski Letters 111, 112; the statement of facts of what appears to be Holmes's argument before Joel Parker is in the Harvard Law School's moot court records; copy OWH Papers, HLS, B65 F6; see 1 Howe 189.

15. The Letters of John Fiske 118–119 (E. F. Fisk ed. 1940), quoted G. Feaver, From Status to Contract 44 (1969); 1 Howe 193; A. E. Sutherland, The Law at Harvard 144–145 (1967). Often quoted as this letter is, it seems fair to say that Fiske was an enthusiast who was also "carried away and *electrified*" by Blackstone, and read Parsons on Contracts "almost like a novel."

16. H. S. Maine, Ancient Law (1861). In this capsule summary I have emphasized the similarities to Holmes's work of twenty years later, The Common Law (1881).

17. J. Austin, The Province of Jurisprudence Determined (1832).

18. E. Tilton, Amiable Autocrat 280 (1947) quoting OWH Sr. to Brownell, May 10, 1865, "privately owned."

19. OWH to Henry Brownell, May 9, 1865, quoted E. Tilton, Amiable Autocrat 280 (1947).

20. A portion of the same letter, copied by Mark Howe, OWH Papers, HLS, quoted 1 Howe 196.

21. H. James, The Notebooks of Henry James 318 (F. O. Matthiessen and K. Murdock eds. 1947).

22. Eleanor Shattuck to Emily Eliot, July 2, 1865, Shattuck Papers, MHS.

23. R. W. Emerson, Complete Writings 1220–1221 (1929); for Bartlett's

speech and the proceedings more generally, see Bail, *Harvard's Commemoration Day, July 21, 1865,* 15 NEW ENG. Q. 256 (1942).

24. See the letters of Henry James to OWH for these dates, in Howe, *The Letters of Henry James to Mr. Justice Holmes,* YALE REV., Spring, 1949, 412–415. See also L. EDEL, HENRY JAMES, THE UNTRIED YEARS 230–238 (1953); HENRY JAMES: A LIFE 75–78 (1985) (but Edel incorrectly has Holmes visiting North Conway in the summer of 1865).

25. See Holmes's diary for 1866, OWH Papers, HLS, B19 F2; 1 HOWE 204.

26. OWH to Felix Frankfurter, March 2, 1930, OWH Papers, HLS.

27. OWH, Speech to the Boston Bar, March 7, 1900, SPEECHES 122.

28. *William C. Endicott,* SPEECHES 127, 128.

29. OWH Diary, entry for April 4, 1867, OWH Papers, HLS, B19 F2.

30. William James to Tom Ward, March 27, 1866, in 1 THE LETTERS OF WILLIAM JAMES 75–76 (H. James ed. 1920).

31. ALH to OWH, July 3, [1866], OWH Papers, HLS, B44 F10.

32. H. JAMES, THE NOTEBOOKS OF HENRY JAMES 318–319 (F. O. Matthiessen and K. Murdock eds. 1947).

33. Holmes apparently was representing his father or the medical school in a dispute concerning lecture fees paid to a Dr. Lombard. On March 8, 1866, Holmes wrote to the dean of the medical school, George B. Shattuck, to say that he waited for a detailed answer from Dr. Cheever, "before making my statement of the claims of the Anatomy Department," which was Dr. Holmes. Shattuck Papers, vol. 23, MHS.

34. The account of Holmes's trip to Europe is drawn from his diary, except where otherwise noted. The diary is in the OWH Papers, HLS, B19 F2; other details in this paragraph are from letters the doctor and Mrs. Holmes wrote to Holmes while he was abroad, OWH Papers, HLS, Box 44.

35. OWH to Harold Laski, February 4, 1927, 2 HOLMES–LASKI LETTERS 918.

36. OWH to Harold Laski, March 4, 1920, 1 HOLMES–LASKI LETTERS 248.

37. OWH Diary, June 11, 1866, OWH Papers, HLS, B19 F2.

38. OWH to Frederick Pollock, June 9, 1930, 2 HOLMES–POLLOCK LETTERS 267. Holmes told several versions of this story. The incident may have occurred on June 10, 1866, at the Cosmopolitan Club, when Holmes's diary has the entry, "introduced to Kinglake & Col & a Frenchman." There probably was no other opportunity for such an exchange until Holmes left London on June 15.

39. The bitterness became more pronounced as he grew older, but even in the 1860s, Stephen's written attacks on his elders in philosophy and religion were often violent and occasionally contemptuous, a trait that Holmes apparently admonished soon after they met. See Leslie Stephen to OWH, July 4, 1870, OWH Papers, HLS; F. MAITLAND, THE LIFE AND LETTERS OF LESLIE STEPHEN 217–218 (1906).

40. Leslie Stephen to OWH, July 28, 1866, OWH Papers, HLS, B50 F6.

41. Thomas Hughes to OWH, December 31, 1866, HLS, quoted 1 HOWE 238.

42. Mark Howe's notes of interview with Learned Hand, OWH Papers, HLS.

43. OWH Diary, July 21, 1866, OWH Papers, HLS, B19 F2.

44. OWH to Baroness Moncheur, September 5, 1915, OWH Papers, HLS.

45. F. MAITLAND, THE LIFE AND LETTERS OF LESLIE STEPHEN 186 (1906).

46. *Id.*

47. The sheet of letter paper on which the notes and poem are written is creased and stained as if it had been folded in a wallet or pocketbook for some time. It carries no date and in the Holmes Papers, HLS, has been filed among miscellaneous memorabilia, B69 F3. The question-game is mentioned in Holmes's diary during the stay at Stonefield, and the poem, aside from answering

the description of the game, appears from the writing to be of this period. The flattering mention of Escot Hall suggests that it was written for an earlier game at Kennaway's, but I have taken the liberty of putting it here. I am obliged to Elisabeth G. Humez for pointing out the similarity of the third stanza to Goethe's "Erinnerung," which was still being memorized by students at Harvard a century later.

CHAPTER 9. THE FIRST VENTURE

1. OWH, MEMOIR OF GEORGE OTIS SHATTUCK 4 (1900); see also *George Otis Shattuck,* SPEECHES 92, 94.

2. Thayer, *Address to the Massachusetts Historical Society,* in OWH, MEMOIR OF GEORGE OTIS SHATTUCK 13 (1900).

3. OWH, MEMOIR OF GEORGE OTIS SHATTUCK 4 (1900); SPEECHES at 92.

4. Thayer, *Address to the Massachusetts Historical Society,* in OWH, MEMOIR OF GEORGE OTIS SHATTUCK 13 (1900).

5. SPEECHES 92.

6. *Id.* at 94.

7. OWH diary, October, 1866, OWH Papers, HLS, B19 F2.

8. George O. Shattuck to OWH, April 1, 1881, OWH Papers, HLS, B49 F37.

9. OWH to Henry Brownell, October 1865, OWH Papers, HLS; see also 1 HOWE 195.

10. I have interpolated from brief entries in Holmes's diary for 1866, OWH Papers, HLS, B19 F2, which show his social engagements. There are regular entries for "Cambridge," which I take to mean a round of calls to friends there.

11. There is a photograph of the house in the Harvard Law Art Collection.

12. OWH Diary entry for November 24, 1866, OWH Papers, HLS, B19 F2.

13. OWH Diary entry for December 6, 1866, OWH Papers, HLS, B19 F2.

14. OWH Diary entries for December 6–29, 1866, OWH Papers, HLS, B19 F2.

15. Adams, *Life of George Cabot Lodge,* reprinted in E. WILSON, THE SHOCK OF RECOGNITION 747, 749–750 (2d ed., 1950).

16. Shattuck Papers, MHS, vol. 23.

17. OWH Diary entry for December 25, 1866, OWH Papers, HLS, B19 F2. Mark Howe misread "Xmas" as "months," see 1 HOWE 254.

18. Mary James to Alice James, January 1867 (?), quoted J. STROUSE, ALICE JAMES 99 (1980).

19. Mary James to Alice James, undated, early 1867(?), James Papers, Houghton.

20. William James to OWH, May 15, 1868, in R. B. PERRY, THE THOUGHT AND CHARACTER OF WILLIAM JAMES 93, 95 (1-vol. ed., 1948).

21. OWH Diary, April 4, 1867, OWH Papers, HLS, B19 F2.

22. Judge Ebenezer Hoar to OWH Sr., November 14, 1867, quoted E. TILTON, AMIABLE AUTOCRAT 291–292 (1947).

23. OWH, *Reports of Cases . . . in the Supreme Court of . . . Iowa,* 3 AM. L. REV. 357 (1867). In the evolutionary scheme Holmes later propounded, judges' ignorance is a source of variation in the law that allows it to evolve.

24. OWH to William James, December 15, 1867, in R. B. PERRY, 1 THE THOUGHT AND CHARACTER OF WILLIAM JAMES 505 (1935).

25. Mary ("Minny") Temple to John Gray, June 27, 1869, James Papers, Houghton.

26. Minny Temple to John Gray, January 27, 1869, James Papers, Houghton.

Henry James's version of this letter in NOTES OF A SON AND BROTHER is somewhat altered.

27. Minny Temple to John Gray, April 2 and November 21, 1869, James Papers, Houghton.

28. Minny Temple to John Gray, "Nov. 1869," James Papers, Houghton.

29. Minny Temple to John Gray, October 24, 1869, James Papers, Houghton.

30. See OWH's review of Story's *Equity Jurisprudence*, 5 AM. L. REV. 115 (Oct. 1870).

31. Little, *The Early Reading of Justice Oliver Wendell Holmes*, 8 HARV. LIBRARY BULL. 163, 180 (1954).

32. The correspondence between Holmes and Thayer is quoted and summarized in 2 HOWE 10–18.

33. See Adams, *Melville Bigelow*, 28 B.U.L. REV. 168 (1921).

CHAPTER 10. TWO PILLARS OF HIS LIFE

1. Marian (Clover) Hooper to Eleanor Shattuck, January 10, 1870, Shattuck Papers, MHS.

2. Mary (Minny) Temple to John Gray, February 16, 1870, James Papers, Houghton.

3. G. ALLEN, WILLIAM JAMES 162 (1967).

4. This episode, a kind of psychological crisis in William James's life, marked a turning for him, and in his recovery he set down a path that quickly diverged from Holmes's.

James described the incident — in which he had a vision of hallucinatory force, followed by months of anxiety — in THE VARIETIES OF RELIGIOUS EXPERIENCE 157–158 (1902); see 1 THE LETTERS OF WILLIAM JAMES 145 (H. James ed. 1920). James seems to have set out toward his own distinctive philosophy after this incident; see R. B. PERRY, THE THOUGHT AND CHARACTER OF WILLIAM JAMES 118–130 (1-vol. ed. 1948). At the same time, and perhaps as part of the same process of recovery, he drifted away from Holmes.

As their thoughts and careers diverged, Holmes and James came to dislike each other's philosophies. But their early friendship has prompted a great deal of speculation about mutual influence, particularly with regard to the "Metaphysical Club." After the crisis of 1870, James organized this informal gathering of philosophers, which at first included Holmes. Except for a bare mention that Holmes had attended its informal meetings, however, little is known about his involvement. See C. PEIRCE, 5 COLLECTED PAPERS 12–13 (1934). Charles Sanders Peirce also attended, and because Peirce and William James were the founders of Pragmatism, some writers have argued that Holmes, too, became a Pragmatist through this early association. Catherine Drinker Bowen made much of the club in her fictionalized biography of Holmes's family, in which she included pages of invented conversation and description of Holmes at the club's meetings. See BOWEN 221–222, 253. The philosopher Morton White, perhaps influenced by Bowen's persuasive descriptions, grouped Holmes with the Metaphysical Club; see M. WHITE, SOCIAL THOUGHT IN AMERICA 62 (1947), and others have followed him. See Fisch, *Justice Holmes, The Prediction Theory of Law and Pragmatism*, 39 J. OF PHILO. 85 (1942); Frank, *A Conflict With Oblivion: Some Observations of the Founders of Legal Pragmatism*, 9 RUTGERS L. REV. 425, 444 (1954); F. R. KELLOGG, FORMATIVE ESSAYS OF JUSTICE HOLMES (1984).

Mark Howe, however, doubted that Holmes was much influenced by the early Pragmatists, see 2 HOWE 75; as did G. Edward White; see White, *Looking at Holmes in the Mirror*, 4 L. & HIST. REV. 440 (1986).

Holmes's instrumental definition of law, as that which courts do, is his closest link with Jamesian Pragmatism. See OWH, *Codes, and the Arrangement of Law*, 5 AM. L. REV. 1 (October, 1870). This essay is so early that it seems unlikely to have been affected by the Metaphysical Club discussions.

Holmes in any case knew little of Peirce's ideas, whatever they may have been in 1870. See OWH to Charles Hartshorne, August 25, 1927, OWH papers, HLS, B52 F29; ("Once in a fertilizing way [Peirce] challenged some assumption that I made, but, alas, I forget what. But in those days I was studying law and soon dropped out of the band"); OWH to President Daniel Coit Gilman of Johns Hopkins, January 9, 1903, OWH Papers, HLS, B52 F29 ("I know Mr. Peirce's philosophy mainly at second hand. . . ."). Nor were they ever close. "I suspected that he regarded outsiders like St. John Green and me [who were not academic philosophers] with contempt or at least indifference." OWH to Felix Frankfurter, March 19, 1927, OWH Papers, HLS, B29 F12.

As to William James, OWH disagreed fundamentally with what he understood of James's ideas. See, among many similar remarks, the following:

> I regard the will to believe as of a piece with the insistence on the discontinuity of the universe which Bill James shares with Cardinal Newman, and which I suspect as induced by the wish to leave room for the interstitial miracle. When we were in our 20s W. James said to me (in substance) that spiritualism was the last chance to spiritualize the world.

OWH to Morris Cohen, March 13, 1925, in L. C. ROSENFIELD, PORTRAIT OF A PHILOSOPHER 351 (1962). Holmes, in short, thought that James's Pragmatism was of a piece with his spiritualism, and had little regard for either.

5. OWH to Nina Gray, August 30, 1914, OWH Papers, HLS, B30 F8.

6. OWH, *Codes, and the Arrangement of the Law*, 5 AM. L. REV. 1, 5 (1870).

7. *Id.*, p.1.

8. Holmes had an early appreciation that thought and motives were often unconscious. It is evident as an assumption underlying his early law writings in the 1870s (see below), and he recalled this having been a settled conviction as early as his talks with William James, presumably before 1870:

> You speak of your reading The Unconscious Mind. As I look on myself as a cosmic ganglion — a manifestation of the unknown substratum — that we call energy — or might as well call it X — . . . . I regard it as somewhat accidental how far the processes of X emerge into consciousness. When we were both young, before all this later talk I used the image of a row of bricks (to Wm. James) on two inclined planes. [Diagram of bricks in a line, down one plane and up the other.] You tip the first brick and the row goes down, the first and the last above the line of consciousness and more may be. . . . Not however that consciousness is a fifth wheel so that Shakespeare might have written his plays without knowing it.

OWH to Ethel Scott, March 9, 1923, OWH Papers, HLS, B49 F24.

Dr. Holmes had his own theory of the unconscious mind; see, e.g., THE PSYCHIATRIC NOVELS OF OLIVER WENDELL HOLMES (C. Oberndorf ed. 1946). As Holmes had formed his own ideas before the doctor published his, it would be difficult to say who influenced whom.

9. OWH to Harold Laski, June 1, 1922, 1 HOLMES–LASKI LETTERS 429–430.

10. The substance of Holmes's lectures on jurisprudence appeared in his review, *"Law Magazine and Review, April 1872,"* 6 AM. L. REV. 723 (1872).

11. G. SANTAYANA, PERSONS AND PLACES 140–141 (1944). The description is from 1872, when the Santayanas moved to 302 Beacon Street.

12. OWH, *Essays on the Form of the Law,* 5 AM. L. REV. 114 (1870).

13. H. ADAMS, THE EDUCATION OF HENRY ADAMS 301 (1918).

14. E. SAMUELS, THE YOUNG HENRY ADAMS 211 (1948).

15. H. ADAMS, THE EDUCATION OF HENRY ADAMS 304 (1918).

16. *Sidney Bartlett, March 23, 1889,* SPEECHES 51, 54. This obituary was more a portrait of Holmes's own ideals than of the deceased.

17. Reviewing a book written by Melville Bigelow, but published as the work of "Judge Isaac Redfield and Melville Bigelow," Holmes said, "Mr. Bigelow has already shown himself so honest and useful a writer that he does not need the aid of an eminent name to commend him to the public." 5 AM. L. REV. 720 (1871). In an earlier review Holmes had been especially caustic about Redfield's willingness to take credit for the work of others. 5 AM. L. REV. 546 (1871). In Holmes's case, James B. Thayer seems to have stepped aside, but not without bitterness. See the discussion in 2 HOWE 11–16. The *Kent,* when published, bore Holmes's name alone as editor, and the acknowledgments show that he was able to hire students to assist him.

18. See preceding note.

19. OWH, *Grain Elevators,* 6 AM. L. REV. 450 (1872).

20. There is no extrinsic evidence that the "Astronomer's" poem was drafted by Holmes, but in other instances Holmes wrote drafts that his father revised before publication. Holmes also sent draft poems to other poets for comment; see his letters to Henry Brownell, above, and it would be surprising if he did not also ask for his father's comments. Several passages in the Astronomer's poem are echoed in Holmes's later speeches, in which he also drew on his Civil War poetry. At a later period of discouragement, for instance, Holmes gave a series of talks in which he meditated on the anonymity of a lawyer's or judge's achievements. Compare, for instance, the Astronomer's

> Must each coral insect leave his sign
> On each poor grain he lent to build the reef,
> As Babel's builders stamped the sunburnt clay,

with Holmes's obituary for Daniel Richardson, his colleague on the bench, in 1890 (SPEECHES 56, 57): "Their true monument is the body of our jurisprudence . . . to which the least may make their contribution, and inscribe it with their name." The Astronomer's questions — Who invented the wheel, etc. — are closely paralleled in *Anonymity and Achievement,* June 3, 1890, SPEECHES 59: "The greater part of the work of the world is anonymous work. . . . Who invented the wheel, or ships, or the city, or contracts. . . . ?" See also *Sidney Bartlett, March 23, 1889,* SPEECHES 51, 54.

The meter is the doctor's, and after the first two installments of the poem, quoted in the text, one hears only the doctor talking, characteristically inveighing against Calvinist bigotry. Even in the later installments, however, there are flashes of Holmes's imagery:

> Alone! No climber of an Alpine cliff,
> No Arctic venturer on the waveless sea,
> Feels the dread stillness round him as it chills
> The heart of him who leaves the slumbering earth
> To watch the silent worlds that crowd the sky.

At the end of the fifth installment there is some battle imagery that also is reminiscent of the younger Holmes's speeches.

21. 3 OWH SR. WORKS 144–146.

22. *Id.* at 172–173. Compare the mysticism and end-of-the-world imagery with, for example, Holmes's *Law and the Court,* February 15, 1893, SPEECHES 168.

23. OWH Sr. Papers, Houghton.

24. E. Tilton, Amiable Autocrat 184 (1947).

25. OWH to William James, May 1, 1878, James Papers, Houghton.

26. Fanny's illness so soon after her marriage is not mentioned in any of the Holmes papers in the United States that have survived, and is not mentioned in any of the published works on the Holmes family. The doctor's July 16, 1872, letter to Carolyn Kellogg, written from Boston, is uncharacteristically distraught and almost illegible, but says nothing about the death of their servant or Fanny's illness. OWH Sr. Papers, Houghton. In a letter of August 23, 1872, to Thornton Hunt, in England, however, the doctor wrote the following:

> My whole household is in trouble and confusion. My wife and myself were called back from Newport to Boston by the illness and unexpected death of one of our most valued and important people in the house; my daughter-in-law is down with rheumatic fever — another woman gives warning that she is going in the very midst of our necessities and there is nobody (in a certain sense) in town, so that we are a desolate little community just at this moment and I feel more like a maid of all work than an author.

Thornton Hunt Papers, Keats House, Hampstead. Hunt misunderstood this somewhat confused account, and on October 4, 1872, the doctor wrote again:

> I should hardly feel that I ought to trouble you with a second letter so soon if I did not fear that I had conveyed an impression of a deeper calamity having befallen than was really the case. It was a most valued and faithful servant whose death was the first of a series of trials and fatigues which have made my summer and early autumn a very hard one to bear. Followed as this was by the severe and long-continued illness of my daughter-in-law and the consequent worry and exhaustion of my wife at the very time when both of us were expecting a little respite and recreation to fit us for the winter's duties—it took a good [deal] of the life out of me as out of all of us. . . . My daughter-in-law has not yet got downstairs, and in the meantime my second son has returned from Europe so far from well that it is a new cause of anxiety for both my wife and myself.
>
> So you see, without what I have any right to call a bereavement, I have yet had a good deal of trouble all around me — to say nothing of repeated indispositions from which I have myself been suffering.

Id. The doctor's other daughter-in-law was with Ned in Europe, and so the illness was Fanny's. Apparently the passion for privacy that Fanny and Wendell shared kept the doctor from mentioning this illness to friends in America.

27. See Kanda and Gifford, *The Kaneko Correspondence,* 37 Monumenta Nipponica 41, 44, n.10 (1982).

28. OWH Diary, OWH Papers, HLS, B19 F2; see Little, *The Early Reading of Justice Oliver Wendell Holmes,* 8 Harv. Library Bull. 163 (1954).

29. OWH Sr. to Thornton Hunt, October 4, 1872, Thornton Hunt Papers, Keats House, Hampstead.

30. *Id.*

31. OWH, *The Arrangement of the Law: Privity,* 7 Am. L. Rev. 46 (1872). Holmes's argument on privity is apparently based on his reading of H. Maine, Ancient Law (1861), supplemented by his own researches.

32. The German school of idealist jurisprudence had developed an opposed view. As the German theory was understood by Holmes, law was an expression of the spirit of a people, and its particulars were exercises of collective will.

Holmes devoted some space in THE COMMON LAW to attacking this theory, and Howe and others have described Holmes's own objective theory of the law as a reaction to Karl Friedrich von Savigny and the Hegelians. But it appears that Holmes's objective theory grew in these early years without reference to the Germans, and perhaps without awareness of them.

From the very start, Holmes's ambition had been to make a philosophical — which is to say scientific — study of the law. See for example, OWH to William James, April 19, 1868: "Law as well as any other series of facts in this world may be approached in the interests of science." R. B. PERRY, THE THOUGHT AND CHARACTER OF WILLIAM JAMES 92 (1948). Cf. Holmes's undergraduate essay on Plato, discussed above, in which he said that modern science would replace Plato's more primitive idealism.

This positivist program alone was enough to put Holmes at odds with the German Idealists when he encountered them, later on. But he had already taken the first important step toward an objective theory by the time of his essay *Privity*.

The first seed of Holmes's theory was probably planted by his effort to digest reported decisions for his law practice, the COMMENTARIES and the AMERICAN LAW REVIEW. Reviewing a digest of federal cases for the LAW REVIEW, Holmes said that a digest should contain only

> an abridgment of the facts with the judgment of the court upon them. . . .
> Just in proportion as a case is new and therefore valuable, no one, not
> even the judges, can be trusted to state the *ratio decidendi*. We believe that
> the very essence of a digest . . . is that it should state cases and not principles.

"*A Digest of the Decisions of the Federal Courts*," 5 AM. L. REV. 539 (April, 1871). Such digests were the data of his scientific study. Their significance was wholly objective — the thoughts of even the judges themselves were irrelevant.

The second step in his argument, formulated clearly for the first time the following year, was to show that these data were like the data of biology and had adaptive significance. The dominant class in a society would succeed in perpetuating itself only if it embodied its objective interests in law. See, e.g., OWH, *The Gas Stokers' Strike*, 7 AM. L. REV. 582 (1873). The final step, taken in articles beginning with *Primitive Notions in Modern Law*, 11 AM. L. REV. 641 (1877) (see below), was to argue that while the basis of judicial decisions was often unconscious, the common law reflected an evolving self-awareness of society, and therefore would increasingly reflect conscious, scientifically determined, objective aims. For an interesting discussion of this last point see Elliott, *Holmes and Evolution*, 13 J. LEGAL STUDIES 113 (1984).

33. 7 AM. L. REV. 652 (1873).

34. This analysis was condensed and published as a long footnote on negligence attached to Kent's chapter on bailments. More than one hundred years later, Alan Watson, in THE EVOLUTION OF LAW (1985), recreated a similar argument, addressing similar questions. Watson concluded that custom became law only when adopted as a rule of decision by the courts; he appeared not to be aware of Holmes's earlier work.

35. OWH to James Fitzjames Stephen, November 17, 1872, OWH Papers, HLS.

CHAPTER 11. *THE COMMON LAW*

1. J. KAY, LOST BOSTON 214 (1980).
2. Quoted O. FRIEDRICH, CLOVER 159 (1979).

3. OWH Sr. to J. L. Motley, in THE CORRESPONDENCE OF JOHN LOTHROP MOTLEY (G. W. Curtis ed. 1900).

4. Little has "received," with a query, rather than "revised." Little, *The Early Reading of Justice Oliver Wendell Holmes,* 8 HARV. LIBRARY BULL. 163, 165 (1954).

5. OWH Diary entry for December 31, 1872, OWH Papers, HLS, B19 F2.

6. OWH Papers, HLS. The witnesses were William E. Perkins, Melville Bigelow, and Russell Gray.

7. Mary James to Henry James, Jr., February 28, 1873, in R. B. PERRY, THE THOUGHT AND CHARACTER OF WILLIAM JAMES 58–59 (1954). Holmes sent the last manuscript for the COMMENTARIES to the printer on February 7, so the dinner may have been more than a few days before the date of the letter, or Holmes may have been carrying proofs rather than manuscript.

8. OWH Diary, OWH Papers, HLS; Little, *The Early Reading of Justice Oliver Wendell Holmes,* 8 HARV. LIBRARY BULL. 163 (1954).

9. OWH's diary entry for March 3, 1873, says, "Fanny read proof alone from and before this date," OWH Papers, HLS.

10. See Holmes's preface to the twelfth edition of James Kent's COMMENTARIES ON AMERICAN LAW (1873).

11. *Id.*

12. See, for instance, the letter from Mary James to her son Henry, December 3, 1873, James Papers, Houghton, quoted 2 HOWE 22: "Fanny Holmes . . . talked of the labor it cost *them* . . . as if it were a common work." (Emphasis in original.)

13. *George Otis Shattuck,* SPEECHES 92, 93–94.

14. OWH to Harold Laski, April 2, 1922, 1 HOLMES–LASKI LETTERS 417; see especially the editor's note to this letter.

15. Richard Henry Dana's journal, MHS, reprinted B. PERRY, RICHARD HENRY DANA 104–105 (1933), quoted 2 HOWE 126.

16. Harold Laski to OWH, April 18, 1932, 2 HOLMES–LASKI LETTERS 1238–1239.

17. OWH to Lewis Einstein, April 26, 1918, HOLMES–EINSTEIN LETTERS 163, 164; see also 2 HOWE 112, n.32.

18. *The Poet at the Breakfast-Table,* 3 OWH SR. WORKS 147; see also BOWEN 272–274.

19. *The Poet at the Breakfast-Table,* 3 OWH SR. WORKS 149. For Holmes's use of the same image, see below.

20. See C. GALTON, HEREDITARY GENIUS (1865); D. KEVLES, IN THE NAME OF EUGENICS (1985).

21. *The Poet at the Breakfast-Table,* 3 OWH SR. WORKS 182.

22. OWH, *The Gas Stokers' Strike,* 7 AM. L. REV. 582 (1873). The first three paragraphs, describing the background of the case, were written by Holmes's cousin, John T. Morse. See Bibliography, above. Holmes's portion does not address the case itself so much as respond to an article in the *Fortnightly Review.*

23. Holmes apparently thought that natural selection operated on classes and races as wholes, rather than on individuals. This is, I believe, contrary to the modern understanding, but Holmes was very much like the English evolutionary historians of the time, in this regard. See J. W. BURROW, EVOLUTION AND SOCIETY 114–115 (1966). Holmes did not read Charles Darwin's works until 1907, and he clung to his own views of evolution all his life. See, among many such examples, OWH to Harold Laski, January 8, 1916, 1 HOLMES–LASKI LETTERS 51–52.

This brief essay is also interesting because it makes pretty plain that Holmes rejected Utilitarian premises as inconsistent with evolutionism, a point that Leslie Stephen made more mildly in his ENGLISH UTILITARIANS (1900). Holmes's own project was to find an analytical system for describing modern law that would be consistent with an evolutionary history. He first succeeded in this in the essays, beginning with *Primitive Notions in Modern Law,* which he collected in THE COMMON LAW, see below.

It is curious that despite Holmes's explicit and repeated rejection of Utilitarianism, some modern writers continue to describe him as in some degree its follower. See, for instance, H. L. POHLMAN, JUSTICE OLIVER WENDELL HOLMES AND UTILITARIAN JURISPRUDENCE 144, 155 (1984). See also Kelley, *A Critical Analysis of Holmes' Theory of Torts,* 61 WASH. U.L.Q. 681, 712–713 (1983); cf. Dudziak, *Oliver Wendell Holmes as a Eugenic Reformer: Rhetoric in the Writing of Constitutional Law,* 71 IOWA L. REV. 833 (1986).

24. For a less sympathetic view, see Rogat, *The Judge as Spectator,* 31 U. CHI. L. REV. 213 (1964).

25. OWH to Mrs. Charles S. Hamlin, October 12, 1930, OWH Papers, HLS, B35 F1.

26. FBH Scrapbook, OWH Papers, HLS, B69 F2.

27. The account of this trip to Europe is taken from Fanny's diaries, OWH Papers, HLS, except as noted.

28. FBH Diary, vol. 1, OWH Papers, HLS, B19 F16; 2 HOWE 97–98.

29. FBH Diary, vol. 2, undated opening pages, OWH Papers, HLS, B73 F10.

30. FBH Diary, vol. 1, OWH Papers, HLS; 2 HOWE 97.

31. FBH Diary, vol. 2, OWH Papers, HLS, B73 F10.

32. See OWH to Harold Laski, June 24, 1926, 2 HOLMES–LASKI LETTERS 849; OWH to Lewis Einstein, August 31, 1928, HOLMES–EINSTEIN LETTERS 289.

33. Fanny's commonplace book, in which she kept recipes, sayings, riddles, and poems, is written more firmly, with fewer misspellings and less eccentricity. OWH Papers, HLS, B73 F9.

34. FBH Diary, vol. 1, OWH Papers, HLS, B19 F16; 2 HOWE 97.

35. *Id.*

36. No further correspondence between the two men has survived, and it appears they did not pursue their acquaintance. By an odd conjunction of mistakes, however, there are two separate accounts of a friendship between Holmes and Maine. Maine's biographer, Feaver, misdates their only meeting to 1871, so that the notes exchanged around Holmes's visit in 1874 appear to him to be evidence of what he calls a "lasting friendship" between the "two scholars." G. FEAVER, FROM STATUS TO CONTRACT 131 (1969). Mark Howe also suggests, more cautiously, that the two men formed a lasting friendship. 2 HOWE 104–105.

All of the evidence for this friendship appears to rest on misdating. In 1873, Holmes had sent Maine — whom he had not yet met — a copy of his *Theory of Torts,* and Maine sent a brief undated note, calling the essay "ingenious and original" (not exactly high praise) and commiserating with Holmes on his having to return to law practice. Both Feaver and Howe misdate this note. Feaver multiplies it into a whole correspondence; Howe dates it improbably to July, 1874, when Fanny and Holmes were traveling on the Continent. Maine's letter refers to his meeting Henry Adams "this summer," which places it in 1873, if nothing else does.

On the eve of his 1874 trip, Holmes sent a set of Kent's *Commentaries* to Maine, who answered with a flattering letter that Fanny pasted into her scrapbook, OWH Papers, HLS, B69 F2. Neither Feaver nor Howe seem to be aware of this second letter, which was the only other letter Maine ever wrote to Holmes. They had no further correspondence after 1874, although Holmes continued to send Maine his articles; see below.

37. The *Alabama* was one of two armored ships built in British ports for

French owners, on behalf of the Confederacy, and which were allowed to sail despite American protests. See H. ADAMS, EDUCATION 167 (1918). They did considerable damage to federal shipping, but the British government disclaimed responsibility. After the war, an arbitration commission directed that Great Britain pay damages to the United States for the *Alabama*'s depredations. Sixteen years later, Holmes wrote an opinion for the Massachusetts Supreme Judicial Court concerning the allocation of the *Alabama* Claims fund, Heard v. Sturgis, 146 Mass. 545 (1890), *reversed sub nom.* Williams v. Heard, 140 U.S. 529 (1891).

38. OWH to Lady Castletown, May 12, 1899, OWH Papers, HLS, B26 F13.

39. Palfrey, *Introduction,* 1 HOLMES–POLLOCK LETTERS xv.

40. OWH to Harold Laski, March 27, 1918, 1 HOLMES–LASKI LETTERS 144. Fanny would not read murder stories or novels in which children were badly treated. *Id.,* 2 HOLMES–LASKI LETTERS 849.

41. FBH Diary, vol. 2, OWH Papers, HLS, B73 F10.

42. *Id.*

43. H. JAMES, THE NOTEBOOKS OF HENRY JAMES 24 (F. O. Matthiessen and K. Murdock eds. 1947).

44. Holmes was a member of the Saturday Club, the Tavern Club, and of "The Club," his generation's equivalent of the Saturday Club. As to The Club, see W. E. Perkins to J. C. Warren, April 10, 1872, in the Warren Papers, MHS:

> The members of this club are as follows — Henry Adams   John Fiske   J. M. Crafts   J. C. Gray, Jr.   C E Grinnell   C. Hale O. W. Holmes, Jr.   H. James Jr   W. James   J. T. Morse Jr. T. S. Perry   J. C. Ropes   A. G. Sedgwick   M. Storey   W. P. Walley   We dine together at Parker's once a month, on the 2d Tuesday.

45. OWH Papers, HLS, B69 F2.

46. Howe notes, OWH conversation with Felix Frankfurter, recounted by Frankfurter, August 10, 1964, OWH Papers, HLS, B54 F5.

47. OWH Papers, HLS, B44 F12.

48. OWH Papers, HLS, B69 F2.

49. The cause of their childlessness, if there was a single cause, is not known with certainty. Mark Howe speculated that Holmes wished not to have children because they would have interfered with his work, and that Fanny accepted his choice, with some sorrow. 2 HOWE 8, 99–100. However, Howe was not aware of Fanny's prolonged illness following her marriage.

The Holmeses' childlessness seems adequately accounted for by Fanny's age and ill health. Fanny deeply regretted her childlessness. Howe interview notes, OWH Papers, HLS, B53 F13. Holmes's feelings are not known. In such circumstances divorce would have been possible, and so Holmes in a certain sense did choose not to be a father. Remarks scattered through Holmes's correspondence suggest that he was torn but remained loyal to Fanny. See, e.g., OWH to Lewis Einstein, August 31, 1928, HOLMES–EINSTEIN LETTERS 289. Fanny's selfless devotion to Holmes was perhaps not so one-sided as it appeared on the surface.

50. See, e.g., L. PAPER, BRANDEIS 21–22 (1983).

51. Kanda and Gifford, *The Kaneko Correspondence,* 37 MONUMENTA NIPPONICA 1, 44 (1982). They have "Shattuck & Holmes," although Holmes did not become a member of the firm until March, 1873. The modern transliteration would be "Inoue," but I give the spelling used then.

52. In 1876, Kaneko was still using his given name, Nao-tsugu, which he changed to Kentaro on his return to Japan in 1878.

53. Howells, *A Sennight of the Centennial*, ATLANTIC MONTHLY, July 1876, p. 97.

54. See, for instance, Enouye's essay in C. LANMAN, THE JAPANESE IN AMERICA (1871).

55. OWH to Kaneko Kentaro, March 21, 1924, Kanda and Gifford, *The Kaneko Correspondence*, 37 MONUMENTA NIPPONICA 414 (1982).

56. OWH to Frederick Pollock, July 27, 1899, 1 HOLMES–POLLOCK LETTERS 96, 97.

57. I. NITOBE, BUSHIDO 16 (1905).

58. *Id.*, p. 16. Some anthropologists in recent years have revived a Hobbesian picture of at least some primitive cultures as in a state of perpetual war. In such a world, revenge is apparently the principal motive for violence, and some recent authors have imagined, if not observed, legal institutions arising as a substitute for blood feuds. See Chagnon, *Life Histories, Blood Revenge, and Warfare in a Tribal Population*, 239 SCIENCE 985 (1988), and sources cited there; see especially notes 12, 13. Holmes's speculations along these lines have been — I don't suppose one can say "confirmed" — at least supported by this research.

59. Holmes, in short, was a structuralist. He later described THE COMMON LAW as a study of the "morphology and transformation of ideas." See OWH, *Law in Science — Science in Law*, COLLECTED LEGAL PAPERS 210, 212–217 (1920). Although there were structuralists among the idealists who followed Kant, Holmes was unusual, perhaps unique in his time, in developing structuralism from a materialist basis.

60. 10 AM. L. REV. 422 (1876).

61. I have paraphrased Holmes somewhat in modern language, since he wrote for his peers in the language of their common work, and even in his own day was difficult for an outsider to follow. Reading Holmes, one often has the sense of plunging into the middle of a conversation between friends who have no need to explain themselves.

62. Emerson Papers, Houghton; copy OWH Papers, HLS, B42 F20.

63. Frederick Pollock to OWH, May 26, 1876, 1 HOLMES–POLLOCK LETTERS 5.

64. C. LANMAN, THE JAPANESE IN AMERICA 58 (1871), quoting an unnamed Japanese student in his twenties, in Washington.

65. Kaneko to OWH, November 7, 1913, Kanda and Gifford, *The Kaneko Correspondence*, 37 MONUMENTA NIPPONICA 302 (1982).

66. OWH to Laski, December 3, 1918, 1 HOLMES–LASKI LETTERS 175. See also F. MAITLAND, THE LIFE AND LETTERS OF LESLIE STEPHEN 289–292 (1906).

67. William James to Henry James, July 5, 1876, in R. B. PERRY, THE THOUGHT AND CHARACTER OF WILLIAM JAMES 99 (1948). In the text, I have used the term *fairness* as shorthand for Holmes's somewhat artificial definition of "culpability."

Holmes's theory of tort liability is now his most famous contribution to the common law in the United States. The idea hinted at in *Primitive Notions in Modern Law — I*, 10 AM. L. REV. 422 (1876), and elaborated in *Trespass and Negligence*, 14 AM. L. REV. 1 (1880) and THE COMMON LAW (1881), is that everyone is held to the conduct expected of an ordinary, reasonable person, stated in objective terms. This is now widely accepted.

Holmes said that this standard of liability was based on a refined sense of culpability, which had supplanted the more primitive impulse of vengeance.

Unless my act is of a nature to threaten others, unless under the circumstances a prudent man would have foreseen the possibility of harm, to make me indemnify my neighbor against the consequences is no more justifiable than to make me do the same thing if I had fallen upon him in a fit, or to compel me to insure him against lightning.

Trespass and Negligence, 14 AM. L. REV. 1, 12 (1880). "Culpable" in Holmes's objective definition is therefore only the reverse of "accidental." Holmes evidently thought that according to modern ideas of social policy it would be unfair to impose liability for accidents, and that the unforeseeable consequences of a person's acts were simply accidents. See Note, *The Origin of the Modern Standard of Due Care in Negligence,* 1976 WASH. U. L. Q. 447, 462–465 (1977).

This analysis allowed Holmes to preserve for a little longer his scheme of duties. Tort law in this scheme imposed a generalized duty to behave prudently toward others, and this arrangement of the law remained implicit in THE COMMON LAW. But there were serious inconsistencies. The *consequences* of departing from this standard were inexplicable. Torts were not punished; courts merely shifted to the actor the cost of any harm to others that might have resulted from his breach of proper care. This was a curious and not necessarily effective way to impose a duty of proper conduct. The inconsistency between the substantive rule of law and the form of damages became even more marked in contract law, where the courts seemed indifferent in most cases to whether a contract was performed or not, so long as the breaching party bore the costs.

In the last essays he prepared for the Lowell Lectures (see below) Holmes overcame this difficulty by stepping entirely out of his original framework and seeing from a new perspective that a lawsuit *began* with damages, with the demand for a shifting of costs, and that the modern plaintiff's demand for recompense amounted to a plea for fairness (instead of vengeance). But he stubbornly preserved his arrangement of the law according to duties, and it was not until his address *The Path of the Law,* written in 1896, that Holmes conceded that his scheme of duties was irrelevant.

Modern commentators, sensing the inconsistency in THE COMMON LAW, have supposed that Holmes had an unstated rationale for the shifting of costs in tort law. See, e.g., Kelley, *A Critical Analysis of Holmes's Theory of Torts,* 61 WASH. U. L. REV. 681 (1983) (Holmes's theory was utilitarian). But this is anachronistic. It remained for much later analysts, notably Richard A. Posner, to work out an economic justification for the shifting of costs.

68. OWH, *Primitive Notions in Modern Law — II,* 11 AM. L. REV. 641 (1877).

69. OWH, *Possession,* 12 AM. L. REV. 688 (1878).

70. *Id.,* p. 701.

71. *Id.,* p. 719.

72. *Id.,* p. 720. Holmes was working out at long last his confusion over the nature of the rights of grain elevator owners and other "bailees."

73. OWH to Arthur Sedgwick, July 12, 1879, OWH Papers, HLS, B35 F2.

74. Frederick Pollock to OWH, November 26, 1878, 1 HOLMES–POLLOCK LETTERS 8.

75. OWH to Frederick Pollock, December 9, 1878, 1 HOLMES–POLLOCK LETTERS 10–11, esp. p. 10, note 2. Shepley, of Portland, Maine, had been a judge of the federal court for the First Circuit, which heard suits from the districts of New England. (There was still an overlapping dual system of federal trial courts, the circuit courts and the district courts.) The leading candidate to replace him was John Lowell, the Massachusetts district court judge before whom Holmes had so often appeared. If Lowell were to be promoted, Holmes might replace him on the district court.

76. See 2 HOWE 130–131.

77. Louis D. Brandeis to Otto Wehle, August 3, 1879, in 1 LETTERS OF LOUIS

D. BRANDEIS 47 (M. Urofsky and D. Levy eds. 1971). Brandeis was Chief Justice Horace Gray's secretary and explained that he could not persuade the chief justice to intervene on behalf of his uncle, Louis Dembitz, who was seeking a federal post, as he had for Holmes.

78. 2 G. HOAR, AUTOBIOGRAPHY OF SEVENTY YEARS 416–419 (1903); 2 HOWE 132.

79. The question apparently was whether Turner Sargent's share of his late father's estate should pass to nephews and nieces, Sargent having died childless, under the terms of a trust established under his father's will, or to Amelia under his own will. See OWH Papers, HLS, B73 F5.

80. EJH to FBH, November 20, 1881, OWH Papers, HLS, B73 F1.

81. Some who knew her in later years in Boston remarked on Fanny's almost purposeful plainness. In Mark Howe's notes of interviews with Charles Curtis, Jr., son of Ellen Curtis, a friend and neighbor of the Holmeses, Curtis speculates that Fanny may have cultivated her plainness as a way of announcing her lack of concern about Holmes's flirtations. Mrs. Frank Wigglesworth, one of Fanny's nieces, described Fanny "as about the plainest woman she had ever seen — making no effort in dress or otherwise. But also full of wit & humor." OWH Papers, HLS, B53 F13. Compare Miss Daintry in Henry James, *A New England Winter*, THE AMERICAN NOVELS AND STORIES OF HENRY JAMES 324 (F. O. Matthiessen and K. Murdock eds. 1948): "She would not for the world have looked better than she thought was right for so plain a woman."

82. Boston Daily Advertiser, April 19, 1880, p. 2, col. 3, quoted 2 HOWE 254.

83. 30 NATION 286 (April 21, 1881), quoted 2 HOWE 255. None of Fanny's embroideries have surfaced, although some perhaps survive. There is a photograph of one in the Harvard Law Art Collection, reproduced 1 HOWE facing page 227, a skillful rendering of a landscape with a Japanese flavor.

84. F. D. BUELL, SATURDAY MORNING CLUB OF BOSTON 36 (1971).

85. OWH to Frederick Pollock, July 16, 1879, 1 HOLMES–POLLOCK LETTERS 11, 12.

86. OWH to James Bryce, August 17, 1879, OWH Papers, HLS, B38 F9.

87. Louis D. Brandeis to Alfred Brandeis, July 31, 1879, 1 LETTERS OF LOUIS D. BRANDEIS 44, 45 (M. Urofsky and D. Levy eds. 1971).

88. OWH, *"United States Reports, Vol. 94"* (book review), 12 AM. L. REV. 354 (1878). These are the Granger cases, see Munn v. Illinois, 94 U.S. 113 (1876).

89. *Common Carriers and the Common Law*, 13 AM. L. REV. 609 (1879). Holmes argued that the strict liability being imposed on common carriers, including the ship owners his firm represented, was a modern innovation and not the ancient doctrine that the courts believed it to be. The innovation, Holmes argued, was made by Chief Justice Holt in the famous English case of *Coggs v. Bernard*, in 1703, for policy reasons that no longer obtained. Holmes argued that if strict liability were to be imposed, it should be on some acceptable policy reason, against which one might argue, rather than a blind repetition of a comparatively recent, policy-based innovation. *Id.* at 630.

90. *Id.* at 631.

91. "Ever since [about 1880] I have recognized the possibility of society consciously taking its destiny into its own hands. The trouble is that it must begin by knowing what it wants, and I am quite sure it would not accept what I think the ideal, or what I think the necessary foundation of reaching any ideal to be reached by such consciously self-determined means." OWH to Franklin Ford, December 29, 1917, in HOLMES–FORD LETTERS 129, 130.

92. See printed invitation and menu in OWH Papers, HLS, B18 F3.

93. OWH to Baroness Moncheur, January 9, 1915, OWH Papers, HLS, B15 F2.

94. *Trespass and Negligence*, 14 AM. L. REV. 1, 15 (1880).

95. *Id.* at 22. Holmes found the "foreseeability" versus "accident" distinction in Brown v. Kendall, 6 Cush. (Mass.) 292 (1850) (Shaw, C.J.), but Holmes's is the first general statement of foreseeability as a rule of liability in negligence, see note 67 above, and is now generally accepted.

96. OWH, THE COMMON LAW 1 (1881). This is the famous opening of the published work. We do not have the text of the lectures, which followed the published text but were greatly simplified.

97. This is not the place for an extended analysis of THE COMMON LAW, which even Holmes's severest critic called "the most important book on law ever written by an American." Rogat, *The Judge as Spectator*, 31 U. CHI. L. REV. 214 (1964). The summary in the text is my own effort to convey the overall argument to a reader or listener; it is not a paraphrase. No short summary could do justice to this long, difficult, and original work. I have somewhat emphasized the analytical framework of Holmes's argument, the classification of "duties," which in the published text is left implicit in the plan of arrangement, and which follows the scheme laid out in his early article on privity.

There is an extensive literature of commentary, which is too diverse to summarize here. The centennial of the publication of THE COMMON LAW called up a new round in the already extensive literature. See, e.g., Touster, *Holmes a Hundred Years Ago*, 10 HOFSTRA L. REV. 673 (1982); White, *The Integrity of Holmes' Jurisprudence*, 10 HOFSTRA L. REV. 633 (1982), which contains a helpful review of the earlier commentary. See also White, *The Rise and Fall of Justice Holmes*, 39 U. CHI. L. REV. 51 (1971).

Unique among nineteenth-century American law books, THE COMMON LAW remains in print, in an excellent 1963 edition by Mark Howe. Howe's preface is a thoughtful and tactful presentation of THE COMMON LAW in relation to Holmes's sources and to later thinking. Howe concludes in this preface that the book must now be read as a work of "philosophy" rather than of legal scholarship.

Perry Miller made a similar point: "*The Common Law* is . . . still the most impressive application to the facade of the law of that method of ascertaining the forces at work which is the essential method of Darwinism." P. MILLER, *Introduction*, in AMERICAN THOUGHT ix, xxxvi (1957).

98. H.L.A. HART, ESSAYS ON JURISPRUDENCE AND PHILOSOPHY 278 (1983).

CHAPTER 12. THE MOVING BANNERS OF A HIDDEN COLUMN

1. OWH to James B. Thayer, March 19, 1893, OWH Papers, HLS, B35 F4.

2. OWH to Mrs. Charles S. Hamlin, October 12, 1930, OWH Papers, HLS; Holmes said he shared the bottle of champagne with Shattuck, but George Shattuck was in Italy at this time.

3. OWH to Frederick Pollock, March 5, 1881, 1 HOLMES–POLLOCK LETTERS 16.

4. George Shattuck to OWH, April 2, 1881, OWH Papers, HLS.

5. See Sutherland, "Reminiscences of Justice Holmes," Arthur E. Sutherland Papers, HLS, B24 F7; OWH to Ethel Scott, May 27, 1910, OWH Papers, HLS, B47 F23; Frankfurter memorandum, Felix Frankfurter Papers, LOC, B146 F2974. Holmes did not explain why he thought he was dying. Frankfurter's memorandum has Holmes saying that "while brushing his teeth, he bled, and said to himself, 'Well, old fellow, your box is being closed." "Brushing his teeth" may be Frankfurter's euphemism; it suggests either more delicacy in telling the tale or more fearfulness at the time than we would expect from Holmes.

6. OWH to Frederick Pollock, April 10, 1881, 1 HOLMES–POLLOCK LETTERS 16, 17.

7. 2 HOWE 259–260.

8. Pollock, *Holmes on the Common Law,* THE SATURDAY REVIEW, June 11, 1881, p. 758.

9. [Dicey], *Holmes's "Common Law,"* THE SPECTATOR, June 3, 1882, p. 745 (emphasis added). This review was published anonymously, but has been identified as Dicey's; see Touster, *Holmes a Hundred Years Ago,* 10 HOFSTRA L. REV. 673, 696, n. 3, and Appendix II at 712 (1982) (where the review is reprinted).

10. George Shattuck to OWH, April 2, 1881, OWH Papers, HLS, B49, F37.

11. Mrs. Glendower Evans to Mark Howe, OWH Papers, HLS; see also L. PAPER, BRANDEIS 28 (1983).

12. The circumstances surrounding Holmes's appointment to the Harvard Law School were reconstructed by Mark Howe; see 2 HOWE 265. The faculty meeting described by him, 2 HOWE 263, suggests the lack of enthusiasm mentioned in the text here.

13. At the time, Holmes spoke of this move as justified and was reasonably happy, although Fanny remarked that he seemed to grow heavier in manner. In later years, he saw it as a wrong turning, "a withdrawal from the fight," very much as he came later to regret leaving his regiment. See, e.g., OWH to Felix Frankfurter, July 15, 1913, OWH Papers, HLS.

14. Holmes was assigned to teach torts, agency and carriers, suretyship and mortgage, jurisprudence, and admiralty. The torts course was taught by the case method from Ames's book. Holmes wrote and later published (see below) three essays to prepare for the courses on agency and suretyship, and apparently delivered them as lectures; the Lowell Lectures made up the bulk of the jurisprudence course. See 2 HOWE 273–274. The published essays are *Early English Equity,* 1 L. Q. REV. 162 (1885); *Agency: I,* 4 HARV. L. REV. 49 (1891), and *Agency: II,* 5 HARV. L. REV. 81 (1891); all three essays were reprinted in COLLECTED LEGAL PAPERS (1920). The essay on equity was one of Holmes's most successful historical researches, although it added nothing to his theoretical system. The two essays on agency were among his weakest efforts.

15. OWH to Frederick Pollock, April 8, 1882, 1 HOLMES–POLLOCK LETTERS; *Twenty Years in Retrospect,* SPEECHES 154, 155. A search by the clerk's office for Justice Frankfurter showed only one recorded appearance by OWH, on January 17, 1879; United States v. Ames, 99 U.S. 35 (1879). See Frankfurter Papers, LOC, B145 F2969; 2 HOWE 128–130. On April 8, 1882, however, OWH wrote to Pollock of his plan to "get a case argued in Washington" before leaving for Europe. It may be that OWH did not go to Washington, after all, in 1882 or, as in 1879 and as I think more likely, another firm with a Supreme Court practice made the principal argument and Holmes attended in a more modest capacity of which there is now no record.

16. This account is drawn from Holmes's trip diary, OWH Papers, HLS, B19, F3, except as otherwise noted.

17. Murlin, *Melville A. Bigelow,* 1 B.U. L. REV. 153, 162 (1921).

18. OWH to James Bryce, December 31, 1882, OWH Papers, HLS; 2 HOWE 280–281. See also OWH to Harold Laski, November 17, 1920, 1 HOLMES–LASKI LETTERS 290, 291: "The choice seemed to be between applying one's theories to practice and details or going into another field" at age forty, with doubts about his ability to make a living and do further creative work.

19. This is Holmes's account of the events. See, e.g., OWH to Lady Castletown, February 26, 1897, OWH Papers, HLS, B39 ("I always supposed he [Shattuck] made me a judge by his advice to the Governor"). There are some difficulties with it. In James B. Thayer's detailed version, based on Shattuck's report to

him, see 2 HOWE 265–270, Shattuck was only the messenger who brought the news to Holmes. There is some evidence for this version. Shattuck had actually written to Governor Long recommending one Judge Bishop for the post, and it was W. C. Russell who wrote to the governor recommending Holmes (see George Shattuck to Governor Long, and W. C. Russell to Long, both December 7, 1882, OWH Papers, HLS, B53 F28 [copies]). Shattuck may have fulfilled some obligation by writing on behalf of Bishop, and when Bishop proved unacceptable privately recommended Holmes. Or Shattuck, as the messenger bringing good news, may have simply allowed Holmes to think he was its author.

What seems most unlikely about Holmes's version is his implication that the appointment came as an entire surprise. Shattuck, knowing of Holmes's ambition, might have put him forward, but it seems unlikely that Russell would have written to the governor without prompting. Holmes, after all, had just accepted a professorship at Harvard. But Holmes never liked to admit any sort of office-seeking, and later would similarly dissemble his eagerness to be appointed to the Supreme Court.

20. Marcus Morton to OWH, December 16, 1882, OWH Papers, HLS, B45 F21.

21. As to Eliot's reaction, see OWH to Frederick Pollock, July 2, 1895, 1 HOLMES–POLLOCK LETTERS 57. As to the faculty's pique, see 2 HOWE 265–270.

22. Brandeis to OWH, December 9, 1882, OWH Papers, HLS, B38 F4, see also 1 LETTERS OF LOUIS D. BRANDEIS 65 (M. Urofsky and D. Levy eds. 1971).

23. OWH Sr. to Carolyn Kellogg, December 13, 1882, OWH Sr. Papers, Houghton. The poem the doctor read at the bar dinner in Holmes's honor is in the OWH Papers, HLS, B52.

24. R. DAVIS, HISTORY OF THE JUDICIARY OF MASSACHUSETTS 25 (1900).

25. OWH to Lewis Einstein, March 31, 1922, HOLMES–EINSTEIN LETTERS 204. In the deleted passage Holmes says, "She [Fanny] sent me to Europe and spent her summer," etc. Holmes's usually reliable memory failed him on this point; his correspondence shows that he did not go abroad in the summer of 1883, and that by January of 1884 he was already receiving letters addressed to 9 Chestnut Street. It was in 1903, when preparing the house at 1720 I Street, in Washington, that Fanny sent him abroad. See below.

26. OWH to Frederick Pollock, August 27, 1883, 1 HOLMES–POLLOCK LETTERS 22.

27. OWH to Frederick Pollock, March 25, 1883, 1 HOLMES–POLLOCK LETTERS 19, 21.

28. The supreme judicial court had original and exclusive jurisdiction of capital crimes, divorce, and equity, and had concurrent original jurisdiction with the superior courts in all matters of law, although the SJC generally left smaller matters to the lower courts to be tried. When acting as a trial court, the SJC occasionally sat *en banc*, but more often a single justice presided over the *nisi prius* proceedings and submitted a report to the full court. Thus, in the famous case of Vegehlan v. Guntner, 167 Mass. 92 (1896), Holmes sat alone as a trial judge in the equity court in Boston, granted a preliminary injunction, and submitted the case with his report to the full court, which granted a final injunction.

The court's *Rules* for 1884, court calendars, and schedules showing the *en banc* and single-justice sittings during Holmes's tenure are among the OWH Papers, HLS, B59. I am also indebted to an undated research memorandum prepared by L. Kinvin Wroth for Mark Howe, OWH Papers, HLS, B59 F2, and sources cited there. See also Loring, *Ought the Full Bench to Be Required to Go Circuit?* 5 MASS. L. Q. 65 (1919).

29. The court heard an average of five cases each day when it sat *en banc*. With two justices usually on circuit, each justice sitting *en banc* would have one

opinion to write for each day. Loring, *Ought the Full Bench to Be Required to Go Circuit?* 5 MASS. L. Q. 65 (1919).

30. "A parol release of a judgment for money, in consideration of payment for a smaller sum, is invalid at common law." Weber v. Conch, 134 Mass. 26 (1883) (Holmes J.).

31. Williams v. Boston Water Power Co., 134 Mass. 406 (1883) (Holmes, J.).

32. Commonwealth v. Fenno, 134 Mass. 217 (1883) (Holmes, J.).

33. Byington v. Simpson, 134 Mass. 169 (1883) (Holmes J.). Holmes relied on his theory of the historical fiction of identity between principal and agent, to allow suit against the wife, although only the husband was a party to the contract.

34. OWH to Frederick Pollock, March 25, 1883, 1 HOLMES–POLLOCK LETTERS 20.

35. *Speech at Dinner of the Boston Bar, March 7, 1900*, SPEECHES 121, 125.

36. Unpublished remarks of U.S. Circuit Judge James M. Morton, Jr., at memorial exercises for Holmes at the Supreme Judicial Court on October 9, 1937, quoted F. FRANKFURTER, MR. JUSTICE HOLMES AND THE SUPREME COURT 16–17 (2d ed., 1961).

37. Jacobs v. Rouse, Equity # 588, Suffolk County, unpublished master's report filed April 18, 1883; see L. Kinvin Wroth, undated research memorandum to Mark Howe, OWH Papers, HLS, B59 F2, App. II.

38. OWH to Frederick Pollock, December 15, 1912, 1 HOLMES–POLLOCK LETTERS 204.

39. *Id.*, August 27, 1883, 1 HOLMES–POLLOCK LETTERS 22.

40. OWH to Lewis Einstein, March 31, 1922, HOLMES–EINSTEIN LETTERS 204, 205.

41. OWH to Felix Frankfurter, OWH Papers, HLS, B29 F8.

42. John Holmes to OWH Sr., September 7, 1883; see Mark Howe's notebook, OWH Papers, HLS, Box 59, entries for 1883.

43. F. FRANKFURTER, MR. JUSTICE HOLMES AND THE SUPREME COURT 55 (1961). I have followed the version Frankfurter published. Among his and Mark Howe's papers is a memorandum with a slightly different account. In the memo, Frankfurter has Holmes saying,

> I remember Cabot Lodge wanting me to run for Governor when I was on the Mass. Bench & I said I didn't want to be Governor & he urged it on me because it would probably make me Senator & I replied, "Why should I give up a deliberate choice of life because taking another job might lead to another that I don't particularly care about?"

Undated, OWH Papers, HLS, B54 F5. There is no indication of when Lodge made this suggestion; I place it in 1883 or 1884 because Dr. Holmes had become a political issue at this time, Governor Ben Butler having opened investigations into the disrespectful use of paupers' corpses in the doctor's anatomy classes, and the issue became a rallying point for Republicans who returned to the State House in 1884.

44. Pittsfield Sun, September 11, 1883, p.2, col.4.

45. Examples of Holmes's jury instructions from 1885 are given in Appendix III of L. K. Wroth's memorandum to Mark Howe, OWH Papers, HLS, B59 F2.

46. See E. SHERMAN, SOME RECOLLECTIONS OF A LONG LIFE 82–104 (1908).

47. OWH to Felix Frankfurter, May 21, 1926, OWH Papers, HLS, B29 F10.

48. OWH to Frederick Pollock, April 9, 1884, 1 HOLMES–POLLOCK LETTERS 24.

49. *The Law, February 5, 1885,* SPEECHES 20, 21.

50. Alice Grenfell to OWH, October 29, 1901, OWH Papers, HLS, B43 F17.

In the letter to which this is the answer, Holmes apparently had told her that he began speaking in the way she admired when he was past forty.

51. *Memorial Day,* SPEECHES 4.

52. *Id.* 4–16.

CHAPTER 13. COURTLY LOVE

1. Theodore Roosevelt to Anna (Bamie) Roosevelt, October 30, 1884, quoted in E. MORRIS, THE RISE OF THEODORE ROOSEVELT 292 (1979).

2. OWH to Frederick Pollock, November 2, 1884, 1 HOLMES–POLLOCK LETTERS 26.

3. Commonwealth v. Peirce, 138 Mass. 165 (1884) (Holmes, J.). Holmes also wrote an interesting opinion in a case concerning a Northampton woman who tripped and fell in the road and suffered a miscarriage. She was only four or five months pregnant, and after a few moments of life the fetus died. Suit was brought on its behalf, or on behalf of the person it might have become, for its wrongful death. In a careful opinion, Holmes said for the court that neither statute nor common law created any liability for the death of a fetus before it reached the stage of viability — the ability to survive independent of its mother. Dietrich v. Northampton, 138 Mass. 14 (1884) (Holmes, J.).

4. Albert Boyden to Mark Howe, July 8, 1942, OWH Papers, HLS, B53 F13.

5. *Id.*

6. H. PEARSON, SON OF NEW ENGLAND: JAMES JACKSON STORROW 23–25 (1932).

7. O. WISTER, ROOSEVELT: THE STORY OF A FRIENDSHIP 130 (1930).

8. *Id.* at 129.

9. See M. A. DEW. HOWE, JOHN JAY CHAPMAN AND HIS LETTERS 59–60 (1937); R. HOVEY, JOHN JAY CHAPMAN: AN AMERICAN MIND 44–45 (1959).

10. John J. Chapman to OWH, March 19, 1887, OWH Papers, HLS, B39 F16. Chapman later reportedly conceived a jealous hatred for Holmes, and at one point contemplated murdering him and committing suicide. Mark Howe interview with R. Hovey, Howe notebook, OWH Papers, HLS, B59. Holmes tried unsuccessfully to find out what was wrong, and wrote repeatedly to Chapman and his family; see letters in OWH Papers, HLS, B39 F16.

11. *The Puritan, February 16, 1886,* SPEECHES 24, 26–27. The next day, Doctor Holmes led the singing of a hymn that he had composed.

12. *One Hundred Days,* 10 OWH SR. WORKS 34.

13. OWH to Simeon Baldwin, June 2, 1886, OWH Papers, HLS.

14. SPEECHES, 32–33.

15. Holmes referred only to his mother's "breakdown," and no other details of her illness have been preserved. Bowen says that Mrs. Holmes's intellect failed, and Bowen's account presumably is based on interviews with friends of the family. The doctor's hasty return from England is described in *One Hundred Days,* 10 OWH SR. WORKS 34.

16. OWH to Frederick Pollock, December 21, 1886, 1 HOLMES–POLLOCK LETTERS 28–29.

17. OWH to Owen Wister, March 25, 1887, OWH Papers, HLS.

18. Barrett Wendell to M. A. DeW. Howe, September 3, 1887, Howe Notebook, OWH Papers, HLS, Box 59.

19. OWH to Frederick Pollock, March 4, 1888, 1 HOLMES–POLLOCK LETTERS 30.

20. OWH to Mrs. Charles Hamlin, October 12, 1930, OWH Papers, HLS,

B35 F1. Holmes says, "I think that happened shortly after my mother's death in February, 1888, but I am not at all sure."

21. OWH to Frederick Pollock, March 4, 1888, 1 HOLMES–POLLOCK LETTERS 30, 32.

22. See Heard v. Sturgis, 146 Mass. 545, 548 (1888) (Holmes, J.); reversed *sub nom.* Williams v. Heard, 140 U.S. 529 (1891). The question before the court was whether an assignment in bankruptcy, made before the 1882 statute, conveyed to his creditors the debtor's claim (against the federal government) for insurance premiums.

Holmes treated this as if it were a case of sovereign immunity, and his citations trace the doctrine from Jean Bodin, a French jurist of the sixteenth century, through Hobbes, Bentham, Austin, and contemporary House of Lords opinions. Since no right or claim against the federal government could exist until created by federal law, there was no legally cognizable property right or claim to convey before 1882.

23. Williams v. Heard, 140 U.S. 529 (1891).

24. Holmes's Journal (the "Black Book") entry for 1888, OWH Papers, HLS; see also *Despondency and Hope,* SPEECHES 106.

25. OWH to Owen Wister, June 8, 1888, OWH Papers, HLS.

26. William James to his sister Alice, October 14, 1888, quoted R. PERRY, THE THOUGHT AND CHARACTER OF WILLIAM JAMES 174 (1954).

27. Ethel Grenfell (later Lady Desborough) to FBH, September 12, 1888; to OWH, January 5, 1889; OWH Papers, HLS.

28. Ethel Grenfell to OWH, May 4, 1889, OWH Papers, HLS. A few weeks after Ethel Grenfell's departure, Sidney Bartlett, a Boston lawyer, died at the age of ninety. Holmes, answering the resolutions of the bar on Bartlett's death, gave a talk that included a passage describing him. *Sidney Bartlett, March 23, 1889,* SPEECHES 51, 53–55. Holmes had the talk printed, and sent a copy to Ethel Grenfell, whose reply makes it plain that she recognized her late uncle in the description: "that 'youthful silver-crowned countenance' and what you said afterward so recalled our happy talk of Boston, of which much has dwelt with me." Ethel Grenfell to OWH, May 4, 1889, OWH Papers, HLS.

29. See OWH Sr. to Mrs. Ward, April 13, 1889, in 2 J. MORSE, LIFE AND LETTERS OF OLIVER WENDELL HOLMES 263 (1896).

30. OWH to Owen Wister, April 14, 1889, OWH Papers, HLS.

31. Kaneko Kentaro to James B. Thayer, August 29, 1889, Kanda and Gifford, *The Kaneko Correspondence,* 37 MONUMENTA NIPPONICA 225 (1982).

32. William James to Henry James, May 12, 1889, in THE LETTERS OF WILLIAM JAMES 285 (H. James ed. 1926).

33. William James, quoted in THE DIARY OF ALICE JAMES 54–55 (L. Edel ed. 1964).

34. OWH to Lady Castletown, February 17, 1898, OWH Papers, HLS, B26 F11.

35. OWH to Harold Laski, March 28, 1920, 1 HOLMES–LASKI LETTERS 253, 254.

36. See "Lord Haldane's Memories," The Times (London), January 14, 1929, p.3, col. 1.

37. Margot Tennant's diary, quoted A. LAMBERT, UNQUIET SOULS 84 (1984).

38. Margot Tennant to OWH, October 23, 1890, OWH Papers, HLS, B37 F18.

39. Margot Tennant to OWH, November 2, 1889, OWH Papers, HLS, B37 F18.

40. OWH to Lady Pollock, August 11, 1895, 1 HOLMES–POLLOCK LETTERS 58, 59.

41. OWH to Lady Burghclere, September 17, 1898, OWH Papers, HLS.

42. Ethel Grenfell to OWH, January 8, 1890, OWH Papers, HLS, B41 F20.

43. OWH to Lady Pollock, August 11, 1895, 1 HOLMES–POLLOCK LETTERS 58, 60.

CHAPTER 14. ANOTHER WAR

1. OWH Sr. to Carolyn Kellogg, OWH Sr. Papers, Houghton.

2. OWH Sr. to Carolyn Kellogg, February 7, 1891, OWH Sr. Papers, Houghton; OWH to Wigmore, February 23, 1893, HLS, B35 F4; see also OWH letters to Owen Wister from this period; the doctor's Friday symphony rehearsals are noted in his appointment books among his papers in Houghton.

3. See, e.g., OWH to Nina Gray, November 19, 1889, OWH Papers, HLS, B31 F3.

4. OWH to Owen Wister, August 21, 1892, OWH Papers, HLS, B35.

5. Boston Post, December 14, 1889. This is signed by a committee of the surviving veterans of the regiment, of which Holmes was a member. It is evidently Holmes's work, and he included a copy in the bound volume he made of his own early essays, OWH Papers, HLS, Paige Box 18.

6. *Over the Teacups,* 4 OWH SR. WORKS 1, 51.

7. Margot Tennant to OWH, November 2, 1889, OWH Papers, HLS, B37 F18.

8. See, for instance, Donnelly v. Boston & Maine R. Co., 157 Mass. 210 (1890). There were a half-dozen such cases in 1890–1891 alone, often with the same defendants and counsel. These were the origin of Holmes's later famous "stop, look and listen" rule, see Baltimore and Ohio R. Co. v. Goodman, 275 U.S. 66 (1927), much criticized at the time and soon overruled, Pokora v. Wabash R. Co., 292 U.S. 98 (1934) (Cardozo, J.).

9. See Coullard v. Tecumseh Mills, 151 Mass. 85 (1890); the reporter set out the tedious exposition of facts.

10. Esmond Shapiro to Mark Howe, August 4, 1942, OWH Papers, HLS, B54 F7; see also Friedman to Mark Howe, June 2, 1955, OWH Papers, HLS, B54 F5.

11. OWH to Frederick Pollock, February 23, 1890, 1 HOLMES–POLLOCK LETTERS 32, 33.

12. *Speech at Bar Dinner, March 7, 1900,* SPEECHES 122, 124.

13. *Daniel S. Richardson, April 15, 1890,* SPEECHES 56–57.

14. See, e.g., *Anonymity and Achievement, June 3, 1890,* SPEECHES 59.

15. OWH to Frederick Pollock, March 22, 1892, 1 HOLMES–POLLOCK LETTERS 35, 37.

16. *William Allen, September 15, 1891,* SPEECHES 65, 67–68.

17. He thought it an affectation to have the book privately printed, and so it was offered for sale; but he equally disliked to see it advertised, and so most of the copies were purchased by him to be given away. OWH to Alfred Zimmern, November 10, 1916, OWH Papers, HLS, "Addenda" (copy; original among Zimmern Papers in the Bodleian).

18. Nina Campbell to OWH, OWH Papers, HLS, B38 F25.

19. Lady Castletown to OWH, February 19, 1892, OWH Papers, HLS, B38 F28.

20. Walt Whitman to OWH, October 24, 1891, HLS, B51 F18. See also Whitman to OWH, July 6, 1899, November 3, 1900, *id.*

21. Louis D. Brandeis to OWH, October 2, 1891, OWH Papers, HLS, B38 F4.

22. OWH to James Bryce, July 17, 1892, OWH Papers, HLS, B39 F4.

23. Commonwealth v. Perry, 155 Mass. 117 (1891).

24. *Id.* at 123 (Holmes, J., dissenting). This is the first expression of Holmes's famous doctrine of deference to the legislature, which would later lead him into dissent on the Supreme Court. See also Opinions of the Justices, 155 Mass. 598, 607 (1892) (the "Coal Yard case") (Holmes, J., dissenting), in which the majority said that a statute authorizing towns to sell wood and coal would be unconstitutional. Holmes dissented, saying, "I see no ground for denying the power of the legislature to enact the laws . . . proposed. The need or expediency of the legislation is not for us to consider."

Plainly implicit in these opinions is the view that Holmes soon made explicit, that except where restrained by some provision of the Constitution, a state legislature had complete legislative authority; that in the legislative sphere it was, like the British Parliament, omnipotent.

Holmes's view is consistent with his usual practice of referring first to English common law. It is identical with the premise of Thomas M. Cooley's CONSTITUTIONAL LIMITATIONS (1868), which Holmes reviewed warmly in the AMERICAN LAW REVIEW when it appeared and used in teaching his course on Constitutional law at Harvard. By 1890, Cooley's was the principal work on the subject:

> In considering the powers which may be exercised by the legislative department of a State, it is natural that we should recur to those possessed by the Parliament of Great Britain, upon which, in a measure, the American legislatures have been modeled.

Id. at 85 (1868). Cooley added, following the weight of judicial authority, that courts would not strike down a statute, even when an explicit constitutional constraint was in question, unless the violation were clear beyond a reasonable doubt. *Id.* at 182–186. Massachusetts Chief Justice Lemuel Shaw was among the authorities for this proposition.

This was Holmes's position, sketched in compressed form in the passage quoted in the text. It was indeed the ordinary, conservative view, only later cast into question by radical property rights advocates.

Two years after Holmes's decision in *Commonwealth v. Perry*, James B. Thayer published a brief article, *The Origin and Scope of the American Doctrine of Constitutional Law*, 7 HARV. L. REV. 17 (1893), in which he emphasized the political importance of the doctrine of judicial deference, amply citing Cooley, as well as Bryce and Dicey on the English constitution. Holmes's dissent in *Perry* was not cited, although Holmes was quoted in another context. Thayer's article is still sometimes cited, and there is a commonly repeated view that Holmes was influenced by it. Thayer sent Holmes a copy, and Holmes certainly agreed with it, as far as it went; but he wrote to Thayer saying that the article relied a little narrowly on a formula based on the separation of powers. Holmes reminded Thayer that it was also important that the state legislatures' powers in legislative matters were unlimited, except where constrained by state or federal constitutions: "State legislature has the power of Parliament —i.e. absolute power, except so far as expressly or by implication it is prohibited by the Constitution." OWH to Thayer, November 2, 1893, OWH Papers, HLS, B35 F4. This, rather than any feature peculiar to the separation of powers, was the principal basis of Holmes's own philosophy.

25. Holmes several times described his meetings with a union leader, but he never gave the man's name or the date of the meetings. I am indebted to Mary Jane Warren for the conjecture, which I think correct, that Frank Foster was the person. Foster was a well-read intellectual, an admirer of Herbert Spencer, and in other ways likely to have been congenial to Holmes. Foster's program, as de-

scribed in his writings of this time, pretty well match those that Holmes attributed to the labor leader he met.

The first mention of the meetings is in Holmes's January, 1893, letter to Frederick Pollock, see below, and it seems likely that they occurred in 1892 and were prompted at least in part by the labor disturbances that year, and perhaps in part by the *Perry* case the year before.

26. OWH to Frederick Pollock, January 20, 1893, 1 HOLMES–POLLOCK LETTERS 44.

27. See, e.g., The Labor Leader, March 10, 1888, p. 2.

28. E. SERGEANT, *Oliver Wendell Holmes,* in FIRE UNDER THE ANDES 323 (1927) (Holmes was the source for this anecdote).

29. See, e.g., *Remarks at Tavern Club, April 24, 1895,* SPEECHES 71. The "one or two laboring men" probably refers to Frank Foster.

30. M. JOSEPHSON, THE ROBBER BARONS 407 (1962).

31. See OWH to Samuel May, a classmate of the doctor, October 8, 1894, in the Harvard Class of 1829 Class Book, p. 328, quoted E. TILTON, AMIABLE AUTOCRAT 438, n. 441 (1947).

32. See OWH Papers, HLS, B73 F14.

33. OWH to James Bryce, November 5, 1894, OWH Papers, HLS, B38 F3.

34. See Mark Howe, notes of interview with Mrs. Arthur Hill, OWH Papers, HLS; quoted 1 HOWE 200, n. i. The date at which Fanny became ill for the second time is not known, but by early 1896 she was sufficiently recovered to suggest that Holmes go abroad; in 1897 she was still better, but not fully recovered. OWH to Lady Pollock, July 20, 1897, 1 HOLMES–POLLOCK LETTERS 75. Fanny probably became ill shortly after the doctor's death, some time in late summer or fall of 1894. Bowen dates the illness to 1896, BOWEN 325, but does not give her source, and she freely invented details of this kind.

35. BOWEN 325, 334–335.

36. OWH Papers, HLS, B44 F12. There is no date on this letter, and placing it here is conjectural.

37. See Holmes's reading list in his Journal, OWH Papers, HLS; OWH to Frederick Pollock, January 20, 1893, 1 HOLMES–POLLOCK LETTERS 44.

38. OWH to Lady Castletown, June 1, 1898, OWH Papers, HLS, B39.

39. Holmes's acceptance of Malthusian doctrine was of long standing, from as far back as his 1873 article, *The Gas Stokers' Strike,* and firmly held all his life. See, among many examples, OWH to Lady Castletown, October 17, 1897, August 19, 1897, OWH Papers, HLS. These were, of course, entirely conventional views, for which Holmes hardly needed to look into books, and which apparently were not based on reading. While Holmes often spoke of Malthus, there is no entry for Malthus's books in Holmes's reading lists until 1914; none for Darwin until 1907.

In 1893, at about the time being discussed, Holmes apparently became alarmed over the prospect of war between the white and colored races. See his letters, and *Paul Bourget* (December 4, 1893), SPEECHES 69, 70. These concerns were prompted by a book, see SPEECHES 163, 165, which evidently was C. H. PEARSON, NATIONAL LIFE AND CHARACTER (1893). Although he often referred to it later, the book does not appear on his reading list, and he may have picked up its ideas from Brooks Adams, who often visited Holmes at Beverly Farms and who, with many other Bostonians, read it that summer. A. BERINGAUSE, BROOKS ADAMS 127 (1955). Pearson predicted the state socialism and the "world . . . cut up into five-acre lots" that Holmes denounced in *The Soldier's Faith,* see below, and predicted "the Twilight of the Gods" for the European races that became Holmes's theme thereafter.

40. OWH to Harold Laski, December 26, 1917, 1 HOLMES–LASKI LETTERS 122.

41. C. PEARSON, NATIONAL LIFE AND CHARACTER 28 (1893). Portions of *The Soldier's Faith* appear to be in direct response to this book; see note 39 above.

42. Margaret Sanger opened the first birth-control clinic in New York City in 1916.

43. See, for instance, OWH to Lady Castletown, August 19, 1897, OWH Papers, HLS, B39 F4. Holmes almost certainly believed that his views were more humane than the conventional hard-mindedness of his class, which would have left the poor to starve. Even today, there is no lack of respectable Malthusians who say that famine should be allowed to run its course when it strikes in Ethiopia or Bangladesh. The brutality with which Holmes expressed his version of this popular philosophy, and his apparently well-developed fantasy about the execution of unfit children, suggest an emotional basis, however, perhaps related to his own childlessness and his sense of having been sent by his parents to die in the Civil War. The experiences of whipping his men to face their death in the Civil War and of sentencing criminals to death presumably played their parts in the development of his feelings.

44. Elmer v. Fessenden, 151 Mass. 359 (1890) (Holmes, J.).

45. Tasker v. Stanley, 153 Mass. 148 (1891) (Holmes, J.).

46. Burt v. Advertiser Newspaper Co., 154 Mass. 238 (1891) (Holmes, J.).

47. The defamation cases, aside from raising the question of the privilege accorded to damaging speech, pointed out another difficulty in Holmes's theory of torts. In several of these cases there were intervening third parties, and in these cases liability depended, not on the behavior of the defendant, but on that of the intervening party.

This was a common problem in negligence cases, where Holmes treated it as a question of foreseeability; the ordinary man was expected to foresee only the lawful behavior of others, and was not held to anticipate wrongdoing. Clifford v. Atlantic Cotton Mills, 146 Mass. 47 (1888); Hayes v. Hyde Park, 153 Mass. 514 (1891). In *Clifford,* as in *Elmer v. Fessenden,* the intervening party was considered a wrongdoer, not to be anticipated. In *Hayes v. Hyde Park,* the intervening third party was innocent, and foreseeable.

In Graves v. Johnson, 156 Mass. 211 (1892), Holmes extended this method of analysis to contract cases. In a suit to enforce a contract to sell wholesale liquor to a buyer in Maine, where resale would be illegal, the defense was the illegality of the contract, on the theory that the illegal resales were foreseeable. But Holmes said, "A man has a right to expect lawful conduct from others. In order to charge him with the consequences of the act of an intervening wrongdoer, you must show that he actually contemplated the act." 156 Mass. 212–213.

American courts generally have not followed Holmes's lead, and have continued to work out their analyses in the opaque language of "proximate cause." Holmes's analysis of foreseeability is, as Frederick Pollock occasionally reminded him, rather finely honed for ordinary work. Holmes's use of the term *foreseeability* to mean the proper course of conduct and events was too old-fashioned and too English for an America in which "foreseeability" soon came to mean mathematical probability.

48. Holmes's Journal, p. 148, OWH Papers, HLS, shows that he began work on *Privilege, Malice and Intent* in the spring of 1894.

49. *Privilege, Malice and Intent,* 8 HARV. L. REV. 1 (1894).

50. *Id.* at 9. This article marks an important new stage in Holmes's thinking, the first extension of his theories into the realm of public law.

In THE COMMON LAW, as an attorney Holmes had described solitary private parties struggling with legal duty. Now Holmes's standpoint had become a judge's, and his task the modern one of regulating complex social relations. The question for Holmes was no longer the defendant's duty, but the judge's. It was no longer enough for him to say, from the counsel table, that judges drew on notions of social policy. Holmes struggled to make himself, as a judge, a conscious instrument of the great social forces brought to bear in his court. His own economic preferences were to be set aside. Much as he disliked and feared the outcome, he could find no general policy in the precedents he was bound to honor that would allow him to deny to capitalists or workers, to Jay Gould or the unions, the privilege to form great combinations, nor to deny the great combines of capital and labor the privilege of waging economic war. Nor from an objective standpoint could he find any argument to support what in any case would be futile — efforts to prevent the struggle between classes. What he did find in the common law were fundamental principles of fairness that were to be applied without regard to the judge's personal loyalties or inclinations.

The article went on to discuss cases in which actual malice would defeat a claim of privilege. These cases seemed to pose a challenge to his system of external, objective standards of liability, and Holmes's program was to confront the challenge squarely and to salvage his system. External standards remained his point of departure, and he repeatedly emphasized that the question of privilege did not arise unless liability by an external standard would otherwise be imposed. This is not so much argued as asserted.

He took the defamation cases first, where liability was based on actual malice. In these he showed that the privileges recognized by courts rested on objective considerations of policy. The law, in Holmes's view, was purely instrumental, and privileges were granted for the sake of some social purpose. (It was at this point in the argument that there was a diversion into the boycott and combination cases.) All that remained, then, was to show that the *defense* of actual malice to a claim of privilege, while apparently an exception to the general rule of external standards, in fact followed from the general rule itself. A privilege to do harm would be withdrawn if exercised for improper motives — not because of some moral judgment upon the motives but because the purpose of the privilege would no longer be served.

The second group of cases consisted of those in which a third person had intervened between the defendant and the eventual harm, sometimes innocently and sometimes not. The defendant was held liable if the intervening party was innocent, by the test of external standards. Here, Holmes salvaged his system by rejecting the usual analysis, which blamed the "last wrongdoer" or the "proximate cause." He substituted his own formula — that a man was not bound to foresee wrongdoing — and then showed that this exemption from the usual requirement of foresight could be defeated, just as a privilege could be defeated, by an intent to cause harm.

The argument is presented as a series of insights, with thoughts set down as they occurred to Holmes, rather than in an orderly exposition, and so is difficult to follow, particularly when the context in which he wrote is no longer present to mind. Despite the article's importance, it has caused a great deal of confusion. A general idea has grown up that Holmes abandoned his earlier insistence on respect for precedent and on objective standards, and gave himself up to pure judicial legislation. See, for instance, Tushnet, *The Logic of Experience: Oliver Wendell Holmes on the Supreme Judicial Court*, 63 VA. L. REV. 975 (1977); White, *The Integrity of Holmes' Jurisprudence*, 10 HOFSTRA L. REV. 633 (1982).

To Holmes, at least, the article was a defense of his system, and not a departure from it. The article extended his common-law analysis into the sphere of public law and laid the basis for his most famous constitutional opinions on due process of law and freedom of speech, see below. Cf. Kellogg, *Common Law and*

Constitutional Theory: The Common Law Origins of Holmes' Constitutional Restraint, 7 GEORGE MASON L. REV. 177 (1984); Vetter, *The Evolution of Holmes: Holmes and Evolution,* 72 CALIF. L. REV. 343, 367 (1984).

51. OWH to Lady Pollock, July 25, 1895, 1 HOLMES–POLLOCK LETTERS 57.

52. *Learning and Science,* SPEECHES 84.

53. *Id.,* 85.

54. *The Soldier's Faith,* SPEECHES 73. This may be Holmes's most famous address. It was criticized at the time, and later, as warlike and jingoistic. Holmes never responded publicly to criticism, but privately he said some years later of this speech:

> For the past two years I have been struck with the question oppressing all sorts of writers, what will become of ideals when historic religion fails? My answer is very simple and probably you know it. Years ago, having the same prepossession, I tried in my speech The Soldier's Faith to bring home by example that men are eternally idealists — (a speech that fools took as advice to young men to wade in gore —) but of course that was not the place to philosophize and give the reason why.

OWH to Clara Stevens, September 3, 1909, OWH Papers, HLS, B15 F25.

55. Theodore Roosevelt to Henry Cabot Lodge, June 5, 1895, 1 SELECTIONS FROM THE CORRESPONDENCE OF THEODORE ROOSEVELT AND HENRY CABOT LODGE 146 (H. C. Lodge ed. 1925).

56. A classmate of Roosevelt's, W. S. Bigelow, invited Holmes to dinner, saying, "Theodore Roosevelt is here for the day, and wants to embrace you in connexion with some recent Jingoid remarks attributed to you." Since Holmes did not ordinarily dine out when Fanny was ill, Roosevelt added a note, "Can't I have a chance just to shake hands with you?" OWH Papers, HLS, B49 F10, no date.

57. Holmes heard this story from the secretary of state, Charles Olney, OWH to Lady Castletown, November 19, 1896, OWH Papers, HLS, B26 F10. On the Venezuela Boundary question President Cleveland took a militant stance that Olney attributed to Holmes's speech, but Holmes thought that absurd.

CHAPTER 15. LADY CASTLETOWN

1. OWH to Nina Gray, September 2, 1895, OWH Papers, HLS, B31 F5.

2. OWH to Nina Gray, July 17, 1896, OWH Papers, HLS, B31 F6.

3. Q. BELL, VIRGINIA WOOLF 78 (1972).

4. OWH to Lady Pollock, April 11, 1897, OWH papers, HLS; 1 HOLMES–POLLOCK LETTERS 72–73.

5. Ethel James to OWH, September 30, 1896, OWH Papers, HLS, B49 F26.

6. Lady Castletown to OWH, "Saturday," no date, OWH Papers, HLS, B38 F28. Holmes's diary places this at July 4, 1896.

7. See OWH to Lady Castletown, August 6, 1897, OWH Papers, HLS.

8. OWH to Lady Pollock, June 11, 1897, 1 HOLMES–POLLOCK LETTERS 72, 73.

9. Margot Asquith to OWH, no date, probably soon after their meeting in the summer of 1894, OWH Papers, HLS, B37 F18.

10. Ethel Grenfell to OWH, no date; from 4 St. James's Square, probably July, 1896, OWH Papers, HLS.

11. This and the following two letters, Henry James to OWH, no date, OWH Papers, HLS. Holmes's diary places these in August, 1896; see also Howe, *The Letters of Henry James to Mr. Justice Holmes,* YALE REV., Spring 1949, p. 410.

12. Henry James to OWH, October 17, 1901, OWH Papers, HLS.

13. OWH diary, OWH Papers, HLS, B19 F3; OWH to Lady Castletown, September 17, 1896, OWH Papers, HLS, B39 F1.

14. A shepherd at Doneraile told Yeats the story of a ghost who showed herself naked until her relatives made clothes and gave them to a beggar. W. B. YEATS, EXPLORATIONS 69 (1962). The story was among those collected by Lady Gregory for *Gods and Men,* published in 1904. It is my fancy to have Holmes talking with Lady Castletown about it in 1896.

15. OWH to Lady Castletown, August 22, 1896, "Saturday, 8 1/2 p.m." (on letterhead of the Queen's Hotel, Queenstown), OWH Papers, HLS, B26 F9.

16. OWH to Lady Castletown, August 23–28, 1896 (the "steamship diary" letter), OWH Papers, HLS, B26 F9.

17. OWH to Lady Castletown, September 5, 1896, OWH Papers, HLS, B26 F9.

18. *Id.*

19. OWH to Lady Castletown, September 17, 1896, OWH Papers, HLS, B39 F1.

20. OWH Papers, HLS, B38 F28. This note in Lady Castletown's hand is on a small square of plain paper and is not dated or signed.

21. Holmes kept with this note some leaves of joe-pye weed (kindly identified for me by Dr. Peter F. Stevens, curator of the Harvard University herbaria). As noted below, Holmes sent Lady Castletown this flowering plant in 1897, and so the date of the letter may be several months later than I have placed it here.

22. OWH to Lady Castletown, September 30, 1896, OWH Papers, HLS, B39 F1.

23. *Id.,* October 7, 1896, OWH Papers, HLS, B26 F9.

24. *Id.,* October 17, 1896, OWH Papers, HLS, B26 F9.

25. *Id.,* November 9, 1896, OWH Papers, HLS, B26 F10.

26. *Id.,* November 21, 1896, OWH Papers, HLS, B39 F1.

27. *Id.,* December 4, 1896, OWH Papers, HLS, B39 F1.

28. *Id.,* December 19, 1896, OWH Papers, HLS, B39 F1.

29. *Id.,* December 28, 1896, OWH Papers, HLS, B26 F10.

30. *Id.,* February 2, 1897, OWH Papers, HLS, B26 F10.

31. *Id.,* February 11, 1897, OWH Papers, HLS, B39 F1.

32. *Id.,* March 5, 1897, OWH Papers, HLS, B39 F1.

33. *Id.,* March 12, 1897, OWH Papers, HLS, B39 F1.

34. *Id.,* March 26, 1897, OWH Papers, HLS, B39 F1.

35. *Id.,* April 10, 1897, OWH Papers, HLS, B39 F1.

36. *Id.*

37. *Id.,* April 30, 1897, OWH Papers, HLS, B39 F1.

38. *Id.,* May 7, 1897, OWH Papers, HLS, B39 F2.

39. *Id.,* May 20, 1897, OWH Papers, HLS, B39 F2.

40. *Id.,* June 3, 1897, OWH Papers, HLS, B39 F3.

41. *Id.,* June 18, 1897, OWH Papers, HLS, B26 F11.

42. *Id.,* June 24, 1897, OWH Papers, HLS, B26 F11.

43. *Id.,* August 9, 1897, OWH Papers, HLS, B39.

44. *Id.,* August 19, 1897, OWH Papers, HLS, B39.

45. *Id.*

46. Although a pink mallow is common, this may have been joe-pye weed, which flowers in the fall. Holmes appears to have sent some to Lady Castletown. She perhaps planted it at Doneraile, and sent back a few leaves. See note 21, above.

47. OWH to Lady Castletown, December 4, 1897, OWH Papers, HLS, B39.

48. *Id.,* December 8, 1897, OWH Papers, HLS, B39.

49. *Id.,* December 17, 1897, OWH Papers, HLS, B39.

50. *Id.*, December 31, 1897, OWH Papers, HLS, B39.
51. *Id.*
52. *Id.*, January 10, 1898, OWH Papers, HLS, B39.
53. *Id.*, February 3, 1898, OWH Papers, HLS, B39.
54. *Id.*
55. *Id.*, May 18, 1898, OWH Papers, HLS, B39.
56. *Id.*, June 6, 1898, OWH Papers, HLS, B39.
57. *Id.*, June 7, 1898, OWH Papers, HLS, B39.
58. *Id.*, September 5, 1898, OWH Papers, HLS, B39.

CHAPTER 16. THE PATH OF THE LAW

1. See Holmes's letters in the fall of 1896 and winter of 1896–1897, to Lady Castletown and to Nina Gray, OWH Papers, HLS, for his popularity at dinner tables. Bowen mentions Holmes's dining out alone while Fanny convalesced, which apparently was still remembered when Bowen interviewed surviving Bostonians, see BOWEN 326, but her single instance of Holmes's dinner conversation — "Zola — Improving, but dull" — is an anachronism. It is evidently taken from Owen Wister's reminiscence of fifteen years earlier, O. WISTER, ROOSEVELT: THE STORY OF A FRIENDSHIP (1930).

2. See, e.g., OWH to Lady Castletown, January 15, 1897, OWH Papers, HLS, B39 F1; *id.*, March 24, 1897; among many such examples.

3. OWH to Lady Castletown, May 20, 1897, OWH Papers, HLS, B39 F1.

4. OWH to Lady Pollock, April 11, 1897, 1 HOLMES–POLLOCK LETTERS 72, 74.

5. See Vegehlan v. Guntner, 167 Mass. 92 (1896). Holmes granted a preliminary injunction as described, heard the case on the merits and then reported the case to the full court for decision on the final order. Holmes's dissent was cited with approval by the House of Lords in *Allen v. Flood,* and so eventually came to be treated as authority in England; see Ware and De Freville, Ltd. v. Motor Trade Assoc., 3 K.B. 40 (1921). The Supreme Court of the United States implicitly adopted his reasoning in American Steel Foundries v. Tri-City Central Trades Council, 257 U.S. 184 (1921); see below.

6. Vegehlan v. Guntner, 167 Mass. 92, 97 (1896).

7. *Id.* at 108.

8. BOWEN 331, presumably from Arthur Hill, whom she lists among her sources. See also Hill, *Oliver Wendell Holmes, Justice of the Supreme Court of the United States,* 39 HARV. GRAD. MAG. 265, 279 (1931).

9. *The Path of the Law,* 10 HARV. L. REV. 457 (1897), reprinted COLLECTED LEGAL PAPERS 167 (1920); an address delivered by Holmes at the dedication of the new hall of the Boston University School of Law on January 8, 1897.

There are no ideas in this talk that one does not find in Holmes's earlier writings and speeches; see Howe, *The Positivism of Mr. Justice Holmes,* 64 HARV. L. REV. 529, 540 (1951); but this is the best and by far the most lucid exposition of his ideas on the nature of the common law, as seen from the young lawyer's perspective.

Perhaps because it speaks so directly to young lawyers, it has been a favorite of the law schools and has been reprinted often. Although the address is often attacked for cynicism, see, e.g., L. FULLER, THE LAW IN QUEST OF ITSELF (1940), generations of young idealists have nurtured their ambitions on it. See, for instance, Justice Benjamin Kaplan, writing in 1980 about his days as a student at Columbia in 1930, *Encounter with Oliver Wendell Holmes, Jr.,* 96 HARV. L. REV. 1828 (1983).

Holmes, as noted earlier, often preached to students about the importance of idealism. The impression of cynicism in this address comes from his strenuous insistence that the student not look at the law in moral terms. This point is emphasized only because Holmes had at last abandoned the framework of "duties," to which he had stubbornly clung during all the years of preparation of THE COMMON LAW and which he finally admitted was superfluous to his analysis there. See OWH to John C. Gray, October 27, 1914, OWH Papers, HLS, B33 F25.

To explain his having abandoned the terminology of duties, Holmes went on at some length, saying that terms borrowed from moral discourse could be misleading. This was not cynicism, only science. As Holmes often pointed out, public morality was one of the *sources* of law, but the terminology of morals was not useful for scientific study. See the exchange between Mark Howe and Henry Hart in 64 HARV. L. REV. 529, 929 and 937 (1951).

The title, "The Path of the Law," is probably a conscious reference to the Tao, a term that connotes both a path to understanding and a way of life; as in Bushido, the Way of the Warrior, a term Holmes almost certainly knew.

In a letter to Lady Castletown, January 11, 1897, OWH Papers, HLS, B30 F1, Holmes said that when delivering this address he departed from his usual practice and read from the written text.

10. *The Path of the Law,* COLLECTED LEGAL PAPERS 167, 202 (1920).

11. OWH to Lady Castletown, February 26, 1897, OWH Papers, HLS, B39.

12. OWH to Lady Castletown, July 15, 1897, OWH Papers, HLS, B26 F11.

13. OWH to Nina Gray, July 25, 1897, OWH Papers, HLS.

14. OWH to Lady Castletown, July 15, 1897, OWH Papers, HLS, B26 F11.

15. OWH to Lady Pollock, July 20, 1897, 1 HOLMES–POLLOCK LETTERS 74, 75.

16. OWH to Lady Castletown, August 19, 1897, OWH Papers, HLS.

17. *Id.,* December 8, 1897, OWH Papers, HLS.

18. *Id.,* February 11, 1898, OWH Papers, HLS.

19. *Id.,* March 8, 1898, OWH Papers, HLS.

20. *Id.,* April 15, 1898, OWH Papers, HLS.

21. *Id.,* April 29, 1898, OWH Papers, HLS.

22. See L. CLIFFORD ("Mrs. W. K. Clifford"), THE LIKENESS OF THE NIGHT (1900).

23. James Bryce to OWH, August 12, 1898, OWH Papers, HLS, B38 F12.

24. OWH to Winston Churchill, July 16, 1898, OWH Papers, HLS, B52.

25. The account of this visit is taken primarily from Holmes's diary, OWH Papers, HLS, B19 F3. The description of Granston Manor is taken from a newspaper story of the time, which is among Holmes's papers. He mentions his illness in letters after he returns home, and some pages of the diary during his visit to Granston Manor and Doneraile are marked with penciled X's. This is apparently in imitation of his father's practice of marking days of illness with crosses or X's, depending on the ailment. On one day he notes explicitly "shingles" and "eczema."

CHAPTER 17. CHIEF JUSTICE

1. *Law in Science, Science in Law,* 12 HARV. L. REV. 443 (1899), reprinted in COLLECTED LEGAL PAPERS 210 (1920). Holmes repeats and elaborates his evolutionary theory, interestingly discussed in Elliott, *Holmes and Evolution: Legal Process as Artificial Intelligence,* 13 J. LEGAL STUDIES 113 (1984); see Chapter 10, note 32, above, but Holmes did not develop any important new ideas in this

address nor attribute any special importance to it. As his unpublished letters make plain, this exposition of his theory is just given as an example of Science for Science's sake: "I have written under high pressure an address which I have to deliver before the N.Y. State Bar Association in January and I have taken delight in there . . . asserting man's right to pursue abstract ends merely to gratify his own appetites. . . . [Man] paints a picture or asks unanswerable fool questions about the universe." OWH to Lady Burghclere, December 2, 1898, OWH Papers, HLS, B38 F14.

2. OWH to Lady Castletown, May 19, 1899, OWH Papers, HLS, B26 F13.

3. *Id.*

4. Lord Castletown to OWH, June 18, 1899, OWH Papers, HLS, B38 F28.

5. OWH to Frederick Pollock, July 27, 1899, 1 HOLMES–POLLOCK LETTERS 96–97.

6. Nina Gray to OWH, July 28, 1899, OWH Papers, HLS, B31 F1.

7. Records of the Supreme Judicial Court, Berkshire Co., Vol. 20, p. 48.

8. The Berkshire Eagle, September 12, 1899, p. 1, col. 5.

9. Horace Gray to OWH (no date), OWH Papers, HLS, B45 F24. See OWH reply, OWH Papers, HLS, B35 F8.

10. Alfred R. Hussey to Mark Howe, August 8, 1942, OWH Papers, HLS, B54 F7. The justices first wore robes in Boston on the first Tuesday in March, 1901, but the incident described occurred in Taunton — apparently an out-of-town tryout — some time before.

11. See, e.g., Plant v. Woods, 176 Mass. 492, 504 (1900) (Holmes, J., dissenting). Holmes also dissented in two cases where his theory of privileges was involved and in which the court held that acts and not motives were always the source of liability, ironically extending Holmes's own doctrine of objective standards past the point to which he would have carried it; Holmes dissented, saying that a privilege was defeated by actual malice. See Rice v. Albee, 164 Mass. 88 (1895); May v. Wood, 172 Mass. 11 (1898). Holmes's view was eventually accepted in Berry v. Donovan, 188 Mass. 353 (1905), which is adverse to labor and holds that combinations of workingmen for a malicious purpose are not lawful. See M. BIGELOW, CENTRALIZATION AND THE LAW 9–11 (1906). Holmes's views of the law, therefore, were not necessarily prolabor. In Plant v. Woods, apparently to dissociate himself from the union, Holmes made a point of spelling out his own economic views, which were Malthusian, and which led him to believe that unions competed with other less favored workers for a share of the limited product. See also OWH, *Economic Elements*, COLLECTED LEGAL PAPERS 279 (1920).

12. OWH to Ellen Curtis, December 4, 1901, OWH Papers, HLS, B35 F9.

13. SPEECHES 122, 123–126.

14. FBH to OWH, June 18, 1900, OWH Papers, HLS, B44 F12.

15. Mark Howe memorandum, "Anecdotes of Austin W. Clarke," May, 1948, OWH Papers, HLS, B54.

16. OWH to Henry James, December 24, 1900, OWH Papers, HLS.

17. Henry James to OWH, no date; OWH Papers, HLS, B45 F1. Holmes's diary shows he received such a telegram on July 21, 1901; OWH Papers, HLS. See also Howe, *The Letters of Henry James to Mr. Justice Holmes*, YALE REV., Spring 1949, at 410, 426.

18. Alice Grenfell to OWH, April 3, 1902, OWH Papers, HLS, B43 F17 (Holmes's letter can be reconstructed from her reply). As to the Upham transaction, see correspondence in OWH Papers, HLS, B51 F5. This is quite different from Bowen's account of a reluctant Holmes being persuaded by Fanny to accept a post that he had not sought. Holmes himself was disingenuous about the matter and disliked any imputation that he had sought the position.

19. Garraty, *Holmes' Appointment to the Supreme Court,* 22 NEW ENG. Q., September 1949, at 291, 295.

20. 1 SELECTIONS FROM THE CORRESPONDENCE OF THEODORE ROOSEVELT AND HENRY CABOT LODGE 517 (H. C. Lodge ed. 1925). Roosevelt did not feel himself bound by the promise McKinley had made to Hemenway; see Judge James M. Morton, unpublished remarks at Holmes memorial October 9, 1937, quoted F. FRANKFURTER, MR. JUSTICE HOLMES AND THE SUPREME COURT 18 (1961).

21. See De Lima v. Bidwell, 182 U.S. 1 (1901); Dooley v. United States, 182 U.S. 222 (1901); Armstrong v. United States, 182 U.S. 243 (1901), and Downes v. Bidwell, 182 U.S. 244 (1901).

22. Downes v. Bidwell, 182 U.S. 244, 287 (1901).

23. Theodore Roosevelt to Henry Cabot Lodge, July 10, 1902, 1 SELECTIONS FROM THE CORRESPONDENCE OF ROOSEVELT AND LODGE 518–519 (H. C. Lodge ed. 1925). In this rambling letter, Roosevelt also mentions the criticisms of Holmes's dissents in labor cases that he has been hearing, but dismisses these.

Felix Frankfurter, in the time after Holmes's death when Frankfurter was to be his biographer, gave a somewhat different account of Holmes's appointment. Omitting the Insular cases from his discussion, he suggested that Holmes was appointed for the apparently Progressive views displayed in his labor dissents. Frankfurter quoted Roosevelt's July 10, 1902, letter to Lodge, but edited out any mention of the colonies, leaving the impression that the Court was narrowly divided on Progressive legislation, which was not the case, and that this issue was paramount in Roosevelt's choice. See F. FRANKFURTER, MR. JUSTICE HOLMES AND THE SUPREME COURT 52–53 (1961) (the cited passage is from lectures delivered in 1938). Bowen gave the same account based on a similarly edited version of Roosevelt's letter, see BOWEN 344–345, apparently relying on Frankfurter; see also A. BICKEL AND B. SCHMIDT, THE JUDICIARY AND RESPONSIBLE GOVERNMENT 7 (1984).

24. See Garraty, *Holmes' Appointment to the Supreme Court,* 22 NEW ENG. Q., September, 1949, at 291, 296.

25. See Holmes's Journal ("the Black Book"), OWH Papers, HLS, p. 140.

26. *Id.*

27. Garraty, *Holmes' Appointment to the Supreme Court,* 22 NEW ENG. Q., September, 1949, at 291, 297.

28. See Editorial, New York Evening Post, August 12, 1902, p. 4.

29. Post, *Judge Oliver Wendell Holmes,* 19 McCLURE'S MAGAZINE 524 (1902).

30. Editorial, Boston Evening Transcript, August 12, 1902, p. 6.

31. Louis D. Brandeis to OWH, September 3, 1902, OWH Papers, HLS, B38 F4.

32. OWH to Louis D. Brandeis, September 4, 1902, quoted L. PAPER, BRANDEIS 26 (1983).

33. SPEECHES 157.

34. W. KING, MELVILLE WESTON FULLER 287 (1950).

35. *Remarks at a Tavern Club Dinner, November 14, 1902,* SPEECHES 150. See similarly, OWH to Clara Stevens, October 17, 1902, OWH papers, HLS ("You feel like a cut flower").

CHAPTER 18. WASHINGTON, D.C.

1. See 1 H. PRINGLE, THE LIFE AND TIMES OF WILLIAM HOWARD TAFT 240–247 (1939) (Pringle does not mention the campaign to oust Fuller); W. KING, MELVILLE WESTON FULLER 304 (1950).

2. Melville Fuller to John Morris, October 16, 1902, copy OWH Papers, HLS, B42 F37; quoted W. KING, MELVILLE WESTON FULLER 282–283 (1950).

3. George Hoar to Melville Fuller, November 5, 1902, quoted W. KING, MELVILLE WESTON FULLER 285 (1950).

4. See Holmes's Journal, OWH Papers, HLS, p. 140; OWH to Owen Wister, December 9, 1902, OWH Papers, HLS. For the farewell to Nina Gray, see the manuscript of Holmes's Ipswich address (published in SPEECHES 136) and the note to Nina Gray attached to it, OWH Papers, HLS, B33 F18.

5. OWH to Ethel Scott, April 25, 1909, OWH Papers, HLS, B49 F23.

6. For Craig's advice, see BOWEN 367; her source was James Doherty, BOWEN 462; but her account of Holmes's arrival in Washington is otherwise inconsistent with Holmes's letters of the time.

7. C. BUTLER, A CENTURY AT THE BAR OF THE SUPREME COURT 65, 66 (1942). Marcus Knowlton had urged Holmes to resign in September, before the Senate had reconvened, apparently out of anxiety to obtain Holmes's seat as chief justice before the outgoing governor of Massachusetts, Winthrop Murray Crane, left office. Holmes was nearly stampeded into resigning before the Senate had confirmed him, but thought better of it and then retained his position in Massachusetts until the last possible moment. Knowlton was then appointed to succeed him.

8. *How the Judges of the Supreme Court of the United States Consult,* 30 AM. L. REV. 903 (1896).

Oral argument w.s far more important than it later became. In the early nineteenth century oral argument was unlimited, following the English fashion, with lengthy readings from the record and from precedents. In England, authorities are read out to the judges in extended argument, and decisions are given from the bench immediately after argument. See, e.g., D. KARLEN, APPELLATE COURTS IN THE UNITED STATES AND ENGLAND (1963). In 1902, the United States Supreme Court was still firmly in the English tradition, and relied more heavily on the spoken than the written word. The justices did not have law clerks, did their own reading and research, and wrote their own opinions, so that, given the volume of work and the bulk of the written records, they were bound to rely heavily on oral arguments and explanations among themselves.

By the 1950s, the justices had acquired offices and clerical staffs, and had come to rely heavily on law clerks to read and digest the written materials. Oral arguments were limited to one hour per side.

At present, each of the justices has four law clerks. While about the same number of cases are argued in a term as in Holmes's day, argument for each party is limited to one half hour. Discussion in the conference room also seems to have taken on less importance, see W. REHNQUIST, THE SUPREME COURT 290–295 (1987). The clerks now often write the opinions under the justices' supervision, *id.* at 298. The written opinions are circulated within each justice's office, and then to the other justices. There is considerable exchange and revision at this stage.

9. R. HIGHSAW, EDWARD DOUGLASS WHITE 35–36 (1981).

10. 188 U.S. 385 (1903).

11. OWH to Ellen Curtis, December 12, 1902, OWH Papers, HLS.

12. OWH to Owen Wister, December 9, 1902, OWH Papers, HLS.

13. OWH to John G. Palfrey, December 27, 1902, OWH Papers, HLS.

14. *Id.*

15. Conferences were and are kept secret, and no one is ever present except the justices, but the procedure has been described in print many times and apparently has not changed greatly since at least Chief Justice Taney's time. See C. E. HUGHES, THE SUPREME COURT OF THE UNITED STATES 58–59 (1936) (cit-

ing sources from Taney's court). Apparently the practice of a separate formal vote taken in reverse order of seniority was abandoned at some point after Chief Justice Hughes described it. The present chief justice records the votes of the justices after the initial discussion, based on their remarks, and apparently no formal vote is taken. W. H. REHNQUIST, THE SUPREME COURT 288–293 (1987).

As to the conferences in Holmes's time, see Justice Brewer, *Working of the United States Supreme Court,* 60 ALBANY L. J. 44 (1899); Remarks of Justice Harlan, in *How the Judges of the Supreme Court of the United States Consult,* 30 AM. L. REV. 903, 904 (1896). For Holmes's work habits, his reliance on notes of oral argument, and the enmity between Harlan and White, see C. E. HUGHES, THE AUTOBIOGRAPHICAL NOTES OF CHARLES EVANS HUGHES 168–175 (1973).

16. When Holmes joined the court, by far the larger part of its jurisdiction was obligatory. Reforms in 1916 and (especially) in 1922 gave the Court some control over its docket by allowing review of large categories of cases through the discretionary writ of certiorari. In 1902, however, most cases came to the Court by writ of error, which the Court was obliged to hear. Direct appeals to the Supreme Court from federal trial courts and a second appeal from the new federal courts of appeals were mandatory in many federal question cases, see Spreckels Sugar Refining Co. v. McClain, 192 U.S. 397 (1904); Act of March 3, Sec. 5, 26 Stat. 827 (1891); as were appeals for the defendant in federal capital criminal cases. Writs of certiorari were introduced in 1891, and greatly expanded in the reform legislation sponsored by Chief Justice Taft in 1925. See generally, F. FRANKFURTER AND J. LANDIS, THE BUSINESS OF THE SUPREME COURT 103–128 (1927); E. SURRENCY, HISTORY OF THE FEDERAL COURTS 240–255 (1987). At present, the Court docket is made up largely of petitions for writs of certiorari, of which it may choose to review perhaps one in fifty.

In the October, 1902, term the Court disposed of only 60 petitions for writs of certiorari, nearly all of them denied, and decided on the merits about 200 cases brought on appeals or writs of error. See 187–188 U.S. (1902–1903).

17. F. BIDDLE, JUSTICE HOLMES, NATURAL LAW, AND THE SUPREME COURT 11 (1961).

18. OWH to Frederick Pollock, December 18, 1902, 1 HOLMES–POLLOCK LETTERS 109.

19. OWH to Ellen Curtis, December 12, 1902, OWH Papers, HLS.

20. From 1889 to 1918, the Court decided about 790 cases in which statutes were attacked under the Due Process and Equal Protection clauses of the Fourteenth Amendment; 2 C. WARREN, THE SUPREME COURT IN UNITED STATES HISTORY 741 (1935 ed.). This is an average of about 26 cases per term, or about one each week of oral argument. Warren did not count Constitutional challenges by criminal defendants, and these were about comparable in number during this period. The Court treated most of these challenges as frivolous, and rejected at least ninety percent (although the Court did accept a larger number of challenges to rate regulations). See Warren, *The Progressiveness of the United States Supreme Court,* 13 COLUM. L. REV. 294 (1913); cf. A. BICKEL AND B. SCHMIDT, THE JUDICIARY AND RESPONSIBLE GOVERNMENT 201, 305–311 (1984) (frivolous and repetitious Constitutional claims 1910–1914).

21. OWH to John G. Palfrey, December 27, 1902, OWH Papers, HLS; see also OWH to Frederick Pollock, December 28, 1902, 1 HOLMES–POLLOCK LETTERS 109.

22. Missouri, Kansas and Tennessee R. Co. v. May, 194 U.S. 267 (1904).

23. *Id.*

24. See Otis v. Parker, 187 U.S. 606 (1903) (Holmes, J.). This was Holmes's first opinion for the Court. He affirmed the federal constitutionality of a California state constitutional provision prohibiting sales of stock on margin.

25. OWH to Nina Gray, February 15, 1903, OWH Papers, HLS.

26. OWH to Ethel Scott, April 24, 1909, OWH Papers, HLS.

27. OWH to Franklin Ford, December 29, 1908, in HOLMES–FORD LETTERS 70, 71.

28. Otis v. Parker, 188 U.S. 606, 608–609 (1903).

29. Holmes's ideas on the Due Process clause were fully formed in his first opinion, less than a month after he took his seat on the Court, and evidently had their roots deep in his previous work in the common law.

A few words to set the context may be helpful. If most lawyers now have any picture of this period, it is of a consistently reactionary Court using "substantive due process" to strike down progressive statutes. In this picture, Holmes is a lonely dissenter from the Court's due process doctrines. Felix Frankfurter and other young admirers of Holmes reinforced this image and perhaps did him a disservice by portraying Holmes as a dissenting liberal, stemming a reactionary tide. See, e.g., F. FRANKFURTER, MR. JUSTICE BRANDEIS 80 (1932).

As Frankfurter himself at times pointed out, however, during Holmes's years the Fuller Court was conservative, in the sense of being restrained, but except for occasional spasms was not reactionary. By and large, the Court upheld social justice legislation attacked by business enterprise under the Fourteenth Amendment. Evenhandedly, although in retrospect perhaps more regrettably, it also turned aside challenges to state criminal convictions and racially discriminatory state laws, except where fundamental principles as then understood were involved. By Charles Warren's count, from 1889 to 1918 the Supreme Court decided 790 cases in which state statutes were attacked under the Due Process or Equal Protection clauses, but in only two cases — Lochner and Coppage, both discussed below and familiar to generations of law students — did the Court strike down social justice legislation in opinions that were widely criticized. Holmes dissented in these two cases, emphasizing — with some reason — that he, rather than the majority, had followed their customary reasoning; and the legal literature of the day tended to make the same point. Hough, for instance, writing in 1919, just before the reaction of the 1920s, expressed the common view when he said the Court had generally approved social justice legislation:

> The direct appeal of property to due process has for the most part failed. . . . The indirect appeal through liberty is still going on. . . . But it is dying, and the courts, when invoked under the due-process clause, are doing little more than easing the patient's dying days.

Hough, Due Process of Law Today, 32 HARV. L. REV. 218 (1919). See also A. PAUL, CONSERVATIVE CRISIS AND THE RULE OF LAW 227, 228 (1976); 2 C. WARREN, THE SUPREME COURT IN UNITED STATES HISTORY 693–694, 741 (revised ed. 1935); A. BICKEL AND B. SCHMIDT, THE JUDICIARY AND RESPONSIBLE GOVERNMENT 201, 309–311 (1984); Warren, The Progressiveness of the Supreme Court, 13 COLUM. L. REV. 294 (1913). See also Frankfurter, The Supreme Court and the Public, FORUM, June 1930, p. 333; E. CORWIN, THE CONSTITUTION AND WHAT IT MEANS TODAY 463 (1978; first ed. 1920).

A helpful characterization of the Court at this time is Laurence H. Tribe's "Model II," in which the Court used substantive — rather than institutional — restraints to check the other branches, see L. TRIBE, AMERICAN CONSTITUTIONAL LAW 567–568 (2d ed. 1988).

If the Court in Holmes's early years was not reactionary, neither did Holmes ever dissent from the doctrine that due process of law had substantive requirements.

Holmes had long accepted that judges would sometimes be obliged to decide cases on legislative grounds. See OWH, THE COMMON LAW 31–32 (M. Howe ed.

1963; first ed. 1881). In *Privilege, Malice and Intent,* 8 HARV. L. REV. 1 (1894), Holmes arrived at the view he clove to thereafter, that when obliged to legislate, a judge should consult the fundamental principles of the evolving common law. See Chapter 14 above.

In his opinion for the Court in *Otis v. Parker,* Holmes adapted these early views to a vigorous method of Constitutional interpretation. He rejected, expressly and somewhat laboriously, Brewer's Natural Law argument: The reasonableness of legislation was not to be judged by the standard of a higher morality above the law. He also rejected a dry literalism of interpretation. The substantive content of the general provisions of the Constitution were to be found in the precedents of the Court itself and the common-law tradition on which they rested. The substantive principles of due process therefore were the "relatively fundamental" rules of right — the evolving and often still unconscious elements of fairness that lay beneath the skin of the common law. In later and better-known opinions, he put this doctrine in more vivid language:

> The provisions of the Constitution are not mathematical formulas that have their essence in form; they are organic living institutions transplanted from English soil. Their significance is vital, not formal; it is to be gathered not simply by taking the words and a dictionary, but by considering their origin and the line of their growth.

Gompers v. United States, 233 U.S. 604, 610 (1914). This is a paraphrase of the famous opening sentence of THE COMMON LAW — "The life of the law has not been logic, it has been experience" — and announces Holmes's consistent method. See Justice Harlan F. Stone's remarks, quoted in A. MASON, HARLAN FISKE STONE 330 (1956).

Except for occasional aberrations like *Lochner,* see below, the Fuller Court during Holmes's years generally followed this restrained method, articulated most clearly in Holmes's frequent opinions for the full Court. The substantive content of the Due Process clause was defined cautiously, case by case, with respect for precedent and for new conditions, and by and large was limited to fundamental principles. See C. E. HUGHES, THE SUPREME COURT OF THE UNITED STATES 193 (1936); Hough, *Due Process of Law Today,* 32 HARV. L. REV. 218 (1919); Powell, *The Judiciality of Minimum-Wage Legislation,* 37 HARV. L. REV. 545 (1924).

Holmes's doctrine, in short, was an effort to establish "neutral principles" of decision in substantive due-process cases, see Wechsler, *Toward Neutral Principles of Constitutional Law,* 73 HARV. L. REV. 1, 19 (1959) (quoting *Otis v. Parker*). See also Frankfurter, *The Constitutional Opinions of Justice Holmes,* 29 HARV. L. REV. 683 (1916).

It would require another book to trace the subsequent history of Holmes's doctrine of substantive due process. Whatever their present usefulness as doctrine, Holmes's Due Process Clause opinions, especially the moving dissents, are frequently read and taught as examples, perhaps the best examples we have, of the passionate objectivity required of judges, even when making a quasi-legislative judgment.

30. Presumably Diamond Glue Co. v. United States, 187 U.S. 611 (1903), and Hanley v. Kansas City Southern R. Co., 187 U.S. 617 (1903), both reported on January 5, 1903, when the Court returned from its recess, see below.

31. OWH to Ellen Curtis, OWH Papers, HLS.

32. See OWH to John Palfrey, December 27, 1902, OWH Papers, HLS ("My first opinion is received with flattering words — I suppose as the baby of the Court").

33. OWH to Melville Fuller, December 28, 1902, OWH Papers, HLS (copy).

34. OWH to Nina Gray, January 4, 1903, OWH Papers, HLS.

35. OWH to Clara [Stevens], January 10, 1903, OWH Papers, HLS.

36. OWH to Frederick Pollock, December 28, 1902, 1 HOLMES-POLLOCK LETTERS 109.

CHAPTER 19. SMILES AND LIES

1. See Otis v. Parker, 187 U.S. 606 (1903); Diamond Glue Co. v. United States, 187 U.S. 611 (1903) (rejecting a Constitutional defense against enforcement of a contract in Wisconsin); and Hanley v. Kansas City Southern R. Co., 187 U.S. 617 (1903) (allowing an injunction against Arkansas' regulation of interstate railroad rates as an impermissible burden on interstate commerce).

2. Mondays were set aside for the wives of Supreme Court justices to be at home; other days were reserved for the cabinet, senior members of the Senate, and ambassadors. Justices of the Supreme Court took precedence over everyone except the President, Vice President, and ambassadors. As the person lower in precedence paid the first call ("On general principles of gravitation," as Holmes liked to say), many people called on the Holmeses when they first arrived in Washington.

3. Bleistein v. Donaldson Lithographing Co., 188 U.S. 239 (1903) (Holmes, J.). This is still a leading opinion on the degree of originality required for a work to receive copyright protection. Considering that Holmes's was the deciding vote in a narrowly divided Court, his opinion had a profound influence on the course of copyright law. See also his prescient concurring opinion in White-Smith Music Co. v. Apollo, 209 U.S. 1 (1908), which provided an argument for extending copyright protection to computer software seventy years later.

4. OWH to Ellen Curtis, February 7, 1903, OWH Papers, HLS.

5. OWH to Felix Frankfurter, March 3, 1928, OWH Papers, HLS, B29 F7.

6. The Lottery Case, 188 U.S. 321, 375 (1903).

7. OWH to Nina Gray, January 16, 1903, OWH Papers, HLS.

8. OWH to Melville Fuller, February 6, 1903 (copy), OWH Papers, HLS; see also W. KING, MELVILLE WESTON FULLER 291 (1950).

9. OWH to Nina Gray, March 2, 1903, OWH Papers, HLS, B31 F12. See also OWH to Melville Fuller, February 5, 1903 (copy), OWH Papers, HLS.

10. See W. KING, MELVILLE WESTON FULLER 291 (1950).

11. *Id.* at 288.

12. Giles v. Harris, 189 U.S. 475, 478 (1903).

13. *Id.* at 481.

14. *Id.*

15. *Id.* at 487–488. Holmes's opinion was a bad one, perhaps his worst, not only in retrospect but in the context of the time.

The plaintiffs had made claims under the Fourteenth and Fifteenth amendments. The circuit court — part of the dual system of trial courts that existed until 1910 — dismissed for want of jurisdiction (apparently the jurisdictional amount was not alleged in the bill) and for want of equity. When the plaintiffs showed their intention of appealing, the circuit court narrowed its ground to want of jurisdiction, presumably to avoid having the case reviewed on its merits in the Supreme Court. 189 U.S. at 493–494 (Harlan, J., dissenting). Holmes, in his opinion for the Court, nevertheless brushed aside the jurisdictional question and decided the case on the merits.

His first argument, which was uncharacteristically specious, perhaps was offered to satisfy another member of the majority, Justice Day, who wrote the opinion in *Giles v. Teasley,* below. This argument, apparently not advanced by counsel, was that if the Alabama constitution were invalid, ordering the plaintiffs to be registered under it would not cure the problem. This is weak, since the new state constitution was not necessarily unconstitutional on its face. Discrimination under the old constitution was assumed. If the past discrimination were remedied by enrolling the plaintiffs as registered voters, this would have gone far to cure the discriminatory effect of the new constitution, at least as to them.

That point was clearly brought out in newspaper accounts based on interviews with an anonymous member of the Court, presumably Harlan. See "Against Negro Voters: Supreme Court Ruling," etc., New York Daily Tribune, April 28, 1903, p. 1, col. 2; "The Supreme Court and the Negro," *id.*, April 29, 1903, p. 8, col. 2. The printed opinions were not made public for some time after the decision was announced, which was unusual.

The second argument, quoted in the text, had at least the merit of honesty. Benno Schmidt, who gave a surprisingly uncritical account in A. BICKEL AND B. SCHMIDT, THE JUDICIARY AND RESPONSIBLE GOVERNMENT (1984), called it "extraordinary" for its frank confession of impotence in the face of an apparent wrong. Loren Miller called it "astounding, almost shocking." L. MILLER, THE PETITIONERS 161 (1966).

Holmes was unwilling to renew the war with the South. But it was not necessary to reach for such ultimates. The Court could simply have ordered the registrars, as individuals, to register the plaintiffs under the new state constitution, which arguably was valid, to remedy past discrimination. At least two members of the Court believed this was an appropriate form of relief. It was all the plaintiffs had asked and it should not have been Holmes's concern, according to his own view of his duty, whether they were wise or would be ultimately successful in their political aims. And, as Holmes had repeatedly said, the power of the federal government would be used to enforce the Court's order.

Holmes's opinion left open the possibility of a suit for damages, but when Giles pushed on this door, it, too, was closed. Giles v. Teasley, 193 U.S. 146 (1904). The opinion by Justice Day was a classic Catch-22: if the discrimination were as severe as alleged, it would be illegal and would have no effect in the eyes of federal law — hence no cognizable damages could be sustained. This was shabby stuff.

16. In re Debs, 158 U.S. 564 (1895) (Brewer, J.).

17. OWH to Nina Gray, May 3, 1903, OWH papers, HLS, B31 F12. Holmes did not mention the Giles case directly in his letters. The opinion was announced on April 27, and this letter, a week later, probably referred to it.

18. OWH to Nina Gray, February 15, 1903, OWH Papers, HLS.

19. OWH to Ellen Curtis, December 21, 1902, OWH Papers, HLS.

20. OWH to Ellen Curtis, January 12, 1903, OWH Papers, HLS.

21. OWH to Ellen Curtis, February 7, 1903, OWH Papers, HLS. This is slightly disingenuous. Chief Justice Fuller was protective of the Court's status, and Holmes sometimes entered into his protocol battles. In 1910, Holmes told the Chief that he would refuse to return to houses where he had been placed below cabinet members at dinner. See OWH to Melville Fuller, May 25, 1910, OWH Papers, HLS, B42.

22. OWH to Ellen Curtis, February 7, 1903, OWH Papers, HLS.

23. BOWEN 376.

24. OWH to Ellen Curtis, January 25, 1903, OWH Papers, HLS.

25. OWH to Nina Gray, January 5, 1903, OWH Papers, HLS, B35 F12.

26. *Id.*

27. OWH to Nina Gray, February 5, 1903, OWH Papers, HLS.

28. OWH to Anna Codman, February 15, 1903, OWH Papers, HLS.

29. OWH to Ellen Curtis, February 7, 1903, OWH Papers, HLS.

30. OWH to Baroness Moncheur, September 9, 1910, OWH Papers, HLS.

31. W. H. H. Llewellyn to Theodore Roosevelt, February 20, 1903 (copy), OWH Papers, HLS, B49 F10.

32. H. PRINGLE, THEODORE ROOSEVELT 185 (1956).

33. See C. CAMPBELL, ANGLO-AMERICAN UNDERSTANDING 319–345 (1957); W. R. THAYER, THEODORE ROOSEVELT (1919) (giving the text of the letter). There appears to be no copy of the letter in Holmes's papers.

34. OWH to Ellen Curtis, March 21, 1903, OWH Papers, HLS.

35. OWH to Anna Codman, February 15, 1903, OWH Papers, HLS.

36. OWH to Ellen Curtis, March 21, 1903, OWH Papers, HLS.

37. Hawaii v. Mankichi, 190 U.S. 197 (1903).

38. Henry James to Frances R. Morse, August 12, 1903, James Papers, Houghton.

39. OWH to Nina Gray, September 24, 1903, OWH Papers, HLS.

40. OWH to Nina Gray, September 26, 1903, OWH Papers, HLS.

41. H. HEUSER, CANON SHEEHAN OF DONERAILE 185 (1923).

42. OWH to Canon Sheehan, "Feb. 1904," HOLMES–SHEEHAN LETTERS 12.

43. OWH to Nina Gray, September 2, 1903, OWH Papers, HLS.

44. OWH to Leslie Scott, October 23, 1903, Leslie Scott Papers, University of Warwick.

45. OWH to Nina Gray, September 26, 1903, OWH Papers, HLS.

46. OWH to Leslie Scott, October 23, 1903, Leslie Scott Papers, University of Warwick.

47. See OWH to Clara Stevens, March 6, 1908, OWH Papers, HLS.

48. Id.

49. OWH to Lewis Einstein, November 23, 1903, OWH Papers, HLS, HOLMES–EINSTEIN LETTERS 6. The house at 1720 I Street was long ago torn down, and the site is occupied by an office building. This description of the house was assembled from numerous sources, principally the published and unpublished reminiscences of Holmes's secretaries, specific bequests in Holmes's will, and the inventory made for his estate. See also BOWEN, who had been in the house; and J. MONAGAN, THE GRAND PANJANDRUM (1988), which contains interviews with surviving law secretaries and a servant of the Holmeses'.

50. OWH to Lewis Einstein, November 29, 1903, HOLMES–EINSTEIN LETTERS 6.

51. OWH to Ellen Curtis, January 2, 1904, OWH Papers, HLS.

52. OWH to Nina Gray, January 16, 1903, OWH Papers, HLS.

53. OWH to Canon Sheehan, "Feb. 1904," HOLMES–SHEEHAN LETTERS 14.

54. OWH to Ellen Curtis, January 24, 1904, OWH Papers, HLS. To which Holmes commented, when Fanny repeated the remark, "Si on n'a pas à qu'on aime il faut aimer ce qu'on a." Id.

55. OWH to Ellen Curtis, April 8, 1904, OWH Papers, HLS.

56. Northern Securities Case, argument for the government, quoted B. MEYER, A HISTORY OF THE NORTHERN SECURITIES CASE 19 (1906).

57. J. P. Morgan, quoted B. H. MEYER, A HISTORY OF THE NORTHERN SECURITIES CASE 24 (1906). By 1909, about one third of industrial (nonfarming) assets were held by the 200 largest corporations. See J. P. BLAIR, ECONOMIC CONCENTRATION 65 (1972).

58. OWH to Harold Laski, July 28, 1916, 1 HOLMES–LASKI LETTERS 8 (Holmes is referring to his views before the First World War).

59. See H. PRINGLE, THEODORE ROOSEVELT 179 (1956); T. ROOSEVELT, THE AUTOBIOGRAPHY OF THEODORE ROOSEVELT 443 (1913).

60. Henry Adams to Elizabeth Cameron, February 23, 1902, 2 LETTERS OF HENRY ADAMS 374 (W. C. Ford ed. 1938).

61. See H. PRINGLE, THEODORE ROOSEVELT 180 (1956). This is Roosevelt's recollection of the meeting, although one must penetrate Roosevelt's bluster. See also his AUTOBIOGRAPHY.

62. See United States v. E. C. Knight Co., 156 U.S. 1 (1895), relying on Kidd v. Pearson, 128 U.S. 1 (1888), which upheld Iowa's prohibition of the manufacture of intoxicating liquors.

63. Northern Sec. Co. v. United States, 193 U.S. 197, 306 (1904) (argument of the attorney general).

64. Holmes's dissent is at Northern Sec. Co. v. United States, 193 U.S. 197, 400 (1904). One mark of the passage of time is that none of the opinions in the case discusses the intent of Congress or refers to legislative history, which would be the dominant considerations today. Another is that only a minority thought the purpose of the antitrust laws was to foster competition: in 1903, the power held by large combines was the dominant question.

Holmes's dissent now seems even more dated than the other opinions, and in its reliance on common-law terms and doctrines seems so archaic as to be difficult to understand. Commentators have said that Holmes's opinion in this case grew out of the same tolerance for combination that he expressed in his Massachusetts labor cases. See, e.g., M. LERNER, THE MIND AND FAITH OF JUSTICE HOLMES 219–222 (1943). Others, like Frankfurter, have tactfully ignored Holmes's *Northern Securities* dissent entirely.

In a general sort of way, Holmes's idea that competition led inevitably to combination — hardly unique to him — formed a background for his opinion. But Holmes was following the precedents of his own court, the usual canons of interpretation (for instance, that terms in a statute that had established meanings at common law were to be given those meanings) and, indeed, the conventional wisdom of the bar. The Harlan opinion, and not Holmes's, seemed the aberration at the time.

Holmes's good friend Frederick Pollock, who had been visiting the United States that fall, agreed to give the *Harvard Law Review* a brief analysis of the common-law issues that Holmes subsequently addressed in his opinion, and concluded precisely as Holmes did: "The mere fact of one corporation owning a majority of the shares in one or more other corporations does not seem to have anything to do with the common law doctrine of restraint of trade." Pollock, *The Merger Case and Restraint of Trade*, 17 HARV. L. REV. 151, 152 (1904). (The article appeared before the case was decided.) See also C. C. Langdell's violent attack, *The Northern Securities Case and the Sherman Anti-Trust Act*, 16 HARV. L. REV. 539 (1904). Holmes was quite genuine in saying that the matter would be obvious if not for the pressure of politics.

> I was told that Taft said my dissent in the Northern Securities case could have been predicted from my opinions in the labor cases. It is not true, so far as my consciousness goes, as I really thought I was interpreting the Sherman Anti-Trust Act without regard to prejudices, but no doubt, the attitude as to one side is correlated with that as to the other.

OWH to Franklin Ford, May 3, 1907, HOLMES–FORD LETTERS 43, 44. Holmes thought and said that Congress could pass a statute reasonably restricting the size of companies in interstate commerce, but hadn't done so. If there is a disingenuous side to his dissent, it is his insistence that Harlan's reading of the statute be taken to its logical and unconstitutional extreme — i.e., authorizing the breakup of every firm or partnership.

65. Undated, quoted W. KING, MELVILLE WESTON FULLER 294 (1950).

66. See Henry Adams to Elizabeth Cameron, March 13, 1904, 2 LETTERS OF HENRY ADAMS (W. C. Ford ed. 1938).

67. Melville Fuller, quoted W. KING, MELVILLE WESTON FULLER 296 (1950).

68. 193 U.S. 197, 400 (1904).

69. Henry Adams to Elizabeth Cameron, March 20, 1904, 2 LETTERS OF HENRY ADAMS 429 (W. C. Ford ed. 1938).

70. OWH to John G. Palfrey, April 1, 1904, OWH Papers, HLS.

71. OWH to Ellen Curtis, April 8, 1904, OWH Papers, HLS.

72. OWH to John G. Palfrey, April 1, 1904, OWH Papers, HLS.

CHAPTER 20. SOLITUDE

1. I. NITOBE, BUSHIDO: THE SOUL OF JAPAN 4–8 (1905). Holmes's reading list for 1904 shows he read the book in the spring of 1904, although the formal publication date is shown as 1905; Kaneko must have brought with him an advance copy, a tactful piece of propaganda. Also touring the United States at this time, perhaps for the same purpose, was Lord Soyen Shaku, abbot of Buddhist monasteries in Kamakura; his talks, translated by D. T. Suzuki, first introduced American audiences to Zen Buddhism. The Lord Abbot's "Memorial Address" has some suggestive parallels to Holmes's Memorial Day talks. SOYEN SHAKU, ZEN FOR AMERICANS 204, 210–211 (1974; first ed. 1906).

2. Kaneko Kentaro to OWH, September 7, 1905, in Kanda and Gifford, *The Kaneko Correspondence*, 37 MONUMENTA NIPPONICA 244 (1982). For Holmes's assistance, see Kaneko to James Thayer, *id.*, at 51; OWH to Melville Fuller, March 30, 1904 (copy), OWH Papers, HLS.

3. OWH Papers, HLS, B54 F14.

4. OWH to Anna Codman, January 20, 1904, OWH Papers, HLS.

5. OWH to Nina Gray, February 8, 1904, OWH Papers, HLS.

6. OWH to Nina Gray, March 21, 1904, OWH Papers, HLS.

7. Mark Howe memorandum of interview with Austin W. Clarke, May, 1948, OWH Papers, HLS, B54 F6.

8. OWH to Nina Gray, July 23, 1904, OWH Papers, HLS.

9. W. KING, MELVILLE WESTON FULLER 299 (1950).

10. OWH to Nina Gray, September 8, 1904, OWH Papers, HLS, B31 F15.

11. Howard v. Fleming, 191 U.S. 126, 129 (1903).

12. City of Joplin v. Southwest Missouri Light Co., 191 U.S. 150 (1903).

13. Atkin v. Kansas, 191 U.S. 207 (1903).

14. See, e.g., Turner v. Williams, 194 U.S. 279 (1904). See also United States v. Sing Tuck, 194 U.S. 161 (1904) (Holmes, J.), a Chinese Exclusion Act case, in which Holmes first stated the doctrine of exhaustion of administrative remedies. I do not believe there would be any serious question, even today, about the correctness of these decisions — however unattractive the immigration laws were — but Holmes has been criticized for them. See Rogat and O'Fallon, *Mr. Justice Holmes, A Dissenting Opinion — The Speech Cases*, 36 STAN. L. REV. 1349 (1984).

15. OWH to Ellen Curtis, November 12, 1904, OWH Papers, HLS.

16. OWH to Nina Gray, December 17, 1904, OWH Papers, HLS.

17. Lincoln v. United States (the *Warner, Barnes* case), 197 U.S. 419 (1905) (Holmes, J.), aff'd on reargument, 202 U.S. 484 (1906) (Fuller, C. J.).

18. William H. Taft to Elihu Root, April 7, 1905, quoted 1 H. PRINGLE, THE LIFE AND TIMES OF WILLIAM HOWARD TAFT 267 (1939).

19. Rasmussen v. United States, 197 U.S. 516 (1905) (White, J.).

20. C. BUTLER, A CENTURY AT THE BAR OF THE SUPREME COURT 93–94 (1942).

21. 2 C. WARREN, THE SUPREME COURT IN UNITED STATES HISTORY 710–711 (1935 ed.).

22. Lincoln v. United States, 202 U.S. 484 (1906).

23. United States v. Heinszen & Co., 206 U.S. 370 (1907).

24. C. BUTLER, A CENTURY AT THE BAR OF THE SUPREME COURT 172 (1942).

25. Lochner v. New York, 198 U.S. 45 (1905). It is not known whose vote shifted, but Fuller's vote is the surprise. Fuller's biographer, noting the inconsistency, says only that "the ten-hour law for bakers seemed to him to be 'featherbedding,' paternalistic, and depriving both the worker and the employer of fundamental liberties." W. L. KING, MELVILLE WESTON FULLER 297 (1950). This just restates the conclusion and does not suggest how Fuller distinguished this case from others in which the Court upheld regulation of hours worked. McKenna, whose father was a bakery owner, and who had grown up in and around bakeries in California, may have persuaded Fuller that bakery work was not dangerous and that the health rationale was a sham. The *Lochner* decision remained an aberration for some years, and was believed to have been silently abandoned until it was revived during the reaction of the 1920s; see below.

26. 198 U.S. 45, 74 (Holmes, J., dissenting).

27. This is now the most famous of Holmes's dissents and one of the most famous opinions in the English language, familiar to generations of law students. The best-known passage in this opinion: "The Fourteenth Amendment does not enact Mr. Herbert Spencer's Social Statics" is, however, just *épater les bourgeois*. Holmes was the only member of the Court who read that sort of book, and the intellectual source of the "liberty" argument, to the extent to which it had an intellectual source, was more likely J. S. Mill's *On Liberty*, which was in the air; see Pound, *Liberty of Contract*, 18 YALE L. J. 454, 460, n. 25 (1909); see also A. V. DICEY, LAW AND PUBLIC OPINION xxvii–xxxii (2d ed. 1914); B. TWISS, LAWYERS AND THE CONSTITUTION 141 (1942). It would be wrong, however, to take the *Lochner* majority's reasoning too seriously as doctrine. After the *Muller* decision, see below, Joseph Choate, acknowledged leader of the New York bar, former ambassador to Great Britain, remarked that he saw no reason why "a big husky Irish washerwoman should not work more than ten hours a day in a laundry if she and her employer so desired," perhaps expressing more frankly the sentiments behind such decisions. Quoted E. SAMUELS, HENRY ADAMS: THE MAJOR PHASE 412 (1964); see also R. BERGER, GOVERNMENT BY JUDICIARY 269 (1977).

28. OWH to Lewis Einstein, April 7, 1905, HOLMES–EINSTEIN LETTERS 13.

29. *Id.,* September 18, 1905, HOLMES–EINSTEIN LETTERS 17, 18.

30. OWH to John Gray, September 3, 1905, OWH Papers, HLS.

31. OWH to Nina Gray, August 26, 1905, OWH Papers, HLS.

32. *Id.,* December 26, 1905, OWH Papers, HLS.

33. *Id.,* March 21, 1906, OWH Papers, HLS.

34. *Id.,* November 9, 1906, OWH Papers, HLS.

35. OWH to Lewis Einstein, November 2, 1905, HOLMES–EINSTEIN LETTERS 20, 21.

36. OWH to Clara Stevens, November 18, 1906, OWH Papers, HLS.

37. OWH to Nina Gray, April 30, 1905, OWH Papers, HLS.

38. See H. G. Wells to FBH, May 13, 1906, OWH Sr. Papers, Houghton.

39. OWH to Clara Stevens, April 14, 1906, OWH Papers, HLS.

40. OWH to Lewis Einstein, June 12, 1906, HOLMES–EINSTEIN LETTERS 22.

41. OWH to Edward Ross, May 6, 1906, OWH Papers, HLS.

42. OWH to John Gray, June 1907, OWH Papers, HLS, B33 F26.

43. FBH to OWH, June 11, 1907, OWH Papers, HLS.

44. OWH to Nina Gray, September 15, 1907, OWH Papers, HLS, B32 F2.

45. OWH to Baroness Moncheur, July 17, 1907, OWH Papers, HLS.

46. Henry Adams to OWH, December 31, 1907, Adams Papers, Houghton.

47. See PROGRESSIVE MASKS: LETTERS OF OLIVER WENDELL HOLMES, JR., AND FRANKLIN FORD (D. Burton ed. 1982). It is interesting and characteristic that Holmes took the celebrated Adams brothers and the obscure Ford more or less on an equal footing.

48. OWH to Ellen Curtis, January 25, 1903, OWH Papers, HLS; see also OWH to Baroness Moncheur, March 5, 1908, OWH Papers, HLS.

49. See OWH to Baroness Moncheur, May 12, 1908, OWH Papers, HLS; Chauncey Belknap's memorandum of a conversation with Holmes, March 30, 1916, OWH Papers, HLS, B54 F5.

50. OWH to Nina Gray, May 30, 1908, OWH Papers, HLS.

51. Mark Howe's memorandum of Thomas Corcoran's talk at the Harvard Law School May 8, 1946, OWH Papers, HLS, B54 F6.

52. Adair v. United States, 208 U.S. 161, 191–192 (1907) (Holmes, J. dissenting).

53. Muller v. Oregon, 208 U.S. 412, 421 (1908); see also 208 U.S. 412, 419–420, n. 1. The "Brandeis Brief" became famous after its success in this case, and signaled a new method of practice and argument on frankly legislative grounds, what was called at the time "sociological jurisprudence." See 2 C. WARREN, THE SUPREME COURT IN UNITED STATES HISTORY 748–749 (1935 ed.). Like other achievements of the Progressive movement, the *Muller* decision is now celebrated without too much thought for its sexist and racist origin.

54. OWH to Clara Stevens, January 6, 1909, OWH Papers, HLS.

55. OWH to Ethel Scott, December 11, 1908, OWH Papers, HLS.

56. OWH to Clara Stevens, March 6, 1909, OWH Papers, HLS.

57. *Id.*

CHAPTER 21. JEU SUI ARNAUT

1. William Moody to OWH, May 19, 1909, OWH Papers, HLS, B45 F25; OWH to Baroness Moncheur, August 27, 1909, OWH Papers, HLS.

2. William H. Taft to Horace Lurton, May, 1909, 1 H. PRINGLE, THE LIFE AND TIMES OF WILLIAM HOWARD TAFT 529–530 (1939); A. BICKEL AND B. SCHMIDT, THE JUDICIARY AND RESPONSIBLE GOVERNMENT 7 (1984).

3. OWH to Baroness Moncheur, May 25, 1909, OWH Papers, HLS, B35 F21.

4. OWH to John Wigmore, August 8, 1909, OWH Papers, HLS.

5. OWH to Baroness Moncheur, May 25, 1909, OWH Papers, HLS, B35 F21.

6. OWH to Charles K. Poe, August 4, 1909, OWH Papers, HLS; OWH to Clara Stevens, September 3, 1909, OWH Papers, HLS; OWH to John Wigmore, August 18, 1909, OWH Papers, HLS.

7. OWH to John Wigmore, August 18, 1909, OWH Papers, HLS. Holmes appears to have made no complete memorandum of the speech.

8. Margot Asquith to OWH, no date, OWH Papers, HLS, B37 F18. This note from 10 Downing Street must date either from the summer of 1909 or from Holmes's last visit in 1913, when Asquith was still prime minister.

9. OWH to John Wigmore, August 18, 1909, OWH Papers, HLS; see also OWH to Canon Sheehan, September 13, 1909, HOLMES–SHEEHAN LETTERS 30 (1976).

10. OWH to Alfred Zimmern, August 24, 1912, OWH Papers, HLS, "Ad-

denda" (copy; orig. in Bodleian). See also OWH to Lewis Einstein, September 10, 1916, HOLMES–EINSTEIN LETTERS 137, 139.

11. See undated notes to Nina Gray and others, OWH Papers, HLS, B36 F33, probably from about 1904–1905; see also OWH to Ethel [Scott], September 13, 1910, OWH Papers, HLS.

12. Holmes's review of Holdsworth's *History of English Law,* volumes 2 and 3, was published in the *Law Quarterly Review* in 1909, reprinted COLLECTED LEGAL PAPERS 285, 289–290 (1920).

13. OWH to Nina Gray, September 29, 1909, OWH Papers, HLS.

14. OWH to Clara Stevens, November 21, 1909, OWH Papers, HLS.

15. OWH to Baroness Moncheur, September 15, 1909, OWH Papers, HLS.

16. *Id.*

17. OWH to Canon Sheehan, September 13, 1909, HOLMES–SHEEHAN LETTERS 30, 31.

18. Ethel Scott had come to the United States, and the Holmeses were seeing her off.

19. OWH to Baroness Moncheur, October 7, 1909, OWH Papers, HLS. See *Law and the Court,* SPEECHES 168, quoted below.

20. Taft tried to get Theodore Roosevelt to appoint Lurton in 1906, and Roosevelt made the gesture of proposing Lurton privately to Lodge and perhaps other senators. But Lodge opposed the appointment — "My objection is fundamental. I do not think you ought to appoint a Democrat to the Supreme Court." A. BICKEL AND B. SCHMIDT, THE JUDICIARY AND RESPONSIBLE GOVERNMENT 8 (1984); see also 2 SELECTIONS FROM THE CORRESPONDENCE OF THEODORE ROOSEVELT AND HENRY CABOT LODGE 228–230 (1925); Roosevelt appointed William Moody instead. Despite all the obstacles, however, Taft was determined to appoint his friend Horace Lurton: "The only pleasure of my administration, as I have contemplated it in the past, has been to commission you a justice of the Supreme Court." Taft to Lurton, December 13, 1909, 1 H. PRINGLE, LIFE AND TIMES OF WILLIAM HOWARD TAFT 531 (1939).

21. E. D. White to OWH, "Monday," no date, from Narragansett; OWH Papers, HLS. From the text of the letter — Peckham is alive, but ill, and the Court is not yet in session — it was written in August or September, 1909. Peckham unexpectedly died in October, and Lurton was given his seat, rather than Moody's. Lurton's nomination was announced on November 30 and was greeted with a predictable storm of opposition from both Republicans and trade union leaders, who thought Lurton too conservative. He was nevertheless approved with little difficulty, on a voice vote in the Senate, December 20. Neither Taft's biographer nor the historians of the Court comment on the disappearance of Senate opposition to such an appointment, and as to Taft's motives have charitably accepted his statement that following the public criticisms in December, Taft reconsidered the nomination, "and became convinced that he was not yielding to 'personal prediliction.'" See A. BICKEL AND B. SCHMIDT, THE JUDICIARY AND RESPONSIBLE GOVERNMENT 8–9 (1984); 1 H. PRINGLE, THE LIFE AND TIMES OF WILLIAM HOWARD TAFT 531 (1939); Watts, *Horace J. Lurton,* in 3 L. FRIEDMAN AND F. ISRAEL, THE JUSTICES OF THE UNITED STATES SUPREME COURT 1847, 1859 (1980).

22. OWH to Leslie Scott, October 24, 1909, OWH Papers, HLS. This was the day of Peckham's death, of which Holmes had not yet learned.

23. OWH to Mme. Nabuco, January 21, 1910, OWH Papers, HLS.

24. OWH to Ethel Scott, October 7, 1909, OWH Papers, HLS.

25. *Id.*

26. OWH to Baroness Moncheur, February 6, 1910, OWH Papers, HLS.

27. OWH to Nina Gray, May 8, 1910, OWH Papers, HLS.

28. Noble State Bank v. Haskell, 219 U.S. 104 (1911) (Holmes, J.). This was one of the few opinions Holmes wrote for the Court with the same freedom and eloquence he gave to his dissents, and it is worth noting that the Court felt obliged to withdraw much of the opinion in response to widespread criticism: "The analysis of the police power, whether correct or not, was intended to indicate an interpretation of what has taken place in the past, not to give a new or wider scope to the power." Noble State Bank v. Haskell, 219 U.S. 575 (1911) (Holmes, J.) (petition for rehearing denied).

29. Dr. Miles Medical Co. v. Park and Sons Co., 220 U.S. 373, 409 (1911) (Holmes, J., dissenting).

30. OWH to Baroness Moncheur, June 7, 1910, OWH Papers, HLS.

31. *Reflections on the Past and Future*, SPEECHES 163, 166–167.

32. *Purgatorio*, xxvi 142. See OWH to Ethel Scott, February 18, 1910, OWH Papers, HLS. The entire passage is as follows:

> *Jeu sui Arnaut, que plor e vau cantan;*
> *consiros vei la passada folor,*
> *e vei jausen lo jorn, qu'esper, denan.*

> *I am Arnaut that weep and go singing;*
> *in thought I see my past madness,*
> *and I see with joy the day which I await before me.*

Purgatorio, xxvi 142–144; from the Temple Classics edition (1903), which may have been the edition Holmes was reading. The translation of verse 142 given in the text is Holmes's own, frequently repeated in his letters of this time. See, e.g., OWH to Ethel Scott, February 18, 1910, OWH Papers, HLS. This passage struck Holmes so forcibly — I do not know any other that he wrote about in the same way — that it may be worth quoting the comments of the Temple edition's editor:

> Arnaut Daniel . . . ca. 1180–1200. . . . He was a master of the so-called *trobar clus*, or obscure style, which revelled besides in difficult rhymes and other complicated devices. As such he was necessarily caviare to the general; and . . . Dante deals with the popular preference for [his inferior contemporary] Guiraut de Bournelh.

Parallels between Holmes and Arnaut are evident. I do not know whether it also struck Holmes that Arnaut was being punished for indulging his lust.

33. See OWH to Ethel Scott, February 18, 1910, OWH Papers, HLS; OWH to Owen Wister, June 3, 1910, *id*. ("I had to rush out of doors and walk it off").

34. OWH to Baroness Moncheur, May 1, 1910, OWH Papers, HLS.

35. OWH to Leslie [Scott], May 23, 1910, OWH Papers, HLS; C. BUTLER, A CENTURY AT THE BAR OF THE SUPREME COURT 179 (1942).

36. OWH to Baroness Moncheur, May 4, 1910, OWH Papers, HLS.

37. 1 M. PUSEY, CHARLES EVANS HUGHES 271–272 (1951). Taft expressed this as his present intention and was careful not to make a promise binding in the future. *Id*.

38. OWH to Owen Wister, June 3, 1910, OWH Papers, HLS.

39. OWH to Baroness Moncheur, July 14, 1910, OWH Papers, HLS; see also W. KING, MELVILLE WESTON FULLER 329 (1950).

40. OWH to Baroness Moncheur, July 14, 1910, OWH Papers, HLS.

41. OWH to Ethel [Scott], July 11, 1910, OWH Papers, HLS.

42. OWH to Judge Putnam, "July 1910," 22 GREEN BAG 528 (1910), reprinted JUSTICE OLIVER WENDELL HOLMES: HIS BOOK NOTICES AND UNCOLLECTED LETTERS AND PAPERS 131, 132 (H. Shriver ed. 1936).

43. OWH to Stephen A. Day, October 14, 1930, OWH Papers, HLS, B42 F37.

44. OWH to Frederick Pollock, September 1, 1910, 1 HOLMES–POLLOCK LETTERS 166, 167.

45. Boston Evening Transcript, September 20, 1910, partially reprinted in S. BENT, JUSTICE OLIVER WENDELL HOLMES 118–119 (1932) (Bent does not indicate his deletions).

46. OWH to Ethel [Scott], September 13, 1910, OWH Papers, HLS.

47. OWH to Frederick Pollock, September 24, 1910, 1 HOLMES–POLLOCK LETTERS 169, 170.

48. OWH to Nina Gray, December 2, 1910, OWH Papers, HLS, B32 F5.

49. OWH to Canon Sheehan, December 15, 1911, HOLMES–SHEEHAN LETTERS 56.

50. OWH to Alice S. Green, September 4, 1910, OWH Papers, HLS.

51. OWH to Ethel Scott, September 24, 1910, OWH Papers, HLS.

52. See THE AUTOBIOGRAPHICAL NOTES OF CHARLES EVANS HUGHES 168 (D. Danelski and J. Tulchin eds. 1973).

53. OWH to Nina Gray, November 20, 1910, OWH Papers, HLS.

54. See W. H. TAFT, OUR CHIEF MAGISTRATE 99–107 (1916); contemporaries describe Taft saying in his speeches, after leaving office, that he had denied Holmes the chief-justiceship because of his opinion in the Philippine Tariff case; but neither A. Bickel and B. Schmidt, in their extended discussion, see THE JUDICIARY AND RESPONSIBLE GOVERNMENT 59–64 (1984), nor Taft's authorized biographer, see 2 H. PRINGLE, THE LIFE AND TIMES OF WILLIAM HOWARD TAFT 533–535 (1939), mention the Philippine Tariff case in connection with the appointment of White. As Holmes was aware, in any case, the lively question was not whether he would be appointed but whether the qualified promise Taft made to Hughes would be honored, and most commentaries have focused on this question. Hughes was suspected of being an insurgent Republican, perhaps of Rooseveltian tendencies, and this undoubtedly helped White's candidacy among the senators. See OWH to Alice S. Green, January 10, 1911, OWH Papers, HLS:

> I suppose Hughes was bitterly disappointed at not getting the place as everyone expected that he would — including, I guess, the President up to the evening before the choice was announced — but there was a great rebellion and it was evident, I imagine, that someone else must be put in.

Pringle concluded, without mentioning the senatorial delegation, that White was simply the better candidate and was favored by the cabinet, members of the Court, and, ironically, by Roosevelt.

55. See A. BICKEL AND B. SCHMIDT, THE JUDICIARY AND RESPONSIBLE GOVERNMENT 64 (1984); THE AUTOBIOGRAPHICAL NOTES OF CHARLES EVANS HUGHES 168–169 (D. Danelski and J. Tulchin eds. 1973).

56. OWH to John Wigmore, May 10, 1916, OWH Papers, HLS.

57. OWH to Baroness Moncheur, December 15, 1910, OWH Papers, HLS.

58. OWH to Alice S. Green, October 14, 1911, OWH Papers, HLS.

59. OWH to Ethel Scott, June 5, 1911, OWH Papers, HLS.

60. *The Class of '61*, SPEECHES 160, 161–162.

61. OWH to Baroness Moncheur, September 15, 1911, OWH Papers, HLS.

62. OWH to Baroness Moncheur, August 28, 1911, OWH Papers, HLS.

63. F. BIDDLE, JUSTICE HOLMES, NATURAL LAW, AND THE SUPREME COURT 9 (1961).

64. This became an annual joke, and although Holmes remained on the Court another twenty years, the phrase was included in his letter to each new secretary.

65. OWH to Baroness Moncheur, April 8, 1912, OWH Papers, HLS.

66. OWH to Lewis Einstein, September 28, 1912, HOLMES–EINSTEIN LET-TERS 71–72.

67. *Reflections on the Past and Future,* SPEECHES 163, 164–165.

68. A. ZIMMERN, THE GREEK COMMONWEALTH (1911). Strum has shown how much this book influenced Brandeis. P. STRUM, LOUIS D. BRANDEIS (1984). To the extent that it held up an ideal, Holmes probably shared it, but, unlike Brandeis, he did not think it likely to be achieved by present efforts.

69. Progressive Party Platform of 1912, in NATIONAL PARTY PLATFORMS 175 (D. Johnson and K. Porter eds. 1975).

70. See, for instance, OWH to James Bryce, January 11, 1914, OWH Papers, HLS, B38 F10:

> I have a good deal of distrust of the present Administration . . . so far as I know [Wilson's] general attitudes I don't believe in them and I equally disbelieve in his pretense of high-mindedness and all that.

For Holmes, who was conscientiously loyal to all things American when speaking to his English friends, these are hard words.

71. OWH to Alice S. Green, December 8, 1912, OWH Papers, HLS, B43.

72. William H. Taft to OWH, December 30, 1913, OWH Papers, HLS, B50 F21.

73. OWH to Canon Sheehan, March 1, 1911, HOLMES–SHEEHAN LETTERS 37.

74. Canon Sheehan to OWH, March 25, 1911, HOLMES–SHEEHAN LETTERS 39.

75. OWH to Frederick Pollock, August 13, 1913, 2 HOLMES–POLLOCK LET-TERS 207–208.

76. *Id.*

77. *Law and the Court,* SPEECHES 168, 172–174. The striking final imagery is similar to a favorite sonnet, "To Night," by Joseph Blanco White, which Holmes read at Fanny's funeral and that was read at his; see below.

CHAPTER 22. THE SKY AFLAME

1. See, e.g., D. ACHESON, MORNING AND NOON 62 (1965); F. BIDDLE, JUS-TICE HOLMES, NATURAL LAW AND THE SUPREME COURT 5, 148–152 (1961).

2. Mark Howe memorandum of interview with Austin W. Clarke, OWH Papers, HLS, B54 F6. Holmes reportedly went right on attending after the shows began to include stripteases; J. LAKE AND H. GIBBO, FOOTLIGHTS, FISTFIGHTS, AND FEMMES 188 (1957), quoted J. MONAGAN, THE GRAND PANJANDRUM 30 (1988).

3. See *Ideals and Doubts,* in COLLECTED LEGAL PAPERS 303.

4. OWH to Baroness Moncheur, March 10, 1916, OWH Papers, HLS. For a description of Frankfurter's circle see, e.g., M. PARRISH, FELIX FRANKFURTER AND HIS TIMES: THE REFORM YEARS (1982). Frankfurter and some of his friends lived in a house near Dupont Circle that Holmes called the "House of Truth." Frankfurter lived there from 1911, when he came to work at the Department of the Interior, until 1913, when he joined the Harvard Law School. He continued to visit Washington regularly during the Wilson administration and returned to the capital when the United States entered the war. Others from the House of Truth who joined Holmes's Monday afternoon circle were Winfred T. Denison ("Dobbin" or "Win"), an assistant attorney general; Loring C. Christie, a Cana-dian graduate of the Harvard Law School; and Lord Eustace Percy, who was on

the staff of the British embassy. Brandeis was an adviser to the Wilson administration and a frequent visitor to the House of Truth (but not, at this period, to I Street).

5. OWH to "D.l.b." [Clara Stevens], July 26, 1914, OWH Papers, HLS.

6. OWH to Lewis Einstein, October 12, 1914, HOLMES–EINSTEIN LETTERS 100, 101. Holmes was correct that, proportionately, losses in battle were less in the First World War than in the Civil War.

7. Otto von Gierke to OWH, "October 1914," OWH Papers, HLS, B43 F4. Von Gierke and his wife had visited the Holmeses in Washington during 1909, and the two men had exchanged reminiscences of army service. The original of this letter, which is in German, and copies of a typescript English translation are in the Holmes papers. It appears that von Gierke sent several copies of the translation so that Holmes could circulate them, which, of course, he did not. Holmes remarked sourly that von Gierke's letter appeared in newspapers before he himself had received it.

8. Enclosure dated November 15, 1914, with letter signed "E. D." [Ethel Desborough] to OWH, December 31, 1914, OWH Papers, HLS.

9. Ethel Desborough to OWH, June 11, 1915, OWH Papers, HLS. See London Times May 28, 1915.

10. See, e.g., Edward White to OWH, August 2, 1915, OWH Papers, HLS.

11. See, for instance, OWH to John Wigmore:

> Doesn't this squashy sentimentality of a big minority of our people about human life make you puke? . . . of pacifists — of people who believe there is an onward and upward — who talk of uplift — who think that something in particular has happened and that the universe is no longer predatory. Oh bring in a basin.

OWH to John Wigmore, November, 1915, OWH Papers, HLS; quoted by R. POLENBERG, FIGHTING FAITHS 211 (1987).

12. OWH to Felix Frankfurter, December 31, 1915, OWH Papers, HLS.

13. Nina Gray to OWH, February 19, 1915, OWH Papers HLS, B31 F1.

14. OWH to John C. Gray, February 21, 1915, OWH Papers, HLS, B33 F26.

15. See *John Chipman Gray,* extracts from Massachusetts Historical Society records, in JUSTICE OLIVER WENDELL HOLMES: HIS BOOK NOTICES AND UNCOLLECTED LETTERS AND PAPERS 133 (H. Shriver ed. 1936).

16. See OWH to Felix Frankfurter, July 5, 1915, OWH Papers, HLS, B29 F3; OWH to Baroness Moncheur, July 6, 1915, OWH Papers, HLS; and other letters of this time.

17. Edward White to OWH, September 11, 1915, OWH Papers, HLS.

18. Henry Adams to Elizabeth Cameron, March 1, 1916, 2 LETTERS OF HENRY ADAMS 638 (W. C. Ford ed. 1938); SELECTED LETTERS OF HENRY ADAMS 270–271 (N. Arvin ed. 1951).

19. OWH to Lady Castletown, September 21, 1915, OWH Papers, HLS, B26 F14.

20. OWH to Lewis Einstein, October 12, 1914, HOLMES–EINSTEIN LETTERS 100, 101.

21. See 2 H. PRINGLE, THE LIFE AND TIMES OF WILLIAM HOWARD TAFT 951 (1939). Taft was aware that his name had been put forward; it is not clear whether he would have accepted less than the chief-justiceship; but he apparently did not discourage the campaign on his behalf.

22. OWH to Clara Stevens, May 13, 1916, OWH Papers, HLS.

23. William H. Taft to James Karger, January 3, 1916, 2 H. PRINGLE, THE LIFE AND TIMES OF WILLIAM HOWARD TAFT 952 (1931).

24. For instance, the Harvard president, A. Lawrence Lowell — who had defended both Frankfurter and Laski when they came under anti-Semitic attack — opposed Brandeis's confirmation.

25. OWH to Clara Stevens, May 13, 1916, OWH Papers, HLS.

26. See A. BICKEL AND B. SCHMIDT, THE JUDICIARY AND RESPONSIBLE GOVERNMENT 373–388 (1984); P. STRUM, LOUIS D. BRANDEIS 296 (1984). Strum argues that Brandeis encountered little anti-Semitism in Boston during his years of practice there. But it was then that animosity toward him accumulated. Fanny, as noted below, was not among his admirers, and her disapproval was perhaps characteristic. See below.

27. OWH to Lady Castletown, June 20, 1916, OWH Papers, HLS, B26 F14.

28. Thomas Corcoran, Holmes's secretary 1926–1927, reported that Fanny did not approve of Brandeis's zeal. She told Corcoran the story of Brandeis's early years in law practice, when Henry Lee Higginson, then of the United Shoe Company, helped introduce Brandeis into Boston society and sent some law business his way. But Brandeis sided with factory workers during a strike at United Shoe. Fanny told Corcoran: "One doesn't do that sort of thing." J. MONAGAN, THE GRAND PANJANDRUM 59 (1988). At his confirmation hearings it was reported that Brandeis first represented United Shoe concerning the leases of their patented machines, and then some years later, after severing all connection with the company, represented opposing parties in the same matter. See A. BICKEL AND B. SCHMIDT, THE JUDICIARY AND RESPONSIBLE GOVERNMENT 373–388 (1984).

29. OWH to Ethel Scott, March 10, 1916, OWH Papers, HLS, B49 F24.

30. Id. See also OWH to Lewis Einstein, March 10, 1916, OWH to Baroness Moncheur, March 10, 1916, OWH Papers, HLS.

31. See 29 HARV. L. REV. 565 (April, 1916).

32. Frankfurter, The Constitutional Opinions of Justice Holmes, 29 HARV. L. REV. 683, 684 (1916).

33. Wigmore, Justice Holmes and the Law of Torts, 29 HARV. L. REV. 601 (1916).

34. OWH to Leslie Scott, May 29, 1916, Leslie Scott Papers, University of Warwick.

35. OWH to Lady Castletown, April 30, 1916, OWH Papers, HLS, B26 F4.

36. Id., June 20, 1916.

37. OWH to Baroness Moncheur, March 10, 1916, OWH Papers, HLS.

38. Mark Howe interview with Austin W. Clarke, May, 1948, OWH Papers, HLS, B54 F6.

39. However, Lady Castletown introduced Lewis Einstein to Holmes, and in 1905, long before he had met Frankfurter, he wrote to Alice Stopford Green about young Dr. Herman Levy: "I always like to play with the young — and always have some pals among the lads who are coming on." OWH to Alice S. Green, OWH Papers, HLS, B43 F14–16. Holmes met others of his Jewish friends, including Paul Warburg, at dinner parties during the Wilson administration.

It was partly Holmes's lack of prejudice that drew so many Jews to him at a time when other doors were closing. But something more seems needed to explain their warm friendships. Despite his patrician connections, Holmes was always somewhat an outsider, and these intellectual, passionate, somewhat aristocratic young men were outsiders, too. See also E. WILSON, PATRIOTIC GORE 784–785 (1962): "Holmes seems to have regarded the intellectual Jew as a special variety of Brahmin."

40. "W. L." [Walter Lippmann], To Justice Holmes, 6 NEW REP. 156 (1916).

41. OWH to Baroness Moncheur, December 30, 1915, OWH Papers, HLS.

42. OWH to Frederick Pollock, February 18, 1917, 1 HOLMES–POLLOCK LETTERS 243, 244.

43. OWH to Harold Laski, May 8, 1918, 1 HOLMES–LASKI LETTERS 152, 153.

44. OWH to Harold Laski, November 1, 1916, 1 HOLMES–LASKI LETTERS 33.

45. OWH to Felix Frankfurter, April 13, 1916, OWH Papers, HLS, B29 F4.

46. *Id.*, April 29, 1916, OWH Papers, HLS, B29 F4.

47. OWH to Felix Frankfurter, December 12, 1915, OWH Papers, HLS, B29 F4.

48. OWH to James Bryce, February 13, 1917, OWH Papers, HLS, B38 F10.

49. OWH to Lady Castletown, February 18, 1916, OWH Papers, HLS, B26 F14.

50. OWH to Felix Frankfurter, March 27, 1917, OWH Papers, HLS. Although addressed to Frankfurter, the remarks quoted here were part of Holmes's long debate with Harold Laski on the nature of sovereignty. See the HOLMES–LASKI LETTERS, *passim.*

51. See, e.g., OWH to Baroness Moncheur, March 10, 1916; to Lady Pollock, July 12, 1916; to Baroness Moncheur, January 22, 1918, OWH Papers, HLS.

52. OWH to Baroness Moncheur, January 22, 1918, OWH Papers, HLS.

53. OWH to James Bryce, April 8, 1918, OWH Papers, HLS, B38 F10.

54. *Id.*

55. OWH to Harold Laski, April 9, 1910, 1 HOLMES–LASKI LETTERS 148, 149.

56. Brooks Adams to OWH, April 8, 1918, OWH Papers, HLS, B37 F1.

57. OWH to Baroness Moncheur, January 22, 1918, OWH Papers, HLS.

58. OWH Papers, HLS, B69 F4.

59. The text of this amendment, known as the Sedition Act of May 16, 1918, is reprinted in Z. CHAFEE, FREEDOM OF SPEECH App. III (1920). It prohibited, among other things, making false statements, or using "disloyal, profane, scurrilous or abusive language about the form of government of the United States, the Constitution . . . or the military or naval forces . . . the flag . . . or the uniform of the Army or Navy." *Id.* at 395.

60. OWH to Frederick Pollock, June 14, 1918, 1 HOLMES–POLLOCK LETTERS 267.

61. Hammer v. Dagenhart, 247 U.S. 251, 277 (1918) (Holmes, J., dissenting).

62. Toledo Newspaper Co. v. United States, 247 U.S. 402, 422 (1918) (Holmes, J., dissenting).

63. OWH to Nina Gray, March 5, 1921, OWH Papers, HLS.

64. William H. Taft to James Bryce, March 24, 1918, 2 H. PRINGLE, THE LIFE AND TIMES OF WILLIAM HOWARD TAFT 908 (1939).

65. William H. Taft to Charles P. Taft II, his son, in France, August 19, 1918, 2 H. PRINGLE, THE LIFE AND TIMES OF WILLIAM HOWARD TAFT 909 (1939).

66. M. PARRISH, FELIX FRANKFURTER AND HIS TIMES 99 (1982).

67. OWH to Harold Laski, November 6, 1918, 1 HOLMES–LASKI LETTERS 169.

68. OWH to Baroness Moncheur, April 4, 1919, OWH Papers, HLS.

69. OWH to Alice S. Green, March 26, 1919, OWH Papers, HLS, B43 F13:

> Some of the lower Judges got rather hysterical and there were some cases in which I should have dissented and in fact had written [dissents], if the Govt. had not wisely dropped them, and the Court had gone the other way.

(The typescript copy in the OWH Papers, HLS, has "country" instead of "Court," from the context obviously a copying error.) This letter has a helpful gloss on the *Schenck* opinion; see below.

70. Schenck v. United States, 249 U.S. 47 (1919). This opinion states the "clear and present danger" test, which is the beginning of modern First Amendment jurisprudence. Although Schenck's conviction was upheld, the opinion stated what was then a liberal view of the First Amendment, at a time when Chief Justice White and many other judges would have applied a much more restrictive test, allowing the government to suppress any speech with a "dangerous tendency." Holmes's statement in *Schenck* would have allowed punishment of speech only when it amounted to an incitement or attempt to commit a crime. See Z. CHAFEE, FREEDOM OF SPEECH (1920). Of the decisions Holmes announced, only the *Debs* decisions drew widespread criticism at the time, and that seems to have been prompted as much by the harsh sentence, which was not subject to review, as by the holding of law.

It is interesting to note, as Chafee pointed out at the time, and Max Lerner some years later, M. LERNER, THE MIND AND FAITH OF JUSTICE HOLMES 293 (1943), that Holmes's reasoning in *Schenck* was an extension of his analysis of common-law attempts. Perhaps more important, *Schenck* is also in the line of descent from Holmes's opinions in defamation and third-party tort-feasor cases, see *Privilege, Malice and Intent,* discussed above. Holmes's First Amendment jurisprudence, in short, grew out of his work in the common law.

In recent years, the *Schenck* opinion has come under criticism for having displayed insufficient sensitivity to First Amendment rights. See Rogat and O'Fallon, *Mr. Justice Holmes: A Dissenting Opinion — The Speech Cases,* 36 STAN. L. REV. 1349 (1984). These criticisms are discussed in connection with Holmes's *Abrams* dissent, below.

71. The cases were Schenck v. United States (and companion cases) 249 U.S. 47 (1919); Frohwerk v. United States, 249 U.S. 204 (1919) (Holmes, J.), and Debs v. United States, 249 U.S. 211 (1919) (Holmes, J.).

72. Debs. v. United States, 249 U.S. 204 (1919) (Holmes, J.).

73. OWH to Baroness Moncheur, April 4, 1919, OWH Papers, HLS; see also OWH to Frederick Pollock, April 27, 1919, 2 HOLMES–POLLOCK LETTERS 11.

74. L. BAKER, BRANDEIS AND FRANKFURTER 221–229 (1984).

75. OWH to A. Lawrence Lowell, June 2, 1919, 1 HOLMES–LASKI LETTERS 211 n.2. Lowell proved to be a supporter of Frankfurter and Pound as well as of Laski.

76. OWH to Ellen Curtis, September 20, 1919, OWH Papers, HLS, B41 F5.

77. See OWH to Ellen Curtis, from 1919 to the 1930s, OWH Papers, HLS, B45 FF5 and 6.

78. OWH to Frederick Pollock, August 21, 1919, 2 HOLMES–POLLOCK LETTERS 22.

79. OWH to Felix Frankfurter, February 11, 1920, OWH Papers, HLS, B36 F5.

80. OWH to Harold Laski, October 26, 1919, 1 HOLMES–LASKI LETTERS 217.

81. *Id.,* February 10, 1920, 1 HOLMES–LASKI LETTERS 239.

82. *Id.,* January 14, 1920, 1 HOLMES–LASKI LETTERS 232.

83. The account of events leading up to the *Abrams* case is taken from the opinions in the case itself and from R. POLENBERG, FIGHTING FAITHS (1987).

84. See *Privilege, Malice and Intent,* 8 HARV. L. REV. (1894), discussed above. The argument developed there — that freedom of speech and freedom of association are necessary if society is to evolve peacefully — is presented in highly compressed form in the *Abrams* dissent.

85. OWH to Frederick Pollock, November 6, 1919, 2 HOLMES–POLLOCK LETTERS 29.

86. D. ACHESON, MORNING AND NOON 119 (1965). Acheson was Brandeis's secretary, and he gives as his source Holmes's secretary, who remained in the adjoining library during the three justices' visit.

87. Abrams v. United States, 250 U.S. 616 (1919). Holmes's dissent in this case has become a definitive gloss upon his earlier opinion for the Court in *Schenck*, and so has become as much a precedent as if it were a holding of the Court. It is at the root of modern First Amendment protections. It has also been called one of the foundation stones of modern liberalism, M. WHITE, SOCIAL THOUGHT IN AMERICA 175–179 (1976). Holmes therefore continues to be criticized by the radical right.

Holmes has also come under strong attack from the left and center in recent years. The argument made is that the *Schenck* opinion, when delivered, was not especially sensitive to First Amendment claims and that only in response to liberal criticism did Holmes change his tune in the *Abrams* and *Gitlow* dissents.

On this theory, Holmes changed his mind about freedom of speech during the summer of 1919: ". . . the Schenck standard was not truly speech-protective; and . . . it was not until the fall of 1919, with his famous dissent in [Abrams], that Holmes put some teeth into the clear and present danger formula." Gunther, *Learned Hand and the Origins of Modern First Amendment Doctrine*, 27 STAN. L. REV. 719 (1975). See also Ragan, *Justice Oliver Wendell Holmes, Zechariah Chafee, Jr., and the Clear and Present Danger Test for Free Speech*, 58 J. AM. HIST. 24 (1971); Rogat and O'Fallon, *Mr. Justice Holmes: A Dissenting Opinion — The Speech Cases*, 36 STAN. L. REV. 1349 (1984); Currie, *The Constitution in the Supreme Court: 1910–1921*, 1985 DUKE L. J. 1111 (1985); H. KALVEN, A WORTHY TRADITION: FREEDOM OF SPEECH IN AMERICA (1988).

Such a profound change in Holmes's thinking, when he was seventy-eight years old, had been a judge for thirty-six years, and had already written several opinions on the same question for a unanimous Supreme Court, calls for an explanation. One would expect dramatic evidence to be put forward. But this is not the case. Professor Gunther says only that the change in Holmes's thinking came about, "at least partly as a result of probing criticisms by acquaintances such as Learned Hand." Gunther, *supra* at 720. Professor Gunther, who is Learned Hand's authorized biographer, might be suspected of being blinded by personal loyalty in this matter, but other authors have seized on and amplified the argument; see, e.g., Gengarelly, *The Abrams Case*, BOSTON BAR J., March, 1981, p. 19 (Part I); and April, 1981 (Part II); R. POLENBERG, FIGHTING FAITHS: THE ABRAMS CASE, THE SUPREME COURT, AND FREE SPEECH 213–228 (1987). As Polenberg's otherwise admirable book is the only history of the *Abrams* case we are likely to have, the Gunther doctrine seems pretty well entrenched.

One may doubt the premise of the argument — that there is a fundamental difference between *Schenck* and *Abrams*. See David Rabban's careful analysis, *The Emergence of Modern First Amendment Doctrine*, 50 U. CHI. L. REV. 1205 (1984) (the only substantive differences in the opinions can be attributed to the differences in the cases themselves, and perhaps to Holmes's reaction to the "Red scare" then in progress).

But even if the *Abrams* dissent set out a different standard from that of *Schenck*, the change was plainly not due to criticism of the *Schenck* decision. Of the critics, Learned Hand is supposed to have been the most pointed, but reading over his very deferential letters and Holmes's replies, one finds it difficult without consulting Hand's own opinion to say just where the criticism lay, and Holmes — as Gunther acknowledges — never quite saw the point on which he and Hand differed. As to the other supposed critics, neither Frankfurter nor Laski criticized *Schenck* on legal grounds. Laski, on the contrary, wrote as follows:

I read your three opinions [*Schenck, Frohwerk,* and *Debs*] with great care, and though I say it with deep regret they are very convincing. . . . I take it you would agree that none of the accused ought to have been prosecuted; but since they have been and the statute is there, the only remedy lies in the field of pardon. Your analogy of a cry of fire in a crowded theater is, I think, excellent.

Harold Laski to OWH, March 18, 1919, 1 HOLMES–LASKI LETTERS 191. The editors of *The New Republic* commented editorially, "Eugene Debs has gone to the West Virginia Penitentiary to begin his ten year sentence. There is no doubt about the legality of his conviction. His Canton Speech clearly violated the Espionage Act." Zechariah Chafee published a long analysis of the *Schenck* opinion, pointing out that it was more protective of free speech than appeared from the result in that case, and correctly presenting Holmes's common-law analysis. In short, the campaign of criticism — aside from the bomb threats and the political vituperation, which if anything would have hardened Holmes in his views — boils down to Hand's tactful suggestions, which Holmes did not pick up, and an article by Ernst Freund in *The New Republic* critical of the opinion. Freund's article indeed stung Holmes, but he called it "poor stuff," and it certainly did not sway him. On the other side of the question were all of Holmes's colleagues, his wife and friends, and everyone in England and America whose opinions about the law he respected. Finally, there is Holmes's letter to Alice Stopford Green, March 26, 1919, well before the supposed campaign to sway him, in which he says that the lower courts were hysterical, that he himself would go as far in favor of free speech as anyone, and that he had written dissents in favor of free speech that were never published because the government dropped the cases. OWH Papers, HLS, B43 F13; see note 69 above.

To a modern eye, Holmes's jurisprudence may have defects. The fundamental objection perhaps is that Holmes did not treat speech, viewed as *action,* as entitled to protections greater than that afforded to other types of behavior. (It was only to *opinion,* considered as such, that Holmes believed the Constitution extended near absolute guarantees.) As the late Harry Kalven said, Holmes washed out the political element entirely. See H. KALVEN, A WORTHY TRADITION (1988); Kalven, *Professor Ernst Freund and Debs v. United States,* 40 U. CHI. L. REV. 235 (1973). The speech of a national party's candidate for President was put on the same footing as a cry of "fire" in a crowded theater, on the same footing as the Yiddish leaflets in *Abrams.*

One encounters the same difficulty, if it is one, in many of Holmes's opinions. He resolutely refused to consider the political context. It seemed incredible to Ernst Freund and perhaps to more recent critics that Holmes should insist on treating Eugene Debs as if he were the defendant in an attempted robbery case, just as it seemed incredible to Justice Harlan that Holmes would insist on treating the Northern Securities Company as if it were a small exporting grocer. But that is what Holmes thought his duty as a judge required of him.

88. Herbert Croly to OWH, November 13, 1919, OWH Papers, HLS.

CHAPTER 23. OLYMPUS

1. J. CHAPPLE, THE LIFE AND TIMES OF WARREN G. HARDING 122 (1924).
2. William H. Taft to Helen Taft, December 26, 1920, 2 H. PRINGLE, THE LIFE AND TIMES OF WILLIAM HOWARD TAFT 955 (1939).
3. OWH to Nina Gray, March 5, 1921, OWH Papers, HLS.
4. *Id.*
5. Sutherland, "Recollections of Justice Holmes," pp. 8–9, Arthur E. Suth-

erland Papers, HLS, B24 F7. Sutherland was Holmes's secretary in 1927–1928; Fanny's routine had not changed for many years.

6. See, for example, Louis Brandeis to Felix Frankfurter, June 2, 1921, 4 LETTERS OF LOUIS D. BRANDEIS 560, 561 (M. Urofsky and D. Levy eds. 1971–1978).

7. See John Lockwood, "Secretary's Memorandum," a sort of orientation paper passed on from one secretary to the next for several years, OWH Papers, HLS, B55 F7; see also OWH's will dated November 13, 1930, OWH Papers, HLS, B55 F10.

8. OWH to Harold Laski, November 17, 1920, 1 HOLMES–LASKI LETTERS 290, 291.

9. *Id.*, November 26, 1920, 1 HOLMES–LASKI LETTERS 294, 295.

10. 25 NEW REP. 294–295 (1921). Holmes had shamelessly primed Cohen for the review, passing on to him praise that others had given at the time the essays were first published. See the Holmes–Cohen Letters of this time, in L. ROSENFIELD, PORTRAIT OF A PHILOSOPHER (1962).

11. OWH to Ellen Curtis, March 17, 1921, OWH Papers, HLS. See also OWH to Harold Laski, March 10, 1921, 1 HOLMES–LASKI LETTERS 318, F. BIDDLE, MR. JUSTICE HOLMES 167–169 (1942). Bowen's account, BOWEN 394, contains additional details I cannot verify.

12. Pound, *Judge Holmes' Contributions to the Science of Law*, 35 HARV. L. REV. 449 (1921).

13. Haldane, *Mr. Justice Holmes*, 26 NEW REP. 34, 36 (1921).

14. OWH to Baroness Moncheur, March 17, 1921, OWH Papers, HLS.

15. See, e.g., OWH to Felix Frankfurter, April 30, 1921, OWH Papers, HLS, B29 F6. Several of the secretaries and Holmes's visitors have described his conversation. Dean Acheson's account seems to capture the quality for young people. See D. ACHESON, MORNING AND NOON 63–64, *et passim* (1965). Chauncey Belknap took shorthand notes of one discourse, March 30, 1916, OWH Papers, HLS, B54 F5. It is interesting to watch the movement of characteristic expressions from conversations to letters, and then to opinions and speeches. Holmes was able to write so quickly in part because he had a fund of well-polished conversation from which to draw.

16. OWH to Felix Frankfurter, December 23, 1921, OWH Papers, HLS, B29 F6.

17. OWH to Harold Laski, October 19, 1920, 1 HOLMES–LASKI LETTERS 287.

18. OWH to Harold Laski, December 22, 1921, 1 HOLMES–LASKI LETTERS 389, 390.

19. OWH to Harold Laski, January 15, 1922, 1 HOLMES–LASKI LETTERS 397–398.

20. *Law and the Court*, February 15, 1913, COLLECTED LEGAL PAPERS 291, 195 (1920).

21. OHW to Harold Laski, November 13, 1921, 1 HOLMES–LASKI LETTERS 381–382. Holmes was particularly moved by the thought of anonymous death. In the spring of 1925, his secretary of that year, W. Barton Leach, Jr., drove Holmes to Arlington, where they visited the mass grave of the unknown soldiers of the Civil War. "Can you imagine a greater gift than that?" Holmes asked. "You not only gave your life, but your identity as well." J. MONAGAN, THE GRAND PANJANDRUM 40 (1988).

22. Edward D. White to OWH, May 9, 1921, OWH Papers, HLS.

23. OWH to Harold Laski, May 8, 1921, 1 HOLMES–LASKI LETTERS 331; *id.*, May 12, 1 HOLMES–LASKI LETTERS 335.

24. Holmes reacted rather coolly, OWH to Lewis Einstein, May 20, 1921, HOLMES–EINSTEIN LETTERS 195.

25. 2 H. PRINGLE, THE LIFE AND TIMES OF WILLIAM HOWARD TAFT 957 (1939).

26. OWH to Harold Laski, May 29, 1921, 1 HOLMES–LASKI LETTERS 338, 339.

27. OWH to Felix Frankfurter, August 30, 1921, OWH Papers, HLS, B29 F6.

28. OWH to Harold Laski, October 21, 1921, 1 HOLMES–LASKI LETTERS 377, 388.

29. *Id.*, November 13, 1921, 1 HOLMES–LASKI LETTERS 381, 382.

30. *Id.*, December 9, 1921, 1 HOLMES–LASKI LETTERS 385, 386.

31. OWH to Felix Frankfurter, April 20, 1921, OWH Papers, HLS, B29 F26. The case is Block v. Hirsh, 256 U.S. 135 (1921) (Holmes, J.). McKenna's rabid dissent, saying that rent control was the door to socialism, 256 U.S. 158.

32. Henry Friendly, quoted L. BAKER, BRANDEIS AND FRANKFURTER 183 (1984).

33. Learned Hand, quoted L. BAKER, BRANDEIS AND FRANKFURTER 35 (1984).

34. See OWH to Harold Laski, December 17, 1920, 1 HOLMES–LASKI LETTERS 297; *id.*, January 12, 1921, 1 HOLMES–LASKI LETTERS 324; OWH, *Introduction*, MR. JUSTICE BRANDEIS: ESSAYS (F. Frankfurter ed. 1932).

35. OWH to Harold Laski, January 12, 1921, 1 HOLMES–LASKI LETTERS 324.

36. OWH to Nina Gray, March 5, 1921, OWH Papers, HLS. In the 1920s, particularly when early efforts to achieve compromise broke down, Brandeis urged Holmes to write dissents, and Holmes did publish dissenting opinions more often than he otherwise would have, as in Leach v. Carlile, 258 U.S. 138, 140 (1922), and Milwaukee Social Democrat Pub. Co. v. Burleson, 255 U.S. 407, 425 (1921). But I have found no evidence at all that Holmes's substantive thought was affected by Brandeis, who was very much his junior in age and judicial experience.

On the mutual influences of the two men, see S. KONEFSKY, THE LEGACY OF HOLMES AND BRANDEIS (1956); on their arriving at similar decisions from different starting points, Freund, *Holmes and Brandeis in Retrospect*, BOSTON BAR J., September–October 1984, p. 7; Hamilton, *The Legal Philosophy of Justices Holmes and Brandeis*, CURRENT HISTORY 654 (1931).

37. See P. STRUM, LOUIS D. BRANDEIS 281–285 (1984). From Brandeis's letters it is plain that he tried for a year after the Zionist conference in the summer of 1920, when he declined the leadership, until the summer of 1921, when he withdrew entirely, to manage the American and World Zionist organizations from behind the scenes, but by the fall of 1921, this had proven impossible and disruptive and had prompted charges of cabal and conspiracy. At the same time, the trade union movement was losing ground under a hostile administration. Apparently Brandeis turned his full attention to making himself more effective on the Court.

38. See OWH to Harold Laski, October 9, 1921, 1 HOLMES–LASKI LETTERS 373, 374.

39. OWH to Harold Laski, January 1, 1923, 1 HOLMES–LASKI LETTERS 469.

40. OWH to Felix Frankfurter, October 23, 1921, OWH Papers, HLS, B29 F6.

41. See exchange of notes between Holmes and Taft, April 2, 1922, William Howard Taft Papers, LOC.

42. William H. Taft to Horace Taft, April 17, 1922, William H. Taft Papers, LOC.

43. *Id.*

44. William H. Taft to Learned Hand, March 3, 1923, 2 H. PRINGLE, THE LIFE AND TIMES OF WILLIAM HOWARD TAFT 969 (1939).

45. William H. Taft to Helen Manning, June 11, 1923, *id.* at 969.

46. OWH to Felix Frankfurter, 1924, OWH Papers, HLS, B29 F8.

47. A. BLAUSTEIN AND R. MERSKY, THE FIRST ONE HUNDRED JUSTICES 140 (1978).

48. Louis D. Brandeis to Felix Frankfurter, April 8, 1922, 5 LETTERS OF LOUIS D. BRANDEIS 50 (M. Urofsky and D. Levy eds. 1971–1978).

49. OWH to Harold Laski, June 1, 1922, 1 HOLMES–LASKI LETTERS 429, 430.

50. OWH to Harold Laski, August 19, 1922, 1 HOLMES–LASKI LETTERS 439. See also OWH to Felix Frankfurter, July 22, 1922 (from Corey Hill Hospital), and August 24, 1922 (from Beverly Farms), OWH Papers, HLS, B29 F7.

51. James McReynolds to OWH, July 11, [1922], OWH Papers, HLS, B45 F25.

52. OWH to Harold Laski, August 19, 1922, 1 HOLMES–LASKI LETTERS 439.

53. OWH to Frederick Pollock, November 9, 1922, 2 HOLMES–POLLOCK LETTERS 104–105.

54. The envelope of papers is among the OWH Papers, HLS, B55 F9, where the War Department papers concerning the burial plot are also found. See also Mark Howe's memorandum of interview with James Nicely (Holmes's secretary 1923–1924), OWH Papers, HLS, B54 F6. Both Holmes and Fanny were buried at Arlington National Cemetery.

55. OWH to Felix Frankfurter, November 27, 1922; December 22, 1922, OWH Papers, HLS, B29 F7.

56. OWH to Harold Laski, December 14, 1922, 1 HOLMES–LASKI LETTERS 462–463.

57. Editorial, *Mr. Justice Holmes,* 33 NEW REP. 84 (1922).

58. Louis D. Brandeis to OWH, December 8, 1922, OWH Papers, HLS, B38 F4.

59. Benjamin Cardozo to OWH, December 4, 1922, OWH Papers, HLS, B38 F27.

60. American Steel Foundries v. Tri-City Central Trades Council, 257 U.S. 184 (1921); see also United Mine Workers v. Coronado Coal Co., 259 U.S. 344 (1922) (Taft, C.J.). These were among the cases that had divided the White Court, were reargued, and then reargued again for the Taft Court. Under Taft they were decided with only Clarke dissenting. But see Truax v. Corrigan, 257 U.S. 312 (1921), in which Taft, writing for the majority, held that states could not constitutionally deprive their courts of the power to halt violent strikes by injunction. There were four dissents with three separate opinions (including one by Holmes).

61. Grogan v. Walker and Sons, 259 U.S. 80 (1922) (Holmes, J.).

62. Lipke v. Lederer, 259 U.S. 557 (1922) (attempted seizure of suspected bootlegger's property under color of a tax); United States v. Stafoff, 260 U.S. 477 (1923) (Holmes, J.) (Congress may not revive repealed criminal statute retroactively). As to the Chinese deportation cases, compare OWH's early comment, *Reply to Correspondent on "The Rights of Chinamen,"* 5 AM. L. REV. 780 (1871), noting that under federal law foreign-born Chinese were not eligible for naturalization and were not "citizens" protected by the Fourteenth Amendment.

63. Bilokumsky v. Tod, 263 U.S. 149 (1923).

64. William H. Taft to OWH, April 23, 1927, OWH Papers, HLS.

65. Buck v. Bell, 274 U.S. 200 (1927) (Holmes, J.). This is Holmes's most notorious opinion, reportedly cited by defendants in the Nuremburg trials. See Gerard, *Capacity to Govern,* 12 HARV. J. OF LAW & PUBLIC POLICY 501 (1989).

The brutality of the language has been especially criticized. Holmes's language was always particularly harsh when he wrote against ordinary instincts, and in this case I suppose his own childlessness added some edge to his language. The regular reappearance in his writings of the theme of necessary sacrifice of children, and the link he makes to the sacrifices made in war, suggests that Holmes unconsciously was repeating his parents' having sent him to war. See Chapter 14, "Another War," above.

There is an extensive literature on *Buck v. Bell*, pointing out among other things that the case was likely collusive, brought on behalf of the state to test the law, so that Carrie Buck was not adequately represented. Neither Carrie Buck nor her children would be considered mentally defective today, and the sterilization was triggered by an I.Q. test that did not and could not reflect the sort of simply inherited characteristic on which the whole business was justified. The elaborate procedural safeguards provided by the Virginia statute were a sham, exhibited in the *Buck* case, to be ignored thereafter. Carrie Buck's sister, for instance, was told she needed an appendectomy and then sterilized without her knowledge. See S. J. GOULD, THE MISMEASURE OF MAN 335–337 (1981). See also Lombardo, *Three Generations, No Imbeciles: New Light on Buck v. Bell*, 60 N.Y.U. L. REV. 30 (1985); Cynkar, *Buck v. Bell: 'Felt Necessities' v. Fundamental Values?*, 81 COLUM. L. REV. 1418 (1918), and sources cited there; Burgdorf and Burgdorf, *The Wicked Witch Is Almost Dead: Buck v. Bell and the Sterilization of Handicapped Persons*, 50 TEMPLE L. Q. 995 (1977). The secondary literature is reviewed in Dudziak, *Oliver Wendell Holmes as a Eugenic Reformer*, 71 IOWA L. REV. 833 (1986).

Most of the objections to the decision are really directed to the statute it upheld or are based on evidence not then available. The brutal administration of the statute in later cases was not before the Court, the legislative judgment that I.Q. was an adequate indicator of heritable defects could not properly have been reversed as a matter of constitutional law, and not even Brandeis — who joined in the decision — could yet imagine a constitutional right of privacy that would have protected Carrie Buck from such intrusions.

By 1942, when hideous events in Europe had ended the vogue for racial hygiene, the Supreme Court struck down an Oklahoma statute that allowed forcible sterilization of felons — a measure that Holmes in his lifetime undoubtedly would have approved, Skinner v. Oklahoma, 316 U.S. 535 (1942); but even then the Court found another rationale — the arbitrary classification of felons violated the Equal Protection clause of the Fourteenth Amendment — and did not overrule Buck v. Bell.

66. Adkins v. Childrens Hospital, 261 U.S. 525, 567 (1923).

67. Gitlow v. New York, 268 U.S. 652, 668 (1925) (Sanford, J.).

68. 268 U.S. at 672, 673 (Holmes, J., dissenting). It appears that at first Taft voted to reverse Gitlow's conviction and considered joining Holmes's dissent. On May 4, Holmes sent Taft a draft passage asking whether he should add it to his dissenting opinion (he did); see William Howard Taft Papers, LOC. He would not have asked Taft's advice unless Taft were considering joining in the dissenting opinion. But when the opinion of the Court was announced on June 8, 1925, only Brandeis joined Holmes's dissent.

69. United States v. Schwimmer, 279 U.S. 644, 654 (1929) (Holmes, J., dissenting).

70. Milwaukee Social Democratic Pub. Co. v. Burleson, 255 U.S. 407, 437 (1921); see also Leach v. Carlile, 258 U.S. 138, 140 (1922) (Holmes and Brandeis, J.J., dissenting).

71. This description of Holmes's routine at about 1925 is constructed from the many published and unpublished reminiscences of the secretaries, particularly those of Arthur Sutherland, "Reminiscences of Justice Holmes," Arthur E.

Sutherland Papers, HLS, B24 F7. Sutherland was Holmes's secretary in 1927–1928. The image of Holmes framed against the window is from A. HISS, REC-OLLECTIONS OF A LONG LIFE 37 (1988). Alger Hiss was Holmes's secretary in 1929–1930.

72. Sutherland, "Reminiscences of Justice Holmes," pp. 6–7, 9–10, Arthur E. Sutherland Papers, HLS, B24 F7.

73. J. MONAGAN, THE GRAND PANJANDRUM 55 (1988).

74. OWH to Harold Laski, May 5, 1928, 1 HOLMES–LASKI LETTERS 498, 499.

75. See OWH to William H. Taft, October 20, 1924, OWH Papers, HLS.

76. As Holmes said to Nina Gray afterward. See OWH Papers, HLS, B33 F28. For a description of the medal and the ceremony, see OWH Papers, HLS, B55 F8.

77. Thomas Corcoran to Felix Frankfurter, December 9, 1926, OWH Papers, HLS, B55 F4. Corcoran was described in the article as Holmes's "Harvard jewel" of a secretary. Fanny thought the whole thing bunk, as Corcoran gleefully told Frankfurter: "Mrs. Holmes has a new password for me. She meets me on the stairs — 'Whose little jewel are you?' — 'I am Justice Holmes' little jewel.' — 'Pass, friend,'" *Id.*

78. Sergeant, *Oliver Wendell Holmes*, 49 NEW REP. 59 (1926), reprinted in E. SERGEANT, FIRE UNDER THE ANDES 307 (1927). In 1926, "Yankee" was a mildly derogatory word when used of a New Englander, suggesting a close-fisted farmer likely to cheat you in the sale of a horse. Holmes — thoroughly English in dress, speech, and habits of thought — when he grew old liked to call himself one of the last Yankees, and Sergeant with this single word transformed an aristocratic tradition into a more comfortably native American nobility. Sergeant's book was a best-seller; this passage was the source of the title for Catherine Drinker Bowen's best-selling *Yankee from Olympus* and indirectly of the successful stage and television play *Magnificent Yankee.*

79. Sutherland, "Reminiscences of Justice Holmes," p. 10, Arthur E. Sutherland Papers, HLS, B24 F7.

CHAPTER 24. FINAL DUTY

1. OWH to Harold Laski, November 13, 1924, 1 HOLMES–LASKI LETTERS 671.

2. See A. MASON, HARLAN FISKE STONE 258 (1956).

3. Myers v. United States, 272 U.S. 52 (1926). Holmes's stinging one-page dissent is at 272 U.S. 277 (1926).

4. William H. Taft to Helen Manning, June 11, 1923, William Howard Taft Papers, LOC, quoted 2 H. PRINGLE, THE LIFE AND TIMES OF WILLIAM HOWARD TAFT 969 (1939).

5. William H. Taft to Horace Taft, June 12, 1928, William H. Taft Papers, LOC.

6. William H. Taft to Horace Taft, November 23, 1925, quoted A. MASON, WILLIAM HOWARD TAFT 228 (1965).

7. OWH to Felix Frankfurter, September 10, 1928, OWH Papers, HLS, B29 F11.

8. OWH to Harold Laski, April 29, 1927, 2 HOLMES—LASKI LETTERS 938.

9. OWH to Felix Frankfurter, May 21, 1926, OWH Papers, HLS, B29 F10.

10. OWH to Ellen Curtis, April 22, 1928, OWH Papers, HLS.

11. William H. Taft to Horace Taft, June 12, 1928, William H. Taft Papers, LOC. The members of the Court had agreed to consider the case solely on the question whether wiretapping was a search-and-seizure within the meaning of

the Fourth Amendment. Taft complained in his letters that in conference Brandeis harped on the Washington state statute forbidding wiretapping. Holmes had originally voted to uphold the conviction, as he did not believe the Fourth Amendment prohibited wiretaps, but Brandeis's insistent discussion of the violation of state law — contrary, Taft thought, to the agreement of the justices — prompted Holmes's dissent on common-law grounds.

12. Olmstead v. United States, 277 U.S. 438, 468 (1928). Taft went on to mention, dismissively, that under Washington law wiretapping was a misdemeanor, but said this had no relevance to admissibility of evidence in a federal trial. *Id.* 468–469.

13. Olmstead v. United States, 277 U.S. 438, 469 (1928) (Holmes, J., dissenting). Cf. Burdean v. McDowell, 256 U.S. 465, 476 (1921) (Brandeis and Holmes, J. J., dissenting) (papers stolen by a private party from criminal defendants and given to federal prosecutors should not be admitted in evidence). The description of Holmes reading is based on Sutherland, "Reminiscences of Justice Holmes," Arthur E. Sutherland Papers, HLS, B24 F7.

Chapter 25. A Ghost on the Battlefield

1. D. Acheson, Morning and Noon 37–38 (1965).
2. Sutherland, "Reminiscences of Justice Holmes," p. 36, Arthur E. Sutherland Papers, HLS, B24 F7.
3. *Id.*
4. A. Hiss, Recollections of a Life 34 (1988).
5. Sutherland, "Reminiscences of Justice Holmes," at p. 42. Arthur E. Sutherland Papers, HLS, B24 F7.
6. Many descriptions of Holmes in his late eighties and early nineties convey this in different ways; see especially Mark Howe's notes of an interview with Learned Hand on June 11, 1942, OWH Papers, HLS, B53 F13.
7. OWH to Felix Frankfurter, January 21, 1929, OWH Papers, HLS, B29 F12.
8. OWH to Felix Frankfurter, July 25, 1921, OWH Papers, HLS, B29 F6.
9. OWH to Felix Frankfurter, November 26, 1921, OWH Papers, HLS, B29 F6. Holmes made similar requests to Laski. Both ignored his requests, as perhaps he expected. After Holmes's death, Laski began work on a book of Holmes's letters, but never completed the task. With Freda Laski's and Felix Frankfurter's assistance, Mark Howe, by then Holmes's authorized biographer, published the complete Holmes–Laski correspondence, see 1 Holmes–Laski Letters v–vi (M. Howe ed., 1953).

Frankfurter kept the letters Holmes sent him — as Holmes kept Frankfurter's — and toward the end of Holmes's life made notes of their conversations at Beverly Farms during summer visits, apparently with the thought of writing Holmes's biography, but he abandoned that plan when he was appointed to the Supreme Court. See Preface to this volume.

10. See, e.g., Sutherland, "Reminiscences of Justice Holmes," p. 17, Arthur E. Sutherland Papers, HLS, B24 F7.
11. OWH to Harlan F. Stone, December 20, 1928, in A. Mason, Harlan Fiske Stone 328 (1956). The case referred to was Williams v. Standard Oil Co., 278 U.S. 235 (1929), in which OWH dissented without opinion.
12. See OWH Papers, HLS, B50 F23.
13. William H. Taft to Horace Taft, November 14, 1929, 2 H. Pringle, The Life and Times of William Howard Taft 967 (1939).
14. William H. Taft to OWH, September 8, 1928, OWH Papers, HLS.

15. A. MASON, HARLAN FISKE STONE 327 (1956).

16. OWH to John Wigmore, February 27, 1929, OWH Papers, HLS, B36 F24.

17. William H. Taft to OWH, April 30, 1929, "10:30 p.m.," OWH Papers, HLS, B45 F26.

18. Helen Manning to Henry Pringle, July 11, 1939, quoted 2 H. PRINGLE, THE LIFE AND TIMES OF WILLIAM HOWARD TAFT 970 (1939). See also J. MONAGAN, THE GRAND PANJANDRUM 64 (1988); BOWEN 403–404. Bowen's source for some details was apparently John Lockwood, Holmes's secretary at the time. She has Taft consulting "Hughes," but the senior Hughes was in New York, and this must be his son, Charles Evans Hughes, Jr., the recently appointed solicitor general.

19. Joseph B. White, "To Night." See J. MONAGAN, THE GRAND PANJANDRUM 64, 146 (1988). Monagan gives no source for this detail. The same sonnet was read at Holmes's own funeral; see "A Sonnet Holmes Loved," Providence Journal, March 11, 1935, where it is printed in full.

20. OWH to Frederick Pollock, May 24, 1929, 2 HOLMES-POLLOCK LETTERS 243.

21. OWH to John Wigmore, May 29, 1929, OWH Papers, HLS, B36 F25.

22. A copy of the probated will is among the OWH Papers, HLS, B55 F10. See also John S. Flannery (the attorney who drafted the will from Holmes's instructions) to Mark Howe, May 13, 1942, OWH Papers, HLS, B54 F8, explaining its provisions.

23. Lockwood, "*I Always Prefer the Original*," 28 U. FLA. L. REV. 394 (1976).

24. OWH to Nina Gray, July 24, 1929, OWH Papers, HLS.

25. William H. Taft to Pierce Butler, September 14, 1929, 2 H. PRINGLE, THE LIFE AND TIMES OF WILLIAM HOWARD TAFT 1044 (1939).

26. William H. Taft to Horace Taft, December 1, 1929, *id.* Justice Sanford lived only a few months longer than Taft, but the others in this group became famous as the "Four Horsemen" during the following decade, forming a strong bloc opposed to much New Deal legislation, prompting President Roosevelt's court-packing plan.

27. OWH to Harold Laski, February 14, 1930, 2 HOLMES–LASKI LETTERS 1223, 1224.

28. See Alger Hiss's 1939 memorandum to Felix Frankfurter, Felix Frankfurter Papers, LOC, B225 F4123. Hiss was Holmes's secretary when Holmes served as acting chief justice and presumably heard the conferences described by Holmes or by the other justices.

29. A. MASON, HARLAN FISKE STONE 276 (1956). Brandeis gave Frankfurter a similar account; see Mark Howe memorandum of talk with Frankfurter, January 2, 1964, OWH Papers, HLS, B54 F5.

30. The Chicago Drainage Canal Case, 281 U.S. 179 (1930). Holmes, while acting Chief, evidently assigned this to himself for the purpose of hearing motions. The case was argued after Charles Evans Hughes became chief justice, but Hughes had been the Special Master whose report was being considered and so recused himself; Holmes, as senior associate, then presumably assigned the opinion to himself.

31. A. MASON, HARLAN FISKE STONE 8 (1956).

32. Farmers Loan & Trust Co. v. Minnesota, 280 U.S. 204 (1930), overruling Blackstone v. Miller, 188 U.S. 189 (1903) (Holmes, J.). See C. BUTLER, A CENTURY AT THE BAR OF THE SUPREME COURT 78 (1942), calling the scene "remarkable."

In Safe Deposit Trust Co. v. Virginia, 280 U.S. 83 (1929), "double taxation" was held unconstitutional, but *Blackstone v. Miller* was carefully and tactfully distinguished. This opinion was written by McReynolds, presumably with guidance from Taft, and delivered by Taft himself on November 25, 1929, one of the last opinions delivered before his final illness. By January of 1930, however, with Taft gone, McReynolds led the Court in expressly overruling *Blackstone v. Miller;* Holmes issued a mild dissent, probably written before he had seen McReynolds's opinion. In Baldwin v. Missouri, 281 U.S. 586 (1930), McReynolds greatly widened the principle of *Farmers' Loan & Trust,* and Holmes dissented much more forcefully.

33. Baldwin v. Missouri, 281 U.S. 586, 595 (1930) (Holmes, J., dissenting).

34. OWH to Charles E. Hughes, February 10, 1930, OWH Papers, HLS, B36 F26; see also 2 M. PUSEY, CHARLES EVANS HUGHES 668 (1951) (where the date of the letter is given as February 12, 1930).

35. OWH to Felix Frankfurter, January 1, 1930, OWH Papers, HLS.

36. A. HISS, RECOLLECTIONS OF A LIFE 37 (1988).

37. OWH to Baroness Moncheur, November 1, 1929, OWH Papers, HLS.

38. OWH to Lewis Einstein, January 16, 1930; HOLMES–EINSTEIN LETTERS 303.

39. See Arthur Wendell to OWH, March 7, 1931, OWH Papers, HLS, B66 F8, apparently answering a query from Holmes.

40. See *Holmes–Cohen Letters* in L. ROSENFIELD, PORTRAIT OF A PHILOSOPHER 443 (1962) (and sources cited there).

41. 281 U.S. v (1930).

42. OWH to Nina Gray, March 21, 1930, OWH Papers, HLS.

43. Hill, *Oliver Wendell Holmes, Justice of the Supreme Court of the United States,* 39 HARV. GRAD. MAG. 265, 269 (1931).

44. OWH Papers, HLS, B31 F2.

45. SPEECHES 178. This is the entire text of the address. At the Harvard Law School Library and the Library of Congress, there are tape recordings of the broadcast. In reading, Holmes repeated the word *death,* as if to say, "Realize, this is truly death," but this does not look so well on the page, and I have given it as he wrote it and not as he read it. The original of the quotation is

Mors aurem vellens, "vivite," ait, "venio."

It is the concluding line of *Copa Surisca* in H. WADDELL, MEDIAEVAL LATIN LYRICS 2, 4 (2d ed. 1930), given to Holmes the previous fall by Alger Hiss. See A. HISS, RECOLLECTIONS OF A LIFE (1988). The translation is presumably Holmes's. The sense of the original poem is "Live and be merry, for tomorrow you may die," which is quite unlike the use Holmes made of the line, but when called to account he said that all was fair in quotation. See Frederick Pollock to OWH, May 4, 1931, 2 HOLMES–POLLOCK LETTERS 285; OWH to Pollock, May 15, 1931, 2 HOLMES–POLLOCK LETTERS 286.

46. OWH to Ellen Curtis, January 9, 1932, OWH Papers, HLS.

47. See AUTOBIOGRAPHICAL NOTES OF CHARLES EVANS HUGHES 299 (D. Danelski and J. Tulchin eds. 1973); 2 M. PUSEY, CHARLES EVANS HUGHES 681 (1951); Mark Howe memorandum of interview with Chief Justice Hughes, OWH Papers, HLS. Hughes recalled getting the statute himself, but H. Chapman Rose, the secretary at that time, recalled being summoned to get it, which seems more likely. See J. MONAGAN, THE GRAND PANJANDRUM 140 (1988).

48. 284 U.S. vii (1932).

49. This is the secretary's account, given to Monagan. J. MONAGAN, THE GRAND PANJANDRUM 140 (1988).

50. Holmes's resignation and the exchange of letters are at 284 U.S. vii (1932).

51. Frankfurter memorandum, September 14, 1932, Felix Frankfurter Papers, LOC, B146 F2974; copy, Grant Gilmore Papers, HLS, B2 F8.

52. Frankfurter memorandum, August 8, 1932, Felix Frankfurter Papers, LOC, B146 F2974; see also Grant Gilmore Papers, HLS, B2 F8.

53. *Id.*

54. Donald Hiss, the secretary at that time, quoted by his brother Alger, in A. HISS, RECOLLECTIONS OF A LIFE 33 (1988). This conversation has long been a staple Holmes anecdote and has appeared in print much embroidered and embellished; I have given here the nucleus, which seems to me likely enough.

55. OWH to Ellen Curtis, December 19, 1933, OWH Papers, HLS, B41 F6.

INDEX

Morse, Robert (cousin), 102, 103, 116
Morton, Marcus, 169, 174, 194, 195
Motley, John Lothrop, 16, 34, 54
Mt. Auburn Cemetery, 200, 323, 349
"Mrs. Jarley's Waxworks," 27
Mugwumps, 156, 185, 221, 236
Murphy, Mary, 175
Museum of Fine Arts (Boston), 155
Mussolini, Benito, 372
Mutsuhito, Emperor of Japan, 132
Myers, Gustavus, 307
My Hunt After "The Captain" (Dr. Holmes), 419*n*
mysticism, 28, 412*n*

Nabuco de Araujo, Joaquín, 287, 297
Napier, Sir Charles, 55
Napoleonic Code, 255
Nation, 102, 155, 164, 236, 337
National Life and Character (Pearson), 202, 445*n*, 446*n*
Natural Law, 423*n*, 457*n*
natural selection, 141, 431*n*
Navy Department, U.S., 5, 225
Nawa Michkazu, 147, 155
negligence, 138, 446*n*
Nelly Baker (steamer), 36
New Deal, 376, 481*n*
New Empire, The (Adams), 236
New England Emigrant Society, 20
New England Guard. *See* Fourth Battalion
Newman, John Henry, Cardinal, 427*n*
Newport News, battle of (1862), 57
New Republic, 318, 320, 325, 328, 332, 337, 338, 350, 355, 474*n*
New York:
    Holmes's trips to, 201, 275, 295–296
    law protecting bakery workers in, 280–282, 352
New York Bar Association, Holmes's speech to (1899), 228, 451*n*–452*n*
New York Court of Appeals, 231
New York Evening Post, 236
New York Times, 343
Niagara Falls, Holmeses' vacation at (1888), 185
Nicholson, James, 175
Nickerson, Albert, 139
Nickerson, Joe, 139
Nineteenth Massachusetts Volunteer Infantry Regiment, 38, 39
Noble (farmer), 12

Northern Pacific, 267
Northern Securities Company, 268–269, 474*n*
Northwestern Law School, 241–242
Norton, Charles Eliot, 151
Noyes, Frances, 311
Nuremburg trials, 477*n*

Oklahoma, sterilization of felons in, 478*n*
"Old Ironsides" (Dr. Holmes), 5
Old Testament, 149
"Oliver Wendell Holmes . . ." (Sergeant), 355, 479*n*
Olney, Charles, 448*n*
Orde, Sir John, 111
Oregon, regulation of women's labor in, 289–290
Origin and Scope of the American Doctrine of Constitutional Law, The (Thayer), 444*n*
Origin of Species (Darwin), 412*n*
Osgood, Mrs., 336
O'Sullivan, John, 49
"Over the Teacups" (Dr. Holmes), 183, 193
ownership, 128, 134
    See also property
Oxford University, Holmes awarded honorary doctorate by, 293–294

Pacifist League, 225
pacifists, 313, 315, 322, 353, 469*n*
Paine, Ned, 79
Palfrey, Francis Winthrop, 37, 38, 53, 54, 56, 63, 64, 65, 68
    death of, 193
Palfrey, John G., xvi, xvii
Pan American Lottery Company, 254
panic of 1873, 141–142
panic of 1929, 373, 375
Papanti, Lorenzo, 117
Paris, Holmes's first trip to (1866), 108
Parker, Horace, 182
Parker, Joel, 96, 98
Parkman, Henry, 138
Parliament, British, 100, 250, 444*n*
Parnell, Charles Stewart, 187, 189
Parsons, Theophilus, 96
Pass, Sergeant, 36
"Path of the Law, The" (Holmes), 223–224, 435*n*, 450*n*–451*n*
Peabody, Joseph, 179, 180, 181

TABLE OF CASES